This ambitious volume marks a huge step in our understanding of the social history of the Great War. Jay Winter and Jean-Louis Robert have gathered a group of scholars of Paris, London and Berlin, who collectively have drawn a coherent and original study of cities at war. The contributors explore notions of well-being in wartime cities – relating to the economy and the question of whether the state of the capitals contributed to victory or defeat. Expert contributors in fields stretching from history, demography, anthropology, economics, and sociology to the history of medicine bring an interdisciplinary approach to the book, as well as representing the best of recent research in their own fields. *Capital Cities at War*, one of the few truly comparative works on the Great War, will transform studies of the conflict, and is likely to become a paradigm for research on other wars.

JAY WINTER is a Fellow of Pembroke College, Cambridge. His previous publications in this series include *Sites of Memory, Sites of Mourning: The Great War in European Cultural History* and (co-edited with Emmanuel Sivan) *War and Remembrance in the Twentieth Century*.

JEAN-LOUIS ROBERT is Professor of History at the University of Orléans. He is the author of *Les ouvriers, la patrie et la Révolution: Paris 1914–1919* (1995).

Studies in the Social and Cultural History of Modern Warfare

Capital cities at war

Studies in the Social and Cultural History of Modern Warfare

In recent years the field of modern history has been enriched by the exploration of two parallel histories. These are the social and cultural history of armed conflict, and the impact of military events on social and cultural history.

Studies in the Social and Cultural History of Modern Warfare intends to present the fruits of this growing area of research, reflecting both the colonization of military history by cultural historians, and the reciprocal interest of military historians in social and cultural history, to the benefit of both. The series will reflect the latest scholarship in European and non-European events from the 1850s to the present day.

Titles in the series

1 *Sites of Memory, Sites of Mourning*
The Great War in European Cultural History
Jay Winter
ISBN 0 521 49682 9

2 *Capital Cities at War*
Paris, London, Berlin 1914–1919
Edited by Jay Winter and Jean-Louis Robert
ISBN 0 521 57171 5 (HB) 0 521 66814 X (PB)

3 *State, Society and Mobilization in Europe during the First World War*
Edited by John Horne
ISBN 0 521 56112 4

4 *A Time of Silence*
Civil War and the Culture of Repression in Franco's Spain, 1936–1945
Michael Richards
ISBN 0 521 59401 4

5 *War and Remembrance in the Twentieth Century*
Edited by Jay Winter and Emmanuel Sivan
ISBN 0 521 64035 0

6 *European Culture in the Great War*
The Arts, Entertainment and Propaganda, 1914–1918
Edited by Aviel Roshwald and Richard Stites
ISBN 0 521 57015 8

7 *The Labour of Loss*
Mourning, Memory and Wartime Bereavement in Australia
Joy Damousi
ISBN 0 521 66004 1 (HB) 0 521 66974 X (PB)

Capital cities at war

Paris, London, Berlin 1914–1919

JAY WINTER
Pembroke College, Cambridge

and

JEAN-LOUIS ROBERT
University of Orléans

Published by the Press Syndicate of the University of Cambridge
The Pitt Building, Trumpington Street, Cambridge CB2 1RP
40 West 20th Street, New York, NY 10011-4211, USA
10 Stamford Road, Oakleigh, Melbourne 3166, Australia

First published 1997
First paperback edition 1999

A catalogue record for this book is available from the British Library

Library of Congress cataloguing in publication data

Winter, J. M.
Capital cities at war: Paris, London, Berlin, 1914–1919 / Jay Winter and Jean-Louis Robert.
p. cm. – (Studies in the social and cultural history of modern warfare)
Includes bibliographical references.
ISBN 0 521 57171 5
1. World War, 1914–1918 – France – Paris. 2. World War, 1914–1918 – England – London. 3. World War, 1914–1918 – Germany – Berlin.
4. Paris (France) – History. 5. London (England) – History. 6. Berlin (Germany) – History. I. Robert, Jean-Louis. II. Title. III. Series.
D523.W578 1996
940 – dc20 96–796 CIP

ISBN 0 521 57171 5 (hardback)
ISBN 0 521 66814 X (paperback)

Transferred to digital printing 2004

VN

Contents

Note on joint authorship

The name of the primary author of each chapter is listed on the table of contents. Here his or her name is italicized, but we include the names of those who researched and wrote parts of each chapter and whose joint research and preparation must be acknowledged to appreciate the collective character of this project.

1 Paris, London, Berlin: *Jay Winter*
2 Paris, London, Berlin on the eve of war: *Jean-Louis Robert*
3 Lost generations: *Adrian Gregory* and Jean-Louis Robert, Joshua Cole, Jay Winter
4 The image of the profiteer: *Jean-Louis Robert* and Jonathan Manning, Armin Triebel, Belinda Davis
5 The transition to war in 1914: *Jon Lawrence* and Martin Dean, Jean-Louis Robert
6 The labour market and industrial mobilization, 1915–1917: *Thierry Bonzon* and Joshua Cole, Jon Lawrence
7 The transition to peace, 1918–1919: *Joshua Cole* and John Lawrence, Jean-Louis Robert
8 Material pressures on the middle classes: *Jon Lawrence* and Jean-Louis Robert, Joshua Cole
9 Wages and purchasing power: *Jonathan Manning* and Joshua Cole, Jean-Louis Robert
10 Transfer payments and social policy: *Thierry Bonzon* and Joshua Cole, Jonathan Manning
11 Feeding the cities: *Thierry Bonzon* and Jonathan Manning, Armin Triebel, *Belinda Davis*
12 Coal and the metropolis: *Armin Triebel* and Jon Lawrence, Thierry Bonzon
13 Housing: *Susanna Magri* and Jon Lawrence, Joshua Cole
14 The 'other war': protecting public health: *Catherine Rollet* and Jay Winter, Joshua Cole
15 The 'other war': setbacks in public health: *Catherine Rollet* and Jay Winter, Joshua Cole

16 Surviving the war: *Jay Winter* and Catherine Rollet, Joshua Cole, Jackie Ariouat
17 Conclusion: *Jean-Louis Robert and Jay Winter*

Acknowledgments of funding
For funding without which this project could not have taken place, we are grateful to the Economic and Social Research Council, the Fritz Thyssen Stiftung, the Historial de la grande guerre, Péronne, Somme, and the Centre nationale de la recherche scientifique's interdisciplinary programme of research on cities. Thanks are due to the editors of the *Economic History Review, European Journal of Population, Annales de démographie historique* and *International Labour and Working-class History,* for the inclusion of material originally published in their journals. All translations were the work of Helen McPhail and Jay Winter. For aid on the bibliography and the index, we are grateful to Bruno Cabanes and Helen MacCartney, respectively.

Figures

Tables

Part 1
Premises

1
Paris, London, Berlin 1914–1919: capital cities at war

Jay Winter

Comparative urban history: Paris, London, Berlin, 1914–1919

In August 1914, the German artist Max Beckmann drew a series of sketches of the crowds gathered in Berlin during the first days of the war. Among them is a drypoint print entitled *Declaration of War 1914*. It shows a group of people trying to get a glimpse of a newspaper with the latest war news. Their faces show a range of reactions, from shock to concern to apparent detachment.[1] This book is about what happened to them, and to people like them living in Paris and London between the outbreak of hostilities in August 1914 and demobilization in 1919.

Nation, city, and community

The history of the Great War has been told time and again within a national framework. Almost all students of the period have been imprisoned, to a greater or lesser degree, within this framework of analysis.[2] Its main drawback is that it tends to conflate into aggregates quite different and frequently contradictory experiences. The best way to penetrate behind the illusory veil of a unitary 'national experience' is to describe the character of community life in wartime.

At first sight, the national bias in the historical literature is curious. Nations do not actually wage wars; groups of people organized in states do. Of course, in an abstract, legal sense, 'France' and 'Britain' waged

1 On the background to this drawing, and other facets of Beckmann's response to the 1914–18 war, see C. Schulz-Hoffman and J. C. Weiss (eds.), *Max Beckmann retrospective* (Munich and New York, 1985), p. 388 and C. W. Haxthausen, 'Beckmann and the First World War' in the same volume, pp. 69–80. See also B. C. Buenger, 'Max Beckmann in the First World War', in R. Rumold and O. K. Werckmeister (eds.), *The ideological crisis of expressionism. The literary and artistic German war colony in Belgium 1914–1918*, Studies in German Literature, Linguistics, and Culture 51 (Columbia, S.C., 1990), pp. 237–75.

2 For examples, see J. M. Winter, *The Great War and the British people* (Basingstoke, 1986); J.-J. Becker, *The Great War and the French people* (Leamington Spa, 1985); J. Kocka, *Facing total war: German society, 1914–1918* (Leamington Spa, 1984).

Fig. 1.1 Max Beckmann, *Declaration of war 1914*

war on 'Germany': a declaration of war was ratified by the appropriately empowered bodies; funds were earmarked, and enabling acts opened the way to armed conflict. But the concrete, visible steps taken by Frenchmen, Germans, or Englishmen to go to war, to provision the men who joined up, and to adjust to the consequences – the human dimension of war – were almost always taken within and expressed through collective life at the local level: communities of volunteers or conscripts; communities of munitions workers; communities of the faithful and bereaved.

We take 'community' to mean social and geographical entities around which ordinary people construct their daily lives. In this sense a neighbourhood is an 'experienced community'; a 'nation', as Benedict Anderson tells us, is an 'imagined community';[3] a city is at the meeting point of the two, with both an imaginative and a visible

[3] Benedict Anderson, *Imagined communities. Reflections on the origins and spread of nationalism* (London, 1983).

existence, one much closer to the neighbourhood than to the nation.[4]

It is not our intention to enter the rhetorical minefield leading to a universal answer to the question as to what constitutes a community. We try to use the term descriptively rather than normatively, thereby avoiding at all costs the kind of warm glow of *Gemütlichkeit* the term 'community' can convey when used uncritically.[5] Nor do we subscribe to any analytical model separating 'community' from 'economic society' and drawing a straight line, called 'modernization', from the one to the other. We use the word 'community' in the way contemporaries did in these cities: to describe the environments – both material and cultural – in which they worked and resided.

The distinction between 'experienced' and 'imagined' communities is best understood as a heuristic device. All experience is imagined in a myriad of ways; it is never a unity, and the cultural dimension of work, wages, and consumption in the urban context is essential to the story we tell in this book. But one of the challenges of such research has been to escape the trap of idealism in social history, to avoid the fashionable current in which only representations exist. Wartime cities were full of such images, but the realities of daily life in wartime all too frequently deflated them by bringing to the fore the physical realities of conscription, shortages, and spiralling food prices. Urban populations faced these tangible, visceral difficulties in one way or another every day of the war. How they did so is essential to an understanding of the differences and overlap between 'imagined' and 'experienced' communities. All we claim is that these levels of perception and adaptation can be explored more effectively on the local than on the national level.

Whereas the history of nations at war has produced a literature of staggering proportions,[6] the history of communities at war is still in its infancy. There is a substantial body of writing on the urban context of wars and civil wars;[7] publications on the American Civil War or the

[4] See D. Feldman and G. Stedman Jones's introduction to *Metropolis London. Histories and representations since 1800* (London, 1989), p. 6.

[5] For a lively demolition of such an approach, see Joanna Bourke, *Working-class cultures in Britain 1890–1940* (London, 1993).

[6] Just to keep up with the recent deluge in this literature is a full-time job. For a sense of its mass and quality, see the summary notices in the journals *War and Society Newsletter*, *Bulletin du centre de recherche de l'Historial de la grande guerre*, and *Militärgeschichtliche Mitteilungen*.

[7] Among the richest collections on this subject are the Bibliothèque de documentation internationale contemporaine in the University of Paris – X, Nanterre, the Bibliothek für Zeitgeschichte in Stuttgart, and the Centre de recherche sur l'histoire des mouvements sociaux et du syndicalisme, at 9 rue Malher, Paris. The centre accommodated meetings of this research group throughout its period of activity.

Paris Commune, for example, fill entire libraries. The range of memoirs about daily life or 'my time' in wartime London, Paris, or Berlin also provides much material of interest to historians.[8] There is as well the evidence of the literary imagination, which provides glimpses, albeit highly subjective ones, of these cities in wartime.[9] But with the exception of studies of revolutionary movements, mostly in Germany and France, the wartime social history of all major European cities, including the great metropolitan centres of Paris, London, and Berlin, has yet to be written.[10]

Capital cities are special cases. They were the 'nerve centres' of the war, the places where the key decisions were taken and confirmed or changed by key political groups and individuals. But they were also like other cities: clusters of quartiers, the identities of which were never subsumed fully by the city as a whole. And within these quartiers, smaller units, many defined by family ties, were where the war was actually lived. In a study of urban history, these more intimate identities and loyalties can never be ignored.

In 1916 a Londoner in uniform was asked whether he was fighting for the empire. His answer was an emphatic yes. What he had in mind was the Empire music hall in Hackney.[11] It is, therefore, essential to attend to the strength of local loyalties expressed in national or imperial phrases, the celebration of mundane and none the less important daily realities in an elevated language of nation, race, and empire. It is certainly true that the history of Paris and Berlin was transformed by the upheavals in the history of their nations, in particular by the war of 1870–1, but even in

[8] For example, see C. E. Cooper, *Behind the lines: one woman's war, 1914–1918* (London, 1982); M. McDonagh, *In London during the Great War* (London, 1935); Roger Martin du Gard, *L'été 1914* (Paris, 1932); R. and D. Glatzer (eds.), *Berliner Leben 1914–1918* (Berlin, 1983); G. Baumer, *Heimatchronik während des Weltkriegs* (Berlin, 1930); W. Eildermann, *Jugend im ersten Weltkrieg. Tagebücher, Briefe, Erinnerungen* (Berlin, 1972).

[9] A. Döblin, *A people betrayed. November 1918: a German revolution*, trans. by J. E. Woods (New York, 1983); L. F. Céline, *Voyage to the end of the night*, trans. by R. Manheim (London, 1988); D. H. Lawrence, *Women in love* (London, 1922), among others.

[10] On Germany, see F. Bay-Heard, *Haupstadt und Staatsumwälzung – Berlin 1918. Problematik und Scheitern der Rätebewegung in der Kommunalverwaltung* (Stuttgart, 1969); R. A. Comfort, *Revolutionary Hamburg. Labor politics in the early Weimar Republic* (Stanford, Calif., 1966); M. Nolan, *Social Democracy and Society. Working-class radicalism in Düsseldorf 1890–1920* (Cambridge, 1981); E. H. Tobin, 'War and the working class: the case of Düsseldorf, 1914–1918', *Central European History*, 18 (1985), pp. 257–98; Gunther Mai, *Kriegswirtschaft und Arbeiterbewegung in Württemberg, 1914–1918* (Stuttgart, 1983). On Paris, see J.-L. Robert, 'Ouvriers et mouvement ouvrier parisien pendant la grande guerre et l'immédiat après-guerre. Histoire et anthropologie', State doctorate, University of Paris – I, 1989, and P. Fridenson (ed.), *The French home front 1914–1918*, (Providence and Oxford, 1992). On other cities, see L. Haimson and C. Tilly (eds.), *Strikes, wars and revolutions in international perspective* (Cambridge, 1992).

[11] P. Gibbs, *Realities of war* (London, 1929), p. 57, as cited in J. G. Fuller, *Troop morale and popular culture in the British and Dominion armies 1914–1918* (Oxford, 1990), p. 36.

these two cities, urban identities, and with them, a sense of place within a district,[12] were never eclipsed by or subsumed completely within national or imperial realities.[13] Some men fought for nation and empire, for King and country. Others fought for their part of London in a way they never fought for England; and even when they saluted England in song and verse, their 'England' was envisioned as a very local and particular place, bounded in many cases by the streets they knew, and the daily lives they led.

All cities are stunningly complex structures, and capital cities are more complex than most. They contain widely diverse populations, the variations among which will be probed at all stages of this study. But one of our key assumptions is that each city was a reality, albeit one full of myth and a mystique carefully cultivated over time by a host of writers, poets, politicians, painters, and tourists. We must not forget, though, that each capital city had a visceral identity, and was not merely a legal artefact created for collecting taxes and organizing the water supply. Each was a complex of urban villages and neighbourhoods whose collective existence was so obvious to its inhabitants that it did not have to be established for them. Others dreamed of 'Paris'; local residents saw a more prosaic, but none the less vivid, urban reality. Those who lived or worked within the boundaries of the twenty arrondissements or in the adjacent suburbs of Paris knew what it was. They could walk from one end to the other on a leisurely day. It took longer to traverse London, but the material sense of a city was shared by millions of Londoners, despite the blurring at the edges of the administrative county into Kentish London or Middlesex. Similarly, being in Berlin was no mystery in 1914. Whether or not the suburban districts of Charlottenberg or Spandau were in Berlin was a matter of administra-

[12] On social differentiation within these cities, see F. Bedarida, 'Urban growth and social structure in nineteenth century Poplar', *London Journal* 1, 2 (1975), pp. 159–88 and, for the twentieth century, two very different neighbourhoods are described in J. White, 'Campbell Bunker: a lumpen community in London between the wars', *History Workshop Journal* (1979), pp. 1–49 and M. Young and P. Willmott, *Family and kinship in East London* (London, 1957); on Paris, among local studies of the Paris region, see P. Jacquemet, *Belleville au XIXème siècle* (Paris, 1984); P. Jacquemet, 'Belleville aux XIXème et XXème siècles', *Annales – Economies, Sociétés, Civilisations*, 30, 4 (1975), pp. 819–43; Annie Fourcaut, 'La banlieue rouge', PhD thesis, University of Paris – I, 1983; and T. Stovall, *The rise of the Paris red belt* (Berkeley, 1990). On Berlin, see H. J. Schwippe, 'Zum Process der sozialräumlichen innerstädtischen Differenzierung im Industrialisierungsprozess des 19. Jahrhunderts: eine faktorialökologische Studie am Beispiel der Stadt Berlin, 1875–1910', in H.-J. Teuteberg (ed.), *Urbanisierung im 19. und 20. Jahrhundert. Historische und geographische Aspekte* (Cologne, 1983), pp. 284–307; and more generally, E. Kaeber, *Berlin im Weltkrieg* (Berlin, 1921).

[13] See S. Rials, *Nouvelle histoire de Paris. De Trochu à Thiers, 1870–1873* (Paris, 1985), W. Ribbe (ed.), *Geschichte Berlin, zweiter Band. Von der Märzrevolution bis zur Gegenwart* (Munich, 1988), and S. E. Rasmussen, *London. The unique city* (London, 1937).

tive nicety, not lived experience, as the incorporation of these and other areas into Greater Berlin in 1920 suggests.

Why select these urban communities? For the obvious reason that to write the history of communities in wartime France, Britain, and Germany without Paris, London, and Berlin would be very odd indeed. Their sheer size invites attention, as does their character as the residence of political, financial, and military leaders. The well-being of these urban conglomerates had a special meaning during the war, and their history – to a varying, though substantial, degree – governed that of the nation as a whole. When the Spartacist uprising failed in Berlin in 1919, it doomed insurrection elsewhere. Had Paris not held out in September 1914 or April 1918, the success of the Allied cause as a whole would have been in doubt. Certainly it would be wrong to read the history of other cities simply as an extension of what happened in the capitals, but no social history of the Great War will be complete without an analysis of metropolitan life during the conflict. That this has never been attempted before is both an indication of the difficulties of such a comparison and a challenge to undertake it.

Strategies of comparison

Comparing these three cities is an attractive and difficult task. Their spatial geometry, their architecture, both public and domestic, varied substantially. Their administrative histories were widely divergent. Yet they also shared structural and functional similarities, and archival and statistical records of sufficient richness to enable rigorous comparisons to be made.

Some parallels are obvious. These cities were centres of the press, transportation, and culture, national, European, and imperial.[14] They were the foci of financial and political power, of commerce and manufacture, and any disruption to essential supplies and services was of immediate concern to those who ran the war.

The administrative history of each capital city presents some striking resemblances to that of the other two. Each city was an administrative unit both distinct from central government and controlled or overseen in a number of important ways. Public order, public health, housing, education, food provisioning in the metropolis, were always on the agendas of municipal, county, and central governments during the war. Who had final authority was a difficult enough question in peacetime; it was an explosive one in wartime.

[14] The literature on cultural exchanges is vast. See for instance, the pathbreaking and elegant study of Donald Olsen, *The city as a work of art: London, Paris, Vienna* (New Haven, 1986), and the catalogue of the Centre Georges Pompidou's remarkable exhibition *Paris–Berlin 1900–1933: rapports et contrastes France–Allemagne* (Paris, 1978).

One reason why these questions have never been answered is that most urban histories respect the conventional boundary of 1914, and therefore either end their narratives with the outbreak of hostilities or leap over the war years entirely.[15] With notable exceptions,[16] scholars in this field have done little to fill this gap.[17]

This is true despite the fact that wartime administrative headaches have left a vast array of sources available for comparative study. Army, police, surveillance, and labour records are particularly abundant for Paris; statistical data are fullest for Berlin; and local authority records are richest for London. This difference in archival materials is no artefact: there is no British series comparable to the collection of police surveillance reports in Paris or in Berlin because the structure of the central state and the links between central and local authority were entirely different. Nevertheless comparisons are rarely possible on the basis of identical sources, and metropolitan history ran along similar lines in wartime. Finding enough coal for Parisians in the winter of 1916–17 was not very different from the same task faced by administrators in London and Berlin. Who had the responsibility to do so varied, as did the degree to which they succeeded. But the choices they faced were much the same.

The physical location of the three cities with respect to the theatre of military operations was of fundamental importance in their wartime history. Here the divergence between Paris – near the front lines – London and Berlin – remote from them – is obvious. But, despite the differences arising from proximity to what the French later called the 'red zone', what is surprising is how many parallels remain within wartime metropolitan history.

We trace these parallels in five sections. After a preliminary presentation of aspects of the social history of the three cities on the eve of the

15 Among valuable studies which treat the war as a terminal date, see L. R. Berlanstein, *The working people of Paris 1871–1914* (Baltimore, 1984). Treating 1918 as the beginning of another tale may have more justification in the case of Berlin. Still, the prior wartime experience is hardly mentioned in B. Grzywalz's otherwise excellent *Arbeit und Bevölkerung im Berlin der Weimarer Zeit* (Berlin, 1988). One East German study (not surprisingly) chose 1917 as the great divide, but its teleology replaced reasoned argument: Kommission zur Erforschung der Geschichte der örtlichen Arbeiterbewegung, *Geschichte der revolutionären Berliner Arbeiterbewegung.* Vol. I: *Von den Anfängen bis 1917;* Vol. II: *Von 1917 bis 1945* (Berlin, 1987).

16 See H.-J. Bieber, *Gewerkschaften in Krieg und Revolution. Arbeiterbewegung, Industrie, Staat und Militär in Deutschland, 1914–1920* (Hamburg, 1981); D. H. Müller, *Gewerkschaftliche Versammlungsdemokratie und Arbeiterdelegierte vor 1918* (Berlin, 1985); J. Bush, *Behind the lines: East End labour 1914–1919* (London, 1984); D. Thom, 'Free from chains? The image of women's labour in London, 1900–1920', in G. D. Feldman and Stedman Jones (eds.), *Metropolis London*, pp. 85–99.

17 An otherwise excellent book by Norma Evenson, *Paris: a century of change, 1878–1978* (New Haven, 1979) refers to the Second World War but not the Great War.

war, we discuss in part 2 the social relations of sacrifice: first, with respect to military mobilization and casualties; and secondly, in terms of wartime caricatures and invective on profiteering.

We then turn to the social history of material life in Paris, London, and Berlin. We trace the history of the social relations of work, wages, and consumption, attending both to quantitative evidence and to the perceptions contemporaries formed of their material condition in wartime. Finally, we describe public health policies and mortality trends among civilians, as a summary measure of the material problems evident in parts 3 to 5. In effect, in this, the first of two volumes, we try to sketch the material constraints operating on these three cities' wartime social and economic history. In the second volume, we describe the ways groups of city-dwellers adapted to wartime conditions within families, quartiers, and social movements.[18]

Citizenship, adaptation, and well-being in wartime

Comparative urban history requires an analytical framework which can identify both convergences and divergences in the experiences of metropolitan populations. The organizing approach of this project is based upon an interpretation of the nature and determinants of adaptation and well-being in wartime cities.

Entitlements, capabilities, and functionings

One of our central arguments is that the nature of citizenship helped determine the efficacy of the war effort of the Allies and limited the efficacy of the war effort of Germany. This, we argue, was visible on the metropolitan level, and operated through the prior existence of what Amartya Sen has called a system of entitlements, a legal and moral framework upon which distributive networks rest.[19] In Paris and London the entitlements of citizenship helped preserve communities at war by enforcing a balance of distribution of necessary goods and services as between civilian and military claimants. In Berlin, a different order of priorities existed. The military came first, and the economy created to service it completely distorted the delicate economic system

[18] We benefited from the participation in our *jours de travail* of many colleagues who offered comments and criticisms on this and other analytical points. Among them are: Christof Conrad, Belinda Davis, Susan Pedersen, Alistair Reid, David Feldman, Cathy Merridale, Antoine Prost, Joanna Bourke, Lara Marks, Libby Schweber, Deborah Thom, Richard Wall, Nick Stargardt, Gareth Stedman Jones, Christian Topolov, Joël Michel, Patrick Fridenson, Françoise Thébaud, Sigrid Stöckel, Dirk Müller, Wolfgang Ernst, Niall Ferguson, Tyler Stovall.

[19] Amartya Sen, *Poverty and famines* (Oxford, 1981).

at home. Our claim is that Allied adaptation and well-being reflected a more equitable and efficient distributive system than existed on the other side of the lines.

To demonstrate this point, we have followed Amartya Sen's innovative framework in departing from the well-established view that the standard of living is a measure of opulence. Instead of aggregating some measure of the value, in monetary or calorific terms, of a basket of consumables, Sen suggests a more fluid and complex approach to the issue of living standards. He urges us to see them in the form of what he terms 'capabilities and functions', of the freedom to be 'able to achieve various personal conditions – to be able to do this or that'.[20] Here health and sickness enter the equation. Once we admit the distinction 'between being "well off" and being "well"', then it follows that 'while well-being is related to being well off they are not the same and may possibly diverge a good deal'.[21]

This approach departs radically from aggregative and absolute measures of well-being. 'The standard of living', Sen holds, 'is not a standard of opulence, even though it is *inter alia* influenced by opulence. It must be directly a matter of the life one leads rather than of the resources and means one has to lead a life.'[22]

> I have . . . called the various living conditions we can or cannot achieve, our 'functionings', and our ability to achieve them, our 'capabilities'. The main point here is that the standard of living is really a matter of functionings and capabilities, and not a matter directly of opulence, commodities or utilities.[23]

Refining the concept further, Sen posits that 'A functioning is an achievement, whereas a capability is the ability to achieve', or in other words, an indication of 'what real opportunities you have regarding the life you may lead'.[24] As one sympathetic critic put it, 'the multidimensional set of available capabilities of a person to function is what the standard of living is about'.[25]

For our purposes, this approach has many advantages. It suggests that the notion of well-being in wartime may be approached fruitfully as a problem of determining capabilities and functionings. That is, we need to discover not one global measure of well-being, but rather to analyse how the war distorted the way in which ordinary people went about their normal lives.

In dealing with the metropolitan experience, we have tried to build

[20] A. Sen, 'The standard of living: lecture I, concepts and critiques', in G. Hawthorn (ed.), *The standard of living* (Cambridge, 1987), pp. 2–3.

[21] Sen, 'Standard of living. I', p. 15. [22] *Ibid.*, p. 16. [23] *Ibid.*

[24] A. Sen, 'The standard of living: lecture II, lives and capabilities', in G. Hawthorn (ed.), *The standard of living* (Cambridge, 1987), p. 36.

[25] John Muellbauer, 'Professor Sen on the standard of living', in Hawthorn (ed.), *The standard of living*, p. 41.

up a general sense of what Sen calls 'capabilities and functionings', consistent with but not identical to indices of real wages or purchasing power. We do not ignore material questions; on the contrary. But we describe clusters of characteristics of urban economic and social life, characteristics which cannot be aggregated into a global quantified indicator of well-being.

Sen cautions against equating the standard of living with the possession of any arbitrarily defined set of goods and services. Instead, he urges scholars to recognize 'the relevance of unaggregated characterisations of functionings and capabilities and of partial orderings of aggregated assessments'.[26] It is for this reason that we have not replicated earlier studies which have aimed at measuring in precise statistical terms the effect of the Allied blockade of Germany, or the response of British and French agriculture to the problem of civilian supply.[27] Such research has thrown light on national developments, but it has produced precisely the confusion of standards of living with aggregate indicators that Sen has urged us to avoid.

Our focus is different. We follow Sen in emphasizing issues of distribution, of fairness, and of injustice, all of which are integral parts of the sense contemporaries had of capabilities and functionings. Freedom for the privileged few is 'unfreedom' for the many. A black market may deliver the goods to those who know how to work it, but it diminishes the standard of living of the many by more than the items it purloins and distributes at exorbitant prices.

Our argument may be summarized as follows. With respect to work, to wages, and to consumption patterns, what Sen calls capabilities and functionings were compromised more in wartime Berlin, than in Paris and London. This contrast was primarily an outcome of different sets of social relations and different meanings of citizenship leading to a different order of priorities about the relative importance of civilian capabilities and functionings as against military needs. That contrast came into focus in the latter half of the war, with the arrival of Hindenburg and Ludendorff in commanding positions both within the armed forces and within German society as a whole in 1916, and at a time when new economic structures were constructed both domestically and internationally by the Allies.

What we have tried to do is to broaden the question of living standards, *à la Sen*, to emphasize the moral and political, rather than the exclusively economic, character of notions of well-being in wartime.

Sen, with Bernard Williams, distinguishes three ways we understand

[26] Sen, 'Standard of living. II', p. 38.

[27] See G. Hardach, *The First World War, 1914–1918. An economic history* (London, 1987); A. Offer, *The First World War. An agrarian Interpretation*; J. M. Winter, *The Great War and the British people*, ch. 7.

well-being. The first relates to what he terms 'agency achievement', or dedication to a cause beyond the personal level; the second to 'personal well-being'; the third, to 'economic well-being'. The standard of living, Williams holds, lies somewhere between the second and the third levels.[28]

The implications of this approach for our study are fundamental. For most of the war, the need to compromise this standard of living, or in other words, to accept sacrifice for the greater good, was a matter of overall consensus. In other words, well-being in wartime entailed all three meanings identified by Sen and Williams above. Most people wanted to win the war, and to dedicate themselves to that effort. Most families had men in uniform, and therefore had a personal interest in daily news as well as in the wider outcome. All were affected by material shortages and pressures. Standards of living therefore involved more than material matters; as long as millions of men were in uniform and at risk of mutilation or death, moral and political arguments came to the fore.[29]

The military dimension

Wartime urban (and indeed national) life was dominated by military mobilization and military losses. A central premise of this study is that urban history was marked at the most fundamental level by the call to arms, and by the attendant anxiety, felt by those who remained at home for 1,500 days, as to the safety and fate of loved ones in uniform. A history of the war period which does not privilege this level of experience is bound to remain superficial.

The horrendous casualties of 1914, followed by the seemingly endless extension of the lists of the wounded and the fallen in the subsequent four years, were fundamental components of the experience of war in Paris, London, and Berlin, as indeed in all other communities. The fear of hearing the knock at the door, or receiving the ritual or stylized letter or telegram, of seeing etched on the face of the mayor, priest, or other official or soldier, the news they had been sent to convey, these were among the most universal and profound experiences of the war, and they lie behind every page of this book.

All other social questions were measured, in part, by reference to the front and the harsh realities faced by the men at the front. Daily newspapers were vital lifelines of information; city-dwellers pored over them to find out something, some hint, about the way the war was going. This did not mean apathy with respect to the organization of

28 B. Williams, 'The standard of living: interests and capabilities', in Hawthorn (ed.), *The standard of living*, pp. 94ff.

29 Sen, 'Reply', in Hawthorn (ed.), *The standard of living*, p. 110.

social life; on the contrary. The shared hardships of the trenches demanded shared hardships at home. Affronts to this sense of justice within a community under siege took many forms. Profiteers were the most conspicuous, but hoarders, tradesmen, *restaurateurs*, coal merchants, farmers, bureaucrats, politicians, staff officers, women all came in for their share of abuse, some deserved, about the 'privileged' position they enjoyed. It mattered little how high death-rates due to disease or enemy bombardment might rise in these cities; their inhabitants still remained 'privileged' as long as the killing went on. The 'privilege' was staying out of the line of fire and therefore staying unmarked and unmaimed.

How civilians wore that badge of 'privilege' was an intensely important subject in wartime. Profiteers wore it brazenly; some came to resemble vultures feeding off the bodies of the dead. Others abused the privilege of relative safety by living conspicuously well. In contrast, the majority of people in these cities acknowledged their civilian status with an austere sense of where they were and where they were not.

Adaptation and the urban community

The two key elements of wartime adaptation followed from the call to arms. Populations had first to adapt to mass mobilization and then to absorb the shock of mass casualties. In doing so, they insisted time and again on the need to share scarce resources and risks. Almost everyone had someone close in the front lines: sons and fathers, uncles and brothers, lovers, friends, colleagues. What happened to them was a permanent uncertainty, one shared by millions of people, whatever their social status or wealth. In this sense, military mobilization and military losses created a sense of a community of those at risk of personal loss which, for a time, transcended – but did not eliminate – pre-war social divisions. The wartime community was one of shared hardships, first and foremost defined by the fate of the men at the front.[30]

There were other definitions of community which came into sharp relief in wartime. Some outsiders were easy to identify, for instance, foreign workers, such as German waiters in Paris, or British students in Berlin. Others presented more difficult choices. If the Kaiser proclaimed in 1914 that now he saw only Germans, it was still true that some were more German than others. Ethnic and national identities within empires were not erased by war, as the abundant evidence of anti-Semitic or

[30] On French mobilization, see Jean-Jacques Becker, *1914. Comment les Français sont entrés dans la guerre* (Paris, 1977); on Britain, see J. M. Winter, *The Great War and the British people*, ch. 2, and P. Simkins, *Kitchener's army: The raising of the New Armies* (London, 1988).

anti-Polish sentiment in Germany and anti-Irish sentiment in Britain suggests.[31]

In addition to problems of ethnicity, there were additional problems related to what may be described as 'marginalized' populations. These were men, women, and children who constituted problem groups, often living at public expense or through philanthropic assistance. They were the elderly, the criminal, the abandoned children, the 'outcasts' of metropolitan Paris, London, and Berlin.

In wartime these groups were a clear charge on the community, in part because they contributed little if anything directly to waging war. Their plight is one of the central features of wartime social history, reflecting the social selection implicit in wartime adaptation to shortages and difficult material conditions. The cry 'fair shares for all' meant fair shares for all entitled to a share. It excluded as well as included, and entailed from the outset a distinction between those at the heart of the community – the soldiers – and those at the margins. Most city-dwellers stood between the two.

In all three cities, public authorities were committed to maintaining the material well-being of the population at home as part of the waging of war. The essential questions were how to do so, and with what degree of necessary deprivation, given the scarcity of goods and services available for home consumption.

Again, the realities of military life dominated this question, as they did all others. There was a clear consensus that living standards for civilians mattered less than provisions and weapons for the men at the front. But to say they mattered less does not mean they were unimportant, or that they could be lowered by fiat. Changes in levels of provisions and services occurred in all three cities, and such shifts in entitlements were accompanied by substantial discussion, debate, and at times, protest. Much of this book will present these quarrels about necessary levels of reduction of what were taken to be 'normal' standards of living in wartime.

Let us return for a moment to the issues raised by Sen and Williams about different meanings of the notion of well-being (see above, pp. 11–13). In many wartime debates, two competing definitions of well-being surfaced. The first may be referred to as well-being on the national level. That entailed defining the conditions of existence of the population in terms of a *national objective*. Here the well-being of the community was measured over time by progress towards victory or (from 1917) towards peace.

[31] This subject has been well researched for London. On the general subject of aliens in wartime, see P. Panayi, *The enemy in our midst. Germans in Britain during the First World War* (Oxford, 1991). The literature on the Irish is vast. For references see Bourke, *Working-class cultures*, ch. 3.

At the same time, well-being was measured in terms of what may be described as *particular objectives*, or the social destinations and personal aspirations of groups and individuals. These were notions of where an individual wanted to wind up after a period of time, a vision, however dimly seen, of a personal or collective future. These hopes and plans had to change during the war, but they were never completely subsumed by it.

To win the war, most people were prepared to undergo shortages, and in Berlin, severe deprivation, but no one completely gave up the notions of well-being grounded in social identities or aspirations. The key to providing a usable and human measure of adaptation and well-being in wartime is to set alongside the national destinations of victory or peace, the complex of individual or group destinations and frustrations in wartime, and then to plot their parallel or conflicting development over time.[32]

That development was the subject of negotiation and renegotiation, at times through official channels, at times on the streets. In each encounter, the clash between national well-being (victory or peace) and the well-being of an individual or a group was reiterated or redefined. The link between the general and the particular, the national and the local, was the popular identification of the community with the nation, and the location of the rhythms of local life within what was understood as a 'national' culture. The pre-1914 history of this process of identification of the particular with the general, of community with nation, is relatively well known.[33] Once that identification was made, then personal or group sacrifices and commitments were placed within the framework of the defence of the larger community of which the individual or collective formed a part.

Strategies of adaptation in wartime involved permutations of identities and loyalties, which could shift radically if one key element changed. For example, the material, and (in many cases) the emotional, support a married woman aged thirty with children enjoyed before the

[32] The stimulating suggestions of Avner Offer and Barry Supple have been very helpful on this point.

[33] On France, see M. Ozouf, *L'école, l'Eglise et la République: 1871–1914* (Paris, 1982); J. Ozouf and F. Furet, *Reading and writing* (Cambridge, 1982); A. Prost, *Histoire de l'enseignement en France (1800–1967)* (Paris, 1975); E. Weber, *Peasants into Frenchmen: the modernization of rural France, 1870–1914* (London, 1979); on Britain, the role of the monarchy in providing this cultural linkage is discussed in R. McKibbin, *The ideologies of class: social relations in Britain 1880–1950* (Oxford, 1990); see the wide-ranging discussion in R. Samuel (ed.), *Patriotism. The making and unmaking of British national identity* (3 vols., London, 1989); on Germany, see the seminal article of J. P. Nettl, 'The German Social Democratic party as a political model', *Past & Present* (April, 1965). The literature on the *Bildungsbürgertum* raises many of the same issues in a middle-class context.

war vanished with news of the death in action of her husband. The recurrence of this personal dimension of the overall catastrophe of the war makes the term 'well-being' of limited value in this study. In wartime, well-being was more easily defined by its absence: a loss of status or provision frequently left deeper traces in popular memory than a gain. The concept of 'distress' may be taken as a rough antonym for 'well-being', and the history of distress in wartime, its character and the attempts at its alleviation, are essential parts of this study.

Even without loss of life, or without the radical changes in family life attendant on the news that a loved-one was coming home, but severely wounded, the very fabric of daily life was repeatedly torn by changes in the material conditions most people had taken for granted in the pre-war period. Each change in diet or heating or housing, for example, presented potential and actual conflicts with the clear, though at times troubled, consensus (until late 1916) about the need to stay the course and see the war through. When hardship had to be endured, it would be accepted if and only if it were seen to be necessary and universal.

The price civilians believed they could and should pay for victory or peace was not limitless. After the failure of the Schlieffen plan in 1914, and the supersession of the war of annihilation by a war of attrition, it made virtually no sense to say that the war had to be won 'no matter what the cost'. The phrase was used time and again, but it was hollow, a mere rhetorical flourish. Everyone knew that the costs did matter. In the army, this was patently obvious. Military units ran out of men; soldiers ran out of ammunition, food, or hope. On the home front, the costs mattered too. Whatever the ration, sometimes no potatoes arrived in Berlin. Strikes showed that the cost did matter, and that at least two identities: national (leading to the abrogation of the right to strike and the suspension of other privileges won over generations) and occupational (tending towards industrial action) coexisted in the minds and behaviour of ordinary people in wartime. At times industrial conflict showed that the notion of 'patriotism' itself was a contested term: both sides used the accusation of 'anti-patriotism' to attack the other. Workers downed tools over ill-treatment or injustices suffered by fellow workers; what was unpatriotic, from their point of view, was not their militancy but rather employers' violations of wartime codes of fairness and decency. Here class-consciousness and patriotism were entirely compatible.[34] Other instances of multiple loyalties producing diametrically different outcomes abound, and support the view that the estimation of costs in wartime cities entailed political and social decisions about how different strata of the population ought to contribute to winning the war. This study tells part of that story.

[34] I am grateful to Joanna Bourke for her comments on this point.

In all three cities, adaptation entailed giving up goods and services which had formed part of the 'normal' basket of consumables of urban domestic life. But it is important to note the subjective character of definitions of normality, and the distance between peacetime conditions and wartime normality.

The subjective dimension of the problem is essential in part because well-being involves affective issues that no historian should reduce to mathematical form; there can be no machines to measure spring in this study. But the subjective is also critical since it raises the fact that much of the sense of well-being in communities in wartime was politically and culturally determined.

Propaganda presented well-being as the diametrical opposite of subjugation to the enemy. Again, the national story here is better known than the urban one.[35] Well-being in Paris was not being in Lille subject to the German army; well-being in London was not having German 'atrocities' not in Belgium but on your doorstep, or in your home.[36]

An important political source of such 'well-being' in wartime was the provision of news and information.[37] State control of information meant control of uncertainty. Confusion or lies could lead to insecurity or panic; thus propaganda and news-reporting contributed directly to popular well-being by giving people the sense that they knew what was going on. This was a risky strategy. 'Selective' reporting could rebound, and lead to deep disillusionment, for example, when the truth of military failure finally hit the Berlin population in the summer of 1918. But even on the other side of the line, well-being was a highly volatile concept, given the unknown survival chances of millions of men in uniform.

35 See M. Sanders and P. Taylor, *British propaganda during the First World War 1914–1918* (London, 1982); H.G. Marquis, 'Words as weapons: propaganda in Britain and Germany during the First World War', *Journal of Contemporary History*, 13, 3 (1978); Becker, *The Great War and the French people*, pt 1. On posters in wartime, see J. M. Winter, 'Nationalism, the visual arts and the myth of war enthusiasm', *History of European Ideas* (1992), and Peter Paret, B. Irwin Lewis, and Paul Paret (eds.), *Persuasive images. Posters of war and revolution* (Princeton, 1992). An unusual and original angle on the history of wartime propaganda governs Stéphane Audoin-Rouzeau's *La guerre des enfants, 1914–1918* (Paris, 1993).

36 J.M. Read, *Atrocity propaganda* (London, 1958).

37 See K. Koszyk, *Deutsche Pressepolitik im Ersten Weltkrieg* (Hamburg, 1978); C. Bellanger *et al.* (eds.), *Histoire générale de la presse française*, vol. V (Paris, 1976); N. Hiley, 'British propaganda and the First World War', in Jean-Jacques Becker, Jay M. Winter, Gerd Krumeich, Annette Becker, and Stéphane Audoin-Rouzeau (eds.), *Guerre et cultures 1914–1918* (Paris, 1994). For a local study of the French press, see R.F. Collins, 'Newspapers of the French left in Provence and Bas-Languedoc during the First World War', PhD thesis, University of Cambridge, 1990, and the same author's 'The development of censorship in World War I France', *Journalism Monographs*, no. 131 (Columbia, S.C., 1992).

A third political component of well-being arose out of pre-war traditions and norms. What people decided they could not do without was neither fixed nor immutable. Such notions could be changed, and were changed, rarely by fiat, more often after intense debate, or by common consent. But there were limits, related to vague notions of 'essential' features of normality, such as an unrationed bread supply or the absence of industrial conscription in London. Both bread rationing and industrial conscription occurred in France, without stirring up the same uproar that threatened their introduction in Britain. At the beginning of the war, the price of bread in Paris was controlled; this hurt the bakers, but defended the well-being of the population as a whole. In London, the free market lasted longer. Striking differences also appeared with respect to military conscription, which operated smoothly in Germany and France, but was revolutionary in Britain.[38] Conscription is but one instance of the way profound moral issues were involved in these complex discussions of the need to depart from 'normal' behaviour in order to win the war.

The urban history of adaptation in wartime is full of instances of the interplay of subjective and objective hardships. To understand such issues, traditional measures of standards of living must be scrutinized, but reliable real wage figures, even if they could be produced, will not in and of themselves suffice as explanatory variables of demographic and other social trends, or more generally, as explanations of the commitment of the population of the three cities to see the war through to victory.[39] A more fruitful approach is to study both quantitative evidence and the wartime reordering of definitions of well-being – some material, some not – of communities and social formations, clustered along class, ethnic, gender, age, or military lines. Essentially we focus on the ways urban populations, whose identities cut across these groups and existed as permutations of them, defined their aspirations and hopes in wartime, their own sense of what Sen calls capabilities and functionings, and how such notions changed over time.

One of the ways in which the moral ambiguities of urban life in wartime were expressed was through caricature. Dailies and weeklies in these three cities printed hundreds of images of the 'profiteer'. By setting up simple polarities of soldier versus civilian, consumer versus merchant or manufacturer, and (at times) men versus supposedly protected or coddled women, these images disclose a major public

[38] See John Horne, *Labour at war: France and Britain 1914–1918* (Oxford, 1991); R. J. Q. Adams and P. Poirier, *The conscription controversy in Great Britain, 1900–1918* (London, 1987); Fridenson (ed.), *The French home front*.

[39] These findings go beyond the approach and data presented in J. M. Winter, *The Great War and the British people*, ch. 7.

debate about sacrifice and well-being in wartime cities.[40] In effect negotiation was conducted in public about what was appropriate behaviour or acceptable levels of consumption in cities where shortages were endemic and (more importantly) where casualty lists grew day after day.

The imagery of 'the profiteer' in wartime journals cannot be equated with popular attitudes. Some of it was clearly self-seeking, and artists – as well as the proprietors and editors who employed them – sought to lead the way; other images were blatantly hypocritical. But there can be little doubt that the press, so visible in metropolitan centres, brought these themes of fairness and inequity to the attention of a mass reading public throughout the war. Who was part of the 'community at war' was a question embedded in the newspapers men and women read day after day. How contemporaries saw these 'communities' – as both imagined and experienced entities – is therefore one of the central themes of this study.

Convergences and divergences

By narrowing the field of analysis to cities, and within cities to communities and *quartiers*, it is possible to trace with some precision the vicissitudes of civilian life and to compare the ways urban administrations and populations adapted to war and its severe demands. We hope thereby to meet the objections of some critics that the analysis of aggregate statistics and experience obscures contradictory evidence of the impact of the war on civilian life.[41] By moving to the urban level, and within that, to the district and (when possible) the street and family level, we have been able to test more completely than ever before the hypothesis that on the Allied side of the line the well-being of the population, defined in terms of capabilities and functionings, was more successfully defended than in Germany. This exercise in urban history

[40] For earlier discussions of the British debate on 'profiteering' see Jay M. Winter, *Socialism and the challenge of war* (London, 1974); B. Waites, *A class society at war. England 1914–1918* (Leamington Spa, 1987); and for a defence, see J. S. Boswell and B. R. Johns, 'Patriots or profiteers? British businessmen and the First World War', *Journal of European Economic History* (1982). J. Kocka's *Facing total war: German society, 1914–1918* (Leamington Spa, 1984) and Barrington Moore's *Injustice. The social bases of obedience and revolt* (London, 1978) point to the German debate. The *locus classicus* for Paris is Robert, 'Ouvriers et mouvement ouvrier'. See also John Horne, '"L'impôt du sang": Republican rhetoric and industrial warfare in France, 1914–1918', *Social History* (1989), pp. 201–23, and, more generally, his *Labour at war: France and Britain 1914–1918* (Oxford, 1991).

[41] L. Bryder, 'The First World War: healthy or hungry?', *History Workshop Journal* (1987), pp. 141–57; and the reply of J. M. Winter, 'Public health and the political economy of war', *History Workshop Journal* (1988), pp. 163–73. The research on Paris, London, and Berlin was conducted after this exchange. The results, discussed in chapter 16, further undermine the position Bryder advances in her 1987 article.

should, therefore, add an important element to the debate over the impact of war on civilian populations, and the components of victory and defeat in the 1914–18 war.[42]

No one would argue for a moment that the war was won or lost solely on the home front. We hold instead that a necessary, though not sufficient, condition of Allied victory was the maintenance of the set of capabilities and functionings of their civilian populations, and the popular recognition that this in fact had been the case. Equally, a necessary, though far from sufficient, explanation of German defeat was the failure of the German authorities to distribute goods and services effectively as between civilian and military claimants, and popular recognition of this failure.

Evidence of the contrast between the two sides in this domain was visible in the mid-years of the war, and was especially marked from early 1917. Consequently, we show the convergence of much of the economic and social history of the three cities in the early years of the war, and the divergence of their experience in the later years of the conflict. A rough divide between 1914–16 and 1917–19 is appropriate in some respects, particularly in demographic history. A more fluid transition from an early phase in 1914–15, a mid-war phase in 1915–17, and a late phase in 1918–19 is a better guide to developments in other facets of urban economic and social affairs. But however we define it chronologically, by the later years of the war the tensions produced by staggering casualty lists and material deprivation grew at an alarming pace, coinciding with the failure of the German High Command to achieve victory in the series of desperate gambles they risked in 1917–18 on the Western front and in the naval war. The population of Berlin had to swallow both bitter pills – the failure of the March 1918 offensive and the failure of the domestic economy to provide even a modicum of the necessities of life – at the same time, in the summer of 1918. Then the majority of the population came to see that the war could not be won, and that further sacrifice could have no justification.

This book tells part of the story of how this came about. It also tells of some of the ways such dire circumstances were avoided in the centres of the Allied war effort. This is not to say that civilians in Paris and London were insulated from the pressures so visible in Berlin in the last phase of the war. It is rather to argue that on the home front those pressures were less intense and the means of coping with them were more successful. Had public authorities in London or Paris faced some of the material, administrative, and political constraints of their Berlin colleagues, they would probably have faced the same crisis.

42 For earlier statements of this position, see J. M. Winter, *The Great War*; and J. M. Winter, 'Some paradoxes of the Great War', in R. M. Wall and J. M. Winter (eds.), *The upheaval of war. Family, work, and welfare in Europe 1914–1918* (Cambridge, 1987).

The fact that they did not have to cope with the same dilemmas suggests that it would be unwise to separate the urban history of the war from the national and international framework which governed it. Urban history has its own rhythms and character, but its decisive features in wartime were a function of decisions taken elsewhere.[43] Consequently, responsibility for the crisis of Berlin in 1917 to 1919 and for the successful containment of the pressures of war in Paris and London lay where responsibility for the entire war lay: in the structures of authority and government, both military and civilian, that is, in the High Commands and in the Cabinets which formally controlled them. In addition, different material outcomes arose from different sets of relations between central and municipal authorities in the three cases.

Ultimately, the contrasts between Paris and London on the one hand, and Berlin on the other, provide in miniature a glimpse of the wider political and economic tests of the war. Those tests exposed different approaches to citizenship, as understood in terms of the entitlements of people to a set of capabilities and functionings necessary for them to go about their daily lives. The Wilhelmine regime failed that test; the Allies on balance passed it.

It is clear that final credit or blame for levels of civilian well-being rested with the Cabinets and General Staffs which ran the war. But at the municipal level the question of agency, of administrative and political responsibility, is necessarily a difficult one. We cannot point a finger at an individual or group and say that he or they made a critical mistake or corrected one just in the nick of time. Errors were indeed made, but the differences between and among these three cities' wartime histories arose more out of structures than out of individual flair or initiative. Those structures were administrative, economic, and (broadly speaking) cultural. In effect, the links that mattered most were those between local authorities and higher authorities on the regional, national, or military levels. In Berlin this relationship was hopelessly fettered by overelaboration producing a system of dizzying complexity. Civil servants in Berlin frequently did the best they could, but no one could make sense of all the intricacies of an administrative network which, by the final phase of the war, came to resemble a maze. In Paris and London, new agencies proliferated too, but they rarely produced the rampant confusion and conflict which became endemic in Berlin as the war dragged on. Why was this so?

Two approaches to this problem may be distinguished. The first emphasizes aggregate wealth and command of imperial supplies. From this point of view, the greater the shortages, the greater the pressure on an already overextended administrative system. After 1915 the Allied

[43] I am grateful for comments on this point by Gareth Stedman Jones.

capitals rarely faced critical material constraints. When they did, as in the case of coal, administrators on national and inter-Allied levels reacted, and the national and international reserves of the Allies were brought into the equation. In this framework, we can see on the local level what such imperial abundance meant for the well-being of civilians in London and in Paris, and what the absence of such reserves meant for Berliners.

The second approach follows recent developments in economic theory in casting doubt on the utility of aggregate measurements. With Sen (as noted above, on pp. 10–11), we approach such crises by defining living standards not through an additive exercise of weights assigned to a basket of consumables, but through an estimation of the way social and political systems provide a cluster of capabilities and functionings which enable people to go about their daily lives. The German system differed radically from that in place in Britain and France in 1914, and even more so, after 1916, with the ascendancy of Hindenburg and Ludendorff to power. Different approaches to the distribution of goods and resources as between military and civilian claimants, he holds, produced different material outcomes for the population as a whole.

This book attempts to show at the urban level the complex interplay between supply and distribution in wartime. Both are interpreted here as facets of the problem of civilian well-being. Material questions dominate this book, but they are discussed always in the context of the social and political system, that is, the system of citizenship, operative at the time.

It is futile to ignore the extent to which citizenship reflects different notions of what has been called *sentiment national*.[44] Here is the point at which the well-being of the individual and the well-being of the collective, in terms of victory or defeat, come together. While economic theory can take us some of the way in understanding the parameters of collective life in wartime, we must not forget what the war was about: a struggle over national destinies.

Questions of fairness and inequality are also important in evaluating the behaviour of administrators and politicians within the national struggle. In Paris and London local and national leaders were able to provide a more equitable distribution of available goods and services than was the case in Berlin, and thereby to avoid for much of the war the damaging atmosphere of suspicion and rancour which poisoned social life in the German capital in the last phase of the conflict. Justice mattered, and in their failure to ensure at least the appearance of fair shares for all, civil authorities lost the trust of the urban population. By

[44] On the notion, see Stéphane Audoin-Rouzeau, *Men at war. National sentiment and trench journalism in France, 1914–1918*, trans. H. MacPhail (Oxford, 1992).

the summer of 1918, Berlin society had fractured into a thousand parts, each trying to find enough food or fuel to survive, each anxiously awaiting news from the front. When the bad news sank in that hopes of victory had vanished, there was nothing left to prop up the regime. It had lost its legitimacy by its failure literally to deliver the goods.

That this contrast can be specified in a number of ways at the metropolitan level is an important part of the story of victory and defeat in the Great War, a story that has never been told before from this point of view. In the first volume of this study we try to describe within a comparative framework the material conditions of urban life. In the second volume, we attend to the ways in which city-dwellers responded to war within their families, their neighbourhoods, and their political and social organizations. This distinction between the two parts of this study should not be taken too far. There is much in volume I about the history of family life and the attempts of rank-and-file members of social movements to address the burning questions of the day. Similarly, in volume II, the material conditions and hardships sketched in volume I will never be marginal to the story of the ways metropolitan populations shaped their own responses to the war.

Together, these two volumes tell a story of harsh realities to which people – sometimes the same people – responded in idealistic and selfish ways. But above all, it is a study of ordinary people, placed under pressures most of us have fortunately never had to face. Brutalization was part of the experience of war.[45] But it is important to remember that most people endured the war, despite the hardships and losses, with their decency, their common humanity intact. Their achievement is worth remembering, when we contemplate the cruel landscape of the history of the Great War.

[45] See George L. Mosse, *Fallen soldiers* (Oxford and New York, 1990).

2
Paris, London, Berlin on the eve of the war

Jean-Louis Robert

The object of this comparison of the three capital cities on the eve of the war is not to present a vast array of the available data on them. To do so would require a book in itself. Instead we offer some reflections which we hope will help to situate the historical issues governing this comparative study. Our aim is to identify the constituent elements of well-being (or ill-being) in the lives of the millions of inhabitants of these metropolitan centres on the eve of the war, and thereby to prepare the ground for later discussions of their adaptive capacity in wartime. In this area, methodological problems abound. Who could say in 1914 whether the rich or the poor were more adaptable, or better suited to face the challenge of war?

Population

Demographic growth

The definition of city limits is a difficult matter in each of the three cases in question. For purposes of comparison, we refer in each case to two urban entities. First there is the city core, defined in 1864 for Paris as the twenty arrondissements; for Berlin, as the 'old Berlin' of urban inner districts, prior to 1920; and in London from 1889, as the twenty-eight metropolitan boroughs. Secondly, there was a larger administrative entity, incorporating the urban core, but extending beyond it. This larger area had its own administrative identity: the Department of the Seine, for Paris; what became 'Great Berlin' in 1920; and 'Greater London'. The rudimentary demographic profile which follows here refers to the larger regions (see figs. 2.1 to 2.3).[1]

[1] For aggregate figures, the sources are: *Census of England and Wales, 1911*; *Recensement de la population de la France, 1911*; *Statistik der Stadt Berlin*, vol. 32. For birth-rates and death-rates, the sources are: for London, London County Council, *London Statistics*; *Registrar-General's Annual Reports for England and Wales*; for Paris, *Annuaire statistique de la ville de Paris et du Département de la Seine*; for Berlin, *Gross-Berlin Statistische Monatsberichte*, 1914–18.

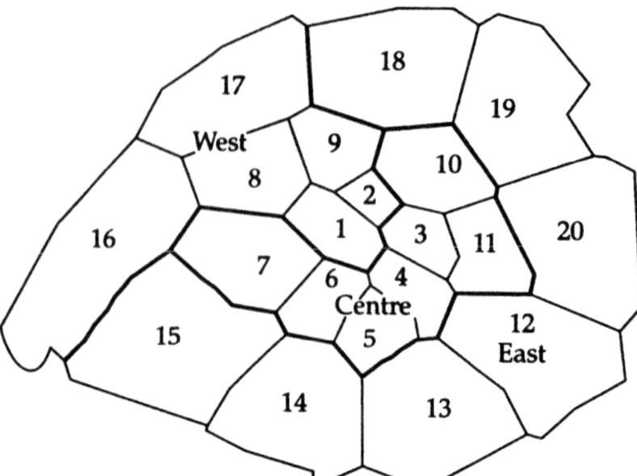

Fig. 2.1 Paris: arrondissements. Source: J.-L. Robert and J. M. Winter, 'Un aspect ignoré'.

Berlin: dynamism and late development

Berlin in 1914 was the least populous of the three urban centres. The German capital had a population of under 4 million. Over 4 million people lived in Paris and its suburbs, and over 7 million in Greater London.

Berliners constituted a smaller part of the overall population of Germany than did the population of either of the other two cities within their national populations. About 6 per cent of the German population lived in the capital, compared to 10 per cent in Paris and 16 per cent in London. National totals (and local proportions concentrated in capital cities) may be misleading; London was the centre of an imperial network of much larger numbers, stretching around the world, whereas Berlin was a provincial city, the capital of Prussia, as much as the capital of the newly established German empire. But the comparison distinguishes national experiences: Great Britain as a long-united kingdom with dependencies around the world, as opposed to Germany, recently united and with a small colonial periphery in the non-European world.

It would be an error, though, to relegate Berlin to the status of a minor European capital, a late developer among metropolitan centres. From the 1870s, Berlin's growth trajectory was much more robust than that of Paris or London. Over five decades, the population of Berlin quadrupled. Growth in Paris and London was about half as rapid in this period. Whereas in 1871 Berlin's population was half that of Paris, by 1914 the two cities were virtually the same size. This growth spurt, unprecedented in European urban history, was not unique to Berlin; a similar trajectory marked the expansion of other German cities in this period. In effect, Berlin's growth was a reflection of the broader urban and industrial transformation of the German economy in the later nine-

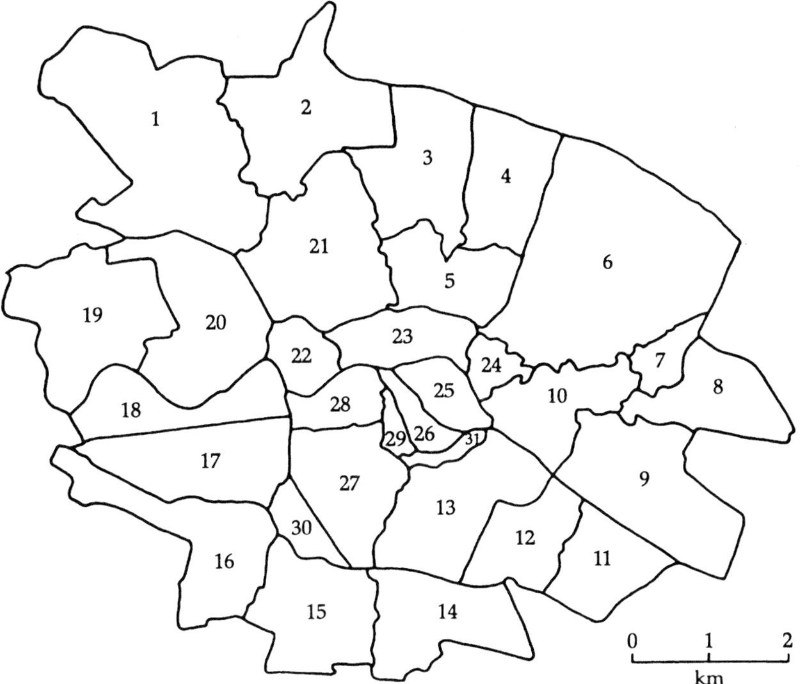

Fig. 2.2 Old Berlin and its districts in 1910.
Key: 1 Wedding 2 Gesundbrunnen 3 Rosenthaler Vorstadt north-west 4 Rosenthaler Vorstadt north-east 5 Rosenthaler Vorstadt south-east 6 Königsviertel north 7 Königsviertel south 8 Stralauer Viertel north-east 9 Stralauer Viertel south-east 10 Stralauer Viertel west 11 Luisenstadt south-east 12 Luisenstadt west 13 Luisenstadt diesseits des Kanals 14 Tempelhofer Vorstadt east 15 Tempelhofer Vorstadt west 16 Schöneberger Vorstadt 17 Untere Friedrichvorstadt 18 Tiergarten Vorstadt 19 Moabit west 20 Moabit east 21 Oranienburger Vorstadt 22 Friedrich-Wilhelm-stadt 23 Spandauer Viertel 24 Königsviertel south-west 25 Berlin 26 Kölln 27 Friedrichstadt 28 Dorotheenstadt 29 Friedrichswerder 30 Obere-Friedrich-vorstadt 31 Neukölln.
Source: Schwippe, 'Zum Prozess der sozialräumlichen innerstädtischen Differenzierung', p. 257.

teenth century.[2] On the eve of the war, Berlin's population represented only 12 per cent of the total German population living in cities of more than 5,000 inhabitants. The growth of Berlin in this period was therefore exceptional among European capitals, but not within Germany itself. Demographic growth was not concentrated in the capital, which in 1914

[2] Jürgen Reulecke and Gerhard Huck, 'Urban history research in Germany: its development and present condition', *Urban History Yearbook* (1981), pp. 39–54; Horst Matzerath, *Urbanisierung in Preussen, 1815–1914* (Berlin, 1985).

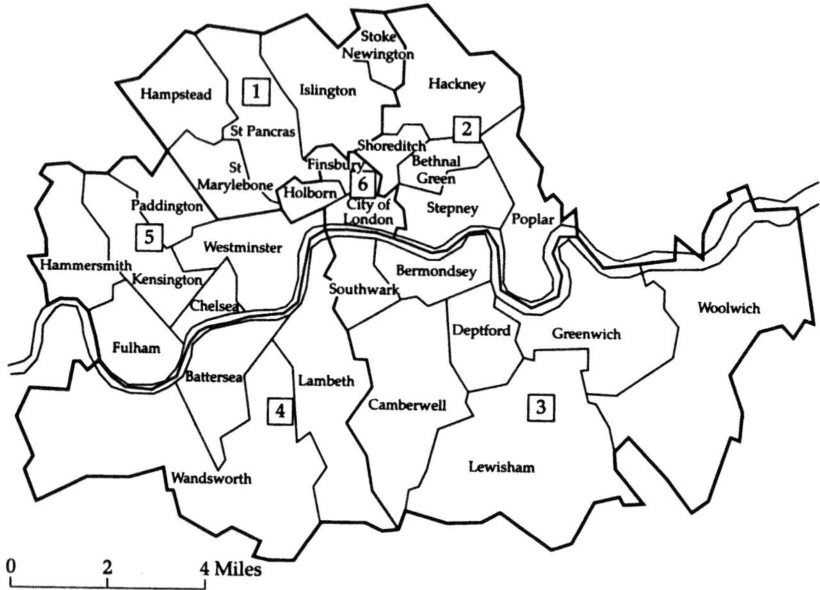

Fig. 2.3 London: boroughs and districts.
Key: Fig. 1 North London 2 East London 3 South-east London 4 South-west London 5 West London 6 Central London

remained a provincial city at the heart of one of the most powerful nations in the world.

London: metropolitan retardation

The most striking demographic feature of London is its sheer size. With 7 million inhabitants, London was a city which dwarfed even Paris and Berlin. The spectacular dimensions of the British capital reflected early industrialization, making Britain the most highly urbanized nation in the world. In 1914, perhaps 70 per cent of the population of England and Wales lived in towns of 5,000 or more inhabitants.[3]

London's massive proportions also mirrored British political power: both imperial, unequalled in the pre-war period, as well as domestic, through the location within the metropolis of the instruments of power and administration of a relatively stable and long-centralized state. With 16 per cent of the total population of England and Wales concentrated within its boundaries, Greater London was an agglomeration of quite exceptional size in this period. Its immense size gave London its specificity, distinguishing its urban history from that of Paris and Berlin.

By the early twentieth century, there were indications that London's period of rapid demographic growth was coming to an end. London's

[3] Paul Bairoch, *De Jéricho à Mexico. Villes et économie dans l'histoire* (Paris, 1985), p. 288.

expansion was certainly inferior to that of Berlin, though this difference was primarily a reflection of the uneven pace of development. More revealing is the comparison between the growth of London and Paris, since the latter was also at the heart of a long-established and centralized state. Taken as a whole, London's nineteenth-century growth was greater than that of Paris, though after 1871 the two cities' growth paths tended to converge. Decadal rates of growth diminished for London from 23 per cent in the period 1871 to 1881, to 18 per cent for 1881 to 1891, to 17 per cent for 1891 to 1901, and to 10 per cent for 1901 to 1911. This demographic retardation is characteristic of large cities, whose pattern of development, as Robson noted, varied from that of smaller ones.[4] In any case, it is clear that Berlin and London represented strikingly divergent histories of urban growth.

Paris: metropolis within the 'désert français'

At first sight, Paris seems to be an intermediate case between London and Berlin. Fully 10 per cent of the national population of France lived in Paris, evenly situated between London (16 per cent) and Berlin (6 per cent). If on the eve of the war Paris resembled Berlin in terms of total population, the French capital also paralleled London in terms of relatively slow rates of growth. The specificity of Paris lay elsewhere. We must place its demographic history in the context, first, of feeble rates of national population growth, much lower in France than in Britain or Germany; and secondly, in the context of slower national rates of urban growth in France. Between 1850 and 1914, the French urban growth rate was 1.3 per cent per year; that of Britain 1.9 per cent, and of Germany, fully 3 per cent.[5] France was a country without a dynamic rate of aggregate or urban growth, reflecting both the character of her industrialization and the enduring strength of her agrarian population. Herein lies the special character of Paris as the dominant element in the urban sector, constituting 30 per cent of the French population living in cities of more than 5,000 people. In contrast, London's population was 23 per cent, and Berlin's 12 per cent, of this national urban population.

No other French city resembled Paris in this period. The Paris region represented an island of growth in a nation with an ageing population, and Paris's robustness added to its symbolic status both within and outside France. During the pre-war period, the so-called 'Belle Epoque', there was some evidence of an upsurge of growth in the capital, insufficient to reach Berlin levels, but spreading metropolitan Paris through a suburban belt until then relatively undeveloped.[6]

[4] B. T. Robson, *Urban growth: an approach* (London, 1973).

[5] J. L. Pinol, *Le monde des villes au XIXe siècle* (Paris, 1991), p. 19.

[6] A. Faure, *Les premiers banlieusards. Aux origines des banlieues de Paris, 1860–1940* (Paris, 1991).

The pre-1914 development of the three cities provided inhabitants of each with grounds for pride. For Berliners, theirs was the 'Chicago' of the European continent, bursting with energy and newcomers.[7] Londoners boasted of living in the greatest European city, perhaps (in a sense) the capital of the world. Parisians felt that theirs was a unique city, certainly without rival in their own country. How many inhabitants shared in such collective satisfaction is a matter for speculation alone.

Urban inhabitants

The demographic structures of the three capital areas reflect different patterns of growth to which we will refer below. Henceforth we concentrate on the population of the inner cities, the core of these urban conglomerates, and not on their periphery. In this way we can identify an urban typology appropriate to each city.

London, city of children

One of the most striking characteristics of London is the proportion of its population of young people, fully 38 per cent under the age of twenty in 1911. This is surprising, given our earlier claim of a slow-down in London's rates of demographic growth in the later nineteenth century. The paradox is resolved in part by noting that by the eve of war in 1914 London had become a relatively minor centre of in-migration. Only 32 per cent of London's population was born outside the Greater London area, compared to over 60 per cent in both Paris and Berlin. This *relative* absence of newcomers and preponderance of families drawn from within London itself contributed to the relative stability of London's social structure. To be a Londoner in the late nineteenth century meant, for most, to be born there and to have one's sense of identity emerge from a particular urban environment, the rhythms of which were perhaps more settled than those of an immigrant city. To be sure, the diminution of migratory movements into London, while marking the city's social structure, did not eliminate or obscure the diversity of its indigenous population, or the ethnic character of some districts, in particular the East End, in which Irish and Eastern European Jews continued to settle throughout this period.

Low rates of in-migration were balanced in part by a relatively high birth-rate. Despite sharing the overall decline in fertility which marked all urban centres in Europe in the last decades of the nineteenth century, London's birth-rate still stood at about 25 per 1,000, and higher still in some working-class districts. It is for this reason that much photo-

[7] Hans Ostwald, *Berlin und die Berlinerin. Eine Kultur- und Sittengeschichte* (Berlin, 1911).

graphic evidence about pre-war London presents the image of a city of children, a theme Dickens had made his own.[8] This old metropolis is therefore the youngest of the three we have studied, a feature of social history both contributing to and reflecting social conditions and family forms.

Paris, city of immigrants

Paris was almost the opposite of London in demographic terms. The under twenty population was less numerous (25 per cent in Paris as opposed to 38 per cent in London), and young adults more numerous. This was the inevitable outcome of the wave of in-migration which marked Paris's demographic development; since most migrants were young adults, it is they who predominated in a city with 62 per cent of its inhabitants born elsewhere. Most were from provincial France, but a growing number came from abroad. About 6 per cent of the total population of Paris was non-French; no other major city had as high a population of 'aliens' in this period.[9] Balancing this inflow was an outflow, especially in times of economic and political crisis, which helped to reduce the net growth of Paris to London levels before the 1914–18 war. In effect, Paris was a city whose development was marked by the high degree of geographic mobility of its inhabitants. This demographic turbulence may have weakened earlier forms of urban sociability, identity, and custom set earlier in the nineteenth century. At the very least, the turnover of the Parisian population presented extremely diverse spatial conditions in which this identity was formed.

To hold a Parisian identity was perfectly consistent with a fully developed sense of one's provincial culture. Newcomers to Paris did not discard the habits of mind of their place of origin. In effect they made it a city of Auvergnats, Berrichons, Bretons.[10]

In contrast to London, Paris's demographic history was marked by a trade-off of high rates of in-migration and a low indigenous birth rate, reaching about 17 per 1,000 on the eve of the 1914–18 war. The decline in fertility was also marked in popular quartiers. In effect, Paris was still an attractive city, a magnet for in-migrants. But given its 'neo-Malthusian' approach to family limitation, and the long-term decline in the Parisian birth-rate, it is not surprising that Paris was perhaps more a city of the ambitious and the present than of the future.

8 In general see H. J. Dyos and Michael Wolff (eds.), *The Victorian city: images and realities*, 2 vols. (London, 1973).

9 See introduction to *Résultats statistiques du Rencensement Général de la population effectué le 6 mai 1911* (Paris, 1913–16).

10 Guy Pourcher, *Le peuplement de Paris, origine régionale, composition sociale, attitudes et motivations*, Cahiers de l'INED no. 43 (Paris, 1963).

Berlin, city of diversity

With 33 per cent under the age of twenty, the age-structure of the population of Berlin rested roughly between that of London and Paris. Berlin's striking demographic growth was the resultant of both vectors we have examined: high in-migration and high fertility. Balancing these factors was a higher death-rate than in either of the other two capitals, though the disparity between Berlin's mortality rates and those of Paris and London was shrinking in the decade prior to the outbreak of war in 1914.

Immigration was formidable; as we have noted, about three of every five Berliners came from elsewhere, in particular from Brandenburg and East Prussia, rather than from Saxony, as had been the case earlier in the nineteenth century. Out-migration was also significant, though it led less to the countryside than to the outside world. Between 1901 and 1910 perhaps 2.6 million people arrived to live in Berlin; about 2.1 million left for other destinations.[11] Those who remained in Berlin helped to form the identity of the city in this, its most robust phase of growth.

Alongside massive migratory movements, Berlin's net population growth rates were bolstered by relatively high birth rates. At 21 per 1,000 Berlin's birth-rate was lower than London's but higher than that of Paris. We may conclude, therefore, that Berlin's dynamism arose from a double process of high migration and high natality.

In 1914 Paris and Berlin were still in a phase of significant in-migration, with a population less settled in its urban environment than was that of London. The skills needed for adaptation evident in a population of urban newcomers in Paris and Berlin were formidable; they would become valuable assets after the outbreak of war. The linkage between demographic development and social stability is never linear, but to ignore the demographic factor is to lose sight of a key element in the cities' social and cultural history.

Industrial and social characteristics

London: financial capital of the world

The general features of the economic profile of the three cities are so well known as to be commonplace. On the eve of the war, London's financial power was unmatched. International commerce, insurance, transport all flowed through London. 'One had to live or at least to work abroad to appreciate to what degree London was part of the daily commercial life of all foreign countries', noted Felix Schuster, one of the great bankers of the City of London.[12] In addition, London was the centre of the stock

[11] E. Bernstein, *Die Geschichte der Berliner Arbeiterbewegung* (Berlin, 1910).

[12] Youssef Cassis, *La City de Londres, 1870–1914* (Paris, 1987), pp. xx–xxi.

and capital markets, and the London Stock Exchange regularly quoted a considerable number of foreign shares. This is hardly surprising, given the massive flow of British capital abroad in the later nineteenth century. Perhaps 40 per cent of all capital outflow from Europe was British in origin, a figure well in advance of French or German venture capital in this period. Underpinning this complex and ubiquitous world market was the gold exchange standard, enabling free convertibility of bills of exchange for gold in London, an achievement unmatched by Paris during a number of turbulent periods in French financial history. This buoyancy in British economic power was not without flaws, as the slow-down in rates of manufacturing output and a declining share in world trade in the late nineteenth century signified. Still the greatest trading power in 1913, Britain was troubled by a deficit on current account – balanced it is true by imperial earnings – and by the growing power of foreign banks, in particular the great German houses.[13] Nevertheless, the vital insurance lifeline to shipping and trade still went through the city of London, and through Lloyds of London in particular. The power of the 'City' (shorthand for British finance) appeared intact on the eve of the Great War.

The international character of London's financial power was unique. The fact that its decisions echoed in Buenos Aires and Bombay had greater impact on the labour force of these cities than on London itself. A comparison with Paris shows the modest imprint of financial power on employment in the two cities. Banking and insurance employed 2.7 per cent of the active population in London; 2.1 per cent in Paris; commerce accounted for 16.6 per cent in London; 14.7 per cent in Paris. The total engaged in the service sector was about the same in the two cities: approaching one-half of the labour force. There is some indication of the significance of the Port of London in the higher proportion engaged in transport in London (12 per cent) compared to Paris (7 per cent). In effect, in the British case, real economic power, like much of the earnings of the City, was invisible, hidden behind the imposing facades of Lombard Street.

In terms of manufacture, the two cities were not far apart, with a slight advantage in terms of labour participation in this sector for Paris. In London roughly 38 per cent was employed in manufacture, with particular concentrations in the food and printing industries. A real difference in the two cities emerges in a comparison of women's work. Roughly one-third of all workers in London were women, a lower proportion than in Paris. The *midinette*, so familiar a figure in Paris, was less well known in London, where female domestic service predomi-

[13] R. Floud and D. McCloskey (eds.), *An economic history of modern Britain*, 2nd edn, (Cambridge, 1994), chs. 1, 7.

nated to a greater degree than in any other European city.[14] In both cities, some preliminary and very tentative steps had also been made in the entry of women into the free professions, teaching and medicine. But for the majority of women workers, domestic service played a traditional mediating role between the classes and districts familiar to students of nineteenth-century cities.[15]

At the heart of the social life of the seat of the British Empire was a handful of men who ran the City of London. In the vicinity of the city, and all along the Thames, dockland drew in a multitude of 'casual' workers, or men and women in 'sweated' trades, locally born, Eastern European or Irish, who for a pittance handled the flow of merchandise passing through the city.[16] This labour force was still remote from a factory proletariat, dominated by the second industrial revolution of the late nineteenth century.

Berlin: industrial power

Comparisons between London and Paris are based on census returns of roughly comparable years and parallel categories of analysis. Unfortunately, the data on Berlin present greater problems for our comparative study. Census returns and social taxonomies for the German capital have their own characteristics, difficult to correlate directly with Parisian and London data. None the less, the major features of social and economic life in Berlin (and their distance from those of Paris and London) can be identified from the available material.

It is clear that pre-war Berlin was more of an industrial city than either Paris or London. A majority of the labour force (between 55 and 60 per cent) was employed in this sector. The corresponding figures for Paris and London are 43 per cent and 38 per cent respectively. If we take account of industrial employment in the suburbs surrounding these cities, the industrial character of Berlin becomes clearer still. The metal and electrical industries employed 15 per cent of the Berlin labour force, compared to 7 and 6 per cent in London and Paris, respectively. The giant operations of the Siemens firm, creating its own industrial city of 100,000 people in Siemensstadt or of the Rathenau firm of AEG in the industrial quartier of Wedding are landmarks of European industrial history. The *Ringbahn*, the network of Berlin's canals, linked industrial enterprises stretching from the south-east to the north-west of the urban region.[17]

[14] Theresa McBride, *The domestic revolution, 1820–1920* (London, 1976).

[15] J.-L. Robert, 'Cours sur culture et société en France 1880–1929', University of Orléans, 1992.

[16] Gordon Phillips and Noel Whiteside, *Casual labour: the unemployment question in the port transport industry, 1880–1970* (Oxford, 1985); and José Harris, *Unemployment and politics: a study in English social policy 1886–1914* (Oxford, 1972).

[17] The following discussion of the industrial character of Berlin is based on: Cyril Buffet,

A visitor to the three cities would have little difficulty in seeing that Berlin was much more of an industrial city, indeed a proletarian city, than either of the other two capitals. Not surprisingly, Berlin had the lowest rates of female participation in extra-domestic employment; perhaps 38 per cent of women aged fifteen and above in Berlin worked outside the home. Much of this industrial activity was geared towards export, a phenomenon in line with the overall robust performance of the German economy as a whole which, after the turn of the century, was approaching the status of the world's leading exporting power.

Only recently the imperial capital, Berlin employed a relatively small proportion of its labour force in the service sector. Roughly 36 to 40 per cent worked here, both for private employers and in the state sector, growing out of the older traditions of Prussian bureaucracy, still buoyant even though Berlin was not the garrison town it had been in the early nineteenth century.[18] Still, the presence of soldiers striding down Unter den Linden was a commonplace feature of the German capital. Less dominant was the service sector, despite the growth of banking and finance after the turn of the century. By 1914 the Berlin stock exchange had surpassed even those of Frankfurt and Cologne, and had become the premier financial market in Germany.[19]

Paris: city of 'midinettes'?

Yet again, we can see how Paris in this period both resembled London and shared some features of the German capital. First, Paris (like London) had a predominant service sector. Fully 50 per cent of the active population was thus employed, a trace perhaps, it should be noted, of the older Jacobin tradition of public service. This may account for the greater role of public employment in the labour force in Paris (12–13 per cent) compared to London (under 10 per cent), a sector traditionally masculine, as in the world of Balzac. As in London, these men worked in a well-defined part of the city, admirably captured by Jules Romains:

> What really marked the centre was its human rhythms . . . the way the streets channelled more than a million men in convergent directions. These streets described an area the absorptive capacity of which appeared unlimited. They stretched from west to east, a kilometre from the river . . . On one side it touched the Opéra. On the other the old *marché du Temple*. The largest part, which absorbed the greatest number, was stuffed into lodgings between *rue Réaumur*

Berlin (Paris, 1993); and F. G. Dreyfus, 'Berlin, capitale du Reich, 1871–1933', in Etienne François et Egon Westerhalt (eds.), *Berlin: capitale, mythe, enjeu* (Nancy, 1987), pp. 55–62.

18 Etienne François, 'Berlin au xviiiè siècle: naissance d'une capitale', in *Berlin: capitale, mythe, enjeu*, pp. 33–42.

19 Dreyfus, 'Berlin', p. 57.

near the Stock Exchange and the *rue du Paradis*. But at night this spongy mass of streets sent out the millions of men saturating it.[20]

As was his wont, Jules Romains exaggerated a phenomenon which, in essence, he described with great shrewdness and clarity.

With 58 per cent of women aged fifteen or more engaged in extra-domestic employment, Paris was one of the great centres of female work at the turn of the twentieth century. *Les glaneuses*, or the gatherers working wherever and however they could, described so well by Michelle Perrot, were indefatigable in Paris.[21] The principal roles they played were in the textile, flower, and millinery trades, covering fully 40 per cent of the female labour force in the French capital. Older trades were more masculine, in particular the furniture and jewellery trades located in the centre and east of Paris. While in general Paris was less of an industrial centre than either London or Berlin, the weight of skilled labour, the *artisanat*, still remained considerable.

These three metropolitan centres, therefore, had different profiles of labour and production, despite the evident similarities of administrative activity appropriate to capital cities. A vast array of employment opened before the newcomer; each city was a centre of possibilities.

At the core of these economic edifices were different key areas: for London, the City and the docks; for Berlin, concentrations of factory labour. The heart of Paris was more diverse, no one sector dominating the rest. Each economic structure had ample space for adaptation at a time of national emergency.

Urban geography: spatial and political dimensions

Territory and power: concentration and dispersal of urban populations

In the three capitals, the city centre, once densely populated, shrank substantially by the twentieth century. The City of London had 130,000 inhabitants in 1851, 20,000 on the eve of the war. Similarly old Berlin had lost half its population in this period; the four central arrondissements of Paris also dwindled both absolutely and relatively with respect to neighbouring districts.

In contrast, suburban growth was formidable, though different administrative definitions of city, county and region in the three cases make direct comparisons difficult.[22] In the case of Berlin, the outer

[20] Jules Romains, *Les hommes de bonnes volontés. Le 6 octobre 1908* (Paris, 1st edn 1932, 1958 edn), p. 190.

[21] Michelle Perrot, 'Les classes populaires urbaines', in F. Braudel and E. Labrousse (eds.), *Histoire économique et sociale de la France* (Paris, 1979), pp. 454–535.

[22] Paul Meuriot, 'De la valeur du terme de banlieue dans certaines métropoles: Paris,

suburbs – integrated in the city only in 1920 – constituted fully 50 per cent of the pre-war population of Greater Berlin. Fully 37 per cent of Greater London's population lived outside the twenty-eight metropolitan boroughs; 30 per cent of the Department of the Seine lived outside the twenty arrondissements.

Some other geographical regularities may be noted in these cities. In all three cities, more prosperous and less densely populated districts were located in the west and south-west of the inner cities. Popular and more densely populated districts were clustered in the north, east, and south-east.

Berlin: replica of the 'incomplete empire'

Spread over 60 square kilometres, pre-war 'old Berlin' was both smaller physically than the other two cities and also had a smaller proportion of the overall urban region. In effect, the Berlin region resembled a cluster of cities, and within them old urban villages loosely linked administratively. Berlin's development was hardly concentric, a feature of its urban history attested to by the fact that the Ring begun by Hobrecht in 1862 was never completed.[23] In this sense, Berlin, the modern city *par excellence*, remained archaic in a number of ways.

Its administrative character was complex. The Berlin region encompassed seven towns (*Städte*) like Charlottenburg, but neighbouring districts (like Steglitz and fifty-nine others) in 1914 were still considered to be rural communes. Dahlem in the south-west still remained a *Gutsbezirk* (rural district), along with twenty-seven others retaining a semi-feudal status. Administering such a complex region presented problems of Byzantine proportions. Some steps towards rationalization were taken before 1914, though it would take six more years to complete the creation of Greater Berlin, measuring 3,500 square kilometres, a city fully four times the size of the old urban centre of 870 square kilometres.[24]

We see here traces both of the administrative complexity of the Kaiserreich and the jealous retention of local loyalties and privileges in districts suspicious of central authorities and worried about absorption in a large amorphous urban entity. Such suspicions were hardly allayed by the construction in both Paris and Berlin of a belt of military fortifications surrounding both cities. The presence of the army was accentuated by the existence of military command centres and emplace-

Berlin et Londres', *Bulletin de l'Institut International de Statistiques* (1915), pp. 320–30; Paul Meuriot, 'Dans quel sens se développent les métropoles européennes', *Journal de la société de statistiques de Paris* (1913), pp. 238–50.

[23] Jean-Louis Cohen, 'Les réformes urbaines à Berlin: deux siècles de chantier', *Critique*, numéro spécial, *Berlin n'est plus une île* (Aug. 1991), pp. 580–95.

[24] Kaeber, *Berlin*.

ments in the suburbs of Paris and Berlin, at Vincennes and Potsdam respectively. The absence of a strong military tradition in Britain is reflected in the absence of a similar base of operations in or near the capital. The navy too was far from London. The only real military presence in London was composed of the ceremonial units of the Horse Guards and the pensioners at Chelsea Hospital.

The system of enfranchisement in Berlin, as in the rest of Germany, was entirely different from that in Paris (with universal male suffrage) or London (with limited male suffrage). The Prussian three-tier voting system was weighted towards property owners and against the propertyless. Not surprisingly, such a system meant that the industrial character of the city of Berlin, however defined, was not reflected fully in its urban administration. Socialists had an uphill road to climb; throughout the war and until 1920, the mayor of the city of Berlin was Adolph Wermuth, candidate of the *bürgerlichen Parteien*.[25]

More than in Paris or London, the system of local politics in Berlin favoured the authority of a mayor elected for twelve years, while the city council was elected every four years. As in Paris and London, superior authorities were entitled to intervene in municipal affairs with respect to certain questions. The King of Prussia confirmed the mayor-elect; a prefect retained control of the police; the Prussian Minister of Finance approved the city budget. More unusual in the case of Berlin was the weight of the President of the *Land* of Brandenburg, who retained the authority to resolve certain disputes. It is still a matter of controversy as to whether or not this bewildering system – then as now understood fully by few – preserved or precluded the autonomy of local power *vis-à-vis* the state.[26]

In effect, we see in microcosm many of the peculiarities of the German political system. In 1914 Berlin, like Germany, was a political entity still in the making, full of contradictory trends, at one and the same time centrifugal and centripetal, moving both towards centralization and retaining local administrative space and power.[27]

London: city, nation, empire

The overlap between metropolitan business and national political power has marked London's history since at least the seventeenth century. Urban districts retained their local character, acknowledged in the 1889 system of elected borough councils in the twenty-eight metropolitan boroughs. Together they formed the County of London, stretching over 300 square kilometres. The surrounding districts were grouped in an even larger unit, Greater London, covering 1,800 square

[25] Adolph Wermuth, *Ein Beamtenleben* (Berlin, 1922).

[26] Volker Rolf Berghahn, *Imperial Germany* (Providence, 1994).

[27] Gerhard Masur, *Imperial Berlin 1871–1918* (London, 1971).

kilometres, and reaching into the eastern county of Kent, the northern county of Middlesex and the southern county of Surrey. Useful for police purposes, the category of 'Greater London' had little political or social meaning for the inhabitants of the metropolis.

The division of administrative responsibilities as between different offices remained complex after 1889.[28] Metropolitan boroughs took over some duties previously performed at parish level, in particular in the fields of public health and public assistance. The Victorian Poor Law was administered by thirty-one local Boards of Guardians, empowered (until 1929) to provide relief for the indigent. Local autonomy extended to other questions as well.[29] For example, the Metropolitan Borough of Stepney refused until 1921 to authorize the construction of an electric tram, the overhead lines of which were deemed unaesthetic. The London County Council was a major employer, controlling parks, schools, transport, gas.[30]

As in the case of Berlin and Paris, the power to control the police escaped local authorities, but in many other ways the 118 members of the London County Council elected for three years were able to act in a manner that mattered at the local level. The system of franchise in local elections was much broader than that at the national level; adult residents of a year or more formed the electorate.

London, in effect, was an immense space occupied by overlapping authorities. While lacking the dizzying complexity of the German system, London's government contained elements of the distant past alongside newer instruments of power. The local and the metropolitan coexisted to provide multiple urban identities for millions of its inhabitants on the eve of the Great War.

Paris: city under surveillance

The Parisian case presents equally baffling complexities. During the Second Empire, the city itself was deemed to cover a terrain of 80 square kilometres, divided into twenty newly numbered arrondissements, curving like the shell of a snail from the old royal core of the city in the 1st arrondissement outwards in widening circles to reach finally the popular districts of the north-east, in the 20th arrondissement. Unlike Berlin or London, there was no 'Greater Paris'. The departmental structure inherited from the Revolution of 1789 remained intact, and the Department of the Seine, covering 480 square kilometres, incorporated

[28] D. Pasquet, *Londres et les ouvriers de Londres* (Paris, 1913). This is a formidable thesis by a French geographer; see also Arthur G. Cook, 'Londres et la gestion de ses affaires municipales', *Journal de la société de statistiques de Paris* (1914), pp. 345–55.

[29] Pasquet, *Londres, passim.*

[30] See Susan Pennybacker, 'The labour policy of the London County Council, 1889–1914', PhD thesis, University of Cambridge, 1981.

both the city of Paris and eighty suburban communes separated from its metropolitan neighbour.

Formally, local power was divided as between Paris and its peripheral communes, through the municipal council of Paris and the general council of the Department of the Seine. But within Paris, the twenty arrondissements, each containing four quartiers, were administrative units beyond the control of the local community. The mayors of these boroughs were civil servants named by the state.

Councillors were elected through a system of universal manhood suffrage. Successful candidates won a majority of votes in a two-stage electoral process. It is important to note that in the case of Paris (and not the surrounding communes), the responsibilities of councillors were strictly limited. Paris had no mayor, but rather a president of the municipal council elected for one year. This official had no control over the police, in marked contrast to provincial practice. Overseeing the municipal council of Paris were two prefects, a prefect for police, scrutinizing issues of public order and political control; and a prefect of the Seine, dealing with other administrative issues. This special form of municipal supervision did not eliminate the room for manoeuvre available to Parisian councillors, who acted in important ways in the fields of public assistance, lighting, roads, and transport.

Paris was overseen as well in a physical way. The French capital was the only one of the three we survey here which preserved in 1914 a system of fortifications creating potential closure in case of attack. London and Berlin had abandoned such defences in the 1860s.[31] Obviously, the retention of such fortifications reflected both geography and the tragic history of the war of 1870–1. But since the suppression of the Paris commune in May 1871, it was apparent that these emplacements were there for internal control as well. Consequently, the physical reality of the Paris region was cut in two, restricting the development of local power and the services it could and had to provide.

The spatial development of the three cities was, therefore, very different. London's situation was the clearest of the three. There was a hierarchy of responsibility, from metropolitan borough to county council, and from there to the local government board, whose president sat in the Cabinet. Local autonomy and local taxation mattered, contributing to numerous heated conflicts over both the rights and the capacity of local communities to provide services for their inhabitants. When the burden of local taxation became (or was felt to become) too heavy around the turn of the century, local residents turned to the central state to accept a larger share of the costs of local provision. In

[31] *Paris démuré* (Paris, 1990); and Jean-Louis Robert, 'Banlieue rouge sang', in Annie Fourcaut (ed.), *La banlieue rouge 1920–1960* (Paris, 1992), pp. 146–59.

these local conflicts may be found the most important impulses towards the creation of what we now call the welfare state.

The case of Berlin was entirely different. The urban network was composed of a patchwork of local authorities, encased in an archaic political system resting on a totally unrepresentative franchise. The links between locality and city, and between both region and province were complex enough; add to these the presence of the army and the central state, and you will begin to appreciate the mosaic of Berlin's administrative history on the eve of the Great War.

The overlap between city and state was most clear-cut in the case of Paris, a city in which surveillance was elevated to an art form. But such watchfulness on the part of external authorities did not preclude the retention of local loyalties. Did the *bellevilloise* identity cease to exist because the mayor of the 20th arrondissement was a civil servant appointed by the central government? Fortunately, administrative control and social experience were never fully synchronized.[32]

Municipal politics and policies

Despite the wide divergence in structures and history, there were some striking parallels among the municipal politics of the three cities on the eve of the Great War. The move to the political right on the municipal level was particularly marked in Paris and London.

The balance of political forces

Since the end of the nineteenth century, the political centre of the municipal council of Paris, previously left Republican, moved to the right. This reflected both the evolution of the city's social structure as well as the burgeoning crisis of Radicalism in the metropolis. Replacing the Radicals was a growing contingent of Socialists, numbering 17 councillors out of 80 in the municipal council of 1914. In the general council of the Department of the Seine, in contrast, the left remained in control, with the Socialist party the largest single group. They were deprived of the presidency of the general council only through the failure of the Radicals to honour the practice of alternating the presidency between majority parties.[33]

In the Parisian suburbs, the Socialists were strong. In the 1914 legislative elections, Socialists captured 10 out of 14 deputies' seats. This contrasted with 12 socialist winners out of 40 in Paris, yielding 22 out of 54 in the Department as a whole. Here is the mark of the alliance of the

32 Jeanne Siwek-Pouydesseau, *Le corps préfectoral sous la Troisième et la Quatrième Républiques* (Paris, 1969).

33 Thierry Bonzon, 'La politique sociale du Conseil municipal de Paris et du Conseil général de la Seine, 1910–20', PhD thesis, University of Paris – 1, forthcoming, 1997.

'Red belt' surrounding Paris and the popular districts of the east of the city, whose socialist representatives stood out among the parliamentarians of the Seine region.[34]

A similar drift to the right was visible in the case of London politics. The progressive alliance, which had controlled the London County Council since 1889, lost it in 1907. But in contrast to Paris, London politics or the alliance of Liberals and Labour were not in the ascendancy in the pre-war period. If anything, the tide was moving towards the Conservatives, whose support was growing even in the working-class East End. In the 1910 elections only two Labour MPs were elected in London, admittedly on the restricted pre-war franchise. But on balance, control of local affairs was firmly in the hands of the moderate right.[35]

In Berlin, as usual, contradictions abound. The electoral system blocked the Socialists from exercising a predominant role in local politics both in Berlin and its periphery. In the Reichstag elections, Socialist candidates won with increasingly large shares of the vote. The six districts of the city, however gerrymandered, had one Social Democratic deputy, and Socialist candidates obtained between 55 and 90 per cent of the vote. What party would not boast about an *average* of 75 per cent support in local areas? 'Berlin is ours', the Social Democrats rightly claimed on the eve of the Great War.[36]

The contrast between London and Berlin was striking: the one with a slender reed of Labour politics in municipal affairs; the other with a powerful base despite much more adverse political conditions. Paris lay between the two, and shared with London a past history of local control by progressive, if not Socialist, alignments. These groups seemed to be losing control of local affairs in both Paris and London on the eve of the war, whereas in Berlin, socialist groups appeared to be in the ascendancy.

Parallels in municipal politics?

Local voting patterns were not identical to national ones, but local electors were influenced by wider political issues too. In addition, municipal interventions were not a matter only of political affiliation, but also of bureaucratic rationalization. Municipal control of urban services seemed most complete in Berlin.[37] In Paris, too, a controlled and centralized system of services was well established. Even on the eve of

[34] Jean-Louis Robert, *Les ouvriers, la patrie et la Révolution, Paris 1914–1919* (Besançon, 1996).

[35] Julia Bush, *Behind the lines: East London labour 1914–1919* (London, 1984).

[36] Paul Meuriot, 'Le Reichstag impérial, 1871–1912, étude de démographie politique', *Journal de la société de statistiques de Paris* (1914), in five parts.

[37] Gaston Cadoux, *La vie des grandes capitales, études comparatives sur Londres, Paris, Berlin* (Paris, 2nd edn 1913).

the war, the municipality renewed its contract with the municipal gas company only on condition that the city progressively took over the use of the concession and that all company workers became municipal employees. Such conditions were hardly politically neutral. In effect, gas lighting was distributed equitably throughout the city.[38]

In London, municipalization of services was a mixed process. The Metropolitan Water Board was established in 1902, but in the case of gas, thirty-six companies served the city, and the County Council controlled lighting only on the Thames and the bridges crossing it. The East End was relatively poorly lit; nocturnal London had a different character in districts of varying wealth.

As in the other two cities, many social services in London were shared by public and philanthropic groups. The establishment of the Salvation Army in Whitechapel in 1878, in one of the most impoverished districts of the city, illustrates this phenomenon, whose spirit and characteristics received an amusing and trenchant treatment in George Bernard Shaw's play *Major Barbara*. The Protestant voluntary tradition was imbedded both in civic action and in charitable work, and helped to mobilize action throughout the metropolis to help care for the denizens of 'Outcast London'.[39]

Housing

Berlin, city of tenements

Legal and tax issues frequently determined urban housing policy. In Berlin private ownership of land was dominant, favouring dense and profitable housing construction. In contrast, some Rhineland municipalities had a broader range of publicly owned property.[40] In Berlin, the parameters of housing were fixed municipally: the width of streets was to be a generous 15 metres and the maximum height of buildings, approximately 18 metres. Such standardization gave the city's domestic housing a uniform character. What were commonly called *Mietskasernen* (literally rented barracks or packed tenements) became the rule in popular housing in Berlin. These constituted buildings of five or six storeys, with inner courtyards extending well beyond the facade, catering (theoretically) for about sixty inhabitants per house.[41]

Another Berlin characteristic was the preponderance of one-

[38] See chapter 11 below.

[39] Gareth Stedman Jones, *Outcast London. A study in the relationship between classes in Victorian society* (Oxford, 1984). [40] Pinol, *Le monde des villes au XIXè siècle*.

[41] M.G. Daunton (ed.), *Housing the workers: a comparative history, 1850–1944* (Leicester, 1990); Hans Teuteberg and J. Klemens Wischermann, *Wohnalltag in Deutschland 1850–1914. Studien der Geschichte der Alltags* (Munich, 1985); and Paul Deschamps, *La formation sociale du Prussien moderne* (Paris, 1916).

roomed apartments. In Luisenstadt, 70 per cent of all apartments were single rooms; the figure was 50 per cent in Wedding, and 49 per cent in old Berlin in 1900. In all these areas, sub-tenancies were normal practice, catering for perhaps one in four residents of the city before the war. Some conditions resembled the older slums of London, and the unhygienic pockets of poverty in Paris, but in other areas of Berlin, the housing stock was at least as good as that in the other two capitals. What distinguished the Berlin case, though, was massive overcrowding. What other explanation is there for the fact that 60,000 Berliners lived in cellars in 1911? Here we see the mark of an extremely mobile and unstable population, recently arrived and frequently in transit.

British experience in urban development was familiar in Berlin, and knowledge of parallel developments helps to account for some more generously endowed developments like Staaken and Siemensstadt, with their small apartments in a more spacious green environment.[42] But such constructions constituted only 5 per cent of all urban building in 1914. To the south-west of the city, around the city's lakes, the bourgeoisie erected comfortable villas far removed from the landscape of the city centre.

The image of Berlin as a tenement city, widespread throughout Europe before the war, was based on reality. But it was a reality complicated in an infinite variety of ways. Behind the high facades of Berlin's streets, a complex network of associations was formed enabling the mass of newcomers to assimilate into urban life.

London, city of tenants and owner-occupiers

Once more in sharp contrast to Berlin, London's urban habitat was much less densely populated. On average eight Londoners (as opposed to sixty Berliners) occupied each dwelling. From the middle of the nineteenth century, urban planning aimed to cleanse the city of its pockets of illness and crime. By 1914, almost all of the slums of Dickens's London had been eradicated. In several waves, private housing came to dominate the city. These dwellings by and large were privately owned or rented or held on long-term (99-year) leases. Houses were rarely sub-divided into Berlin-like cells. Much land was in the hands of a small group of proprietors and institutions, many with aristocratic connections. In the majority of cases, it was not in their interests to create very dense housing, as in the case of Berlin, catering for a massive immigrant community.[43]

[42] Ilse Costas, 'Management and labour in the Siemens plants in Berlin, 1896–1920', in L. Haimson and G. Sapelli (eds.), *Strikes, social conflict and the First World War. An international perspective* (Milan, 1991).

[43] Harold Carter and C. Roy Lewis, *An urban geography of England and Wales in the*

Fully 76 per cent of households lived in individual houses, mostly rented. In contrast 20 per cent lived in apartments and 7 per cent in rooms adjacent to shops or offices. The dimensions of such accommodation varied greatly, but popular housing was generally of two types. One was extremely simple, composed of a kitchen downstairs and a bedroom above, or a small house shared by two families, one on the ground floor, one a floor above. For the fortunate, housing was available in the new 'garden cities', much admired in Paris and Berlin. In sum, on the eve of the 1914–18 war, London was a massive city with a relatively low rate of overcrowding (however defined), the housing stock of which, while far from flawless, compared favourably both with that of continental cities and of the provincial cities of England and Wales.

Two worrying problems remained on the eve of the war. The first was the level of rents, which roughly were double or treble that of Paris. Consequently, Londoners had to devote a much larger part of their earnings to housing. Secondly, urban renewal caused major problems of displacement. Between 1902 and 1913, 70,000 lodgings in working-class districts were demolished, but only 15,000 new units were constructed in the same period.[44] It was inevitable that there would be a housing shortage, reflected in the fact that in 1914 only 1 per cent of the housing stock was unoccupied. We have noted that the period of London's massive growth was over, but housing problems remained a chronic headache, which (as we shall see) intensified during the war.

Parisian contrasts

Once more Paris appears to be a city midway between London and Berlin. More crowded than London, Paris accommodated on average thirty-four people per dwelling. Like Berlin, Paris was a city the majority of whose inhabitants lived in rented apartments. In the suburbs, separate owner-occupied houses did exist and flourish, before the post-war vogue of housing estates.

The specificity of the case of Paris rests on the convergence, first of the older character of its housing stock (compared to Berlin), and, secondly, of the absence of a policy, similar to that undertaken in London, of destroying unsanitary districts. The real estate market in Paris is as yet not well researched, but what we know points to high mobility and complex manipulations of real property.[45]

Paris more than London was an overcrowded city. Fully 43 per cent of lodgings were deemed to be overcrowded, and most of these were

nineteenth century (London, 1990); Richard Rodger, *Housing in urban Britain 1780–1914* (London, 1989).

[44] S. Merrett, *State housing in Britain* (London, 1979).

[45] For urban housing in Paris, see Christian Topalov, *Le logement en France, histoire d'une marchandise impossible* (Paris, 1987).

insanitary as well. Some progress was registered through municipal action, though, especially in terms of the modernization of heating, lighting, waste and garbage removal, and water supply.

Another special feature of the Paris case was the sharp contrast between the east and west of the city with respect to the quality of construction. In the east, the poor quality and dimensions of housing walls built in the second half of the nineteenth century precluded the construction of multi-storeyed dwellings. In the west of the city, beautiful dwellings constructed in stone could support easily five, six or even seven storeys. Here is one of the sources of the imbalance between the west, with an abundance of housing units, and the east, with a serious shortage.

For purposes of comparison, it may be useful to envision three types of housing in the pre-war period: the London house, detached or semi-detached; the one-roomed flat in Berlin; and the diverse apartments of Paris. Certainly, the individual household in London describes a fundamental element in what Londoners understood as well-being. Different standards applied on the continent; in smaller quarters, Parisians were not necessarily less satisfied with their accommodation. Overcrowding on the Berlin scale was clearly undesirable. But the density of Paris offered some compensations: access to leisure, a shared urban culture and social life. In effect, the Parisian worker paid less attention than his London counterpart to housing and the comforts it provided.

Health and social morphology

It was a commonplace that in these three cities there was a degree of social and spatial inequality in mortality rates, especially those of infants and those suffering from tuberculosis.[46] In both respects, Paris was the worst off of the three capital cities. In terms of progress in public health at the end of the nineteenth century, Paris lagged behind the others. Berlin, starting at a higher level of mortality, made great strides in this period, bypassing Paris and in certain cases even approaching London levels of life expectancy.

One observer caught these developments well, on the eve of the war:

> if, with mediocre water supply, three times the population, poor air, a sky filled with clouds polluted by oil fumes, London has a rate of infant mortality lower than that of Paris, where the air is often pure and radiant, where the climate is more temperate, where the water and food are superior, this must arise from the hygienic and moral merits of the English household.[47]

[46] T. H. C. Stevenson, 'The social distribution of mortality from different causes in England and Wales, 1910–12', *Biometrika*, 15 (1923), pp. 382–400.

[47] Cadoux, *La vie des grandes capitales*, p. xxx.

Whatever the effect of morality, better housing, public hygiene and probably better nutrition lay behind the fact that at all ages female mortality was lower in London than in Paris. For all ages, the death-rate in Paris was 15 to 17 per 1,000. In Berlin, the rate was 13 to 15, and in London, 11 to 13 per 1,000 (see appendix).

This interpretation of London's superior social conditions, in particular her healthier domestic arrangements, as the source of the higher life expectancy of her population, is of some, though limited, utility. After all, the population of Berlin was even more overcrowded, but still survived at higher rates than did that of Paris. What is missing is a sense of the importance of health policy in London and Berlin, and the advantages accruing to these cities rather than to Paris, where such policies were less well developed (see chapter 14).

For fundamentally conservative reasons, an incipient 'welfare state', entailing national insurance, had been in place for decades in Berlin by the time of the 1914–18 war. Similar policies had moved from local to national provision in Britain through the National Insurance Act of 1911. In contrast, French social policy remained hesitant and uncoordinated in 1914.

Culture and images

It would be unwise to argue for the existence of a common urban culture in these three cities, without major qualification with respect to quartier, gender, class, profession, generation, and origin. The only acceptable generalization about these cities is the diversity of possible lives which were lived in them, regardless of whether or not we consider Paris socially a more varied city than, say, Berlin. Both unrepresentative instances and gross generalities must be avoided in an attempt to described the ambience of these cities on the eve of the 1914–18 war.

Some observations, even of a partial kind, may be helpful in introducing cultural elements to this survey of the pre-war urban landscape. We know that Parisian and Berlin workers used an important part of their disposable income for social expenditure in their quartiers, for example, clothes and drink. In contrast, rent and furnishings commanded a larger part of working-class expenditure in London.[48] Among other differences were a greater expenditure on bread in London, on meat in Paris, and (as the stereotypes had it) on meat and sausages in Berlin. Studies of local dialects distinguish different parts of these cities as well.[49] Among elites, nuances concerning taste and

48 Maurice Halbwachs, *La classe ouvrière et les niveaux de vie* (Paris, 1912).

49 Lionel Richard, 'Identité contradictoire', in L. Richard (ed.), *Berlin 1919–1933. Gigantisme, crise sociale et avant-garde: l'incarnation extrême de la modernité* (Paris, 1991), pp. 14–43.

sociability can be made. For example, the hierarchy of London clubs corresponded to an entire world of social discrimination. And as between these cities, clichés travelled. It was no accident that Berlin cabarets had Parisian names; music as well as art travelled between the capitals with great rapidity. Apollinaire brought news of cubism to Berlin in 1912; Rilke came to Paris to write poetry in an elegant hotel in the Faubourg St. Germain, now the Musée Rodin; Emile Zola escaped from a prison sentence during the Dreyfus affair and hid in a suburban district of south London.

Such linkages, both personal and cultural, existed and grew apace in the pre-war period. But for our purposes, it may be useful to isolate two areas in which the specificities of each city may be identified: what the French like to call 'collective memory'[50] and the image contemporaries themselves formed about these cities.

Berlin, red and uniform?

Berlin attracted much comment in the pre-war period. Reports proliferated about this explosive city, this European Chicago. Foreign observers frequently returned to a number of salient points, in particular, the idea of an incomplete capital city, poorly administered by the rest of Germany. No doubt there was in pre-war Germany a degree of nostalgia for the past, for the small, independent cities of human proportions, which had fostered German culture in the nineteenth century. Berlin had something of a bad press among Germans, a phenomenon which antedated the creation of the Kaiserreich. Consider these words of Heine:

> Berlin, Berlin, great city of misery!
> In you, there is nothing to find but anguish and martyrdom . . .
> They have the stiff march of the stilted
> They respect rights as if they were candles
> One says that they have swallowed the staff
> With which they will beat you later on.[51]

An urban population docile and disciplined, according to some; to others a city functioning 'with the regularity of a motor', a city where (unlike Walter Benjamin's Paris) people do not promenade.[52]

Much of this commentary centred around Berlin's 'modernity', its

[50] Halbwachs, *La mémoire collective* (Paris, 1950).
[51] Heinrich Heine, as cited in Marc Henry, *Trois villes: Vienne, Munich, Berlin* (Paris, 1917).
[52] *Ibid.*

characteristic (in Simmel's phrase) 'to live only in the present'.[53] Left behind was its past as a Prussian city hidden in the immense tracts of the North German plains, and marked by its feudal inheritance. 'Under an entirely modern head, an entirely Gothic body', according to one essayist.[54] And to recall the tradition of the sergeant-king who punished strollers! Modernity, to be sure, was here, but it was cast within a particular tradition.

This was hardly the only image of the city to be disseminated in the pre-war years. To others Berlin was (as all cities are) the imaginative creation of its inhabitants, and from this point of view, Berlin was a city of fascination, prefiguring at the turn of the century the Berlin of the 1920s. If Berlin was not yet fully the intellectual capital of Germany – a title hotly disputed by Munich as well as a number of Rhineland cities – it was already something of an artistic capital, with flourishing avant-garde art and reviews. Its claims to world status as a scientific centre were hard to contest, with the foundation in 1909 in Dahlem of the Kaiser Wilhelm Society, later the Max Planck Institute. At the turn of the century, Berlin was the city which had furnished by far the most winners of the Nobel prize in science. It was also a city with a thriving Jewish culture, contributing handsomely to all aspects of life. In music in particular, Berlin came to rival even Vienna.[55]

Another image of pre-war Berlin which had lasting force was that of a red city. We have already noted the massive turnout in local and Reichstag elections of the Social Democratic party (SPD) on the eve of the war, reflecting the spread of a special working-class political culture. Social democracy had its adherents among middle-class groups, and in particular among intellectuals, who saw it as a vision of modernity.[56] The only truly national party, the SPD gave voice to those who dreamed of the transformation of the city into a real capital of a unified and democratic nation.

To others Berlin was a city 'sullen' or 'new, ugly and characterless'.[57] These insults distorted the nature of a city with a very unusual history, marked by the encounter of the political and military leaders of the Kaiserreich, a growing urban bourgeoisie, and avant-garde workers and intellectuals – an encounter whose history had not yet fully unfolded on the eve of the war.[58]

53 G. Simmel, as cited in Georg Lohmann, 'La confrontation de Georg Simmel avec une métropole: Berlin', *Critique* (1991), pp. 623–42.

54 Jules Huret, *En Allemagne, Berlin* (Paris, 1909).

55 L. Richard, 'Identité contradictoire', pp. 14–43. See also, part 3 of François and Westerholt (eds.), *Berlin: capitale, mythe, enjeu.*

56 E. Bernstein, *Die Geschichte der Berliner Arbeiterbewegung* (Berlin, 1910).

57 Henry, *Trois villes.*

58 Franz Hessel, *Promenades dans Berlin*, trans. by Jean-Michel Beloeil (Grenoble, 1989). First appeared in Berlin in 1929 under the title *Spazieren in Berlin.*

London, healthy and stable?

Much more is known about Victorian than about Edwardian London. The extremes of wealth and squalor, the mélange of moral uprightness and depravity of the Jack the Ripper variety, of Victorian times, had diminished at least in degree after the turn of the century. The images of night refuges, of child prostitution, of the starving and the hanged gave to the spectre of Victorian London more than a little Gothic flavour. By 1914 how much had vanished, like a bad dream? City planners certainly prayed that it would. Consider the wording of the Town Planning Act of 1910: 'The bill aims in broad outline at and hopes to secure, the home healthy, the house beautiful, the town pleasant, the city dignified and the suburb salubrious.'[59] Here was a social space defined by notions of health, sobriety, and a kind of urban aesthetic: beautiful neighbourhoods, human cities. Behind these words lay much nostalgia for an imaginary rural past in a society long used to urban conditions, grown (as in the case of London) to gigantic proportions. The dream of the green landscape, the cottage farm, the culture of a pastoral society maintaining 'older' values, all had weight in pre-war London.[60]

Thus to some the dangerous city of Dickens and the turbulent years of mid-century had given way (at least in their imagination) to another London, well-ordered, clean, healthy, like a vast urban village. The urban revolts of the 1880s, described by Stedman Jones,[61] were a thing of the past, replaced by calmer and more regular urban rhythms, attesting to the resolution of the struggle for subsistence in earlier generations. Neither social conflict nor the danger of revolt had vanished entirely. During the dock strike of 1911 the Home Secretary, Winston Churchill, despatched mounted troops throughout the East End, both to protect the docks and send a message to the working-class population. In the same period suffragette agitation gravitated towards London because that was where the key decisions were taken on votes for women. But such conflicts were national rather than strictly London-based. For real turbulence, the observer of pre-war Britain would have to turn away from London and travel across the Irish Sea.

Within London itself, civic pride took on a tangible form, in the growth of national ceremonies as well as in the appearance of statuary and architecture, erected with the gravity appropriate for the capital of the Empire.[62] But such public theatre should not obscure the persistence of a sadder, more desperate side to London life. As George Orwell told of entering London a bit later:

59 J. B. Collingworth, *Town and country planning in Britain* (London, 1982), p. 4.

60 F. H. Dodds and C. Colls, *Englishness* (London, 1992).

61 Stedman Jones, *Outcast London*, ch. 1.

62 E. J. Hobsbawm and T. Ranger (eds.), *The invention of tradition* (Cambridge, 1983).

> Mile after mile of ugly houses, inhabited by men living a dull and honest life. And further on, there was London proper, stretching along never-ending streets, eight million people, each of whom lives his little life without a hope of changing it.[63]

A city where the force of habit had turned into instinct. We should recall that it was London, and not Berlin, New York, or Moscow which inspired Orwell's novel *1984*. These views of a writer of the 1930s, responding to the economic crisis of the interwar years, were not unknown before the Great War among some intellectuals. D. H. Lawrence found London an abomination.[64] But among wider circles, London did not inspire such fear or loathing, and some of the same vision of progress animating the German labour movement was present, albeit in a less theoretically developed form, in London too.

This image of London triumphant, and perhaps a bit smug in self-satisfaction, is surely a partial one, obscuring tensions and conflicts which would emerge during the war. But to miss the pride of Londoners in their own city and its complex landscape is to miss much of importance about the pre-war British world.

Paris: Revolution, Nation, Republic

Paris was neither the financial bastion of London nor the industrial powerhouse of Berlin. It played an essential role in European cultural life, though one contested in primacy by a number of other European cities. The special place of Paris in European social history resided more in its symbolic functions on the one hand, and in what the French prefer to call *l'imaginaire*, on the other.

It was no accident that the Universal Exposition of 1889–90 (as indeed that of 1938 under the Popular Front) took place in Paris, marking the centenary of an event still exceptional in European history. To celebrate the Republic was to celebrate Paris, its revolutions, its popular emotions. The feeling evoked by the events of 1870–1 were still alive in 1914, as close to contemporaries then as is the Second World War to us today (1996). Such symbolism and the collective memory of a common and tragic past were ubiquitous. Republican display left its architectural traces throughout the city: the Eiffel Tower, the Grand Palais, the Petit Palais, the Gare d'Orsay and Les Invalides, the Hôtel de Ville itself. The city hall is filled with murals of a didactic nature, teaching us the values of Republican progress, in which science and justice are the triumphant heralds of an active and vigilant populace. The Republic in this

63 George Orwell, *Coming up for air* in *Collected Works* (London, 1986 edn), vol. VII, pp. 14–40.

64 D. H. Lawrence, *Sons and lovers* (London, 1913), p. 98.

symbolic world is the nation, the people alert and dominant. If one sets aside the glaring exception of the political rights of women, France had since 1848 been the champion of universal suffrage. Paris, Republican heartland, site of decisive insurrections, core of the nation, is also in 1914 the symbolic home of this Republican trilogy echoing through the world.

Paris's symbolic status was enhanced by the political centralization set in motion in the 1790s, and by the selective memory of foreigners, who (as Henri Hauser noted) in their imagination, used a conjuring trick to reduce France to Paris and the Riviera.[65] Such a vision had little room for industrial Paris, growing rapidly (as we have noted) before the war. But this deforming mirror[66] of the reality of Parisian life created symbols which mattered to Parisians themselves. A sense of living at the heart of a city of style, of memory, of daring was part of urban citizenship too.

Paris was represented in a host of ways as the city of sophistication, of pleasure, of the good life as well. Here was the place to promenade and to be seen to promenade, as a host of witnesses noted.[67] Social life was lived in part on the streets and in the cafés, replicated in part in Berlin, but not in London.

The other side of the story of Parisian life, as we have noted, was more sombre. Of our three cities, Paris was the unhealthiest. Tuberculosis and alcoholism were urban plagues, not merely the invention of reformers. Still, the landscape of sensuality was there, recapitulating the earlier history of Paris as the centre of Court pleasure and the Enlightenment. It may not be implausible to suggest a return to these images in the early twentieth century. The sensuality of impressionist painting reinforces this idea. Renoir, after all, presented a memorable image of popular pleasures in his celebrated *Moulin de la Galette*. Paris appears there as a site of sensuality, with echoes of a more degraded kind not far away. We are not entirely in the realm of the *imaginaire* when we note that Paris was a magnet for prostitution[68] and for illegitimate births. Perhaps one-third of all births occurred outside wedlock on the eve of the war. Here is the meeting point of pleasure and poverty (see chapter 16). In sum, Paris retained its imaginative status as a free city, but one which knew little of the world around it.

This introduction can only provide a hint as to the richness of the social history of these three cities. It goes against the grain of our profession to use later developments to describe earlier ones. In effect, each of these cities in 1914 faced a myriad of possible futures, and the

[65] Henri Hauser, *Le problème du régionalisme* (Paris, 1924).

[66] Suzanna Barrows, *Miroirs déformants* (Paris, 1990).

[67] Walter Benjamin, *Passagen: Walter Benjamins Urgeschichte des neunzehnten Jahrhunderts*, ed. Norbert Bolz and Bernd Witte (Munich, 1984).

[68] See Alain Corbin, *Les filles de noce* (Paris, 1990).

parting of the ways arose more out of events than out of predetermined structures. This sense of the possible is perhaps the characteristic most clearly shared in these three cities. In these metropolitan centres, these 'Molochs', millions were exposed to a regime of rapid change, of a range of experience and impression, of a sense of grandeur and cosmopolitan life.[69] In this sense, Parisians, Berliners, and Londoners shared certain psychological strategies of adaptation to their environment; they may have conjured up a sense of well-being more linked to accommodation than to happiness. Perhaps this reticence, this constraint on hopes, unintentionally provided the residents of these capital cities with a better preparation for the disaster which was to follow than anyone could have known at the time.

69 'Moloch' is G. Simmel's phrase, in 'Les grandes villes et la vie de l'esprit', which appeared in 1903 in the *Jahrbuch der Gehestiftung*, and appeared in French in *Philosophie de la modernité: la femme, la ville, l'individualisme*, trans. by J. L. Vieillard-Baron (Paris, 1989), pp. 233–52.

Part 2
The social relations of sacrifice

3

Lost generations: the impact of military casualties on Paris, London, and Berlin

Adrian Gregory

For communities at war, military casualties predominate. The fundamental reality is loss of life and limb. All other considerations are secondary. If communities are viewed as the sphere in which the distribution of privileges and goods is negotiated through legal and political channels, then no decision is as important as the one which determines who will live and who will die violently. Those who volunteer or who are conscripted and lay down their lives for the common good become the moral touchstone by which others are judged. Death in war stands as the counterpoint to the pursuit of self-interest, the antithesis of shirking, hoarding, and profiteering. The death of the soldier or sailor is the exemplary sacrifice which has the moral power to evoke material sacrifice. The needs of 'total war'[1] subverted the dominant idea of political economy, the idea that the common good was served by the pursuit of self-interest. In its place it resurrected new forms of older ideals, those of Christian martyrdom and 'republican' civic humanism in which self-interest was *contrasted* to the common good.

The particular communities studied here occupied a unique place in their societies, aspects of which were described in chapter 2. When discussing casualties, the first question is whether or not the three capitals' inhabitants suffered military losses to a similar degree and in a similar chronological rhythm as did the nation as a whole. Put bluntly, when it came to the universal burden of death, did London, Paris, and Berlin pull their weight?

Any answer must be qualified, due to the unevenness of the statistical and administrative evidence available on each city. Full data on urban casualties were published in Berlin, but not in Paris or London. We have attempted to derive these data for the Allied capitals from partial sources, described below. For London, we have used the Roll of Honour

[1] Trevor Wilson has argued that this term is meaningless, that all it describes is a 'bloody big war'. This is to ignore the crucial aspect of ideological transformation that a 'total war' brings about. The difference is not merely quantitative but qualitative. T. Wilson, *The myriad faces of war* (Cambridge, 1986), p. 669.

of the London County Council, which provides much biographical detail on the men in the employment of the Council who died in the war. For Paris, we have consulted the Roll of Honour of the *commune* of Clichy, just north of the boundaries of the city. Here too rich biographical detail enables us to draw some inferences about the social composition of casualties in an area not unlike many other parts of Paris. The use of these sources was governed by the absence of alternatives. There are no other materials known to us which could establish plausible estimates of war losses in these cities. This is the first such attempt, and must be treated with the caution needed in all exploratory ventures.[2]

With these caveats in mind, we have presented our findings under the following heads. The first part of the chapter is statistical. First, we present estimates of the dimensions of the 'Lost Generation' in London, Paris, and Berlin. Secondly, we discuss the contrast between the voluntary system in London and conscription in the other two cities, and its implications for the chronology of urban losses. Thirdly, we describe the distribution by age and occupation of urban war losses. In the second half of the chapter, we present evidence as to the impact of casualties on this scale within urban communities and on some aspects of the treatment of the wounded. Here our treatment is not comprehensive, but relies on partial information to point to the presence of casualties within these three cities.

Demographic outlines

Summary tables 3.1 and 3.2 present estimates of military participation from the three metropolitan centres during the 1914–1918 war. They throw considerable light on the question as to whether city-dwellers contributed their share of soldiers and bore their share of casualties. On balance the answer seems to be that rates of mobilization in Paris and London were in line with those in France and Britain as a whole. But whereas 80 per cent of German males of military age were mobilized, only 60 per cent of the same cohort in Berlin were in uniform. It is possible that the Berlin statistics exclude men from the city who enlisted elsewhere. But even if this added a further 10 per cent to the proportion of the eligible cohort in uniform, it would still mean that the proportion of Berliners in uniform was below the national average. This is an important finding, with implications both for casualties and for relations between soldiers and civilians, both during and after the war.

Of those mobilized, Parisians suffered casualties slightly lower than the national average; Londoners, slightly higher. Given estimation

[2] Thanks are due to Peter Simkins and Wilhelm Deist for their advice on this point.

Table 3.1. *Military participation and military losses: the male population of Paris, London, and Berlin, 1914–1918*

City	Total male population	Males aged 15 to 49	Enlistment	Deaths on active service
Paris (Department of the Seine)	2,000,000	1,100,000	880,000	123,000
London (Greater London)	3,400,000	1,900,000	1,050,000	131,000
Berlin (Stadt)	995,000	600,000	350,000	54,000

Table 3.2. *Military participation and military losses: percentage enlisted and killed, Paris, London, and Berlin, compared to France, Britain, and Germany, 1914–1918*

City	Percentage enlisted of total of military age	Percentage killed of men mobilized	Percentage killed of total of military age
Paris	80.0	14.0	11.2
London	55.0	12.5	6.9
Berlin	59.0	15.4	9.0
France	79.0	16.8	13.3
Britain	53.0	11.8	6.3
Germany	81.0	15.4	12.5

errors, it is probably safe to conclude that the Allied capitals were not far from the national average in terms of war losses. Death-rates in uniform were higher in Paris than in London, as they were in France as compared to Britain as a whole. The gap between Paris and London was about 4 per cent; on the national level, the gap was somewhat larger, at 7 per cent. In Berlin, fewer eligible men went, but those who did so suffered casualties above the national average. This may have reflected the social composition of enlistment and rank, though again estimation errors require us to treat these distinctions with caution.

What is not at issue is the sheer scale of the slaughter. Table 3.1 indicates that approximately 300,000 men from these three cities died during the war. This is an underestimate of loss of life on active service in these metropolitan regions, since the Berlin figures refer only to the pre-1920 inner city. Had we been able to include deaths from the surrounding region, incorporated after the war in 'Greater Berlin', the total figure for deaths in these three metropolitan regions would probably have reached 350,000 or more. Whatever the precise figure, the reality was clear. The war was an unprecedented catastrophe, the shadow of which was cast over urban social history for decades after the Armistice.

Estimates of military participation

To evaluate the findings stated above, it is necessary to follow the logic of their calculation. We posited alternative assumptions about the value, in manpower terms, of the populations of the capital cities to the war effort and hence of the likelihood of casualties amongst their inhabitants. One view has it that the capital cities were large economies with an inevitable surplus of dispensable or substitutable military-age male labour. Populations were generally younger than the national average, they had manual dexterity and educational standards higher than the average, and were more exposed to nationalist and imperial propaganda. Younger, keener, more skilful, surely these were the kind of men that the armed forces would want in large numbers?

The opposing view questions the validity of these arguments. The cities had industries and services indispensable to the war effort; the men involved could not easily be replaced. Indeed many spheres needed to expand, creating a demand for male labour which withdrew available manpower. The grinding poverty caused by endemic unemployment and casual employment took its toll on the health of a substantial minority of the population. This view concedes that the urban population was more educated and skilful, but even when this didn't exempt them from military service altogether, it would keep them away from being used as cannon fodder. These cities had concentrations of indifferent or politically unreliable ethnic minorities, men who tried to evade military service or be rejected. Finally the urban working class was regarded with suspicion by the military authorities who had no faith in their discipline or their stamina in combat and who positively feared their potential for political subversion. In Germany in particular, 'The officer corps were terrified by the spectre of a mass army of Social Democrats who would disobey orders and turn their weapons against the existing state.'[3] This view is consistent with an under-

[3] V. R. Berghahn, *Germany and the approach of war in 1914* (London, 1973), pp. 16–17: for Britain see G. Dallas and D. Gill, *The unknown army* (London, 1985), pp. 18–19: 'The Army considered the health of city dwellers to be poor and their natures unsuited to military service.' For France, see J.-J. Becker, *Le carnet B: les pouvoirs publics et l'antimilitarisme pendant la guerre* (Paris, 1973). As Becker demonstrates, these fears proved groundless in 1914.

representation of city-dwellers in uniform and with their concentration in service arms away from the firing line.

Our research has led us to confirm parts of both hypotheses. What mattered was the interplay between the urban economies of these cities and the specific structure of military recruitment adopted in them.

The relative size of the three cities was crucial. With 16 per cent of Britons living in the London conurbation, it was inconceivable that the male population would not be drawn into the armed forces in large numbers. Any large-scale expansion of the armed forces was still-born without Londoners.

The French army, desperately short of manpower in its need to match German numbers and burdened with an ageing population, could not ignore the 10 per cent of young Frenchmen living in the Paris region before 1914. By contrast, the German army could have expanded without calling up any Berliners at all. It would have been politically disastrous to exempt the Prussian capital totally from the imperial effort, but the low requirement of Berliners and their subsequent return to industry was a measure of German demographic strength. Nevertheless, relative size was only one element in the story.

Social structure also played a part in determining the composition of armies. The commanders of the three nations would have agreed that rural labourers and peasants represented the ideal infantry soldiers. Inured to open-air living and physical labour and presumed to be deferential, they were perceived as more useful and more malleable as front-line soldiers. Yet availability differed vastly among the three nations.

It is well known that the largest single occupational group among French war dead was agricultural labourers. Not surprisingly, largely agricultural military districts, such as Orléans, Le Mans, Rennes, and Limoges suffered the highest losses relative to men enlisted.[4] A French peasant of military age may have been twice as likely to die in Horizon Blue as his industrial contemporary.

The British had no such rural reservoir of manpower to draw upon. The only substantial peasantry in the United Kingdom, that of rural Ireland, was alienated by ham-fisted recruiting, although the urban inhabitants of Ireland, regardless of confession, responded to the call for recruits. The British mainland rural population had been in long-term decline since the 1870s, emigrating to Dominions or migrating to the cities. Even before 1900, the recruitment of the army had been directed, by necessity rather than choice, towards the towns. With the outbreak of war, the volunteers who came forward were overwhelmingly urban. Kitchener, the Minister of War, was left with Hobson's choice. London

[4] J.-J. Becker, *The Great War and the French people* (Oxford and Providence, 1985), pp. 332–3.

clerks and sweatshop workers were not ideal infantrymen, but neither were Sheffield knifegrinders or Lancashire spinners.

These broad structural considerations substantially determined the numbers participating in the conflict and the proportion of metropolitan inhabitants in the front lines, but the interaction of the urban labour market and manpower planning (or its absence) had a further role to play, one that will be dealt with in the subsequent sections concerning the chronology of casualties, age structure, and occupational variations.

Estimates of London's military participation

Obtaining the relevant figures was more difficult than one would expect. There are no straightforward and authoritative sources that can be used. Relatively speaking, London is the most difficult case for estimating both recruitment and the death toll. Enlistment records for the city are patchy, to some degree accurate from August 1914 to July 1915[5] and again during 1918, but difficult to obtain for most of the war.

An estimate for war deaths of residents of the British capital has never been attempted. The supplement to the decennial census of 1921 subsumes the war dead callously in the category of 'out-migration'.[6] The supplement to the Registrar General's return for July 1918[7] provides a starting point for estimating the scale of recruitment. In this supplement the number of Londoners absent on military service was estimated by comparing a population estimate based on birth-rates with a population based on civilian death-rates. The assumption made was that servicemen remained an active part of the population with respect to the birth-rate only. Dubious as this assumption may seem, it does yield a figure consistent with the fragmentary evidence available from other sources. The figure for servicemen resident in London but absent from the city in mid-1918 was approximately 475,000 for the Administrative County of London and 790,000 for Greater London.[8]

This figure cannot be the total because of three categories it inevitably excludes: (1) those who died or were taken prisoner before mid-1918 on active service (largely excluded from the birth-rate estimate); (2) those wounded or sick and discharged (and therefore represented in the civilian death-rate); (3) those conscripted later than early 1918. Adequate allowance for each category must be made. A reasonable postulate is that at least 100,000 Londoners fell into the first category prior to mid-1918. Study of the demobilization statistics of the British

[5] London Intelligence Committee Reports, monthly. However the trade biases of these reports mean that they are not definitive. The Parliamentary Recruiting Committee also kept records for the period.

[6] See J. M. Winter, *The Great War and the British people* (London, 1986), ch. 3.

[7] *Registrar General's Report for England and Wales, 1918*, PP 1920, vol. X, Cmd 608.

[8] *Ibid.*

Army suggests a similar number of discharged men.[9] Finally, at least 50,000 men were recruited too late to influence the mid-1918 estimate. A conservative estimate, therefore, is that approximately 1,050,000 men from Greater London served in British forces during the Great War.

Of these men approximately 130,000 were killed or died on active service. This figure is based on the principle that if a reliable figure can be found for a part of the London population, then the total for London can be extrapolated from it. Two independent sources indicate that the percentage of Londoners killed whilst serving as other ranks in the London Regiment represented broadly 20 per cent of the total of Londoners who died on active service.[10] From this a global approximation of the London death toll can be obtained. Roughly 80 per cent of the other ranks who died with the London Regiment were resident in Greater London. This means that 26,000 Londoners died whilst serving in the ranks of this unit.[11] If this is 20 per cent of the total Greater London death toll, then the total for London was approximately 130,000.

About half of the Greater Londoners of military age served. Of those who served, approximately 12 per cent died. Both these figures are very close to the national average. They provide the grounds for arguing that London's military participation was roughly in line with that of the nation as a whole.

Estimates of Parisian military participation

For the Paris military district – larger than both Paris and the Department of the Seine – the conventional figure is that 1,083,000 men served and 114,200 were killed. This figure suggests that perhaps 80 per cent of the men of military age served and that 10.5 per cent of these men were killed or died. However both figures are likely to be an underestimate. Paris had large numbers of recent migrants who were called up to serve in their native military districts. The figure also excludes officers.

A re-examination of the statistics for Paris was necessary in order to test the accuracy of the published statistics. The district of Clichy may provide clues in this respect. Clichy was reasonably representative of the experience of Paris as a whole. It had a socially mixed population, a wide occupational spread and was close enough to the suburbs

9 E. Spears, *Statistics of the military effort of the British Empire* (London, 1922), p. 417.

10 *The London County Council Roll of Honour* (London, printed in two volumes 1915–16 and resumed 1919–20) yields 19 per cent in this category on a large and broad occupational base. The four fragmentary London volumes of the privately produced *National Roll of Honour* (London, 1915–22) show a similar 1 in 5 ratio. Both these sources are partial and potentially biased, but they are broad enough and large enough to be used.

11 *Soldiers died in the Great War, vol. 76r: London Regiment, Inns of Court OTC and the Honourable Artillery Company* (London, 1920; repr. Polstead, 1988).

(adjacent to the 17th arrondissement) to be influenced by the expansion of wartime industry.

By examining the 16,000 names on the pre-war electoral register, it was possible to trace part of the mobilizable population of Clichy: the 6,680 men of military classes 1890 to 1913. This was then compared with the death toll recorded in the *Livre d'Or* (Roll of Honour) which lists Clichy residents killed or who died on active service.[12] Such an examination revises the official participation ratio upwards. In the same military mobilization classes nationally, the number of men killed was 12.9 per cent. For Clichy the total is 11.5 per cent. In other words the discrepancy between Paris and the nation may have been less than the 1924 statistics published by Huber would suggest. There is a larger gap in the lower age groups, and the 'Clicheans' below voting age are not incorporated in this figure. Nevertheless the figure for both war deaths and war service of Parisians should be revised upwards. The real proportion of deaths to men serving is closer to 14 per cent and the estimate of men serving may be at least 100,000 too low. Figures at least as high as 880,000 serving soldiers from the Department of the Seine and 123,000 war dead are nearer the mark for this population. These figures suggest that Parisian men were sheltered compared to their rural counterparts but that the difference was less than has been assumed.

Military participation: the Berlin case

Berlin has the best statistical record on this question. The statistics published under the Weimar Republic for the historical record of the previous regime state that 53,605 Berliners died in uniform (see table 3.1).[13] Total recruitment of Berliners for the forces is more difficult to establish. In a work published in 1921, the total number of enlisted men, non-commissioned officers, and officers billeted in Berlin is listed. The figure divides those who were billeted after their initial mobilization from those who were billeted in the city for special training (*Durchmarschtruppen*). The former category is of interest here. Most of those billeted in the city were local residents who had just been conscripted or who had volunteered. Although the figure includes some Allied troops, it may be assumed that the number was negligible. The figure obviously excludes naval personnel and men enlisted in other recruitment areas, but it provides a rough order of magnitude. The total number of troops billeted in Berlin (city) between 1 August 1914 and 31 March 1919 was 309,532. They stayed on average about two weeks each.[14]

12 For received wisdom, see M. Huber, *La population de la France pendant la guerre* (Paris, 1931), p. 426. Huber gave this figure, but with reservations. For our estimates on Clichy, all figures are derived from *Le livre d'Or*, published in Desormeaux, *Clichy*.

13 *Statistik des Deutschen Reichs*, vol. 276, pp. li–lvi.

14 Kaeber, *Berlin*, p. 35.

It is unclear from internal evidence whether this figure best represents enlistment for Berlin proper or for Greater Berlin. Supporting evidence suggests that it may be accurate for Berlin narrowly defined. The net change in the male population of Stadt Berlin between 1913 and 1918 indicates a loss of male population of 332,226. Given civilian population movements and male mortality, this figure is in line with the estimate of 310,000 soldiers present in Berlin during the war.

We must exercise some caution before concluding that the total of soldiers billeted in the city represents the Berlin population serving during the Great War. We must recognize that among those who served were professional soldiers and young men of the mobilization classes of 1911 to 1914 then doing their military service. These men probably would not have been billeted in the city when general mobilization took place, but went straight to their units in the field. The size of this population is impossible to estimate. In Berlin in 1913 there were 86,893 men aged between twenty and twenty-four.[15] Given standards of medical fitness and other restrictions on active service, a conservative estimate would have it that perhaps half or roughly 40,000 of these men also served, though they were missed by the billeting statistics. Adding this figure to our previous estimate provides a total of roughly 350,000 Berliners in uniform during the Great War. Handled with care, this estimate provides at least an order of magnitude for military participation in Berlin during the conflict.

A further examination of military statistics reveals that Berlin's casualties were on average older than those in other parts of Germany. Being older, they were more likely to be married too: of the 54,000 men who died, 19,000 left widows behind. In other words, younger, single men in Berlin stayed out of uniform more than did the same cohort in other parts of Germany. Whereas in Germany as a whole, about half of those who died were under the age of twenty-five, in Berlin, roughly 40 per cent was in this age group. Hamburg's 'Lost Generation' had a similar age profile, whereas more rural Bavaria and Prussia as a whole followed the national norm.

Conclusion

This roundabout method of calculating enlistments and casualties in Paris, London, and Berlin offers the only comparative estimates available on the incidence of military participation in the metropolitan centres. In comparative terms, Berlin registered low mobilization but casualties at about the national rate. Both Paris and London followed the national pattern of mobilization. In terms of percentage killed of those

[15] *Statistik der Stadt Berlin*, 1915–1920, p. 190; on the size of the 1913 male cohort, see *Statistik der Stadt Berlin*, 1912–1914, pp. 26–9.

who served, Paris suffered slightly lower than average war losses; London, slightly higher. But both Allied capitals were roughly in line with the national experience.

The special case of London: the voluntary system

Any comparison of the three cities must start with a fundamental point. Berlin and Paris in 1914 were the capital cities of societies with conscription; London was not. That the voluntary enlistment system had survived in Britain in the years prior to the Great War was an historical anomaly. No other major European power offered its citizens or subjects the right to choose whether or not to serve in the armed forces. More remarkable still was the fact that Britain retained this policy through a year of involvement in continental warfare. Various explanations can be put forward for the British refusal to enter the world of mass conscript armies. The strategic interests of Britain for a century had been defined principally in colonial terms, creating a reliance on a capital-intensive rather than a manpower-intensive navy and an increasing use of the Indian army as an imperial policeman. The need for extra-continental mobility had militated in favour of a small but long-service regular army. The desire to avoid paying the economic or political costs of larger land forces had created a climate opposed to the extension of military service.

Nevertheless the pressure for compulsory enlistment mounted during the Edwardian period. The British army was small and overstretched, urbanization and emigration had undermined its recruiting base amongst the rural populations of Britain and Ireland. Furthermore the appearance of the German naval threat had raised the spectre of invasion and the need to fight a war on land. Finally the secret clauses of the Entente Cordiale committed Britain to send an army to France. The result was the growth of political pressure for 'national service'.

That this pressure was resisted may be credited in part to the nature of the London labour market. The social structure of recruitment for the regular British army changed dramatically in the late nineteenth century to a point where roughly half the rank and file were drawn from the lowest stratum of urban life, the unskilled, casual labour and domestic service. The army of 1914 did not reflect the structure of the nation as a whole, preponderantly a nation of miners, ship builders, and 'manufacturing hands'. It did reflect the structure of the poorer areas of the great cities and particularly London.[16]

London was a double asset for the army in that it provided the right

[16] E. M. Spiers, 'The regular army in 1914', in I. Beckett (ed.), *A nation in arms* (Manchester, 1985), pp. 37–62, esp. p. 45.

occupational structure for dealing with the problem of reservists. Long service and little useful training damaged the later job prospects of men discharged from the forces. These men had missed apprenticeships in manufacturing and were often in poor health. London, with its huge tertiary sector, provided a refuge for such men. It was a centre of domestic service, portering, and a host of uniformed jobs (post office, police, transport, commissionaires), where a military background was an asset. For example, on 4 August 1914 the *Daily Mail* stated that over 1,000 metropolitan policemen had been called to the colours.[17] It is difficult to know precisely how many ex-servicemen settled in London, but it is reasonable to assume that they far outnumbered the already substantial numbers who originated there.

In London too the prominence of the white-collar sector had given rise to a substantial amateur military tradition. With the foundation of the Territorial Army in 1909, London was earmarked to provide the manpower for two divisions, and this understates the real significance of Greater London in volunteer units by about a third. Large numbers of the London middle classes had volunteered for the Yeomanry during the Boer War, and London units had been prominent in indicating their willingness to serve overseas. At the outbreak of war London Territorial units were quickly committed to the European war.

Chronologies of war losses

Paris

At the outbreak of war three French military classes were with the colours, those of 1911 to 1913. On mobilization they were joined by the classes of 1896 to 1910. In September they were supplemented by the twenty-year-olds of the class of 1914, and by the end of the year the classes of 1892 to 1895 and of 1915 had been called up. In April 1915 the class of 1916 was called up, as were the classes of 1889 to 1891. By spring 1915 the French army had theoretically incorporated 80 per cent of French males aged between eighteen and forty-six years of age, ranging from 60 per cent of the older groups to 90 per cent of the youngest. Exemptions were provided for the chronically ill (often consumptive), the disabled, and fathers of six or more children (unusual in Paris!). Only 1.5 per cent of the population dodged the draft.

In practice certain occupations, crucial to the war effort, were partially protected from mobilization at the start. Some – such as the 80 per cent of railway workers and postal workers who avoided military service or the 33 per cent of tax-collectors and policemen who were exempt – would have been prominent in Paris; others – such as miners – would not.

[17] *Daily Mail*, 4 August 1914, p. 3.

To examine the chronology of casualties for Paris, the Clichy sample has been taken as broadly representative. The months of death of Clichy residents can be tabulated to provide an overview of when Parisian casualties occurred. The results are displayed in fig. 3.1.

In the opening months of the war workers in manufacturing industry took their chances with the rest. There was no anticipation of a long war with the concomitant industrial mobilization entailed. As a result, Parisians participated fully, perhaps even disproportionately, in the opening clashes of the Frontiers and the Marne. The high casualties for September 1914 in the Clichy sample suggest that Parisians fought desperately as the German armies closed in on their families and that they continued to fight tenaciously until the invading force was repulsed a safe distance.

High casualties were sustained in the offensives of spring and autumn 1915, but a clear change is observable by February 1916. During the worst of the Battle of Verdun, the casualties for Clichy remained at relatively low levels. Even when they rose in the autumn of 1916 as French armies attacked at Verdun and on the Somme, they remained low in absolute terms.

At these points Clichy diverged from the nation. Why? The most plausible answer is that skilled men were being released from the army to build and operate the vast defence industries which grew from mid-1915 in the Paris region. Indeed this is indicated by the relatively low casualties in 1916–1917 reported in the *Livre d'Or* for Clichy. As many Parisian workers were removed from the firing line to work in the growing industries, the proportion of Parisians in the army dropped and so too did Parisian casualties. By June 1917, 36 per cent of the workers under the Ministère de l'armamente and the Sous-secrétariat de l'aviation were recalled servicemen, a total of over 611,000. Many of these, particularly in the aircraft industry, were working in the Paris region. For example, at the Blériot factory at Suresnes 1,000 of the 1,420 employees were recalled servicemen.[18]

The casualties continued to drop in 1917, reflecting both the protection of workers and the ending of offensive operations in the wake of the Nivelle offensive. It is worth noting that London's casualties rose during this period, reflecting the shift of the offensive burden on the Western front to Britain from France.

In 1918 casualties rose once more, reflecting the renewed defence of Paris and the counter-offensive of summer and autumn 1918. In addition we must take into account the release of factory workers for service under the *loi Mourier*, under which the army had the right to

[18] Archives Nationales (AN) F22/11334, Commission inter-ministérielle de la main d'oeuvre, 1 July 1917; Robert, 'Ouvriers et mouvement ouvrier', vol. I, p. 88.

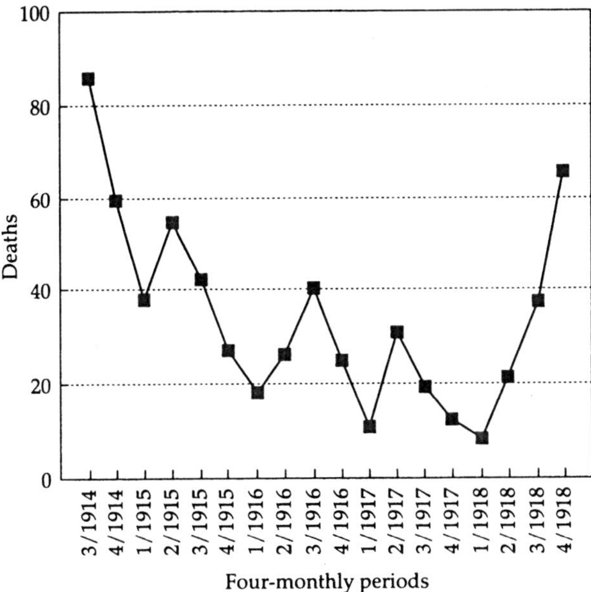

Fig. 3.1 Deaths on military service, Clichy, 1914 to 1918, by four-monthly periods

recall to the front industrial workers between the ages of twenty-four and thirty-five who had been removed from active service in 1914 and 1915.[19] Finally the ravages of the bitter fighting at the end of the war, as well as the pandemic of influenza, rendered October 1918 the third worst month of the war.

Berlin

There were certain broad similarities between French and German patterns of enlistment and military participation. Every German male was eligible for military service between the ages of seventeen and forty-five. At the age of twenty he could be called up for two years' regular service (or three in the cavalry). In 1914 this meant that the classes of 1912 and 1913 were with the colours before mobilization. For the next five years all men served with the regular reserve. At mobilization the 'regular' army consisted of the classes of 1907 to 1913. However, to the surprise of their opponents, the Germans rapidly mobilized their 'reserve forces' and put them straight into action. These consisted of men in the first and second 'Ban' of the *Landwehr*, for which Germans were eligible up to the age of thirty-nine. Such was the demographic strength of Germany that the army had been able to be

[19] J. Horne, 'L'impôt du sang', pp. 220–1.

selective in terms of recruitment both with respect to physical fitness and political reliability (as well as affording the luxury of two, rather than three, years of full service). It seems probable that in the initial months of the war a substantial part of the available manpower was not called, and among them were thousands of Berliners.

In theory, the organization of the German army was federal. Bavaria, for example, retained a separate army structure under the loose control of the Prussian War Ministry. Organization remained strongly regional. Berlin was the centre of the III corps district (Brandenburg). It could be assumed, therefore, that the bulk of Berliners mobilized at the outbreak of war served in one of the four divisions recruited in this area, the 5th and 6th Divisions (III Brandenburg corps) and the 5th and 6th Reserve (III Reserve corps). However Prussia as a whole (together with Alsace Lorraine) also contributed the manpower for the Prussian Guard, in which many Berliners served. This regional recruiting system and the fact that Berliners served predominantly in a small number of units present convergences with London and divergences from Paris. Parisians would probably be recruited by specific regiments, but these regiments were spread throughout the army's divisions, with a consequent spreading of casualties.

Among the units which recruited Berliners were elite troops. In 1914 the 5th Division was with Von Kluck's army and served successively at Charleroi, the Marne, and the Aisne; the 6th was at Mons, the Marne, and the Aisne. All the units associated with Berlin fought on the Western front in 1914 and in some of the bitterest fighting. The reserve units fought at Antwerp and on the Yser, the Prussian Guard at Ypres. The use of these units as assault forces continued. The III corps was the force which took Fort Douaumont at Verdun and subsequently suffered ghastly casualties in the May offensives. Its units were then transferred to the bitter struggles on the Somme.[20]

As the war progressed, other units emerged with a Berlin component. A second group of divisions was formed in October 1914, and the regiments comprising some of these 201 to 206 Infantry were Berlin recruited. Also important amongst the middle classes were volunteer regiments, drawn partially from the first 'Ban' of the *Ersatzreserve*. These were comprised largely of young men below the age of twenty who volunteered before they were called up. Famed for their (heavily romanticized) assault at Langemark, these regiments appear to have

[20] For the above discussion, see A. Horne, *The price of glory. Verdun 1916* (London, 1962), pp. 105–24, 189. For unit histories see *Histories of two hundred and fifty one divisions of the German army which participated in the war (1914–1918) compiled from the records of the intelligence section of the general staff, American Expeditionary Forces* (Chaumont 1919; repr., London Stamp Exchange, 1989), pp. iii, 109–10, 112–14, 128–31, 132–3 and throughout.

appealed to the middle-class students of Berlin.[21] Many graduates of the Kaiser Wilhelm Gymnasium listed in the school's Roll of Honour served with them. This accounts for the high casualties in the chart of casualties by month for October 1914.

Many newcomers to Berlin would have served in the units of the districts from which they originated. The Gymnasium students served in a broad range of units as officers; nevertheless a sufficiently large number served in III corps to justify considering the chronology of their casualties: 1915 was a bad year, with serious casualties incurred on both the Eastern and Western fronts; May 1916 represents a late peak. After that casualties remain at a relatively low level, particularly in the autumn and winter of 1917.

The casualties of present and former pupils of the Kaiser Wilhelm Gymnasium total roughly 20 per cent killed of all who served, suggesting heavy casualties for Berlin as a whole. But in fact Berlin was a workers' city, and in wartime Berliners in uniform were an active minority. The heavily industrialized nature of the city meant that even at the outset proportionately fewer Berliners were conscripted than Parisians (27 per cent as opposed to 30 per cent in September), and it seems that the recall of Berlin workers to man war-related industries began early. Indeed, many workers may not have gone in the first place, since the War Ministry was forced to attempt to comb out younger men as early as April 1915.[22]

A total of 92,400 workers was recalled to Berlin in the course of the war.[23] Furthermore at the outbreak of war 33 per cent of the Berlin population (compared to 38 per cent in London and 25 per cent in Paris) was below military age. It may well be the case that, despite volunteering, many of the classes of 1914 to 1919 were drawn directly into war-related industries rather than called up into the armed forces.

This lower rate of military mobilization had important implications both for the chronology and age structure of Berlin casualties. Exemptions from military service grew exponentially in the middle years of the war for industrial workers. At the end of 1915, 600,000 fit men, 'liable to field duty' (KV) were exempted in Germany. In early 1916 this grew to 740,000.[24] The Prussian War Ministry held this figure in check until autumn 1916, when the Hindenburg Programme with its emphasis on substituting machines for men was instituted. From September 1916 to July 1917 the number of fit men exempted rose to 1 million.[25] By January 1918 the number of KV exemptions had risen to 1.2 million, and a total of

[21] The volunteers were less dominant at the battle (actually fought at Bixchoote) than legend suggested. See G. Mosse, *Fallen Soldiers* (New York, 1990), p. 71.

[22] G. D. Feldman, *Army, industry and labor in Germany, 1914–1918* (Oxford, 1992), p. 68.

[23] *Statistik des Deutschen Reichs*, vol. 406, pp. 2–5.

[24] G. D. Feldman, *Army, industry and labor*, p 73.

[25] *Ibid.*, p. 301.

2.3. million men of military age were exempted. The belated attempt of the High Command to comb out 30,000 men[26] between October and December 1917 was a drop in the ocean.

Berlin represents a special case, in that its industrial character limited the degree to which its male population was mobilized. The city did have a heavily engaged minority in elite military units, which reflected its Prussian history. These men suffered high casualties. Other groups stayed put, manning the war industries, perhaps creating a wider gap in Berlin than in London or Paris between those who fought and those who stayed at home.

London

For London there is no district such as Clichy which might be considered representative in order to assemble a chronology of military death for the city. Residential separation was extreme in class terms, and some alternative data base must be sought. The Roll of Honour of the London County Council (LCC) is an attractive alternative. The wide range of residential areas and occupations of LCC employees allows the construction of a chronology that may cautiously suggest the experience of the metropolis as a whole. About 1,000 deaths among this population may be reliably analysed for this purpose.

There are flaws in these data. LCC employees were older than average and more likely to have seen previous military service. Some working-class occupations were under-represented. Nevertheless the figures do show certain features which other evidence implies are applicable to the metropolis as a whole. If the LCC losses are plotted against the national chronology of losses,[27] then two points immediately appear. First, there is a robust correlation between the two graphs; and, secondly, there are clear deviations which can be traced to particular features of the war Londoners fought (see fig. 3.2).

In terms of the chronology of losses, the London pattern departed from that of Berlin and Paris. The continental cities suffered their major casualties early in the war. By contrast the medial date of death amongst LCC employees was November 1916, and there is reason to believe that this would have been later for Londoners as a whole, since a high proportion of LCC casualties were army reservists, thrown into the fighting early in the war. Most Londoners who died on active service did so later in the war.[28]

In effect, Paris and Berlin suffered the worst haemorrhaging in 1914

[26] *Ibid.*, p. 417.

[27] Compiled by mapping the monthly military losses in all theatres (published in the *Statistics of the Military Effort of the British Empire during the Great War* (London, 1922) and adding known large incidents of naval loss).

[28] More research is needed on the social history of reservists.

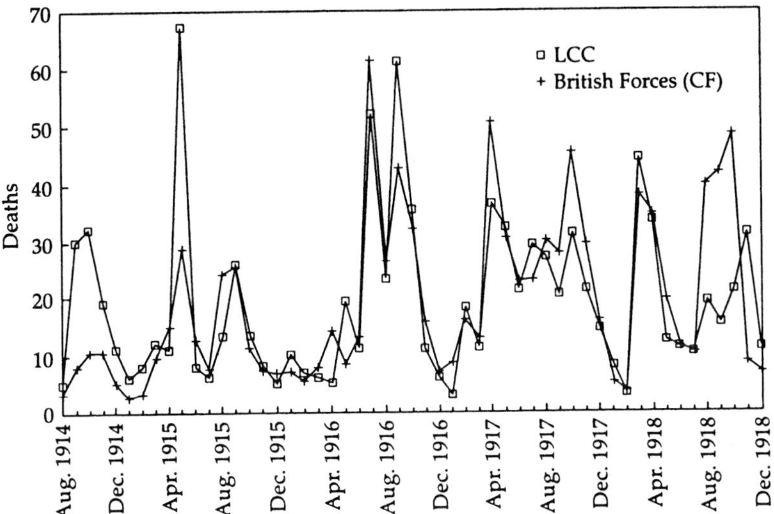

Fig. 3.2 LCC war deaths, 1914 to 1919, compared to a counterfactual estimate of British war losses

and 1915, whereas London suffered more in late 1916, 1917, and 1918. Yet London deviates from the British national total in the same direction as Paris and Berlin from their respective nations: towards earlier casualties. About 32 per cent of the LCC casualties were sustained before the opening of the Somme offensive (1 July 1916), compared with 20 per cent of British casualties.

Conscription did not begin in Britain until early 1916. Prior to this date, London's casualties were exclusively volunteers or reservists (peacetime volunteers) and remained predominantly volunteers for a great deal longer, perhaps even up to the end of the war. The first Londoners involved were regulars and reservists. Of the regular army at the outbreak of war it seems reasonable to estimate that some 20,000 came from London. Of the 120,000 or so army reservists called up on 2 August, it seems reasonable to assume that as many as 40,000 were resident in London. Once naval reservists are added, it seems possible that 80,000 Londoners were in uniform by 4 August 1914. This had an effect on casualties: 1,200 sailors, mostly reservists, died with the sinking of three cruisers in the North Sea in September 1914. Casualties amongst the mostly reservist infantry of the British Expeditionary Force (BEF) were massive in the first four months of the war. If London was disproportionately involved, then its casualties were also disproportionately heavy.

Londoners were heavily represented amongst the earliest volunteers. Perhaps half the volunteers in the first week following Kitchener's appeal came from the metropolis.[29] This reflected the fact that many who responded initially were of a similar type to those recruited by the army in peacetime; it also suggested the better organization of London recruiting, the faster flow of information about the war in the capital, and the disruption of commercial life – the Stock Exchange closed at the outbreak of war. It is probably not coincidental that the first 'pals' battalion recruited in London was the 'stockbrokers' battalion'.

London volunteers were utilized in a different fashion from those of the provinces. Whilst the provinces were forming the New Army divisions, Londoners were channelled principally into existing structures. The London Regiment, with its large establishment of part-time troops and its particular social composition, expanded massively in the first months of the war. London eventually raised four divisions of territorials. Roughly 20 per cent of Londoners who died in the war served in the ranks in one or other of the battalions of the London Regiment.[30] If officers and men in territorial support units are included, it is likely that some 25 per cent of Londoners who served were in one or other of the London divisions. These divisions remained principally composed of Londoners to the end of the war; unlike other territorial forces they did not markedly dilute their regional recruiting.[31]

In summary, perhaps 25 per cent of Londoners served with London divisions, in which they constituted the overwhelming majority. The other 75 per cent were scattered relatively evenly through the armed forces as a whole, but with a high component of high-risk groups, particularly reservists and officers. Therefore the chronology of London deaths reflects three points: (1) high initial casualties; (2) a particular reflection of high casualties when the London divisions were engaged in fighting; but (3) a tendency broadly to mirror national losses.

This is precisely the picture presented by a frequency analysis of LCC employee deaths by month. The peak in May 1915 reflects the disastrous assault on Festubert by the London regiments. The peak in September 1916 represents the casualties sustained by the 47th and 56th London divisions in the battle of Fleurs-Courcellette on the Somme. On the other hand, the peaks for 1914 represent reservist casualties and the peaks for July 1916, April–May 1917, October 1917, and March 1918 represent the losses sustained by the army as a whole in the Somme offensive, Arras, Passchendaele, and the 1918 German spring offensive.

The most serious deviation from this pattern occurred in autumn 1918, where LCC losses were far below the national figure, determined

[29] Simkins, *Kitchener's army*, p. 49.

[30] Based on percentages in *LCC Roll of Honour* and in the London volumes of the (very partial) *National Roll of Honour* (London, 1915–22).

[31] Ian Beckett, 'The territorial force', in Beckett (ed.), *A nation in arms*, pp. 128–63, esp. p. 147.

both by offensive action and increasingly by the ravages of influenza. This reflects the absence of substantial numbers of conscripts in the LCC death toll. Only four LCC casualties enlisted in 1918. This is partly an institutional bias: local government was a protected occupation. But it also reflects the more general failure of conscription to uncover surplus manpower in London. By autumn 1918 the British army had become largely a conscript force, yet the London area failed to provide many field-service fit (grade 1) conscripts for the army. The reports on the fitness of recruits in 1918 show that the entire county area of London yielded only 65,000 Londoners for the army in both grades 1 and 2 between January and October. Almost half of those recruited were not fit for any combatant role.[32]

Each city therefore reflected national experience in the chronology of loss whilst simultaneously deviating from it. All three cities suffered heavy casualties earlier than the national average, more markedly in the case of Paris than the other two. This leads to the theme of the next two sections in which we try to discover who these casualties were.

Which generation lost?

In establishing the age structure of death for the three cities it is once again necessary to utilize a range of sources not directly comparable. The French sources usually refer to 'generations', that is, birth cohorts, in calculating death-rates. The British sources refer to age at death, which is hardly surprising given the absence of conscription before the war. It is inevitable that comparisons will be limited due to the variety of evidence available.

For Clichy the limitations of an examination based on the electoral register are immediately apparent. The electoral register only includes men of voting age and therefore automatically excludes the younger military classes who were an important segment of the casualties. But even allowing for this bias, it is clear that, over time, casualties grew older. In 1914, 8 per cent of the men who died belonged to the classes of 1899 and earlier (men over the age of thirty-five). By 1915 this had risen to 20 per cent, and thereafter this figure rose to 30 per cent. The youngest classes – those of 1910 to 1913 (under the age of twenty-five) suffered 33 per cent of the casualties in 1914, falling to 20 per cent subsequently. The number of casualties in the classes of 1914 and after is impossible to estimate. The Clichy figures suggest that the young bore the brunt of casualties in 1914, but thereafter older soldiers predominated in the lists of the fallen.

32 'Report on the physical examination of men of military age by National Service Medical Boards', PP 1919, vol. xxvi, Cmd 504.

There is additional evidence that Parisian casualties were older than average for France as a whole. In the Archives Nationales, there are nominal lists of all Parisians who died on active service. Amongst the officers of the 1st arrondissement who died, the average age at death was thirty-one. Amongst the other ranks of the 4th arrondissement the average age of death was thirty-three. These records appear to be incomplete and possibly unrepresentative, but they are suggestive. They support the argument that metropolitan casualties were older than average, a finding consistent with the evidence available for Clichy.[33] Amongst the employees of a Paris textile firm, for which we have complete figures, the average age at death was twenty-nine.[34]

To assess the charge that the heaviest burden of war casualties were borne by older cohorts, we must turn to evidence on Berlin and London. For London precise figures are difficult to establish. Just as the Clichy data are of limited use in this context, the London County Council figures are suspect. The LCC Roll of Honour gives a median age for the dead of over thirty.[35] The nature of LCC employment would suggest that this may reflect employment rather than casualties. An alternative method is to use the age of death amongst Londoners who died of disease and wounds and were buried in London cemeteries between 1914 and 1919. This gives an older-than-average age structure.[36] Some of these men died of illness, and may have been too old for combat. Nevertheless, it seems likely that Londoners who died in the armed forces during the war were several years older than the national average, around the age of twenty-seven as opposed to twenty-three. Put another way, 74 per cent of British losses were aged under thirty, but only 56 per cent of the London sample we have examined were in this cohort.[37]

The best statistics we have are the meticulous figures for Berlin. These strongly confirm that the average metropolitan casualty was older than his provincial counterpart. In Germany as a whole 49 per cent of those who died in the war were aged twenty-five or below, but for Berlin the figure was only 41 per cent. Other data point to the same conclusion: 38 per cent of Germans killed were between the ages of twenty-six and thirty-five, a figure identical to that for Prussia as a whole. In contrast, 40 per cent of Berliners belonged to this older age group. Above the age of thirty-five the disparity is striking: 13 per cent of all Germans and 19 per cent of Berliners belonged to the older classes (see fig. 3.3 and tables 3.3 and 3.4).

[33] AN, F7 12453. *Livre d'Or*, analysed by Jay Winter.

[34] AN, F7 12453. *Livre d'Or*, Liste des employés de la Maison Rabaudi Fils, 7 rue du Quatre Septembre, Paris, analysed by Jay Winter.

[35] *LCC Roll of Honour*, 1,000 valid cases.

[36] National Inventory of War Memorials: Registers of Streatham, Mitcham, and Bethnal Green war cemeteries.

[37] See J. M. Winter, *The Great War*, ch. 3.

Table 3.3. *Age distribution of total military losses, Germany, 1914 to 1919*

Age-group	Germany	Berlin	Prussia	Westfalen	Bavaria	Hamburg
15–20	155,953	4,613	98,714	8,635	14,574	2,814
20–25	674,331	17,256	416,785	47,670	72,639	13,077
25–30	389,904	12,592	242,302	27,638	40,853	8,674
30–35	247,760	9.073	153,762	16,270	25,282	6,315
35–40	147,567	6,005	91,583	8,535	14,096	3,966
40–45	58,600	2,997	37,938	2,335	4,498	1,571
45–50	14,510	853	9,612	509	815	445
50–55	1,292	75	765	31	116	57
55–60	734	30	450	20	68	32
60+	500	24	270	4	61	20
Unknown	690	87	628	35	11	8
Total	1,691,841	53,605	1,052,809	111,682	172,945	36,937
Single	1,163,199	33,626	720,411	79,475	129,875	24,178
Married	518,351	19,336	326,240	31,728	42,211	12,389
Widowed	7,772	399	4,862	421	700	225
Divorced	2,192	244	1,296	58	159	145
Unknown	327	0				

Source: Statistik des Deutschen Reiches, V. 276, pp. li–lvi.

Table 3.4. *Percentage distribution of German war losses, 1914, according to age and marital status*

Age-group	Germany	Berlin	Prussia	Westfalen	Bavaria	Hamburg
15–20	9.2	8.6	9.4	7.7	8.4	7.6
20–5	39.9	32.2	39.6	42.7	42.0	35.4
25–30	23.0	23.5	23.0	24.7	23.6	23.5
30–35	14.6	16.9	14.6	14.6	14.6	17.1
35–40	8.7	11.2	8.7	7.6	8.1	10.7
40–45	3.5	5.6	3.6	2.1	2.6	4.2
45–50	0.9	1.6	0.9	0.5	0.5	1.2
50–55	0.1	0.1	0.1	0.0	0.1	0.2
55–60	0.0	0.1	0.0	0.0	0.0	0.0
60+	0.0	0.0	0.0	0.0	0.0	0.1
Unknown	0.0	0.2	0.1	0.0	0.0	0.0
Total	100.0	100.0	100.0	100.0	100.0	100.0
Single	68.8	62.7	68.4	71.2	75.1	65.4
Married	30.6	36.1	31.0	28.4	24.4	33.5
Widowed	0.5	0.7	0.5	0.4	0.4	0.6
Divorced	0.1	0.5	0.1	0.1	0.1	0.4
Unknown	0.0	0.0	0.0	0.0	0.0	0.0

Source: Statistik des Deutschen Reiches, V. 276, pp. li–lvi.

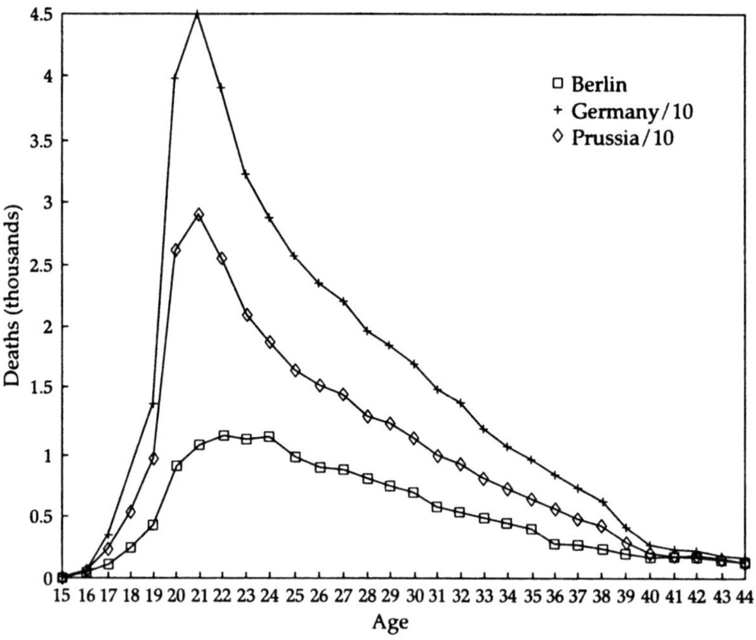

Fig. 3.3 Age distribution of German war losses: Berlin, Prussia, Germany, 1915 (15 to 44)

The weight of available evidence from all three cities points to the conclusion that metropolitan casualties as a group were older than their provincial counterparts. Yet this conclusion is strongly counter-intuitive. Metropolitan populations were younger than that of the nations to which they belonged. How can the paradox be explained? Two solutions can be put forward. One is imbedded in the available evidence. Young immigrants between the ages of eighteen and twenty-five have probably escaped the records in all three cities. The second explanation addresses the paradox directly. In London 38 per cent of the population was below military age in 1914; in Berlin and Paris, the figure was 33 per cent and 25 per cent respectively. Although there was under-age volunteering in all three cities, it may be assumed that the vast majority of those between the ages of fourteen and twenty remained in civilian employment in the first year of the war. Because of the growth of war industries in all three cities, it is likely that many of these male youths were drawn into such employment. Once they were employed in 'protected' industries, they were less likely to be released for military service.

A paradoxical conclusion follows. The youthful profile of the cities had the peculiar effect of placing a disproportionate burden on the middle-aged inhabitants. And indeed, in some cases, on still older men.

Both the Clichy and the *LCC Rolls of Honour* show that a small, but significant, number of volunteers died above the supposed maximum military age. Similarly, Berlin had twice as many casualties aged fifty plus as the whole of Westphalia. The 'Lost Generation' of all three cities had a sprinkling of men in their fifties. In the case of Paris these would be men who could have remembered the siege of 1870, and who might be expected to have a heightened sense of patriotism. Londoners aged fifty and over included a number who had served as volunteers in the South African war. More generally, the bulk of metropolitan casualties would have been broadly between twenty-five and forty years of age. These were men born between 1875 and 1890, the last of the 'Victorians' coming of age around the turn of the century, men brought up in a more certain age than their younger counterparts.[38] They were in 1914 men with settled lives, who did not simply rush off in the heat of the outbreak of war. They knew what they were doing. Significantly, many would have been husbands and fathers. The Berlin casualties were 20 per cent more likely to be married than the national average. Nearly 20,000 had wives, and a measurable percentage were widowed or divorced. This unusual age structure of casualties, older than average, had a direct bearing on the destruction of families and the upheaval inevitably occasioned by loss of life in war.

By death divided?

Was the burden of death in uniform equally distributed among urban social groups in the three cities? Given the unevenness and ambiguities in data on occupation in Berlin, a full comparative treatment of this question is beyond the scope of this study. Instead we limit our remarks primarily to Paris and London, with some comment where appropriate on Berlin.

In all three cities there was resentment during the war over the notion that certain groups, particularly industrial workers, had evaded the 'blood tax' levied on the population as a whole. Were these cities havens for shirkers within particular occupation groups?

The *LCC Roll of Honour* provides useful evidence on this contention. Enlistment was roughly 60 per cent manual, ranging from park sweepers to skilled mechanics, and roughly 40 per cent non-manual, ranging from office-boys to doctors, architects, and solicitors. An analysis of casualties shows a slightly greater risk to the non-manual part of the labour force (see table 3.5). Fragmentary evidence on Berlin municipal employees shows the same pattern of higher losses among officials (*Beamte*) than among manual workers (*Arbeiter*).

[38] On the concept of a generation of 1914, see R. Wohl, *The generation of 1914* (London, 1979), though this study reinforces the view that it was youth which dominated war losses.

The problem remains that the general classes of white-collar and blue-collar labour hide as much as they reveal. If risk is analysed by occupation, a more nuanced picture emerges. Casualties by occupation varied according to a series of factors. One of the most important was the age profile in the occupation. This dictated the likelihood of serving in the firing line. Equally significant was the degree of protection from military enlistment of workers and those engaged in essential public services, like the railways. This affected time spent at risk. In Berlin and Paris this meant likelihood of recall for war work on the home front. In Britain this was more likely to relate to the number of territorials or reservists in an occupation and therefore the likelihood of serving very early in the war. Next was usefulness of skills to the army. This decided the likelihood of use in a non-combatant capacity or in a lower-risk role. Drivers, for example, were more likely to be used in a support arm than the infantry; mechanics would often be used in a maintenance capacity. The health profile of an occupational group would matter. Unskilled but fit manual workers would be sent to the trenches, but many urban inhabitants developed occupational diseases rendering them unfit for the front line. The educational standards and social prestige of certain occupations often determined the likelihood of serving in high-risk roles, such as officers and air-crews. In the British case, the expansion of the voluntary army forced a wholesale recruiting effort for suitable 'temporary' officers many of whom were drawn from the middle classes and filled prestigious London battalions like the London Rifle Brigade, the Honourable Artillery Company, and the Artists' Rifles. Finally there were intangibles such as the patriotism, enthusiasm, or caution associated with different classes and occupations.

A wide variety of options emerged in wartime, with differing risks attached to them. Most of these qualifying variables worked to limit the time spent in the front line by sections – and only some sections – of the urban working class.

The figures reported in table 3.5 define the casualty rate as a percentage of those who served. If these figures are applied to the total workforce, the discrepancies widen. Thus in the British case, 63 per cent of the workforce in finance and commerce had enlisted by July 1918, compared with 45 per cent in manufacturing. In banking alone the figure was almost 80 per cent in uniform. Therefore the corrected figures would suggest that some 4 to 5 per cent of the total pre-war work force in manufacturing died during the war compared with 16 per cent of the workforce in banking.[39]

The statistics for Clichy (table 3.6) are based on a different denominator. Those at risk are men whose names appear on the electoral register

[39] See J. M. Winter, *The Great War*, ch. 2.

Table 3.5. *London's military participation and war losses, for London County Council employees, and for some other groups of employees, in rank order of proportion of those who died in the war*

Occupation	Enlistment	Deaths	% deaths
School caretakers	138	24	17.3
Bank employees	2,800	440	15.7
Park services employees	424	61	14.3
Insurance employees	108	15	13.8
London			12.3
Teachers	2,353	273	11.6
Dock workers	3,629	403	11.1
LCC	21,861	2,357	10.8
Asylum workers	943	97	10.3
Gas workers	4,024	417	10.3
Post-office workers	436	43	9.9
Tramway workers	3,507	334	9.5
Electricity workers	2,000	162	8.1
Fire brigade/ambulance workers	345	27	7.8

Sources: LCC Record of Service; Lloyds of London Roll of Honour; Croydon, Wimbledon, Northwood, and Kensington Post Office Memorials; *South Metropolitan Gas Company Roll of Honour; Port of London Authority Roll of Honour; Institute of Electrical Engineers Roll of Honour; National Provincial and Union Bank Roll of Honour; National Westminster and Parrs Bank Roll of Honour.*

in 1914. Given the near universality of conscription, and the low rate of non-compliance with orders to join up, these totals describe the number of men in Clichy eligible for military service on the eve of the war.

One common feature of casualties by occupation in all three cities was the high proportion of casualties amongst clerks. The replacement over time of the male clerk 'with the copperplate handwriting . . . by the female ledger clerk and the shorthand typist'[40] may have been accelerated by high war casualties among male clerks.

Teachers may also have been a high-risk group. In Berlin over 30 per cent of the staff of the Kaiser Wilhelm Gymnasium (an elite school) was killed compared with 20 per cent of the former pupils. The figure of 20 per cent for the former Gymnasium pupils is also relevant at this point, in that most worked in the financial and commercial sectors, which suffered almost identically high casualty rates in British forces. It is also worth noting that the average age of those listed amongst the former casualties of the Gymnasium was substantially lower than the Berlin

[40] Peter Dewey, 'The new warfare and economic mobilization' in John Turner (ed.), *Britain and the First World War* (London, 1988), p. 76.

Table 3.6. *Clichy: military participation and war losses by occupation, in rank order of percentage killed of men of military age*

Occupation	Mobilizable	Deaths	% deaths
Printing workers	261	50	19.2
Unskilled workers	1,086	161	14.8
Wine merchants/café and restaurant workers	173	25	14.5
Merchants/shopkeepers (not food trades)	121	17	14.0
Building workers	892	124	13.9
Miscellaneous	52	7	13.5
White-collar workers/domestic servants	773	99	12.8
Clichy	6,680	765	11.5
Paris			11.3
Manufacturing workers (not metal trades)	594	65	10.9
Taxi drivers and chauffeurs	220	23	10.5
Gardeners	50	5	10.0
Food-provision workers	221	21	9.5
Metal trades workers (skilled and semi-skilled)	1,041	88	8.5
Public service workers	893	63	7.1
Free professionals, managers, students	222	14	6.3
Landlords	22	1	4.5
Businessmen with workshops/factories	59	2	3.4

Sources: A. Desormeaux, *Clichy pendant la guerre* (Paris, 1920), pp. 535–58; Archives de Paris, Porte de Bagnolet, Liste électorale de Clichy, 1914.

average. This again suggests that the upward age bias was accounted for by the exemption of the youngest manual workers.

One reason for this slaughter of the middle and lower middle classes may have been the number who served as officers. Of the 477 employees of London County Westminster and Parr's Bank who died serving in British forces, no less than 207 or 43 per cent were officers.[41] In the British case the prodigal use of subalterns in tactical situations produced very heavy losses amongst the urban middle classes. Some facets of patriotism or even the 'jingoistic' nature of some aspects of middle-class

[41] London County Westminster and Parrs Bank: 'Names of members of staff who, have given their lives for their country in the great war 1914–1918'. Courtesy of Catherine Moriarty and the National Inventory of War Memorials project at the Imperial War Museum.

culture may have contributed to the high losses. This may help to account for high losses, for example, amongst Paris publicans, many of whom were much older than average. Amongst the younger middle classes, the legendary bravery (and tactical naivety) of German volunteers had counterparts in all three nations.

Against this may be set the low figures for casualties amongst employers and members of the free professions in Clichy. These were substantially lower than average. This cannot be explained by the fact that these men were older than average; in fact when weighted for age, statistics on these groups emerge as even more strikingly under-represented in terms of high casualties. Thus intellectuals and professionals suffered less than 60 per cent of the casualties that their age structure would imply. Employers were even more sheltered, suffering only 41 per cent of expected casualties by age (compared with a 67 per cent under-representation for metal-workers). Admittedly some valuable professional services would logically be kept out of the front line (such as doctors). Some of this evidence points to the possibility that the well-off in Paris were the worst shirkers of all. The evidence (such as it is) for Berlin and London resists this interpretation. The professional classes of London suffered heavily, as the rolls of honour for elite educational establishments also suggest.

In absolute rather than in proportionate terms the majority of metropolitan casualties came from the working class. In this sense, the pre-war social commentators who claimed that in a European war it would be the workers who would be killed were proved right. Yet at the same time it was clear that certain sub-groups were relatively sheltered from the slaughter. Those with skills particularly relevant to munitions production, first and foremost engineering workers, were protected. By contrast the unskilled and casual labourers went to the front, when physically fit to do so. Thus park keepers in London suffered casualties comparable with the high losses amongst lawyers. Similarly printers and building workers in Paris and dockers in London registered casualty rates noticeably higher than engineers and transport workers. In London the situation was complicated by the nature of the pre-war army and the presence of reservists. In Paris the public-sector employee was heavily protected as vital to civil administration. By contrast, in London he was likely to be a regular serviceman and therefore disproportionately likely to be called up in the early stages of the war.

Precise figures for Berlin occupations are difficult to evaluate and compare with Paris and London statistics. However the percentage of German men of various occupational groups who were blinded during the war shows a similar under-representation of industrial workers: only 12 per cent of the total war-blind fell into this category, despite a much higher percentage of industrial workers in the population as a whole.[42]

Behind the rhetoric of 'nations in arms' there were real and substantial inequalities in all three countries. The soldiers' war was more central to some groups than to others; the clerk and the building worker saw more of the 'sharp end' than the railwayman and the lathe operator. This existential gap generated tensions, imbedded in which were powerful political implications. The heavy sacrifices of the active minority of Berliners, their resentment at the risks they had taken and the deaths of their comrades were the immediate background to the *Freikorps'* war against 'shirking' industrial militants. Similarly the apparently sheltered position of some Parisian industrial employers and some shopkeepers, including butchers and bakers, added force to unrest in that city as the charge of 'shirker' was added to that of 'profiteer'. At the same time divisions among blue-collar groups added other divisions within the overall population, thereby weakening the overall split between those who served and those who didn't.

The British volunteer system (and it seems that most Londoners were volunteers) helped to safeguard political stability in London by creating a remarkably equitable distribution of the risks of military service. This is another apparent paradox, for the voluntary system was criticized by its conscriptionist opponents as being an unfair system which sheltered shirkers.[43] Yet it is noticeable that the inequalities of age and occupation outlined above appear less sharp in the case of London than in the case of the other two cities. Differences of losses between occupations appear relatively small, except amongst occupations with a high proportion of either regular reservists or officers.

Conscription from the outset was concerned principally with the requirements of military efficiency. Both the German and French governments recalled key workers from 1915 on. By contrast, in the British case many workers in key industries volunteered. The government had no moral right to recall these men and utilize them in the factories whilst in uniform, nor would the trade unions have permitted it. The army would have resisted the mass discharge of soldiers back into civilian life. As a result the wholesale release of munitions workers which was so important in creating the discrepancies in France and Germany did not happen in Britain until late in the war and even then only on a small scale.

The volunteer system created a sense of equity in other respects, not least in maintaining for the first eighteen months of the war the belief that the choice to serve was in the hands of the individual rather than the state. The nuanced nature of recruiting in London with its dozens of local and associational military units also gave the individual a sense of

[42] R. W. Whalen, *Bitter wounds: German victims of the Great War, 1914–1939* (Ithaca, N.Y., 1984), p. 45. [43] See J. M. Winter, *The Great War*, ch. 2.

control over the nature and style of his military service. Leaving to the individual the decision whether to serve or not to serve produced inefficiencies in the war effort, and the problems of manpower planning were not tackled effectively until 1918 in Britain. None the less the greater sense of equity that the system created was of incalculable benefit to the war effort. As it turned out, there was little surplus manpower in London for conscription to sweep up; it is even possible that the voluntary system led to more Londoners serving than through a more rationally applied manpower budget.

In conclusion the casualties sustained by soldiers from these three capital cities were not identical to those of the three nations for whom they fought. The Berlin case had the chief defining characteristics of lower initial military mobilization. In Paris, everyone joined up in 1914. In London, the voluntary system produced an army more middle-class and white-collar than the nation as a whole.

Each city's 'Lost Generation' resembled the losses of the other two. The metropolitan way of life was little disrupted by military casualties, because of the innate demographic vitality of the cities and the diversity of their populations. In London, the absence of military preparations before 1914 meant that it would be many months before the British army would undertake major operations in the field; this postponed deaths until later in the war. In Paris and Berlin the shock came earlier.

The sheer size of these cities, alongside lower urban than rural casualty rates, helps us to understand why the sense of abiding gloom that accompanies *monument aux morts* in rural France has no metropolitan equivalent. Likewise, in the case of London, there was no single date which had the emotive power of 1 July in Belfast or Bradford, when (following the opening of the Somme offensive in 1916) bereavement suddenly struck whole terraced streets. Yet the reality of metropolitan loss and its visible manifestation were deeply engrained in the fabric of urban life. It is to this subject we turn next.

By grief united?

To My Mother – 1916

If I should fall, grieve not that one so weak
And poor as I
Should die.
Nay, though thy heart should break
Think only this: when at dusk they speak
Of sons and brothers of another one,
Then thou canst say – I too had a son
He died for England's sake.

Rifleman Donald Cox, London Rifle Brigade[44]

[44] M. Stephen (ed.), *Never such innocence: a new anthology of Great War verse* (London, 1988), pp. 69–70.

Statistical analysis of casualty figures suggests divisions and inequalities between groups, but casualties were suffered individually. It may be true to state that schoolteachers in London died in higher proportions than tramway workers, but what mattered was that practically every school lost a teacher and each tram depot lost workers. Every street, rich or poor, in each of the cities, had its casualties. This was the underlying unity of experience.

A death in war is not a number, it is a life cut short. Some examples from the *London County Council Roll of Honour* illustrate the pain endured and the diversity of possibilities foreclosed. Death could come early. Richard Medhurst worked as an oiler and cleaner at Deptford pumping station after serving twelve years with the navy in which he had enlisted as a youth. He was recalled in August 1914 to serve on the cruiser HMS Cressy. On 22 September 1914 at 7.15 in the morning the ship was hit by a mine whilst attempting to pick up survivors from two other cruisers. The Cressy sank in 35 minutes. Medhurst, a stoker, drowned; he was thirty-three years old.[45]

Death was never far from the front lines. William Curtis was born in 1888 in Carlisle. He trained as a teacher at St Mark's Chelsea and in 1911 became an assistant teacher at Mandeville Street school in Clapton. In September 1914 he enlisted in the Civil Service Rifles. At the attack on Festubert on 25 May 1915 he volunteered with seven other men to precede the main assault in a bombing party. Whilst attacking an enemy trench with hand grenades, he was shot dead, with three of his comrades. The survivors received the military medal.[46]

Death could be arbitrary. Walter Plumridge left school at fourteen and worked as a printer. In 1907 he joined the Royal Horse Artillery. Transferring to the reserves in January 1914, he joined the LCC as a second-grade attendant at Long Grove mental hospital. He was recalled in August 1914 and sent to France. He took part in almost every large battle from Mons onwards and was promoted to bombardier, turning down the offer of a commission. On 21 March 1918 he was killed by a direct hit on his gun position.[47]

In the same period of the war Albert Broad died. He worked as a boy gardener at Battersea park. He took a great interest in the flowers and animal life and was an enthusiastic woodworker in his spare time. Called up in 1917, he was sent to join the 4th battalion of the Royal Fusiliers in France in March 1918. Three weeks after arriving he was killed instantly by a shell. He was nineteen years old.[48]

[45] *LCC Roll of Honour* II, pp. 5–6, pp. 10–11.
[46] *LCC Roll of Honour* XXI, pp. 7–8.
[47] *LCC Roll of Honour* LXVI, pp. 14–15.
[48] *LCC Roll of Honour* LXVI, p. 23.

Death could be haphazard. Men died in train accidents, middle-aged men collapsed on guard duty, one man drowned whilst punting at Oxford on leave. Dozens died of disease: influenza, dysentery, and typhoid. Some died of malnutrition in prisoner-of-war camps, some were killed immediately after surrendering. One man died in Holland after being repatriated, having spent almost four years as a prisoner.

Men died protecting the empire. Simon Cohen was born in Zuslov in Russia in 1885. His parents brought him to England at the age of five. After working for his father as a provision merchant for a few years and spending some time in Montreal, he passed the open competitive examination and joined the Clerk of Council Department of the LCC in 1911. He was fond of outdoor sports and was a leader for the Jewish Lads' Brigade. He spoke French, German, and Hebrew and held certificates in commerce. In 1914 he attempted to join the army but was rejected on grounds of eyesight. In October 1914 he was finally accepted by the 1st London Sanitary Company. He saw service at Ypres and Neuve Chapelle, was promoted to sergeant and wounded. Invalided home in 1915 he was recalled and drafted to Egypt to serve with the Egyptian Labour Corps. Due to his ability to master Arabic he was promoted to captain. In 1919, he was about to be demobilized when he was shot dead by 'unknown assailants'. There is a disconcerting Levantine modernity about the incident.[49]

The impact of war could fall with particular savagery on a close-knit community. The alumni of the Kaiser Wilhelm Gymnasium suffered terribly. Curt Kiekebusch was born in 1896. He volunteered on 13 August 1914 and was sent to the front on 1 October 1914. By 22 October he was dead of wounds sustained in a grenade explosion near Cerny. His elder brother, Werner, was turned down repeatedly for military service because his chest measurement was below standard. Eventually he was accepted by his late brother's regiment. In February 1916 he was sent to Flanders and in May 1916 was promoted to lieutenant. He fought on the Somme at Barleux, Moquet farm and at Courcelette (perhaps against some of the men of the LCC). In November 1916 after winning the Iron Cross second class, he was invalided back to recuperate from heart problems, but in July 1917 he returned and won the Iron Cross first class at Poelcapelle. On 21 March 1918 he was killed on the first day of the great offensive against the British, dying at Rollot, not far from Walter Plumridge, whom he had faced unknowingly for several years.

Lothar Bahr was born in 1896, he volunteered for an infantry regiment on 17 August 1914 and was sent to the front on 3 October. Hospitalized with an ear infection at the end of the year, he was sent to an animal and food procurement centre in Tourcoing where he spent

[49] *LCC Roll of Honour* LXV, pp. 19–20.

most of 1915 before being accepted for officer training in November 1915. In January 1916 he was sent to Verdun where he was killed on 5 May in the fierce fighting at 'Toter Mann' (Mort homme). His best friend was already dead; Rudolf Flügel had received a head wound in February 1915. He was sent to a hospital in Dortmund and had been visited regularly by his family. He had seemed on the road to recovery when an infection set in. He died on 15 August 1915. For the Flügel family this was the second loss of the war. Rudolf's brother Otto had volunteered three days before him and had been killed along with many other volunteers at Dixmuiden on 21 October 1914. It is easy to imagine the anxiety of the family concerning the third and eldest brother, Max. Max fought on the Eastern front and was wounded near Dunsburg in September 1915. In April 1917, he was redrafted and sent to fight on the Western front at the Chemin des Dames and Winterberg. In July 1918 he became severely ill with a lung infection. He survived.[50]

These individual cases show how the war was lived at the level of the family, a theme to be treated at length in volume II of this study. But social and collective responses to military losses mattered too. Each city had to adapt rapidly to an unanticipated scale of loss as early as 1914. The losses of Parisians in the first six weeks of the war may have exceeded the city's entire losses during the Franco-Prussian war. Even London, which was relatively less involved in 1914 than the other two capital cities, suffered a shock for which numerous colonial wars could not have prepared the city. More Englishmen were killed at Le Cateau than in any battle since the seventeenth century. And that was just the beginning.

The reaction was immediate. By 1 September 1914 the Duchess of Devonshire had made a public appeal that those bereaved by the war should not wear traditional mourning dress. The *Pall Mall Gazette* approved of the appeal, stating that although 'we have yet to receive those lists that everyone awaits and everyone dreads, we must consider beforehand how they should be received'. The editorial acknowledged that 'it is of no use trying to stifle human nature. Hearts will break and tears will flow. However willing the sacrifice, whatever the pride in the hero, there is none who in the inner chamber will not weep for the dead.'[51]

It is important to note that the process of commemoration almost preceded the notification of mass casualties. Even as the first battle of Ypres began, the *Pall Mall Gazette* had a story about how rolls of honour should be prepared, 'A medieval art revived'.[52] The LCC authorized the serial publication of a roll of honour for its employees early in 1915. In

50 W. Masche, *Kriegsgeschichte der Schüler und Lehrer des Kaiser Wilhelms-Real Gymnasium zu Berlin* (Berlin, 1919).

51 *Pall Mall Gazette*, 1 Sept. 1914, p. 1.

52 *Pall Mall Gazette*, 24 Oct. 1914, p. 3.

fact publication was suspended in autumn 1916 by order of the censor.[53] By November 1914 the London department store Selfridges had a mahogany *Roll of Honour* for its 250 men serving and a wreath had been placed by it honouring the first employee to die in the war.[54]

Not all members of the community responded well to the need to respect grief. On October 1915, two railway employees were sentenced at Marylebone police court for the theft of possessions which were being sent to the relatives of dead officers.[55] Equally, not all the bereaved themselves behaved in a decorous fashion. A woman charged with drunk and disorderly behaviour at a West London magistrates' court in 1915 claimed in her defence that she had lost her husband and nearly all her family during the war.[56]

By 1916 the impact of heavy casualties was being felt throughout London and had received visible confirmation in the presence of street shrines. The idea of commemorating those who were serving and particularly those who had died appears to have originated in the East End of London. The idea is a natural extension of the roll of honour and a halfway house between the roll and the permanent war memorial. The first street shrine seems to have been unveiled in Hackney in August 1915.[57] By the end of the year it had been joined by shrines in Stepney, Clerkenwell, Kennington, Finsbury, Ealing, Hendon, and Tottenham.[58] Street shrines were a form of commemoration particular to London and one that cut across class boundaries. Most areas of the metropolis had at least one shrine; even fashionable Bloomsbury followed suit in December 1917.[59] Few parishes went as far as Camberwell, which had ten street shrines by January 1916 and a further four under construction.[60] The street shrines served as focal points for private contemplation, for religious services, and perhaps most importantly as a surrogate tomb, an integral part of the grieving process.[61] The street-shrine movement reached its apogee in 1918 when it culminated in the erection of a great shrine in Hyde Park. Built at the instigation of Messrs. Higham and Walton, it became a focus of pilgrimage in the months of August and September in reaction to the massive losses of spring 1918 and the growing death toll of the autumn. It was permanently covered with wreaths, perhaps as many as 10,000.[62] On 2 September it was announced that the shrine would be made permanent.[63] In the event it was superseded by

53 *LCC Roll of Honour*, Preface. 54 *Pall Mall Gazette*, 16 Nov. 1914, p. 5.

55 *Pall Mall Gazette*, 23 Oct. 1915, p. 5. 56 *Pall Mall Gazette*, 30 Oct. 1915, p. 2.

57 *The Times*, 11 Aug. 1916, p. 11.

58 *The Times*, 4 Nov. 1916, p. 3; 31 Oct. 1916, p. 5; 4 Nov. 1916, p. 3; 16 Oct. 1916, p. 5; 10 Nov. 1916, p. 3; 26 Dec. 1916, p. 3; 7 Dec. 1916, p. 9; 8 Dec. 1916, p. 5.

59 *The Times*, 4 Dec. 1917, p. 5.

60 C. Moriarty, 'Christian iconography and first world war memorials', *Imperial War Museum Review*, no. 6 (1990), pp. 63–75, p. 67. 61 *Ibid.*, p. 68.

62 *The Times*, 2 Aug. 1918, p. 3; 5 Aug. 1918, p. 4; 7 Aug. 1918, p. 7; 19 Aug. 1918, p. 10; 22 Aug. 1918, p. 6. 63 *Pall Mall Gazette*, 2 Sept. 1918, p. 5.

the Cenotaph, designed by Lutyens for the Peace procession of 19 July 1919.

Paris also had its public commemorations. In Clichy, a particular ritual was associated with the burial of soldiers who had died in the local requisitioned hospital. If the body was not reclaimed by the soldier's family (the first case concerned an Algerian), then the funeral was held in the Clichy cemetery. The ritual changed little in four years. The mayor or a representative went to the hospital to claim the body and the funeral cortège crossed Clichy to the cemetery where the mayor gave a short speech at the graveside. In the early years of the war the cortège and the burial attracted substantial crowds of local people, but as the war progressed the numbers shrank. In 1914–15 the inhabitants of Paris were willing to demonstrate solidarity with their defenders, but as the years went by, the sense of immediate threat diminished, and it may have become harder to mobilize public emotion on behalf of total strangers. A similar rise in indifference was demonstrated by diminishing contributions to war-related charities, from the 39,702 francs donated to the '75 fund' and other charities in Clichy in 1915 to the feeble response of 9,191 francs in 1917.[64]

More direct in its ability to provide an outlet for local emotion was the observance of All Saints Day, 1 November (*Toussaint*). On this occasion the local population placed flowers on the military graves in the cemetery. Civic dignitaries assembled and led a procession to the cemetery. The mayor delivered a classical oration on the virtues of dying for the country. However, this date was also the moment for the manifestation of public sorrow. Many women publicly broke down. So powerful were the emotions released on this occasion that there were fears that it might undermine civic morale, and in 1916 the prefect of police actually banned processions. Public pressure forced a reversal, and in 1917–1918 processions resumed.

In Berlin, the ritual of contributing to charities through purchasing the right to hammer a nail in a 'nail memorial' provided a similar occasion for marking the fallen and their families. Church services and black-edged notices in the press also gave the local community the news that it was time to offer respects and where possible assistance to stricken families. Further research is necessary, though, before concluding that the same or similar commemorative practices existed in Berlin as in Paris and London. It is possible that rituals of remembrance in Berlin had less of a civic character than in Paris or London, and more of a military character, reflecting regimental and military traditions.[65]

[64] Desormeaux, *Clichy*, *passim*.

[65] See J. M. Winter, *Sites of memory, sites of mourning. The Great War in European cultural history* (Cambridge, 1995), ch. 4. See also J.-J. Becker, Jay M. Winter, Gerd Krumeich, Annette Becker, and Stéphane Audoin-Rouzeau (eds.), *La très grande guerre* (Paris, 1994).

Whilst it is possible to delineate the salient points of public grief, private grief and the methods of coping with it are harder to gauge. That grief was widespread was obvious. In 1916 a public-health officer claimed that whilst labour conditions for women in Woolwich had improved and whilst food and money was available in abundance, war conditions had been unfavourable to women's health because of the widespread anxiety and grief. Although statistical measurements may not support this judgement, the way a qualified contemporary perceived the situation should not be discounted lightly. Families were devastated by loss.

The first news that a London family would have of the death (or only too frequently disappearance) of a relative was a stark letter or telegram from the War Office or Admiralty. The casualty department appears to have had a bad reputation for the offhand manner with which it dealt with inquiries. A letter to the press in 1917 complained: 'I have had my ears stuffed within the last few days with too true tales of the hauteur of these officials, displayed not only in personal interviews, but painfully manifest in letters to legitimate inquiries and applicants.'[66] By the time this letter was written, reform was under way. Rudyard Kipling had been commissioned to write a new form of consolatory letter, an activity for which he was doubly qualified, as poet of army and empire and father of a son missing, presumed dead. The government also authorized a scheme, in November 1917, by which a memorial plaque would be sent to the next of kin of each man killed in the war.[67]

A similar process occurred in Paris. At the outbreak of the war an impersonal communication was sent directly to the families through the post. This produced many heart-rending scenes of grief and shock. The intention had been that the mayor would come and break the news to the family, but the chaos and pressures of the first months of the war and the sheer number of casualties had caused the municipal system to break down. By late 1914 the correct procedure was reinstated. News of loss was first sent to the town hall and the mayor or his surrogate was appointed to go to the home concerned and break the news personally with an official expression of regret. This small gesture was at least an acknowledgement that families had a right to be treated with more respect and support than contained in a bureaucratic letter at such a traumatic moment.

Ultimately it was personal condolences rather than any official initiative that mattered. Officers made a point of writing to the relatives of men killed; when an officer was killed his family could expect letters from fellow officers and men. Relatives wanted to know the circumstan-

66 *Pall Mall Gazette*, 5 Sept. 1916, p. 9; 4 Oct. 1917, p. 3.

67 *Pall Mall Gazette*, 21 Nov. 1917, p. 4; 22 Nov. 1917, p. 5.

ces in which death had occurred.[68] The widow of William Cowan, an old soldier who had re-enlisted in 1914, placed an advertisement in a newspaper for particulars of her husband's death. She received a letter from a comrade.[69] Over fifty years after the war John Tucker met a relative of one of the men he had served with. The family had kept the letter they had been sent by the man's officer after his death:

> With deep and personal regret I have to inform you of the death in action of 3302, sergt. F. S. Osborn 1/13th London Regt. He was killed about 3.45 on the morning of the 19th inst. A raid was in progress and sergt. Osborn was in charge of the leading party when the raiders were spotted by the German sentries. He charged one of them, was wounded in the chest and staggered back . . . He was removed on a stretcher but remained unconscious and died before he reached our lines. He died the best death possible, the death of a fine soldier and a very gallant gentleman . . . Please accept my sincere sympathy at his death and believe me, I am as sorrowful at his death as anyone can be who is related to him . . .
>
> Yours truly (sgd)
> E. F. Clarke,
> Captain.[70]

That this letter was valued by the family both for the information it contained and for the sentiment expressed was clearly shown by the way it was treated as an heirloom.

In November 1916, Ernst Strassmann wrote to his parents in Berlin describing the death of his brother on the Somme:

> Do not grieve too much. We should be thankful that we had him with us so long, that he was joyful and hopeful to the end, that he fought heart and soul and that his soldier's death was painless . . . Those who give their lives for us give us and the whole nation life . . . That is why to die for the Fatherland is the highest fulfilment in life.[71]

Whatever this message meant to the Strassmanns, its force rested on a common belief that the war was worth fighting and that sacrifices were shared by all. Londoners were never forced to face the possibility that the sacrifices were in vain, except for a few trying weeks in the spring of 1918. Similarly Parisians were able to see their losses as being the brutal but necessary price of an inevitable victory. For some, the price of that victory was simply too high. Both war-weariness and pacifist sentiment spread from 1917 under this heavy burden. But in Berlin the situation

[68] Sometimes the information would never come: of the 200 or so men who died in the 2/2nd, 2/4th and 18th battalions of the London regiment on 21 March 1918, not one has an individual marked grave. M. Middlebrook, *The Kaiser's battle: 21 March 1918: the first day of the German spring offensive* (London, 1978), p. 320.

[69] *LCC Roll of Honour* VI, p. 8.

[70] Cited in J. Tucker, *Johnny get your gun* (New York, 1958), pp. 100–1.

[71] P. Witkop (ed.), *Kriegsbriefe gefallener Studenten* (Munich, 1928), p. 255.

was worse. Only there was the population forced to face the dreadful double reality of bereavement and defeat, one aggravated by the obvious perversion of the ideals of common sacrifice that occurred during the difficult last year of the war.

Heroes and victims

The wounded: hospitals and treatment

This brief survey of the effects of military participation and war losses on the three capital cities can only hint at the multiple levels in which the conflict marked and disfigured the life of these three cities. The subject of the presence of the wounded in Paris, London, and Berlin deserves a book in itself. Here we restrict our treatment to some aspects of the history of healing and recuperation in these cities, and offer particular detail on London.

The presence of the wounded, sick, and convalescent as well as those invalided out of the armed forces was one of the visible signs of the growing intensity of the conflict in wartime capitals as well as one of the points of contact between home front and the front lines. Berlin hospitals accommodated 253,000 wounded men during the course of the war. The vast majority of these were accommodated by the Rudolf Virchow hospital (which alone accounted for over 200,000 of those treated) and the large military hospital at Busch, a small community just outside Berlin, which treated some 30,000 men.[72] If the men were accommodated in hospitals for approximately a month on average, then there was an average of just under 5,000 wounded men in the Berlin hospitals at any given time. However it seems likely that the flow of the wounded in and out of these cities was more uneven.[73] Unlike Paris or London, Berlin was remote from the main battlefronts after 1914.

With 30,780 beds for other ranks and 5,884 beds for officers, London provided a little over 10 per cent of the total United Kingdom hospital beds for military use in 1918 and almost 31 per cent of the total of beds for officers.[74] The expansion of hospital accommodation for the armed forces increased exponentially throughout the war both in London and the provinces. At the outbreak of war there were approximately 7,000 equipped beds in about 150 military hospitals. Of these perhaps 1,500 beds were in the area of Greater London, the largest military hospitals in the capital being the Herbert Hospital at Woolwich with 629 beds and Queen Alexandra's Military Hospital with over 200.[75] This accommodation was woefully inadequate for a large-scale European war. Fortu-

72 Kaeber, *Berlin*, p. 502. 73 *Ibid*.

74 W. G. MacPherson, *Official history of the medical services*, vol. I (London, 1921), p. 94.

75 Macpherson, *Medical services*, p. 71.

nately, plans existed for the creation of 'Territorial Force General Hospitals' utilizing the resources of existing civil hospitals. Four such hospitals were created on mobilization. Thus King's College Hospital became the nucleus of the Fourth London General Hospital.[76] By early 1915 a fifth hospital had been added, when St Thomas's became the fifth London General Hospital.

The Territorial Force General Hospitals were the first line of additional medical services and they expanded beyond the premises initially provided. By 1917 the five had become hospital complexes involving civil hospitals and a variety of other accommodation.

The 1st London (Camberwell) provided beds for 231 officers and 1,390 other ranks in three civil hospitals, in LCC schools and in huts in Myatts Park. The 2nd London (Chelsea) used four civil hospitals, an LCC secondary school and St Mark's College, providing 170 beds for officers and 1,352 for other ranks. The 3rd London (Wandsworth) used no less than eight civil hospitals as well as the Royal Victoria Patriotic School and adjoining huts, housing 897 officers and 1,503 other ranks. The 4th London (Denmark Hill) was based on King's College Hospital but also used the resources of the Maudsley Civil Asylum and the Italian, Popular, and West London Hospitals. It also used huts in Ruskin park. This hospital dealt with 478 officers and 1,693 other ranks. Finally the 5th London (Lambeth) used St Thomas's and the Red Cross Hospital to accommodate 62 officers and 600 other ranks.[77] In total these hospitals provided beds for 1,838 officers and 6,438 other ranks.

It soon became clear that the scale of casualties would require more hospital space than the existing hospitals, both civil and military, could provide, even when supplemented by local schools and by hutted accommodation. Part of the answer was the voluntary provision of accommodation in large private buildings, as described below. But the immediate necessity of crisis obviously drew attention to existing public buildings. Poor Law institutions became the mainstay of this second wave of hospital provision: 'war hospitals'. These were official military hospitals under War Office control and were an important part of total provision in London. Poor Law infirmaries were commandeered at East Dulwich, Bethnal Green, Endell Street, Fulham, and Holborn. Workhouses were taken at Bermondsey, Hammersmith, Lewisham, Mile End, Mitcham, and Tooting, and three hospitals were occupied in Hampstead. These buildings were either hospital equipped or readily converted. In most cases they would also provide some of the staff needed to run the hospital.[78] Between them they housed 68 officers and

[76] *Pall Mall Gazette*, 20 Oct. 1914, p. 7. [77] Macpherson, *Medical services*, p. 74.

[78] B. Abel-Smith, *The hospitals, 1800–1948* (London, 1963), pp. 259–61.

10,170 other ranks by 1917.[79] The smallest of these hospitals, Endell Street in Bloomsbury, dealt with a theoretical maximum of 573 patients from 1916, but 'at times of pressure when the billeting of convalescent men was allowed, the numbers on the register approximated to 800'.[80] Most of these war hospitals retained staff from their civilian use and initially at least some of their patients. This made them unpopular with troops sensitive to the stigma of the Poor Law.[81]

Of the London District's 36,664 hospital beds available, about 20,000 were provided for military use under War Office auspices.[82] What of the remainder? Large numbers of voluntary hospitals came into existence during the war.[83] As the system became regularized, they were divided into Category A and Category B hospitals from 1915. These hospitals received capitation payments from the War Office for each soldier accommodated, Category A hospitals receiving more.[84]

The principal use of these hospitals was the accommodation of convalescents. The proportion of such hospitals in the London area was high and as the hutted camps were not used for officer convalescents, this goes a considerable way towards explaining the high proportion of officers' beds in the London total. As a general rule, by 1917 soldiers were 'retained in general hospital' only 'so long as they require specialized treatment or observation' and were 'immediately evacuated to the cheaper auxiliary hospitals' as soon as possible.[85] Conditions in voluntary hospitals were more relaxed, with more generous visiting hours and men allowed to smoke in the wards.[86] In Kensington Officers' Home there were two bathrooms on every floor and most of the accommodation was in single rooms.[87] Even more luxurious was some of the provision made in 1915: 'several of the principal London Hotels have set aside rooms for the use of single officers and suites for the married'.[88] Not all of these institutions were philanthropic; indeed, in 1916 some private nursing homes in London were accused of enriching themselves by contracting to take military personnel and using volunt-

[79] Macpherson, *Medical services*, p. 82.

[80] F. Murray, *Women as army surgeons* (London, 1920), p. 137.

[81] Abel-Smith, *Hospitals*, pp. 259–61. On staff see P. Mitchell (ed.), *Memoranda on army general hospital administration* (London, 1917), pp. 25–6.

[82] Permanent military hospitals expanded capacity threefold, Abel-Smith, *Hospitals*, p. 267.

[83] For Red Cross convalescent homes see E. Charles Vivian and J. E. Hodder Williams, *The way of the Red Cross* (London, 1915), p. 269.

[84] Abel-Smith, *Hospitals*, p. 265.

[85] Mitchell, *Memoranda*, p. 26.

[86] Abel-Smith, *Hospitals*, p. 272.

[87] Abel-Smith, *Hospitals*, p. 273. It is unclear whether this refers to the officers' hospitals at Moray House and Aubrey House which were used from 1916 onwards, see F.M. Gladstone, *Aubrey House Kensington 1698–1920* (London, 1922), p. 55.

[88] Vivian and Hodder Williams, *Red Cross*, p. 270.

ary staff to cut overheads on their usual business, a particularly distasteful form of profiteering, depriving soldiers and exploiting civilian good will.[89]

As a volunteer nurse with the 1st London hospital, Vera Brittain describes working at a commandeered college, 'one of the few dignified buildings in the dismal, dreary, dirty wilderness of South East London'. Adaptation was difficult for a woman from the provincial middle classes with no previous medical experience. The professional nurses were, 'still suspicious of the young semi-trained amateurs upon whose assistance they were beginning to realise with dismay, they would be obliged to depend for the duration of the war'.[90] She had to leave the inadequate hostel in which she was housed at 6.15 a.m. to be on duty by 7.30 a.m. and worked until 8.00 p.m., with a weekly half-day holiday, 'which we gave up willingly enough whenever a convoy came in or the ward was filled with bad cases'.[91]

On 4 July 1916 'began the immense convoys which came without cessation for about a fortnight and continued at short intervals for the whole of that sultry month and the first part of August'. Throughout those 'busy and strenuous days' the wards 'sweltered beneath their roofs of corrugated iron; the prevailing odour of wounds and stinking streets lingered perpetually'. By the evening of 4 July Brittain's forty-bed hut was 'filled beyond capacity with acute surgical cases'.[92]

In contrast, Endell Street hospital belonged to the large category of war hospitals which were housed in Poor Law premises. It was housed in the disused infirmary of St Giles, Bloomsbury, a central location convenient for the main railway stations. Used solely for other ranks, it was typical of the response to the hospital crisis of 1915 when it was apparent that pre-war provision was insufficient. What was extraordinary about the hospital was that its medical staff consisted entirely of women. For this reason a detailed account of the hospital's operation was published by one of its founders in 1920, less than a year after it had closed.

On commandeering the building,

> extensive structural alterations were necessary. Lifts capable of carrying stretchers were put in; the sanitation was renewed, and electric light and modern cooking apparatus were installed . . . The fittings of padded rooms and curious pieces of furniture, designed to restrain the insane came out of the lunacy block . . . ward kitchens and bathrooms were installed on every floor;

[89] Abel-Smith, *Hospitals*, p. 282.

[90] V. Brittain, *Testament of youth* (London, 1933), p. 206.

[91] *Ibid.*, pp. 207–9.

[92] *Ibid.*, pp. 279–81.

and operating theatres, X-ray room, laboratories, dispensaries and store rooms were completed.[93]

Relations with the Board of Guardians were strained as the hospital staff tried to get them to remove unnecessary stores.[94] Nevertheless by May 1915 the hospital was ready to open with seventeen wards and a staff of 180 for 520 cases.[95]

The wards had 'ample window space' and though the beds were closer than was 'usual or desirable in civilian hospitals, there was plenty of fresh air and light . . . great trouble was taken to make the Endell Street hospital look gay and comfortable. Every ward had its flowers and its red blue and scarlet blankets gave it colour . . . its table and screen covers . . . an air of comfort.' Nevertheless the electric lighting was faulty and it took a long correspondence to receive standard lights so that the patients could read or play cards.[96] Because of the proximity of the railway station, the hospital received a high proportion of serious cases. 'As a rule every bed emptied during the day filled at night.'[97] The monthly turnover varied between 400 and 800 cases.[98] In all, 26,000 patients passed through the hospital including over 2,000 Canadians, over 2,000 Australians and about 200 Americans.[99] Sixty of the beds were reserved for medical cases and the rest were surgical.[100] In 1915, before the introduction of steel helmets, there were numerous head wounds. Surprisingly, these men seem to have recovered well, perhaps because those with the most severe wounds were unlikely to survive as far as the hospital. There was always a large number of compound fractures: in 1917, 154 fractured thighs at one time. Apparently these were exacting cases. One man had his humerus smashed into a hundred pieces, but recovered completely.[101]

Seven thousand operations were conducted in the operating theatre, not counting minor operations performed in the wards.[102] In the medical wards there were many cases of rheumatism, gastric ulcers, and pleurisy as well as gas poisoning, malaria, and 'mental disturbance'.[103] During the Spanish flu epidemic in 1918, critical pneumonia cases reached sixty per day. In November and December 1918 twenty-four men died.[104]

The patients' dining-room was a 'somewhat gloomy place' but this scarcely mattered as the majority of patients took their meals in bed. A recreation room housed a library, billiard table, and stage.[105] The hospital operated under army discipline. Non-commissioned officers

[93] Murray, *Women as army surgeons*, p. 125. [94] *Ibid.*, pp. 130–2.
[95] *Ibid.*, pp. 136–7. [96] *Ibid.*, pp. 137–8. [97] *Ibid.*, pp. 144–5.
[98] *Ibid.*, p. 175. [99] *Ibid.*, p. 146. [100] *Ibid.*, p. 161.
[101] *Ibid.*, p. 162. [102] *Ibid.*, pp. 163–4. [103] *Ibid.*, p. 170. [104] *Ibid.*, p. 172.
[105] *Ibid.*, p. 139.

amongst the patients were responsible for ward discipline and were answerable to the Doctor in Charge who had been granted an honorary commission. In 1915 and 1916 other ranks were not allowed off hospital premises unaccompanied. As a result volunteers organized extensive official outings for the convalescent.[106] Subsequently the rule was rescinded and convalescents were allowed out on their own until 5 p.m. The most advanced convalescent cases were sent to the VAD (Voluntary Aid Detachment) auxiliary hospitals at Dollis Hill and Highgate, which 'were a great source of pleasure and benefit to the men . . . who were well cared for and very happy in them'.[107]

Partly because of its central location the hospital was continually thronged with visitors. They fell into two categories: family and friends visiting specific patients, and well-wishers volunteering out of a sense of duty to visit the sick. According to the history of the hospital, 'The relatives were very brave and very pathetic. The men clung to their mothers and many a careworn weary woman sat night after night by the side of her son, grateful to be there.'[108] Relatives seem to have had more or less unlimited access, friends were allowed to visit on three days per week.[109]

The entertainment efforts of the hospital were remarkable. More than a thousand artistes visited the hospital each year. Between May 1915 and May 1919, 511 entertainments were held, including 260 concerts in the recreation room, 70 ward concerts, 95 orchestras, 52 plays, and 4 pantomimes.

Other visitors came as a matter of duty. The King and Queen visited on one occasion and the Queen Mother, Queen Alexandra, was a frequent visitor. Generally the hospital was overwhelmed with visitors, all of whom were determined 'to speak one word of kindness to the poor fellows or as one lady wrote "bring one ray of pleasure to the poor mutilated darlings"'.[110]

War casualties: solidarities, rights, obligations

Maintaining the support of the community for the wounded was as vital for the war effort as the provision of men and munitions. Society had implicitly contracted to care for the well-being of the wounded soldier

106 In the early days of the war the social elite went to elaborate lengths to escort wounded soldiers on outings. According to a newspaper story from autumn 1914, 'some of our wounded in the hospitals are being taken out for afternoon drives by people who have carriages. Yesterday a fine equipage with a pair of high stepping horses crossed Trafalgar Square and went down the Strand with two ladies and three wounded soldiers, and the crowd at Charing Cross gave them a hearty cheer.' *Pall Mall Gazette*, 6 Oct. 1914, p. 5.

107 Murray, *Women as army surgeons*, pp. 176–7.

108 *Ibid.*, p. 173. 109 *Ibid.*, p. 182. 110 *Ibid.*, p. 185.

in August 1914. A failure to live up to that promise would have opened rifts in society and between the forces and civilians. Despite the angry polemics of some war poets, this split did not occur in Britain. One possible reason is the nature of the voluntary system itself. We have noted that the majority of Londoners in uniform were volunteers; their links to the home front were never severed.[111]

Paris and Berlin also saw a blossoming of voluntary activity. This subject will be treated in volume II, where we shall discuss organizational pressure on public policy with respect to the wounded, widows, orphans, and other war victims. Here our intention is to suggest that the wounded were present in these metropolitan centres. They could not be ignored. They demanded attention, and at least in the short term, they got it.

In Paris, foreign residents were responsible for the hospital of Maison Blanche and the rehabilitation school at the Grand Palais. Maurice Barrès instituted a fund for clothes and prosthetics through subscriptions collected in *L'Echo de Paris*. Even if, as in London, the motivations of these self-appointed friends of the wounded were not entirely pure, their help was undeniably important.[112]

Nevertheless, in Paris some of the war wounded took matters into their own hands. Paris was particularly important as a visible concentration of the permanently maimed, in part because of the concentration of specialized medical services in the city. By 1916 a number of veterans' lobbies had come into existence including the Association fraternelle des anciens combattants de la Marne, the Union amicale des mutilés et réformés de la préfecture de la Seine and a mutual-aid society sponsored by the railwaymen's union and approved by the Ministry of Labour.[113] Military hospitals strictly controlled propaganda by such organizations but the numerous voluntary hospitals proved a fertile recruiting ground. One of the most influential organizations, the Association générale de mutilés de la guerre (AGMG) was created under the auspices of the specialist hospital for amputees at the Maison Blanche in August 1918. It had 1,000 members by March 1916 and by December 1918 the number had risen to 13,875.[114] The influence of the association was disseminated through its twelve page monthly publication, *Journal des mutilés, reformés et blessés de guerre*, begun in May 1916. Largely concerned with providing advice on pensions, rights, and benefits, it grew to cover a wide range of topics and interests. Politically

111 John Fuller, *Troop morale and popular culture in the British and Dominion armies, 1914–1918* (Oxford, 1990).

112 A. Prost, *Les anciens combattants et la société française, 1914–1939* (Paris, 3 vols., 1977), vol. I, p. 29.

113 Prost, *Anciens combattants*, vol. I, p. 30.

114 *Ibid.*, p. 29.

moderate, the association disseminated an ideology of mutual assistance and self-help, although it is clear that some members were angry and dissatisfied with the state and the general public.[115]

A more radical voice emerged as the war progressed. In February 1917 the foundation of the Union nationale des mutilés et reformés (UNMR), which represented the more outspoken provincial associations, challenged the moderation of the ACMG with a more militant campaigning stance. In the aftermath of the Chemins des Dames offensive the militants gained influence and confidence.

On 11 November 1917 the UNMR organized a congress at the Grand Palais at which 125 local societies were represented and which was attended by 1,500 seriously wounded delegates.[116] The congress was successful as a lobby in pressuring the government on the question of pensions as a natural right of the war wounded. The congress demanded that the community should consider 'whether it does not have a simple moral duty vis-à-vis the wounded', and re-emphasized that 'war wounds give a genuine right to reparation for harm that results by virtue of the infirmity caused' and 'this right should constitute the foundation of the new legislation on pensions'.[117] At the end of the war, the hope was that the defeated powers would pay for the damage they had caused.

In Germany the mounting pressure on the war economy placed the wounded in an even more vulnerable position. Indeed, as early as December 1914 there had been signs that potential tensions would emerge if things became difficult. A wounded soldier wrote a letter to the Socialist newspaper *Vorwärts* complaining of an incident in a Berlin theatre. Two fashionably dressed women had seen a nurse changing the dressing on an amputee's leg stump. One of them had whispered to the other: 'God isn't that disgusting! They could have left that one behind.'[118] Such crass remarks may have been heard on rare occasions in London and Paris as well. But the growing difficulties on the German home front from 1916 on indicated that trouble was bound to come. In the next chapter, we shall continue the presentation of evidence about the confrontation of civilians and soldiers in these three cities.

Berlin became the centre of a political agitation on the part of wounded veterans. In May 1917, Erich Kuttner, a Berlin lawyer wounded at Verdun, organized a meeting to protest at the inadequacy of provision for the wounded and the bereaved. He was responding to the attempts of the annexationist right to co-opt the anger of veterans for their own ends. Instead Kuttner's organization, the Bund der Kriegsbeschädigten und Kriegsteilnehmer aligned themselves with the Social

[115] *Ibid.*, pp. 36–7.

[116] *Ibid.*, p. 41. [117] *Ibid.*, p. 42, n. 152. [118] Whalen, *Bitter wounds*, p. 49.

Democrats in the demand that war profiteers should be made to pay for welfare. In Berlin the Bund grew in strength throughout 1917. After Kuttner was posted to Königsberg it was led by Karl Tiedt, a radically minded bohemian. The organization clashed with both the military authorities and the Fatherland party.[119]

On 7 January 1918 the disabled veterans were physically attacked by right-wing militants in Berlin's Alexanderplatz when they heckled a Fatherland party rally. In the bitter uproar that followed, Kuttner organized a public protest in which veterans mailed their decorations to Admiral Tirpitz. This led to his being banned from political activity.

The politics of disabled veterans tended towards the left in Berlin during the final year of the war, in contrast to provincial organizations, which frequently had a more centrist or right-wing slant. In the immediate post-war period the movement split, with Tiedt aligning himself with the Communists in January 1919 against Kuttner and the Social Democratic mainstream.[120]

One crucial point seems to have created the difference between Berlin on the one hand and London and Paris on the other. The wounded soldiers who returned to Berlin re-entered a civil society under much more extreme pressure than their counterparts faced in Paris and London. Not only had civilian hardship in Berlin reached levels unknown in the Allied capitals, but the percentage of Berliners killed on active service was also higher than the same rate for Parisians and Londoners in uniform (see table 3.2).[121] In all three cities, voluntary action had done a great deal to ameliorate the condition of veterans from the outset of the war. But by 1917, the German people, including the hard-pressed middle classes, had neither the time nor the money to engage in benevolent activity, and by 1918 many veterans were reduced to begging in the streets.[122]

Crippled German veterans were caught in a double bind. The privileging of the needs of the war economy rendered many of them superfluous, and the strains that the growth of the military-industrial complex created undermined the sense of mutual responsibility that might have assisted them. Benevolence had become a luxury in a nation on the breadline; the same was true in Paris from 1917. Yet the outcome of the war meant that their claim for decent treatment was more difficult to sustain than similar claims among wounded veterans of the British and French armies. In a revolutionary situation, the state had little time (or money) for men on crutches. Still the plight of the wounded was a standing reproach which could not but damage the morale of the people.

[119] *Ibid.*, pp. 123–5. [120] *Ibid.*, p. 125. [121] *Ibid.*, p. 104. [122] *Ibid.*, pp. 97–8.

Conclusions

The subject of military participation and war losses is rightly at the centre of any consideration of urban social history during the war. Let us summarize our main findings. First, urban populations suffered casualties close to, though slightly below, the national average. The contemporary image of the urban 'shirker' was, therefore, an exaggeration, which arose out of the relatively low rate of enlistment of young workers. The metropolitan 'Lost Generation' was older than that of other communities. Young city-dwellers were less likely to die in uniform than young rural workers. This difference in the age-structure of losses was more important in generating the image of urban 'shirking' than the levels or proportions of losses sustained in these cities.

Secondly, while white-collar workers generally suffered slightly higher casualty rates than their blue-collar neighbours, there were very wide variations within these groups. Some manual and non-manual workers were privileged, in the sense of staying out of the line of fire; others were not. Here is another instance of the fracturing of occupational categories into smaller fragments, each with its own wartime history. Those useful to munitions production in particular and to the war economy in general suffered less than others.

Thirdly, total military casualties did not interfere with the long-term demographic growth of the capital cities. London would have lost as many young men to emigration as it did to the war; the losses suffered by Paris and Berlin were more than compensated by the results of industrial growth and economic expansion.

None the less, the human cost of the fighting was all too evident in the capitals in the 1920s. Otto Dix portrayed the broken veterans begging on the streets of Berlin in his savage and satirical paintings. In London and Paris there were the annual ceremonies at the Cenotaph and the Arc de Triomphe on 11 November. To this day signs on the Paris Metro reserving seats for the war mutilated and the annual sale of poppies for charity in London are reminders of the fate of that generation.

The weight of these losses created images of unity and obligation as well as undercurrents of tension in all three cities. Yet ultimately the knowledge of victory provided the means of overcoming the tensions in the Allied capitals. In Berlin the wounds were to fester.

It may be useful to locate these findings in the overall history of the adaptation of metropolitan populations to war. Here contrasts as between the city's military participation parallel similar contrasts in other domains. London's history is one of continuities and a slow but effective adaptation to demands for more and more recruits. The voluntary system produced a relatively narrow variance of the proportion mobilized between occupational groups. Londoners bore approximately their fair share of casualties. But given the fact that London's casualties were later and lower than those suffered by Parisians and Berliners, there were bound to be fewer tensions in the British capital, both between civilian social groups and between soldiers and civilians as a whole.

In contrast, Parisian mobilization and losses were brutal and immediate. The bloodbath of 1914 took its toll in the French capital in a way unknown in London. After the first year of the war, casualty rates diminished for Parisians, though in aggregate the French capital suffered the greatest losses of the three cities under review. Given the sharp inequalities in the incidence of war losses in different occupational groups, and given the high toll of war deaths, tensions between different parts of the Parisian community and between soldiers and civilians were inevitable.

Berlin's war losses resembled those of Paris in the shock of the early phase of fighting. While relatively fewer men were mobilized in Berlin than in Paris, Berliners in uniform suffered relatively high casualty rates. Given the strength of industry in Berlin, it is not surprising that thousands of young men in Berlin were protected from the worst of the fighting through deferment in order to work in munitions production. But those Berliners who did join up bore a disproportionate share of casualties. Here was one source of the tension between front and rear which carried on well after the Armistice, and further poisoned the post-war history of the Weimar Republic.

4
The image of the profiteer

Jean-Louis Robert

Sacrifice was configured both as a material reality and a moral necessity. To understand it, citizens elaborated a complex moral language, which both set limits on well-being and helped define its social and individual meaning. The press helped propagate this discourse through caricature and comment. Through both we can see how decency constituted a social good even (or perhaps especially) under conditions of material deprivation. This attribute infused discussions of capabilities, duties, and entitlements in wartime, when moral exhortation was the stock in trade of the press. The first and foremost carrier of this kind of social good was the soldier, whose comportment constituted the prototype of citizenship, and on whose fortitude the well-being of the community and nation as a whole reposed.

The image of the soldier was central to the moral language of the press in the Great War. We are not concerned here with this image as a force in political debate, either patriotic, nationalist, or (from 1917) pacifist. Rather, we focus on images of right behaviour, starting with the soldier, who was at the heart of the system of values underpinning morale on the home front.

Diametrically opposed to the soldier, the man of sacrifice, were those who benefited from the war without risking their hides. First and foremost here were the profiteers, people who put their personal interest over the collective destiny of the nation and of the people among whom they lived. The critique of the profiteer described an arc linking (at one end) extremes of admirable and (at the other end) extremes of deplorable behaviour in wartime. In the antinomian moral universe of war, the profiteer stood out as a clear symbol of who not to be and what not to do; for this reason, and on account of the abundance of caricatures presenting this issue, we concentrate in this chapter on this one vehicle of moral comment in Paris, London, and Berlin during the war. We reach here the other side of the story presented in chapter 3 on military participation, and use cartoons to disclose the way contemporaries juxtaposed forms of moral behaviour, personal conduct, and social comportment during the 1914–1918 war.

To study the moral language of the home front also helps us to decipher some of the complex features of the social relations of material life described in the chapters which follow. The key point is that those relations were based on notions of sacrifice shared by all. Why examine this issue through caricatures? Because they describe a set of widely disseminated images of social groups and the issues which concerned them. Together they enable us to construct the way contemporaries envisioned and represented the system of social relations in which they lived.

Representations are no substitute for other kinds of evidence or analysis, but social history without them is likely to be incomplete. Representations provided a framework of meaning for sacrifice, for material hardships and the redistribution of wealth. This is self-evident in the discussion in chapter 3 on the 'Lost Generation'; it will be present in later chapters too. Images projected signs and commonly understood codes of the period. Whether or not munitions makers took unfair advantage of their wartime position and reaped huge profits is a controversial matter; there is a rich literature on it.[1] Contemporaries had their own strong views on the subject. They *knew* that profiteers were at work, and that their wealth was ill-gotten; that belief was illustrated (as well as stimulated) by caricature.

There is an aesthetic aspect to this material which must not be ignored. Some cartoonists were powerful because they were accomplished artists; others appealed because of their humorous angle on events. The subject was serious, but it wasn't always treated seriously. When handled with care,[2] caricatures are valuable evidence of some of the essential characteristics of systems of representation, operating through symbol, emblem, and accusation. Of course, this evidence is only part of the story, and in the second volume of this study we will discuss other forums of moral discourse in wartime, which also drew upon imagery for its strength.[3]

Sources

This analysis rests on the premise that the press and its readership were in a dialectical relationship. Each affects the other; the press could not

1 For a start, see Kocka, *Facing Total War*, and Boswell and Johns, 'Patriots or profiteers?'

2 The best reference work on the study of caricatures has been produced by the Groupe d'études sur l'image fixe, in their journal *L'Image fixe*, 1 (1987), pp. 1–34. See also N. Gérôme (ed.), *Archives sensibles. Images et objets du monde industriel et ouvrier* (Paris, 1995), and closer to the history of art, Marie-Claude Vettraino-Soulard, *Lire une image* (Paris, 1993).

3 For this point with respect to the Parisian labour movement, see Robert, 'Ouvriers et mouvement ouvrier', ch. 4.

sustain images outside of its readers' range of reference. As many scholars have recognized, it is futile to ask simply if the press forms or follows opinion. In contrast there appeared in recent years some sophisticated work using the press to construct elements of what French scholars like to call *mentalités*.[4] This category is particularly difficult to fix in wartime, but in any event our interest lies elsewhere: in the elucidation of the signs and common language understood at the time by the readers of these newspapers and weeklies. We need as well to establish the importance of caricatures and sketches in newspapers and magazines. In the daily press, images, caricatures, or photographs drew the readers' attention; a drawing or sketch was less salient, sometimes less charged with symbols and, on occasion, cruder in quality. For weekly magazines, drawings served to attract the potential buyer, and the larger the potential audience, the more elaborate and refined they were.

The publications examined here varied substantially in character and in political outlook. It is therefore necessary to introduce them in more detail. *Le Petit Journal* was a newspaper which had dominated the Parisian press for much of the nineteenth century, and which in 1914 was still one of the most robust papers in the capital. Leaning politically to the right, its readership was strong in the middle classes, among shopkeepers and among artisans. The paper conventionally represented the middle classes according to the older model of 'Monsieur Prudhomme', timorous and undynamic. The paper printed few caricatures of war profiteers, and in particular few of industrialists. This lacuna may not have been an accident: one of the most important shareholders in the newspaper was Louis Loucheur, Minister of Commerce from 1917.

L'Intransigeant was a popular paper with a working-class Parisian readership. Its design was dynamic, with many caricatures. Its political orientation was left of centre, and entirely patriotic during the war. Many of its cartoons about profiteers mixed this imagery with that of the feminine.

In addition to these two sources, material has been culled from three papers associated with the labour movement, though they have been less useful than one might have thought, a weakness perhaps associated with censorship or self-censorship. *L'Humanité*, the paper of the Socialist party, had many caricatures before the war, but few during it. *La Bataille* was the organ of the Confédération générale du travail and, like *L'Humanité*, its voice was solidly behind *union sacrée*. The readership of *La Bataille* was composed of trade unionists, to whom social criticism was essential reading. *La Bataille* launched a series of drawings entitled

[4] See the sophisticated discussion of the need to go beyond this question in the conclusion to Becker, *1914*, and Stéphane Audoin-Rouzeau, *A travers leurs journaux: 14–18, Les combattants des tranchées* (Paris, 1986). Both share the view that the press is reflective.

'The pillory of the profiteers', full of allusions to the French Revolution, but after 1916, possibly for financial reasons, caricatures vanished from this paper. Finally there was *Le Populaire,* appearing from 1916, which described the pacifist left of the labour movement. Not surprisingly, this paper provided the greatest number of caricatures vilifying the profiteer, munitions makers, shopkeepers, or the bourgeoisie fleeing the city during the March 1918 German offensive.

For London, the most useful source was the *Daily Herald* (at that time *The Herald*), throughout the war a Socialist and pacifist paper. Its early critique of the profiteer grew directly out of its pre-war preoccupations. Despite a restricted circulation, this paper is the richest source of imagery on this subject. *The Herald* showed little evidence of self-censorship and produced some of the most violent and dramatic images of war profiteers we have.

John Bull, in contrast, was a right-of-centre popular weekly. Its circulation grew rapidly during the war, rising from 135,000 in 1916 to 2.5 million in 1918. Chauvinist in outlook, the paper (and its editor, Horatio Bottomley) championed the 'common man', his wisdom and good sense. His cause was their cause; his enemies were their enemies, especially those who made life harder for civilians and in particular for soldiers' families. *John Bull* pilloried bureaucrats, big businessmen, industrialists, big traders, but spared the shopkeepers who formed an important part of its readership.

Punch was an old-established elite satirical review, aiming at the leisured and educated classes, eager for gossip about polite society. Here too we find in wartime some reference to the profiteer, as well as some sympathy for the hardships faced by the old middle classes and not faced by the *nouveaux riches,* who did so well in wartime.

In Berlin, four journals provided evidence about images of the profiteer. The *Berliner Illustrierte Zeitung* was a mass-circulation paper, with a readership of over 1 million. It used drawings liberally, but had relatively few caricatures. Published by the Ullstein group, it was conservative politically. It represented the patriotic sentiment of the majority of the German population on the outbreak of the war.

Ulk was a popular weekly supplement to the *Berliner Tageblatt,* a mass-circulation liberal newspaper published by the Mosse group. It had few images of profiteers, and those dealing with the subject were usually ambiguous. The satirical Berlin weekly review *Kladderadatsch* was also a Mosse publication. As in the case of *Ulk,* images of the profiteer were rarely used; on the other hand, the bureaucracy came in for its share of abuse. Finally, there was *Simplicissimus,* published in Munich, but read widely in Berlin. With a relatively small circulation of about 100,000, it was more critical than the other journals, more aesthetically conscious, and shared a sense of national tragedy towards the end of the war.

It is apparent that we are dealing with a heterogeneous sample of press opinion in visual form. We have used dailies, weeklies, mass-circulation and elite papers; we have consulted publications with different political points of view. In the best of all possible worlds, comparisons between similar publications in different cities could be made. But the relative paucity of evidence over the short term means that we have insufficient material to offer rigorously comparative time series open to the analysis of variance and correlation.

Instead of a quantitative analysis, we try to identify normative systems and symbols appearing in the wartime press. That the Socialist press attacks employers more than the Conservative press is not our concern; what matters more is the common denominator linking these disparate sources. That link is the expression of a normative language about sacrifice and privilege in wartime.

Moral obligation on the home front

To invoke a sense of duty during the Great War was both a propaganda device and a spontaneous expression of conscience among millions of people with loved ones in combat.[5] This appeal to conscience was not simply a matter of national sentiment, since it invoked moral categories separating those who behaved well and those who behaved badly on *your* side. This is the locus of images of the profiteer. One prime instance is 'the nightmare of the profiteer' – the angel of peace – in *Kladderadatsch* on 31 December 1916 (fig. 4.1), or more wryly the *Punch* caricature of 8 November 1916, in which the profiteer's child asks, 'Daddy, who did you do in the Great War?' (fig. 4.2).

The soldier plays a double role of authority, as in the appeals for civilian wealth or effort – for instance, in *Le Petit Journal* of 26 December 1916 on 'new taxes and the poilu's opinion' – on the one hand, and in the evocation of the hardships of trench life as a reason for austerity on the home front, on the other.

Those who fight and those who are privileged

It is rare to see together in caricatures a soldier and a non-combatant civilian male, since this juxtaposition was potentially volatile. Why one group bled and another group prospered was a question best postponed in the interests of solidarity. Soldiers are particularly rare in caricature in the Berlin press, where the question was perhaps more dangerous than in Paris or London. Caricaturists in *The Herald* or *John Bull* could, however, dare to put the question. On 17 June 1916, just two

[5] See John Horne (ed.), *Forms of mobilization during the First World War* (in press), and B. Waites, 'Moral economy in wartime', in P. Liddle (ed.), *Home fires and foreign fields* (London, 1985).

Fig. 4.1 The nightmare of the profiteer, *Kladderadatsch*, 31 December 1916

Fig. 4.2 'Father, who did you do in the Great War?', *Punch*, 8 November 1916

weeks *before* the disaster of the Somme offensive, *The Herald* showed the profiteer writing the names of the dead in a ledger. On 27 May 1916, *John Bull* has the head of 'Grabban Squeeze' shipping company, with millions of 'extra war profits' sitting fat and smug on one side of a drawing, the other side of which is composed of three crosses askew in a foreign field (fig. 4.3). A few months later, on 2 September 1916, the paper shows a food profiteer reaping a 'rich harvest' alongside his colleague, the grim reaper. A similar identification of the profiteer as devourer of men can be seen in the image of the shark in *La Bataille* on 11 February 1916, a few days before the Battle of Verdun began.

More generally, caricatures juxtapose the soldiers' virtues with the mediocrity or egotism of some civilians, the cowardice of others, the incompetence or indifference of bureaucrats, the rapacity of merchants who sell to soldiers (as in *La Bataille* of 26 January 1916). The imagery here is less normative than negative, in decrying greed or meanness, though it does suggest a sense of the growing gap between front and home front in the middle years of the war. What is missing is mutual sympathy and comprehension. The soldier scoffs at hardship at home, while the civilian betrays indifference or scorn about what the soldiers have been through. One instance is the reply of a bourgeois at the seaside to a war invalid. 'Certainly, certainly, but you are a hero' (*Le Populaire*, 3 September 1918, fig. 4.4). The balance of opinion is always on the soldiers' side.

Cartoons carry one particular moral norm in wartime: aside from material aid to the war effort, always inferior to what soldiers have to give, the civilian is enjoined to show some degree of humanity, of comprehension, of solidarity with the soldier. At the heart of wartime systems of normative representation is a repeated insistence on the need for civilians to retain this level of human sympathy for the men at the front.

Another link between the profiteer and the combatant is that of the family, mostly through the figure of the woman and child, as in the *Daily Herald* (of 11 August 1914), sometimes through the widow, draped in black (*The Herald*, 2 October 1915). More rare is the case of the son of the soldier juxtaposed to the children of the rich (*Le Petit Journal*, 8 May 1915, fig. 4.5). Through the family, the link between privilege and sacrifice becomes immediately apparent to the reader. The merchant, the proprietor, the boss are in touch not with soldiers but with their families. It is clear who is sacrificing and who is not. Here criticism is fierce, and social tensions find vivid expression.

Duty and conscience

Caricatures have both a negative and a positive function. Their criticism of social and individual behaviour is expressed through a visual language based on widely understood signs establishing, through negative reference, what positive and valued behaviour on the home front ought to be.

Beyond the idea of an equality of sacrifice, caricatures project norms

Fig. 4.3 'Profit – and loss', *John Bull*, 27 May 1916

Fig. 4.4 'Certainly, certainly, but you are a hero', *Le Populaire*, 3 September 1918

Fig. 4.5 'Soldier's son', *Le Petit Journal*, 8 May 1915

which are not exclusively related to wartime conditions, but which take on special emphases related to the conflict.[6] The first is a rejection of base materialism, frivolous enjoyment, unrestrained pleasure (*L'Intransigeant*, 26 March 1917, *Le Petit Journal*, 30 April 1917), or of empty-headedness. Frequently the guilty party is a woman, a moral nullity, as in *The Herald* of 31 October 1914, showing two fashionable ladies doing their bit for the war by putting the dogs on the servants' diet (fig. 4.6), or a bourgeois couple, probably *nouveaux riches*, concerned that the quartier doesn't have to know that they are still eating oysters and lobster (*L'Intransigeant*, 21 January 1917), or again through the image of a woman of substance about to take her dog for a walk in her limousine (*Kladderadatsch*, 17 March 1918). Here are instances of what not to do, and, by inversion, we can see what would be a more austere form of behaviour appropriate to the war.

Austerity is the direct opposite of profiteering, the egotism and

[6] For pre-war caricatures, see Eduard Fuchs, *Die Karikatur der europäischen Völker von 1848 bis zur Gegenwart* (2 vols., Berlin, 1904), and E. Fuchs, *Der Weltkrieg in der Karikatur* (Berlin, 1916), vol. I. See also Stéphane Michaud, Jean-Yves Mollier, and Nicole Savy (eds.), *Usages de l'image au XIXè siècle* (Paris, 1992); *Draw! Political cartoons from left to right* (Washington, 1991); Ursula Koch, *Der Teufel in Berlin. Von der Märzrevolution bis zu Bismarcks Entlassung. Illustrierte politische Witzblätter einer Metropole, 1840–1890* (Cologne, 1991).

"Yes darling, one feels that it is one's duty to set an example of self-denial to the people– I have put Fido and all the dear dogs on the same food as the servants."

Fig. 4.6 'Sacrifice', *The Herald*, 31 October 1914

insatiable rapacity of which offered caricaturists a field day in wartime. 'John Bull' tells a striking Welsh miner on 24 July 1915: 'I know the rapacity of your employers, and suffer from it like yourself. But you and I will stop their little game later on. Meanwhile, go back to the pit, my lad, and play the *big* game, for Comrade, King and Country!' (fig. 4.7). In *L'Intransigeant* of 30 August 1917, a wine merchant at the front refuses to lower his prices for soldiers back from battle. Profiteers were hard-hearted men, without pity for ordinary people, as seen in the cruelty shown by a landlord to the wife of a soldier just called to the front in *The Herald*'s comment on 'Rent and duty' of 23 October 1915 (fig. 4.8), just when rent control was enacted (see chapter 13), or by the profiteer's trampling on the bodies of fallen men in *The Herald* of 20 February 1915 (fig. 4.9). Through his false patriotism, his cosmopolitanism, his indifference (or even hostility) to the chances for peace, the profiteer represents everything the soldier is not. Profiteering is fraternity turned inside out. It is also Mephistophelean logic, providing elaborate self-justification to soothe troubled consciences. *The Herald* of 6 March 1915 shows an industrialist picking the pocket of a worker, and then, to add insult to injury, claims that anyone objecting to this practice is a 'shirker'.

Fig. 4.7 'To the Welsh miner', *John Bull*, 24 July 1915

RENT AND DUTY!

The Landlord,
"No, my misguided woman, patriotism demands that we shall raise your rent! Is it not obviously the landlord's duty to leave his tenants as little as possible with which to deplete our country's food supply by wasteful and excessive purchase?"

Fig. 4.8 'Rent and duty!', *The Herald*, 23 October 1915

Simplicissimus of 20 March 1915 shows a similar contempt among businessmen for ordinary people.

What could be more useful as an inversion of the soldier's courage than images of the cowardly and indolent bourgeois fleeing Paris during the German offensive of 1918 (*L'Intransigeant*, 22 April 1918)?

Fig. 4.9 'Poster appeal to profiteers', *The Herald*, 20 February 1915

L'Intransigeant of 10 May 1918 shows a couple by the seaside in their '*trop petits trous*' bemoaning the absence of danger they left behind in Paris. You might die of a German shell in Paris, but you could die of boredom in the beach. On 12 October 1918 the same paper showed a well-dressed young man sadly musing on the fact that he had decided

Fig. 4.10 'The dream world of the war supplier', *Kladderadatsch*, 10 December 1916

to join up, but now it was too late. Sloth, again silently juxtaposed to the soldiers' fate, is the theme of *Kladderadatsch* of 10 December 1916. Using a well-known motif of Breughel, the artist presents a Berlin butcher asleep on his hams (fig. 4.10).

Special attention was paid to the *nouveaux riches*, on account of their pretentiousness, their bad taste, their ostentation and vulgarity. *Punch* had fun at the expense of wives of 'the war profiteer species', ill-bred and ridiculously dressed, buying items they didn't recognize at whatever the price just for the sake of throwing their money around (6 November 1918 and 13 March 1918). That this image was widespread can be gauged from

Fig. 4.11 'M. Nouveauriche moves in', *L'Intransigeant*, 26 January 1917

similar treatments in *Ulk* (28 June 1918), in the *Berliner Illustrierte* (26 April 1917), and in *L'Intransigeant* (26 January 1917, fig. 4.11). In this last, entitled 'Monsieur Nouveauriche moves in', the man in question wants to put a vermeil statue of 'the war' prominently on his new mantelpiece. The same vulgarity is visible in female form in the *La Bataille* series: 'The pillory of the profiteer' (7 February 1916). The message is clear: parvenus moved up in the world as the soldiers sank deeper into the mud.

In contrast, there were many icons of good citizenship in wartime. They dwelt on hardship and sacrifice specific to the war, but also presented an image of a better society, more austere, simpler, more altruistic, more communitarian. Juxtaposed to the soldier's exertions, those of the civilian are valorized not through violence, but through sobriety, solidarity, and a sense of fairness in everyday life.

Fig. 4.12 'The leeches and their victim', *John Bull*, 23 June 1917

Representations of social relations

In a variety of ways, caricatures describe social tensions. We have focused until now on tensions between front and rear; of equal importance were tensions between different social groups on the home front. One salient juxtaposition was between consumers and tradesmen or proprietors – producers, middlemen, shopkeepers, property owners. This binary image took precedence over, but did not eliminate totally, the common pre-war antagonism between capital and labour.

This is hardly surprising, given the commitment of the press to minimize older social conflicts in the interests of *l'union sacrée*. With some exceptions, strikes were either played down or went unreported. By concentrating on the large bloc of consumers as a unity, the press presented a fluid society, where common interests – food, fuel, housing – took precedence over particular claims.

It is true that the Labour press continued to project pre-war slogans in wartime forms. *The Herald* insisted that 'Labour repudiates profiteers' on 2 September 1916; John Bull muses 'and they wonder at "Labour unrest"' in showing a working man bitten by no fewer than five profiteer-leeches (23 June 1917, fig. 4.12). In *Le Populaire* of 19 April 1918, a classic fat, middle-aged employer berates a young working woman worker for wanting to leave work at 6 p.m., snorting at her, 'what do you do in the evenings?' The same humiliation is doled out by the 'hirer' in the same paper earlier in the war, on 30 January 1916. Occasionally distinctions are made between honest employers and profiteers, but the possibilities of an alliance of the productive nation against the unproductive parasites are rarely evoked. In the London press, elements of continuity with pre-war radical rhetoric are more evident than in Paris or Berlin.

The pillorying of profiteers and middlemen makes sense only against the backdrop of the constant struggle for provisions in these three cities, as indeed in the three nations as a whole. The difficulties faced by consumers, discussed below in chapters 11–13, were so commonplace that caricature operated on unspoken assumptions about the hardships ordinary people faced in the course of their daily lives.

It is important to note that the social profile of the profiteer is rarely precise or specific. The *nouveaux riches* rose from all groups, and were identifiable not by their origins but by their bad taste and their vulgar ostentatiousness. How they made their money in wartime is also unclear. Whether they were merchants, speculators or in the munitions trades is left unanswered in the caricatures on the theme in the Mosse publications *Ulk* and in *Kladderadatsch* (see for example, 25 February 1917).

The profiteer and the consumer

One critical opposition in caricature is between the consumer – usually a woman and child, the family of a soldier – on the one hand, and the tradesman, on the other. The whole chain of production and distribution, with each link taking its cut of the final price and profit, is the subject of criticism. Some urban prejudice against farmers' supposedly nefarious practices appeared, as in *Ulk* of 22 November 1918, at a time when the nation as a whole was *in extremis*. Earlier in the war we meet the peasant or the farmer, guilty of selling his products at too high a price (*La Bataille*, 20 March 1916; *Ulk*, 19 March 1915) on the black market, or just hoarding them. These farmers are usually shown as living well (*La Bataille*, 8 February 1916), without necessarily the same opulence or grossness as the urban profiteer.

These images disclose the outlines of a social rift between town and country, as in *Ulk*, of 2 August 1918 (fig. 4.13), where a well-fed farmer's family, digging into a feast, feels some sympathy for their urban guests, and suggests closing the window so that the aroma of their sausages won't tantalize the city people looking forlornly in at them. The opposition of peasant and Parisian is explicit in *La Bataille* of 24 June 1916, as it is between farmers and workers in the British case of *The Herald* of 6 February 1917, showing a young worker feeding 'war profits' to British farmers, under the title 'A little child shall feed them'.

In contrast to the producers of food, who come in for much criticism, there are few images of those who make other essential items of household consumption like clothes or shoes. Despite severe shortages

Fig. 4.13 'Guest-free, meat-free', *Ulk*, 2 August 1918

here, their manufacturers escaped the censure through caricature visited on their rural compatriots.

Another guilty part is that of the middleman, clearly but rarely realized, as in *La Bataille* of 27 April 1916 (fig. 4.14). In *John Bull* of 14 July 1917, he is the shipping profiteer; in *Simplicissimus* of 19 May 1915, he is the hoarder, or 'potato patriot'. The wholesaler does even better than the farmer, and it is he who has all the gross features of the profiteer: big belly, cigar, pig-like coarse face.

Still another kind of profiteer is the merchant, modest or substantial, in direct contact with his customers. To *L'Intransigeant* of 31 May 1916, he is the grocer; elsewhere he is the butcher or the coal merchant (*Le Petit Journal*, 31 January and 3 February 1917); in all cases, the store owner hoards his merchandise within his shop, as if expecting a cunning thief to pry and find out the truth of his claim that he has no stock; the intention is to sell it when the price goes up still further (*Kladderadatsch*, 11 June 1916; *Punch*, 24 February 1915; *Berliner Illustrierte*, 25 September 1916). In a cartoon in *Ulk* for 22 November 1918, the food profiteer's nightmare is falling prices. Given the future of inflation in Germany, he could have slept in peace. Some speculators added to the soldiers' hardships by selling dear to the army or directly to the men in uniform.

Fig. 4.14 'The intermediary', *La Bataille*, 27 April 1916

Most merely added to the difficulties of ordinary civilians, of varying means (*Punch*, 12 August 1914).

The landlord is an additional category of profiteer identified in wartime caricature. Of time-honoured pre-war vintage, this social type of rent-gouger took on the form of the 'vulture' in *La Bataille* of 21 February 1915 (fig. 4.15). He can be found in the British press too.

The social relations of consumption described in these sources furnished an abundant array of overlapping conflicts and solidarities. In *La Bataille* of 2 June 1916 (fig. 4.16), three different kinds of profiteers hover threateningly over a poor housewife: a farmer, a shopkeeper, and an unidentified rich man, each proclaiming his innocence of profiteering. Here we can see the opposition of town/country, consumer/shopkeeper, and poor/rich in but one cartoon. These divisions are both old and new, and enable us to anticipate in the following chapters much

— Je vous ai doublé votre loyer? C'est possible, mais j'ai toujours entendu dire que les locataires de Levallois paieraient.....

Fig. 4.15 'The vulture', *La Bataille*, 21 February 1915

discussion of the dislocation and recombination of adversarial relationships in all three wartime cities.

The munitions maker

Continuities in the British case are clear. The Labour journal *The Herald* felt no obligation to deviate from its single-minded pursuit of the employer or industrialist as profiteer *par excellence*. But this category was reformed quickly to represent the special case of the armaments maker and army supplier. Here even more centrist publications found an easy target: the merchant of death, the man whose profit grows with the casualty lists. His profit comes less from exploiting the worker than from forcing prices up to the detriment of the well-being of the whole community (*Punch*, 5 April 1916). In *Kladderadatsch* for 24 March 1918, just a week after the launching of the massive German offensive on the Western front, the Daimler limousine is driven by a chauffeur who

Fig. 4.16 'No profit', *La Bataille*, 2 June 1916

dwarfs the officers in his charge. The French manufacturer in *Le Populaire* of 7 June 1918 is delighted at the renewal of the war of movement; there's money in it for him.

Here the war profiteer is set against the community as a whole, rather than against any one section of it. It isn't what he does which is wrong – at least for the vast majority outside the pacifist movement. His fault is in using the war crisis to squeeze every penny out of the public coffers.

The bureaucracy

Of only slightly less culpability in this gallery of wrongdoers is the bureaucracy. In all three cities, and especially in Berlin, the nobility of the desk was excoriated. Its members were not profiteers, but rather incompetents who could not or would not help soldiers or their families. In *L'Intransigeant* of 16 September 1916 (fig. 4.17), a bureaucrat asks a

La forme

DESSIN DE DHARN.

— *Avez-vous votre certificat de blessures ?*

Fig. 4.17 'The form', *L'Intransigeant*, 16 September 1916

man with a bandaged face and apparently no arms for his medical certificate, to certify the obvious – that he really was wounded. *Kladderadatsch* (21 October 1917, fig. 4.18) lampooned the Teutonic warrior-bureaucrat; less charitable was *L'Humanité* of 19 December 1915, in portraying a bureaucrat more interested in roasting his own carcass on a good coal fire than in arranging for the transport of refrigerated meat for the population as a whole. *Kladderadatsch* of 29 October 1916 displays indispensable chairs for the work of public servants, indispensable, that is, for their long naps.

Equal sacrifice

Linking the public consciousness of casualties and of an improper distribution of material hardship in wartime is the notion of fairness, defined not in precise terms but revealed by its gross abuse. We can see what is out of bounds in any number of caricatures. In *L'Intransigeant* of 10 March 1917, an old woman rightly complains that she has to queue in winter for products freely available for those who can afford to buy them in a tea shop. In *Le Petit Journal* of 19 June 1917, a rich boy with his

Fig. 4.18 'Paper war', *Kladderadatsch*, 21 October 1917

mother is on the way home from shopping; jam is leaking from his bag. He sees a poor boy watching and asks the well-dressed mother, 'is he waiting for us to give him our "jam card"?' In *Kladderadatsch* of 7 November 1917, it is the railway owners whose fares make them millionaires at the expense of the general public. The message is clear: for everyone who goes without, someone is growing fat.

Divergences: Paris, London, Berlin

So far we have insisted on convergences in the systems of wartime representations of equality and privilege in popular caricatures. It is important to note national emphases, traditions, and styles within these regularities.

London continuities

It is not our intention to claim that these images are representative or exhaustive of the repertoire of caricatures appearing in the press in wartime. What we can suggest, though, is that pre-war styles and symbols were mobilized in different ways. That *The Herald* in 1914 to 1915 carried on its pre-war style of 'employer bashing' may seem unremarkable in the British context, but it would have been shocking in Paris or Berlin, where events and political commitments had rapidly moved on. Here is an eloquent example of 'business as usual' among polemical illustrators, separating British caricature artists from German or French. That many of *The Herald* cartoons were the work of the Australian artist Frank Dyson enables us further to nuance this distinction. In Australia, as in Britain, workers' commitment to the war effort was entirely consistent with very rough treatment of employers seen by their workmen to be giving them a raw deal.[7]

In the British case, the force of tradition was sufficiently strong to empower week after week the repetition of pre-war political messages in the form of cartoons only barely adapted to wartime conditions. The difference is only slight between a pre-war caricature of the profiteer in the *Daily Herald* of 22 January 1914, one dealing with 'war clouds' on 1 August 1914, and a later one on war profiteers of 11 August 1914 (already cited). In the following months, little was added to the stock figure, easily identifiable as a vulgar capitalist, doing well out of the war. This suggests both a precocious attention to the problems of the profiteer in 1914–1915 and a loss of originality in the later years of the war. Continuity has its cost in faded familiarity. In contrast, the profiteer becomes more visible in the press of Paris and Berlin the longer the war went on.

Paris and the moral message of military service

In Paris, representations of the soldier overlapped with those concerning war profiteers. It would be necessary to present a much more systematic survey of the press before commenting rigorously on the image of the soldier in the Parisian press. On the basis of the evidence at hand, as well as advertisements, it appears that the soldier was more

[7] See R. Dare, 'Australie et l'éclatement de la guerre de '14', *Guerres mondiales et conflits contemporains* (1995), pp. 323–54.

present in Parisian caricature than in those of the other two cities. This is hardly surprising, given the vast military population in the city in transit to the front to the north and east as well as *en route* home, and the ubiquity of discussions of national defence. But it is also likely that the prominence of the soldier in popular imagery discloses a sharper contrast between front and home front than in the British case. Consider *L'Intransigeant* of 19 August 1918, emphasizing the safety of civilians, or *Le Petit Journal*'s presentation of a frivolous woman complaining to a wounded soldier that she too had been hit by a ball, a tennis ball. Consider too *La Bataille* of 28 January 1916, presenting a mean-minded wine merchant quarrelling with soldiers. The press touched a sensitive point with these images, but one which hardly exaggerated the seriousness of the moral issue of proper civilian comportment when millions of men were bleeding and dying just 100 kilometres from Paris. Above all, a nation with a Jacobin tradition of the *levée en masse* could easily draw upon the image of the soldier as the embodiment of the Republican ideal. The same was not possible in either Germany, with an imperial army, or in Britain, which had no similar traditions of military service.

Berlin and the men who ran the war

The system of representations in Berlin almost never presented the common soldier juxtaposed to the war profiteer. It is almost as if the subject of the army (as opposed to civilians) suffering from price gouging was simply unthinkable. In contrast there is a surfeit of images of bureaucrats, as well as a concentration on a theme absent in Paris or London (both in image and in reality): the black market. In the French and British capitals, the consuming public is unified; in Berlin it is divided between those with the know-how to use the black market and those who refuse or who are unable to do so. The press suggests that Berlin society was more fragmented, more divided, more individualistic than that of London or Paris, as well as more conscious or open about its illegal practices. In *Ulk* of 25 October 1918 (fig. 4.19), five different people are shown before the magistrates, each charged with some kind of black-market practice.

The normality of petty law-breaking pointed not only to the breakdown of collective solidarity, but the conditions that produced it informed images in Berlin rarely found in Paris or London. These pointed an accusing finger not at Britain or France, but at the 'internal enemy'. This is the title of a cartoon in *Simplicissimus* of 21 June 1916, in which a dragon hovers over both civilians and soldiers (fig. 4.20). In the same journal, earlier in the war, on 19 April 1915 (fig. 4.21), there is a rare instance of anti-Semitism in wartime caricature: an identifiable Jew is surrounded by his comrades in profit if not in faith.

Fig. 4.19 'Sins of the day', *Ulk*, 25 October 1918

Fig. 4.20 'The inner enemy', *Simplicissimus*, 21 June 1916

Fig. 4.21 'War profiteer', *Simplicissimus*, 19 April 1915

Conclusions

We have established clearly that the critique of privilege was common to public discourse in the metropolitan press. Beyond the shibboleths of propaganda, there was a moral code expressed time and again in these cities. It pointed out at a time of unimaginable sacrifice at the front that civilians had to live with one eye, as it were, fixed on the men who weren't there. This normative code ruled out of bounds in wartime a whole panoply of sins: dissoluteness, frivolousness, the display of conspicuous wealth, egotism, cynicism, vulgarity, an uncompromising search for personal advantage, sloth, incompetence.

Shirkers were both those who ducked national service and those who behaved as if blood was not flowing at the front. The study of caricatures demonstrates that well-being meant not living well in a material sense, but living well in a moral sense. Austerity was both valued and unavoidable in a major war; it was how one lived with it which disclosed an individual's and a nation's moral character. In effect, shortages of goods were tolerable; a shortage of human decency was not.

Wartime caricatures disclosed a new adversarial language in metropolitan life. Most studies of propaganda concentrate on the vilification of the enemy. What they miss is the way caricature redefined the internal social order. We have seen some old bifurcations take on new forms; together with new divisions, they describe many of the tensions of wartime urban life. In different ways and at different times they arrayed home versus the front; city versus countryside; men versus women; consumers versus merchants; munitions makers versus the rest; the *nouveau riche* versus the ordinary man; as well as the time-honoured opposition of capital and labour. Most of these images focus on the question of consumption, and the shortages of basic commodities which affected different groups in different ways. This is not surprising, since it is precisely what the readership experienced. But if this evidence reinforces our sense of material grievance, it also provides good grounds for concluding that the Great War crystallized a set of moral codes, which can be seen in the popular press. These codes described rules governing the economy of sacrifice as well as identifying and excoriating those whose behaviour made a mockery of the 'Lost Generation'.

Part 3
The social relations of labour

5 The transition to war in 1914

Jon Lawrence

The outbreak of war brought a sharp fall in economic activity and employment in all combatant countries, and in all three capital cities. By mid-1915, however, both Berlin and London were enjoying near boom conditions, while Paris remained in the grip of a severe unemployment crisis. The central concern of this chapter will be to account for these very different economic trajectories during the transition to war. Why should Berlin and London, with their radically different economic structures, have adapted successfully to the challenge of war, while Paris slid into a period of prolonged economic and social crisis? Was the crisis of the Parisian economy purely the product of war-time factors: its proximity to the front, the 'flight of the bourgeoisie', and the loss of its industrial hinterland to the north? Or were there more long-term factors which uniquely inhibited the adaptation of the Parisian economy? In other words, this chapter will ask whether structural or contingent factors were more important in determining the effects of the outbreak of war on the economies of the three cities.

As we have already seen, the three capital cities were politically, economically, and socially distinct in 1914. Berlin had only been the capital of a united Germany for a little over forty years, and it retained many of the characteristics of a large provincial manufacturing centre. A significantly smaller proportion of the workforce was engaged in the administrative, financial, transport, and service sectors than in either London or Paris. The manufacturing sector accounted for almost 60 per cent of the pre-war workforce, compared with approximately 40 per cent in both London and Paris. Moreover, capital goods industries such as metals and machine making were much more important in Berlin than in either London or Paris, where production tended to be geared to satisfying the consumer demands of the home, and especially the metropolitan, market (see chapter 2).

In many respects, it was Paris and London, with their large state bureaucracies and developed financial communities, which had most in common economically and socially, while Berlin remained much more heavily dependent on its staple manufacturing industries. Yet, as we have noted, by December 1914, the radically different economies of Berlin and London were both adapting relatively smoothly to the demands of total war, while Paris had been plunged into a profound social and economic crisis.

To understand this contrast we turn predominantly to two types of source material: unemployment statistics and surveys of employment. Although these were never compiled in precisely the same way for the three cities, they do provide the basis for a comparison of economic trends during the first months of the conflict. Unemployment statistics are most comprehensive for Paris, but they do not start until October 1914, and it is not until January 1915 that they are available on a trade-by-trade basis. Even then, they record only the total number of people unemployed in each trade, not the percentage unemployed. This can be estimated, but not without some error since the only base-figures available are those from the 1911 census, which, besides being three years out of date, were also based on a slightly different system of classifying occupations. Moreover, although an allowance can be made for the number of men called up from the pre-war workforce of each trade, it is not possible to estimate how many workers transferred from one trade to another. Since the transition to war was a period of unusually high mobility of labour, this inevitably introduces a second source of error into the figures reproduced in table 5.6. As we have already seen, unemployment statistics for Berlin and London refer to a smaller proportion of the workforce. The Berlin figures refer solely to trade unionists (perhaps one-third of the city's total workforce), while those for London are a composite based on trade-union returns from the printing and book trades, and government returns for all workers in trades covered by the National Insurance Act of 1911: building, engineering, shipbuilding, and vehicle building. Neither series can therefore be considered representative; they indicate, not absolute levels of unemployment, but broad trends in the unemployment experience of the two cities. In addition, it should be noted that the London data refer to the metropolitan area as a whole, rather than just to the administrative County of London.

If the unemployment statistics for London are relatively weak, the employment surveys for the city are remarkably comprehensive. Between 22 August 1914 and 31 July 1915, the London Intelligence Committee of the Local Government Board produced eight detailed statistical surveys of employment in the capital.[1] They were undertaken

[1] BLPES, Local Government Board, London Intelligence Committee Papers, 9 vols., Aug. 1914–July 1915 (hereafter LIC), unpublished, held at the British Library of Political and Economic Science, London.

in cooperation with the Board of Trade, and relied on the voluntary returns of selected employers to provide a representative sample of the experience of all firms. From the beginning the sample used was a large one, covering approximately 65 per cent of employees in large firms (those with more than 100 employees) and 10 per cent of employees in small firms by early September. The importance (and difficulty) of securing accurate returns from small firms was fully recognized. The Committee used Home Office lists of London workshops and factories to ensure the representativeness of its sample, which by mid-September had increased to cover nearly 18 per cent of the workforce in small firms.[2] Although it seems likely that in the first months of the war the sample method may have led the authorities to underestimate the number of firms which ceased trading (since they could be mistaken for companies failing to reply to the Committee's circulars),[3] these surveys remain a valuable guide to changing patterns of employment for which there is no equivalent in either Paris or Berlin.

For Paris we have the results of fifteen detailed surveys of the Inspecteur du Travail concerning the number of workshops still open and the total numbers of workers still employed. These reports vary in scope and content, but they can be used to form a working estimate of employment trends. The Berlin data, produced monthly in the *Monatsberichte Gross-Berlin*, are stronger, but they are still inferior to the London employment statistics, because they refer only to firms with more than twenty-five employees (a serious problem, since we know from the London data that there was a significant transfer of workers from small to large firms during the first months of the war). More comprehensive data exist for parts of Berlin, but their value is limited because they do not form part of a continuous series, and because their representativeness remains open to question.[4]

The differences in the sources available for the three cities are thus considerable, but, as long as these differences are kept in mind, they do not preclude a comparative analysis of the impact of war on the urban economies of Paris, London, and Berlin. This is the purpose of the remainder of this chapter, and of the succeeding chapters on the metropolitan labour market in the periods 1915 to 1917 and 1918 to 1919.

Clearly in an analysis which focuses on the impact of war on the

2 LIC, vol I, p. 112 and vol. II, p. 240.

3 See BLPES, London, Board of Trade, 'Report on the state of employment in the United Kingdom in April 1918', pp. 6–7, for a discussion of this problem with reference to national employment surveys.

4 For the series on Parisian employment, see Robert, 'Ouvriers et mouvement ouvrier', ch. 2. For an example of such a local employment survey see State Archive Potsdam, Province Brandenburg (hereafter SA Potsdam, BP), Rep. 30, Tit. 35, no. 1465, Berlin SO, 10 Oct. 1914.

urban labour market it is important to begin by characterizing the state of employment in the three cities on the eve of war. Unfortunately it is all but impossible to talk with any precision about pre-war unemployment levels. As we have seen, in Paris the collection of reliable unemployment statistics grew out of the unemployment crisis of 1914; there are no pre-war data. In contrast, Berlin and London do offer pre-war series, although in both cases they are based primarily on the experience of organized male workers. Between 1910 and 1914 Berlin trade unions reported an average unemployment rate of 4.8 per cent, somewhat lower than the average rate of 6.0 per cent suggested by London trade society returns.[5] However, in July 1914 the Berlin series reported that unemployment was significantly above this long-term average at 6.5 per cent, whereas in London the unemployment rate among trade unionists was historically low, at 4.6 per cent. Whilst we cannot treat these figures as representative of wider unemployment rates in the two cities,[6] they do suggest that their respective economies entered the war at very different points in the trade cycle.

It would be wrong, however, to conclude from official unemployment figures that Berlin entered the war with a larger surplus of unemployed labour than London, for the London labour market was characterized by chronic casualization. Employment by the day, or even by the hour, remained commonplace in most London trades.[7] High production costs, unstable markets, and abundant supplies of labour, encouraged London employers to concentrate on highly flexible, labour-intensive production techniques rather than to invest capital in fixed plant and machinery. Employers often reduced costs further by extensive use of outworking – especially in the clothing trades.

In Paris casualization was much less important. Relatively low wage rates for manual workers meant that employers had little incentive to hire casual labour, especially since labour was in any case less plentiful than in London as a result of the lower long-term birth-rate. The Parisian labour market was still highly fluid, but its instability owed more to the rapid turnover of workers moving from job to job than to the arbitrary power of the employer to hire and fire.[8] In Berlin, casualization was

[5] Berlin figures refer to six trades: metals, wood, textiles, transport, general factory employment, and office work; London figures are based on the returns of six occupation groups: carpenters, plumbers, engineers, shipbuilders, printers, and bookbinders. See *Monatsberichte Gross-Berlin*, 1913–14; Board of Trade, *Labour Gazette*.

[6] Returns made under the National Insurance Act of 1911 recorded a higher rate of 7.1 per cent in July 1914 – even though these too were confined primarily to skilled male workers (their wider coverage among the casualized building trades probably explains the discrepancy).

[7] See N. B. Dearle, *Problems of unemployment in the London building trade* (London, 1908); Stedman Jones, *Outcast London*, part 1; C. Booth (ed.), *Life and labour of the people of London*, 9 vols. (1892–7), vols. IV and IX, pp. 197–213 and 326–61.

[8] C. Charle, *Histoire sociale de la France au XIXème siècle* (Paris, 1991).

even less widespread, not least because production costs remained low and capital goods industries could therefore continue to prosper alongside consumer industries and the service sector.[9]

The immediate impact of the outbreak of war

The outbreak of war in August 1914 brought economic dislocation and increased unemployment to the capital cities of all the major combatant countries. In Berlin unemployment amongst male trade unionists rose from 6 per cent to 19 per cent in the first two weeks of the conflict and was probably even more severe amongst unorganized workers.[10] The rise in London was more modest, with unemployment rates amongst workers covered by the National Insurance Act increasing from 7 per cent to 10 per cent during August.[11]

Although Parisian unemployment statistics are not available before October 1914, it is clear from other sources that dislocation was even more severe in the French capital. Estimates produced by the Inspecteur du Travail during August 1914 suggest that employment levels in Paris had fallen by a remarkable 70 per cent since the beginning of the war, and that 68 per cent of workshops in the Paris region had closed altogether.[12] Unofficial estimates of unemployment in the capital suggest that up to 600,000 Parisians were without work within a few weeks of the outbreak of war.[13] These figures find confirmation in the official returns on workplace accidents which show that only 4,961 accidents occurred in the Paris region during August and September 1914, compared with 27,106 in the same period during 1913 (a fall of 82 per cent).[14]

The contraction of employment was not as severe in either Berlin or London. Indeed, in London overall industrial employment appears to have contracted by less than 10 per cent by late August, and by only 13 per cent at its low-point in mid-September.

Although the Berlin statistics are much less comprehensive than those for London, the monthly survey of employment published in the *Monatsberichte Gross-Berlin* shows that by early September industrial employment in the greater Berlin area had fallen by more than 24 per cent (table 5.1). However, because the survey covers only firms with

[9] See *Dokumente aus geheimen Archiven*, vol. IV (Berlin, 1914–18), p. xiii. However, by 1914 the rapid growth of Berlin since unification was beginning to undermine some of its historic cost advantages – and especially to force up rental and food costs.

[10] *Monatsberichte Gross-Berlin*, 1914.

[11] Board of Trade, *Labour Gazette*, Aug. and Sept. 1914.

[12] Calculated from figures in *Bulletin du Ministère du Travail*; see Robert, 'Ouvriers et mouvement ouvrier', ch. 2.

[13] A. Fontaine, *French industry during the war* (New Haven, 1926), p. 22.

[14] *Bulletin du Ministère du Travail*, May–June 1915.

Table 5.1. *The contraction of industrial employment (male and female) in Paris, London, and Berlin at the outbreak of war in 1914 (July 1914 = 100)*

Date	Paris	London	Berlin
Mid-Aug. 1914	—	91	—
Late Aug./early Sept. 1914	29	—	76[a]
Mid-Sept. 1914	—	87	—

Note: [a]Refers only to firms with more than twenty-five employees (see text).
Sources: Bulletin du Ministère du Travail, 1914–20; BLPES, Local Government Board, London Intelligence Committee Papers, I and II; *Monatsberichte Gross-Berlin*, 1914–15.

more than twenty-five workers, this may understate the aggregate fall in employment. When the Factory Inspectorate for north Berlin carried out a survey of local firms in early September 1914, it found that most of the firms that had closed down were small businesses.[15] Similarly, the only source presently available that gives details of the changing pattern of employment across firms of all sizes shows a much more substantial contraction than that revealed in the *Monatsberichte Gross-Berlin*. This survey of industrial employment in south-east Berlin found an overall contraction of employment of more than 39 per cent in mid-October, compared with a figure of only 22.5 per cent in the *Monatsberichte* for October (table 5.2). It may be that south-east Berlin was particularly hit by the outbreak of war, but in any case the more detailed survey confirms the war's greater impact on small firms.[16]

Even when small firms are included, however, it is clear that the contraction of employment was much less severe in Berlin than in Paris. Thus, whereas the Parisian inspectorate claimed that at least 68 per cent of firms in the Paris region had closed since the beginning of the war, the local report for north Berlin found that only 19 per cent of the district's firms had closed *over the previous twelve months*.[17] Even so, it found few firms unaffected by the outbreak of war – nearly 85 per cent of the companies still trading were found to be operating some form of short-time work.[18]

[15] SA Potsdam, BP, Rep. 30, Tit. 35, no. 1465, Gewerbeinspektion N, 12 Sept. 1914. The report also noted that many firms in the fashion and luxury goods trades had been forced to close. [16] *Ibid.*, Berlin SO, 10 Oct. 1914.

[17] *Ibid.*, Gewerbeinspektion N, 12 Sept. 1914. A year later the Paris factory inspectorate reported that 38 per cent of firms remained closed.

[18] *Ibid.* According to the report only 12 per cent of the firms still open were working a normal week, 4 per cent were working overtime, 34 per cent had reduced the working day by between 2 and $4\frac{1}{2}$ hours, and 15 per cent were working just one or two days per week. There are no details of the hours worked in the remaining firms (34 per cent of those open), but presumably these too were working short-time.

Table 5.2. *An index of industrial employment in south-east Berlin, 10 October 1914 (July 1914 = 100)*

Industry	Employed in Oct. 1914
Leather	141
Clothing	88
Textiles	87
Food	87
Machines	52
Wood	51
Metalwork	44
Printing	35
Paper	23
All trades surveyed	61

Source: State Archiv Potsdam BP, Rep. 30, Tit. 35, no. 1465, Berlin SO, 10 Oct. 1914.

The contraction of employment in Berlin was markedly uneven between trades (table 5.2). In part this reflected the composition of each trade's pre-war workforce by sex and age, since one of the main causes of the contraction of employment was the mass mobilization of young male workers into the armed forces. But it also reflected the very uneven impact of the war on different trades. Thus, although the leather industry, printing trade, and paper industry all employed roughly equal numbers of men and women, their experience of the transition to war was very different.[19] In the leather trade the sudden demand for military accoutrement work led to a rapid expansion of employment, while in the printing and paper trades the interruption of raw-material supplies and the curtailment of civilian demand appears to have led to a massive collapse.

Although the first Parisian statistics to be broken down by trade date from January 1915, it is noticeable that they too suggest considerable variation by trade. Only 11.1 per cent of workers in commerce and banking are recorded as unemployed compared with 46.5 per cent of those in fine metal work and 45.2 per cent of those in printing.[20] The story is similar for London, although no trade suffered as severely as the paper industry in south-east Berlin or fine metal work in Paris. Worst hit during August 1914 was the cycle and motor trade. Employment in small firms fell by 46 per cent during the month – and whilst enlistment accounted for no more than one-sixth of this fall, it would be wrong to imagine that the rest were simply thrown into unemployment. Even in August 1914 many were able to find work in larger engineering firms

[19] *Monatsberichte Gross-Berlin*, 1913, pp. v and vi.

[20] See below, table 5.6.

able to benefit from government war contracts. Indeed, by the end of August London's large engineering firms had already seen an 11.5 per cent *net increase* in employment (after allowing for enlistment).[21]

It should be clear already that the initial impact of war was far less severe in London than in either Berlin or Paris. Undoubtedly the major reason for this was simply that mobilization was on a much more modest scale in Britain than in either France or Germany. By late September approximately 300,000 Parisian males had been drafted into the armed forces (roughly 30 per cent of the total male workforce). In Berlin the comparable figure was approximately 28 per cent by early September,[22] but in London perhaps 6 per cent of the male workforce enlisted during August (including reservists), and only 8.2 per cent had done so by mid-September. It was not until July 1915 that enlistment in London exceeded 20 per cent of the pre-war male workforce, by which time much higher enlistment rates had been registered in both Paris and Berlin.[23]

Mass mobilization by state decree placed an incalculably greater burden on the urban economies of Berlin and Paris during the first month of war than did the voluntary scheme embraced in Britain to supplement the British Expeditionary Force. The enlistment of so many workers was itself guaranteed to cause a significant contraction of employment in both Paris and Berlin during 1914. Unfortunately it is difficult to gauge precisely what proportion of the fall in employment in the two cities can be attributed directly to mobilization, because in neither case are employment statistics disaggregated by sex. In Paris the overall fall in employment, at approximately 70 per cent, was clearly far too great to be attributed solely to mobilization, but even in Berlin the threefold increase in male unemployment would suggest that the contraction of employment cannot be attributed solely to the direct effects of mass mobilization.

Mobilization, however, had an indirect as well as a direct impact on the overall level of employment in the three cities. The men who enlisted in the respective armed forces were overwhelmingly young and probably included a high proportion of the most productive workers in

21 LIC, vol. I, pp. 115–16. This figure would have been higher still if the committee's surveys had included government factories such as the Woolwich Arsenal, which absorbed large numbers of skilled engineering workers in the first months of the war. See PRO, SUPP 5/1051, 'Statement of employees in O. F. Woolwich from week ending 1.8.1914 to week ending 5.2.1916'.

22 *Korrespondenzblatt der Gewerkschaften*, 1914, p. 562, which shows that 27.7 per cent of Germany's unionized workers had been called up by early September 1914.

23 LIC, vol. IX, p. 229, and *Jahresberichte der Gewerbeaufsichten*, 1914–18, p. 75. For Paris the estimates were calculated from the statistics for French male age groups serving, and the mobilization orders by age. On this question see J. Maurin, *Armée, guerre, société: soldats Languedociens, 1889–1919* (Paris, 1982).

many industries. In France the sixteen *classes* of 1896–1910 and 1914 were all mobilized by the government during the first month of the war (the *classes* of 1911 to 1913 were already under arms).[24] Moreover, within each *class* the rate of mobilization varied between 80 and 85 per cent; clearly the Parisian economy had been almost wholly denuded of young male workers by the end of August 1914. Not surprisingly many firms found that they had lost so many key workers that it was impossible, at least in the short term, to maintain production. Worse still, many of those enlisted in both Paris and Berlin were small employers who consequently were forced to close their workshops and lay off their hands.[25]

These difficulties were compounded further by the fact that, in both France and Germany, the transport network was placed largely at the disposal of the military authorities to carry men and materials to the front. In addition, municipal transport, including the Métro, virtually ceased to operate in Paris during the crisis. As a result many firms found themselves cut off both from their sources of supply and from non-local markets. Inevitably the problem was most acute for export-orientated industries such as the Berlin piano trade, where employment fell from 600 to 50 at the outbreak of war, or Siemens, which lost foreign orders for 5.8 million light bulbs.[26]

Significantly, when the London Intelligence Committee held an enquiry into the causes of the dislocation of trade in early September 1914, few firms pointed to mobilization as a factor in their difficulties (see table 5.3). Instead the enquiry concluded that the primary cause of the 'depression' in trade was the disruption of peacetime markets, either as a result of diminished demand, or of specific wartime conditions (for instance the loss of enemy markets and the closure of the Baltic ports).[27] To a lesser extent war conditions also had a direct impact on many trades through shortages of raw material, lack of inland or overseas transport, and the restriction of credit facilities. As in Paris and Berlin, mobilization played its part in transport difficulties, and also to some extent in the collapse of normal patterns of demand, but its overall importance was much less than in the other capitals. Indeed, it should already be clear that at this stage the war as a whole impinged much less directly on civilian life in Britain than it did on life in France, Germany, or for that matter Russia and Austria-Hungary.

In London almost a third of all small firms (those with fewer than 100

[24] For a discussion of the impact of mobilization on French industry see Fontaine, *French industry*, pp. 22–39.

[25] See *Ibid.*, p. 22 and *Jahresberichte der Preussischen Gewerberäte*, p. 69.

[26] *Jahresberichte der Gewerbeaufsichten*, p. 224 and G. Siemens, *Der Weg der Elektrotechnik* (Munich, 1961), p. 69.

[27] LIC, vol. II ('Report on the causes of depression in various trades'), pp. 25–39.

Table 5.3. *Percentage of all London firms identifying certain causes of trade depression, early September 1914*

Cause of depression	Large firms[a]	Small firms
Lack of orders	60	61
Lack of material	36	24
Stoppage of exports	36	16
Lack of inland transport	25	7
Financial difficulties		32
Shipping difficulties	17	8
Other difficulties		6
No complaint to make	12	13
No answer given	1	4

Notes: The column percentages total to more than 100 because many firms referred to two or more causes of depression.
[a]More than 100 employees.
Source: BLPES, Local Government Board, London Intelligence Committee Papers, II ('Report on the causes of depression'), p. 26.

employees) reported that their trade was suffering because of a shortage of credit (table 5.3). Indeed it would appear that many small London firms were unable to weather the initial period of dislocation because they could not obtain sufficient credit either to produce for stock, or to invest in the new productive capacity which would allow them to tap new wartime patterns of demand. As a result, it was small rather than large firms that were most severely hit during the first months of the war in London (see table 5.4). Remarkably, as early as mid-August, at the height of the initial crisis, there had already been a 2 per cent net *increase* in male employment in large firms, after allowing for enlistment, compared with a net contraction of 4 per cent in small firms (table 5.4, D1 and D2). By mid-September this had become a 3.5 per cent net increase for large firms and a 6.5 per cent net contraction for small ones. Hence there are strong grounds for believing that London experienced a significant transfer of workers from small to large firms during the first six weeks of the war.

One factor in this transfer of labour in London may well have been the greater propensity of small firms to lay off workers rather than to put them on short-time (table 5.4, A1-B1 and A2-B2). There are no comparable statistics for Paris or Berlin, but, as we have already seen, there is considerable evidence from both cities that small firms suffered disproportionately from the dislocation of August–September 1914. It therefore seems likely that these cities would have experienced a similar transference of labour from small to large firms, though perhaps more

Table 5.4. *The course of employment in industrial firms in London, August to September 1914 (percentages)*

	Male workers							
	Large firms				Small firms			
	On short-time (A1)	Fall in employment (B1)	Joined forces (C1)	Net change in employment (D1)	On short-time (A2)	Fall in employment (B2)	Joined forces (C2)	Net change in employment (D2)
Aug. 1914	18.5	4.0	6.0	+2.0	18.0	10.0	6.0	−4.0
Sept. 1914	12.5	6.5	10.0	+3.5	16.5	17.0	10.5	−6.5

	Female workers			
	Large firms		Small firms	
	On short-time (A1)	Fall in employment (B1)	On short-time (A2)	Fall in employment (B2)
Aug. 1914	41.0	6.0	24.0	8.5
Sept. 1914	31.0	7.0	29.0	12.0

Note: All figures are percentages of workers employed in July 1914.
Source: BLPES, London Intelligence Committee Papers, II, p. 245.

slowly than in London because of the greater disruption caused by mobilization.

Political responses

Having looked briefly at the nature of the immediate crisis in the three cities, we will now examine how government authorities, local and national, responded to the challenge of financial crisis and economic dislocation in the first months of the war. This section therefore will explore two main areas of government policy during the immediate crisis: financial affairs and social welfare.

Ironically, an examination of government responses to the war suggests that intervention occurred in inverse relationship to the seriousness of the social crisis in the three cities. In London, where the crisis was least severe, government agencies were most active in the pursuit of the twin objectives of alleviating distress and returning economic life to its normal channels. In Paris, where the crisis was most severe, relief work was underfunded (although unemployment and separation allowances *were* paid), and measures to stabilize the economy were sacrificed to the immediate goal of national defence.

This ordering of priorities was not, however, as perverse as may at first appear. For France, the military crisis was so extreme that not only did it overshadow all other considerations, but it guaranteed that the military would have an absolute call on all resources whether human, material, or financial. In many respects German government circles were dominated by a similar outlook, although since the military crisis was less desperate, there was a less single-minded devotion to military interests over all others. In Britain the greater remoteness of the conflict, encapsulated in the semi-official slogan of 'business as usual', meant that government at all levels felt better able to devote attention to ameliorating the social and economic consequences of war.

In Paris, as in Berlin and London, the period of ultimatum and counter-ultimatum which led up to the outbreak of war was one of extreme financial uncertainty. Prices on the Paris Bourse fell sharply during the last week of July, while public uncertainty was reflected in a general movement to withdraw funds from the banks.[28] The period of economic crisis therefore preceded the formal outbreak of war, especially in France where the fear of invasion was perhaps greatest. On 31 July the French government introduced a series of bold measures to halt the mounting crisis. Settlement day on the Bourse was deferred to avert the failure of many firms unable to meet their obligations. At the

[28] Marcel Poëte, 'La physionomie de Paris pendant la guerre', in H. Sellier, A. Bruggeman, and M. Poëte (eds.), *Paris pendant la guerre* (Paris, 1926), pp. 69–87.

same time the government announced a moratorium on bills of exchange, and announced that bank deposits would be limited to withdrawals of 250 Francs and 5 per cent of the total balance.[29] At this time the Banque de France still possessed considerable financial assets in both cash and bills, but, unlike the Bank of England or the Reichsbank, it was not free to use its reserves to restore economic confidence because of a secret agreement which pledged the bank to help finance general mobilization.[30] Under this agreement the bank was obliged to find the massive sum of 2,900 million francs, and thus had virtually no funds available to maintain liquidity within the domestic economy. This presented a stark political choice in which national defence was given absolute priority over the needs of civilian life. In many respects it is this choice which lies behind the unparalleled collapse of industrial employment in Paris during the first weeks of war. The government's financial restrictions were so severe that not only did credit become virtually unavailable, but cash itself became scarce. The result was that many firms faced such a severe liquidity crisis that they were simply forced to close down.[31]

Although both Britain and Germany also faced a period of considerable financial uncertainty during the immediate pre-war period, neither country's political leaders were forced to make similarly stark choices between civilian and military requirements. On Friday 31 July both the London and Berlin stock markets ceased trading in response to the mounting sense of crisis throughout Europe. London, as the centre of the world's money and commodity trading markets, was affected particularly severely by the near total collapse of international commerce.[32] Between 28 July and 1 August the Bank of England had raised its base (or re-discount) rate from 3 per cent to 10 per cent in an attempt to halt cash withdrawals. On Sunday 2 August the Chancellor of the Exchequer, Lloyd George, met representatives of the Bank of England and the main joint-stock banks to develop a concerted strategy for avoiding prolonged financial crisis in the event of war. The result was a series of measures designed both to diffuse the immediate crisis (including the closure of all banks until 7 August, and a moratorium on all debts and obligations exceeding £5), and to restabilize the economy (including a reduction of interest rates to 6 per cent, the classification of

29 G. Bonnefous, *La Grande Guerre* (Paris, 1957), pp. 70–2.

30 This agreement had been negotiated in November 1911 – in the wake of the Agadir crisis. See M. Marion, *Histoire financière de la France depuis 1715*, 6 vols. (Paris, 1927–31).

31 For instance see *Le Temps*, 1 Sept. 1914, 'Pour la reprise de travail'.

32 According to the *Bankers' Magazine*, 98 (Sept. 1914), p. 323, by August 1914 the London money markets were already in total chaos thanks to the breakdown of foreign remittances. Interestingly the French moratorium on bills was said to have proved especially destabilizing.

government £1 and 10s notes and postal orders as legal tender, and the coining of additional silver).[33]

In contrast to the French case, the British government's policies were designed to control the financial crisis without plunging the economy into a severe liquidity crisis.[34] The reserves of the Bank of England were used, not to underwrite mobilization, but to cover the cash liabilities of the great joint-stock banks. As a result the Bank's reserves fell by £17 million during the week 29 July to 5 August, or from 51 per cent of total liabilities to just 14.5 per cent. In all the government accepted liabilities on about £500 million of securities – a vast sum which only makes sense when understood as part of the wider strategy of 'the Free Trade war': whereby the British authorities envisaged that their primary contribution to the Allied war effort would be economic and naval, rather than military.[35]

The financial crisis was less severe in Germany, perhaps partly because, as a net debtor, Germany was less affected by the near-suspension of international commercial transactions. Even so, the last week of July placed severe pressure on German banking reserves, culminating, on 31 July, in the decision to suspend convertibility in an attempt to preserve the large gold reserves which had been deliberately built up over the preceding five or six years.[36] On 1 August the Reichsbank raised the discount rate from 5 to 6 per cent, but there was no move to introduce a moratorium on debts.[37] On the contrary, the government implemented a series of policies designed specifically to restore liquidity to the economy. Since at least 1909, the German authorities had been aware of this problem, and had been trying to increase the use of paper money within the economy. They had also drawn up plans for easing the financial and economic crisis likely to be caused by a major European war. Whereas French plans involved exacerbating the liquidity crisis by withdrawing large sums from the economy to help finance mobilization, the German plans involved greatly increasing the quantity of small denomination bank notes in circulation, and releasing 550 million Marks to help small businesses hit

33 *Bankers' Magazine*, 98 (Sept. 1914), pp. 317–38, 'The great crisis'.

34 A second block of measures followed on the 13 August 1914 – these were designed to relieve the continuing liquidity crisis on London's discount and commodity markets; *Ibid.*, pp. 333–4.

35 S. Pollard, *The development of the British economy, 1914–1980* (3rd edn, London, 1983), p. 35. On the 'Free Trade war' see D. French, *British economic and strategic planning, 1905–1915* (London, 1982) and 'Allies, rivals and enemies: British strategy and war aims during the First World War', in J. Turner (ed.), *Britain and the First World War* (London, 1988), pp. 22–35.

36 For a discussion of the background to the German financial crisis see R. Zilch, *Die Reichsbank und die finanzielle Kriegsvorbereitung, 1907 bis 1914* (Berlin, 1987).

37 *Berliner Börsen-Courier*, 1 Aug. 1914.

by the crisis.[38] This money was distributed through a network of local lending institutions, and was intended to help firms overcome the short-term cash-flow problems caused by the sudden collapse of normal patterns of supply and demand.[39] Its distribution was premised on the assumption that the war would be short and victorious – and that victory would more than cover the cost of any emergency measures deemed necessary to preserve domestic stability. Interestingly, there were widespread calls for similar arrangements to help small firms in Britain, but no legislation was introduced. Given the large number of small firms citing 'financial difficulties' as the main cause of trade depression (table 5.3), this may help to explain the significant decline of employment among small London workshops during the first months of the war.

Thus the contrasting responses of national governments to the financial crisis which accompanied the outbreak of war had an important influence on the pattern of economic dislocation identified for each of the capital cities. Government decisions also played a vital part in determining the extent and duration of the social crisis in Berlin, Paris, and London. In all three countries politicians were quick to recognize that existing, predominantly charitable, mechanisms for social provision could not cope with distress on the scale that the war would bring. Indeed in France and Germany many private charities ceased to function altogether in the initial upheaval of war. Within days Britain, France, and Germany had each introduced an *ad hoc* system of social payments to provide for the families of men mobilized into the armed forces, and to relieve the distress caused by war-related unemployment.

We will discuss these policies in detail in chapter 9, but a few introductory points may be helpful here. These new schemes were broadly similar in the three countries: each relied on local government and charitable agencies to deliver relief to those in need, and each assumed that benefits should be non-contributory, and should offer no more than the bare minimum necessary for survival. In Germany and France the need for decisive government action was particularly great because many traditional forms of private welfare provision had collapsed under the strain of war.

Although the genesis and purpose of the governments' welfare schemes may have been similar, they had very different results in the three capitals. In Berlin and London welfare provision appears to have operated relatively smoothly, albeit after an initial period of administrative confusion, but in Paris government attempts to relieve distress had largely collapsed by late August. As the war came to the outskirts of the French capital, both local and national government suspended their

[38] Zilch, *Die Reichsbank*. [39] *Berliner Börsen-Courier*, 20 Aug. and 31 Dec. 1914.

operations, but the administrative structure surrounding the prefects and the military authorities was still in place. The main civil authorities such as the Conseil Général de la Seine did not meet between 14 August and late December 1914.[40] In addition the Commission de Travail, set up by the central government in August 1914 specifically to deal with the capital's severe economic crisis, was suspended a month later during the confusion which accompanied the withdrawal of the government to Bordeaux.[41] Nevertheless social provision continued through mayor's offices, both at the communal and arrondissement levels. At these mayoral offices Parisians received both unemployment and military allowances. In addition communal kitchens operated to provide food for residents of each arrondissement. These measures were sponsored both by the majors and by local socialist organizations.[42]

In Berlin and London, welfare agencies were not placed under comparable pressure. Local government, in particular, continued to play an active part in the relief of distress. Indeed, in Berlin the municipal authorities introduced their own welfare measures including, in late August, a supplement to the basic state unemployment and dependants' benefits, which was intended to compensate for the high cost of living in the capital, and in October a scheme of rent support for war families.[43] In London the twenty-eight metropolitan borough councils formed local representative committees under the direction of the government's Committee for the Prevention and Relief of Distress. These local committees had a broad membership including councillors, employers, administrators, charity workers, and trade unionists, and were charged with distributing grants from the centrally organized National Relief Fund, inaugurated by the Prince of Wales as a special war charity.[44] Thus welfare in London was a mixture of both national and local, and public and private effort. It was far from perfect: many

[40] T. Bonzon, 'La politique sociale du Conseil Municipal de Paris et du Conseil Général de la Seine pendant la Grande Guerre', unpublished DEA. thesis, University of Paris – I, 1994.

[41] On the Commission de travail see R. Picard, *Le mouvement syndical pendant la guerre* (Paris, 1927). On the reticence of the Préfecture de la Seine to continue public works see the declaration of Léon Jouhaux to the congress of the Confédération Générale du Travail (CGT) in July 1918, in CGT, *Compte-rendu des travaux de la CGT* (Paris, 1919), p. 226.

[42] Robert, 'Ouvriers et mouvement ouvrier', esp. chs. 2–5.

[43] See *GemeindeBlatt Berlin*, 1914, p. 375; *Berliner Morgenpost*, 28 Aug. 1914; E. Kaeber, *Berlin im Weltkrieg: fünf Jahre städtischer Kriegsarbeit* (Berlin, 1921), pp. 49–50; and Stadtarchiv Berlin, Rep. 00-02/2 316, 'Stadtverordnetenversammlung Vorlagen', 1914, p. 837 (13 Oct. 1914).

[44] See 'Memorandum on the steps taken for the prevention and relief of distress due to the war' (PP 1914, LXXI), p. 877; and 'Report on the special work of the Local Government Board arising out of the war up to 31st December 1914' (PP 1914–16, XXV), pp. 300, 305–6.

Table 5.5. *An index of the course of employment in the Paris region and in France, July 1914 to October 1915 (July 1914 = 100)*

	July 1914	Aug. 1914	Oct. 1914	Jan. 1915	April 1915	July 1915	Oct. 1915
Paris	100	29	33	50	57	63	73
France	100	34	44	56	63	67	74

Source: Constructed from a series in *Bulletin du Ministère du Travail*, 1914–15; see Robert, 'Ouvriers et mouvement ouvrier', ch. 2.

committees appear to have been remarkably complacent about local distress (especially amongst women workers),[45] but, like the efforts of the Berlin municipal authorities, their work remains impressive.

Economic crisis in Paris

If the French government's decision to give the army absolute priority over financial resources all but guaranteed that France would suffer more severe economic dislocation than the other nations during the first weeks of the conflict, the rapid success of the subsequent German offensive through Belgium and northern France made it equally certain that there would be no speedy recovery of economic fortunes during the autumn. By October 1914, after the German offensive had been halted at the Battle of the Marne, the first official unemployment returns revealed that more than 300,000 Parisians were without work. The real total was probably even higher, since these returns excluded anyone in receipt of a refugee's or soldier's dependant's allowance.[46] Three months later, in January 1915, there were still 230,000 officially out of work, despite the continued mobilization of male workers into the armed forces. These figures represent a level of unemployment not witnessed in either Berlin or London.

By early 1915 the Parisian experience of employment was already beginning to converge towards that of France as a whole (table 5.5). The period of divergence was between August and October 1914, when employment rose by nearly a third nationally, but hardly improved in Paris. To understand this divergence of experience we must look not to the structural weaknesses of the Parisian economy, but to contingent

45 See *Women's Dreadnought*, 31 Oct., 7 Nov., and 12 Dec. 1914. For a different perspective see *Toynbee Record*, 27, 1 (Nov. 1914), pp. 10–12: 'The Borough of Stepney and the relief of distress', and pp. 15–23: 'Unemployment amongst women in Stepney'.

46 A. Fonvieille, 'Etude critique du régime des allocations aux familles des militaires soutiens indispensables', unpublished Ph.D thesis in Law, University of Montpellier, 1919.

factors arising directly out of the war itself. Above all, we must again stress the importance of the proximity of Paris to the front, and hence to the effects of the German offensive. At the height of the military crisis in August and September 1914, Paris seemed in imminent danger of falling to the advancing German armies. The city suffered its first aerial bombardment on 30 August 1914 and on 2 September almost the entire administrative machinery of government departed for Bordeaux to protect it from the advancing enemy, staying there until 9 December 1914 (by which time the front had been stabilized north of the capital). The government of Paris was effectively placed in the hands of the army, who proceeded to redirect the entire life of the city towards one end: the defence of the nation in its moment of crisis. From the taxi-cabs used to ferry soldiers and munitions to and from the Marne to the navvies working on the city's fortifications, all Paris was part of the battle to stem the German advance.[47] Inevitably this total concentration of the capital's resources on the war and on the city's defence occurred at the expense of the economic restructuring that would have been necessary to overcome the dislocation of the immediate crisis.

The Parisian economy was also affected badly by the loss of Belgium and large parts of northern France to the invading German armies. Suddenly the capital's major source of raw materials and semi-processed goods was gone, along with one of the most important markets for its skilled finishing trades. On the eve of the war the area directly affected by invasion accounted for approximately two-thirds of French manufactured iron and steel production, three-quarters of coal and coke production, four-fifths of pig-iron and woollen production, and over 90 per cent of the output of linen goods and copper.[48] The French economy as a whole was seriously weakened by the loss of this vital productive capacity, much of it in the key war industries, but Paris was particularly badly hit because of its proximity to, and consequent integration with, the northern industrial region.[49]

Another factor retarding recovery during this period was the massive exodus from the capital during the military crisis. An analysis of the results of a census carried out during September 1914 suggests that only 1.8 million people were still resident in Paris at this time; more than 1 million fewer than on the eve of the war.[50] Assuming that approximately 300,000 of these had been mobilized, that still leaves more than 700,000 civilians who had fled the capital. From the census it appears

[47] See Becker, *1914*.

[48] Fontaine, *French industry*, pp. 16–17. These figures refer not just to the territories lost to the enemy, but also to adjacent areas under fire or otherwise disorganized by military action.

[49] See Centre de Documentation d'Histoire des Techniques, *Evolution de la géographie industrielle de Paris et la proche banlieue au XIXème siècle* (Paris, 1991).

[50] *Annuaire Statistique de la ville de Paris et du Département de la Seine, 1914*, pp. 652–4.

that approximately 220,000 of these were children under fifteen years old, while the remainder was made up of 310,000 women and 200,000 men. Moreover, these figures almost certainly underestimate the exodus because large numbers of refugees from northern France and Belgium were flooding into Paris at the time this census was taken.

This voluntary evacuation was particularly heavy among the Parisian bourgeoisie, and resulted in the depopulation of many of the wealthiest districts such as the 16th arrondissement and Neuilly-sur-Seine.[51] Indeed most of the capital's great commercial banks and its 'quality' newspapers such as *Le Figaro* and *Le Temps* followed the Government to Bordeaux during September. As a consequence Paris became effectively a workers' city during the worst months of the crisis. The cost of this social transformation was, however, very high, since the flight of the bourgeoisie meant the flight of bourgeois capital. This retarded recovery in two main ways. First, it hit the already depressed finished-goods and service industries by removing many of their most affluent customers. Second, many of the small businessmen who fled the city during the autumn closed their workshops before leaving, despite appeals from the Inspecteur du Travail to keep them open.[52]

In the absence of direct information about the impact of economic dislocation on different trades during the autumn of 1914, we must again turn to the unemployment returns of January 1915. These figures are worth examining in some detail, since they underline the uneven impact of the employment crisis in Paris.[53] In marked contrast to the situation in London and Berlin, there was little difference in the pattern of employment of men and women during January 1915 (table 5.6). In a few trades female unemployment appears to have been exceptionally high (chemicals 83 per cent, printing 75 per cent), but overall the rates for men and women were almost identical. Much more marked was the difference between the situation of manual and non-manual workers. In the service sector unemployment rates appear to have ranged between 10 and 20 per cent, but in the industrial sector they were generally around 30 per cent, rising to between 40 and 50 per cent in trades such as building, printing, and the luxury crafts. It may be that unemployment rates amongst non-manual workers were deflated by the after-effects of the September exodus (though most Parisians returned once the immediate crisis had passed), but this would still not alter the fact that within Paris the experience of unemployment was overwhelmingly an experience of manual workers.

The crisis was most severe in the city's consumer-orientated trades

[51] See Robert, 'Ouvriers et mouvement ouvrier', map 5, p. 1311.

[52] *Bulletin du Ministère du Travail*, Jan.–Mar. 1915.

[53] *Ibid.*, Jan. 1915 – for a discussion of the problems inherent in translating these data into unemployment *rates* see above, pp. 136–7.

affected by the flight of the bourgeoisie, and by the collapse of working-class purchasing power through enlistment and unemployment.[54] The apparent exception of the clothing trade could be the result of underestimation caused by the informal employment structures of the sector, which tended to obscure unemployment (especially amongst outworkers) from the official gaze. On the other hand, it may be that, like the leather trade, clothing was better placed than other consumer trades to transfer from civilian to military production. Certainly in Berlin and London sections of the clothing industry such as tailoring were amongst the first trades to enjoy boom conditions during the autumn of 1914.

Thus Paris, unlike Berlin or London, came close to fulfilling the predictions of pre-war commentators such as Norman Angell, who argued that a major European war would plunge advanced western societies into a period of prolonged social and economic chaos.[55] The severity of the Parisian crisis is probably revealed most fully by the collapse of employment in industries catering predominantly for the civilian population, such as printing and food. There is, however, some uncertainty about the definition of the food industry used in the construction of the Parisian unemployment statistics. At the national level food production was the industry least affected by the contraction of employment during August 1914, and by January 1915 employment in the industry stood at 68 per cent of its pre-war level, despite heavy male enlistment into the armed forces.[56] The food industry was also relatively little affected by the outbreak of war in Berlin and London. Significantly, statistics for industrial accidents in the food industry of the Paris region do not show a fall over pre-war levels commensurate with the contraction of employment suggested in table 5.6. By the first quarter of 1915 industrial accidents were only 24 per cent below their level for the same period in 1914, by far the lowest fall for any industry in the Paris region.[57] One explanation for this discrepancy may be that the Parisian unemployment figures included workers in the food service industries, or even domestic cooks, as well as those employed in the manufacture of food and drink. Indeed, by mid-December 1914 employment in the London food industry had declined by only 7.5 per cent, compared with perhaps 40 per cent in Paris a month later.[58]

[54] Although the collapse of working-class purchasing power was partially allayed by the introduction of basic unemployment and separation allowances in August.

[55] N. Angell, *The great illusion: a study of the relation of military power in nations to their economic and social advantage* (London, 1910); discussed in H. Weinroth, 'Norman Angell and *The great illusion*: an episode in pre-1914 pacifism', *Historical Journal*, 17, 3 (1974), pp. 551–74; see also A. J. A. Morris, *Radicalism against war, 1906–1914: the advocacy of peace and retrenchment* (London, 1972).

[56] *Bulletin du Ministère du Travail*, Jan.–Mar. 1915.

[57] *Ibid.*, May–June 1915. [58] LIC, vol. VI, pp. 9–28.

Table 5.6. *An estimate of unemployment by trade in Paris, January 1915*[a]

Trade	Male workers: Unemployed (no.)	Male workers: Unemployed (%)	Female workers: Unemployed (no.)	Female workers: Unemployed (%)	Men and women: Total unemployed as % of July 1914 workforce
Food[b]	4,504	31	5,129	57	41.3
Building	17,262	45	7	—	40.9
Clothing[c]	8,840	35	43,827	17	19.0
Fine metal work	5,784	65	5,361	36	46.5
Printing	5,316	29	7,459	75	45.2
Wood	10,202	32	3,875	67	36.9
Chemicals	2,815	26	2,149	83	37.0
Leather	3,217	15	2,525	13	14.4
Engineering[d]	9,288	15	2,579	35	17.3
Commerce and banking	15,377	9	15,364	14	11.1
Professions	4,263	10	5,757	15	12.6
Service[e]	7,281	37	32,428	19	21.1
Total	94,149	20	126,460	20	20.0

Notes: [a]Col. 2, col. 4, and col. 5 represent the number unemployed as a percentage of the *estimated* number employed in July 1914 (after allowance for enlistment into the armed forces). This calculation therefore makes no allowance for movement between trades after July 1914 (see text).
[b]Food may include the food service industries as well as manufacture.
[c]Clothing and textiles sector.
[d]Engineering, electrical, and metal trades.
[e]Domestic service.
Source: Bulletin du Ministère du Travail, Jan.–March 1915.

To summarize, therefore, the severe and prolonged employment crisis in Paris during the autumn of 1914 must be understood in terms, not of structural weakness, but of immediate and overwhelming war-related factors of which the proximity to the front was undoubtedly the greatest. When combined with the destabilizing impact that mass mobilization and financial collapse had had in August, one need hardly look further for an explanation of why the economic crisis associated with the transition to war was so much greater, and so much more protracted, in Paris than in either London or Berlin. Structural factors may have played a secondary role, especially in prolonging the crisis after the immediate threat to Paris had passed, but they did not determine the nature of the Parisian crisis of 1914.[59] It could be argued, however, that the massive exodus from Paris, which did so much to

[59] Robert, 'Ouvriers et mouvement ouvrier', ch. 1, *passim*.

prolong the crisis in the French capital, had its roots in structural factors. The exodus reflected the long-established tradition of people not born in the city to return to the provinces in times of crisis. Had fewer Parisians been born outside the city, the exodus might well have been less extreme.

Rapid stabilization in London and Berlin

It is evident that Berlin and London did not face a grave economic crisis during the autumn of 1914. For instance, trade-union returns for Berlin show that unemployment peaked in early September, falling sharply thereafter, so that by January 1915 male unemployment was already below pre-war levels (table 5.7). Female unemployment rates took much longer to return to pre-war levels, although again they fell continuously from October 1914 (these figures may be unrepresentative because so few women were members of trade unions at this time). The story was broadly similar in London, although here unemployment never rose as sharply, and was already below pre-war levels by December 1914 amongst insured workers (table 5.7).[60]

On the basis of its statistical surveys of the state of employment in London, the Local Government Board's London Intelligence Committee concluded that the low-point of the recession was reached by 22 August, the date of its first comprehensive employment survey.[61] At first sight this may seem a classic example of official optimism. As we have seen, male unemployment continued to rise until mid-September, while other indices of social distress peaked even later. For instance, in London boroughs as diverse as Shoreditch and Stoke Newington the numbers of children receiving free school meals because of poverty continued to rise until early October.[62] However, the committee's statement was concerned neither with unemployment, nor with social distress, but with economic activity as measured by aggregate employment levels. Its optimism was therefore based on the substantial reduction in the number of workers on short-time between the August and September surveys. In mid-August 1914, 45 per cent of women and 16 per cent of men were either on short-time or had been laid off. By September these figures had fallen to 36 per cent for women, although

[60] Despite the fact that nearly two-thirds of the insured workers in London worked in the building industry, which was hit hard by the war, and also suffered from historically high rates of seasonal unemployment in the winter months.

[61] LIC, vol. I (22 Aug. 1914), p. 28; *Ibid.*, vol. II (5 Sept. 1914), pp. 11–24, and (12 Sept. 1914), pp. 133–6.

[62] *Ibid.*, vols. I–III ('Reports on the highest number of necessitous children fed, by borough' – recorded weekly throughout August to October 1914, and published as Appendix C of the main employment reports).

Table 5.7. *Unemployment rates in Berlin and London, July 1914 to April 1915*

	Greater Berlin[a]		London[b]
	Male trade unionists unemployed (%)	Female trade unionists unemployed (%)	Insured workers unemployed (%)
July 1914	6.3	2.4	7.1
Aug. 1914	19.2	12.4	9.6
Sept. 1914	19.9	18.8	10.0
Oct. 1914	14.5	17.9	8.2
Nov. 1914	10.5	13.6	7.7
Dec. 1914	7.2	10.7	5.9
Jan. 1915	5.5	9.8	4.7
Feb. 1915	3.6	7.0	3.9
April 1915	1.5	4.7	1.8

Notes: [a]Trade unions in six sectors: metal, wood, transport, textiles, factories, and office work.
[b]Building workers, engineers, shipbuilders, and vehicle builders in the London region covered by National Insurance.
Sources: Monatsberichte Gross-Berlin, 1914–15; Board of Trade, *Labour Gazette*, Aug. 1914–May 1915.

there had been a slight increase amongst men to 16.5 per cent.[63] Thereafter the improvement was rapid, so that by mid-October only 21 per cent of the pre-war female workforce was either on short-time or unemployed, and only 9.5 per cent of the male workforce.[64]

There are no comparable statistics for aggregate employment in Berlin, but it seems unlikely that the recovery set in as early, due mainly to the greater impact of mobilization. However, there is no doubt that by the spring of 1915 Berlin (like London) was suffering, not from the problems of unemployment and social distress, but from acute labour shortages in all sectors of the economy. This is borne out by Berlin factory inspectors' reports which by March 1915 had ceased to mention problems of unemployment, and were focusing instead on the complaints of employers about the high wages demanded by scarce skilled workers.[65] It also finds statistical corroboration, not only in the low

[63] *Ibid.*, vol. II ('Statistical survey of employment – mid-September'), pp. 240–1. Figures refer to manual and non-manual workers, but exclude building, railways, docks, the professions, government employees, and domestic service.

[64] *Ibid.*, vol. III ('Statistical survey of employment – mid-October'), p. 260.

[65] SA Potsdam, BP, Rep. 30, Tit. 35, no. 1466: Reports from factory inspectorates in north-west, east and south-east Berlin, and the adjacent town of Neukölln (March, 1915).

unemployment rates seen in table 5.7, but also in the employment survey of April 1915 conducted by the Berlin city factory inspectorate. The results of this survey are summarized in tables 5.8 and 5.9. Similar data for London are included for comparative purposes, although it should be noted that the Berlin statistics concern only employees of large firms, whereas the London statistics are comprehensive for the sectors covered (hence the much greater numbers involved in the London data).

By April 1915 Berlin had seen a major shift of both male and female workers into large industrial firms (tables 5.8 and 5.9). Female employment in this sector had increased by 50 per cent since July 1914, while male employment was up 36 per cent in net terms. However, only a few trades such as chemicals, metalwork, machines, and leather seem to have benefitted from this movement of labour. In most Berlin trades employment in large firms either remained static or fell during the first nine months of war. Clearly the dynamic trades were those boosted by massive war contracts, while largely civilian trades such as printing, paper, laundries, and even clothing all lost workers.[66]

The basic pattern of labour-force mobility was similar in London, although the aggregate shifts in employment appear to have been considerably lower. Partly, this reflects the fact that the London data cover firms of all sizes, and so are not boosted by the transference of workers from small to large firms. However, even if one looked only at large firms, defined as those with over 100 employees in the London data, the increase in employment would be much less than that revealed in the Berlin returns (2.5 per cent for women, and 6.4 per cent for men in April 1915 in the industrial and commercial sectors combined, see tables 5.8 and 5.9).[67] A number of factors may explain this contrast, including the spur to labour mobility provided by greater dislocation in Berlin during the immediate crisis, the pre-war strength of Berlin's metal and machine industries, and the more rapid emergence of a war economy in Germany than in Britain, where the real turning point came only after the formation of the Ministry of Munitions in May 1915.[68]

The stabilization of the Berlin and London economies during the

[66] A survey of firms in south-east Berlin in October 1914 found that military contracts were most common among firms in the leather trades, metalwork, textiles, machines and wood-working (in that order): SA Potsdam, BP, Rep. 30 Tit. 35, no. 1465, Berlin SO, 10 Oct. 1914.

[67] LIC, vol. VIII ('Statistical survey of employment – April 16th 1915'), p. 3.

[68] See G. D. Feldman, *Army, industry and labor in Germany, 1914–1918* (Princeton, 1966); C. Trebilcock, 'War and the failure of industrial mobilisation, 1899 and 1914', in Jay M. Winter (ed.), *War and economic development: essays in memory of David Joslin* (Cambridge, 1975), pp. 139–64; D. French, 'The rise and fall of "Business as usual"' in K. Burk (ed.), *War and the state: the transformation of British government, 1914–1919* (London, 1982); and J. Turner, *British politics and the Great War* (London, 1992), pp. 4, 55–61.

Table 5.8. *The fluctuation of female industrial employment in Berlin and London, July 1914 to April 1915*

Trade group	Berlin: Estimate of number employed, July 1914 (large firms)[a]	Berlin: Change over period to 1 April 1915 (%)	London: Estimate of number employed, July 1914[b]	London: Change over period to 16 April 1915 (%)
Mining and quarrying	1,238	−26	—	—
Metalwork	2,031	+95	7,700	+12
Machines and instruments	14,325	+92	7,500	+10
Chemicals	1,576	+292	6,500	+4
Textiles	5,568	−13	—	—
Clothing	1,992	−17	153,300	−5
Leather	898	+8	12,000	−21
Paper	569	−34	18,300	−9
Printing	1,187	−44	17,800	−5
Wood	176	+58	7,500	+2
Food and drink	2,984	+33	20,000	0
Laundries	943	−15	36,500	−13
Total	33,487	+50	287,100	−4

Notes: [a]Berlin figures refer only to women over sixteen in firms employing fifty or more persons.
[b]London figures refer to all female workers in each trade group.
Sources: Jahresberichte der Gewerbeaufsichten, 1914–18, pp. 76–7; BLPES, London Intelligence Committee Papers, VIII (April 1915).

autumn of 1914 cannot, therefore, be attributed to the same social and economic processes. In Berlin it was undoubtedly the powerful metalworking and machine-making industries which led recovery – once they had been able to re-organize production, both to offset the impact of mobilization, and to meet the new pattern of war-related demand. In London the essential war industries (metals, machines, and chemicals) were all much weaker than in Berlin. Indeed, in mid-February 1915, government war contracts had created more jobs in London, in aggregate terms, in clothing and related trades than in all the essential war industries combined.[69] As a result of this relative weakness in metals and engineering, government contracts provided work for only one-fifth of male industrial workers in London compared with one-third in

[69] See LIC, vol. VII ('Statistical survey of employment – 12th February 1915'), p. 19. This report suggests that the war industries employed the equivalent of 45,644 full-time workers, compared with a figure of 47,987 for the clothing, leather, and fur sectors.

Table 5.9. *The fluctuation of male industrial employment in Berlin and London, July 1914 to April 1915*

	Berlin				London			
Trade group	(1) Estimate of number employed in July 1914 (large firms)[a]	(2) Percentage of col. 1 total employed on 1 April 1915	(3) Percentage of col. 1 total called up	(4) Net change in employment since July 1914 (%)	(5) Estimate of number employed in July 1914 (large firms)[a]	(6) Percentage of col. 1 total employed on 1 April 1915	(7) Percentage of col. 1 total enlisted	(8) Net change in employment since July 1914 (%)
Mining and quarrying	5,693	35	40	−24	—	—	—	—
Metalwork	12,587	127	45	+72	27,800	91	17	+8
Machines and instruments	64,445	97	41	+38	98,300	91	17	+8
Chemicals	7,331	149	41	+90	17,600	93	18	+11
Textiles	3,133	78	21	−1	—	—	—	—
Clothing	1,621	69	22	−9	67,100	87	14	+1
Leather	1,358	93	40	+33	18,200	102	17	+19
Paper	788	64	17	−18	8,400	81	19	0
Printing	1,549	54	27	−19	61,300	84	14	−2
Wood	3,328	55	25	−20	51,300	79	17	−5
Food and drink	3,971	91	38	+29	41,700	90	18	+8
Building	1,930	54	34	−12	117,000	85	14	−1
Laundries	880	63	18	−18	5,100	86	30	+15
Total	108,614	97	39	+36	513,800	87	16	+3

Notes: [a]Berlin figures refer only to men over sixteen in firms employing twenty-five or more persons.
[b]London figures refer to all male workers in each trade group.
Sources: Jahresberichte der Gewerbeaufsichten, 1914–18, p. 75; BLPES, London Intelligence Committee Papers, VIII (April 1915).

Britain as a whole.[70] This may therefore help to explain why male unemployment fell more slowly in London than in either Berlin (see table 5.7), or the wider British economy.[71]

However, the London economy had advantages as well as disadvantages when compared with Berlin, and it is these which help to explain why it negotiated the transition to war relatively successfully. For instance, London benefitted from the stabilizing influence of its large service and transport sectors, since both proved far less vulnerable to dislocation than manufacturing. In September 1914 only 65 per cent of male workers and 57 per cent of female workers in the industrial sector were still employed full-time (compared with July 1914). The comparable figures for the commercial and service sector were 84 per cent and 88 per cent respectively. By December 1914 male industrial employment was already showing a net increase, but amongst women there was still a net contraction of employment of 5.5 per cent, compared with a contraction of only 1.5 per cent in the commercial sector.[72] There are no precise figures for employment in transport, government service, or the Post Office, but two reports on labour mobility during the transition to war suggest that these sectors were all actively recruiting labour, especially male labour, during this period.[73]

There is also evidence that the traditional flexibility of the London labour market and London industry helped to facilitate processes of adaptation necessary to meet the challenges of the new wartime economy. In particular, the labour, rather than capital, intensive basis of much London industry meant that it was often relatively inexpensive to shift output into new production areas. This argument is hard to verify, but it is clear that in tailoring, boot making, leather working, and other consumer trades London manufacturers were very quick to adapt their production processes in anticipation of government contracts – there is even an example of an umbrella factory re-tooling to produce gun components.[74]

[70] *Ibid.*, p. 4, and LIC, vol. VIII ('Statistical survey of employment – 16th April 1915'), p. 4; compared with BLPES, Board of Trade, 'Supplementary report on the state of employment in February [1915]', p. 6. The two reports differ slightly in their estimate of female workers on government contracts, but the figure was probably 17 per cent in London compared with 21 per cent nationally.

[71] Taking a weighted average of trade-union and National Insurance figures, unemployment nationwide fell from 6.6 per cent in August 1914 to 1.8 per cent in February 1915. In London it fell from 10.2 per cent in August to 3.5 per cent the following February; Board of Trade, *Labour Gazette*, Sept. 1914–March 1915.

[72] LIC, vol. V ('Statistical survey of employment – 11th December 1914'), pp. 11–12.

[73] LIC, vol. VII ('Report on transference of trade based on trade returns relating to February 12th, 1915'), pp. 158–75; and Board of Trade, 'Supplementary report – February [1915]', pp. 6–9.

[74] See *Ibid.*, pp. 6–9; Board of Trade, 'Report on the course of employment in the United Kingdom from July 1914 to July 1915': also *Toynbee Record*, 27, 1 (Nov. 1914).

Conclusion

It is clear that we must look primarily to contingent, war-related factors, rather than to structural factors, as the key determinants of dislocation and recovery in the urban economies of Paris, Berlin, and London in 1914. This is most apparent in the case of Paris, where normal civilian life was all but destroyed in 1914 by two successive crises of war: first, by the colossal effort to mobilize all resources, human, material, and financial, for the anticipated 'short war' with Germany, and then by the dire consequences of military action which brought war to the gates of the city. Within the course of two months Paris had lost a third of its male workforce through mobilization, a further 40 per cent of its population through flight, the government and most of the civil administration had been removed and it had seen the near-collapse of both credit and the cash economy. Moreover, those who remained in the capital were living effectively in an armed camp in which the defence of the nation took absolute priority over all other concerns.

This unparalleled crisis cannot be explained solely by reference to the pre-war structure of the Parisian economy. There are some reasons for believing that the effects of mobilization and financial collapse were exacerbated by the relatively small scale of industry in Paris (many small workshops never re-opened after the crisis). But the German occupation of Belgium and northern France, the traditional industrial hinterland of Paris, was a more important factor prolonging the crisis during 1915.

The limitation of structural explanations is underlined by the strong similarities in the experience of Berlin and London during the first months of the war, despite the fact that their economies were radically different. Both cities experienced an initial period of severe dislocation (worse in Berlin because of heavier mobilization), followed by a sustained recovery which had brought acute labour shortages by spring 1915. Contrary to the pre-war expectations of commentators such as Norman Angell, the transition to war in Berlin and London would appear to demonstrate that, when war itself did not impinge directly on urban life, adaptation could prove remarkably smooth, whatever the pre-war economic structure.

Structural factors are not, however, irrelevant; they account for many essential features, not of the crisis period, but of the subsequent recovery. We can only understand the radically different processes of recovery in Berlin and London by reference to the pre-war economic structure of the two cities. Thus in Berlin recovery was led by the rapid expansion of the city's pre-war base in heavy industries like metalworking, machines and chemicals. In contrast, London's recovery was largely the result of the rapid adaptation of its traditional consumer industries to war production, and the buoyancy of employment in the large public-service and transport sectors.

The process of adaptation and recovery was far from complete by early 1915, even in Berlin and London. In both cities female employment was still below its pre-war level, especially in the manufacturing sector, and the war industries which would come to dominate economic life were as yet in their infancy. Neither city had yet developed a fully fledged war economy, nor had there yet been any significant dilution of the predominantly male character of the industrial labour force. Paris was even further from developing a war economy at this point. There were still 230,000 officially unemployed in January 1915, a figure that was to fall only slowly over the following twelve months. Indeed, as we shall see in the next chapter, it was only in the latter half of 1916 that the rapid growth of the new war industries, largely in the suburbs, finally began to absorb the slack in the Parisian labour market.

6
The labour market and industrial mobilization, 1915–1917

Thierry Bonzon

Introduction

After the initial crisis of 1914–1915, which to different degrees disturbed the labour market in the three capital cities, their urban populations entered a period of massive mobilization. Given the presence of a highly skilled labour force, transport and communications networks, and central political and financial institutions, Paris, London, and Berlin were repositories of economic assets essential to the war effort.

Three processes governed the reorganization of the metropolitan labour market: the expansion of industrial activity to fulfil war contracts for goods ranging from shells to military uniforms; the rapid growth in urban activity in general, such as food and fuel provision for the civil population; and the concomitant recession in consumer-goods production. The outcome was an unprecedented social and occupational reordering of production, which changed not only the labour market but the very appearance of the three capital cities themselves.

We should note that on the eve of the war these cities were very large reservoirs of labour. For the Department of the Seine the overall estimate of the number of wage-earners in 1914 was 1,750,000.[1] The order of magnitude of the labour force in Greater Berlin was similar. There were more than 1,400,000 workers registered in Krankenkasse (national health-insurance bureaux) in July 1914.[2] A London County Council (LCC) estimate for July 1914 gives a figure of close to 1,400,000 workers in the twenty-eight metropolitan boroughs under the jurisdiction of the LCC.[3] These are almost certainly underestimates, given the exclusion of domestic workers and many women workers whose employment went unreported before the war.

[1] For Paris, the estimate is given by Robert, 'Ouvriers et mouvement ouvrier', p. 65.

[2] *Gross-Berlin Monatsberichte*, 1914–18.

[3] Cf. BLPES, Local Government Board, London Intelligence Committee Paper, and Board of Trade, State of Employment Reports (excluding domestic service, the professions and the self-employed for men and domestic service, homeworkers, transport, government, the professions and the self-employed for women).

As we have seen in chapter 5, the immediate impact of the outbreak of war in Paris and Berlin was very different. So was the trajectory of labour-market activity in 1915 to 1917. Massive unemployment characterized the first months of the war in Paris, and remained a chronic problem over the next year. By early 1917, unemployment was eliminated. Conversely, the Berlin labour market was marked by great tensions after the middle of 1916, tensions which were exacerbated by the implementation of the Hindenburg Programme and the Auxiliary Service Law in December 1916. In other words, a comparison between Paris and Berlin disclosed a Parisian crisis related to the transition from peace to a war economy in 1914 to 1915, followed by a Berlin crisis related to the total social and economic mobilization of the labour force, starting in 1916 and continuing until after the Armistice. In this sphere as elsewhere, London's wartime history was more uniform than that of the other two cities. Its instabilities were real, though modest, in comparison to the other two.

The war upset all the major elements of the labour market. It challenged pre-war patterns of recruitment; income; hours of work; demarcation disputes and definitions of skill; geographical mobility; and the link between work and leisure time. These constraints, born of industrial mobilization, affected individuals and social groups in the three cities in complex and contrasting ways. For some, the gaps created by mobilization and the circumstances of full employment meant opportunities for unexpected gains in income and social standing. For others, such as skilled workmen in Paris, the war completely disrupted their working lives. For most workers, the period was one of harsh challenges and a sharp reorganization of social relationships at work. Adaptation to these manifold challenges lies at the heart of this chapter.

To what extent was the restructuring of the labour market, and its attendant costs, accepted by individuals and social groups in the three cities? To answer this question, we must address the specific characteristics of the transformation of the labour process in each of the three cities, the scale and timing of change, and the pattern of employment which flowed from it. We must consider too the mobility of different sectors in these great conurbations, and the way in which the relocation of work reconfigured urban space, with important effects on housing, transport, and leisure, all essential elements of urban well-being in war-time.

Contrasting urban patterns

Local distribution

Not surprisingly, the shape of the urban economy shifted with the demands of munitions production. As table 6.1 shows, in London

Table 6.1. *An index of the evolution of employment by sector (July 1914 = 100)*

	France (01/1918)	Estimate for Paris region (01/1918)	London (07/1918)	Berlin (01/1918)
Food	73	98	97	52
Chemicals	119	159	147	99
Printing	56	75	75	64
Clothing[a]	83	111	86	57
Leather	84	112	—	100
Timber	88	118	85	57
Metal-working[b]	163	218	165	142
Construction	52	70	64	31
Transport	100	134	—	59
Commerce	92	96	—	69
Public service	—	—	88	—
Government factories	—	—	1,145	232

Sources: Bulletin du Ministère du Travail; BLPES, Board of Trade, *State of Employment Report,* July 1918; *Gross-Berlin Monatsberichte,* 1914–19.
Note: For Paris, the figures are estimates, which are probably too high. Still the order of magnitude of change as among the three cities is the significant point.
[a]Berlin: textiles and clothing.
[b]Berlin: metal-working and mechanical engineering.

Table 6.2. *An index of the growth in numbers employed in the Paris region and in establishments with more than twenty-five employees in Greater Berlin (July 1914 = 100)*

	01/15	08/15	01/16	08/16	01/17	08/17	01/18	08/18
Greater Berlin	84	88	89	94	101	108	109	105
	01/15	07/15	01/16	07/16	01/17	07/17	01/18	07/18
Paris region	50	63	78	93	121	120	126	115

Sources: Bulletin du Ministère du Travail; Gross-Berlin Monatsberichte, 1915–19.

expansion was most marked in government factories, in metal-working, and in the chemical industries. Employment grew by 130 per cent in these three sectors, which were directly dependent on war contracts, while it diminished by 20 per cent for all other trades. Growth in the numbers employed was particularly spectacular in government factories. Their workforce – admittedly modest in July 1914 – increased more than tenfold, from 11,000 to 126,000 workers in four years. These public-sector workers constituted 22.5 per cent of LCC employment in July 1914, fully 45.5 per cent four years later. In July 1918 the global groups of all metal industries and all government factories represented 27 and 25 per cent of industrial employment respectively, as compared to 18.5 and 1.5 per cent four years earlier.[4]

The same pattern of development can be seen in Berlin in the sectors linked to war contracts. Metal-working and mechanical engineering grew by 42 per cent between 1914 and 1918; government factories grew by 130 per cent over the same period. These sectors were employers on the grand scale. The growing role of these activities in industrial employment is indicated by the net growth in the total workforce for establishments with more than 25 workers: from 33 to 43 per cent in metal working/mechanical engineering, from 12 to 26 per cent in state-owned manufacturing.[5] Comparable changes occurred in Paris, where the workforce employed in metal-working and the chemical industry rose by approximately 100 and 50 per cent respectively between 1914 and January 1918.

Conversely, examination of sectors unconnected with war industries shows a drop in employment, with sharp variations among the three capitals. Thus the erosion of skills which were not involved directly in the war effort is clear in Paris, in the domestic building trade which in January 1918 employed only 70 per cent of its pre-war workforce, or in printing and the most delicate metal-working trades. These trades, far from returning to pre-war levels of activity, underwent a profound crisis which can be seen, again in 1918, in the existence of a residual level of unemployment (see table 6.6). London also experienced a similar erosion, with construction and the paper industry at levels 36 and 25 per cent below their July 1914 levels.

The situation was very different in Berlin. Table 6.3 shows that in Paris the number of workers employed in sectors not directly engaged in war production – transport and food – fluctuated around pre-war levels. In contrast, in the German capital the crisis in these areas of employment only deepened as the war continued. The timber trade sustained its level of employment at half the total of July 1914. Employment in construction, commerce and the food industry fell spectacularly. In the latter two areas, which played a key role in sustaining the material well-being of urban populations, it declined sharply from the second half of 1916. In commerce, a decline of 20 per cent in employment between 1914 and 1916 became a decline in 34 per cent below pre-war levels by mid-1918. In the food trade, the drop was

[4] Board of Trade, *State of Employment Report*, July 1914.

[5] *Gross-Berlin Monatsberichte*, 1914.

31 per cent in the first two years of the war; and 54 per cent between July 1914 and August 1918 (see table 6.4).

The situation was much worse than in Paris, where the level of employment in the food industry had declined by only 2 per cent as of January 1918, or in London, where by July 1918 the food industry also had virtually recovered its July 1914 level. This contrast between Paris and London on the one hand and Berlin on the other is still more marked in respect of transport: while by mid-1916 Paris had regained levels of employment comparable to 1914, transport in Berlin had lost 40 per cent of its workforce (see tables 6.3 and 6.4). Here we see clear evidence of the more effective adaptation of the Allied metropolitan economies to the demands of total war. They had greater capacity to increase war production without sacrificing elements essential to the well-being of metropolitan populations.

Change over time

Patterns of mobilization also differed in the three nations and had decisive effects on the labour market in their capitals. The key variable, of course, was conscription: thus only 20 per cent of London's male workforce was in uniform in July 1915, as compared to much higher levels of enlistment in Paris and Berlin. In the case of Paris, as we have seen, it was the most active elements in the urban economy which were affected: all military classes for the years 1896 to 1914 (ages twenty to thirty-eight in 1914) inclusive were mobilized at the end of the first months of the war. Only after 1916 did the situation in London resemble that in the other two cities. By July 1918 an estimated 250,000 London industrial workers – or 46 per cent of the male workforce employed in July 1914 – had been mobilized.[6]

As we have seen in chapter 5, Paris faced a severe initial crisis in 1914. A year later, the city's labour market went through a complex restructuring process on a very large scale. Three phases can be distinguished in the reshaping of the Paris labour market from 1915 to 1917. The first was a recovery from the early wartime economic crisis. Until mid-1915 the number of wage-earners grew briskly, from 50 per cent of pre-war levels of employment in January 1915 to 63 per cent eight months later (see table 6.2). Here there is an early indication of the dynamism of certain industrial sectors, in particular the dozen automobile manufacturers in the Groupe régional de fabricants d'obus de Paris (shell

[6] For early mobilization, see Jon Lawrence, Martin Dean, and Jean-Louis Robert, 'The outbreak of war and the urban economy: Paris, Berlin and London in 1914', *Economic History Review*, 45, 3 (August 1992), pp. 564–93; for 1918, see N. B. Dearle, *The labor cost of the World War to Great Britain in 1914–1922. A statistical analysis* (New Haven, 1940), p. 16.

Table 6.3. *An index of numbers employed in firms in France and in the Paris region, by branch, according to studies by the French Ministry of Labour (index figures for Paris in parentheses) (July 1914 = 100)*

	01/15	07/15	01/16	07/16	01/17	07/17	01/18	07/18
Food	68 (61)	74 (70)	76 (78)	81 (87)	79 (104)	83 (104)	73 (98)	66 (83)
Chemicals	67 (60)	79 (74)	94 (96)	104 (112)	118 (155)	120 (150)	119 (159)	116 (147)
Printing	42 (38)	48 (45)	50 (51)	54 (58)	56 (73)	55 (69)	56 (75)	57 (72)
Clothing	55 (49)	66 (62)	72 (74)	77 (83)	78 (102)	79 (99)	83 (111)	85 (107)
Leather	63 (56)	71 (67)	77 (79)	83 (90)	83 (109)	85 (106)	84 (112)	83 (105)
Timber	39 (35)	50 (47)	61 (63)	71 (77)	80 (105)	84 (105)	88 (118)	93 (117)
Metal-working	63 (56)	82 (77)	112 (115)	135 (145)	159 (209)	167 (209)	163 (218)	153 (193)
Fine metals	25 (22)	38 (36)	48 (49)	60 (65)	63 (83)	68 (85)	68 (91)	66 (83)
Construction	26 (23)	33 (31)	39 (40)	44 (47)	46 (60)	51 (64)	52 (70)	60 (76)
Transport	63 (56)	79 (74)	91 (93)	96 (104)	98 (129)	97 (121)	100 (134)	98 (124)
Commerce	56 (50)	62 (58)	68 (70)	70 (76)	69 (91)	72 (90)	72 (96)	73 (92)

Source: Bulletin du Ministère du Travail, 1914–1919.

Table 6.4. *An index of the level of employment in establishments with more than twenty-five employees, in Greater Berlin, by sector (July 1914 = 100)*

	01/15	08/15	01/16	08/16	01/17	08/17	01/18	08/18
Food	86	82	80	69	60	52	52	46
Chemicals	72	71	76	92	90	92	99	98
Printing	66	64	65	66	65	63	64	60
Clothing	69	82	77	77	67	61	57	52
Leather	114	102	98	83	79	85	100	92
Timber	50	51	56	55	52	54	57	52
Metal-working	86	95	93	107	128	141	142	133
Construction	51	56	47	52	39	43	31	35
Transport	70	66	65	65	61	61	59	59
Commerce	79	78	81	79	76	71	69	66
Government factories	135	143	154	161	182	217	232	234

Source: Gross-Berlin Monatsberichte, 1914–19.

Table 6.5. *An estimate of unemployment in Paris in January 1916*

	Men		Women	
	Number out of work	Unemployment rate (%)	Number out of work	Unemployment rate (%)
Food	334	3	1,027	11
Construction	2,484	8	0	0
Textiles/clothing	1,371	6	27,940	11
Industrial art	1,121	15	2,238	15
Printing	739	5	2,366	24
Timber/joinery	1,368	5	1,577	27
Chemicals	220	2	482	19
Leather/rubber	252	1	763	4
Metals/electrical	778	2	837	11
Commerce	3,764	3	7,612	7
Professions	1,981	6	5,314	14
Domestic service	1,721	10	24,569	15
Total	16,133	4	74,725	12

Source: Bulletin du Ministère du Travail, 1915–19.

manufacturers), initiated by the Comité des forges (the Metal-industry Employers' Association), presided over by Louis Renault.[7]

[7] On the role and attitude of Paris employers, see Robert Pinot, *Le Comité des Forges au service de la nation* (Paris, 1919); Patrick Fridenson, *Histoire des usines Renault. Naissance de la grande industrie, 1898–1939* (Paris, 1972), and Henry Donald Peiter, 'Men of good-will: French businessmen and the First World War', PhD thesis, University of Michigan, 1973.

Table 6.6. *An estimate of unemployment in Paris in February 1918*

	Men		Women	
	Number out of work	Unemployment rate (%)	Number out of work	Unemployment rate (%)
Food	47	0	95	9
Construction	273	1	2	0
Textiles/clothing	158	1	3,978	1
Industrial art	106	1	436	3
Printing	104	1	285	3
Timber/joinery	217	1	308	5
Chemicals	56	1	143	6
Leather/rubber	48	0	222	1
Metals/electricals	81	0	179	2
Commerce	352	0	1,090	1
Professions	264	1	831	2
Domestic service	254	2	4,101	2
Total	1,960	—	11,670	—

Source: Bulletin du Ministère du Travail, 1915–19.

A second phase of restructuring took place from October 1915 to July 1916, marked by a slower rate of growth in numbers employed in the Paris region. This placed limits, according to the Paris regional inspector in June 1916, on the growth of war industry. 'In the present state of affairs it is no longer possible for the industrialists to increase their production substantially', he noted.[8] But that was not the only problem. Although persistent transport problems continued to affect production, it was above all the 'scarcity or total lack of primary materials'[9] that delayed the recovery of sectors which were not high on the list of the priority war industries.

At the same time the earlier reduction of levels of unemployment could not be sustained. Although for the half-year from January to July 1915 the drop in unemployment was 51 per cent, no further gains were registered throughout the period July 1915 to July 1916; and unemployment still stood at 90,000 in January 1916. Full reallocation of available labour only occurred from the summer of 1916.

This was when unemployment finally faded away. After the beginning of 1917, it affected only those engaged in a few sectors: skilled workers who could not retrain, domestic staff, and to a lesser degree employees in the liberal professions (table 6.6). By January 1917 employment levels in the Paris region exceeded the 1914 figure (table 6.2). This change reflected broader developments in the inter-Allied

[8] *Bulletin du Ministère du travail,* June 1916, p. 217. [9] *Ibid.*

Table 6.7. *An estimate of the rate of unemployment (%) in London, 1914 to 1918*[a]

Jan.–March 14	April–June 14	July–Sept. 14	Oct.–Dec. 14
8.1	6.0	8.7	6.8
Jan.–March 15	April–June 15	July–Sept. 15	Oct.–Dec. 15
3.8	2.0	2.5	2.4
Jan.–March 16	April–June 16	July–Sept. 16	Oct.–Dec. 16
1.9	1.4	1.2	1.3
Jan.–March 17	April–June 17	July–Sept. 17	Oct.–Dec. 17
1.4	1.2	1.0	1.2
Jan.–March 18	April–June 18	July–Sept. 18	—
1.2	1.2	1.0	

[a]Percentages represent averages based on monthly trade-union and National Insurance returns for London or the London area; trades covered: building, mechanical engineering, vehicle building, printing, shipbuilding and bookbinding. Vehicle-building dropped from the series in February 1915; printing and bookbinding dropped out in February 1918.
Source: Board of Trade, *Labour Gazette*, February 1914–January 1919.

system of supply. For example, coal supplies for the industrial suburbs improved sharply from 1916, thereby enabling industrial employment and output to rise.[10]

Matters were very different in London, where the initial shock of war was much less severe, and recovery from it less of a problem. According to sources quoted by the Local Government Board's London Intelligence Committee, the level of unemployment in the capital dropped from 9.9 per cent in September 1914 to 2.6 per cent in July 1915.[11] Such a speedy return to pre-war levels also put an end to the work hitherto undertaken by this committee.

At the beginning of 1916 unemployment in London fell below 2 per cent (see table 6.7), a figure never attained in peacetime. Although these figures only cover a limited number of trades (mechanical engineering, vehicle-building, shipbuilding, printing, and book-binding), the situation for most of London's workforce cannot have been very different. An exception was the winter of 1916–1917, when the dockers suffered from a decline in shipping on the Thames, and some areas of trade suffered shortages. In this period, London's restructuring was less violent, partly due to the mildness of the initial disruption of labour, partly due to the absence of conscription. But it also reflects a greater

[10] Archives de la Seine, O.R. 7 230.

[11] Based on a weighted average of National Insurance and Trade Union returns published in the Board of Trade *Labour Gazette* and referring overwhelmingly to male workers. By this measure, unemployment had been lower earlier in the spring of 1915: in April and May it stood at 1.9 per cent.

fluidity in the labour market (in contrast to Paris) and consequently a smoother transition to wartime production.

This mobility benefited industries servicing war contracts, at the expense of sectors not directly affected by industrial mobilization. In 1915 these sectors began to suffer labour shortages: this particularly affected the service sector, which had difficulty in keeping staff, a point which made a distinct impression on contemporaries. John Gray reported that

> The world became topsy-turvy. Old standards fell away. Barmaids and potmen came and went more quickly than ever before, and one morning my beloved Mrs A. announced she was leaving us to 'make munitions' . . . My brother left the local photographers for the local munition works, exchanging his wage of a few shillings a week for one of several pounds. My sister said goodbye to hairdressing and took her place behind the bar, for barmaids soon became very hard to obtain and harder still to keep.[12]

Within the sector of war manufacturing the competition between companies for workers encouraged mobility. Thus, until the introduction of 'leaving certificates', many factories in south-east London lost workers to the high wages at the Woolwich Arsenal: in certain extreme cases there was a complete turnover of staff in the space of three months.[13]

On the level of the London labour market as a whole, the shift of civilian labour towards companies engaged in war work was extensive and prompt. Thus in July 1915, although nearly 20 per cent of the industrial labour force was mobilized, the level of industrial employment was only 9 per cent below the pre-war figure. More than 60,000 men and women had joined the industrial sector.[14] Subsequently, the expansion of munitions factories between mid-1915 and 1916 and the gradual inflow of women workers intensified the restructuring process. Certainly the absence in London of the severe shock experienced in Paris in the first days of the war helped greatly. When the Military Service Acts took effect, their consequences for the labour market were less severe, and did not appear likely to upset the labour market to any great extent.

In Berlin the restructuring of the labour market was marked first by a period of rapid expansion in industries concerned with war contracts from the first months of the war (see table 6.4). In particular, increased production in the metal-working sector is clearly identifiable, beginning

12 J. Gray, *Gin and bitters* (London, 1938), p. 102.

13 As cited in *History of the Ministry of Munitions*, VIII, part 2, p. 177.

14 BLPES, London Government Board: London Intelligence Committee Report. The figures shown here provide an estimate of the reduction in mobility towards war manufacturing to the extent that, notably, the figures for the industrial labour force include the building industry.

in the second half of 1916 and covering 1917. The numbers employed in metal-working and mechanical engineering grew considerably between August 1916 and August 1917, passing from 7 per cent to 41 per cent above pre-war levels. Above all, the late summer of 1916 marked a clear divide; thereafter metal-working was well above the pre-war level.

This turning point in German war production was related first to the timing of military events. The enormous needs of weaponry and munitions created by the Battle of Verdun and the vigour and unexpected intensity of the Allied offensive on the Somme led the Ministry of War to a prompt upwards revision (during August 1916) of its armaments manufacturing programme. The second factor is well known because of its political implications:[15] the shift of control over munitions manufacturing from the Ministry of War to the Kriegsamt, under General Groener and the Military Command (OHL). Since the end of August the German GHQ had been under Hindenburg and Ludendorff's direction, in a slide towards a quasi-'military dictatorship' of the economy. This was welcomed by industrialists, who believed that it would serve their interests better than the old Ministry of War had done hitherto. Incorporating the change of policy, the programme drawn up by Hindenburg promptly after taking office insisted on the mobilization of all available resources. The theory on which he worked was simple: the only way to compensate for the progressive numerical inferiority of German troops on the Western Front was an ambitious armaments programme. Production targets were systematically revised upwards (aiming to double the quantity of explosives and mortars, and treble the number of machine guns) and the time needed to achieve them revised downwards.

This plan translated into an unprecedented mobilization and militarization of the German economy and society: all energies had to be devoted to the success of the Hindenburg Programme. At the same time as the Auxiliary Service Law (December 1916) established total mobilization of the workforce at the heart of the war effort, the Ständige Ausschuss für Zusammenlegungen (SAZ) was charged with overseeing the conversion of businesses to meet military demands, or their closure.[16] In this way more than 2,000 Berlin firms acquired additional workers – generally between 20 and 100 each – as part of the auxiliary service system.[17]

The importance of this turning point in the war is marked by figures

[15] See in particular Gerald D. Feldman, *Army, industry and labor*, pp. 150–68, and Hardach, *The First World War*, pp. 62–71.

[16] On this point, see Feldman, *Army, industry and labor*, pp. 273–83.

[17] Two exceptions were the firms of Siemens and Halske and Siemens-Schuckertwerke in Spandau, which received 9,529 and 11,362 workers respectively. Brandenburg, Landeshauptarchiv Pr.Br.Rep.30 Berlin C. n. 1915, *Vaterländischer Hilfsdienst*, pp. 403 ff.

concerning the principal private employment bureau for the metal trades in Berlin – the Arbeitsnachweis des Verbandes Berliner Metallindustrieller – as shown in table 6.8. It should be noted, though, that the rise in demand preceded the implementation of the Hindenburg Programme. Increasing numbers of vacancies were evident from the middle of 1916, an immediate reaction to the Battle of the Somme: the pressure on the labour market operated sooner than is generally recognized. From the summer of 1916, and despite significant fluctuations, the curve of vacancies rose steadily. In July and August 1917 nearly 10,000 posts per month were on offer in Berlin in the metal trades. This figure was approximately 30 per cent of the labour force in this sector at that time.[18]

In the same period the gap between vacancies and applicants increased spectacularly from February 1917. At the worst moment, in July 1917, there was a shortage of nearly 6,000 workers.[19] These figures illustrate the acute labour shortage, particularly for skilled workers, which marked the Berlin labour market in the second half of the war.

On the other side of the line, the situation was acutely different. Figures recorded by the Office départemental de placement de la Seine (table 6.9)[20] show how job vacancies reached a plateau in November 1916. In addition, from December 1916 the demand for jobs always exceeded vacancies, which is precisely the opposite of the situation in Berlin.

In the German capital considerable tensions arose after the labour market was geared to war production. In Paris, tensions arose before that process of restructuring. In other words, the transformation of work in Paris concluded a period of crisis; in Berlin, it initiated a period of intense and increasing difficulties.[21]

Mobility

Dimensions of the problem

In all three capitals, mobility lay at the heart of the restructuring of the labour market. The expansion of industries linked to military contracts required both (1) major movements of labour to productive sectors; and (2) the control of labour once allocated in the most efficient manner.

[18] According to figures in the *Gross-Berlin Monatsberichte*, 1914–19, referring only to companies with more than twenty-five employees. [19] *Ibid.*

[20] This deals only with unskilled workers, who were mostly employed in munitions factories. It should be noted that the Office began to operate only in November 1915, and the reading of the graph therefore requires care. In effect, we should note that at the outset the fumblings of this institution arose from the small number of personnel covered by departmental placements up to the end of 1916.

[21] See chapter 11 below.

Table 6.8. *Activity in the employment exchange for the Association of Metal-working Industries in Berlin (Arbeitsnachweis des Verbandes Berliner Metallindustrieller), April 1915 to November 1917*

	Seeking employment			Vacancies			Taken on		
	Men	Women	Total	Men	Women	Total	Men	Women	Total
04/1915	6,000	469	6,469	4,874	461	5,335	4,874	461	5,335
05/1915	4,319	592	4,911	3,851	585	4,436	3,851	585	4,436
06/1915	4,961	1,094	6,055	4,193	1,091	5,284	4,193	1,091	5,284
07/1915	4,518	1,026	5,544	3,840	1,017	4,857	3,840	1,017	4,857
08/1915	4,134	884	5,018	3,644	881	4,525	3,644	881	4,525
09/1915	3,962	810	4,772	3,710	806	4,516	3,710	806	4,516
10/1915	4,291	538	4,829	3,890	537	4,427	3,890	537	4,427
11/1915	3,648	408	4,056	3,323	408	3,731	3,323	408	3,731
12/1915	1,882	536	2,418	1,782	436	2,218	1,782	436	2,218
01/1916	2,750	632	3,382	3,862	533	4,395	2,440	392	2,832
02/1916	2,763	744	3,507	3,873	542	4,415	2,288	497	2,785
03/1916	3,030	776	3,806	4,215	694	4,909	2,700	557	3,257
04/1916	2,093	671	2,764	2,806	530	3,336	1,810	527	2,337
05/1916	2,378	864	3,242	3,160	807	3,967	2,117	784	2,901
06/1916	2,350	966	3,316	3,232	971	4,203	2,094	813	2,907
07/1916	3,115	1,094	4,209	4,329	1,246	5,575	2,873	968	3,841
08/1916	2,896	1,231	4,127	5,309	1,664	6,973	2,665	1,178	3,843
09/1916	3,205	2,375	5,580	5,231	2,564	7,795	2,611	1,928	4,539
10/1916	3,197	2,713	5,910	4,563	2,517	7,080	2,538	1,946	4,484
11/1916	3,339	2,545	5,884	4,255	2,115	6,370	2,463	1,599	4,062
12/1916	2,660	2,188	4,848	3,158	2,336	5,494	1.960	1,329	3,289
01/1917	3,469	2,705	6,174	3,344	3,192	6,536	2,599	1,942	4,541
02/1917	3,077	2,253	5,330	4,284	2,811	7,095	2,146	1,386	3,532

03/1917	2,959	2,464	5,423	4,616	3,792	8,408	2.034	1,624	3,658
04/1917	2,148	2,124	4,272	3,375	3,565	6,940	1,800	2,024	3,824
05/1917	2,425	1,933	4,358	3,414	4,367	7,781	2,033	1,828	3,921
06/1917	2,527	1,411	3,938	4,346	4,725	9,071	2,263	1,301	3,564
07/1917	2,394	1,611	4,005	5,036	4,829	9,865	2,115	1,487	3,602
08/1917	2,309	2,576	4,885	4,996	4,893	9,889	1,883	2,403	4,286
09/1917	2,381	2,701	5,082	4,356	3,502	7,858	1,953	1,903	3,856
10/1917	2,271	2,085	4,356	4,348	3,042	7,390	1,967	2,112	4,079
11/1917	1,717	2,059	3,776	3,425	1,598	5,023	1,368	1,034	2,402

Source: Reichsarbeitsblatt, 1916–17.

These two demands met with hostility amongst some working people, because they challenged the very identity of work, the freedom of the worker in his job, and certain trade-union rights such as control of entry into a trade.

In Paris the importance accorded to a skill was fundamental. The Union des syndicats ouvriers de la Seine, with 200 unions in 1914, consisted essentially of craft unions. Skilled trades flourished in the Paris area. They combined craftsmanship, drawn from a period of qualification for entry into the trade, and pride in a corporate post that was the foundation of a strong worker identity. The link between qualification and skill was challenged by the Ministry of Armaments' judgement that the professional skill necessary to work in a munitions factory could be acquired in two or three months. The newcomers' lack of professional experience and their vulnerability to agreeing to inferior working conditions and wages were worrying enough. But skilled men also expressed the fear that an increase in the numbers of workers would mean loss of identity. All these arguments fostered workers' resistance to job mobility, seen as an attack on the privilege of skill.[22]

In London, too, craft traditions were built into trade-union structures and traditions, particularly in the Amalgamated Society of Engineers (ASE).[23] The practice of the 'closed shop', union control of recruitment and apprenticeship procedures, and union benefits guaranteeing the wages of the skilled workforce were obstacles to wartime changes in the skill composition of the labour force and to its physical transformation.

High rates of turnover collided with two entrenched positions: workers' commitment to freedom of movement and their defence of their rights within the workplace itself. For example, on the eve of the war building workers in Paris, facing an employer's boycott, left their worksite for a better arrangement with an employer who would pay union wages.[24]

The Berlin case presented entirely different headaches. Traditionally an area of high labour mobility, appropriate to a city of inmigration, Berlin's labour market from 1915 to 1917 shows a paradoxical situation: relatively low military mobilization *and* a shortage of manpower for war production. The resolution of this apparent contradiction is twofold. On the one hand, the German war economy was obliged to expand beyond its capacity; on the other hand, the army

22 *Bulletin des usines de guerre*, no. 5 (29 May 1916) and no. 49 (2 April 1917). On this and the preceding point, cf. Robert, 'Ouvriers et mouvement ouvrier', vol. II, pp. 322–60.

23 See J. B. Jefferys, *The story of the engineers, 1800–1945* (London, 1946), vol. I.

24 Gérard Noiriel, *Les ouvriers en France aux 19ème et 20ème siècles* (Paris, 1988).

required more and more men for the gigantic operations extending from the English Channel to the Ukraine. Without a system of *arbitrage*, of ordering of priorities, both sides' demands went unfulfilled. In manpower terms, the army was stretched the longer the war went on, and the war industry was unable to find sufficient workers, raw materials, and transport to cope with spiralling orders for munitions and military equipment. Bottlenecks appeared everywhere, and though heroic efforts were made in Berlin as elsewhere to provide the men in uniform with the weapons and supplies they needed, problems proliferated. What was at fault was not the will to work for victory, but the system designed to achieve it.

Forms of control of labour mobility

By challenging pre-war practices in the name of national defence, the restructuring of the labour market in the three cities introduced a tension constraining – and in fact capable of undermining – the mobilization process. The workers' agreement to accept sacrifices for the sake of victory was genuine, but limited. In many cases they brought their own point of view on the question of mobility to negotiations on the way war production was organized and expanded.

There is one respect in which the organization of labour in Paris differed sharply from that in the other two capitals. In Paris, control of the workforce was resolved in a radical fashion, by the placement of enlisted men in war factories. 'Militarization' is too strong a word for this process, since the workers in question enjoyed the same rights to pay as enlisted men. Still, unlike London or Berlin, in Paris workers manned war factories while technically still in uniform. There the recall of the skilled workforce from the front was initially an emergency measure, imprecisely regulated and based on an initiative of the Ironmasters' Federation, the Comité des forges.[25] But in May 1915, matters moved swiftly with the installation of Albert Thomas as Under-Secretary of State for Munitions. He took a clear stand in the conflict between the needs of industrial rationalization and the imperatives embedded in the republican ideal of equality in the face of military service – the 'blood tax'. He defined the status of the skilled worker in uniform reassigned to a war factory. Such a worker was not discharged; he remained mobilized, but was under the supervision of the civilian

[25] The role of employers' organizations, particularly the Comité des forges, of which the secretary-general Robert Pinot was the privileged confidante of the war ministry, should be emphasized. Faced with the shortage of skilled workers, he divided them between the industrialists of the Groupe de Paris (led by Louis Renault) the mobilized metal-workers and inspected depots on the home front. See Pinot, *Le Comité des Forges*.

authority of the Ministry of Armaments, largely staffed by socialists working with Albert Thomas.

This definition of factory work as an alternative form of military service was central to the rhetoric of French industrial mobilization.[26] Subsequently, the constant opposition of Thomas and his colleague and later successor, Louis Loucheur, to returning any workers – even shirkers – to the front, demonstrates the protection afforded to mobilized workers in war factories. Their service was regulated by two pieces of legislation. First came the *loi Dalbiez* of 1915, specifying the conditions under which skilled workers could be returned from the front to war factories. Commissions were established with trade-union representation to examine the qualifications of each returned man. Secondly came the *loi Mourier* of 1917, a measure designed to respond to public dissatisfaction about the supposedly privileged status of metal-workers in war factories. This law enabled their recall to active military service. In fact, it was not systematically applied.[27]

This military element in the workforce of war factories became a distinctive feature of the restructuring of the Paris labour market. Approximately 35 per cent of the workforce of Paris munitions factories,[28] or nearly 150,000 workers in 1917–1918, were technically still in uniform.[29] With 90 per cent classified as *professionnels*, these workers occupied the most skilled posts; they accounted for 44 to 45 per cent of the workforce in factories producing engines, aircraft, and tanks and only 18 per cent in factories manufacturing shells or grenades. These percentages at times reached very high levels. At the Peugeot works at Levallois-Perret, there were 680 mobilized men out of 923 employees; at the Blériot factory at Suresnes, 1,000 out of 1,420 were mobilized workers.[30]

Nothing like this could be found in Berlin, where the skilled workers recalled from the front by the *Zurückstellung* process – 90,000 at the end of 1917[31] – simply were exempted from military service, thus benefiting from the same status as their civilian colleagues. The Paris structure of military regulation of labour, initiated by Albert Thomas, the architect of

26 See John Horne, '"L'Impôt du sang"', pp. 207–8.

27 See J. Horne, *ibid*.

28 See, Robert, 'Ouvriers et mouvement ouvrier', vol. I, p. 88. The statistics for employees mobilized have been calculated by the author from a sample of 165 war factories or workshops employing more than 180,000 workers.

29 It is not possible to give more than a very rough estimate of the workforce in establishments engaged in war work.

30 Robert, 'Ouvriers et mouvement ouvrier', Annexe, Fédération des usines de guerre.

31 The *Zurückstellung* system allowed 700 workers to return to Berlin in 1914, 21,400 in 1915, 24,900 in 1916, 27,600 in 1917, and 18,900 in 1918. From: Brandenburg, Landeshauptarchiv (LHA), Pr.Br.Rep.30 Berlin C, Jahresberichte der Gewerbe-Aufsicht, n. 1958, p. 232.

the system of munitions production, was unique among the three capitals.[32]

In London and Berlin – and, to a lesser extent, in Paris – there were similarities in strategies designed to limit labour mobility. In the case of London, the Munitions of War Act of July 1915 was particularly important. Anticipating the practice of dilution, it authorized the state to direct metal-workers to war factories and to control their mobility while there through the system of 'leaving certificates'. Under this system, skilled workers could not change jobs without permission – in the form of a leaving certificate – from their previous employer. Any worker breaking this rule was banned from working for six weeks. Though they retained a right of appeal to an *ad hoc* tribunal, workers saw the system as draconian. Of all cases that went to appeal, only 26 per cent went in favour of the workers.[33]

Across Britain as a whole, no less than 2 million workers – 30 per cent of the industrial workforce – were directly affected. Here the political sacrifice was delineated clearly. By accepting the Munitions Act, the British labour movement agreed to the abrogation of the right to strike for the duration of the conflict.

In Berlin the restriction of turnover came after a period of extreme fluidity of the labour market in the early months of the war. An unexpected shortage of munitions overwhelmed industrialists, with military orders distributed in the greatest confusion. Many companies whose work was based on war contracts introduced a high-wage policy with the aim of seizing market share from their competitors. Such practices reduced the Berlin metal-working industry to a state of virtual chaos by the end of 1914 and led industrial managers to demand control of labour turnover. This last was provided by the Kriegsausschuss für die Metallbetriebe Gross-Berlins, which granted the necessary leave to any worker who wished to move to another, better-paid job.[34]

The same preoccupation re-appeared – in a minor key this time – in Paris, with the opening of the Office départemental du placement et de la statistique du travail de la Seine. Established by decision of the Conseil général of the Department of the Seine in June 1915, the bureau was the first attempt to regulate the labour market in Paris. It had two aims: to ensure physical mobility for workers and to ensure continuity and stability of employment. Labour interests were reflected in regulations favouring the unemployed. But if a man out of work refused

32 And far removed from the Italian system, where 'militarization' is indeed the accurate description of labour policy. See Giovanna Procacci, *Stato e classe operaia in Italia durante la prima guerra mondiale* (Milan, 1983).

33 See G. Rubin, *War, law and labour: the Munitions Acts, state regulation and the unions* (Oxford, 1987), p. 203.

34 See G. D. Feldman, *Army, industry and labor*, pp. 76–7.

without cause a job designated by the local labour bureau, he risked losing unemployment benefit. The statistical records of these bureaux made it possible to identify workers with what might have been a penchant to leave work.[35]

Regulation: forms and limitations

The development of such methods of controlling labour mobility was part of the process of bringing trade unions into the regulatory network of the war economy. Such institutions provided a setting for negotiations over the scale of sacrifice accepted by labour in the interest of national defence.

In Paris particularly, the war was the occasion of the inclusion of unions in a network of joint commissions. This was in contrast to the pre-war policy of the Confédération Générale du Travail (CGT) to avoid any policy of presence or collaboration with management or the state. One such wartime institution was the Commission paritaire pour l'application de la loi Dalbiez which regulated the sensitive question of the allocation of mobilized men to munitions factories: another was the Commission mixte chargée d'étudier le maintien du travail dans le Département de la Seine.[36] The latter was also the basis of the Office départemental du placement et de la statistique du travail de la Seine, which scrupulously obeyed the principles of worker participation in management.

In Germany the Kriegsausschuss für die Metallbetriebe Gross-Berlins, established in February 1915, was also the site of labour participation in the war economy. This committee of management and trade unions met each week to assess the requests of workers who wished to move to another factory. They thereby operated as mediators between workers' hopes of better pay and managers' needs for a stable workforce.[37] With the enactment of the law on auxiliary service in December 1916, worker representation was assured within the Feststellungsausschuss für den Bezirk des Oberkommandos in den Marken, the commission charged with controlling the assignment of workers to war factories.[38] In London, the same functions were elaborated under the

[35] See the reports drawn up by the Socialist conseillers généraux Henri Sellier and Emile Deslandres, on the introduction and then the operation of the departmental bureaux. In particular, see Conseil général de la Seine, Rapports et Documents, no. 6, 26 June 1915, and no. 8, 30 November 1918.

[36] The proceedings of the Commission sessions appear in the Ministère du travail et de la Prévoyance sociale, *Travaux des Commissions mixtes départementales pour le maintien du travail national*, vols. 1–5, *1915–1918* (Paris, 1916–18).

[37] Cf. G. D. Feldman, *Army, industry and labor*, pp. 77–8, and *Jahres- und Kassenberichte der Gewerkschaftskommission Berlins und Umgegend*, 25 (1914), pp. 59–60.

[38] Brandenburg, LHA, Pr.Br.Rep.30 Berlin C, no. 1915, Vaterländischer Hilfsdienst, pp. 65, 145, 199, 221, 226.

Munitions of War Act, through which trade unionists served on the Central Munitions Labour Supply Committee, the body advising the Ministry of Munitions on dilution.

The negotiation process was strictly limited in character and extent. Differences between the parties remained and were clearly visible in London over the painful question of 'leaving certificates'. With the introduction of conscription, from January 1916, the practice of leaving certificates introduced certain managerial evasions. Since the fear of being refused leave to move or of having an exemption from military service removed was entirely genuine, many industrial managers played on this feeling to impose severe work conditions on their employees. With the combined application of the Military Service Act and the Munitions of War Acts, a slide towards an informal system of industrial constraint – with affinities with industrial conscription – began to operate. The fear of a transfer to the front acted as a guarantee of labour discipline at the workplace.[39] This authoritarian tendency in the system of the control of labour mobility finally brought about its abolition in October 1917. Pressure from the ASE, echoing the claims of the shop-stewards' movement, produced telling arguments that the leaving-certificate system undermined rather than strengthened munitions production.

We must caution against painting too monochromatic a picture of labour attitudes on this question. In Paris the drive to maximize production was championed by officials who joined the mixed commissions. These were men representing labour at the national, federal, or departmental level. On the shop floor, in contrast, among rank-and-file trade unionists, different attitudes predominated. For militants the most important aim was to avoid dividing workers through piece-rate payment and through overtime.[40]

Similarly, negotiations with the various Parisian trade unions over the opening of branches of the Office départemental du placement et de la statistique du travail de la Seine were not always conclusive. Thus the absence of such a placement office in the building trade was a mark of resistance to change in a sector where worker placement was already well organized and labour turnover was substantial.[41]

Feminization of the labour force

All three nations were faced with a delicate balance between the needs at the front and those at home, and difficult relationships developed between industrialists and the army over the distribution of available manpower. In France, where universal liability to conscription – 'the

39 Rubin, *War, law and labour*, p. 225.

40 See Robert, 'Ouvriers et mouvement ouvrier', vol. III and in particular pp. 734–9 and 744–9. 41 *Ibid.*, vol. II.

blood tax' – was a fundamental value of Republican culture, the presence of mobilized men in munitions factories was bound to breed resentment about the safe havens occupied by these supposed 'shirkers'. Underlying the question of male employment throughout the war was the reality of trench warfare. The presence of the poilu lay behind the *loi Dalbiez* of 1915; it also raised temperatures at home. Protests over injustice were set in the context of the terrible hardships endured by combatants who remained at the front.

The recall of soldiers to work in war factories presented complex difficulties for the organization of an efficient labour force. Aside from the recall of soldiers, other workers were mobilized: foreign workers in Paris; prisoners of war in Berlin; the young, the old, and above all women of all ages in all three cities.

Women played a considerable role in the restructuring of the labour market, but it was in Berlin that the feminization of branches of work linked to war contracts proceeded most rapidly.[42] In Paris, the drive to recruit women to work came later in the war. Statistics in table 6.5 show that 12 per cent of the female labour force – compared to 4 per cent of men – were still unemployed in January 1916. Here we see evidence of the weight of female labour in the pre-war urban economy and of the difficulty of adapting these workers from dressmaking and domestic work to the needs of the new war factories.

After 1916 female unemployment declined rapidly as both the level of unemployment benefit and the rise in the cost of living drew more women workers into the war factories. The monetary value of unemployment benefit was held at a low level.[43] While enabling the poorest to survive, it was a powerful incentive for others to find work. In general, this strategy of supporting incomes followed the recommendation of the Commission mixte chargée d'étudier les questions relatives au maintien du travail dans le Département de la Seine to relaunch the economy through increased consumption.[44]

Similarly with separation allowances: rates set in November 1915[45] by the Conseil général were left unaltered until April 1917 and then increased from 1.25 francs plus 0.75 francs per child per day to 1.50 francs

[42] For an examination of this question, see D. Thom, 'Women and work in wartime Britain' in R. Wall and J. Winter (eds.), *The upheaval of war: family, work and welfare in Europe, 1914–1918* (Cambridge, 1988); D. Thom, 'The ideology of women's work in Britain, 1914–1924', PhD thesis, Thames Polytechnic, 1982; G. Braybon, *Women workers in the First World War* (London, 1981).

[43] A law of 5 Aug. 1914 fixed the benefit at 1.25 francs per day plus 0.50 franc per child under the age of sixteen, with a maximum of 2.50 francs per family, until April 1918. See Robert, 'Ouvriers et mouvement ouvrier', vol. II.

[44] Ministère du travail et de la Prévoyance sociale, *Travaux des Commissions mixtes départementales pour le maintien du travail national.*

[45] Conseil général de la Seine, Procès-verbaux, 12 November 1915, p. 586.

plus 1 franc per child. Such benefits could not be enjoyed by those in receipt of unemployment allowances. Maintaining grants without increases encouraged the search for additional family income, all the more urgent as the cost of living spiralled, essentially from the third quarter of 1916 and above all with the drastic rise in prices in the spring of 1917.[46]

From 1916, as women increasingly joined the labour market, the question arose of adding separation allowances to wages. Criticized at one moment for their excessive tendency to withhold allowances from women workers[47] – thus discouraging wives of mobilized men from joining munitions factories[48] – these local commissions were called to order by the prefect in June 1916.[49] At a time of robust expansion of war industries, it was important to attract women workers by giving some guarantee that they could retain both wages and benefits.

This considered policy of encouragement to join the workforce brought results. In November 1915 only 738 out of 3,500 workers in the Citroën factory were women, but by the end of the war they constituted half of its 11,700-strong workforce. In the Department of the Seine as a whole, women made up nearly one-third of the labour force in munitions factories in 1917–1918, and half of all wage-earners in the Department, as against slightly less than 40 per cent in 1914.[50]

Faced with the expansion of female employment and the shortage of labour, any doubts management may have had about recruiting these workers faded away. André Citroën, for example, believed in the need to organize production so as to employ as many women as possible. To him, the expansion of female employment went hand in hand with the adoption of Taylorism, or scientific management. In this new system, Parisian women occupied the least-skilled positions; still at Citroën, they represented more than 90 per cent of shell-assembly workers, and certain unskilled operations such as checking were 100 per cent female-staffed.[51]

46 On this point, see the graph in Robert, 'Ouvriers et mouvement ouvrier', vol. I. p. 126.

47 Cf. the Paris Socialist conseiller Alphonse Loyau in a session of the city council: 'every day the canton commissions report the removal of many women from the lists, having found employment, usually in a munitions factory . . . As soon as their wages exceed 3 francs per day, their grant is withdrawn'. Conseil municipal de Paris, Procès-verbaux, 15 April 1916, p. 252.

48 Alphonse Loyau: 'The exercise of such a policy, Sir, means sowing discouragement, giving birth to rage and resentment. It also harms economic activity, which needs workers who are currently lacking . . . it is putting a premium on laziness.' Conseil municipal de Paris, Procès-verbaux, 15 April 1916, p. 252.

49 Cf. Conseil général de la Seine, Procès-verbaux, 21 June 1916, p. 195.

50 Robert, 'Ouvriers et mouvement ouvrier', vol. I, p. 88 and vol. II, p. 457.

51 Sylvie Schweitzer, 'Organisation du travail, politique patronale et pratiques ouvrières aux usines Citroën, 1915–1935', State doctoral thesis, University of Paris – VIII, 1980.

The Citroën factory, however, was not typical. The labour force employed in munitions factories came from a wide range of backgrounds. Although women were well represented in production areas requiring a lesser degree of skill (chemicals, munitions, electrical industries), male civilians predominated in two types of manufacturing which required either physical strength (heavy industry, chemicals) or a high level of training (timber, aviation). Here construction workers served because of their strength and older men from traditional trades brought craft traditions to new tasks.[52]

Finally, it should be noted that the Ministry of Labour went to considerable lengths to ensure acceptable conditions for the integration of this labour force into factory work. To this aim the Comité du travail féminin was set up in April 1916 by Albert Thomas. From then on the ministry issued numerous edicts with precise regulations affecting work stations and rest periods, forbidding night work, or stating hygienic requirements. The question of work by pregnant or breast-feeding women was faced directly. Here French pronatalism came to the fore. The law of August 1917 on breast-feeding rooms – favouring assistance to women at work rather than their exclusion from war work – is no doubt the best illustration of this consensus, discussed in chapter 14.

This emphasis on the need to encourage the birth-rate in France contrasts sharply with the very different attitudes adopted in Britain by the Health of Munition Workers Committee of the Ministry of Munitions. Far from allowing mothers to combine maternity and work in the factory, this committee took a firm stand against the expansion of crèches at work and strongly discouraged young mothers from working.[53]

The demands of the war economy eventually overcame such scruples. By July 1918, the proportion of female workers in the labour force in sectors most directly connected to the war effort (metal-working, chemicals, and government factories) was similar in London and in Paris. By then, women occupied a full third of all jobs.[54] Some caution is needed before assuming a similar situation on both sides of the Channel. British data are derived from Board of Trade statistics based on industry rather than occupation. Many women registered as having gone into industry were in fact working in offices; thus several motor-trade firms quickly decided to transfer their male office workers to manufacturing and to replace them by recruiting women.

The 'feminization' of the industrial labour force in London should

[52] On this point, see Robert, 'Ouvriers et mouvement ouvrier', vol. I, pp. 88–9.

[53] See Susan Pedersen, 'Social policy and the reconstruction of family in Britain and France, 1900–1945', PhD thesis, Harvard University, 1989, pp. 91–110.

[54] Board of Trade, *State of employment report*, July 1918.

not be overestimated. Only a few sectors, such as food, textiles, and chemicals, took on more women than men. Conversely, in the metal-working industry, between July 1814 and July 1918, the number of male jobs grew by 99,000 as against only 47,000 for women.[55]

Further, the absorption of this new workforce appears to have been slow and uneven. Employers' reluctance to take on women was clearly evident until the munitions crisis of May 1915. In April 1915 male employment in London had grown by 70,000 since July 1914, compared with a rise of only 1,000 for women. Despite the determined attitude of the Ministry of Munitions, many government factories were very slow to take on female staff; the Royal Gunpowder Factory at Waltham Abbey did not employ any women at all until April 1916. Later still, several government establishments employed very few women.[56] No doubt we see here traces of the bitter trade-union resistance to dilution by women workers; management reluctance; and the ambiguous attitude of the Ministry of Munitions. There may also be evidence of the strong British adherence to the ideal of the 'male bread-winner' – not unknown on the Continent – which tended to restrict women's social life to the narrow confines of domesticity.[57]

These were limits to a process that had a logic of its own. The war needed more workers: some of them had to be women. By mid-1915 anyone could see that this was so. From the spring of 1915, the increase in levels of female employment was more rapid: in the space of three months, 36,000 women went into industry, finance, and commerce. In December 1915 the Board of Trade noted widespread shortages of women workers and at many of its meetings discussed how to persuade more women – particularly those with work experience – to join the workforce.[58]

In 1916–1917 the development of new government-controlled war factories drew more women into the war economy. Nationally, the total number of female workers in the branches covered by the Board of

[55] Board of Trade, *State of employment reports, July 1918* (1918 totals represent estimates based on the result of a survey of employment trends across Greater London). See also *Census of England and Wales, 1911*, and PRO, SUPP 5/1051 (Woolwich Arsenal); Dearle, *Labor cost*; BLPES, Local Government Board, *London Intelligence Committee Reports*, August 1914 to July 1915.

[56] They made up 14 per cent of the labour force at H. M. Hackney Wick in January 1917, 15 per cent at Royal Enfield in April 1918, and there were no women in the TNT factory (government TNT purifying plant) at Rainham in January 1918. See *History of the Ministry of Munitions*, VIII, part 2.

[57] See Pedersen, 'Social policy', pp. 91–102. This concept is not unknown, nor in the Paris workers' movement. On this point, see Jean-Louis Robert, 'La C.G.T. et la famille ouvrière, 1914–1918: première approche', *Le Mouvement social*, no. 116 (July–September 1981), pp. 47–66.

[58] Board of Trade, *State of employment report*, mid-December 1915, pp. 3–8.

Trade enquiry grew by 19 per cent (162 per cent for metal-working, chemicals, and munitions). No statistics of this kind exist for London, but a few examples show a comparable change. At the Woolwich Arsenal the number of women employed grew from 195 in June 1915 to 11,000 in July 1916 and to more than 25,000 a year later.[59] In the same area, the London General Omnibus Company experienced similar growth in its female workforce: from 226 at the beginning of the war to 2,417 in December 1916 and 3,225 in April 1917.[60]

If we assume that London followed the national pattern of expansion, it can be estimated that the female labour-force grew by 25 per cent during the war, slightly less than in Paris, where it was probably close to 30 per cent. The war continued to provide opportunities for significant growth in the female workforce, even though this expansion was mostly in sectors where female employment was already well established before the war. No doubt some women were unemployed in July 1914, while others, younger women, were looking for their first job; the majority were probably women changing jobs or returning to work after years at home.

Matters were very different in Berlin: in December 1917, the proportion of women in the three sectors of metal-working, chemicals and machine tools was more than 50 per cent.[61] The expansion of female employment in industry was particularly striking in the German capital, reaching levels unknown in the other two cities and appearing to form an essential pillar of Berlin's industrial mobilization. Thus the numbers of female workers increased by 279 per cent in the machine-tool industry and by 116 per cent in metal-working between 1914 and December 1917. A wider assessment, based on statistics of the health-insurance system, suggests that the growth in women's work in Berlin was of the order of 38 per cent.[62]

Sectoral distinctions abound. In the chemical industry, more women than men were at work as early as April 1916. By 1918, 60 per cent of the labour force was female. The same linear growth in female labour took place in mechanical construction. In metal-working, in contrast, the growth in numbers of women workers was irregular; the number of females did not overtake the numbers of male workers in this vital sector. Although the Hindenburg Programme brought about a general growth in the labour force as a whole, and in the number of female workers in particular after the final months of 1916, its effects remained moderate.

On this point, the statistics of the Berlin metal-working industries'

[59] PRO, SUPP 5/63.

[60] *Women, war and society collection* (Adam Matthews publications, Taunton, 1990), Reel 41: 36/9 and 36/13.

[61] This only relates to factories with more than twenty-five employees. *Gross-Berlin Statistische Monatsberichte*, 1914–18. [62] *Ibid.*

Table 6.9. *Activity in the Departmental labour exchange bureau in the Department of the Seine, unskilled male labour section, November 1915 to October 1918*

	Seeking work	Vacancies	Taken on
11/1915	134	134	15
12/1915	416	770	101
01/1916	284	393	93
02/1916	316	486	138
03/1916	521	510	245
04/1916	533	373	231
05/1916	670	691	282
06/1916	565	681	159
07/1916	742	733	438
08/1916	844	986	421
09/1916	898	902	529
10/1916	1,245	1,471	637
11/1916	2,862	2,754	1,062
12/1916	4,066	2,457	1,554
01/1917	5,141	2,226	1,487
02/1917	8,980	1,570	1,495
03/1917	7,135	1,835	1,395
04/1917	7,622	1,518	1,291
05/1917	7,635	1,923	1,518
06/1917	8,154	1,575	1,520
07/1917	5,797	1,616	1,397
08/1917	5,511	1,629	1,579
09/1917	4,947	1,799	1,682
10/1917	5,808	1,827	1,744
11/1917	6,089	1,717	1,609
12/1917	5,670	1,589	1,570
01/1918	5,945	1,430	1,402
02/1918	5,703	2,700	2,177
03/1918	4,722	1,903	1,835
04/1918	4,761	2,287	2,197
05/1918	4,372	2,209	2,181
06/1918	5,270	2,516	2,493
07/1918	6,224	3,022	2,862
08/1918	5,098	2,703	2,549
09/1918	5,584	2,646	2,417
10/1918	5,113	2,343	1,981

Source: Conseil général de la Seine, Rapports et documents, no. 8, 30/11/1918, pp. 273–4.

labour exchange offer fuller information. Until the middle of 1916 vacancies for women workers remained few, although there was a great shortage of male workers (table 6.8); managers of metal-working factories were anxious above all to recruit a skilled (and therefore male) work-force. In November 1916 a report from the Verband Märkischer

Arbeitsnachweise remarked that 'the shortage of workers is reaching such proportions that it exceeds the capacity of the placement system to satisfy industrial needs'.[63] By July this severe shortage affected the working conditions of skilled metal-workers: significant extensions of working hours were noted almost everywhere.[64]

From August–September 1916 onwards, on the other hand, the demand for women workers grew particularly strongly, trebling in the space of a year. Although at first job-seekers matched vacancies, after February 1917 the gap between the two became much greater. Here we find evidence in the vital metal-working industry of a labour shortage preventing the realization on the urban level of plans drawn up by fiat by military authorities on the national level. Planning went on without regard to conditions on the ground where the weapons of war had to be produced.

Here is the urban face of the contradictions produced by the Hindenburg Programme. By late 1916 women spent hours trying to find food for their families (see chapter 11 below). On top of this, their employment in war factories further complicated the management of Berlin households. There were many cases of women working in war factories having to leave their jobs under the pressure of the search for food. Such multiple burdens underline the fact that higher wages could not make up for the stress, exhaustion, and uncertainty of wartime metropolitan life.

The price paid by women for working in war factories was in this respect much higher in Berlin than in the two other capitals. The health policy of the Ministry of Armaments in Paris does not seem to have had an equivalent in Berlin. True, the employment of women in a factory was subject to restrictive regulations, with night work, for example, requiring a special dispensation; but a report from the Gewerbe-Aufsicht stressed that many women were taken on for this kind of work whatever the regulations, and exhaustion at work was common because these women, some of whom had recently been delivered or had very young children, suffered from malnutrition.[65] Here we see the intersection of the two levels of hardship in Berlin life: one – long and dreary hours in munitions production – shared by Parisians and Londoners; the other, material shortages and bureaucratic regulations of a Talmudic complexity. For women workers in Berlin, getting through the week was a considerable achievement. Their mobilization presented them with hardships at least as severe, and in some ways worse, than those faced by women in Paris and London.

[63] *Reichsarbeitsblatt*, 1916, vol. 14, 12, p. 974.

[64] *Ibid*., 1916, vol. 14, p. 638.

[65] Brandenburg, LHA, Pr.Br.Rep.30 Berlin C, Jahresberichte der Gewerbe-Aufsicht, no. 1958, pp. 269–75.

Spatial restructuring of the labour market

The aspects of job mobility described above occurred against the backdrop of the creation of new factories or the conversion of older establishments within these cities, but more generally in the suburbs. The development of these new industrial centres radically altered the world of work in these cities in wartime.

In Paris, the dimensions of the new war sector were so great as to transform the conurbation into a veritable arsenal. Paris was the site of this concentration of war production for many reasons. First, the capital lay at an ideal distance from the front, neither too near – risking the inconvenience of accurate and continuous German bombardment or the effects of nearby fighting – nor too far; transport of munitions to the combat zone could be simple and swift. Paris also met the need for a centre of communication to link the city with the armies via a dense and centralized network of railways. Finally, the Parisian tradition of metal-working and metal-finishing was a vital asset for the project of building new war factories.

Thøese establishments profoundly and permanently modified the pattern of industry in Paris. They were located on the edge of the city (with Citroën in the 15th arrondissement) and mostly in the inner suburbs, where 75 per cent of war-related factory work took place. They brought together substantial numbers of workers: 22,000 at Renault in Boulogne-Billancourt, 6,000 in the Puteaux arsenal, 5,200 in the cartridge factory at Vincennes, 11,000 with Delaunay-Belleville at Saint-Denis. The emergence of new centres of economic activity in the suburbs was spectacular. In Suresnes, the number of factories in the mechanical and metal-working sectors grew from eight to twenty-five between 1915 and 1919, while the number of their workers increased elevenfold.[66] The centre of gravity of economic activity thus tended to shift from the old industrial quartiers of Paris (Faubourg Saint-Antoine in the 11th and Belleville in the 20th arrondissements) towards the new industrial belt surrounding the city.

These new factories were intended to draw labour to live in the vicinity of their workplace, but such was not always the case. The moratorium on rents helped to prevent tenants from moving their residence for the duration of the war. Consequently improved public transportation within the conurbation – a very slow process[67] – was an

[66] See Kaizo Isobe, 'Problèmes d'évolution économique et d'urbanisme dans la banlieue ouest de Paris: Puteaux et Suresnes pendant la guerre de 1914–1919 et pendant l'entre-deux-guerres', PhD thesis, University of Paris – IV, 1982.

[67] The reports of the Conseil municipal de Paris and Conseil général de la Seine are full of references to the incessant interventions on this theme by councillors. For references in the popular press, see *La banlieue ouest*, *Le journal de St Denis*, among others.

essential prerequisite of the restructuring of the Paris labour market. Reluctance to accept geographic mobility constrained job mobility in wartime. The consequences of leaving a familiar craft and local ties to work in the war factories made this no easy task. This is part of the explanation for the 'stickiness' of the wartime labour market and, in Paris, for the persistence of female unemployment as late as 1916 (see table 6.5).

In London the expansion of war industries was based on the Thames and its important maritime trade. The British capital was also crucially important as a dispatch centre, sending arms, munitions, reinforcements, and supplies of all kinds to the troops on the Western front. To meet this demand London could draw upon a large potential reserve of female workers.

Within Greater London, the geographic spread of industries controlled by the Ministry of Munitions was vast. The periphery was important, lying farther out than the Berlin or Parisian equivalent, where war factories clustered closely round the capital. These workshops and factories lay outside the domain of the London County Council with some significant exceptions: the Woolwich Arsenal and a few more modest establishments such as the Clement Talbot aircraft factory in Ladbroke Grove (with 2,000 workers at the beginning of 1918) or the TNT factory at Hackney Wick (with nearly 1,500 workers at the beginning of 1917).

Considerations of local safety undoubtedly influenced the peripheral urban siting of potentially dangerous industries. The Silvertown disaster, which caused the death of more than seventy people in January 1917, was clear proof of the risks of such establishments on old overcrowded industrial sites, and encouraged greater care. The explosives factory at Hackney Wick closed in April 1917, and in early 1918 munitions filling operations at Southwark were suspended.

Yet these sites were not so much a departure from as a deepening of pre-war trends. The 1914–1918 war extended the spread of London's industrial suburbs,[68] particularly in the northern and western districts, a development which long antedated the war.

Four zones profited from war-related industrial development. To the north, the valley of the River Lea, a tributary of the Thames, constituted an important axis of war production employing at least 25,000 workers. It had large works, such as the Royal Small Arms factories at Enfield (10,000 employees in March 1917) and the Royal Gunpowder factory at Waltham (more than 5,000 employees in May 1917). The zone extending in the west from Willesden to Hayes, passing through Acton and Ealing,

[68] D. H. Smith, *The industries of Greater London: being a survey of the recent industrialisation of the northern and western sectors of Greater London* (London, 1933), pp. 41, 81, 97, 106–9, 169; and P. G. Hall, *The industries of London since 1861* (London, 1961), pp. 137–8.

constituted a looser zone, more dispersed and less important (with about 15,000 workers in 1917). Finally, apart from the small centre at Croydon to the south, there was the arsenal at Woolwich on the lower Thames, constituting an industrial centre with more than 70,000 workers at the end of 1917 – or between 8 and 10 per cent of the industrial workforce employed by London County Council.

Woolwich was within the boundaries of the LCC; the other factories were well outside its administrative borders. This concentration of labour in Woolwich made great demands on space, and the spectacular growth in numbers – a sevenfold increase between 1914 and December 1917 – inevitably meant heavy in-migration. Estimates suggest that perhaps 27,000 newcomers settled in the Metropolitan Borough of Woolwich; therefore, at least 35,000 people were affected by population movements from the south-eastern counties around London to the vicinity of the Arsenal. The management of these population flows required some ingenuity, including the use of the Thames for transport to the Arsenal, and the provision of buses, trains, and special trams, with appropriate timetables, for the benefit of the labour force and the munitions effort as a whole.

In Berlin the most striking spatial development was the growth of the formidable concentration of war factories at Spandau, just outside 'old Berlin's' municipal borders. According to health-insurance statistics, nearly 120,000 workers were employed there in January 1918, or approximately 9 per cent of the total labour force of Greater Berlin. Spandau was, moreover, the only district showing a noticeable increase in numbers of workers. While everywhere else the pre-war population was only just exceeded after 1917, the increase at Spandau was an impressive 100 per cent, or an increase of some 60,000 people.[69] This spatial concentration of labour suggests a sharper division between the effects of the war on different districts of the city. Berlin's industrial concentration appears to have been more weighted towards one area than were developments in the Parisian and London regions. In all three cities, major transport problems were posed by these shifts, but the headaches in Berlin – as usual – were probably greater than in the other two cities.

Conclusion

Examination of the restructuring processes in the labour market in the three capitals reveals three different experiences. The chronology, for example, is different in each case. The Paris labour market experienced a slow, massive reshaping, after the major economic and social crisis of

[69] *Gross-Berlin Monatsberichte*, 1914–18.

the first months of the war. By January 1917 the re-gearing of labour had occurred. The total number of people employed in the Paris region was 20 per cent greater than before the war. In Berlin the limits of restructuring and expansion were reached by early 1917; thereafter no further growth was possible. Indeed in key sectors such as food, the labour force shrank progressively from 1916 on. In London, in contrast, no such problems emerged. Restructuring took place more easily and with relatively fewer of the difficulties faced in Paris early in the war and in Berlin later on.

In London the tardy introduction of conscription undoubtedly enabled the labour market to adapt more smoothly to the war economy. Older habits of recruitment of labour and its migration carried on in the early phase of the war. From 1916, London moved closer to Paris and Berlin, but the history of the labour market in the three cities never converged fully.

Paris and London shared certain characteristics. In both cities the role of political decisions at the national level was of prime importance. The decision was taken very early in France, at the highest levels of government, to give industrial mobilization top priority and therefore allocate labour to arms factories despite the opposing claims of the military authorities. From May 1915 the policy of the Ministry of Munitions was clear. They oversaw the formation of mixed commissions of management and labour to implement the deployment of a militarized labour force in war factories, and to bring more women into the munitions sector.

The contrast between French strategy and German ideas on the mobilization of labour is striking. The French choice was a risky one, but at least it was a workable scheme. The German authorities were unable or unwilling to decide clearly between industrial mobilization and the military demands of national defence. The principal political decision affecting the labour market – the Hindenburg Programme – was taken in late 1916, at a time when the restructuring of the Paris labour market had already taken place. It was a leap in the dark, and created deep and disturbing fissures in the Berlin labour force, as it did in the rest of German society.

The implementation of the Hindenburg Programme took place at a very difficult moment. Food shortages were bad enough, and held back the fielding of a more efficient labour force, as is evident in the reduced productivity of night-shift workers. But then came further problems of transport, housing and heating. In effect, the attempt to realize the full mobilization at the heart of the Auxiliary Labour Law of December 1916 took no account of the rigidity of an urban labour market with a smaller reserve of manpower in key positions from 1917 onwards.

Finally, there were supply constraints to contend with. Shortages of fuel and primary materials due to the blockade and administrative failings, particularly in transport, had a direct effect on the utilization of labour in Berlin. In contrast, industrial mobilization in Paris was aided and abetted, especially from late 1916, by massive imports of British coal. The introduction of an international supply network, dwarfing the urban economy, made all the difference in putting labour to work in Paris.

In microcosm, the failure to solve the labour problem in Berlin reveals the structural and material weaknesses within the German economy as a whole. In contrast, in London and Paris the transition to war was managed with some difficulty, but the longer the war went on, the more clear-cut was the Allied advantage in terms of creating a labour force geared to the demands of the war economy. Here political decisions had their echoes, and Berlin suffered with the rest of Germany the consequences of the Hindenburg Programme.

The effects of this war-induced industrial reorganization were long-lasting in all three cities. In Paris in particular, it both broke up and restructured communities of workers and the working class as a whole.[70] At an individual level the war produced a myriad of choices, destroying some livelihoods no doubt but also creating many opportunities for new forms of work in new parts of the urban environment. Many women found their working lives transformed during the conflict. With one notable exception, the feminization of the workforce was limited strictly to wartime: in all three cities, women who moved into the service sector stayed there after the war. But that is a story best told after we have considered the final phase of the wartime distribution of the labour force, that related to demobilization.

[70] Robert, 'Ouvriers et mouvement ouvrier'.

7
The transition to peace, 1918–1919

Joshua Cole

The end of hostilities and the demobilization of Europe's armies after November 1918 inaugurated a period of economic transition that was just as dramatic as the crisis of mobilization in 1914–1915. Nevertheless, the changes that had taken place in Paris, London, and Berlin in over four years of total war ensured that the transition to peace would not bear any simple resemblance to mobilization in reverse, that is, a return to the pre-war situation. All three cities had been transformed by the demands of the war economy, albeit to varying degrees. Older patterns of employment had been disrupted, new industries had been developed, and the state had intervened in the economic life of each city in unprecedented ways. This chapter will explore the crises of demobilization in each city in order to determine the extent to which the dislocation caused by the war continued into the immediate post-war period.

In assessing the changes which accompanied the demobilization, some historians have emphasized the quick abandonment of government control during the difficult years 1919 and 1920, and pointed to the apparent victory of free-market policies in the post-war period, at the expense of organized labour.[1] Other historians have questioned the view which posits a stark opposition between wartime economic interventionism and post-war *laissez-faire* in Western Europe, and noted instead several significant arenas of continuity between the period before and immediately following the Armistice of 11 November 1918.[2]

[1] In this connection see Susan Armitage, *The politics of decontrol: Britain and the United States* (London, 1969), pp. 10–20; Paul Johnson, *Land fit for heroes: the planning of British reconstruction, 1916–1919* (Chicago, 1968), pp. 249–84, 285–337, and 451–4; Gerald D. Feldman, 'Economic and social problems of the German demobilization, 1918–1919', *Journal of Modern History*, 47 (March 1975), p. 2; Charles Maier, *Recasting bourgeois Europe: stabilization in France, Germany and Italy in the decade of World War I* (Princeton, 1975), ch. 3: 'The limits of economic restructuring', pp. 135–231; and R. F. Kuisel, *Capitalism and the state in modern France: renovation and economic management in the twentieth century* (Cambridge, 1981), pp. 51–9.

[2] For examples of such arguments see especially John Horne, *Labour at war* (Oxford, 1991) and the articles in Patrick Fridenson (ed.), *The French home front, 1914–1918* (Providence, 1992).

John Horne has argued, for example, that the move toward government decontrol in France and Britain stimulated the representatives of organized labour to direct their efforts towards more easily acceptable reformist goals, such as the eight-hour day.[3] Meanwhile, Gunther Mai has posited that the activist labour policy of the German Demobilization Office was an important factor in delaying the economic crisis which eventually overtook Germany in 1923–1924, and was thus an important part of political stability in the immediate post-war months.[4] Thus, although the supporters of the decontrol argument can certainly point to long-term trends to support their claims, it remains difficult to make global generalizations about the role of the state in the reconversion of the economy to peaceful ends during the years 1919 and 1920.

Our urban focus has allowed us to shift the grounds of the debate somewhat, and the following chapter concentrates on the particular effects of military demobilization on the labour markets of Paris, London, and Berlin during the crucial months of late 1918 and 1919. By determining the extent to which the situation at the urban level conformed or did not conform to the general picture of post-war economic dislocation in each country, we will be able to ascertain whether the respective capitals benefited or were put at a disadvantage by the policies followed at the national level. Our approach does not seek to determine whether the advocates of decontrol or continued economic supervision carried the day, but rather to assess the effects that the eventual compromises between the two sides had upon the capitals of France, Britain, and Germany. The possibility that urban areas may have had different priorities or interests during 1919 is all the more significant given Rodney Lowe's suggestion that problems with reconversion in Britain arose because the programmes for social support that accompanied demobilization came into conflict with the needs of British industry.[5] The potential for conflict between an anti-revolutionary social policy on the one hand and a recovery-minded economic policy on the other, was all the more acute in the capitals

[3] Horne, *Labour at war*, ch. 9, 'The reckoning: l'Après-guerre and the longer term legacy', esp. pp. 357–62. For a comparative discussion of the eight-hour day in the post-war period see Gary Cross, 'Worktime in international discontinuity', in G. Cross (ed.), *Worktime and industrialization. An international history* (Philadelphia, 1988), pp. 163ff.

[4] Gunther Mai, 'Arbeitsmarktregulierung oder Sozialpolitik? Die personelle Demobilmachung in Deutschland 1918 bis 1920/1924' in G. D. Feldman, C.-L. Holtfrerich, G. Ritter, P.-C. Witt (eds.), *Die Anpassung an die Inflation* (Berlin, 1986), pp. 203–36, here p. 233.

[5] Rodney Lowe, 'The erosion of state intervention in Britain, 1917–24', *Economic History Review*, 31, 2 (1978), pp. 270–86, here p. 284. See also G. D. Feldman's comments on Lowe's argument in G. D. Feldman, 'Die Demobilmachung und die Sozialordnung der Zwischenkriegszeit in Europa', *Geschichte und Gesellschaft*, 9 (1983), pp. 156–77, here p. 173.

because of the tendency for post-war social instability to be aggravated in large urban areas.

The first and most socially disruptive phase of demobilization involved bringing home the troops and re-absorbing them into the domestic economy, either by creating new jobs or by replacing the women, foreign workers, and older men who had been hired 'for the duration'. Policy makers in Britain, France, and Germany realized that this phase would necessarily cause a sharp but temporary increase in unemployment. This crisis was most pronounced in Greater Berlin, where post-war unemployment peaked in February 1919 at 235,540 men and women, declining to 70,733 by the end of the year.[6] Unemployment figures for London are incomplete for this period, but national figures for Britain suggest that post-war unemployment reached its apex in February 1919 for women and non-military men, and that the rates for ex-servicemen continued to rise until May 1919 when the last troops were released.[7] A reasonable estimate of the number of unemployed in London at the peak of the crisis would be in the neighbourhood of 100,000 men and women; in spite of these high numbers however, it was generally agreed that the demobilization in Britain was not the catastrophe that many had feared.[8] In France, a two-step demobilization process slowed the release of soldiers from active duty and alleviated the pressure on the labour market. As a result, the post-war jobless level in Paris peaked in April 1919 at just 77,514 men and women, and it declined to only 1,200 by December, out of a total workforce of about 1.6 million.[9] This evidence of an extremely severe unemployment crisis in Berlin, a sharp increase in unemployment in London, and a more

[6] Brandenburg Landeshauptarchiv (henceforth LHA), Pr.Br.Rep.30 Berlin C. n. 1959, Jahresberichte der Gewerbe-Aufsicht, p 15. It remains difficult to gauge the severity of the post-war economic crisis in Germany. The figures on unemployment in 1919 are incomplete and imprecise, and almost certainly under-reported. Furthermore, the figures contain little indication of other weaknesses in the labour market, such as short-time work, or redundant and 'make-work' in certain industries which padded employment rolls without contributing significantly to increased productivity. Even the definition of 'unemployment' itself seems to have been ambiguous in this period, as the lack of a consistent statistic in the official publications of the period indicates. See Richard Bessel, 'Unemployment and demobilization in Germany after the First World War', in Richard Evans and Dick Geary (eds.), *The German unemployed, experiences and consequences of mass unemployment from the Weimar Republic to the Third Reich* (London, 1987), pp. 25–6, 30–31; Gerald D. Feldman, 'Economic and social problems', p. 23; and Gerald D. Feldman, 'Saxony, the Reich, and the problem of unemployment in the German inflation', *Archiv für Sozialgeschichte*, 29 (1989), p. 105.

[7] See N. B. Dearle, *The labour cost of the world war*, pp. 159–67. See also figures from Dearle reproduced in table 7.1.

[8] David Englander, 'Die Demobilmachung in Grossbritannien nach dem ersten Weltkrieg', *Geschichte und Gesellschaft*, 9 (1983), pp. 195–210, here pp. 202–3.

[9] Robert, 'Ouvriers et mouvement ouvrier', p. 1845.

attenuated period of relatively high unemployment in Paris highlights the differences in each of the three cities at the end of the war (see table 7.1). Coming as it did after four years of war and unprecedented civilian hardship, this pressure on the workforce also meant that the demobilization process contained the potential for a great deal of conflict. Strikes were frequent in 1919 in Paris and London, despite the fact that demobilization was accomplished relatively smoothly in the Allied capitals. In defeated Berlin, of course, the tensions between ex-soldiers, workers, and a discredited regime found expression in the revolution of 9 November 1918 and the street battles of January and March 1919. These events will be analysed in volume II.

Given the expectations of a surge in unemployment, an important part of demobilization plans in all three cities was the establishment of temporary systems for the distribution of unemployment benefits to workers who suddenly found themselves out of a job and for ex-soldiers who had difficulty in finding one. In Britain the most severe social consequences of the transition to peace were to be offset by the introduction of the 'out-of-work donation', paid to all civilian workers, ex-servicemen, and their dependants.[10] In Germany, the *Reichsverordnung* of 13 November 1918 made it clear that the responsibility for the dispensation of unemployment support would be largely left to the individual municipalities. Half of the funds would be provided by the national government, one-quarter would come from the provincial or state treasuries (from the Prussian administration, in Berlin's case), and the remainder would be paid for by the city itself.[11] In France, responsibility for unemployment support had been in the hands of municipal administrations since the beginning of the war. The recognition of government responsibility for the lot of the returning soldier and the women who had been hired only for the duration of the war was an important step in all three countries toward the development of a permanent system which recognized the principle of 'work or maintenance'.

The second and more long-term problem of the transition was the actual reconversion of the war economy to peaceful ends, a task which required the investment of new capital and the reopening of consumer markets that had been eclipsed by the demands of war. Here the story is

[10] *History of Ministry of Munitions* (London, 1922–3), vol. VI, part II, p. 84; A. C. Pigou, *Aspects of British economic history, 1918–1925* (London, 1947), pp. 28–9; B. Gilbert, *British social policy, 1914–1939* (London, 1970), pp. 59–63; S. Pedersen, 'Gender, welfare and citizenship in Britain during the Great War', *American Historical Review*, 95, 4 (Oct. 1990), pp. 1005–6; W. R. Garside, *British unemployment policy, 1919–1939: a study in public policy* (Cambridge, 1990), pp. 34–9.

[11] *Reichsgesetzblatt*, no. 6530 (1918), pp. 1395–1408. On the development of the German unemployment system see also G. D. Feldman, 'Saxony, the Reich, and the problem of unemployment', pp. 109–16.

quite different in each of our three cities. After an initial 'breathing space' immediately after the armistice, London benefited from a post-war boom in the British economy which lasted from approximately April 1919 to April 1920. During this period wages, prices, and the money supply all rose dramatically. This unprecedented inflationary boom appears to have been driven primarily by the desire of industrialists, wholesalers, and retailers to rebuild depleted stocks of raw materials and finished goods, and to a lesser extent to renew machinery.[12] Post-war restocking and the satisfaction of suppressed wartime demand were necessarily short-term in their effects, however, and the post-war boom in London was followed successively by a slump at the end of 1920 and a period of serious stagnation which lasted until the end of 1922. The end of the boom also marked the beginning of a new period of high unemployment.

In France, production levels did not increase substantially during the period 1919 to 1921, despite a parallel period of inflation similar to that experienced in Britain.[13] The difficulties of reconversion in Paris during this period had their roots in the wartime neglect of commercial services which had accompanied the command economy, and in delays in reinvigorating this traditionally weak sector in France once the war was over. These obstacles to a smooth transition were compounded by shortages of raw materials and a serious crisis of liquidity in early 1919. Uncertainty about the increased militancy of Parisian workers during the spring and early summer of 1919 also contributed to caution on the part of investors. Confidence did not improve until the victory of the Bloc National in the legislative elections of November 1919, significantly demonstrating that political stability was viewed as the real sign of a return to peace and normality in France.[14] In 1921, the same international slump which had ended Britain's post-war boom was also felt in France, but after 1922 French production levels increased rapidly, outstripped only by the United States among Western industrial nations.[15]

The history of reconversion in Berlin should be distinguished from that of Paris and London for several reasons. Obviously, the chaos which accompanied the revolution hampered any attempts to find political solutions to the crisis of demobilization. Furthermore, the

[12] On the periodization of the post-war economy in Britain see Pigou, *Aspects*, p. 70. For a reassessment of this view see J. A. Dowie, '1919–1920 is in need of attention', *Economic History Review*, 28 (August 1975), pp. 429–50; and S. N. Broadberry, *The British economy between the wars: a macroeconomic survey* (Oxford, 1986), chs. 8 and 9.

[13] Charles Gide and William Oualid, *Le bilan de la guerre pour la France* (Paris and New Haven, 1931), pp. 277, 314–16.

[14] Kuisel, *Capitalism and the state*, pp. 62–6. Maier, *Recasting*, pp. 91–109.

[15] Gide and Oualid, *Le bilan de la guerre*, p. 276.

continuation of the Allied blockade until the summer of 1919 meant that the wartime shortage of fuel and raw materials would continue to be a severe problem for industry during the first year of peace. The coal shortage was especially acute: between 1 April 1918 and 31 March 1919 Berlin industry received 54 per cent less coal than the previous year, and the situation was compounded by the loss of minerals and ores mined in Alsace and Lorraine.[16] Similarly, the confiscation of transportation vehicles by the Allied forces, especially railway carriages, forced Berlin's public transportation network to cut its service by a third in January because of lack of locomotives, despite the fact that they were carrying nearly a million passengers a day.[17]

Most importantly, however, the peculiar circumstances of the German post-war inflation created a very different environment for the reconversion of industry than in the other two capitals. Although British monetary policy permitted a short inflationary boom throughout much of 1919 and early 1920, and a similar phenomenon occurred in France, the Allied powers subsequently followed strict deflationary policies, contributing to the slump of 1920/1. A combination of factors led economic policy makers in Berlin to back monetary interventions which allowed Germany to maintain an exchange rate favourable to exports, in the interest of both capturing markets abroad and encouraging employment at home.[18] Even during the temporary lull in inflation – the

[16] Report to Berlin City Council by Dr Körte, the Director of the Kohlenstelle *Groß*-Berlin, August 1919. Landesarchiv Berlin, Aussenstelle Breite Strasse (henceforth LAB (STA)), Rep. 00/02-1 2189, Akten der Stadtverordneten-Versammlung zu Berlin betreffend die auf die Umwälzung bzw. die Übergangswirtschaft bezüglichen Vorlagen und Anträge, 1918–1920, p. 116. Körte noted that between 1 April 1917 and 31 March 1918 Berlin had received 789,000 hundredweight bags of coal briquets for household use, 200,000 tons of coal for gas works, and 38,000 tons for electric works. Between 1 April 1918 and 31 March 1919 this figure fell to 576,000 bags for household use, 29,000 tons for gas works, and 8,000 tons for electric works, decreases of 27 per cent, 86 per cent, and 79 per cent respectively.

[17] *Die wirtschaftliche Demobilmachung*, 7 (9 January 1919), p. 52. The Allies demanded 5,000 locomotives (out of a total of 30,000), 150,000 rail cars (out of 570,000) and 5,000 trucks as a part of the Armistice terms. In addition, they received all of the rolling stock in Alsace-Lorraine. See Friedrich Hesse, *Die Deutsche Wirtschaftslage von 1914 bis 1923* (Jena, 1938), p. 143. Apparently, however, the German trains were in such poor repair that the Allies only took a fraction of their original demands. See 'Verkehrslage Ende Dezember 1918', *Die wirtschaftliche Demobilmachung*, 2 (3 Jan. 1919), p. 18.

[18] Gerald D. Feldman, 'The political economy of Germany's relative stabilization during the 1920/21 world depression', in G. Feldman, C.-L. Holtfrerich, G. A. Ritter, and P.-C. Witt (eds.), *Die Deutsche Inflation. Eine Zwischenbilanz* (Berlin, 1982), p. 188. See also Peter-Christian Witt, 'Staatliche Wirtschaftspolitik in Deutschland 1918 bis 1923: Entwicklung und Zerstörung einer modernen wirtschaftspolitischen Strategie', in *ibid.*, pp. 153–79. Witt argues that the early stages of inflation between 1918 and 1922 resulted from a calculated attempt by the government to implement a policy of social and economic stabilization.

so-called period of 'relative stabilization' from mid 1920 until the resumption of rapid currency depreciation in the summer of 1921 – there was little interest among German economic policy makers in achieving real currency stability, especially as the reparations question had not yet been settled. Of course, the easy access to credit made the inflation very advantageous to industrialists, who were able to invest in new machinery on favourable terms.[19] On the national level, inflation allowed Germany to escape the high levels of unemployment suffered in the post-war depression in France and England. For Berlin, on the other hand, where large numbers of unemployed workers continued to be dependent upon municipal support at fixed rates, inflation contributed to the misery and exhaustion of the urban population and led to an increasingly poisoned political atmosphere.

Within these different national contexts, the positions of organized labour, industrial leaders, and government also varied. In France and Britain, representatives of labour were excluded from post-war governments and their influence on demobilization and reconversion could come only through negotiation or the threat of disruption.[20] A willingness to use this threat by the Confédération Générale du Travail (CGT) in France was responsible for the passage of the eight-hour-day law in late April 1919. In Britain, by contrast, the same goal – the 48-hour week – was accomplished at the local level through accords between unions and employers in early 1919, despite the fact that a national law on the eight-hour day was never passed.[21] In Germany, where the defeat brought members of the Socialist party into government for the first time, similar reforms were enacted through the corporate structure set up by the Stinnes–Legien agreement of 15 November 1918. This accord recognized the trade unions as legitimate representatives of Germany's workers, put an end to company unions, guaranteed parity between workers and employers on the committees which were set as part of the new *Arbeitsgemeinschaft*, and, finally, established the eight-hour day.[22]

[19] G. D. Feldman, 'Economic and social problems of the German demobilization', p. 23.

[20] John Horne, *Labour at war*, p. 351. [21] *Ibid.*, pp. 360–1.

[22] On the Stinnes–Legien agreement, see Gerald D. Feldman, 'Das deutsche Unternehmertum zwischen Krieg und Revolution: Die Entstehung des Stinnes-Legien-Abkommens', in G. D. Feldman, *Vom Weltkrieg zur Weltwirtschaftskrise. Studien zur deutschen Wirtschafts- und Sozialgeschichte 1914–1932* (Göttingen, 1984), pp. 100–27; Maier, *Recasting*, pp. 58–65. H. A. Winkler, *Von der Revolution zur Stabilisierung in der Weimarer Republik, 1918–1924. Arbeiter und Arbeiterbewegung in der Weimarer Republik 1918 bis 1924* (Berlin, 1984), pp. 75–9; U. Kluge, *Die Deutsche Revolution 1918–1919: Staat, Politik und Gesellschaft zwischen Weltkrieg und Kapp-Putsch* (Frankfurt am Main, 1988), pp. 72–4; and R. Rürup, 'Demokratische Revolution und "dritter Weg". Die deutsche Diskussion', *Geschichte und Gesellschaft*, 9 (1983), pp. 278–301. The prohibition on longer working hours was suspended in December 1923, and the principle of overtime for work over eight hours per day was not established until April 1927. See Maier, *Recasting*, p. 512.

These successes allowed labour leaders in all three cities to hope that the gains made by unions during the war years would become permanent.

Preparations for peace

In all three countries, planning for post-war economic reconstruction meant constructing a system capable of bringing millions of soldiers home, retraining them if necessary, and finding them employment. Simultaneously, such planning meant making a decision on how many of the wartime innovations would become permanent, and which would be allowed to lapse. In Britain, there was little support for continued state intervention in the economy and even labour leaders were content to assert their own autonomy and their desire for free and untrammelled negotiations with representatives of industry. In France, the success of the wartime alliance between business and the state won more adherents, but in the end the advocates of non-intervention carried the day. In Germany, where the defeat had made pre-Armistice plans for reconstruction obsolete before the fact, the situation was less clear, and revolutionaries, labour leaders, government officials, and military personnel found themselves thrown together in an improvised system where the pressures of the moment fostered cooperation between groups and individuals with otherwise incompatible beliefs.

Since early 1917 government departments in the British capital had been drawing up plans for handling the transition to peace and for initiating a period of post-war reconstruction.[23] The Ministry of Munitions had plans for organizing the demobilization of civilian workers 'constantly under consideration' from spring 1917, and in early 1918 even began to discharge staff in response to a falling demand for munitions and severe restrictions on raw material imports.[24] The German spring offensive put an end to this first wave of redundancies, but by April 1918 it had been agreed between the Ministry of Munitions and the Ministry of Reconstruction that 'plans for terminating contracts must be framed on the broad principle that materials, manufacturing capacity and labour should be diverted at the earliest possible moment from the production of useless munitions to peace

[23] BLPES, PP 1918, vol. XIII Cmd 9093 Condition of industry after the war reports, and K.O. Morgan and J. Morgan, *Portrait of a progressive: the political career of Christopher, Viscount Addison* (Oxford, 1980). On the widespread discussion of various demobilization plans see S. Graubard, 'Military demobilization in Great Britain following the First World War, *Journal of Modern History*, 19, 4 (1947), pp. 1–18.

[24] *History of the Ministry of Munitions*, vol. VI, part 2: 'The control of industrial manpower, 1917–1918', pp. 77–81.

industry'.[25] Government officials recognized that this policy would carry a high price in terms of unemployment, especially since it would coincide with rapid demobilization from the armed forces, but argued that it was none the less preferable to a slow transition in which scarce national resources would be wasted in producing unwanted war material.[26]

The move towards decontrol was not uncontested in Britain, and there was considerable discussion of corporatist solutions to the problems of demobilization and reconversion. The initial popularity of such innovations as the Joint Industrial Councils (also called Whitley Councils, after the Speaker of the House, John Whitley), which would allow for labour's participation in management, foundered shortly after the Armistice for lack of organization and government support, however, and the discussion produced little in the way of concrete results.[27] In the end, continued government supervision was considered only in such areas as the coal industry, and rail and shipping transport.[28]

In France, the war economy in 1918 was second to none. This very success made speculation about the nature of the post-war economy more open to debate and, in fact, post-war planning was a virtual obsession of policy makers during the period 1916–1918. Having produced more tanks and aircraft than any other belligerent power, could the French capitalize on their undeniable success in the peace which would follow? The question appeared all the more vital in the light of the widely held belief that the war would be followed by a period of intense economic competition with Germany.[29] In Paris, planners looked to the city's gigantic new industrial base to play a leading role in the development of modern technologies, especially in the areas of precision mechanics, aviation, and automobiles. At the same time, however, Paris's older craft industries in such sectors as furniture or clothing had already been in decline even before the war due to foreign competition, and the hope was expressed that these too could be reinvigorated in the new post-war order.

Trade unionists and the leaders of the CGT supported a continuation of wartime controls in the post-war period. Their programme, announced in November 1916, envisioned an intensified mobilization of industry based upon the application of modern technologies and the full participation of workers in the management of the economy. Socialist

[25] *Ibid.*, p. 83. Contracts for shells, bombs, ammunition, etc. were to be terminated within two to four weeks. See also Pigou, *Aspects*, pp. 117–26; Armitage, *The politics of decontrol*, p. 10; and R.H. Tawney, 'The abolition of economic controls, 1918–1921', *Economic History Review*, 13 (1943), pp. 1–30, on the wider movement to ensure a rapid return to free market conditions.

[26] *History of the Ministry of Munitions*, vol. VI, part 2, pp. 83–4, and Pigou, *Aspects*, pp. 22–5.

[27] On Whitley Councils see Johnson, *Land fit for heroes*, pp. 48–51, 156, 158–65, 201, 376–82.

[28] John Horne, *Labour at war*, p. 358. On the question of continued government intervention in the shipping, coal, and railway sectors in Britain see Armitage, *The politics of decontrol*, chs. 2–4.

[29] John Horne, *Labour at War*, p. 128.

members of the Assembly also favoured continued cooperation between government and industry, although they were notably less enthusiastic about post-war reforms than the labour representatives. A lack of cooperation between labour and Socialist politicians eventually prevented these plans from being realized, however, and Albert Thomas's successor (from 1917) at the Ministry of Armaments, Louis Loucheur (who also headed the Ministry of Industrial Reconstruction after January 1919) eventually chose an approach more favourable to private enterprise. Loucheur considered, and then vetoed, plans to use state contracts as a centrepiece of post-war reconstruction. After this, supporters of an increased role for the state in the economy, such as Etienne Clémentel at the Ministry of Commerce, were given scant attention.[30]

The situation in Berlin was of course very different. The Berlin economy had reached its wartime peak employment levels in December 1917; after this point the shortage of labour and raw materials limited further expansion. Furthermore, the great Berlin strike of January 1918, in which more than 200,000 workers participated, dramatically illustrated the extent to which the city had become divided through the hardship of war.[31] Although there was widespread unrest in Paris too, the tensions within Berlin's economy had reached both their material and political limits.

The original German preparations for demobilization, drawn up by Rathenau and Moellendorf in 1917–1918, foresaw the extension of many state controls into the post-war period.[32] Based upon an anticipated orderly release of troops by profession according to economic necessity,

30 *Ibid.*, pp. 135–41, 147–52, 357. See also Kuisel, *Capitalism and the state*, ch. 2, pp. 34–50, and ch. 3, pp. 59–62. For a revised assessment of the attitudes of the French ministers see John Godfrey, *Capitalism at war: industrial policy and bureaucracy in France, 1914–1918* (Leamington Spa, 1987), pp. 188–99; and Patrick Fridenson, 'Introduction: a new view of France at war', in P. Fridenson (ed.), *The French home front*, pp. 5–6.

31 Stephen Bailey, 'The Berlin strike of January 1918', *Central European History*, 13, 2 (June 1980), pp. 158–74.

32 G. D. Feldman, 'Economic and social problems', pp. 5–6. Already in August 1916 the Reichskommissar für Übergangswirtschaft (National Office for the Transition Economy) had been established, and throughout 1917 and 1918 the Labor Ministry entertained proposals and suggestions from unions and industry leaders for meeting the anticipated crisis of adaptation to peace. Organizations such as the Bund Deutscher Frauenvereine (Alliance of German Womens' Unions) and the Katholischer Frauenbund (Catholic Womens' Group) drew up plans for assisting the women who would be laid off from their wartime employment, while trade-union associations, such as the Generalkommission der Gewerkschaften Deutschlands (Directing Commission of German Unions), and the Hauptausschuss nationaler Arbeiter- und Berufsverbände Deutschlands (Directorial Committee of the National Workers' and employees' Association of Germany) challenged the government to establish clear guidelines for the distribution of food and scarce raw materials, for regulating working hours, as well as assistance to the unemployed and aid in finding housing. Bundesarchiv Potsdam (henceforth BAP), Rep. 39.01, n. 1734, 'Die Überleitung in die Friedenswirtschaft', pp. 2–6, 89–92, 112–14, 135–42.

these plans were rendered impractical by the Armistice agreement and the fall of the regime. According to the terms of the Armistice, all military forces were to be removed from foreign territory within fourteen days, and the west bank of the Rhine was to be clear of German troops by early December. War Minister Scheüch's decree of 16 November 1918 ruled that only those soldiers born before 1876 were to be released immediately, followed by the classes of 1877 to 1879 at the end of the month. All soldiers coming originally from Alsace-Lorraine received immediate leave to return to their families.[33] Scheüch's plan called for the gradual release of those soldiers born in 1880 or later, but in practice it was difficult to prevent units from melting away in the confusion of the retreat and the revolution.[34]

On 12 November 1918, the Reich Ministry for Economic Demobilization (RFWD), was set up under the direction of Colonel Joseph Koeth.[35] Koeth's Demobilization Office established a network of local Demobilization Commissions; the Demobilization Commission for Greater Berlin, which encompassed Charlottenburg, Spandau, Schöneberg, Lichtenberg, and Neukölln, was established on 21 November. In principle, there was to be parity between representatives of labour and industry on the Demobilization Commissions, but members from both groups were appointed by the RFWD rather than elected by their respective constituencies.[36] The measures to be taken by these commissions included the immediate revision of current war contracts, and the precise determination of the state of goods that were still under production. All goods that were finished as of 10 November were to be paid for in full. Problems encountered in the difficult task of reconvert-

[33] *Reichsanzeiger*, 275 (21 November 1918). Reproduced in Gerhard A. Ritter and Susanne Miller (eds.), *Die Deutsche Revolution 1918–1919. Dokumente* (Frankfurt, 1983), pp. 221–2.

[34] Among military and municipal authorities there was a great deal of anxiety that the flood of homecoming troops would contribute to the instability of German cities, especially in Berlin. Members of the III Army Command supported recruitment of soldiers for agricultural labour in the provinces, expressing the fear that 'the discharged will stream to Berlin looking for employment and expecting to be as well-paid as munitions workers. When they don't find such work, further unrest will be unavoidable' (BAP, Rep. 32.01 1, p. 104). On the lack of discipline during the demobilization see also Mai, 'Arbeitsmarktregulierung oder Sozialpolitik?', pp. 205–6.

[35] Koeth had been Director of the War Raw Materials Department (KRA) and was widely viewed at the time of his appointment to the Demobilization Office as being favourable to industry. Nevertheless, he was later perceived by employers as being too conciliatory towards labour, and he eventually lost their support. In April 1919, once the first troops were back in Germany, Koeth's office was disbanded and its operations absorbed into the Labour Ministry. See G. D. Feldman, 'Economic and social problems', p. 15; W. J. Mommsen (ed.), 'Die Organisierung des Friedens: Demobilmachung 1918–1920', *Geschichte und Gesellschaft*, 9 (1983), n. 2; and Detlev Peukert, *Die Weimarer Republik. Krisenjahre der klassischen Moderne* (Frankfurt, 1987), pp. 57–9.

[36] Frauke Bey-Heard, *Hauptstadt und Staatsumwälzung, Berlin 1919. Problematik und Scheitern der Rätebewegung in der Kommunalverwaltung* (Stuttgart, 1969), p. 115.

ing industry to a peacetime footing would be mediated by a new corporate body, the so-called Zentral Arbeitsgemeinschaft set up under the terms of the Stinnes–Legien agreement, which provided for the participation of both labour and employers in the demobilization process. Within the locally organized Arbeitsgemeinschaft every branch of industry would have its own committee (Fachausschuss) which would work in tandem with the district Demobilization Commission to deal with such difficult problems as the distribution of raw materials, the regulation of work hours, pricing, and wages. Wherever possible, production was to be redirected and maintained as a prop for sustaining employment levels. Koeth's office was even ready to renegotiate government prices in some industries in order to maintain production as a hedge against further unemployment.[37] In spite of the political chaos which accompanied the revolution, Koeth's Demobilization Commissions and the Arbeitsgemeinschaft functioned surprisingly smoothly; cooperation between officials, employers and labour leaders was facilitated by the widely shared desire to normalize the economic situation as quickly as possible.[38]

Demobilization in France, Britain, and Germany thus required that the respective governments take a position on two primary questions: would labour be allowed a voice in the management process and in defining the specifics of industrial reconversion? Would the state take an active role in guiding the transition to peacetime production? Officials in the victorious countries were confident enough in the fragile social consensus which existed in France and Britain to answer a qualified no on both counts. In Germany, on the other hand, the threat of a complete descent into chaos forced the Kaiser's successors to grant many concessions to labour leaders, and to consider a more conciliatory approach. In all three cases the decisions taken in 1919 were made with special consideration of the situation in the three capitals, where the unemployment crises of January–April 1919 were most strongly felt and where the threat of unrest was greatest. Were these policies justified on the basis of the crisis posed by demobilization in each case? In order to answer this question we will now turn to the actual crisis of unemployment in each city.

The unemployment crisis of 1919

The relative severity of the post-war unemployment crisis in London and Paris was primarily a function of their respective plans for releasing soldiers from military service. The intensity of the Berlin crisis, on the other hand, reflected the weaknesses inherent in the German war

[37] See letter from Koeth, 3 December 1918, 'An alle Demobilmachungskommissare und Beschaffungsstellen sowie alle Gruppen . . . ', BAP, Rep. 32.01, n. 1, pp. 165–7.

[38] Peukert, *Die Weimarer Republik*, p. 58.

economy, the chaos of defeat, and the tendency of released soldiers, repatriated Germans from occupied territories, and refugees to gather in the German capital. In London and Berlin the peak level of unemployment arrived early, in February and March 1919; in Paris the apex was not reached until April. In all three cases, however, the worst period of unemployment was over by the summer of 1919. Paris's level of unemployment fell most quickly, while the number of jobless in London declined more slowly, and was never completely absorbed throughout the post-war boom of April 1919 to April 1920. Berlin's level of unemployment also declined significantly after reaching its peak in February 1919, and the increases in male employment were substantial between October 1918 and April 1919. Nevertheless, the recovery was slow and there were worrisome signs of stagnation in some sectors, especially in the powerful metals and machine branch.

The case of London will be examined first. In November 1918, the British workforce as a whole already included more than 820,000 workers who had been demobilized from the armed forces, a further 4,500,000 remained under arms, the vast majority of whom had to be reabsorbed into civilian life and the civilian labour market during the next eighteen months.[39] The government attempted to control this process of demobilization by giving priority to men who had definite offers of employment (the so-called 'slip men'), but the fear of serious unrest within the home army meant that many had to be released with no immediate prospect of employment in civilian life.[40] Estimates based on national insurance and out-of-work donation returns for the period of the post-war demobilization suggest that between May 1919 and May 1920 – virtually the whole of the period of the post-war boom – more than 70 per cent of the male unemployed in Britain were ex-servicemen.[41] Many were either partially disabled men unable to find work in their old trades, or young men who had no established trade to which they could return. The government introduced a series of training schemes and voluntary agreements with employers in the hope of improving prospects for these men, but it seems likely that the onset of the slump in late 1920 did much to undermine their efforts. As late as 1921 the British Legion claimed that 80 per cent of the unemployed were ex-servicemen.[42]

[39] Dearle, *Labor cost of the world war*, pp. 29–30. Also see S. Graubard, 'Military demobilization in Great Britain' and K. Jeffery, 'The post-war army' in I. Beckett and K. Simpson (eds.), *A nation in arms: a social study of the British army in the First World War* (Manchester, 1985), pp. 212–15. A small proportion of these soldiers would have been self-employed, and some would almost certainly have been too disabled to compete in the labour market, government schemes to aid their re-employment notwithstanding.

[40] See A. Rothstein, *The Soldiers' Strikes of 1919* (London, 1980).

[41] Dearle, *The labor cost of the world war*, pp. 159–67.

[42] S.R. Ward (ed.), *The war generation* (Port Washington, N.Y., 1975), p. 22.

Dearle's estimates show (table 7.1, column 1) that unemployment in Britain reached its peak in March and April 1919, declining thereafter as the post-war boom began. Unemployment in London appears to have followed broadly the same pattern, although good data are lacking. Nevertheless, partial data from specific branches of the labour market indicate that London's experience was not markedly different from that of the country as a whole. National Insurance returns suggest that in the engineering industry unemployment rose from about 1.4 per cent at the Armistice to 14.4 per cent in March 1919, but had fallen back to 6.4 per cent by August 1919. The London building trades followed a similar cycle with unemployment rising from 1 per cent at the Armistice, to 13.8 per cent in February, before falling back to 3.6 per cent by August 1919, although this movement was accentuated by the normal seasonal pattern of employment in the building trade (table 7.1, columns 2 and 3).

In France, on the other hand, a more gradual system of military demobilization ensured that the impact on the labour market would be less severe. The first wave of homecoming soldiers arrived on 1 December 1918 when all men aged fifty to fifty-two were discharged. Every ten days another birth cohort was released, such that between December and 3 April 1919 all soldiers thirty-three and older had been given leave to return home. The younger cohorts, aged twenty-two to thirty-two, were eventually released after the signing of the peace treaty, between July and October 1919. Given that the younger veterans were not released until later, demobilization in Paris did not place quite the same pressure on the labour market as in London, and this pressure was especially attenuated after April, once the first wave of discharges had been accomplished.[43]

Of course, the increase in unemployment did appear substantial to the Parisians themselves. The total number registered as unemployed in Paris soared from 11,665 in late December 1918 to 77,514 in early April 1919, an increase of approximately 66,000 in just over twelve weeks (see table 7.1, column 4). This increase in the early weeks of 1919 is not as large as one may have supposed under the circumstances, however. A more severe disturbance to employment patterns seems to have been largely avoided due to the efforts of the Departmental Placement Office of the Seine, which succeeded in finding employment for 99,000 workers in 1918 and 177,000 in 1919.[44] This office was maintained after the war and proved to be an efficient and indispensable addition to the

[43] The first phase of demobilization affected only the classes of 1887 to 1906, some 2,500,000 men altogether. The second phase of demobilization, concerning the classes of 1907 to 1917, brought a further 2,000,000 soldiers back to civilian life. See Antoine Prost, *Les anciens combattants et la société française, 1914–1939*, vol. I (Paris, 1977), p. 48.

[44] The same office had found employment for 16,000 workers in 1916 and 47,000 in 1917. See note 43.

Table 7.1. *Number unemployed in Paris and Berlin, and percentage unemployed in two sectors of the London labour market, November 1918 to December 1920*

Date	Britain	London Engineering (%)	London Building (%)	Paris	Berlin	Greater Berlin
Nov. 1918	69,807	1	1	9,440	10,342	—
Dec. 1918	380,695	7	6	11,665	48,705	—
Jan. 1919	678,703	11	7	—	106,371	—
Feb. 1919	948,620	13	14	37,221	182,641	275,000
Mar. 1919	1,060,245	14	14	—	185,845	—
Apr. 1919	1,093,328	11	13	77,514	175,021	—
May 1919	771,211	12	10	—	161,228	208,000
June 1919	606,125	8	6	—	139,497	—
July 1919	495,884	8	5	—	112,056	—
Aug. 1919	478,084	6	4	26,629	94,711	—
Sept. 1919	403,003	6	3	—	82,202	—
Oct. 1919	479,427	7	4	—	75,832	—
Nov. 1919	544,899	7	6	—	64,748	—
Dec. 1919	593,085	10	7	1,266	51,167	70,000
Jan. 1920	580,786	11	7	—	—	—
Feb. 1920	455,091	9	5	—	—	—
Mar. 1920	379,206	7	3	—	—	—
Apr. 1920	334,849	7	2	—	—	—
May 1920	310,326	7	3	—	—	—
June 1920	290,315	7	4	—	—	—
July 1920	271,879	7	3	—	—	—
Aug. 1920	276,099	7	5	—	34,054	—
Sept. 1920	334,810	7	—	—	—	78,415
Oct. 1920	583,885	—	—	—	—	81,467
Nov. 1920	—	—	—	—	—	87,609
Dec. 1920	—	—	—	—	—	94,670

Sources: Berlin: Nov. 1918–April 1919 – *Die wirtschaftliche Demobilmachung*, vol. 2, no. 67 (1919), p. 575; May 1919–Dec. 1919 – Brandenburg, LHA, Pr.Br.Rep.30 Berlin C, no. 1959, *Jahresberichte der Gewerbe-Aufsicht*, p. 15; Aug. 1920 – *Reichsarbeitsblatt*, vol. 1 (1920/21), p. 4; Sept. 1920–Dec. 1920 – *Reichsarbeitsblatt*, vol. 1 (1920/1), *passim*. Paris: Robert, 'Ouvriers et mouvement ouvrier', vol. 2, p. 359. London: Board of Trade, *Labour Gazette*, 1919–21.

urban administration. Shortened working hours, which had sunk below seven hours per day in some cases even before the eight-hour law of April 1919, also served to alleviate some of the strain on the labour market. The cumulative effect of these different factors is demonstrated in the steady decline in the unemployment figure after April 1919. The figure was more than halved by October 1919, and it was down to 1,200 in December. In May 1920 only seventy people remained on the unemployment lists in Paris.

Other factors certainly played a role in minimizing the rise in unemployment in Paris. Almost half of the women employed in munitions factories had already left their jobs by January 1919, a double effect of a government indemnity system and the willingness of other women to return to their pre-war occupations. A storm of circulars and official measures was aimed at the elimination of female industrial labour: the hiring of women was forbidden in state-owned establishments and openings in private firms were reserved for demobilized soldiers. The trade unions cooperated with this effort, and were quick to assert that women's labour constituted unwelcome competition, bringing wages down and disrupting family life. The pressure seems to have worked: in March 1919 a government report noted that of 91,000 men who had worked in war industry 62,000 were still employed, while only 20,700 women remained from the 48,000 who had once worked the assembly lines. Also remarkable was the massive layoff of foreign workers who had played their part in the war effort. By the end of November 1918 only 4 per cent of the colonial workers remained in France, and of these the greater part had stayed behind illegally. The forced departure of the colonial workers was particularly abrupt and brutal, so much the more so because their presence was seen by officials to be a provocation to the returning veterans.[45] When one adds to these factors the demobilization of those workers enlisted from the provinces to work in Parisian munitions factories, then one can explain the relatively low increase in male unemployment in Paris during this period.

In Berlin, the chaos which accompanied the Armistice caused an extremely rapid increase in unemployment. By the end of November 1918 there were already over 10,000 unemployed workers in the city; six weeks later, in early January, the figure was well over 100,000. According to the published reports of the Demobilization Office, the number of unemployed in the city did not peak until March, when a

[45] Nevertheless, this hard-line policy with respect to colonial and immigrant workers did not last. Already before the end of 1919 it had become necessary to have recourse to immigrant labour, demonstrating that the lessons of the war were to have their effect on employment patterns in the 1920s and 1930s.

figure of 185,845 jobless workers was recorded.[46] On 21 February 1919 the total figure for Greater Berlin stood at 276,420.[47] Just over two months later, the figure for Berlin proper had only subsided to 161,228, and in that same month, May 1919, 208,174 people registered their search for jobs at the Greater Berlin Labour Exchange. It should be noted that these figures are most likely to be underestimates, as in many cases non-union workers were not counted, and the registration of unemployed women was notoriously incomplete. The intensity of the crisis in Berlin can be gauged by the comments of one observer, who estimated that of the 1,041,000 unemployed workers in Germany in early March 1919, 275,000 were in the capital.[48]

Despite the fact that Berlin's unemployment figures declined after February 1919 in a manner similar to that in Paris and London, the intensity of the crisis in Berlin meant that substantial numbers of workers were still left jobless at the end of the year. In December 1919 there were still 51,168 jobless workers in Berlin proper, and over 70,000 in the greater metropolitan area (see table 7.1, columns 5 and 6). This picture of a severe crisis in unemployment in Berlin stands in sharp contrast to the situation in Germany as a whole, where unemployment peaked in January 1919 and had largely subsided by April. Richard Bessel has pointed out that those areas which were net population losers during the war (Berlin's population fell by nearly 16 per cent between 1914 and 1918) often became centres of unemployment after the war as those who had left returned home.[49] In fact, between 1 November 1918 and 31 January 1919 Berlin had a net in-migration of over 230,000 people. Although this group contained many returning soldiers, one should recognize as well that Berlin was a natural destination for refugees from the lost territories, and for foreigners of German extraction who followed the troops home.[50]

The most significant factor in alleviating this pressure on the German capital was the *Reichsverordnung* of 28 March 1919, which aimed at forcing people to return to their pre-war residences. The version of the decree passed by the Greater Berlin Demobilization Commission

[46] Brandenburg LHA, Pr.Br.Rep.30 Berlin C, n. 1959, Jahresberichte der Gewerbe-Aufsicht, p. 15.

[47] *Die Wirtschaftliche Demobilmachung*, 2 (21 Feb. 1919). See also figures given in Klaus Dettmer, *Arbeitslose in Berlin. Zur politischen Geschichte der Arbeitslosenbewegung zwischen 1918 und 1923*, dissertation, Freie Universität Berlin, 1977, pp. 51–7.

[48] Friedrich Reichardt, *Die Entlassung Auswärtiger* (Berlin, 1919), p. VI.

[49] Bessel, 'Unemployment and demobilization', p. 31. Bessel points to Saxony as another example of an area which had lost population during the war and which subsequently became a centre for unemployment in the post-war period.

[50] Robert Scholz, 'Die Auswirkung der Inflation auf das Sozial- und Wohlfahrtswesen der neuen Stadtgemeinde Berlin', in G. D. Feldman, C.-L. Holtfrerich, G. A. Ritter, and P.-C. Witt (eds.), *Konsequenzen der Inflation* (Berlin, 1989), pp. 45–75, here p. 58.

ordered that those who had moved to their current residence after 1 August 1914 should return to their pre-war homes, and it enforced this provision by limiting the amount to time that they could receive unemployment benefits while remaining in Berlin to only four weeks. In Berlin the payment was later limited further, to only two weeks. Berlin's labour market was one of the principal beneficiaries of this order, and one historian has estimated that it may have opened up as many as 40,000 jobs in the capital, compared with 10,000 in Nuremberg, 2,500 in Frankfurt and 1,000 in Düsseldorf.[51] Also contributing to the alleviation of unemployment were the many public works projects financed by the various municipalities of Greater Berlin; these projects were primarily emergency, stopgap measures, however, and had little long-term effect upon the labour market in the city.[52]

Unemployment figures are a useful gauge of the relative severity of the dislocation caused by demobilization in the three cities, but they are more meaningful when used in conjunction with data on employment in the different branches of industry.[53] For London, two comprehensive surveys of employment carried out by the Board of Trade in January and April 1919 provide the necessary data. If we look first at employment patterns in the three main sectors of employment: industry, commerce, and transport, we can see that change was far from even

[51] Bey-Heard, *Hauptstadt*, pp. 117–18. See also Ernst Kaeber, *Berlin im Weltkriege* (Berlin, 1921), p. 16.

[52] Plans to absorb Berlin's oversupply of available labour into public works projects had some initial success, as evidenced by a March report on a project to extend the underground rail service in Neukölln. Public buildings were another important area of employment support, and during 1919 a tuberculosis sanitarium for children was built in Berlin, a Labour Office and a hospital extension were constructed in Lichtenberg, while Neukölln built a welfare office and a nursing home. In Schöneberg, the roofs of 300 private buildings were repaired through such public works funds and labour, while in Charlottenburg workers were hired to refurbish the city's schools. Street repairs, especially in Charlottenburg and Lichterfelde, employed up to 10,000 workers for an average of four and a half months each during this period, while an additional 5,700 were employed in the extension of water mains and plumbing facilities in Neukölln, Tempelhof, Lichterfelde, Spandau, Grunewald, and Berlin itself. All told, such projects employed approximately 30,000 people throughout 1919 and early 1920, although rarely for longer than four or five months at a time. Furthermore, these projects were often hindered by the same difficulties in obtaining raw materials that faced private industry. See *Reichsarbeitsblatt*, 17, 4 (April 1919), p. 288; and 'Zur Sonderaktion für die Gross-Berliner Erwerbslosen', *Reichsarbeitsblatt*, 1, 5 (May 1920), pp. 179–80.

[53] In the context of civilian and military demobilization, trade-based unemployment statistics can be misleading since they take no account of the net flow of workers in or out of different occupations. For example, a shrinking workforce (employed and unemployed) could cause a decline in unemployment in a given sector, thus reflecting a movement of labour into other areas of the economy. Likewise, unemployment could decline in sectors whose total workforce was expanding, if the expansion was fast enough to absorb the number of new workers seeking employment in that sector.

Table 7.2. *The course of employment in major sectors of the London economy, November 1918 to April 1919 (November 1918 = 100)*

Sector	11 Nov. 1918	31 Jan. 1919	30 Apr. 1919
Industry	100	88.7	90.6
Males	100	96.6	106.2
Females	100	80.3	73.1
Commerce[a]	100	102.7	102.4
Males	100	108.0	124.9
Females	100	98.3	94.6
Transport[b]	100	103.2	125.4
Males	100	106.9	144.4
Females	100	93.4	72.8
All '28' trades	100	92.1	95.7

Notes: [a]Excludes all local government workers.
[b]Tramway and bus services only.
Source: Board of Trade, *State of Employment Reports for January 31st 1919 and the end of April 1919.*

(table 7.2). First, it can be seen that while male employment was generally on the increase, female employment declined in all sectors. This was undoubtedly a direct result of the reabsorption of ex-servicemen into the labour market, and the release of women (partly voluntary, partly not) from jobs that they had held 'for the duration'. It is noticeable that the release of women was considerably greater in the industrial and transport sectors than in commerce, where uniquely the increased wartime employment of women became a permanent feature. There was also a much more rapid increase in male employment in transport than in industry. This reflects the fact that London industries had absorbed large numbers of male as well as female employees during the war, many of whom were now being released, while the transport sector had experienced both a considerable net fall in employment and the large-scale replacement of male labour by women workers.[54]

Aggregate statistics of employment and unemployment can, however, provide only a very partial insight into the dramatic processes of adaptation which characterized the immediate post-war period in London. As well as the first waves of servicemen who had to be reabsorbed into the labour market, there were also thousands of former war-workers anxious to find employment in civilian industries. In addition, significant numbers of workers were displaced from their

[54] See chapter 6.

employment by the implementation of the Restoration of Pre-War Practices Act. The result was rapid and dramatic shifts in the distribution of the London labour force (see table 7.3). As with the transport sector, trades which had seen the greatest contraction of employment during the war, which now saw the greatest net increases. Particularly dynamic were industries such as food and drink, printing, and clothing where normal patterns of demand had been constrained by wartime austerity and the government's determination to give priority to the major war industries over scarce raw materials and labour power.[55] In these trades substantial increases in male employment levels were *not* accompanied by any significant fall in the numbers of women workers. In all other industries female employment appears to have fallen substantially in the immediate post-war period, with the largest falls occurring in the main war industries such as metals and chemicals (female employment in the building trade was never extensive, and declined especially rapidly after the war). As one might expect, the most substantial falls occurred in the government's own war factories, where nearly 80 per cent of women, and over 40 per cent of men had been released by the end of April 1919 (table 7.3).

By April 1919 male employment had increased in all London industries other than these government munitions factories, although it rose by only 2 per cent in the case of the metal and engineering trades, which appear to have been shedding wartime recruits almost as quickly as they reabsorbed ex-servicemen. Since male industrial employment had actually been about 3 per cent below its wartime level at the end of January 1919, this would suggest that the last three months of the 'breathing space' (November 1918 to March 1919) witnessed a 10 per cent net increase in male employment (table 7.3). Much of this increase was probably at the expense of women workers brought into industry 'for the duration', but none the less it does suggest the resilience of the post-war London economy.

Data on post-war employment in Berlin were published in the *Gross-Berlin Statistische Monatsberichte* and although they indicate some rough similarities to the situation in London, the differences are significant. Given the intensity of the unemployment crisis, the Berlin economy shows signs of a remarkable dynamism in the first few months of peace, although this dynamism may be merely a sign of how far the situation had deteriorated before the Armistice (see table 7.3). As in the British capital, the sectors of the Berlin economy which had suffered the worst contraction during the war were the quickest to expand after November 1918, especially printing and paper manufacture, and the food, wood,

[55] P. Dewey, 'Military recruiting and the British labour force during the First World War', *Historical Journal*, 27, 1 (1984), pp. 199–223.

Table 7.3. *An index of employment levels for men and women in Greater Berlin and London, by industrial sector, October/November 1918 to April/December 1919 (October 1918 = 100 for Berlin; November 1918 = 100 for London)*

		Males				Females				Total			
Trade	City	1918	1/19	4/19	12/19	1918	1/19	4/19	12/19	1918	1/19	4/19	12/19
Paper and printing	London	100	108	132	—	100	103	101	—	100	—	—	—
	Berlin	100	144	162	315	100	100	92	99	100	118	121	132
Food	London	100	103	131	—	100	95	96	—	100	—	—	—
	Berlin	100	149	167	264	100	100	99	78	100	122	130	136
Clothing	London	100	109	124	—	100	101	100	—	100	—	—	—
	Berlin	100	118	136	590	100	84	88	100	100	91	96	113
Wood	London	100	99	123	—	100	75	67	—	100	—	—	—
	Berlin	100	114	136	203	100	85	79	95	100	106	119	143
Building	London	100	107	118	—	100	80	49	—	100	—	—	—
	Berlin	100	116	145	184	100	68	61	56	100	106	127	146
Chemicals	London	100	87	114	—	100	55	65	—	100	—	—	—
	Berlin	100	125	132	238	100	84	61	64	100	100	89	93
Metals and machines	London	100	94	102	—	100	66	53	—	100	—	—	—
	Berlin	100	104	96	134	100	73	53	47	100	89	75	69
Government factories	London	100	74	59	—	100	42	21	—	100	—	—	—
	Berlin	100	123	147	179	100	90	65	36	100	105	100	80
Commerce	London	100	108	125	—	100	98	95	—	100	—	—	—
	Berlin	100	151	179	441	100	99	97	95	100	113	119	116
Transport	London	100	107	144	—	100	93	73	—	100	—	—	—
	Berlin	100	155	197	236	100	89	44	21	100	127	133	137
Total	London	100	97	106	—	100	80	73	—	100	—	—	—
	Berlin	100	117	126	191	100	84	67	57	100	99	94	98

Sources: London: Board of Trade, *State of Employment Reports*, 31 Jan. 1919 and April 1919. Berlin: *Gross-Berlin Statistische Monatsberichte*, vol. 5, no. 12, pp. 30–5.

and transport industries. In these four sectors the absorption of returning troops was rapid in Berlin, far outstripping the pace of expansion observed in London.[56] The increase in male employment in the Berlin chemical industry also stands out: an increase of 25 per cent between October 1918 and January 1919, while in London the figure fell 13 per cent. A further important difference is the 47 per cent *increase* in male employment in Berlin's state-owned factories between October 1918 and April 1919, at a time when London's government factories cut back on male employment by 41 per cent. Similarly, whereas female employment in London's government factories fell almost 80 per cent, state factories in Berlin limited their cuts to only 35 per cent. These differences indicate the extent to which the government in Berlin was committed to propping up employment in the state-owned enterprises in an attempt to lessen the impact of the defeat on the working population.[57]

The reason such measures were necessary was obvious. The backbone of Berlin's industrial economy, the metals and machines sector, continued to release workers in large numbers throughout 1919. In fact, employment in this sector, which had been almost 30 per cent higher than its July 1914 level in October 1918 had sunk to a level 10 per cent *lower* than its pre-war level by December 1919 (see table 7.4). By the latter date, male employment had increased by 34 per cent since October 1918, but the number of men who joined the workforce in this sector could not make up for the large numbers of women who left employment. The reasons for the slow recovery in this sector were the continued shortage of raw materials, especially a lack of coal, and a wave of strikes which hit the Berlin factories in September and October 1919.[58]

[56] This disparity between London and Berlin may be exaggerated slightly by the fact that the base for comparison is the October 1918 figure for Berlin and November 1918 for London. Nevertheless, the fact that London may have already begun to absorb some of its returning troops in November (thereby decreasing the percentage change observed by January) should not distract from the basic assertion made here, that certain sectors of Berlin's economy were able to absorb the returning soldiers relatively rapidly. The fact that the Berlin figures are for firms employing more than twenty-five workers may also account for some of the disparity.

[57] The situation in the Berlin munitions industry was quite varied in the weeks and months after the Armistice. For example, in the week of 17–25 January 1919 the Artillerie-Depot Spandau had yet to suffer any layoffs and was still operating eight-hour shifts. The Firma R. Linka, also in Spandau, had let go of some workers, but was still employing 300 women in the manufacture of explosives for mineworkers on five-hour shifts. The Firma Garbaty in Pankow, also a military contractor, had yet to let go of any of its 800 women employees and was able to keep production going seven hours per day. In contrast, however, the Deutsche Maschinenbau AG in Wildau was being completely shut down by degrees, letting go of its 300 women employees. Likewise, the large rubber manufacturer, Runge-Werke in Spandau, was laying off all women and was down to three to four-hour shifts. BAP, Rep. 32.01, n. 18/1, pp. 220–1.

[58] See *Reichsarbeitsblatt*, 17, 10 (October 1919), p. 757 and 11 (November 1919), p. 833.

Table 7.4. *An index of levels of employment in post-war Berlin, in firms with 25+ employees (July 1914 = 100)*

Trade	July 1914	Oct. 1918	Jan. 1919	Apr. 1919	June 1919	Aug. 1919	Oct. 1919	Dec. 1919
Agriculture and gardening	100	68	59	72	84	85	84	76
Brick and stone	100	39	47	48	55	62	60	58
Metalwork and machines	100	129	114	96	97	97	94	89
Chemicals	100	97	97	97	89	92	90	90
Lighting and soap	100	71	87	90	92	96	101	103
Textiles and clothing	100	52	47	50	52	54	56	59
Printing and paper	100	60	71	73	76	76	75	80
Leather	100	93	60	57	57	55	62	61
Wood	100	53	56	63	48	68	72	75
Foods	100	46	56	59	58	57	57	54
Cleaning	100	50	55	56	58	58	55	56
Building	100	32	34	41	48	51	49	47
Commerce	100	65	73	77	77	75	75	76
Transport	100	58	74	77	79	80	80	80
Hotels and restaurants	100	59	56	60	63	66	67	69
Music and theatre	100	52	63	63	66	64	65	61
State	100	235	246	239	222	219	204	189
Other	100	108	109	111	113	113	110	92
Total	100	103	102	97	96	97	94	91

Source: Gross-Berlin Statistische Monatsberichte, vol. 5, no. 12 (1919), pp. 30–5.

As in London, Berlin's female employment declined abruptly after the Armistice, especially in the war-related industries and in transport, while remaining relatively constant in commerce. The release of women in the transport sector was worse in Berlin: a decline of 56 per cent by April 1919, compared to 27 per cent in London. The number of women employed in the Berlin metals and machine trades fell 47 per cent between October 1918 and April 1919, and figures for London show a similar decline. During the same period the Berlin chemical branch lost 39 per cent of its female employees, while the corresponding sector in London fell by 35 per cent. But while female employment in London's textile and clothing sector remained relatively constant throughout this period, the number of women employed in Berlin in this sector fell considerably, by about 16 per cent. In London, the end of the war brought new life to these sectors; in Berlin, on the other hand, the continuation of the Allied blockade, disorder in Eastern Europe, and a subsequent shortage of raw materials prolonged the stagnation of the textile branch.

Nevertheless, not all the Berlin women who entered the industrial workforce during the war left immediately after the Armistice. The decline was more gradual, such that the figure for women's employment in the metals and machine sector was still 38 per cent higher in December 1919 than the pre-war level (72,079 in December 1919 compared to 52,065 in July 1914). Similarly, the number of women who entered the transport sector during the war declined substantially after the Armistice (almost 80 per cent between October 1918 and December 1919), but not completely, and the figure in December 1919 was still almost 60 per cent higher than the pre-war level.

A further cause of this more gradual decline in female employment was almost certainly the shortage of manpower resulting from military losses; this factor played a role in all three cities. Its extent is difficult to determine, given the resumption of internal and international migration after the war. But since over 50,000 Berliners died on active military service, there were inevitable gaps in the labour force which in the short term some women filled.

Unfortunately, it is not possible to compare employment levels in Paris to those of Berlin and London for these months. Nevertheless, certain conclusions are possible. When the total number employed in the Paris region is indexed against a base of 100 for 1914, one finds a level of 120 for the period 1917–1918, falling to 110 in January 1919 and 91 in July 1919, after which point it begins to climb again. Of course, the decline in the first six months of 1919 was very uneven in its distribution throughout the economy and, as in Berlin and London, it concerned primarily employment in metal manufacture, machines, and chemicals. By June 1919 several of the most important Parisian war factories had seen their employment lists fall to 40 per cent of the peaks registered for the boom years of 1917 to 1918. Some factories closed their doors completely for periods of up to several weeks. As in the British and German capitals, however, those sectors which had been most affected by the war, such as printing and the building trades, were stimulated into renewal by the cease in hostilities.[59]

In all three cities, then, the crisis was traumatic but ultimately of short duration. The rise in unemployment was sharpest in London and Berlin, while authorities in Paris were more successful in minimizing the deleterious effects of the transition upon the urban labour market. The release of women from wartime employment was pronounced in all

[59] Robert, 'Ouvriers et mouvement ouvrier', p. 1846.

three cities and was especially abrupt in Paris. In Berlin, on the other hand, there is evidence that the decline in female employment was more gradual and did not entirely return to pre-war levels by the end of 1919. In London the textile and clothing trades rebounded or held steady after the Armistice, whereas in Berlin the continued shortage of raw materials resulting from the blockade drove this sector further into decline. Finally, state-owned factories in London witnessed sharp drops in both male and female employment, while in Berlin this decline only affected female workers, and male employment in state-owned factories actually increased substantially after November 1918.

In general, the labour outlook in 1919 was distorted by the effects of military mobilization and military losses. As we have seen in chapter 3, the total war dead for Greater London and the Department of the Seine each exceeded 100,000; over 50,000 Berliners were also killed or died on active service. Casualty rates varied as between armies and service branches, but a conservative estimate of the ratio of the wounded to men killed is of the order of 2:1. This yields a further estimate of 500,000 wounded men whose transition to peacetime work was inevitably problematic. How far these casualties distorted the labour market is impossible to say; to ignore their presence is an absurdity.

Economic policy and the transition

Did the policies followed at the national level help or hinder the economic recovery of London, Paris, and Berlin in the post-war period? The labour market in London certainly benefitted in the short run from British monetary policy in the spring of 1919. From the point of view of the common soldier, however, the measures put forth by the Ministry of Labour to reintegrate the veteran into British society promised more than they eventually delivered. In Paris, the government's quick withdrawal from the economy after the Armistice had mixed results for the labour market in Paris. If Parisian labourers could congratulate themselves upon gaining the long-sought eight-hour bill, they also found the government to be increasingly unsympathetic to their demands. Only in Germany, however, are we presented with a situation where the needs and priorities of the capital city came into direct conflict with a policy implemented at the national level.

In March 1919 the British government extended the wartime prohibition on the export of gold coin and bullion, thereby postponing the return of Britain to the Gold Standard.[60] This policy was designed to prevent the Bank of England from imposing a high discount rate to

[60] S. Howson, *Domestic monetary management in Britain, 1919–1938* (Cambridge, 1975), pp. 11–23.

defend its gold reserve, since this would have constricted credit severely, and made it impossible for the economy to reabsorb the large numbers of men still to be demobilized from the armed forces. Had the government not stayed off gold, there would have been no post-war boom, and the economy would have been plunged into an early and severe recession. In November 1919 the British authorities attempted to halt rapid monetary expansion by raising the Bank of England discount rate from 5 per cent (its wartime level) to 6 per cent. This policy had little effect, but it was not until 15 April 1920 that the Bank raised the discount rate by a further 1 per cent, by which time it could be said that the post-war boom was already largely played out. Thus, for the whole period of the post-war boom, government monetary policy exerted very little restraining influence on economic activity. Credit remained cheap and plentiful so that firms were able to borrow heavily to finance restocking and retooling.[61] In addition, the rapid removal of government wartime controls over industry, raw materials, and prices further limited the scope for any central restraining influence. As a result, the post-war optimism of industrialists was given free rein, new investment was heavy, and production costs soared, until, early in 1920, the once-and-for-all demand associated with restocking, deferred civilian consumption, and the replacement of equipment damaged or worn out during the war began to decline.

In so far as the nation benefitted from the post-war boom, so too did the London economy. But if British monetary policy played an effective role in absorbing the worst of the immediate unemployment caused by demobilization, less can be said for the various schemes put forth by the Ministry of Labour to reintegrate the veteran into the peacetime economy. The ministry's Industrial Training Scheme, which aimed at retraining wounded soldiers for industrial labour met with some success, and claimed to have placed as many as two-thirds of the 100,000 veterans who participated. A lack of cooperation from trade unions, who feared a loss of their right to certify skilled labour as a result of the retraining schemes, hindered the Ministry's efforts, however, and led to considerable disillusionment on the part of the veterans themselves.[62]

The same series of decisions which gave rise to the post-war boom in Britain also set off a great deal of monetary instability in France. In March 1919 the British Treasury also declared a halt to the advances it had been paying to the French government throughout the war. The devaluation of the franc followed; the rate of exchange rose from 5.45 to the dollar in March 1919 to 11 to the dollar by the end of the year.[63] Within this inflationary context, the Ministry of Industrial Reconstruc-

[61] Pigou, *Aspects*, pp. 176–83.

[62] Englander, 'Demobilmachung in Grossbritannien', pp. 204–6.

[63] Gide and Oualid, *Le bilan de la guerre*, pp. 315ff.

tion, under Louis Loucheur, attempted to negotiate the return to a free market. This propensity to return to the *status quo ante bellum* was clearly in the collective mind of the Paris Municipal Council. Until the Armistice, the Municipal Council made a practice of supporting the propositions of the minority Socialists calling for a more interventionist policy. After 11 November, however, the council did an about-face, and voted against such propositions, throwing its weight instead behind a series of actions which favoured the freedom of commerce and enterprise. At issue were socialist-sponsored measures to maintain price controls in the transport sector, and extensions on municipal spending. In the same spirit, Clemenceau refused to concede to the establishment of the Economic and Social Council called for by the CGT. Even in the tumultuous months between January and July 1919, when there were 171 strikes in Paris, the state intervened in the conflicts only on 22 occasions, including the times when it intervened with force.[64]

This reticence on the part of the state was all the more remarkable in Paris, where the militancy of the working populations was especially vexing to both employers and officials. Paris metal-workers, for example, played a central role in the wave of strikes in May and June of 1919. Although the April 17 agreement on the eight-hour day had been settled at the national level, the details of the accords were left to be negotiated locally, and Paris workers were angry to discover that real wages were to be maintained not through pay increases but in concessions to mechanization and automation, which would increase production. When the union representatives demanded a further reduction of the work week to forty-four hours, the employers balked and 165,000 workers went on strike. As Horne recounts the story, the factory owners quickly took advantage of the situation by declaring a lockout and using the work stoppage as an opportunity to retool the workshops.[65] This outcome shows the complexity of the situation in Paris during the period immediately following the Armistice.

The depth of the crisis in Berlin and the continued political uncertainty of 1919 placed the municipal administration in a difficult position, halfway between the radical demands of the revolution's leaders and the desire of the Demobilization Office to create a climate favourable to private enterprise. Unlike the situations in Paris and London, where city government was never thrown into question, the crisis in Berlin revealed the limits of the municipal government's authority. On 18 November, Mayor Wermuth told the City Council that he had been in contact with the workers' and soldiers' councils who controlled the city after the revolution of the 9th, and that he would continue to perform his

[64] Robert, 'Ouvriers et mouvement ouvrier', p. 1834.
[65] John Horne, *Labour at war*, pp. 371–2.

administrative functions.[66] In fact, the burden quickly became too much for Wermuth's administration to handle on its own. On 3 December 1918 the Demobilization Commission for Berlin extended its jurisdiction to all localities covered by the Greater Berlin Bread Rationing Cooperative, and one month later the same commission decreed that the cost of supporting the increasing numbers of unemployed in the city should be more equally distributed among the various constituent parts of Greater Berlin.[67] Thus, although an avowed goal of the demobilization authorities was decontrol of economic activity, the process worked toward a greater political integration of Greater Berlin, and presaged the absorption of the surrounding suburbs into a newly enlarged municipality in October 1920.

The conflict between the Koeth's Demobilization Office and the municipal government came to a climax over the issue of unemployment benefits. The absence of a national minimum level of support meant that urban areas, whose local wage rates were higher, would also have the highest level of unemployment payments. Berlin city officials appealed to the national and state level authorities for a change in the regulation, in the interest of removing a further incentive for the unemployed to gather in the capital. On 12 December 1918 Mayor Wermuth wrote an urgent letter to Koeth complaining about the arrangement, stating that 'it is not so much a matter of the greater financial burden [faced by the Berlin administration] but the extraordinary danger of having so many idle workers in large urban areas'.[68] Claiming that the Reich and Prussian authorities had been generous with advice but had not provided any practical assistance to the problems of the cities, Wermuth called for a national minimum unemployment rate of 3.0 marks per day (Berlin's was 4.0 marks at the time) to be implemented immediately. He acknowledged that agrarian interests were opposed to such a minimum, as it would discourage attempts to recruit workers for farm work in the countryside, but he justified the demand on the grounds that the cities had suffered more

[66] LAB (STA), Rep. 00/02-1, n. 2189. Akten der Stadtverordneten-Versammlung zu Berlin betreffend die auf die Umwälzung bzw. die Übergangswirtschaft bezüglichen Vorlagen und Anträge, 1918–20, p. 9. Wermuth's pledge stood in stark contrast to the lack of planning on the part of the City Council. Already in January 1918 one of its members had predicted the crisis that the end of the war would bring and had proposed the creation of a 'Central Office for the Transition Economy', which would deal with unemployment and anticipated housing shortages. The measure was defeated by the Liberal coalition that dominated the council, ostensibly because the city did not need another office, and because the existing administration was sufficient. See LAB (STA) Rep. 00/02-1 2148 Akten der Stadtverordneten-Versammlung zu Berlin, betreffend Allgemeine *Maßnahmen* aus *Anlaß* des Krieges, pp. 6–10. On the lack of planning at the municipal level for the demobilization see Scholz, 'Die Auswirkung der Inflation', p. 54.

[67] Kaeber, *Berlin*, p. 58.

[68] BAP, Rep. 32.01, n. 20, p. 193.

during the war than rural areas, and that it would be a mistake to abandon them now that the crisis had reached boiling point.[69]

It took several more communications from Mayor Wermuth, in which his frustration and anger became more and more evident,[70] before a response came from Koeth rejecting his plea for a national minimum in unemployment support. Koeth wrote that a national minimum had been considered, but that there was no evidence that higher-rate levels in cities were a contributing factor to the larger number of unemployed who gathered there. Furthermore, he pointed out that a rate of 3.0 marks per day would be a strong disincentive for workers to accept jobs in smaller towns where the local wage rates were not much higher. Finally, and this is perhaps where his real concern lay, Koeth wrote that such a measure would be extremely difficult to retract once the crisis had passed, and that it was for this reason preferable to remain with the old system, whereby each community would set its own rates.[71]

While these debates were dividing the representatives of the national and municipal administrations, city spending on unemployment support in Berlin went from 5.7 million marks in December, 1918 to 26.6 million marks in February, 1919. By the summer of 1919 it had tapered off to about 12 million marks per month. In all, the city spent over 232 million marks on unemployment support in the first year of peace.[72] Did high levels of unemployment benefits encourage unemployment during this period, as some historians have claimed? After the Berlin rate rise in January 1919, an official from the Charlottenburg Magistrate wrote to Koeth complaining that the new levels had approached or even exceeded the wages of unskilled workers, and low-level office employees:

> The support payment has thus certainly become a premium for the idle; [the measure] will cause the workers to lose all fear of a further deterioration in their circumstances – in fact, it may make [such deterioration] more desirable – and it will certainly reinforce the tendency toward strikes and unreasonable wage demands.[73]

69 Wermuth wrote: 'The war weighed heaviest on the cities in every respect, and not only financially – much more so than in the countryside or smaller towns. It would be a serious mistake to avoid measures that would achieve a more just distribution of unemployment on such grounds', *ibid.*, p. 194.

70 See for example his letter of 16 December in BAP, Rep. 32.01, n. 19, pp. 63–4.

71 BAP, Rep. 32.01, n. 20, p. 210.

72 Kaeber, *Berlin*, pp. 364–5, 367. According to Kaeber, unemployed men received 4 marks per day in November and December 1918 while women received 3. For married men an extra supplement of 1 mark was added. In April the rates were set at 6 marks per day for single men, 7 for married men, and 3.5 for women. A 2 mark supplement was available for those with children. These rates remained steady throughout 1919, despite rising prices of food and daily needs.

73 BAP, Rep. 32.01, n. 20, p. 239; see also pp. 247–8. Koeth felt obliged to respond to the

Raising the rates in Berlin did put pressure on other communities to follow suit, as union officials demanded that local rates keep up with neighbouring jurisdictions.[74] Furthermore, high rates of unemployment benefits pushed up the wages on public works projects, and made job openings in agriculture or mining seem considerably less attractive. It is likely, however, that unemployment benefits were only a disincentive for accepting work in the very early stages of demobilization, and even then only in the major cities, such as Berlin.[75] The fact that the unemployment rates quickly fell behind the rapid increases in the cost of living soon became a more serious problem: in Berlin the rates did not change between April 1919 and February 1920, during which time the value of the mark plummeted from approximately thirteen to ninety-nine to the dollar.

Koeth and the national authorities at the Demobilization Office were willing to tolerate the risk of greater unrest in the capital in the interest of maintaining an atmosphere favourable to business interests in the country as a whole. Berlin's very particularity, and its atmosphere of continued crisis and social conflict, gave the officials from the Demobilization Office little incentive to seek administrative cures for a problem that would clearly overwhelm any political solutions arrived at in the short term. For Mayor Wermuth and the municipal administration, on the other hand, the unwillingness of the national authorities to extend special assistance to the city left them effectively powerless in the face of an economic crisis that threatened to drain the city's finances and bring production to a halt. Ironically, the process which brought the capital in line with the experience of the country as a whole was not one of increased stabilization, but rather the destabilizing inflationary crisis of 1922–1923, which first threatened employment in both the capital and the country, and then brought the two to a common collapse in late 1923.

Conclusion

Military demobilization in London and Paris, although traumatic enough for the individuals whose jobs were at stake, did not differ greatly from the overall experience of their respective nations, and in this light, neither city can be said to have been put at a disadvantage by their respective governments' policies. In fact, the diversity of the

Charlottenburg official's accusation that he had capitulated to the demands of radicals by claiming that the decision to raise the rates had already been arrived at by the Greater Berlin Demobilization Commission, before meeting with the representatives of the unemployed.

74 Officials from other communities protested as well. See BAP, Rep. 32.01, n. 20, p. 279. See also G. D. Feldman, 'Saxony, the Reich, and the problem of unemployment', p. 110.

75 G. D. Feldman, *ibid*., pp. 111–13.

London economy allowed it to weather the transition from wartime production with relative success, and there is evidence that this diversity allowed London to fare better than the country as a whole in the slump that set in after the summer of 1920. Because of this diversity, increases in employment in the food, paper and printing, clothing and commerce sectors helped to offset the layoffs in the industries associated with the war effort. In Paris, the two-step demobilization process, combined with the efficiency of the departmental placement bureaux served to alleviate the effects of large-scale unemployment and allowed the government to control labour protests with merely a few strategic concessions. In Berlin, on the other hand, the unemployment caused by demobilization reached much higher levels than in the rest of the country, and the city's reliance upon heavy industry proved to be a burden because smaller consumer industries were not able to compensate for the falling off of demand in the metals and machine sectors. The transition to peace in the old German capital was much more painful and embittered than the transition to war had been less than a decade before.

Part 4
The social relations of incomes

8
Material pressures on the middle classes

Jon Lawrence

Introduction

This chapter examines the impact of the war on sections of Berlin, London, and Paris society outside the manual working class. It is therefore concerned with vast and heterogeneous populations – ranging from lowly junior clerks to company managers; from small shopkeepers to powerful industrial magnates; or from poor widows living on income from a few government bonds to wealthy rentiers drawing income from extensive holdings in stocks and shares or in real estate. In all three cities this last group tended to possess substantial land and property in the country – so that in a sense its identity was as much rural as urban. Indeed, in London 'fashionable society' remained dominated by the upper gentry down to the Great War.[1] Although, according to British sensibilities, this elite was almost the antithesis of 'middle-class', they will be included none the less in this discussion for the sake of comparability.[2]

Given the remarkable diversity of the metropolitan 'middle classes', it is hardly surprising that their experience of war was highly diverse – not only because of objective differences in levels of wartime hardship, but also because individuals handled these hardships in varied ways, influenced partly by the distinctive cultural traditions of different social or religious groups, and partly by more individual psychological factors. In particular we must never forget that war often brought personal tragedy – in the form of bereavement – that could wholly overshadow material experiences of hardship or prosperity.

As this chapter will demonstrate, for the middle classes, the lottery of the wartime economy offered the prospects of great riches for some alongside crippling losses for many others. In all three cities the normal

1 F. M. L. Thompson, *English landed society in the nineteenth century* (London, 1963); F. M. L. Thompson, 'Britain', in D. Spring (ed.), *European landed aristocracy* (Baltimore, 1980).

2 See Oscar Wilde's *The importance of being earnest* (London, 1898), for the purest satire of this position. Mockery is abundant on landed pretensions in E. M. Forster's *Howard's End* (London, 1908).

mechanisms whereby middle-class families sought to minimize the inherent risks of a capitalist economy collapsed. Almost without exception, the capital value and the income derived from traditional 'safe' investments such as government stock, debentures, and property conspicuously failed to keep pace with rapid price inflation – indeed often such securities actually recorded significant falls in *nominal* value. In contrast, there were also many people in Berlin, London, and Paris who managed to amass vast fortunes from speculative investments in raw materials or from their activities in the war industries. War dramatically disrupted the normal 'rules of the game' throughout the economy. It was no longer just the 'unseen hand' of the market which determined winners and losers – in each country the demands of mobilizing for war forced the state to make unprecedented interventions into economy and society. This was clearest in the case of the housing market, where government action to control rents or to improve security of tenure undermined rental incomes for many landlords, while others continued to make huge profits from uncontrolled properties. This politicization of the market, which extended to many other fields including raw material supplies and pricing policies, greatly increased the scope for wartime grievances to take a strongly political form, and helps to explain the vehemence of the post-war middle-class reaction in all three cities.

'On the eve'

After centuries as the focal point of national political power and of 'fashionable society', both London and Paris possessed heavy concentrations of wealth and income. Over 7 per cent of the Parisian population owned fortunes of more than 50,000 francs (compared with a national average of under 3 per cent), and it was generally believed that more than two-thirds of the 'super-rich' – those with personal fortunes over 5 million francs – lived in Paris.[3] In turn London and its environs accounted for more than 44 per cent of all income assessed by the Inland Revenue even though it contained only 16 per cent of the national population.[4] In contrast Berlin possessed a much smaller elite – with only 5.5 per cent of the population earning over 3,000 marks on the eve of the war despite the fact that some contemporary authorities believed that even for inclusion in the *Mittelstand* one needed an annual

[3] Adeline Daumard, 'La bourgeoisie', in G. Duby and E. Labrousse (eds.), *Histoire économique de la France* (Paris, 1980), vol. VI, pp. 103–6.

[4] W. D. Rubinstein, *Elites and the wealthy in modern British history: essays in social and economic history* (Brighton, 1987), chs. 2 and 4.

income of at least 2,700 marks.[5] Significantly, just 5.7 per cent of the Berlin workforce worked in domestic service during the 1900s, compared with 9.9 per cent in London, and 8.5 per cent in Paris – again suggesting a significantly smaller 'bourgeois' population in the German capital.[6]

Perhaps inevitably it is very difficult to find directly comparable statistics on the 'middle-class' workforce of the three cities, and all but impossible to talk with any precision about the numbers who were independently wealthy – that is, living on investment income, rather than on incomes derived from employment or profits. In Britain, census statistics do not distinguish between employers, employees, and the self-employed – making it impossible to include businessmen and women from the industrial and service sectors in any estimate of the total 'middle-class' population (see table 8.1). This is a major problem because we know that the 'small master' was an important feature of the London economy, especially in the so-called 'sweated trades' of the central and eastern industrial districts.[7] Even so, the small master was undoubtedly more common in both Paris and Berlin, where artisanal traditions, though declining, remained very powerful. Hence the large number of 'independent' workers recorded in Berlin, almost two-thirds of whom worked in industry (especially the clothing trades), and the fact that only one-sixth of the chefs d'établissements recorded in the Parisian census ran or owned companies with more than five workers (table 8.1). If we exclude small masters because of their absence from the London data, and perhaps also because many would have shared the material conditions and lifestyles of manual workers, we can estimate that, on the eve of the war, approximately 26 per cent of Berliners, 28 per cent of Parisians, and 31 per cent of Londoners were engaged in non-manual occupations. However, it should be remembered that the decades immediately before the Great War saw a major migration of non-manual workers into the suburban districts which had grown up on the outskirts of all three cities. For instance the highest concentrations of Londoners employed in commerce and finance were to be found not

[5] For a discussion of the parameters of the *Mittelstand* see G. Schmoller, *Was verstehen wir unter dem Mittelstand?* (Göttingen, 1897); L. D. Pesl, 'Mittelstandsfragen. Der gewerbliche und kaufmännische Mittelstand', in *Grundriss der Sozialökonomik*, vol. IX (Tübingen, 1926), pp. 72–9; and H. Tobis, *Das Mittelstandsproblem der Nachkriegzeit und seine Statistische Erfassung* (Grimmen in Pommern, 1920), pp. 5–6. For information on Berlin incomes before and during the war see *Statistisches Jahrbuch der Stadt Berlin*, vol. 34 (1915–19), p. 849.

[6] *Population Census of England and Wales, 1911; Résultats statistiques de recensement général de la population effectué le 5 mars 1911*, vols. II and III.

[7] Stedman Jones, *Outcast London*; A. L. Bowley, 'The survival of small firms in London', *Economica*, 1 (1921), pp. 113–15.

Table 8.1. *A rough estimate of the structure of middle-class occupations in Berlin, London, and Paris before the Great War (figures to nearest 1,000)*

Sector	Number employed	% total workforce
Paris (1911)		
Government non-manual[a]	60,000	3
Liberal professions	50,000	3
Private non-manual[b]	140,000	8
Commercial occupations	200,000	12
Small masters (<6 workers)[c]	150,000	9
Employers (>5 workers)	30,000	2
Total 'middle-class'	630,000	37
Excluding 'small masters'	480,000	28
London (1911)		
Government non-manual[a]	117,000	5
Liberal professions	90,000	4
Private non-manual[d]	196,000	9
Private traders[e]	275,000	13
Employers/masters[f]	N/A	
Total 'middle class'	678,000	31
Berlin (1907)		
Government non-manual and professions	76,000	8
Private non-manual[g]	92,000	10
'Independent' (commercial)[h]	66,000	7
'Independent' (industrial)	96,000	10
Total 'middle class'	330,000	35
Excluding small masters (est.)	234,000	24

Notes: [a]Includes teachers.
[b]Includes banking and finance.
[c]'Chefs d'établissements' with fewer than 6 employees.
[d]Includes railway clerks and officials, telegraph and telephone workers, and dock officials.
[e]Includes all 'dealers', plus restaurant and inn keepers and 'builders'.
[f]The census makes no distinction between employers, employees, and the self-employed for most trades – e.g. many of the 65,000 tailors recorded in the census would have been small masters, but they cannot be included in this estimate of the middle classes – in contrast to both Paris and Berlin.
[g]Includes shop assistants.
[h]Includes only self-employed workers in commerce, e.g. shopkeepers, factors, etc.
Source: Census of England and Wales, 1911; Recensement général de la population de la France, 1911; Statistik des Deutschen Reichs, vol. 207, p. 29.

in west or south-west London, but in the new suburbs of Middlesex and Essex such as Ilford, Hornsey, and Southgate.[8]

The impact of war

This section will examine the impact of the war on the three main sources of middle-class income: salaries, profits, and investments. It will also look at the changing distribution of wealth during the war and the immediate post-war period. First, however, we must look in some detail at the forces which determined the real value of wealth and income in each of the three cities – namely, inflation and taxation. At the beginning of the war France had the least-developed system of direct taxation, having introduced an income tax only in July 1914. In contrast Britain, increasingly recognized as the first modern 'fiscal state', had operated a direct tax on incomes for nearly a century.[9] Combined with a 'supertax' on high incomes, and duties on inherited wealth, such direct taxes represented almost half of all state revenues, compared with 11 per cent in Germany and 22 per cent in France.[10] During the war all three countries sought to strengthen fiscal policy in order to offset the massive cost of the conflict. Initially France had set her new income tax at a flat rate of just 2 per cent; by 1920 the maximum tax rate stood at 50 per cent.[11] In all, French taxes are estimated to have covered 15 per cent of total government expenditure during the Great War.[12] The German effort to strengthen fiscal policy was less pronounced – four special taxes on war profits were introduced between June 1916 and November 1919. In all the authorities raised just 12.6 billion marks from taxation, tolls, and other sources of revenue between 1914 and 1918, or 7.3 per cent of the total expenditure of 171 billion marks.[13] This massive shortfall – representing almost 93 per cent of wartime expenditure – had to be met through printing currency and through issuing treasury bonds. British taxpayers experienced a much more sharply increased

[8] London County Council, *London Statistics* (1920–1), vol. 25, plate 7, between pages 48 and 49.

[9] On the early growth of British taxation and state expenditure, see J. Brewer, *The sinews of power: war money and the English state, 1688–1783* (1989); P. K. O'Brien and P. A. Hunt, 'The rise of the fiscal state in Britain, 1485–1815', *Historical Research* (June 1993). On the nineteenth-century state, see P. Harling and P. Mandler, 'From "fiscal military" state to laissez-faire state, 1760–1850', *Journal of British Studies*, 32, 1 (Jan. 1993), pp. 44–70; and on the twentieth-century, see J. Cronin, *The politics of state expansion: war, state and society in twentieth-century Britain* (London, 1991).

[10] *Bulletin de la statistique générale de la France*, XIV (1925), p. 423, ('Progression des impôts de 1913 à 1925 en France et en divers pays').

[11] *Ibid.*, pp. 416–17, ('Progression des impôts').

[12] G. Hardach, *The First World War, 1914–1918* (London, 1977), p. 162.

[13] W. Prion, 'Die Finanzen des Reiches (Kriegsanleihen, Inflation)' in G. Anschütz, F. Berolzheimer, *et al.* (eds.), *Handbuch der Politik*, V, 4, *Der Wirtschaftliche Wiederaufbau* (Berlin and Leipzig, 1921), pp. 2–3.

direct tax burden than their German counterparts – especially after 1916 – but even so estimates suggest that 70 per cent of wartime expenditure had to be met from government borrowing.[14] At the beginning of the war the standard rate of income tax had been 1s 2d in the pound on incomes over £3,000 (an effective tax rate of approximately 6 per cent). By 1918–1919 it stood at 6s in the pound on incomes over £2,500 (a rate of 30 per cent) – rates of 'supertax' were also increased sharply so that on incomes over £150,000 per annum an effective rate of nearly 52 per cent applied. Moreover, after 1916 the threshold for income tax was reduced from £160 to £130. Combined with wage-inflation this had the effect of trebling the number of income-taxpayers – for the first time in half a century significant numbers of manual workers were expected to pay income tax.[15]

As table 8.2 demonstrates, price inflation was considerable in all three countries.[16] Even official figures suggest that Germans suffered most from rising prices – despite the fact that the figures take no account of the exorbitant prices on the black market. Little notice should therefore be taken of the apparent stability of prices in Germany between January 1917 and the Armistice, since by this time many basic commodities were only available at 'unofficial' black market prices thanks to the twin effects of the blockade and the diversion of resources to the war effort under the Hindenburg Programme (see chapters 7 and 12). Prices in France and Britain rose broadly in tandem throughout the war (slightly faster in Britain between 1914 and 1916, slightly slower thereafter). By the Armistice basic commodities had more than doubled in price, while many 'luxury' goods had become all but unavailable.

Salaried employees

In broad terms the war appears to have had a similar effect on salaried employment in all three cities. This can be characterized as follows: heavy enlistment of young male workers into the armed forces, leading to the large-scale absorption of new workers during the war (many of them women); and retention of many of these workers after the war,

14 J. C. Stamp, *Taxation during the war* (London, 1932), p. 154, and 'Memorandum on the cost of the war' dated 31 March 1922, PRO T172/1310, cited in B. Waites, *A class society at war: England 1914–1918* (Leamington Spa, 1987), p. 106. These figures take account of all receipts collected on wartime incomes, not only those actually received between 1914 and 1918.

15 See Waites, *Class society at war*, pp. 106–8, and R. C. Whiting, 'Taxation and the working class, 1915–24', *Historical Journal*, 33, 4 (1990).

16 The sources surrounding calculations of price movements in wartime, and the general problems associated with estimating inflationary pressures, will be dealt with in chapter 9. Real wage calculations require careful attention to such matters; we have therefore left the matter in the chapter on wages rather than in the present discussion of middle-class incomes.

Table 8.2. *An index of official prices recorded in Paris, Britain, and Germany, July 1914–September 1921 (July 1914 = 100)*

	Paris[a]	Percentage change in prices over half year	*Britain*[b]	Percentage change in prices over half year	*Germany*[c]	Percentage change in prices over half year
July 1914	100	—	100	—	100	—
Jan.–Mar. 1915	115	15	115	15	124	24
July–Sept. 1915	120	4	125	9	155	25
Jan.–Mar. 1916	133	11	137	10	176	13
July–Sept. 1916	133	0	150	9	212	20
Jan.–Mar. 1917	148	11	168	12	215	1
July–Sept. 1917	183	24	182	8	217	1
Jan.–Mar. 1918	203	11	190	4	225	4
July–Sept. 1918	225	11	208	9	236	5
Jan.–Mar. 1919	256	14	218	5	259	10
July–Sept. 1919	256	0	213	−2	348	34
Jan.–Mar. 1920	—	—	231	8	—	—
July–Sept. 1920	—	—	262	13	—	—
Jan.–Mar. 1921	—	—	252	−4	—	—
July.–Sept. 1921	—	—	220	−13	—	—

Notes and sources: [a]Paris prices derived from survey of a Parisian consumer cooperative in *Bulletin de la statistique générale de la France* (1915–20).
[b]British prices are based on a survey of the Board of Trade, published in its *Labour Gazette* regularly from 1914 to 1921. The index is based on a fixed basket of commodities deemed to represent pre-war typical working-class expenditure on food, rent, clothing, and fuel.
[c]German prices are derived from G. Bry, *Wages in Germany, 1871–1945* (Princeton, 1960); see ch. 9 for details of series (recalculated at July 1914 = 100). The absence of change in 1917 and 1918 in this series is the best indication of the unreality of official estimates of price movements.

thanks to a rapid expansion of overall employment. During the war, non-manual earnings appear to have fallen significantly behind the course of both retail prices and average manual earnings in all three cities. After the war manual/non-manual differentials were largely restored to their pre-war level, at least in Britain and France, but there appears to have been a permanent narrowing of differentials among non-manual workers, with lower-grade workers seeing their salaries rise by up to three times the rate of their senior colleagues.

In Britain enlistment from commercial and financial occupations was equivalent to 63 per cent of the pre-war male workforce by July 1918 (although this figure included enlisted men who had not been employed in the sector in July 1914, and men who had subsequently been discharged back into civilian employment). Even so, the comparable figure for male enlistment from all sectors was significantly lower, at 46 per cent of the pre-war male workforce.[17] On the basis of national figures one would expect that in London 110,000 women and 75,000 men would have found new jobs in either finance and commerce or government employment by the end of the war. In fact the figure was almost certainly much higher, given the concentration of major financial institutions and government ministries in central London – the Ministry of Munitions alone employed over 25,000 at its London headquarters by 1918.

Even after the transition to peace the 'salariat'[18] in the three cities was not only much larger than before the war, but had clearly grown much faster than pre-war trends would have suggested. In London commercial and financial employment grew from 180,000 in 1911 to 241,000 in 1921 – an increase of 34 per cent, compared with an increase of just 12 per cent between 1901 and 1911. Figures for Paris are imprecise but suggest that employment in the financial sector rose at an *annual* rate of 12.5 per cent between 1914 and 1921 (from 45,000 to 100,400), compared with a pre-war annual rate of 3.3 per cent (from 35,000 in 1906 to 45,500 in 1914). In contrast, retail employment actually fell between 1914 and 1921, although it had been growing steadily before the war.[19] Boundary changes prevent a direct comparison for pre- and post-war Berlin, but the 1925 census suggests that 30 per cent of the active population of greater Berlin was employed in non-manual occupations (public and private), compared with approximately 18 per cent for the old city before the war.[20] National data for Germany confirm this trend, suggesting that the *Angestellte* (salaried non-manual workers) increased by 96 per cent between 1913 and 1928 (from 2.8 million to 5.5 million workers).[21]

Moving on to the question of income, it is clear that, at least during

[17] BLPES Board of Trade, Report on the State of Employment in July 1918, p. 5 – these figures refer to the United Kingdom as a whole, including Ireland where conscription was never implemented. They are broadly comparable with figures derived from military sources – see J. M. Winter, *The Great War*, p. 75. Assuming a male workforce of 13 million (*ibid.*, p. 43) these figures give a total enlistment rate of 47.3 per cent.

[18] In English, the term excludes working-class incomes, paid by the hour, day, and week, in order to specify those with regular incomes by and large from non-manual labour. The category *salarié* or *salariat* in French includes all those who earn a wage. The more inclusive French usage does not distinguish between social position. Here we follow the more discriminating English categorization of 'salary' for middle-class incomes and 'wages' for working-class incomes.

[19] Robert, 'Ouvriers et mouvement ouvrier', ch. 2. In 1906 employment in the retail and wholesale sector stood at 481,000; by 1914 this had risen to 579,800, but by 1921 employment had fallen back to 522,500.

[20] *Statistik des Deutschen Reichs* (1926), vol. 406, pp. 2–5.

[21] M. Victor, *Verbürgerlichung des Proletariats und Proletarisierung des Mittelstandes* (Berlin, 1931), p. 23.

the war, the buoyancy of white-collar employment was not translated into any significant growth in earnings. Although salary data are scarce for all three cities, there is evidence that many non-manual workers enjoyed only modest salary increases throughout the war – indeed many received no increases at all. In Britain, no civil servant was eligible for a cost-of-living increase (or War Bonus) until July 1916, when the authorities agreed to sanction increases of 4s for men earning less than £2 per week, and 3s for men earning between £2 and £3 per week.[22] A man earning £3 per week therefore received an increase of 5 per cent, although by this time retail prices had already risen 50 per cent above their pre-war level. Thereafter War Bonuses were gradually extended to the higher grades within the civil service – again with increases related *inversely* to pre-war salaries, thereby underlining the subsistence principle behind the awards. In May 1917 a War Bonus of 5s per week was paid to all male civil servants earning between £3 per week and £250 per year, while those on pre-war salaries of 30s or less received an extra 9s (30 per cent, compared with price increases of approximately 80 per cent). Six months later all employees on under £500 per annum were brought under the War Bonus scheme – although those on the higher grades received increases of no more than 10 per cent on pre-war salary scales. Interestingly, the government was much more generous towards salaried employees such as draughtsmen and architects who worked closely with manual workers – offering them War Bonuses in line with those awarded to war workers in order to avoid workplace friction.[23] It was not until 1918 that high-ranking civil servants received any salary increases to compensate for the rapid rise in the cost of living. Moreover, as late as July 1920 – when prices stood at approximately 160 per cent above their pre-war level – a Head of Department could expect to receive only 25 per cent more than in 1914.[24] This represented a fall of 52 per cent in the real value of top public salaries – or 63 per cent, after allowing for higher rates of income tax.

Perhaps inevitably wartime salary data for the private sector are more patchy, but some branch records do survive for London. From the salary records of the Cornhill branch of the Midland Bank it is possible to trace the impact of the war on two distinct groups of bank employees: male clerks employed throughout the war, and female clerks hired

[22] PP 1918, LCd 9017, vol. VII, 'Conciliation and Arbitration Board for Government Employees. Record of Proceedings for 1917', p. 5; women on the same salaries were awarded increases of 2s and 1s 6d respectively.

[23] *Ibid.*, p. 5 – men earning £2 or less per week now received 14s per week, women received 9s.

[24] This, however, did still represent an increase of almost £10 per week – probably sufficient to stave off destitution – PP 1921, Cmd 1188, vol. IX, 'Report of the Committee Appointed to Advise as to the Salaries of the Principal Posts in the Civil Service', p. 3.

during the war.[25] The records suggest that the salaries of both groups of bank workers failed to keep pace with rising prices during the war, but that male clerks fared much worse than traditionally lower-paid female staff. Even at the end of the war the average male clerk earned almost three times as much as the average female clerk, but his salary had fallen by 41 per cent in real terms, whereas hers had fallen by just 9 per cent (see table 8.3). After the war both male and female clerks won salary increases in excess of the current rate of inflation, but in 1920 the salary of a male clerk at the Cornhill bank was still worth just 66 per cent of its 1914 value, whereas female clerical salaries had risen by 3 per cent in real terms. It was only after the slump of 1920–1922, when prices fell much faster than salaries (but not faster than wages), that male clerical workers re-established pre-war differentials over manual workers. Hence, although Guy Routh's figures for the mid-1920s show that most grades of clerical workers in Britain had made clear gains since 1914, despite the rise in prices, we should not assume that the war itself had been an easy time for the 'salariat'. Interestingly, Routh also records a significant narrowing of differentials *among* clerical workers, both between higher and lower grades in the same occupation, and between clerks employed in different occupations. For instance, before the war the salary of a railway clerk was approximately half that of a well-paid commercial clerk. By the mid-1920s their salaries were almost the same.[26]

Although data for Paris and Berlin are more patchy, there is considerable evidence that non-manual salaries followed a broadly similar pattern in the two cities. Certainly the majority of government officials in Paris seem to have suffered a sharp fall in real incomes during the war. As in London, higher-grade workers generally fared worst, while the lowest-grade clerks and assistants received proportionally much larger increases in recognition both of material hardships and of recruitment problems among junior staff. For instance, in 1918 the real income of a director in the Ministry of Justice had fallen by 50 per cent, whereas the income of an administrative assistant had fallen by just 5 per cent (see table 8.4). By 1920 most grades in the ministry had improved their position somewhat, but the salary of a director was still worth only 60 per cent of its 1914 value, whereas an assistant's salary had risen 47 per cent in real terms. There also appears to have been a significant narrowing of differentials within the armed forces and the magistracy, but not as between teachers,

[25] Midland Bank Group Archives, 'Salary Register, Midland Bank, Cornhill Branch', Ref: AA 166 1. Unfortunately the salary records of female clerks already employed in 1914 are incomplete.

[26] G. Routh, *Occupation and pay in Great Britain, 1900–1960* (Cambridge, 1965), p. 79; the main group to fall behind the rate of inflation was male business clerks.

Table 8.3. *Changes in the annual salary of male and female bank clerks at a City of London bank, 1914 to 1920*

Year	Average salary of male clerks employed continuously, 1914–1920[a] £/yr	Deflated index[b]	Average salary of *all* Temporary female clerks £/yr	Deflated index[b] (1914 = 100)
1914	221	100	52	100
1915	231	83	65	100
1916	242	73	68	87
1917	257	64	81	86
1918	270	59	99	91
1919	325	69	127	114
1920	383[c]	66	141	103

Notes: [a]All bank clerks earning £300 or less per annum at the beginning of the war and remaining in employment until 1920.
[b]Deflated according to Board of Trade cost-of-living index – see table 8.2.
[c]Figure adjusted to compensate for the retirement of the two highest-paid clerks during 1920 – it is assumed that they would have received rises in line with other male clerks at the branch.
Source: Midland Bank Group Archives, 'Salary Register, Midland Bank, Cornhill Branch', Ref. AA 166 1.

where all grades appear to have seen their real income fall by about one-third.[27]

In Berlin white-collar workers (*Angestellte*) appear to have suffered more than most during the initial economic crisis associated with mobilization in 1914. Layoffs were common among clerks and junior managers, and many of those who kept their jobs were forced to take pay cuts – average male earnings fell by 2 per cent among the *Angestellte* during the first year of the war (female earnings fell by 4 per cent over the same period).[28] With price inflation of 55 per cent in the first year of the war, this represented a massive decline in the purchasing power of salaried employees. Moreover, even when the economy began to grow rapidly under the stimulus of government munitions contracts, industrial companies were much more anxious to hire additional skilled

[27] E. Martin Saint-Léon, 'La bourgeoisie française et la vie chère', *Le Musée Social* (1 Jan. 1921), pp. 34–8.

[28] Derived from figures for Germany in A. Günther, *Kriegslöhne und Preise und ihr Einfluss auf Kaufkraft und Lebenskosten* (Jena, 1919), pp. 43–4. See also J. Kocka, *Die Angestellten in der deutschen Geschichte, 1850–1980: vom Privatbeamten zum angestellten Arbeitnehmer* (Göttingen, 1981), p. 146.

Table 8.4. *Changes in the annual salary of government officials in Paris, 1914 to 1920*

	Salary in francs per year		Index (defl. 1918)	Salary 1920	Index (defl. 1920)
	1914	1918			
Ministry of Justice, central administration[a]					
Director	15,000	16,920	50	31,720	60
Head clerk, 1st class	9,000	12,720	63	18,720	59
Head clerk, 3rd class	7,000	10,720	68	16,720	68
Principal clerk	4,500	6,720	66	12,720	81
Clerk, 2nd class	3,000	5,220	77	8,720	83
Administrative assistant	1,500	3,220	95	7,720	147
Military officers[b]					
Marshall	30,600	—	—	42,240	39
Colonel	11,664	—	—	23,160	57
Captain (after 8 yrs)	6,276	—	—	15,060	69
Lieutenant (after 8 yrs)	4,776	—	—	12,204	73
Teachers (Paris)[a]					
Agg.,[c] 1st class	8,000	—	—	17,820	64
Agg., 6th class	5,500	—	—	12,820	66
Elementary, 6th class	4,000	—	—	9,220	66
Paris magistracy[a]					
1st president, Court of Cassation	30,000	—	—	36,720	35
Prosecutor, Paris Appeal Court	13,200	—	—	20,720	45
Magistrate, 1st Class (Seine)	10,000	—	—	17,720	51
Deputy Prosecutor, 1st Class	5,000	—	—	11,720	67
Deputy Prosecutor, 3rd Class	2,800	—	—	8,720	89

Notes: [a]Assumes an inflation supplement of 720 francs, and residence supplement of 1,200 francs for 1918 and 1920 – there were also special supplements worth 360–480 francs per month per child.
[b]Salaries for 1920 include all supplements, including bonus paid to married officers.
[c]'Agg.' means with state certificate for passing the *Agrégation* examinations.
Source: Martin Saint-Léon, 'La bourgeoisie française et la vie chère', pp. 34–8.

craftsmen, than to expand their clerical staff. In Berlin, Siemens increased its workforce by over one-third during the war, but the white-collar workforce increased by only 10 per cent.[29]

According to one right-wing pressure group representing members of the *Angestellte*, the average salary of its members had risen by just 18 per

[29] J. Kocka, 'Weltkrieg und Mittelstand. Handwerker und Angestellte in Deutschland, 1914–1918', *Francia*, 2 (1975), p. 440.

Table 8.5. *Changes in the annual salary of government officials in Berlin, 1914 to 1918*

Income class	Salary (Marks/yr) 1914	Deflated Index (1914 = 100) 1917	1917	Deflated Index (1914 = 100) 1918	1918
Class 1 (top)	14,680	15,680	49	15,980	46
Class 2 (top)	7,000	7,980	52	8,200	50
Class 3 (top)	5,000	5,780	53	6,000	51
Class 4 (top)	3,000	3,600	55	3,900	55
Class 4 (bottom)	1,500	2,100	64	2,400	68

Note: Officials with dependent children could claim an additional supplement of 10 per cent on basic salaries.
Source: Kaeber, *Berlin*, p. 552.

cent between August 1914 and July 1917, whilst even the *official* price index suggested that the cost-of-living had risen by nearly 120 per cent (table 8.2).[30] As chapter 9 demonstrates, manual wages were rising much more quickly during this period, with workers in Berlin war industries enjoying increases of up to 100 per cent – almost enough to keep pace with the cost-of-living. As in London and Paris, higher-grade workers suffered a particularly sharp fall in real earnings. National figures suggest that between 1913 and 1918 high-ranking officials averaged increases of 47 per cent, middle-ranking officials received 72 per cent, and their junior colleagues 118 per cent.[31] Using official cost-of-living figures this represented a decline of almost 40 per cent in the real earnings of higher officials, compared with only 8 per cent for junior employees. However, given the widespread dependence on the black market, where prices were often ten times pre-war levels, the decline in living standards was almost certainly much greater for all groups.

For Berlin itself our main information relates to government officials working for the Berlin, Prussian, and Reich authorities. The Berlin municipality introduced a special war-related supplement for junior grades in the spring of 1915, although it was far too little to restore employees' pre-war living standards.[32] Later, the Berlin authorities extended the scheme to officials earning up to 9,000 Marks per annum, and introduced additional supplements for those with dependants. However, all grades of Berlin government officials had still experienced a significant fall in living standards by 1917–1918 (table 8.5). Interestingly, there appears to have been less narrowing of differentials than in

[30] Kocka, *Die Angestellten*, p. 145.
[31] Kocka, 'Weltkrieg und Mittelstand', p. 439.
[32] Kaeber, *Berlin*, pp. 551–3.

either Paris or London, with even junior officials experiencing falls of between one third and a half in pre-war living standards even when calculated using official estimates of the cost of living. Kaeber notes that public-sector manual workers fared much better than their salaried colleagues, and suggests that the authorities felt compelled to match wage rises in private industry. He concludes that many members of the municipal, Prussian, and Reich bureaucracies were only able to survive the war by living off their pre-war savings and other capital assets.[33] Clearly the war represented a severe crisis for the Berlin 'salariat' – especially once it became apparent that the patient acceptance of hardship through four years of war had been in vain.

Professionals and businessmen

Defined by its source of income, not its occupation, this fraction of the middle classes is perhaps the most heterogeneous. It includes members of the liberal professions, such as barristers and doctors, who relied upon fees rather than salaries for their income; anyone involved in trading, from the poorest street vendor to international commodity brokers; and finally all types of 'industrial capitalist' from the self-employed master-craftsman to the wealthy armaments magnate (but not salaried employees or shareholders).

Perhaps inevitably this is the area where our knowledge of the impact of the war is weakest. As chapter 4 on the image of the profiteer makes clear, profit-making was not a neutral activity during the war – as a result, we need to be very cautious when assessing the scarce material available on wartime profits in the three cities. The war created great opportunities for individuals to make large fortunes through commerce and industry – the popular demonology of *nouveaux riches* coal merchants and farmers, or millionaire shipping magnates and munitions contractors was not wholly without foundation. At the same time war also brought ruin to many small and large businesses in all three cities.

Professionals

Evidence from France suggests that the war had relatively little impact on professional incomes. According to A. Daumard, professional workers such as lawyers and doctors were generally able to increase fees sufficiently to keep up with the rising cost of living.[34] Certainly the review of private income undertaken by Dugé de Bernouville in 1937 suggests that between 1913 and 1920 the income derived from the 'liberal professions' declined by just 10 per cent in real terms (table 8.6),

[33] *Ibid.*, p. 552.

[34] Daumard, 'La bourgeoisie', pp. xx–xxi.

compared with falls of over 60 per cent for incomes from property, and for the income of higher civil servants. Data for Germany are more sketchy, but Hans Tobis, writing in 1920, commented that the war had seen a significant fall in the income of both doctors and lawyers, although he attributed this at least in part to long-term trends, notably the growing competition from new groups of salaried workers such as company accountants and notaries or health workers with the Krankenkasse.[35]

In Britain living standards of most professional workers probably fell over the period 1914 to 1922, although not by more than about 10 per cent. Routh suggests that some professional workers made substantial gains over the period – the median real income of barristers rose by 50 per cent, while among solicitors and doctors the lowest-paid quarter of the profession recorded gains of approximately 30 and 25 per cent (again in real terms).[36] This pattern of gains for junior workers was repeated among most of the professions, and was almost certainly the result of the severe shortage of young, newly qualified men, caused by a combination of heavy wartime casualties and the suspension of normal training programmes during the war.[37]

Unfortunately these figures tell us little about the course of professional incomes during the war itself. They also shed little light on the experience of economically more marginal professional groups such as writers and artists. In Britain, it was precisely these people that the Professional Classes War Relief Council considered worst affected by the dislocation of war. Established early in the war to help maintain the social standing and 'respectability' of hard-hit professional families, the council found that many of its cases involved men whose income had completely vanished with the outbreak of war. Musicians, artists, and actors suffered from the widespread desire to economize on entertainment, while journalists, writers, and architects all suffered from the knock-on effects of raw-material shortages which curtailed the publishing and construction industries.[38]

35 Tobis, *Das Mittelstandsproblem*, pp. 80–7.

36 Calculated from Routh, *Occupation and pay*, pp. 62 and 104.

37 See A. Offer, *Property and politics, 1870–1914: landownership, law, ideology and urban development in England* (Cambridge, 1981), pp. 64–5, on the impact of the war on solicitors' prospects, and Waites, *Class society at war*, p. 92 (table 3.5), which confirms the trend towards narrowing differentials. However, Routh, *Occupation and pay*, p. 62, suggests that junior barristers may have experienced a fall in real income of up to 15 per cent.

38 For discussion of the Council's activities see *Charity Organisation Review* (Feb. 1916 and May 1917). See also *Estates Gazette* (13 July 1918), which stresses the plight of architects due to the collapse of civil building projects, and the utilitarian nature of much war-related construction.

Table 8.6. *The impact of the war on various forms of wealth and income in France, Germany, and the United Kingdom, circa 1913 to 1920*

France

	1913	1920	Deflated index[b] (1913 = 100)	1923	Deflated index (1913 = 100)	1925–26	Deflated index (1913 = 100)
Sources of income (1,000m Francs)							
Salaries	15.7	57.4	104				
Securities	4.5	11.8	75				
Property	2.6	3.5	38				
Agriculture	8.4	18.5	63				
Industry and commerce	4.0	14.6	104				
Liberal professions	0.6	1.9	90				
Forms of wealth							
Average estate	100					175	43
Average Seine	100					118	29
Shares	100	156	45				
Dividends	100	170	48				
Municipal stock[g]	100			63	19[h]		
Russian stock	100			25	7[h]		
Neutral stock[i]	100			280	85[h]		

United Kingdom

	1913	1920	Deflated index[b] (1913 = 100)
Sources of income (£m)			
Employment	1,160	3,525	118
Rental income	249	259	40
Trading profits	693	1,430	80
Forms of wealth			
Total estates[d]	£246m	£327m	48
London property[e]	£44.5m	£48.4m	50
Share index	100	170	66
Dividends (indexed)[f]	100	182	87
£100 $2\frac{1}{2}$% Consols	£73.3	£47.8	25

Germany[a]

	1913	1920	Deflated index[b] (1913 = 100)
Sources of income (1,000m marks)			
Employment	23.0	44.0	77
'Independent'	26.0	24.0	37

Notes: [a]Pre- and post-war comparison is almost impossible for Germany given the changes to both territory and currency; relative shifts in the importance of different sources of income and wealth are more revealing.

[b]Deflators used: France: see table 8.2; UK: Board of Trade cost-of-living index; Berlin: see table 8.2.

[c]Post-war estate values are from 1925–6 assessments.

[d]Total property assessed for estate duties, probate, etc., 1913–14 and 1920–1 (deflator for Jan. 1921 applied).

[e]Based on quinquennial valuations of 1911 and 1921 (appropriate deflators applied).

[f]Average dividends for 1914 and 1919 (appropriate deflators applied).

[g]Ville de Paris 3% 1910 and 2% 1899 and Foncieres 3% 1903 and 1912.

[h]Value of stock at the end of 1923 (appropriate deflator applied). 1920: 352; 1923: 329; 1925–6: 407. Jeanne Singer–Kérel, *Le coût de la vie à Paris de 1840 à 1954* (Paris, 1961).

[i]Swiss 3% 1890, Swedish $3\frac{1}{2}$% 1895 and Japanese 4% 1905.

Source: L. Dugé de Bernouville, 'Les revenus privés, 1913–1936', *Revue d'économique politique* (June 1937); C. Feinstein, *National income, expenditure and output of the United Kingdom, 1855–1965* (Cambridge, 1972); *Statistical Abstract for the United Kingdom* (72nd edn) 1913–1927 (PP 1928–9 Cmd 3253, vol. XXI); *The Economist*, 26 July 1919; H. Parkinson, *Ordinary shares: a manual for investors* (3rd edn, London, 1949); London County Council, *London Statistics*, 1923–4; L. de Chilly, 'La classe moyenne en France après la guerre, 1918–1924. Sa crise: causes, conséquences et remèdes' (doctoral thesis, Faculté de Droit de Paris, 1924); *Bulletin de Statistique et de législation comparée*, vol. 74 (1913), pp. 710–15; vol. 77 (1915), pp. 294–9; vol. 102 (1927), pp. 74–9; vol. 103 (1928), pp. 66–71. G. D. Feldman, *The great disorder. Politics, economics, and society in the German inflation 1914–24* (Oxford, 1993), p. 218.

By July 1918 the Professional Classes War Relief Council claimed to have helped more than 10,000 families, primarily by paying for children's school fees, placing older children in 'suitable' positions, and helping with medical costs in pregnancy. Assistance was therefore designed, not to maintain middle-class living standards, but to prevent parental hardship having a long-term impact on the social standing of professional families. In other words, the relief council assumed that wartime hardship would have to be endured, and directed its efforts towards ensuring that hardship was only 'for the duration' – a generation of middle-class children could not be rendered *declassé* by the war effort. This ethos – summed up in the council's claim that it offered not charity, but a chance for families 'adversely affected by the prevailing conditions to tide over until the coming of better times' – could probably stand as the common sentiment of middle-class groups in all three cities.

Retail and wholesale tradesmen

For anyone involved in buying and selling the war was a time of great uncertainty. For many it was also a time of great opportunity thanks to the scarcity of many basic commodities and raw materials. This was classically true in the case of the massive 'black market' which developed in Berlin after 1916. Here traders willing to operate outside the law could make enormous profits by satisfying the demands of a hard-pressed civilian population. In contrast, whilst a black market certainly existed in both London and Paris, it did not usually impinge directly on the daily struggle for survival.[39] In both Paris and London most traders sought to keep on the right side of the law most of the time. Indeed, wartime emergency legislation came to be the primary arbiter of the fortunes of small traders in both cities. For instance, in Paris rigorous price controls on bread severely squeezed bakers' profits, while grocers and coal dealers were free to charge inflated market prices. In London the introduction of selective rationing on food and fuel during 1917 and 1918 had similar consequences (see chapters 13 and 14). However, small traders were not only affected by the arbitrariness of state intervention; many also suffered from the weakness of wartime distribution systems, and from the declining purchasing power of their traditional customers. Recent research on local price levels in suburban Paris has shown that in fourteen working-class districts retail prices rose by 164 per cent between 1913 and 1918, whereas in eight wealthy districts they rose by only 137 per cent over the same period.[40] Given the higher overheads of

[39] See E. Smithies, *The black economy in England since 1914* (Dublin, 1984), pp. 19–37; J. Gray, *Gin and bitters* (London, 1938), p. 111. No systematic study of black marketeering in Paris has been begun, possibly because of the paucity of sources, or because of the evanescence of the practice.

traders based in prosperous districts, these results suggest a significant squeeze on wartime profit levels in these areas. On the other hand, distribution problems were often more acute in poorer neighbourhoods. It was coal merchants and 'trolley-men' in East London who suffered most during the coal famine of 1916–1917, while West End merchants continued to be able to get their supplies directly from the main rail depots. Similarly, it was East End grocers who suffered most during the potato famine in the spring of 1917.[41]

Businessmen in industry

The war involved considerable hardship for the owners of many small workshops. The initial dislocation associated with mobilization appears to have affected them much more severely than larger employers, so that in all three cities the war brought an immediate and permanent shift of economic resources and manpower from small to large firms.[42] In Paris many of the small masters who closed their workshops and fled the city in September 1914 never reopened for business. In Berlin and London the decline of small firms was less dramatic, but there is no doubt that they had considerable difficulty both in securing war contracts from government agencies, and in retaining skilled workers, given the competitive wages paid in the war industries. In London the plight of the 'one-man business' became a particular issue after the introduction of conscription in 1916. In all three cities small firms found it unusually difficult to recruit young workers to fill apprenticeships – traditionally a vital element in the workshop economy. For instance, figures from the Berlin Chamber of Commerce record apprenticeships among member firms declining from 41,000 in 1914 to just 7,800 in 1918.[43] The story was not, however, wholly negative. As the demands for war *materiel* expanded, so many small firms were able to obtain lucrative sub-contracts from larger companies unable to meet their government orders. Though officially discouraged, such sub-contracting flourished in all three cities, providing a vital lifeline for many small firms able to adapt production to the demands of war.[44] But in sectors where adaptation was difficult, such as the luxury fine-craft trades of both Paris and London, the war brought real hardship from which post-war recovery was only partial.

The corollary of this was that large-scale heavy industry enjoyed a

[40] Figures calculated by J.-L. Robert, from the 'Enquête sur les prix de détails des communes de la banlieue de Paris', *Bulletin de la Statistique générale de la France* (1913–19). In 1913 retail prices had been 10 per cent lower in working-class districts than in wealthy districts; by 1918 they were actually higher in the working-class districts, though only marginally so. [41] See chapter 11.

[42] See ch. 5, p. 140. [43] Kocka, 'Weltkrieg und Mittelstand', p. 446.

[44] See ch. 6, p. 173.

period of unparalleled prosperity in all three cities. Despite innovative wartime accounting techniques designed to reduce tax liabilities and avoid the ignominy of 'profiteering' charges, the profit levels and dividends declared by most large munitions firms still give some indication of this wartime prosperity. Nowhere was this dynamism more apparent than in the industrial suburbs around Paris, where firms such as Renault and Citroën mushroomed into massive industrial combines (see chapter 6). As Patrick Fridenson has demonstrated, the war stimulated a rapid acceleration in the accumulation of industrial capital in France, especially in the Paris region.[45] Progress was less dramatic in London, but even so the capital value of most metal-working and engineering firms rose dramatically during the war (table 8.7). Indeed the rapid fortunes made by war contractors became a commonplace in London 'Society' – as *Punch* acknowledged in a cartoon from April 1916. A well-to-do couple see two people in a chauffeur-driven Rolls-Royce:

She: 'Good gracious! The Brown-Smiths!! I thought they were so poor.'
He: 'Yes. But, you see, he's been supplying the Government with shells for quite a fortnight!'[46]

Rentiers and investment income

Income from investments took many forms, from the modest setting aside of small sums of disposable income to the acquisition and manipulation of vast portfolios. It is necessary to bear in mind that many of those with investment income were not wealthy, though fortunes were made and lost on the Stock Exchange every day.

For our purposes, a preliminary distinction may be useful. We may separate so-called 'safe' investments, favoured because they offered a guaranteed income with minimal risk to capital, and 'speculative' investments, where returns could be much greater, but the capital invested was much less secure. 'Safe' investments included government 'securities' such as pre-war British 2½% Consols, but also loans raised by foreign powers such as the Russian stock popular with small investors in France before the Great War. Municipalities also issued stock which guaranteed a fixed income and reconversion at a specified date (e.g. Ville de Paris 3% issued in 1910), while the Debenture Stock and Preference Shares issued by railway companies and other large firms followed similar principles. In addition many middle-class families held considerable assets on deposit with banks or building societies, while some also relied on property as a source of rental income.

Naturally investment income varied between the three cities, and

[45] Fridenson, *Histoire des usines Renault*. [46] *Punch*, 5 April 1916.

Table 8.7. *An index of the changing value of ordinary shares in a sample of British and German public companies, by sector, 1914 to 1918 (1914=100)*

Sector	Britain	Germany
Metals and engineering	300	87
Chemicals etc.[a]	259	102
Coal mines (domestic)	180	91
Food and drink	160	81
Textiles and clothing	153	115
Overseas Investment Co.	145	80
Insurance	124	53
Utilities and tramways	89	70
Sample size	44	32

Note: The index is based on an average of the *highest* price recorded for the ordinary shares of each company during each calendar year.
[a]Includes oil and rubber companies.
Source: F.C. Mathieson & Sons, *Stock exchanges (London and provincial) ten-year record of prices and dividends, 1909–1918* (12th edn, London, 1919); *Statistisches Jahrbuch der Stadt Berlin*, vol. 32, pp. 356–61; vol. 33, pp. 360–71.

between different types of investment, but as a general rule such 'safe' investments were expected to yield an income of between 3 and 5 per cent on total capital. Londoners reliant upon rental income probably enjoyed a significantly lower yield than this before the war, thanks to a prolonged slump in the housing market and near-stagnant rents.[47] Few investments yielded more than 5 per cent unless they were of a more speculative nature. According to a survey by *The Economist*, companies listed on the London Stock Exchange paid an average dividend of 10.4 per cent on ordinary capital in 1914, but this varied from as little as 0.9 per cent paid to the shareholders of canal and dock concerns, to as much as 25.2 per cent to those who held shares in oil companies.[48] Such variations were typical of 'speculative' investments, as too was the constant danger of company failure – when everything invested could be lost.

Thanks to Adeline Daumard we have a particularly detailed picture of the investment holdings of the Parisian bourgeoisie.[49] These show that Parisians in 1914 held a much higher proportion of their total wealth in the form of stocks and shares than the French population as a whole (51.4 per cent compared to a national figure of 29.6 per cent, table 8.8). It also shows that their holdings were much more cosmopolitan,

[47] Offer, *Property and politics*, pp. 264–7. [48] *The Economist*, 26 July 1919, p. 125.
[49] Daumard, 'La bourgeoisie'.

Table 8.8. *The structure of wealth in Paris, 1914 and 1928, expressed as percentage of total wealth*

Source	France 1914	Paris 1914	Paris 1928
'Safe' investments			
Property	45.1	31.1	25.1
Cash etc.[a]	19.3	13.5	18.7
Personally	4.4	2.5	5.6
Government stock	9.9	21.2	9.6
Foreign	(4.2)	(10.2)	(2.8)
Domestic	(5.7)	(11.0)	(6.8)
Debenture stock	11.1	12.7	11.0
Foreign	(2.4)	(3.8)	(2.6)
Domestic	(8.7)	(8.9)	(8.4)
Total 'safe'	89.8	81.0	70.0
'Speculative' investments			
Shares	8.6	17.5	26.6
Foreign	(1.9)	(5.1)	(6.2)
Domestic	(6.7)	(12.4)	(20.4)
Business	1.6	1.5	3.4

Note: [a]Includes currency, debts, deposits, savings accounts, and insurance.
Source: Daumard, 'La bourgeoisie'.

with nearly 20 per cent of all wealth held in foreign stocks and shares, compared with the national figure of 8.5 per cent. Safe investments clearly predominated, with public and debenture stock twice as popular as shares, while almost half of all wealth was held in property or in cash.

The pattern of Parisian wealth-holding changed dramatically during and after the Great War. By 1928, the foreign holdings had almost halved in value, and the holding of government bonds had fallen even more sharply. In contrast business capital, personal wealth, cash holdings, and shares were all more important than before the war. Overall, there appears to have been a significant shift from 'passive' to 'active' capital – a shift reflecting the wartime buoyancy of industrial and commercial profits compared to all forms of fixed investment. Again this pattern held true for all three cities, as the summary data on income and wealth presented in table 8.6 illustrate. In each case the value of most traditional 'safe' investments collapsed dramatically during the war. Perhaps not surprisingly the stock issued by the former Tsarist government collapsed most precipitously. Repudiated by the new regime, it no longer yielded any income, and had virtually no market value. French municipal stock had also fallen dramatically in value (by one-third in monetary value and by about 60 per cent in real terms), and British government Consols fell by 78 per cent in real terms (see table 8.6). Property values held up marginally better: they appear to have fallen by 43 per cent in real terms in London by 1921. Thanks to wartime legislation controlling rents and improving security of tenure, rental incomes appear to have fallen more sharply – down 62 per cent in France and 65 per cent in Britain according to national income data. In contrast, income from employment/salaries and from business profits appears to have retained its value more successfully according to the same data. There are also signs that share dividends performed much better than most other forms of investment income, especially in Britain (see table 8.6). Finally, data on personal estates suggest that the real value of personal fortunes almost certainly declined dramatically in all three countries between 1914 and 1920. Again the data are strongest for France, where we can see that assessments of 22,500 personal estates left in the Department of the Seine during 1925–1926 record an average estate of 110,000 francs, compared with an average of 94,000 francs for 18,000 estates left during the period 1912 to 1913.[50] In real terms this represents a fall of approximately 70 per cent in total personal wealth, much more dramatic than the national figure of 57 per cent (also for 1925 to 1926), or the figure suggested by the *aggregate* value of estates left in Britain between 1920 and 1921: which suggests a fall of 45 per cent, in real terms, since 1913 to 1914 (see table 8.6).

Clearly, in global terms, the Great War had an impact on the wealth and income of middle-class families to the degree that they were dependent on investments, especially where those investments were in fixed securities that inevitably failed to keep pace with rapid wartime inflation. This was especially true in Paris and Berlin because of the severity of the post-war inflation – in Britain the slump of 1920–1922 did much to re-establish the economic position of the rentier middle-class – though it by no means brought about a complete restoration.[51] Within this global picture, however, there was scope for great variation in individual fortunes depending on the exact nature of investments held. Again wartime emergency legislation and other forms of government intervention played an important part in determining 'winners' and 'losers'. For instance, in both Britain and France, only certain types of property came within the scope of government rent controls – London landlords letting more expensive properties remained free to charge a market rent throughout the war, as did owners of commercial and industrial property in Paris. Between 1914 and 1923 the rent on such property rose, on average, by 100 per cent, whereas the rent on

[50] *Bulletin de Statistique et de législation comparée*, vol. 74 (1913), pp. 710–15, vol. 102 (1977), pp. 74–9. [51] See McKibbin, *The ideologies of class* (Oxford, 1990), ch. 9.

residential property remained stagnant.[52] Comparison with Berlin is once more limited, due to problems of comparable sources and of the precise measurement of inflation.

The influence of government policy on share prices and dividends was more subtle, but there is little doubt that the allocation of war contracts, and decisions over the allocation of scarce raw materials, had a direct impact, both on the profitability of companies and on the performance of their stocks and shares. The shares of some favoured munitions companies rose phenomenally during the war – for instance, shares in the Projectile Company registered a twelvefold increase between 1914 and 1918, as did shares in the French munitions firm Hotchkiss. In contrast, shares in publishing firms fared badly as they struggled to survive drastic shortages of paper and other raw materials. For instance, by 1918 shares in *The Gentlewoman* magazine had fallen to just 32 per cent of their pre-war value – in *real* terms their value had fallen by 86 per cent. Overall a survey of British companies by *The Economist* in 1919 suggested that companies dealing in rubber, iron and steel, engineering, shipping, oil, and nitrates consistently paid above average dividends on ordinary capital during the war.[53] In general terms shares performed less well in France (see table 8.9), but even so the exact balance of a portfolio remained crucial to determining the profit and loss account for individual investors.

Conclusions

This survey of the impact of the war on different forms of middle-class wealth and income has demonstrated that the war brought real hardship for large sections of the non-manual population, including the 'salariat', sections of the professions, 'small masters', and the vast majority of families dependent upon investment incomes. The degree of hardship varied from group to group, and from city to city, but large numbers of previously prosperous individuals were forced to accept a much reduced standard of living, and in the worst cases were forced to the margins of subsistence.

For most, such material hardship was a wholly alien experience. The rationale of middle-class investment patterns had always been to minimize risk and instability – suddenly this strategy was thrown into disarray as war disrupted the normal patterns of economic life. Like their national governments, large numbers of middle-class families were forced to live off their accumulated capital to get through the war. For most this was painful, but not disastrous – families could, after all, take comfort from their visible contribution to the wartime 'economy of

[52] See chapter 13 below. [53] *The Economist*, 26 July 1919, p. 125.

Table 8.9. *An index of the movement of share prices on the London and Paris stock exchanges, 1914 to 1921 (1914* = 100)

Date	Paris	London
June 1914	100	100
1915	79	95
1916	84	108
1917	101	122
1918	108	146
1919	121	172
1920	154	172
1921	—	117

Source: Paris, see table 8.6; London: H. Parkinson, *Ordinary shares: a manual for investors* (3rd edn, London, 1948).

sacrifice'. It is surely this which explains why, despite very real material deprivations, one finds so little organized political dissent among the middle classes of all three cities between 1914 and 1918.

Some might suggest that this was because these diverse and profoundly individualist sections of society were intrinsically incapable of concerted activity – but this is to fall into the mistake of taking their own rhetoric at face value. The political voice of the middle classes was far from silent during the immediate post-war period, as the activities of groups such as the Middle Classes Union and the Anti-Waste League testify in Britain, or the Liberal party in Germany. The post-war period was characterized by a strident 'middle-class reaction' in all three countries, and in each case the capital can be considered to have been at the epicentre of the return of conservative power. To some extent there was also a common political language in the three countries, which portrayed the middle-class public as increasingly crushed between big business on the one hand and organized labour on the other. There were, however, also major differences in the political temperament of the three countries, differences which were shaped both by their very different long-term political traditions, and by their very different experience of the result of wartime material deprivations. In Britain and France there was undoubtedly a sense that sacrifices had not been equal, and that business and labour were unduly favoured in government circles, but there remained considerable solace in the claim that the middle classes had played an unequal part in the achievement of victory.[54] In Germany there could be no such solace; only recriminations. Indeed one could argue that an important element in Germany's ultimate defeat was the fact that, from 1916 onwards, it became

[54] E.g. C. F. G. Masterman, *England after war: a study* (London, n.d. [1922]), p. 72.

increasingly difficult for any section of the population to sustain the belief that the acute material hardships of the home front served a wider collective purpose. As early as May 1916 a Berlin diarist, Pastor Falck, noted that,

> As of today one can only buy meat with bread tickets that have a special mark. In the next few days a proper meat ration ticket will be made available. For a pound of good sweets you must pay 6–8 Marks. In the meantime, metal-workers are making up to 250 M per week through overtime. Workers, black marketeers, and war contractors have money to burn. And next to them the officers aren't doing too badly either. The middle class, above all the clerks [*Beamtenschaft*] are living in want, and have to pinch and scrape to get by.[55]

Things would get much worse for the *Beamtenschaft* and their like over the next two years, as the implications of the Hindenburg Programme worked themselves out amidst worsening shortages of many raw materials and foodstuffs.[56] Certainly, if we were to survey the fortunes of the middle-class populations of the three cities from the perspective of the mid-1920s, we would have to conclude that materially it was the Berlin middle class that suffered most after 1914. Only in Berlin can we truly talk of the war decade as a social and economic disaster for the middle classes. In contrast, by the mid-1920s the London middle classes had largely recovered their pre-war social and economic position – thanks in part to the strongly deflationary economic policies followed by government. Paris charted a middle course: investment incomes and capital assets were undermined by the continuation of inflation, but the middle classes as a whole were not reduced to the desperate conditions of men and women of their social standing in Berlin.

[55] P. Falck, unpublished diary, Bundesarchiv Potsdam – 2.3.1.2, Sachthem. Sammlung 92, Krieg 1914–1918, n. 266, p. 96.

[56] These developments are examined in greater detail in chapter 11 on the social relations of consumption in the three cities, and will also form the heart of the second volume of this study on family, quartier, and social movements in these three capital cities.

9
Wages and purchasing power

Jonathan Manning

Data on wages are essential to an analysis of wartime material conditions. But can these statistics be used without falling into the trap described by Sen as the construction of empty taxonomies conventionally known as 'living standards'?[1] To be sure, wages and incomes form part of the notion of 'capabilities' and 'functionings' adumbrated by Sen. But his work on the Bengal famine of 1943 added an additional and essential dimension to the problem of 'capabilities': the dimension of inflation, which in Berlin in 1916–18 as in Bengal in 1943, soared out of control.[2] Under conditions of spiralling inflation, the very notion of 'living standards' is problematic. But even when less severe price movements occurred, the simple correlation between wages and prices is remote from Sen's concept of 'capabilities', since real wages are not equivalents of the degree to which urban populations responded individually or collectively to rapid economic fluctuations.

This is especially the case in wartime. How do we quantify uncertainty, introduced violently with a price spiral that appeared to be able to spin out of sight? What point of reference could contemporaries have used? The inflation of the Napoleonic wars was robust, though over decades, not months, and besides, that experience had passed into history long before 1914. In the Berlin case, we have the further difficulty of the black market, the ubiquity of which casts serious doubts on the utility of official price series. How can we deflate money wages for illegal purchases, themselves a necessity in a system in which first priority went not to civilians but to the army? How can we calculate the transaction costs to a family of hours spent queuing for produce that was theirs by right but unavailable in the shops none the less?

The calculation of real wages in wartime is impossible for a second set of reasons. The free market in wages, unfettered or semi-controlled competition for limited positions in the labour market, was a luxury

[1] See Sen, *Poverty and Famines.*

[2] *Ibid.*, ch. 3.

these three nations could not afford after 1914. Everyone was forced to make sacrifices in wartime, but that common bond produced a powerful logic to redefine the notion of citizenship in terms of a minimum wage, or a minimum level of support for those unable to earn it.

This is an important part of the logic behind state intervention in the labour market. To produce munitions of war, the state had to fashion a very special labour market, supported by social expenditure where necessary. It is for this reason that we discuss earnings in this chapter and then turn to transfer payments in the next. Together they tell the story of the formulation of new rules of behaviour in the marketplace, which accorded to wage-earners rights they had not enjoyed in the past.

In all three cities we shall see that the notion of a minimum wage or a minimum level of earnings had important effects both on pay relativities and differentials, or in other words, on the social relations of wages.

Another point that may help to locate this chapter in the overall study is the notion of sacrifice. Everyone on the home front accepted hardship in their daily lives, in the certainty that whatever they faced paled in comparison with conditions in the trenches. Whatever the grumblings about suddenly rich workers, the truth was that everyone gave up something in wartime, and many gave up all they had. The fixing of sacrifice is the essential feature of what we have described in chapter 1 as the negotiation between well-being understood as an individual trajectory and well-being taken as collective destiny. In wartime the collective mattered; for some it was all that mattered; for most, the collective and the personal overlapped in complicated and unprecedented ways.

Above all, the collective task was producing the weapons of war. To do so required profound changes in the way in which work was organized and in the structure of pay. These changes certainly did not preclude inequalities and injustices in remuneration and work practices. But more importantly, wartime conditions reordered hierarchies of pay according to branch, profession, skill, gender, and age. Not surprisingly, munitions workers were privileged and, among them, especially metal-workers. But the pressure to increase output favoured intensified production on a mass scale through the use of semi-skilled and unskilled labour, wherever such man- or womanpower could be found.

Wage-bargaining formed part of the wartime break-up and reordering of pre-war work hierarchies. The fluidity of the situation was remarkable. We can speak of a veritable kaleidoscope of changing positions and family earnings, varying in terms of whether a man had been mobilized, whether multiple family members worked in a munitions factory, or changed their profession or level of skill, whether women worked for pay at home or at a distance. The permutations of these wartime trajectories were endless.

Such fluidity in the social relations of earnings easily led to a sense of injustice among some about the supposedly privileged position of some munitions workers. As we have seen in chapter 4, newspaper caricatures used wartime enrichment, be it at the top or bottom of the business hierarchy, as the antithesis of the sacrifice of the soldier. Such tensions are inevitable in such a highly malleable work situation, and should not be taken as ascriptive, popular expressions of what was deemed to be moral and immoral behaviour in wartime.

These moral notions are not embedded in the material on wages, prices, and earnings we discuss in this chapter. Instead it is best to see these data as the outcome of the changing social relations of work under the highly unusual conditions of war.

We concentrate here on three key branches of urban industrial activity – construction, clothing, and metal-work – in order to answer the following questions. Where was wage-bargaining located in the broader discussion about comportment in wartime, about the need to balance the logic of the marketplace with notions of citizenship? What can we learn about the notion of acceptable levels of civilian sacrifice in wartime? How varied are the three case studies with respect to both questions?

Data on the three sectors we have analysed help demonstrate the variables determining pay levels. In no sense do they indicate aggregate experience. If anything, the variation in experience in these three sectors was so substantial as to enable us to conclude that there was not one but many trajectories of earning power even in the same urban space.

The cost of living

Once more, we must emphasize the uncertainties introduced by war. To calculate an index of the cost of living over time, a set of items must be chosen which do not vary substantially in quantity or in quality. Nothing could be further from the truth between 1914 and 1918. Consumer behaviour had to change to accommodate drastic shifts in imports and inputs. Potatoes turned into turnips when the need required; white bread turned grey, when the extraction rate of wheat was changed. Ersatz products proliferated. Rationing complicated matters further, especially under transport conditions that precluded the arrival of rationed goods to markets which, legally, were entitled to them. At other times, goods vanished for more nefarious dealings, familiar to Berliners, though less so to Londoners or Parisians.

For all these reasons, the recourse to 'a basket of consumables' in cost-of-living analysis and to official price series are invitations to distortion. In chapter 8, we presented a table of Berlin prices which, though officially sanctioned, ventured into the realm of the imaginary.

They indicated that prices remained high but constant in 1917 and 1918. Berliners would have laughed their heads off had they been told that inflation was modest or non-existent. When statistics fly in the face of a multiplicity of evidence, it is the data which must be treated with the highest scepticism.

Yet we must use them *faute de mieux*, and also because they formed part of public discourse on the issue of well-being in wartime. One such source, to be handled with care to be sure, was the Sumner Committee estimates on British working-class consumer expenditure in 1918.[3] The authors of this report followed precedent, in particular weightings within households budgets based on an enquiry conducted in 1904.[4]

As official moratoria were established on working-class housing rents in France and Britain, the importance of food in the measures of the cost of living grew significantly. The Board of Trade weighted food as 60 per cent of household budgets which covered a wide range of items (food, clothing, rent, fuel, light).[5] In France, consumption figures were founded on two investigations into working-class budgets carried out in 1896 and 1905, although by using cooperative shops (Cooperative de Consommation) as its source of prices, the index tended to under-represent the true cost of living since the Cooperative lagged behind other retailers in raising its prices.[6] Bread was the most important item in food expenditure, and despite modest price fluctuations in wartime, it had a profound effect on the overall cost of living.[7] There are several price series for the Paris region; the series presented here is an average of urban and suburban data (see table 9.1).

Although the British figures are national, the advent of price-fixing and food control in 1917 offers a more reliable indication of the rise in prices, especially when the Board of Trade index covers such a wide range of items. While the increases in both indices of the cost of living in Berlin clearly outstrip price rises in Paris and London, the extent of the black market, particularly in the later stages of the war, suggest that these figures seriously underestimate the true cost of living in Berlin (see table 9.1).[8]

[3] PP 1918, VII, cmd 8980, *Report of the Committee appointed to enquire into the report upon (i) the actual increase since June 1914 in the Cost of Living to the working classes and (ii) any counterbalancing factors (apart from increases of wages) which may have arisen under War conditions.*

[4] Board of Trade, *Labour Gazette*, August 1919, p. 318.

[5] Board of Trade, *Labour Gazette*, August 1919, p. 318.

[6] M. Halbwachs, 'Prix de détail', *Bulletin de la Statistique générale de la France* (Oct. 1915–July 1920).

[7] M. Halbwachs, 'Budget de familles ouvrières et paysannes en France en 1907', *Bulletin de la Statistique générale de la France* (Oct. 1914), pp. 47–83.

[8] For Berlin, the cost-of-living estimate is made by adjusting the annual figures given by the Reichsamt to the monthly progression given by Calwer's figures on food prices. The

Table 9.1. *Official estimates of the cost of living, 1914 to 1919, in Paris, London, and Berlin (1914 = 100 in Paris and London; 1913 = 100 in Berlin)*

	Paris	London		Berlin	
Quarter	Cost of living	Cost of living	Food	Cost of living	Food
1914 July	100	100	100	98	99
Oct.–Dec.	100	110	114	108	111
1915 Jan.–Mar.	115	115	121	122	199
Apr.–Jun.	—	122	127	140	127
Jul.–Sep.	120	125	134	152	135
Oct.–Dec.	—	132	142	156	136
1916 Jan.–Mar.	133	137	147	173	141
Apr.–Jun.	134	143	154	203	159
Jul.–Sep.	133	150	162	208	181
Oct.–Dec.	140	160	177	206	198
1917 Jan.–Mar.	148	168	189	211	224
Apr.–Jun.	168	177	198	212	246
Jul.–Sep.	183	182	204	213	262
Oct.–Dec.	190	183	203	216	279
1918 Jan.–Mar.	203	190	207	221	293
Apr.–Jun.	223	198	207	223	304
Jul.–Sep.	225	208	215	231	317
Oct.–Dec.	246	223	230	243	338
1919 Jan.–Mar.	256	218	227	254	356
Apr.–Jun.	263	207	208	288	376
Jul.–Sep.	256	213	214	341	412
Oct.–Dec.	282	223	229	420	515

Sources: G. Bry, *Wages in Germany, 1871–1945*, pp. 440–5; M. Halbwachs, 'Prix de détail', in *Bulletin de la Statistique générale de la France*, October 1915 to July 1920; Board of Trade, *Labour Gazette*, August 1919, p. 318, April 1920, p. 229.

It is important to remember that the figures for all three cities were published by the respective governments, and are therefore likely to under-represent inflation, not only to maintain domestic morale, but also since acknowledgement of higher rates led automatically to demands for higher wages in state-run sectors. Nevertheless, we must respect the professionalism of the statistical branches of government offices in all three cities, composed of people determined to provide objective judgements.

These problems in presenting comparative price series become much

adjustment is merely a graphic interpolation, and can only be considered a rough approximation of the cost of living. Adapted from Bry, *Wages in Germany, 1871–1945*, pp. 440–5.

worse when we attempt to convert them into deflators for real-wage indices. Then we confront the full frailty of the available statistical material. In the case of London and Paris, we present data on wages and the price level as a whole. For Berlin, we relate wage data to the price of food, more sensitive than a global figure to the intrusion of the black market.

Examination of the cost-of-living indices (table 9.1) discloses further important issues. While there is firm evidence that the cost of living at least doubled in all three cities, both the nature and chronology of the rises show important variations. The average quarterly increase was smallest in Paris until 1916, superseded only modestly by London and Berlin. The German capital was in no sense in a disadvantageous position *vis-à-vis* the Allied capitals at this time, especially with respect to food products. From the summer of 1916, the trajectories of the three cities diverge. Berlin prices rise at a rate much greater than that of London or Paris. A 10 per cent increase in London was matched and exceeded by an increase in prices of 20 per cent in Paris, but of fully 30 per cent in the cost of living and of 26 per cent in food prices in Berlin. These comparisons are innocent of the full impact of the German black market.

In 1917, the ravages of inflation appeared worse in Paris than in London. From February to May 1917, prices in the French capital rose by 14 per cent, the same figure as that registered for Berlin food prices between May and August 1916. Here is the source of much of the labour unrest of 1917.

Wage movements in three branches of employment

Construction

The wartime story of the construction industry was one of a difficult period involving a reordering of wage hierarchies, and a movement into other industries. Military mobilization directly affected the number of builders who remained in the trade, since the munitions industries provided a particularly tempting lure for unskilled labourers who could almost double their wages by moving into semi-skilled armaments work by the end of 1916. In all three cities the wages of workers skilled in traditional construction techniques, such as masons, failed to rise as rapidly as those of their colleagues, who also registered a decline in their purchasing power.

The outbreak of war had a negative impact on the building trades of the three cities. In Berlin it compounded a downturn in the construction cycle, which had already caused high unemployment and widespread dissatisfaction over wage levels earlier in the summer of 1914. After the declaration of war almost all private building projects ceased, and the soaring price of raw materials did nothing to resuscitate trade, although carpenters did benefit from the building of barracks and other military installations around the city. In London, unemployment among builders initially doubled, but the immediate need for both armaments factories and accommodation for munitions workers, together with a strong flow of volunteers for the British army, brought a swift upturn in their fortunes, and from March 1915 until the Armistice the proportion of out-of-work (insured) builders stayed well below 2 per cent.[9] Despite little movement in the construction industry in Paris, wages were stable in Paris at the outbreak of the war, an unfavourable situation under conditions of inflation.

Builders enjoyed certain advantages over male colleagues in other industries. Construction workers required both physical strength and specific skills, attributes which protected them from the dilution of labour, for unlike engineering factories, building sites rarely employed female workers. In addition, the competition for all available labour from the burgeoning munitions industries saw employers offer higher wages and benefits to retain their workforce. For perhaps the first time in its history, London experienced a shortage of unskilled labour, and the militancy of the construction workforce which remained with the trade forced up wages even more for the unskilled. Moreover, the functional nature of the new construction projects saw some branches of the building trade benefit more that others. Building war workshops and factories was a job for carpenters more than stone-masons.

During the war, unskilled labourers' salaries fared best in all three cities, despite suffering a poor start in London. Their actual earnings remained inferior to those of their skilled colleagues. For those on the lowest wages, of course, there was little room for economy, and they required greater measures merely to maintain subsistence. In Berlin (table 9.2) this was explicitly recognized as war-related supplements (*Kriegsteuerungszulage*), introduced in the spring of 1916, offered increases of 14 pfennigs per hour to unskilled building workers, 3 pfennigs per hour more than their skilled colleagues.[10] This assistance meant that their wages at least kept pace with the rate of inflation for all goods, though not for food products.

In London the granting of incentives effectively meant flat-rate bonuses, which favoured the lower paid to a greater extent. As the official *History of the Ministry of Munitions* acknowledged, 'Earnings were driven up by the grant of extras, meals, fares, lodging money, [and] special bonuses.'[11] When accommodation costs of up to 17s 6d per

[9] LCC, *London Statistics 1915–20*, vol. 26, 1921, p. 85.

[10] *Jahres- und Kassenberichte der Gewerkschaftskommission Berlins und Umgegend*, vol. 27 (1916), p. 39.

[11] *History of the Ministry of Munitions* (1922), vol. V, part 1, p. 209.

Table 9.2. *Berlin: hourly wage rates (in marks) of skilled and unskilled construction workers, for a nine-hour day, and an index of wage rates, 1914 to 1918, and for an eight-hour day from 21 November 1918 (1913–14 = 100)*

	Skilled		Unskilled	
1913–14	0.84	100	0.57	100
04/1914	0.82	98	0.64	112
04/1915	0.84	100	0.64	112
09/1916	0.98	117	0.81	142
12/1917	1.60	190	1.48	260
10/1918	1.80	214	1.68	295
12/1919	3.20	381	3.00	526

Source: Adapted from Bry, *Wages in Germany*, table A-38, p. 437.

week were awarded to workers on remote sites, this represented an important supplement to the weekly pay packet.

At the other end of the skills ladder conditions were very different. Masons registered only modest rises throughout the war in both Paris and London (tables 9.3 and 9.4). New construction projects – especially war factories – had little demand for skilled stone-workers, as emphasis lay more on the functional nature of the buildings. London wage rises for masons perpetually lagged behind those granted to carpenters and bricklayers, although the divide was never more than 5 per cent, and in real terms masons kept narrowly ahead. In Paris, on the other hand, masons' wages fell below their pre-war level until 1916, and from June 1916 wage relationships were overturned as bricklayers' and carpenters' wages overtook those of the more skilled masons. By June 1919, wages in the French capital had struck a new balance; all skilled workers in the trade received 20 francs per day. Labourers were still in last place, but they had narrowed the wage gap, and only their wages had kept pace with the inflationary cost of living.

The Berlin building unions' sense of achievement in winning the battle to have cost-of-living increases written into workers' contracts soon turned to disappointment and frustration when it became clear that the war supplements failed to offer long-term protection against rapid price inflation.[12] Mid-war wage rises reflected a decline in competition due to the conscription of building workers – of 11,800 members of Berlin building trade unions, 6,215 were in uniform in 1915.[13] In addition wage gains followed the implementation of the

[12] *Jahres- und Kassenberichte der Gewerkschaftskommission Berlins und Umgegend*, vol. 27 (1916), p. 39.

[13] *Jahres- und Kassenberichte der Gewerkschaftskommission Berlins und Umgegend*, vol. 25 (1914), p. 35; vol. 26 (1915), pp. 43–5.

Table 9.3. *Paris: daily salaries, in francs, for a ten-hour day for 1914 to 1918, and for an eight-hour day in 1919, and an index of salaries (1914 = 100)*

	Mason		Bricklayer		Carpenter		Labourer	
1914	10	100	9.5	100	10	100	5.25	100
06/1916	9	90	9.5	100	10	100	—	—
08/1916	9	90	10	105	10	100	—	—
12/1916	9	90	10.75	113	11.25	112	5.5	105
04/1917	—	—	15	158	12	120	—	—
06/1917	—	—	14	147	14	140	8	152
12/1917	14	140	16	168	15	150	9.5	181
06/1918	14	140	16	168	15	150	—	—
06/1919	20	200	20	211	20	200	13.6	259

Source: Bulletin du Ministère du Travail, 1914–19.

Table 9.4. *Increases in men's wages in the London building trades, 1914 to 1919, pence per hour, and an index of wages (June 1914 = 100)*

Date of increase		Mason		Bricklayer or carpenter		Labourer	
For war work	For non-war work	Pence	Index	Pence	Index	Pence	Index
6/1914	—	12.25	100	11.5	100	8	100
12/1915	—	—	—	11.5	100	7.5	94
7/1916	—	13.25	108	12.5	109	9	113
4/1917	6/1917	14.25	116	13.5	117	10	125
10/1917	1/1918	16	131	15.25	133	11.75	147
1/1918	5/1918	18[a]	147	16.16[a]	149	13.22[a]	165
7/1918	9/1918	19.97[b]	146	19.12[c]	167	15.2[d]	190
2/1919	—	21.75	178	21	193	17	213

[a]12.5 per cent increase.
[b]17.75p + 12.5 per cent.
[c]17p + 12.5 per cent.
[d]13.5p + 12.5 per cent increase.
Sources: Bowley, *Prices and wages*, p. 116; *London Statistics 1915–20*, p. 61.

Hindenburg Programme in December 1916, leading to major construction projects in the munitions industries. But such improvements were short lived. As in Paris, the unskilled did better than the skilled workers: the wage differential between them narrowed from 47 per cent to just 7 per cent, but the serious shortages of raw materials which developed in the spring of 1918 brought back the threat of unemployment to the

Berlin building trades.

There are interesting parallels in the fortunes of builders in the three capitals. None of the sectors studied here recorded any wage rise until at least mid-1916, except unskilled German workers, despite rises in the cost of living which varied from 30 to 100 per cent. From that point onwards, only the wages of unskilled labourers kept pace with inflation. In London, workers employed on sites officially recognized as 'war work', a distinction introduced in April 1917, enjoyed wage rises before colleagues on other sites, which helped them in the battle against inflation, but the rises were soon forwarded to their fellow workers.

It is important to note that in Paris, despite the independent character of each building site, there was a tendency towards the appearance of if not fixed, at least 'normal' wages. This arose out of public notice on the press of work contracted out by the municipality. The rate of pay in these projects tended to become the quasi-official rate throughout the trade. This benefit failed, though, to defend Parisian building workers against the wartime price spiral.

The clothing trades

The clothing trade provides a prime example of the various fortunes of female labour during the war.[14] In many ways it represented a similar story to all other trades, with the poorly paid catching up their better-paid colleagues, but the salaries of some women clothing workers at the start of the war were so low that very substantial wage increases were required to maintain parity with a pre-war standard of living. In Berlin, wages in this sector provided less than half the adequate income to survive, and as demand for clothing tumbled, only comprehensive war supplements could provide a living wage. The situation in both Paris and London was less drastic, yet the wartime chronology of wage rises lagged seriously behind inflation, and only in the post-war period were gains made.

Encompassing an extremely broad range of skill and wage levels, from the relatively well-paid Parisian seamstresses and furriers to the wretched 'sweated' labour of home-workers in all three cities, the clothing trade suffered immediate set backs with the declaration of war. The rapid decline of the luxury-goods market hit Parisian workers hard, while the curtailment of foreign trade caused further unemployment in a depressed Berlin market. Only the introduction of massive military contracts for uniforms offered a means of stabilizing the employment

[14] For example, women outnumbered men by fourteen to one in the London shirt-and-collar trade. LCC *London Statistics 1915–20*, p. 64.

Table 9.5. *Women's wages in the London clothing industry, 1914–1918, pence per hour or weekly wage, and an index of wages (July 1914 or July 1915 = 100)*

	Date						
Trade	1914	7/15	12/16	2/17	11/17	3/18	11/18
Tailoring[a] (pence per hour)							
(minimum)	3.25d	3.5d	3.5d	4d	5.5[b]	7[b]	7d
Index	100	108	108	123	169	215	215
Shirt and collar[a] (pence per hour)							
(minimum)	—	3.5d	3.5d	4d	5.5[b]	7[b]	8
Index	—	100	100	114	157	200	229
All trades (shillings and pence per week)							
(average weekly earnings)	—	17s 5d	18s 8d	21s	22s 8d	23s 11d	28s 5d
Index	—	100	107	121	130	137	163
Millinery workers (shillings and pence per week)							
'Competent hands'	12s to 18s			24s			
Index	100			200			
'First hands'	18s to 25s			30s			
Index	100			167			
'Copyists'	25s			30s			
Index	100			120			

[a]Trade Board minima.
[b]Committee on Production awards.
Sources: Wages, prices and profits; Prices and wages in the United Kingdom, 1914–20, pp. 52–3; London County Council, *London Statistics* 1915–20, p. 64; D.M. Barton, 'The course of women's wages', *Journal of the Royal Statistical Society* (July 1919), pp. 508–44.

and wage situations. Economic survival during the war depended on the ability of the different branches of the clothing industry to adapt to the manufacture of new products as well as items of essential civilian consumption.

The most poorly paid clothing workers had always been amongst the lowest-paid workers of any trade. In London (table 9.5) the Trades Board Act of 1912 had imposed minimum wages of 3.25d per hour for ready-made tailoring, which had helped to introduce a degree of security to poorly paid clothing workers. Low levels of unionization and bargaining power in Paris, Berlin, and London, however, continued to leave women vulnerable to reductions in their wages.[15] Unemployment at the outbreak of war in Berlin enabled employers to reduce piece-rates, while in 1915 wages in Paris had halved for both first-hand seamstresses and hand workers in the fur trade (see table 9.6).

War contracts offered some hope of guaranteeing employment for

[15] *Jahres- und Kassenberichte der Gewerkschaftskommission Berlins und Umgegend*, vol. 26 (1915), p. 47.

Table 9.6. *Paris: minimum daily wage rate (in francs) for women clothing workers in Paris, 1914 to 1919, and an index of wage rates (1914 = 100)*

	1914	1915	9/1916	6/1917	1/1918	3/1918	5/1918	9/1918	10/1918	1919
Furrier (apprentice)	1	—	3	3.5	3.75	—	4.25	5	—	7
	100	—	300	350	375		425	500		700
Worker (manual)	3	1.5	3	4	4	—	6	9	—	13
	100	50	100	133	133		200	300		433
Machinist	4	3	4	5	5	—	7	10	—	14
	100	75	100	125	125		175	250		350
Seamstress (apprentice)	0.5	—	—	1	1.25	2.75	—	—	3.5	4
	100			200	250	550			700	800
First hand	4	2	—	4.75	5	8	—	—	10	12
	100	50		119	125	200			250	300
Milliner (apprentice)	0.5	—	—	1	—	—	—	4.8	—	4.8
	100			200				960		960
First hand	3	1.5	—	5	—	—	—	9.6	—	10.8
	100	50		167				320		360

Note: The final column for the year 1919, represents the highest level the minimum salary reached up to September 1919, even if the increases occurred earlier in the year.

women for the duration of the war. The conditions imposed by employers, however, ensured that work in this field would always be arduous. There was no protection of piece-rates for clothing, as there was in munitions manufacture. In London, the *Women's Dreadnought* under the 'Army Contracts and Sweating', reported cases dealt with by the Public Health Officers of Bethnal Green, including one where the manufacture of soldiers' flannel belts was paid at 8d per dozen, yet it took three hours to produce twelve belts. In a twelve-hour day a worker earned only 2 shillings.[16]

In Berlin attempts were made to stabilize the fortunes of piece-workers. They were to be paid 75 per cent of the contract price per item, but important deductions would be made from this sum to cover not only insurance, but even the cost of sewing materials such as thread. There were even cases of unscrupulous employers charging women rent for their work space in a factory.[17] Later in the war the receipt of 75 per cent of the contract price actually proved to be a serious handicap to the wages of piece-workers, for the growing ersatz economy saw the introduction of paper-based materials which reduced the price per item – and therefore earnings – yet involved no significant reduction in either labour or time.

Attempts were made to secure reasonable wages for Parisian home-workers. In March 1916, the Department of the Seine tried to enforce a minimum wage of 50 centimes per hour, but this would have taken the wages of home-workers above those paid to factory and workshop employees. The measure encountered fierce resistance from employers, and eventually they agreed upon the lower level of 30 centimes per hour.[18]

In Paris the imposition of minimum wage levels was of great importance. An inspection of five factories in April 1916 revealed that almost all the workers were paid the absolute minimum wage.[19] Moreover, despite a 33 per cent rise in prices, little was done to improve these minima except on behalf of apprentices (those in the third and final year of their training), who would have found it difficult to survive without significant wage rises. The rises awarded to apprentices, however, were much greater than those awarded to their skilled colleagues, and between 1914 and 1919 apprentices' wages had risen by between 600 and 700 per cent. For less skilled workers in the fur, tailoring, and millinery trades, salaries were halved during 1915, and did not regain

16 *Women's Dreadnought*, 26 Dec. 1914.

17 Brandenburg LHA, Pr.Br.Rep.30 Berlin C, Jahresberichte der Gewerbe-Aufsicht, n. 1956, pp. 322–3.

18 'Enquêtes sur les salaires en 1920 et 1921', *Bulletin de la Statistique générale de France* (July, 1921), pp. 341–2.

19 *Bulletin du Ministère du Travail* (Jan., Feb., and March 1926), p. 15.

their pre-war level until September 1916. Increases came only in May and June 1917. This had a dramatic effect on the wage hierarchy within sectors of the trade, and even after significant post-Armistice rises for all clothing workers, the wage differentials between workers in the same branch had diminished substantially.

Wage statistics for London are less conclusive, but seem to indicate a similar pattern. Average earnings, as opposed to wages, in the shirt-and-collar trade demonstrated a gradual but consistent rise throughout the war, and exceeded the legal minimum wage rate until November 1916. Committee on Production wartime awards in the autumn of 1917, and spring of 1918 took minimum hourly rates to 8d, but do not seem to have been reflected in greater earnings, or in improvements for better-paid workers. It appears they were introduced as compensation for a reduction in working hours, maintaining earnings in a shorter working week. In April 1919, the Ministry of Labour finally intervened, enforcing a trade-wide minimum rate in the clothing industry of 7d per hour (28s for a 48-hour week), although this undercut some of the individual agreements reached between the Committee on Production and certain branches of the London clothing trades.[20]

If the fortunes of clothing workers in Paris and London experienced an upturn, however slight, in 1916, the opposite was true for Berlin. Diminished demand forced the authorities to limit working hours for tailors to 40 hours per week, although in theory wages were assured at 80 per cent of their usual level. Wage increases of 10 per cent for homeworkers and 7 per cent for finishers (*Zwischenarbeiter*) hardly compensated them for work restrictions which limited them to 70 per cent of their previous workload. In addition few of these guarantees were either in place or respected by employers, who by the end of 1916 began to neglect them whatever their liability. The result was a 'considerable drop in income'.[21] In May 1916 the first war-welfare allowances (*Kriegsfürsorge*) for unemployed and underpaid clothing and textile workers were introduced by a consortium of 87 communities in Greater Berlin.[22] Clothing workers increasingly depended on these supplements which stood at 115 per cent of piece-work rates and 90 per cent of the hourly rates for time-workers by the end of 1918.[23]

Assessed in real terms against any of a number of cost-of-living

[20] London assistants and tailoresses reached an agreement in August 1918 securing 37s 6d per week. D.M. Barton, 'The Course of Women's Wages', *Journal of the Royal Statistical Society* (July 1919), pp. 529–33.

[21] *Jahres- und Kassenberichte der Gewerkschaftskommission Berlins und Umgegend*, vol. 27 (1916), p. 42.

[22] *Ibid.*, p. 44.

[23] *Jahres- und Kassenberichte der Gewerkschaftskommission Berlins und Umgegend*, vol. 28 (1917), p. 55.

indices, it is clear that life for clothing workers was financially difficult in all three capital cities. This was particularly true early in the war. Only modest wage rises had been achieved by Londoners and by Parisian skilled workers by December 1916, while in Berlin at this time wages fell. Maintaining an adequate salary depended upon finding work in firms working on war contracts, favouring output over quality. This helps to account for the gains by Parisian apprentices. The lesser-skilled, lower-paid London milliners' wages rose more rapidly than those of their more skilled colleagues (as in the Parisian hat trade), and like the apprentices they were the best prepared to adapt to wartime needs. Here we can see the impact on the reordering of wage hierarchies of the workings of the war economy, justifying the payment of a minimum wage to those in poorly paid trades.

Metal and munitions work

The massive war-time growth area of the economies of Paris, Berlin, and London occurred in the manufacture of armaments. The numbers employed in munitions factories grew dramatically, and stories of both the fabulous wages and wealth earned by arms workers became legion. In Jules Romains' *Verdun*, Edmond and Georgette Maillecottin were said to earn 2,000 francs a month between them, almost six times a reasonable pre-war working-class wage, and more than five times the standard earnings of a skilled turner in 1916.[24] A reporter for the Berlin factory inspectorate noted after the war that 'The living standard of the Berlin working class (*Berliner Arbeiterschaft*) was considerably raised during the war'.[25] He offered slight evidence to support his statement: for example, young workers could apparently afford to rent rooms by themselves instead of sharing them, and they could now afford to attend the cinema and theatre. Such views were widely held in the aftermath of the war.

Were they accurate? By the end of 1914, the demand for weapons and ammunition rose meteorically and factories worked around the clock to supply the armed forces. Opportunities for good pay were there. Despite well-documented wage series for munitions workers, an appraisal of actual earnings is obscured by the need to convert wage rates into earnings. Pay came from many sources of output. Intensity of production was the rule. Overtime, night, and Sunday work were paid at anything from time-and-a-quarter to time-and-a-half, while the prevalence of piece-rates and premium bonus systems of payment all raise elements of doubt about precise estimates of pay. The wage series

[24] Romains, *Verdun*, p. 467.

[25] Brandenburg LHA, Pr.Br.Rep.30 Berlin C, Jahresberichte der Gewerbe-Aufsicht, n. 1958, pp. 323–4.

Table 9.7. *London: weekly wages in shillings, 1914 to 1918, and an index of wages (July 1914 = 100)*

	Fitters/turners		Patternmakers		Machinists	
07/1914	40	100	45/9	100	32	100
11/1914	43	108	48/9	107	35	109
04/1915	47	118	52/9	115	39	122
11/1916	50	125	55/9	122	42	131
04/1917	55	138	60/9	133	—	—
08/1917	58	145	63/9	139	—	—
10/1917[a]	58 + 12.5%	151	63/9 + 12.5%	157	—	—
12/1917	63 + 12.5%	177	68/9 + 12.5%	169	—	—
08/1918	66/6 + 12.5%	187	72/3 + 12.5%	178	—	—
12/1918	71/6 + 12.5%	201	77/3 + 12.5%	190	—	—

[a]Following the National Agreement on General Wage Application, signed by the Engineering Employers Federation and forty-eight trade unions, in February 1917, increases determined by the Committee on Production were universally applied to all male munitions workers over the age of eighteen. The 12.5% increase was only on the standard weekly wage, and did not apply to overtime.
Source: Trade union figures supplied to Labour Research Department, *Wages, prices and profits*, p. 48; *Prices and Wages in the United Kingdom*, pp. 127, 128.

we present here for all three cities are not to be relied upon for a precise picture of earnings, but more for an illustration of wage boundaries. Given the necessary caution in handling these data, we still may discern that wage differentials among skilled, semi-skilled, and unskilled workers narrowed in Paris and London, but remained more solid in Berlin (see tables 9.7, 9.10 and 9.12).

It does seem clear, however, that the massive demand for munitions workers had a favourable impact on all munitions salaries. By late 1914 recruitment of 'War Munitions Volunteers' had become an important part of the British war effort. Initially this targeted 'only men skilled in engineering and kindred trades', but after the shell scandal of May 1915, the burgeoning armaments factories began to welcome all available labour, be it male or female, skilled, semi-skilled, or unskilled. A factory inspectorate in Berlin noted that by March 1915 demand for workers was so great that wage supplements of 35-50 per cent were not uncommon, and in some cases reached as high as 80 per cent, as employers sought to retain their own workers and attract others.[26]

Sustaining a high and consistent output of munitions required the regulation of labour in the three cities. In Berlin the military authorities instituted a system of voluntary leaving certificates which requested

[26] Brandenburg LHA, Pr.Br.Rep.30 Berlin C, n. 1466, Berichte über die Lage der Industrie, 1915–21, p. 15.

Table 9.8. *Paris: an index of standard daily wages in francs, 1914 to 1919 (1914 = 100)*

	Metal-worker (*ajusteur*)		Turner		Blacksmith		Pattern-maker	
1914	9.5	100	9.2	100	9	100	8.5	100
12/1914	10	105	10.5	114	9.3	103	—	—
12/1916	12.15	128	12.1	132	10.9	121	11.4	134
03/1917	13.25	140	13.7	149	13.5	150	13	153
09/1917	13.75	145	14.5	158	13.7	152	13.6	160
11/1917	14.75	155	15.5	168	15	167	14.5	171
07/1918	16.4	173	17.25	187	16.6	184	16.2	191
04/1919	23.8	251	26	283	25.2	280	23.2	273

Source: Tarifs de salaires et conventions collectives pendant la guerre.

Table 9.9. *Paris: an index of minimum daily wages for skilled workers, in francs, 1914 to 1919 (1914 = 100)*

	Metal-worker (*ajusteur*)		Turner		Blacksmith		Pattern-maker	
1914	8	100	8	100	8	100	8	100
12/1915	5.5	69	5.5	69	6	75	—	—
12/1916	8	100	8	100	8	100	8	100
03/1917	10	125	10	125	9.5	119	10	125
09/1917	10	125	10	125	9.5	119	10	125
11/1917	11	137	11	137	11	137	11	137
07/1918	12.5	156	12.5	156	12.5	156	12.5	156
04/1919	17.65	221	18	225	18	225	17.65	221

Source: Tarifs de salaires et conventions collectives pendant la guerre.

employers to hire only those workers who had permission from their previous workplace to change jobs. This did not stop the bonuses, mentioned above, but it curtailed the freedom of labour to such an extent that a War Commission for the Greater Berlin Metal Trades was founded in the spring of 1915, to mediate between workers' demands for the right to work wherever wages were highest, and the employers' requirements of a stable workforce.[27] In London the Munitions of War Act of 1915 imposed even tighter controls. Leaving certificates became compulsory, and a change of employer without permission was possible only after a period of six weeks' unemployment.

[27] *Jahres- und Kassenberichte der Gewerkschaftskommission Berlins und Umgegend*, vol. 25 (1914), pp. 59–60.

Table 9.10. *London: minimum weekly time-rates (in shillings) for British women munitions workers, 1914 to 1918, and an index of wage-rates (1914/15 = 100)*

	On women's work			On men's work		
	Rate	Hours	Index	Rate	Hours	Index
12/1914	12	54	100	—	—	—
10/1915	—	—	—	20	54	100 (National factory)
11/1915	16	54	133	—	—	—
02/1916	—	—	—	20	54	100 (Controlled estimate)
07/1916	20	54	167	20	54	100
01/1917	—	—	—	20	48	100
				[23s 6d	54	117.5]
4/1917[a]	24s 9d	54	206	24s	48	120
				[27s 6d	54	137.5]
8/1917	27s 3d	54	227	26s 6d	48	132.5
				[30s	54	150]
12/1917	30s 9d	54	256	30s	48	150
				[33s 6d	54	167.5]
8/1918	35s 9d	54	298	35s	47	175
				[38s 6d	54	192.5]

[a]Until March 1917, women doing skilled men's work received the same increases. From April 1917, they were awarded separate increases.
Source: PP1919, Cmd 135, vol. XXXI, 'Report of the War Cabinet Committee on Women in Industry'. A. L. Bowley, *Prices and Wages in the United Kingdom*, Oxford, 1921, pp. 186–7.

Although relatively successful, these measure were very unpopular. Official London wages (table 9.7) recorded an increase of only 25 per cent by the end of 1916, compared to a rise in prices of 60 per cent. The sentiment that labour was the only commodity whose price the government had sought to control provoked hostility throughout the war, featuring prominently in the findings of the 1917 Inquiry into Industrial Unrest.[28] On the other hand, it appears that these controls had less effect during the second half of the war. A government memorandum noted that: 'In essential trades the men, rapidly growing bolder, are in a position practically to dictate what wages they shall receive.'[29]

In Berlin and Paris, salaries in munitions factories reflected different conditions. Demand for labour pushed wages up, but the return of soldiers to man war factories in the Paris region added an additional variable: these men were paid civilian wages but they were technically under military discipline. Officials in the munitions industries made

[28] 'Industrial Unrest: reports of the Commission of Inquiry into Industrial Unrest, London and South-Eastern Areas', PP 1917–1918, Cd 8666, vol. XV, p. 120.

[29] Public Record Office (PRO), LAB 2/250/1, Memo from Campbell to Wolff, 21/11/1917.

sure that this special status was not used to threaten militants with a return to the front; in fact many of these men were at the forefront of shop-floor struggles in wartime.

Of a variety of payment systems in all three capitals, piece-rates were by far the most lucrative wage arrangements. There was no limit to the demand for armaments and, as production targets were perpetually increased, the greater the output the better the earnings of piece-rate workers. Moreover, the drive for maximum production led the German authorities to abolish employers' pre-war rights to reduce piece-rates when earnings reached a certain threshold, and thus increased earnings at the expense of the manufactures' overall profit.[30] The Minister of Munitions, Lloyd George, guaranteed the payment of pre-war piece-rates, and as these were based on massively inferior production targets they could offer very generous earning opportunities. Without the establishment of uniform national piece-rates, however, the benefit proved to be solely for workers in factories which had manufactured munitions before the war.

There were important differences in the payment systems in the three cities. In Paris (tables 9.8 and 9.9) skilled workers were paid according to piece-rates, and unskilled workers paid according to time-rates.[31] This arrangement certainly raises questions over what was deemed 'skilled' work, but in London it ensured the stability of the pre-war wage hierarchy. In London and Berlin, skilled workers were employed on supervisory roles, and therefore only time-rate payment was suitable.[32] Semi-skilled and unskilled workers enjoyed the apparently more lucrative piece-rate system, in some cases upsetting the traditional wage hierarchy, as the Inquiry into Industrial Unrest discovered: 'The earnings of the skilled man are much less on a whole than the earnings of the semi-skilled piece-workers'.[33] Steps were taken to right this 'topsy-turvy arrangement' in October 1917, with the award of a 12.5 per cent wage rise to time-workers just three months later, suggesting that the differences between the two systems was not so great. This point finds corroboration in data on the earnings of workers at both national Shell and Projectile Factories in April 1918 (table 9.11), where foremen (undoubtedly employed on supervisory functions and thus paid time-rates) earned approximately 40 per cent more than machine operators (who were far more likely to have been paid on piece-rates).[34]

[30] P. Quante, *Lohnpolitik und Lohnentwicklung im Kriege* (Berlin, 1920), p. 329.

[31] The GIMM (*Groupe des Industries Métallurgiques, Mécaniques et Connexes*) inquiry of 1920 revealed that only 13 per cent of unskilled workers were paid piece-rates, as opposed to 73 per cent of turners and pattern-makers (*décolleteurs*).

[32] Thanks are due to Elisabeth Domansky for help on this point.

[33] *Industrial Unrest: Reports of the Commission of Enquiry into Industrial Unrest*, p. 3.

[34] War Cabinet Committee on Women in industry, PP 1919, Cmd 135, XXXI, p. 121.

Table 9.11. *London: average weekly wages and earnings in April 1918, in fifteen national projectile factories (5,107 men and 12,939 women) and thirty national shell factories (20,750 men and 20,686 women)*

Job	Shell factories						Projectile factories					
	Wages			Earnings			Wages			Earnings		
Men	£	s	d	£	s	d	£	s	d	£	s	d
Foremen	4	16	6	6	13	4	5	5	10	6	12	7
Fitters	3	12	0	5	1	8	3	8	5	4	19	8
Turners	3	9	2	5	1	8	3	1	10	6	2	10
Machine operators	2	9	9	3	15	0	2	11	7	4	12	8
Labourers	2	9	0	3	10	0	2	12	6	4	2	6
Average	2	19	3	4	6	6	2	19	1	4	14	8
Women												
Forewomen	2	2	1	2	10	10	2	9	8	3	4	2
Tool room workers	1	12	2	1	14	9	1	11	1	1	19	5
Machine operators	1	12	1	2	2	7	1	14	1	3	2	5
Labourers	1	11	4	1	17	9	1	14	1	2	6	3
Average	1	12	8	2	2	4	1	14	8	2	16	8

Source: PP 1919, Cmd 135, vol. XXXI, 'Report of the War Cabinet Committee on Women in Industry', p. 121.

If munitions work proved particularly lucrative to any workers, it was to women. Despite employers' refusals to recognize female labour as anything but unskilled, and their reluctance to acknowledge equal work when women were substituted for men, women did make substantial gains. In Britain Circular L2, issued in October 1915, guaranteed women doing men's work exactly the same time-rates or piece-rates (table 9.10). If the principle was clear, the practice was confused, since there were numerous loopholes whereby employers could claim that women had not directly replaced men. For example, women rarely had the necessary engineering experience to set up a machine. The circular was more concerned with preventing the undercutting of male rates than ensuring a fair deal for women, but it implicitly acknowledged that women could do skilled work.

It was not until May 1916 that some women in Berlin (table 9.12) managed to win promotion from Category 3 work, which involved some semi-skilled practices. Their earnings, however, had already risen significantly from mid-1915 through a series of war-supplements which favoured lower-paid employees. In Paris (table 9.13) directives from the French Minister of Armaments secured wage rises for women munitions workers, but they did so relatively late in the war, in March 1917.

Table 9.12. *Berlin: an index of average hourly wages (in pfennigs) for semi-skilled, unskilled and piece-work, for women, in Berlin metal-work factories, 1914 to 1918 (July 1914 = 100)*

	Verband Berliner Semi-skilled		Verband Berliner Unskilled		Seimenswerks Semi-skilled		AEG, *et al.* Piece-work	
04–06/1914	—	—	—	—	40	100	—	—
07/1914	41	100	32	100	—	—	44	100
01–03/1915	—	—	—	—	45	113	—	—
04/1915	—	—	—	—	—	—	50	114
12/1915	52	141	37	130	—	—	—	—
01–03/1916	—	—	—	—	49	123	—	—
05/1916	—	—	—	—	—	—	70	159
12/1916	62	151	48	150	—	—	74	168
02/1917	—	—	—	—	63	158	—	—
01–03/1917	—	—	—	—	—	—	83	189
06/1917	69	168	64	200	—	—	—	—
07–09/1917	—	—	—	—	78	195	—	—
12/1917	87	212	75	234	—	—	87	198
03/1918	90	220	79	247	—	—	—	—
06/1918	93	227	80	250	—	—	—	—
09/1918	94	229	86	269	—	—	—	—
12/1918	111	271	90	281	—	—	—	—

Source: Quante, *Lohnpolitik und Lohnentwicklung im Kriege.*

Table 9.13. *Paris: average and minimum salaries for women metal-workers, 1914–1919, and an index of salaries (1914 = 100)*

	1914	7/15	12/15	12/16	3/17	11/17	7/18	4/19
Semi-skilled								
Average	3.75	—	3.75	6	7.5	9.5	10.5	12.5
	100		100	160	200	253	280	333
Minimum	3.5	2.3	3.5	4.5	6.5	8	9	10.5
	100	67	100	129	186	229	257	300
Unskilled								
Average	3.25	—	3.25	5	7.5	8.5	9.5	11.5
	100		100	154	231	261	292	354
Minimum	2.9	2	3	4	6.5	7.5	8.5	10.5
	100	69	103	138	224	259	293	362

Source: Tarifs de salaires et conventions collectives pendant la guerre.

The earnings of semi-skilled women workers rose more rapidly than did those of unskilled women until the spring of 1917; the reverse was true thereafter. In general, from early 1917 the rise in women's wages in Parisian war factories outstripped the rise in prices.

The fate of munitions workers may have been generally favourable, but there was no uniform story to tell for all workers. Paid on piece-rates, skilled Parisian munitions workers saw their minimum wages rise slowly during the war. The delays functioned as an incentive to the maintenance of high output levels. Fluctuations in their earnings paralleled price movements. In contrast, the pre-war wage hierarchy was upset from the spring of 1917 when blacksmiths and turners overtook metal-workers, establishing a lead which remained well after the Armistice. Conclusions for London are less clear cut, with high wages current in almost all branches of the armaments industry, yet only the less-skilled workers appeared to have made any improvements in their purchasing power. This would suggest a narrowing of wage hierarchies through a twofold movement: the skilled falling back, and the semi-skilled and unskilled (especially women) catching up. Figures for the National Shell and Projectile Factories in the spring of 1918 suggest, however, that the hierarchy of earnings had been much less affected than the wage levels imply. Since skilled workers were employed on time-rates, they were probably able to work longer hours on supervisory duties less exacting on their health than the repetitive piece-work employment of semi-skilled or unskilled men. Moreover, these statistics reveal that, whatever the gains made by women armaments workers, both their wages and earnings remained substantially below those of their male counterparts.

In Berlin, wages of munitions workers depended both upon their branch of manufacture and their skill level. In the metal trades major wage advances were made by skilled workers who thereby increased the wage differential over unskilled male labourers from 27 per cent to 43 per cent in the course of the war. In the explosives trade there was a much more even advance of wages for all workers. Among German women munitions workers, the semi-skilled enjoyed higher wages and greater increases than the unskilled until after December 1916, when the unskilled recorded an important advance. In real terms, these women continued to lag behind the semi-skilled for the rest of the war. The same was true with respect to the sexual division of pay. The pay of women munitions workers in Berlin rose more slowly than did male wages, further compromising the position of women at a time of massive price inflation.

The comprehensive system of wage-supplements in Berlin narrowed incomes to a degree greater than wage levels suggest. These payments were made only in state-owned factories, although the effect they had on wages could not be ignored by private manufacturers.[35] The first benefit to be introduced was the War-time Assistance for Children

[35] Quante, *Lohnpolitik*, p. 329.

(*Kinderkriegsbeihilfe*) of October 1915, which helped to support the families of all munitions workers earning less than 160 marks per month. This was followed by two more supplements, the War-time Family Assistance and the War Expenses Bonus, both of which were also means-tested. These were particularly important benefits for women workers, who earned much less than their male colleagues. When the War Expenses Bonus was introduced, 6,722 women out of approximately 7,000 at the Feuerwerks Laboratorium Spandau initially qualified.[36] By the end of the war, these supplements could increase the income of an unskilled worker with two children by as much as one-third.[37]

Wages and competition

If the sole criterion for considering wages was take-home pay at the end of the week, then it is clear that munitions workers suffered least during the war. This is not to say that wage movements matched price movements, but it does suggest that of all workers in the three capital cities their earnings were least diminished by wartime inflation.

This is the global picture, but we must nuance it with respect to city, time, and sector. The outbreak of war brought a striking loss of purchasing power for all workers in Paris. Builders struggled to maintain their pre-war salaries, some clothing workers saw their wages halved, and even the wages of women munitions workers fell by one-third. Mapped against price rises early in the war, these static wage conditions translated into serious shortfalls in purchasing power. By February 1916 seamstresses were still 60 per cent below their pre-war level, and even successful armaments workers had experienced a reduction in purchasing power of around 20 per cent. By the end of 1917, however, certain sections of the workforce had made major improvements in their purchasing power, especially unskilled women munitions workers who had made advances of close to 40 per cent compared to the pre-war period. This compared favourably with both male munitions workers (who only later in the war reached parity with their pre-war purchasing power) and especially with women working in other industries.

Thus, if 'winning' meant simply keeping abreast of inflation, and avoiding wartime impoverishment through the eclipse of wage rises by price rises, then there is no difficulty in identifying the 'winners': apprentices in the clothing trades and women munitions workers. While the wages of all Parisian clothing workers had caught up with inflation by October 1918, the length of the period spent catching up

[36] *Ibid.*, pp. 329, 341–2. [37] *Ibid.*, pp. 342, 375.

made the war a very hard time for almost all except apprentices. In 1917 and 1918, employers in the clothing trades had to increase wages in order to preserve their labour force; thus the indirect effect of munitions salaries was to raise female wages across the board.

In London, munitions workers initially were able to protect the value of their earnings. Despite a rise in the cost-of-living of 22 per cent, their salaries kept abreast of inflation well into 1915, another indication of stability and continuity in the social history of the British war effort. Gradually, however, government efforts to restrict wage rises through the Munitions of War Act began to take effect, and by 1916 the wages of male armaments workers had joined the wages of workers in all other trades in falling below their pre-war purchasing power. Increases in hourly rates were cancelled out by a reduction in the working week for shirt-and-collar workers, and for women workers in London only the munitions trade offered generous earning opportunities. The wage differential between men and women narrowed, though women's wages were still substantially lower. In comparison to the wages current in traditional spheres of female employment (such as domestic service and home-work), the advances were dramatic. Indeed, for women doing women's work, wage rises (meagre before 1914) never approached wartime inflation (see tables 9.5–9.6); the gains came in the munitions sector.

To ensure continuity of production and minimize labour disputes, from 1917 the Committee on Production began to award nationwide wage increases. Initially these were only for war workers, although the awards soon spread to other branches of less essential work. These flat-rate increases helped the more poorly paid workers more, and key benefits were granted to women workers. The first was a reduction in the age of majority from 21 to 18, so that more women were paid adult rather than youth wages. Secondly, minimal hourly rates were guaranteed, even for piece-workers. This proved to be a major wartime gain for women (as the War Cabinet report on women in industry noted), since 'It had not even been conceded to the male workers in Woolwich Arsenal in pre-war days.'[38]

In Berlin those who maintained adequate incomes were those in receipt of war bonuses. For clothing workers these were essential supplements to all branches and skill levels since the reduction of available work seriously affected wages during the war. In the construction trade, on the other hand, bonuses were targeted for unskilled employees providing some protection against the steep rises in the cost of living, and offering some incentive to remain as builders rather than

[38] *Report of the War Cabinet Committee on Women in Industry*, PP 1919, Cmd 135, vol. XXXI, p. 124.

pursue work in the munitions trade. The result was a reordering of the skill differential of wages, especially beneficial for the unskilled.

Wage hierarchies within the Berlin munitions industries remained much more stable than in the other two cities. Movements in the wages of women workers failed to match those for their male colleagues; the sex differential of pay remained level in the explosives trade, and changed to the disadvantage of women in the metal industry.

With respect to the skill differential of wages, in the metals trades skilled workers actually increased the wage differential between themselves and all other workers (table 9.14), although in the explosives trade wage rises were much more even for all workers. Compared to workers in other trades, however, employment in the Berlin armaments industries was by far the best option for maintaining purchasing power. When food commodities became particularly scarce, the ability of large companies such as Siemens to commandeer supplies and sell directly to their own workforce proved to be an important advantage for workers in the struggle to keep up with the cost of living.

Standards of living

We have argued in chapter 1 that the well-being of the population is not measured by a simple progression of purchasing power. Especially in wartime, the intensity of labour was critical. Wages were payment for hours worked and effort spent, so that if only harder work and longer hours enabled workers to maintain the real value of earnings, then merely to remain on a level with rising prices entailed hardship. Ashley's formulation is particularly apposite to wartime conditions: 'overtime earnings are earnings for which the employees have given not only additional work but work which involves additional strain'.[39] Thus simply to reproduce pre-war levels of production was inadequate in wartime.

Both patriotism and financial necessity contributed to workers' willingness to accept a longer working week. One observer of wartime London reported that 'Sunday work is optional in theory, but compulsory in practice; and women are obliged to consent in order to meet the high cost of living.'[40] Similar cases of long hours – up to sixty hours per week – were common in both Paris and Berlin. For skilled engineers and metal-workers in Berlin, twelve-hour days were far from unusual, and even seventeen-hour days not infrequent. When the Factory Inspectorate wanted to calculate weekly earnings in 1915, they based their calculations on an *average* 57-hour week (six ten-hour shifts, with a

[39] London School of Economics (BLPES), Sumner Committee working papers, R(0)43 f332, no. 108.

[40] B. Drake, *Women in the engineering trades* (London, 1917), p. 53.

Table 9.14. *Berlin: an index of average hourly wages (in pfennigs), by trade according to the Berlin Employers' Association (Verband Berliner Metallindustrieller), 1914 to 1918 (June 1914 = 100)*

	Skilled				Semi-skilled					
	Machine metal-worker		Fitter		Machine worker		Driller		Unskilled Warehouse worker	
06/1914	75	100	82	100	57	100	70	100	54	100
12/1915	114	152	111	135	92	144	100	143	65	120
12/1916	168	224	152	185	120	211	138	197	79	146
06/1917	196	261	164	200	144	253	156	223	92	170
12/1917	218	291	207	252	166	291	182	260	108	200
06/1918	242	323	221	270	177	311	197	281	114	238
12/1918	283	377	253	309	210	368	237	339	151	280

half-hour lunch break).[41] In Paris the eight-hour day was not introduced until May 1919, though restrictions on working hours were in place by 1917. Workers in war factories had Sundays off from May 1917. In Paris, limiting the working week was one means of protecting the health of women workers, and thereby promoting a revival of the birth-rate, a constant preoccupation of wartime propaganda.

With maximum output the goal of all manufacturers during the war, the relation between productivity and the health of the workforce was only gradually appreciated. British inquiries into working practices discovered that a shorter working day actually led to an increase in both hours worked – through a dramatic reduction in lost time – and in total output.[42] This led to measures to end Sunday work (Direcular L86 of April 1917), and eventually to reduce shifts from twelve to eight hours, for, as the inquiry discovered, 'No employer who has once adopted the shorter scale of hours ever desires to return to a longer period.'[43] It was not only hours spent at a factory, however, which took their toll on workers' health, for increasing numbers of people were travelling further and further on a daily basis to take up jobs in munitions sites, often on overcrowded transport.[44]

41 Brandenburg LHA, Pr.Br.Rep.30 Berlin C, Jahresberichte der Gewerbe-Aufsicht, n. 1958, pp. 258–9. Brandenburg LHA, Pr.Br.Rep.30 Berlin C, Berichte über die Lage der Industrie, n. 1466, p. 12.

42 In one test case, workers on a twelve-hour day produced 262 units, those on a ten-hour day 276 units, and those on an eight-hour day, 316 units. 'Second Interim Report on an Investigation of Industrial Fatigue by Physiological Methods', PP 1916, Cmd 8335, vol. XI, p. 44.

43 Ministry of Munitions: Health of Munitions Workers Committee. Memorandum No. 5. Hours of Work. PP 1916, Cmd 8186, vol. XXIII, p. 5.

44 Ministry of Munitions: 'Health of Munition Workers Committee. Final Report.

A reduction of hours, however, required an increase in hourly wage rates to compensate for the loss of earnings. In London this was clearly done, with clothing workers awarded significant rises to their minimal rates from 1917 onwards. In Paris, on the other hand, employers do not appear to have recognized the shortfall in income caused by reducing hours. Moves towards the curtailment of overtime, together with the introduction of 'la semaine anglaise', in May 1917, which abolished Saturday afternoon work for women, had a serious impact on earnings, and form part of the explanation for the spring strikes of 1917, occurring at a time of soaring prices.[45]

One partial measure of the real value of incomes during the war is the amount of disposable income available to workers. The evidence, however, tends to be anecdotal, although certain statistics point the same way. In all three cities contemporary accounts single out munitions workers as the principal beneficiaries of generous wages and of lavish expenditure. We have already noted the account of the Berlin factory inspector who saw greater attendance at the cinema and theatre by the working classes. In London John Gray had no difficulty in distinguishing a munitions worker, 'There was no mistaking the flashy fur coats and the fashionable high-legged coloured boots of the women, or the gaudy suits and caps of the men, and the money-to-burn manners of both.'[46]

Evidence from the archives of the Midland Bank suggests that there was indeed a degree of surplus income among munitions workers, for deposits in the Woolwich Branch (Woolwich was the main armaments manufacturing district of London) rose by 543 per cent compared to only 93 per cent for the Rotherhithe Branch, situated in another area of the capital. These data suggest a particularly buoyant economy for the Woolwich area, but it is impossible to know which workers in particular were able to increase their savings.[47]

In Berlin the military authorities actually introduced a plan restricting workers under the age of eighteen from receiving more than 18 marks per week, the rest of their earnings to be placed in savings accounts. By April 1918 there were deposits of 8.75 million marks, of which only 3.375 million were paid out during the war.[48] Here again there are grounds for assuming that at various periods of the war some

Industrial health and efficiency', PP 1918, Cmd 9065, vol. XII, p. 32. Report from the Select Committee on Transport (Metropolitan Area)', PP 1919, Cmd 9978, vol. VII, p. 399. [45] Robert, 'Ouvriers et mouvement ouvrier', vol. VI.

[46] Gray, *Gin and bitters*, p. 104.

[47] We are grateful to the Midland Bank archivist for unpublished information on both deposit and current accounts at selected branches, 1913–19. *Midland Bank Group Archives*.

[48] Brandenburg LHA, Pr.Br.Rep.30 Berlin C, Jahresberichte der Gewerbe-Aufsicht, n. 1956, pp. 282–4.

of the workers in the three capitals enjoyed an income which had not only kept pace with their pre-war purchasing power, but in fact had exceeded it. This improvement, however, needed to come from a relatively high starting point, and was much less significant for workers whose initial income was lower. Thus, the move from domestic labour and home-work to munitions factories brought with it an important and sizeable wage increase for poorly paid women, even before they had been granted their first wage rise. Outside war-work, for those who remained with their traditional trade, there do not appear to be accounts of either spending sprees or conspicuous expenditure, and this includes Parisian clothing apprentices who had been awarded pay rises of over 800 per cent. Their total income still left little margin for extravagance.

There were two flaws in the cost-of-living index. The first was that it did not adequately reflect price movements, which were more volatile than wages. The second was that different social groups had different minimal forms of expenditure. House rent posed less of a problem to families with more than one working adult. The loss of a major wage-earner to the armed forces did not necessarily spell disaster for a household. There was one fewer person to provide for, and in any case, separation allowances offered some compensation. Any reduction in the family income might be further offset by letting out the absent man's room. In munitions areas the sum received was in some cases sufficient to cover the rent of the entire property (the rent moratorium applied only to households, not to sub-let rooms).[49]

Conclusion

This sketch of the available evidence on wages and earnings in wartime only broaches the question as to the impact of war on the economic situation of the mass of the working population. The array of situations and factors which could affect the income of an individual during the Great War extended well beyond the workplace. If many workers were now working excessive hours and enduring the prolonged stress of munitions production, others were glad of the available employment. Carters and hawkers, and most notably London dock-workers no longer had to suffer the vagaries of the casual-labour system, and many men enjoyed regular employment and a regular salary for the first time in their lives.[50] Similarly, unemployment figures for builders remained extremely low for the war period.

This is not to say, however, that the period of the Great War was anything but difficult for the majority of workers in Paris, Berlin and

[49] Pember-Reeves, *Round about a pound a week* (London, Virago, 1979), p. 97.

[50] G. Phillips and N. Whiteside, *Casual labour. The unemployment question in the port transport industry 1880–1970* (Oxford, 1985), pp. 82, 125.

London. Even in the better-paid munitions industries wage rises followed rather than anticipated increases in the cost of living,[51] and in non-war-related work no rises were awarded until 1916. Those uninvolved with the war economy were impoverished during the conflict. A sense of the rapid progress made by women and young workers moving into the armaments trade has to be tempered by a recognition of the long-term sacrifices they made. They left school early, received no comprehensive training, followed no formal apprenticeship, and when the signing of the Armistice signalled the end of the demand for armaments, they were the first to be cast into unemployment. Boys who under ordinary circumstances would have completed an education or trade apprenticeship found themselves after the war unqualified, unskilled, and unemployed.

Writing in 1919, Hammond's conclusion for England seems applicable to all three capital cities:

> When pay for over-time, Sundays and holidays, besides the greater regularity of employment, are taken into consideration, perhaps the economic situation of the English working man or working woman is not materially worse than before the war, but if so, this means that it requires more effort to maintain the same standard of living. As a matter of fact, the old standard is not being maintained, but substitutes have been made for commodities largely consumed before the war.[52]

The war presented civilians with a host of material problems, and wages could only form part of the solution. Shortages appeared irregularly in all three cities. The worst were in Berlin. Faced by the black market, it was better to be wealthy than poor, but money was no guarantee of access to goods. Uncertainty dominated material life in Berlin.

In the other two capitals, too, the strain of longer working hours had material consequences. Workers' health was a precarious commodity, and fatigue threatened both earnings and productive capacity. One observer noted that output fell in the night shift at the National Projectile Factory at London's Hackney Marshes, 'due to the fact that women had to stand in food queues during the day'.[53]

Daily life was a test of wits and stamina, and the struggle to find affordable food and fuel placed an even heavier strain on citizens with smaller budgets. Against this backdrop, we have to weight the significance of rising money incomes, and narrowing wage hierarchies. On balance, the costs of such improvement were heavy. In the Great War there were few 'winners'. Perhaps the most sober conclusion is that

[51] Labour Research Department, *Wages, prices and profits* (London, 1922), p. 46.

[52] M.B. Hammond, *British labour conditions and legislation during the war* (Oxford, 1919), p. 201.

[53] *History of the Ministry of Munitions* (1923), vol. VIII, part 2, p. 140.

during the conflict some workers lost less than others. Moreover, those who achieved the principal wartime material gains were the first to lose them after the Armistice: women munitions workers.

The post-war period did, however, reveal improvements in the conditions of employment in all three cities. Hours of work were dramatically reduced towards a standard 48-hour week, and workers were now guaranteed minimal time rates even when employed on piece-rates. The levelling up of wages brought important improvements to those who were chronically underpaid before the war, such as Parisian clothing apprentices, and home workers in the three cities. Concern over the health of munitions workers led to inquiries and greater awareness of how to improve working conditions. More regular breaks, and the massive development of factory canteens, were welcome benefits to the health of manufacturing workers.[54]

What is the sum of all these vectors? There is no simple answer, but certain features of wages and earnings in wartime stand out. Some workers earned enough to purchase household necessities without difficulty; most were less fortunate. Some were better off during the war, with respect to regularity and levels of earnings, than before 1914. It cannot be ignored, however, that these advances resulted from four years of instability and strain, starting (especially in Paris) with a surge of unemployment and loss of earnings, and later requiring longer and longer hours and harder work to support the national war effort.

The overall impression is one of precariousness and uncertainty. On balance, the suspension of the free market in labour, described in chapters 5–7, benefited especially the poorest and most irregularly employed sections of the pre-war population. Better-off workers had variable fortunes in wartime, none approaching the exaggerated claims as to workers' conspicuous consumption circulating in the popular press.

In effect, everyone made some kind of sacrifice in wartime, even if the degree of hardship varied substantially over time and sector. There is no one story to tell in terms of wages in wartime, but within the overall picture one general point emerges. The balance between the rights of citizenship and the workings of the labour market was never stable, but in Berlin it was more unstable than in the Allied capitals. On the Allied side of the line, though at great cost in terms of effort and endurance, incomes for most workers were sufficient to defend what Sen calls 'functionings' and 'capabilities'. In Berlin, increasingly after 1916, this was not the case.

The sheer scale of inflation, which in Berlin in the second half of the

[54] Mathilde Dubesset, Françoise Thébaud, and Catherine Vincent, 'The munitionnettes of the Seine', in P. Fridenson (ed.), *The French home front* (Oxford, 1992), ch. 12.

war dwarfed price rises in London and Paris, meant that Berlin workers could not possibly command wages which would enable them regularly to purchase even a modicum of household necessities. What did citizenship mean in this situation? Entitlements were paper realities. Civil rights were no guarantee of survival, as the flourishing black market in Berlin (significantly absent in Paris and London) attested.

In each city, there were those who suffered more than others. Wartime social policy is a reflection of both administrative and popular sensitivity to the fragility of the material situation of the mass of the population and of the wartime consensus as to the need to supplement wages, especially for those with men in the armed forces. The panoply of transfer payments promulgated in wartime, to which we now turn, was necessary because, at a time of massive inflation, wage levels in all three cities were an insufficient and at times misleading guide to well-being in wartime. How these policies were framed and with what effect is the subject of the next chapter.

10
Transfer payments and social policy

Thierry Bonzon

Introduction

The outbreak of the Great War powerfully disrupted the domestic life of millions of urban residents. The mobilization during the first months of the war of 30 per cent of the male labour force in Paris and 28 per cent in Berlin, and the voluntary enlistment of 15 per cent of London workers,[1] reduced household income because men's work was the principal source of family income in all three cities.[2] When social policy considered family welfare at the turn of the century, the need to fit male incomes to family needs was a widely held assumption.[3] The war made this a matter of urgent necessity. In Paris, the scale of the employment crisis, the very slow restructuring of the labour market and the persistence of high levels of unemployment all weighed particularly heavily on domestic life.[4] Later the unprecedented rise in the cost of living, the difficulty of finding basic provisions in all three capital cities – but especially in Berlin[5] – made the redirection of income to family needs a prime factor in the management of the war on the home front.

The reshaping of the labour market in these three cities, with an increase in the number and a change in the deployment of women workers, as well as the introduction of wages policies, had profound implications for the urban population.[6] This chapter surveys the

[1] Estimates for the end of September 1914. Cf. Jon Lawrence, Martin Dean, and Jean-Louis Robert, 'The outbreak of war and the urban economy: Paris, Berlin, and London in 1914', *Economic History Review*, 45, 3 (1992), p. 574.

[2] In 1911 58 per cent of women in Paris over the age of 15 worked outside the home; the figure for London was 43 per cent, against only 38 per cent in Berlin in 1910. The proportion of men over the age of 15 who were employed stood at 92, 93 and 87 per cent for the three cities respectively. Cf. Lawrence, Dean, and Robert, 'The outbreak of war', table 1, pp. 566–7.

[3] On this point, see the work of Susan Pedersen, notably her PhD thesis, 'Social policy and the reconstruction of the family in Britain and France, 1900–1945', PhD thesis, Harvard University, 1989.

[4] See above, chs. 5 and 6.

[5] See below, chs. 11 and 12.

[6] See above, ch. 8.

essential part in the maintenance of household incomes played by redistributive social policies.[7]

In Paris, London, and Berlin, three sectors contributed to social transfer payments: the state, local authorities, and an array of private groups, communities and institutions. The role of the last, although still not sufficiently well known, was in many ways fundamental, and the many forms of group identity in the three cities expressed through this work deserve closer study.[8] In each city the overlap among these three elements formed a specific configuration of central importance in pre-war social policy. That relationship was destabilized by war. This chapter addresses the question, how did social policy evolve, both in principal and in practice, during a war in which pressures on households grew ever greater?

At the level of the capital cities, the scale of the problems to be resolved and the gravity of the political, military, and economic situation required a fundamental reorganization of social policy admin-

[7] To disencumber the text, and to shorten the tabular material in it, the following is a list of sources from which evidence on social policy has been drawn.

For Paris: Conseil municipal de Paris, Rapports et Documents, nos. 49 and 60 (1915), nos. 20 and 95 (1919); *Annuaire statistique de la Ville de Paris* (1914–1919); Conseil municipal de Paris, Procès verbaux, 10 Dec. 1915, 13 Nov. 1916, 8 Dec. 1916, 12 Nov. 1917, 16 Nov. 1917; *Journal officiel*, 12 March 1918; Antoine Prost, *Les anciens combattants et la société française, 1914–1939* (Paris, 1977), vol. I.

For London: Report of the Departmental committee on Old Age Pensions, PP 1919, XXVII, Cmd 410; Scheme of the Lords Commissioners of his Majesty's Treasury for the award of additional allowances to old age pensioners suffering special hardship owing to the war, PP 1916, XXIII, Cd 8373; Administrative concessions made to old age pensioners, PP 1916, XXIII, Cd 8320. London County Council, *London Statistics, 1915–1920* (London, 1921); G. Thomas, 'State maintenance for women during the First World War: the case of separation allowances and pensions' (PhD thesis, University of Sussex, 1989); F. Tilyard, *Unemployment insurance in Great Britain, 1911–1948* (Leigh-on-Sea, 1949); Board of Trade, *Labour Gazette*, Oct. 1914, Aug. 1915; Ministry of Labour, Final Report of the Committee of Inquiry into the scheme of out-of-work donation, PP 1919, XXX, Cmd 305; J. M. Hogge and T. H. Garside, *War pensions and allowances* (London, 1918); Report of the Administration of the national Relief Fund, PP 1914–16, XXXI, Cd 7756; PP 1917–18, XVII, Cd 8449.

For Berlin: Kaeber, *Berlin*; Julius Parst, *Gesetzliche Kriegsfürsorge Invaliden – und Hinterbliebenen – Fürsorge* (Berlin, 1915); *Berliner Fürsorge-Arbeit während des Krieges* (Berlin, 1916).

[8] The development and the role of private bodies during the war, and in particular the work of the churches, remains under-researched, though everyone acknowledges their importance. Some recent work has revealed urban solidarities by stressing the mobilization of particular social groups, for example, Parisian workers. See Jean-Louis Robert, 'Mobilisations militantes à Paris pendant la grande guerre', paper presented to the conference on Mobilizing for total war: society and state in Europe 1914–1918, Dublin, 23–25 June 1993.

istered by local, regional, or national public authorities. This fuelled a process of concentration which challenged the triangular configuration described above. It led to an unprecedented expansion in public expenditure as the public sector took over social payments, such as separation allowances, unemployment benefit, and military pensions.

The fundamental shift may be described in the following terms. Before the war, the German system of social insurance was nationally determined and locally administered. As a system of right it was in advance of that available in Britain or France. But under the pressure of war and of material shortages, German rights became privileges, whereas British and French privileges became rights. There are qualifications which must be made in this overall interpretation, but it provides a basis upon which to construct a more nuanced history of social policy in wartime.

In the Allied capitals, the 'threshold effect' of war is apparent.[9] It was not only that a threshold of benefits was passed, but also a threshold of taxation necessary to maintain such transfer payments. The case of France is instructive. From 1914–17, a decision to impose an income tax was postponed. In 1917, that difficult step became unavoidable. After the war, income tax stayed, and brought in its wake the means to deliver a package of transfer payments, which constituted a redistribution of income from the middle classes to the poorest citizens, to supplement, match, or replace traditional forms of aid based on individual charity or patronage.

The aim of the regulatory procedures introduced in wartime was to restrict the extent of sacrifices required of the poorest and most vulnerable social groups. Intended to correct the effects of the market by intervening between wage movements on one side and inflation on the other, they were the subject of constant negotiation between social groups, their representatives, and central or local authorities. How this negotiation was conducted is a subject for the second volume of this study. Here we investigate how far social transfers in wartime attained their aim: to guarantee to all a minimum standard of living at a time of rapid price inflation and material shortages.

Social policy was undoubtedly a weapon capable of strengthening social cohesion on the home front, and measures were defined in terms of precise targets. They traced the clear outlines of a social geography of rights, defined both by inclusion and exclusion. They thereby helped to create a hierarchical image of society organized in concentric circles, defining and/or deepening the concept of urban citizenship by reference to contribution to the war effort. This topography of citizenship

[9] Alan T. Peacock and Jack Wiseman, assisted by Jindrich Vevenka, *The growth of public expenditure in the United Kingdom* (London, 1961).

needs to be explored first, in each city, before we turn to particular policy measures.

The concept of citizenship built up by these social policies imposed responsibilities which were emphasized time and again during the war: the responsibilities of national defence, of forming and maintaining the armies, of accepting sacrifice and casualties, of the 'blood tax'.[10] But the sacrifices required were so painful and unprecedented and their social distribution so varied that the pressures of war on the home front seemed more likely to destroy social cohesion than to fortify it.

The aim of social policy was to reaffirm the bonds of citizenship by reformulating the package of rights due to urban residents tested by the war. In many respects the success of the authorities' attempts to replace the notion of benefit as a privilege with the idea of benefit as a citizen's right, and a right that could be exercised not only in theory but in practice, was an essential element in shoring up the endurance of urban populations in the hard years of the war.

In the first two years of the war, all three cities' populations knew hardship, but conditions were no worse in Berlin than in Paris or London. In some respects, as we have noted in chapter 5, Parisians had the hardest time in 1914-15. After 1916, Berlin was the worst off. In contrast, in the last two years of the war, while major problems existed – for instance, with respect to the supply of coal – most urban residents in Paris and London were assured of access to basic necessities as of right. In Berlin, however, such was the scale of material and administrative problems that this commitment remained only a pious hope. On the metropolitan level, the authorities could do little to affect overall levels of consumption, and their failure was found to shake social cohesion to a degree which undermined the legitimacy and the authority of the regime. In the German capital, rights were reduced to privileges, and privileges were a function of who knew whom and who could operate the black market most effectively. That story we tell in volume II of this study.

Social provision and social policy in 1914

To highlight the contrast in the wartime history of social policy, a brief examination of social benefits available to metropolitan populations in 1914 is essential. Here we can see clear divergences among the cities. With respect to retirement pay, unemployment benefit, and access by right to medical care, Paris was well behind Berlin or London on the eve of the war.

[10] John Horne, 'L'impôt du sang'.

From 1889 those over the age of sixty-five in Germany were entitled to a pension. In Britain old-age pensions were introduced in 1908, and supported 610,000 people by the following year. The law on French workers' and peasants' retirement pensions was introduced in 1910. This established a system funded by compulsory contributions from workers and employers, topped up modestly by state funds. The scheme was pared down due to the combined hostility of employers and the Confédération Générale du Travail (CGT): the principle of compulsory insurance was quickly abandoned. A year before the war it covered only 50 per cent of potentially insurable people and the sums distributed were negligible.

In France there was no health-insurance system, in marked contrast to the scheme developed out of Bismarck's legislation in 1883, through which all full-time industrial workers in Berlin subscribed to a Krankenkasse (national health-insurance office). In Britain the National Insurance Act was passed in 1911, providing all workers with a minimum base of health insurance. That minimum was not available by right to French citizens before the 1914-18 war; care for the poor through Assistance Publique partly filled this vacuum.

The same contrast was evident in protection against unemployment. On the eve of the war, London workers without work in a number of 'precarious trades', especially on the docks, could rely on unemployment benefit distributed under the National Insurance Act of 1911. Berliners, especially male industrial workers, were covered through the national scheme of social insurance, organized and administered at the provincial and local level. At the same time, the unemployed Parisian worker had to seek trade-union or mutual-aid support, or turn to charity.

This contrast helps account for the difference in the sphere of family policy between the British and German model of wage bargaining and the French model. In effect, in London and Berlin workers bargained for higher wages as individuals in the labour market. In Paris they bargained as heads of families.[11] The same different approach marked unemployment benefit. In London and Berlin, the issue was the man out of work. In Paris the issue was tied up with the size of the unemployed worker's family.[12]

The mix between the central state, the municipal authorities, and private associations was different in the three cities. The rule of thumb is that the state was least evident in the French case. In Britain, the pre-war balance between local authority and central authority was clear: the weight was more heavily on the side of local authority. The German system was national in law and provincial and municipal in reality. The

[11] Susan Pedersen 'Social policy', ch. 1, pp. 27–73.

[12] See Susan Pedersen, 'Gender, welfare and citizenship in Britain during the Great War', *American Historical Review*, 95, 4 (1990), pp. 983–1006.

balance between the two was contested, both before and during the war, as we shall see in volume II.[13]

Fiscal conservatism helps to account for French retardation in social policy. Maternity benefit and aid to *familles nombreuses* were introduced by law in 1913, but both reflected the outlook of French conservatives, at one and the same time pronatalist – favouring a rise in the birth rate – and unwilling to authorize major expenditure to help raise the birthrate. In France, political resistance to the imposition of taxes encouraged support for mutual-aid bureaux which distributed unemployment aid (under the law of 1905). This placed private enterprise rather than state agencies at the centre of social provision. Similarly, in Paris the special association between local and state authorities' finance was a constant element; thus the financing of the law of 1905 covering aid for 'the old, the infirm and the incurable' was funded 30 per cent by the state and the Department, the remaining 70 per cent being a charge on the city of Paris whose income was secured through a cluster of local taxes, the *octroi*.

In London and Berlin as well, the link between private activity and public intervention was intrinsic to social policy.[14] In the British capital it was expressed through the work of groups such as the Charity Organization Society or the Salvation Army. The central state never displaced local authorities or philanthropic organizations as the focus of aid for the sick, the unemployed, the elderly. This was also true with respect to Berlin.

On the eve of the war traditional systems of social aid (in which aid remained subject to the recipient proving that his or her need was legitimate) overlapped with policies of benefit by right. In all three capital cities the two systems coexisted. In the French capital, even though the right of certain categories of people to aid was recognized without question (as with respect to maternity benefit), the payment of many grants rested on the judgement of the Charity Board of the local *mairie* (as, notably, for the 1913 law on aid for large families). In London some measures tended to stigmatize the beneficiary and others, more developed than in Paris, aimed at instituting the right of support for fixed categories. This applied particularly to unemployment insurance. In Berlin, many workers, women in particular, fell through the social net created by the Bismarckian system of social insurance. We must beware of mistaking national legislation for urban reality in the field of social policy, then as now.

Social policy and transfer payments during the war

In each of the three cities, from August 1914 social policy measures were framed to help support those suffering from some facets of war-related

[13] We are grateful to Elisabeth Domansky for discussions on this point.

[14] See José Harris, *Public lives, private virtues* (Oxford, 1993).

deprivation: the wives and dependants of mobilized men; disabled veterans; war widows; and the unemployed.

Separation allowances initially were the most important facet of wartime transfer payments. Such payments affected a substantial part of the population of each city. These allowances took the form of family-based benefits, compensating for the interruption in the income of the head of the family. In Berlin immediately and in London after some confusion, these payments were a right to the families of all soldiers (except for officers). In Paris these payments closely resembled a form of traditional aid: proof of need was required to justify the payment of the allowance. Local committees considering requests issued a decree fixing a maximum income level above which a wife could not receive benefit: this was established at around 4 francs per day. The work of the local committees was on several occasions subjected to the same criticisms from socialists as had been directed previously to traditional charitable institutions which scrutinized carefully anyone asking for benefit.[15]

To what extent did the military allowance compensate for the loss of the mobilized man's wages (taking into account, of course, the changed size of the household in wartime)? This question can be posed with respect to all three cities. A comparison of two sets of wages and household size in the three cities shows that the income per head in January 1915 was higher in London: the decrease there was clearly less than in Berlin and much less than in Paris (between 3 and 37 per cent for London; between 21 and 72 per cent for Paris). Family-based benefits and the military allowance took sufficient account of household size to favour the largest families in comparison with childless couples, whatever the husband's wages before mobilization. In Paris the gap between the childless and the *famille nombreuse* even reached 50 per cent in certain cases. Finally, the lower level of grant in Berlin and Paris penalized households where the husband's wage was more substantial.

An initial approach based on the size of the grants alone (tables 10.1, 10.2 and 10.3) appears to show a more favourable situation in London, where the sums allocated were larger, regardless of household size. The policy on military allowances clearly favoured large families in all three cities. Thus in Paris and Berlin, in January 1915, a mother of three children received twice as much money as did a childless soldier's wife. This preference increased throughout the war, becoming more marked in Paris (the multiplier was 2.5 for London and Berlin, but 3 for Paris); this should not be surprising in view of the vitality of the pronatalist movement in France.

[15] Alphonse Loyau attacked the excessive rigour of the committees: 'Every day the canton committees rule out many women who have found a job, usually in munitions factories . . . as soon as their wages exceed 3 francs per day, their benefit allowance is withdrawn.' Conseil municipal de Paris, *Procès-verbaux*, 15 April 1916, p. 260.

Table 10.1. *Separation allowances in Paris, 1914 to 1919, in francs, compared to a monthly wage for skilled men and for semi-skilled women in the metal trades, according to family size, and an index of the rise in the cost of living (1914 = 100)*

Date	Rate of pay (francs): skilled men/day	Male earnings per month (francs)	Rate of pay (francs): semi-skilled per day	Woman's earnings per month (francs)	Monthly separation allowance: childless	Monthly separation allowance: 3 children	Indexed cost of living (1914 = 100)
August 1914	9.5	228	3.75	90	37.5	82.5	100
January 1915	10	240	—	—	37.5	82.5	115
July 1915	—	—	—	—	37.5	82.5	120
January 1916	12.15	291.6	3.75	90	37.5	105	133
July 1916	—	—	—	—	37.5	105	133
January 1917	13.25	318	6	144	37.5	105	148
July 1917	13.75	330	7.5	180	37.5	105	183
January 1918	14.75	354	9.5	228	45	135	203
July 1918	16.4	393.6	10.5	252	45	135	225
January 1919	23.8	571.2	12.5	300	45	135	256
July 1919	—	—	—	—	—	—	256

Sources: Wages: chapter 9, tables 9, 12; prices and allowances: see note 7.

Table 10.2. *Separation allowances in London, 1914 to 1919, compared to a monthly wage for skilled men and for semi-skilled women in the metal trades, according to family size, and an index of the rise in the cost of living (1914 = 100)*

Date	Rate of pay: (shillings) skilled men/week	Male earnings per month (shillings)	Woman's pay (shillings/pence) semi-skilled per week	Woman's earnings per month (shillings)	Separation allowance: childless (shillings/(month)	Monthly separation allowance: 3 children	Indexed cost of living (1914 = 100)
August 1914	40	160	12	48	50	86	100
January 1915	43	172	—	—	—	—	115
July 1915	47	188	—	—	—	—	125
January 1916	—	—	16	64	—	—	137
July 1916	—	—	—	—	—	—	150
January 1917	50	200	—	—	50	110	168
July 1917	58	232	24/9	99	—	—	182
January 1918	71	284	30/9	123	—	—	190
July 1918	75	300	35/9	143	—	—	208
January 1919	80	320	—	—	50	134	218
July 1919	—	—	—	—	—	—	213

Sources: Wages: chapter 9, tables 9,12; prices and allowances: see note 7.

Table 10.3. *Separation allowances in Berlin, 1914 to 1919, compared to a monthly wage for skilled men and for semi-skilled women in the metal trades, according to family size, and an index of the rise in the cost of living (1914 = 100)*

Date	Men's rate of pay: skilled/hour (Pfennigs)	Male earnings per month (Marks/ Pfennigs)	Women's rate of pay semi-skilled per hour (Pfennigs)	Woman's earnings per month (Marks/ Pfennigs)	Monthly separation allowance: childless	Monthly separation allowance: 3 children	Indexed cost of living (1914 = 100)
August 1914	75	162	41	88.56	18	48	100
January 1915	—	—	—	—	24	54	119
July 1915	—	—	—	—	—	—	135
January 1916	114	246.24	52	112.32	30	75	141
July 1916	—	—	—	—	—	—	191
January 1917	168	362.88	62	133.92	40	100	224
July 1917	196	423.36	69	149.04	—	—	262
January 1918	218	470.88	87	187.92	50	110	293
July 1918	242	522.72	93	200.88	—	—	317
January 1919	283	611.28	111	239.76	60	120	356
July 1919	—	—	—	—	—	—	412

Note: The length of the average working week is estimated at 54 hours.
Sources: Wages: chapter 9, tables 9, 12; prices and allowances: see note 7.

The distinction between material benefit and its real value with respect to purchasing power appears in indices shown in real terms in tables 10.1, 10.2, and 10.3. They emphasize the range of circumstances operating in the three capitals. For a woman without children whose husband was at the Front, the contrast between Berlin on the one hand and Paris and London on the other was striking. In Berlin, separation allowances retained their value: they rose from 18 to 40 marks between 1914 and 1917; in Paris and London, 1914 and 1917 levels were identical. At no time during the war did the authorities in the Allied capitals take adequate steps in favour of women without children whose husbands were mobilized. However, we should not be too optimistic about the situation in Berlin. The absolute level of separation allowances in Berlin was relatively low; though they retained their value, they were still inadequate for many women throughout the war.

For those with several children to care for, the situation varied less sharply between the cities. First, the benefits were increased, though insufficiently to prevent a loss of pre-war purchasing power as inflation outstripped benefits. Secondly, the differences among the three cities were smaller, and on several occasions during the war there was a visible effort to help these families. None the less, over the period as a whole, it was only in London that revisions of the grant enabled it to maintain roughly the same purchasing power in January 1919 as it had had in August 1914. In Paris and Berlin, on the other hand, the purchasing power of separation allowances fell in step, as the rate of inflation increased rapidly.

In Paris the increasing cost of household provisions – and particularly the surge in prices in the spring of 1917 – hit hard at the real value of the benefit, which remained stable between July 1916 and late 1917. However, the rise in the allowance in January 1918 brought some improvement. Conversely, in Berlin the increase in the allowance introduced in January 1918 brought no relief from the pressure of inflation, in the face of which the authorities were impotent.

On balance, quantitative surveys of military allowances reveal fairly strong contrasts: a higher level in London than in Paris or above all Berlin; privilege accorded to large families in London and Paris; better cost-of-living indexation in Berlin for married women without children, better levels of benefit in London than in Paris for women with several children to care for.

Yet these initial conclusions require some qualification. First we must consider the problems raised by the way cost-of-living assessments were carried out in Berlin. The official figures available do not take account of black-market prices, which are known to have been very much greater than official prices. They therefore tend to underestimate considerably the real price rise in food experienced by the consumer, particularly after 1916. On the other hand, those in receipt of family allowances also had access to other forms of support or benefits.

These supplementary benefits were concerned primarily with housing and rents, which was the subject of state intervention in all three cities. Thus in Berlin, throughout the war – after October 1914 – the mobilized man's family received housing aid (*Mietbeihilfe*). At the beginning of the war the aid was substantial: it represented a 75 per cent increase on the military grant. However, as it was not revalued later, it became derisory and by November 1918 it represented only a 15 per cent addition to the grant which had itself substantially depreciated in value. In London a similar measure operated from March 1917. More substantial than in Berlin, it could reach £2 per week and further increased the contrast between London and Berlin.

Rent control was an essential pillar of social policy in wartime. In London a freeze on rents – if they were less than £35 per year – was imposed at their August 1914 level. In all three cities, industrial warfare required this brutal suppression of the rights of possessive individualism. The importance of this measure for the families of Paris mobilized men goes without saying; renewed every quarter after 14 August 1914 and controlling all rents under 1,000 francs, the law of 3 March 1918 ratified this great social transfer to the detriment of the middle classes.

Finally, still in Paris, the free distribution of coal and potatoes organized by the city was a form of aid equivalent in monetary terms to some 10 francs per month every winter, or an increase in the military grant of about 25 per cent for a married woman without children in January 1917, a little less (22 per cent) two years later. This was a form of benefit available to all, not just to those with husbands in uniform.

The two surges of unemployment in the three cities, at the outset and after the war, led the authorities to intervene to improve or consolidate the existing support systems. In Paris unemployment benefit was first organized by the local authorities in a totally improvised manner; it was not until the end of August that a series of circulars regulated the operation of this new state-subsidized service and gave unemployment allowances their distinctive pattern. In Berlin a law of 1 September 1914 allowed the unemployed to benefit from allowances (*Arbeitslosenfürsorge*) during the capital's first period of unemployment, and in November 1918 a similar system was introduced (*Erwerbslosenfürsorge*) which aimed to compensate the unemployed during demobilization. London had a similar system, with its Emergency Grant, introduced in October 1914 (which operated until the end of May 1915) and the Out-of-Work Grant instituted at the end of November 1918.

Comparison of unemployment benefit levels shows the lowest levels in Berlin; but it should be stressed that these sums were supplemented by contributions from trade unions and professional organizations, and from provincial insurance offices, the levels and regularity of which remain unknown. Although the family-based French allowances distributed larger benefits in cases with dependent children, a woman without work whose husband was mobilized could not retain both military and unemployment grants.

Above all, in all three cities, the end of the war and the period of demobilization brought a spectacular revision of grants: the rate at the beginning of the war was doubled in Paris and Berlin, trebled in London. The loss in income for the unemployment-grant recipient compared to the income which he could expect if he were taken on for work diminished sharply: from 52 to 35 per cent for a Parisian unskilled construction worker with three children, from 69 to 28 per cent for comparable circumstances in London. Obviously, the low levels of benefit at the beginning of the war were an incitement to join the labour market while in 1919 it was a matter above all of avoiding social upheaval. In all, there were few major differences among the three capitals in this facet of the history of social policy.

Last but not least were war widows. Here the history of social policy in the three cities also parallel. The grants paid to war widows at the beginning of the war were roughly similar for the wife of a private soldier – slightly higher in Paris (47 francs per month against 25 marks in Berlin and 20 shillings in London). The situation in London was improved by July 1915, when the widows' pension was doubled, and by September 1919, when it was doubled again. The progression was a little less if the widow had three dependent children, but the base figure was also higher – double the amount in 1914. Further, in London there is evidence of a real determination to ensure an adequate level of benefit for war widows. This is hardly surprising, given the way they symbolized in their private lives the sacrifice the nation as a whole was making. Berlin was no exception here. An effort was made to provide for war widows, though benefit levels could not keep up with the cost of living.

Legislation concerning disabled men was full of regulations of varying degrees of complexity. It is not our intention to specify in detail the various elements making up the allowance, nor the procedures leading up to its definition in each country. But it is nevertheless important to stress a series of universal problems. The question of whether a medical condition was 'service attributable' was one of the most delicate. Could the increased severity of previous illness during leave from the front be grounds for compensation? Although this was accepted in Germany, resistance in France was strong and the painful problem of tuberculosis sufferers led to the elaboration of a special statute, that of the 'Discharge No. 2'. As described by Antoine Prost,[16] the extreme complexity of the legislation must be recognized. Until March 1919 the granting of a pension for disability and discharge from the army were in opposition to each other. There was a myriad of qualifications concerning the attribution of a condition to the nature of military service, the determination as to whether or not it was incurable, how grave it was, and how it affected the disabled man's ability to support himself in civilian life. Incomprehensible to the ordinary citizen, this legislation, and the tedious administrative procedures which it engendered, created a feeling of disorientation and dissatisfaction all the greater because of frequent cases of manifest injustice.

Recognizing the peculiarities of the three national systems, we are still able to offer a few general comparisons. The system of allowances arising from military mobilization, including associated measures (rent freezes and free distributions by the Paris city authorities), worked moderately well in London and, to a lesser degree, in Paris. In Berlin the authorities' inability to maintain the real value of benefits was clearly evident in the case of large families and the unemployed.

During the demobilization period, the contrast between increased grants in Paris and London on one hand and continuing inadequate levels in Berlin proved once more that in Germany public authorities were incapable of introducing transfer payments which in the eyes of urban residents, would guarantee access to minimum levels of consumption. An examination of benefits for invalids and war widows reinforces the same contrast: limited though real compensation in Paris and London; inadequate compensation for war-related deprivation in Berlin.

The war and social benefits: passing through a threshold?

The introduction of these social benefits in all three cases, led to a redistribution of roles between city, state, and the traditional aid agencies. This was true in all three cases. Social tension in wartime had to be controlled; in this effort public authorities on the municipal level played an important role. Although they did not vanish entirely, the worlds of philanthropy and traditional forms of aid were placed in a much more subordinate position in the framework of social policy than had been the case before the war.

London in August 1914 had no administrative organization capable of managing the system of separation allowances. To fill the gap, initially the War Office – as the body paying the allowances – charged the private voluntary organization the Soldiers' and Sailors' Families

16 Antoine Prost, *Les anciens combattants et la société française 1914–1939* (Paris, 1977), vol. I.

Association (SSFA) with organizing their distribution. This combination demonstrated the private/public partnership which was repeated right down to the premises used by SSFA representatives. They occupied the Local Distress Committees established at the beginning of the war at the instigation of the Local Government Board. Given the huge pressure of numbers eligible for benefit, it is not surprising that this arrangement quickly reached crisis point. Only later was a relatively efficient administrative system introduced.

The work of SSFA was not restricted to the simple distribution of allowances, but represented the traditional role of charitable organizations. Subject to checks, inquiries into morals and home visits, and forced to hear advice on domestic management, the benefit recipients were liable to see their grant withdrawn under pretext of drunkenness or infidelity. Such practices aroused numerous attacks from the labour movement, on the grounds that the distribution of a state allowance via a charitable organization was intolerable.[17] Finally, after the introduction of a parliamentary inquiry, the SSFA's role was much reduced when the Ministry of Pensions adopted the grant system in 1917. Then separation allowances became an entirely public measure financed directly by the Treasury and administered by the Ministry of Pensions.

In London unemployment benefits developed in similar fashion. At the beginning of the war the government was content to rely largely on private charitable organizations (notably the Prince of Wales' Relief Fund) which were closely associated with the local distress committees. The situation in force at demobilization, a moment matching the crisis of 1914, was a striking contrast with the first months of the war. The Out-of-Work Donation, introduced on 25 November 1918, left no room for philanthropic activity and settled the state's responsibility in the world of social-transfer payments.

Although the procedure in Paris was perhaps less spectacular, it was none the less unmistakably different after the war. As local authorities took on responsibility for unemployment, powerfully backed by governmental intervention with the creation of the Fonds de chômage de la ville de Paris and the Office départemental de placement de la Seine, private organizations were marginalized. Above all, this concentration in the hands of public powers represented a change in the logic of policy. Public intervention in the sphere of social benefits opened the door to the creation of a broader structure of citizens' rights. In Paris, for example, the allocation of separation allowances changed. Initially its grant was not a right and depended on independent assessment by the members of local commissions. Over time it was subordinated to general rules, precise regulations which restricted arbitrary acts. Obtaining the unemployment benefit correspondingly evolved towards a

[17] Susan Pedersen, 'Social policy', ch. 2, pp. 121–3.

right for all those who had lost their jobs because of the war. Finally, the regulations affecting the selection of beneficiaries of free distribution of goods by the Paris municipal authorities were substantially reassessed in a session of the city council on 8 December 1916. Until then benefits in kind were disbursed by benefit offices – which were concerned with the 'most needy'. Thereafter, the principle of distribution by right carried the day. From a practical point of view, this decision entailed a radical alteration in the character of distribution. What had been a matter of allocating a sack of coal after inquiry into the recipient's circumstances, leading inevitably to numerous recriminations, became a preliminary assessment of all beneficiaries, enabling the allocation to each household of quantities in line with the stock available. Equity replaced moral scrutiny, at least in wartime.

Thus the system of transfer payments created by the war simultaneously reflected a relative reduction in philanthropy and revealed an eclipse of its methods. Privilege was replaced by the affirmation of a right. That right was the basis of social-transfer payments, justifying the distribution of goods paid for by the public as a whole for the welfare of the less well-off sections of the community.

The evolution of legislation on disability pensions in France is the best illustration of this change. At the beginning of the war the pension was above all a gesture, a manifestation of national solidarity for a man marked physically by the war, a form of charitable aid. It expressed no right to compensation since mutilation was seen as part of the risk which accompanied the 'blood tax' imposed by the regime. However, the law of December 1916 acknowledged military responsibility for disability, and a little more than two years later the law of March 1919 included the right to compensation in its rubric.

This elaboration of a basket of rights, paid for through the transfer of wealth from the community as a whole to those in need of assistance, was inaugurated during the war under the guidance of both local and national authorities. This system – visible in all three cities – contributed powerfully to strengthening closer social ties among citizens and shoring up the legitimacy of the public powers. Above all it constructed a notion of citizenship which defined itself by the access of urban populations to minimum levels of essential goods.

The novelty of this idea in London is apparent in comparison with Paris, the soul of Republican tradition. The urban dimension should be emphasized here. In Paris municipal institutions played a determining role, even if they were sometimes only the agent of governmental intervention. In Paris the various benefits were distributed at the arrondissement's benefit bureau, free coal was collected from the municipal coal-yard, and it was at the municipal butchers' shops that meat could be bought at a low price.

This shift in the nature of urban citizenship was of long-term importance in all three cities. Only in Paris and London did resources match rights, enabling the authorities to deliver the goods. In Berlin, whatever the will, local authorities could only deliver what they had, and the longer the war dragged on, that was never enough.

Conclusion

The war was therefore a moment of significance in the reorganization of social benefits, especially in London and Paris. The situation in the three cities at the beginning of the century was characterized by a plurality of systems in fluid and often contradictory situations. The outbreak of war precipitated the adoption of responsibility for social benefits by public authorities and the marginalization of philanthropic activity. This concentration effect of welfare[18] was inevitable in view of the impact of the war and the scale of operations introduced. It also determined a second effect, a threshold effect, increasing irreversibly the financial responsibility of public authorities and the level of taxation necessary to fulfil these obligations.

In all three cities authorities aimed at replacing privileges by rights. In Paris and London they were able to do so. In Berlin, the authorities were powerless to oversee the creation of a new definition of urban citizenship, defined in part by the right of access to a minimum of essential goods and services. That achievement was limited to the Allied capitals.

The system of benefits set in place during the war contributed to the construction of a new urban social structure. Those whose sacrifice was directly linked to the war effort earned the greatest right to social benefits. The disabled and war widows featured to differing degrees at the heart of the social-transfer payments. Others, like the elderly, were not so lucky. Thus we must be cautious before generalizing about the impact of these new wartime social policies. There were those marginalized as much as those given pride of place. But on balance, especially in the Allied capitals, the new system helped to shore up social cohesion in wartime.

We must supplement this story with respect to the fortunes of middle-class families and other social groups. But in sum the story seems clear. In Berlin, a pre-war system in some respects in advance of that in Paris and London turned from a system of rights to a system of privileges, especially for those able to work the black market. In the Allied capitals, privileges became rights, with lasting consequences for the history of social policy in this century.

[18] Peacock and Wiseman, *The growth of public expenditure*, ch. 8.

Part 5
The social relations of consumption

11
Feeding the cities

Thierry Bonzon and Belinda Davis

Introduction

Recent research on how the Great War affected food supplies and patterns of consumption in the combatant nations has concentrated on policies and conditions in aggregate or in scattered urban environments.[1] Provisioning the three capital cities during the 1914–18 conflict was similar in kind to the problems faced in other areas. But in the case of Paris, London, and Berlin, the scale of the problem was immense. The varied success in adequately provisioning the people played a role in the ultimate outcome of the war itself. Issues not only of food supplies necessary to absolute physical survival, but also of indigenous food culture, equitable distribution, and the states' legitimacy as measured by their responses to hardships were central to both popular and policy discussions of the 'food question'.

Paris, London, and Berlin, with their millions of inhabitants, demanded vast amounts of food: 3.6 million people to be fed in greater

[1] Cf. P.E. Dewey, 'Food production and policy in the United Kingdom, 1914–1918', *Transactions of the Royal Historical Society*, 30 (1980), pp. 71–89. Work on the effects of the blockade on Germany includes the following: A.Bell, *A History of the blockade of Germany and the countries associated with her in the Great War, Austria-Hungary, Bulgaria, and Turkey, 1914–1918* (London, 1937); Paul Vincent, *The politics of hunger* (Athens, Ohio, 1985); Lothar Burchardt, *Friedenswirtschaft und Kriegsvorsorge* (Boppard am Rhein, 1968); and Offer, *An agrarian interpretation*. Contemporary accounts include George Schreiner, *The iron ration* (New York, 1918); as well as E. Blücher von Wahlstatt, *An English wife in Berlin* (New York, 1920); and Cooper, *Behind the Lines*. The effects of the Allied blockade on the immediate post-war period are the subject of a recent survey by N.P. Howard, 'The social and political consequences of the Allied blockade of Germany, 1918–1919', *German History*, 11, 2 (1993), pp. 161–88. Rhineland-Westphalia has been studied by Anne Roerkohl, *Hungerblockade und Heimatfront* (Stuttgart, 1991). For other urban cases, see J.P. Bott, 'The German food crisis of World War I: the cases of Coblenz and Cologne' (PhD thesis, University of Missouri, 1981), and Tobin, (War and the working class), pp. 257–98, as well as V. Ullrich, *Kriegsalltag: Hamburg im Ersten Weltkrieg* (Cologne, 1982), for insight into the situation in Hamburg. With the exception of the publications from the Carnegie Foundation in the 1920s, there are no such works relating to French cities.

Berlin in 1914, over 4 million in the Paris region, and more than 7.2 million in the colossal conurbation of London.[2] With 6 per cent of the national population in Berlin, 10 per cent in Paris and a staggering 16 per cent in London, these urban concentrations – each unique in its own country – demanded complex supply and distribution systems simply to stay afloat. In Paris, supply was a spectacular and noisy affair in the heart of the city: the 'Stomach of Paris', with its supporting apparatus congesting the city centre, was also an anthropomorphic symbol for the life of the city as a whole. The vast social mix of the three cities, the great variety of their characteristic trades, and the presence of public institutions (charitable and aid organizations in particular, but also schools, universities, hospitals, and military barracks) added to the uniquely diverse character of metropolitan demand.

The capitals' demand for food was enormous; but, in wartime, it was also highly variable. In Paris and Berlin, mobilization brought a double shift. Rising numbers of Berliner and Parisian men left for the front.[3] At the same time, workers, especially women, flocked in from the countryside and small towns to these two cities;[4] and, by mid-war, German propaganda simultaneously and contradictorily exhorted workers to work in the capital's munitions industry, and to leave the city to reap much-needed crops for which adequate rural labour was lacking. From the start of the war, refugees from the eastern provinces also added to Berlin's swollen population. But fluctuations in population numbers varied all the more spectacularly in Paris, because it was close to the war zone. In September 1914 alone, a massive influx of refugees followed the departure from the city of a third of the indigenous population of the Department of the Seine.[5] Thereafter, the arrival of fresh refugees, of which there were more than 100,000 in the Department of the Seine on 31 October 1915, and foreign or provincial workers attracted by the prospects of work in war factories, increased the urban population

[2] These figures are from census reports in 1910 for Berlin, and in 1911 for Paris and London. The geographical entities concerned are 'Greater Berlin' defined in 1921, the Metropolitan Police District and City of London, and the Department of the Seine for Paris.

[3] In Paris the number of mobilized men reached 300,000 by the end of September 1914. Henri Sellier suggests 700,000 to 800,000 for the Department in June 1915, while the number of men recalled may be estimated at 100,000 in 1915. In Berlin, 200,000 men were at the front in 1915 while, conversely, between 1915 and 1918 the *Zurückstellung* (recall for factory work) system brought back nearly 100,000 workers. On this point, see Lawrence, Dean, and Robert, 'The outbreak of war and the urban economy', p. 574, and see ch. 3 above.

[4] On female migration during the war, see Ute Daniel, *Arbeiterfrauen in der Kriegsgesellschaft: Beruf, Familie und Politik im Ersten Weltkrieg* (Göttingen, 1989), p. 98.

[5] The results of the census carried out at the request of the military authorities in September 1914 were published in the *Annuaire statistique de la ville de Paris et du Département de la Seine, 1914*, pp. 929 ff.

considerably.[6] At the time of the German spring offensive in 1918, another exodus of Parisians took place,[7] but after the Armistice and throughout the demobilization period an even greater population crowded into the city. One Paris councillor suggested that the population of the Department of the Seine had fluctuated between 2 million and 5 million.[8] The constant flow of men on leave or *en route* to the front added a further dimension to these large-scale movements.

These tidal flows of population inevitably strained the food supply of each capital city. The situation in Berlin was all the more delicate because its extraordinarily rapid population growth in the two pre-war decades was not matched by an expansion of food production in adjacent districts.[9] Further, high tariffs on grain set in 1902 – the state's bargain with rural producers in order to win their support for a naval build-up – substantially increased the cost of basic foods, penalizing the poorest urban consumers, and leading to agitation in working-class districts of Berlin, particularly in 1903 and 1911.[10]

For many people in the Allied capitals, too, food supply was a precarious matter. In Britain concern about levels of consumption led industrialist and social reformer Seebohm Rowntree to formulate the notion of 'the poverty line', and to show that one-third of the urban working classes lived below his stipulated nutritional minimum. In London, the development of the casual labour system made matters desperate for a growing population, and islands of poverty were well established in pre-war Paris.[11]

In all three cities, problems of food supply were made visible by the

[6] In 1917 the estimates carried out for distribution of sugar-ration cards showed Paris with more inhabitants than in 1914: See Robert, 'Ouvriers', vol. I, p. 69.

[7] See ch. 16.

[8] Cf. Conseil municipal de Paris, Procès-verbaux, 30 May 1919, p. 699.

[9] We should remember that the population of greater Berlin grew from 827,000 inhabitants in 1871 to nearly 4,000,000 on the eve of the war, a rate of growth unmatched in Paris or London (see above, chapter 2). On population in Germany during the war, see R. Meerwarth, A. Günther, and W. Zimmerman, *Die Einwirkung des Krieges auf Bevölkerungsbewegung, Einkommen und Lebenshaltung in Deutschland* (Stuttgart, 1932). On agricultural production on the eve of the war compared with the war period, see, along with Burchardt, *Friedenswirtschaft*, F. Aeroboe, *Der Einfluss des Krieges auf die Landwirtschaftliche Produktion in Deutschland* (Stuttgart, 1927); and J. Flemming, *Landwirtschaftliche Interessen und Demokratie* (Bonn, 1978).

[10] The expansion of the Social Democratic party in the 1903 and 1912 elections can be seen in the light of these waves of protest. See on this topic William C. Mathews, 'The German Social Democrats and the inflation: food, foreign trade and the politics of stabilization 1914–1920' (PhD thesis, University of California, Riverside, 1982), ch. 1.

[11] Berlanstein, *Working people of Paris*; Stedman Jones, *Outcast London*; Margaret Anne Crowther, *The workhouse system, 1834–1929; the history of an English social institution* (London, 1983). On German workers' protest emerging from the effects of the tariffs, see e.g. T. Lindenberger, 'Die Fleischrevolte am Wedding. Lebensmittelversorgung und Politik in Berlin am Vorabend des Ersten Weltkrieges', in Manfred Gailus and Heinrich Volkmann (eds.), *Der Kampf um das tägliche Brot* (Opladen, 1994), pp. 282–304.

proximity of the institutions and agents of political power and, in Paris, by revolutionary gestures associated with demands for food. Long before the Russian Revolution of October 1917, political leaders were sensitive to the political implication of such questions. With the outbreak of war, and the subsequent restructuring of the labour force (see chapter 6), the need to feed the domestic population was complicated by the demands of a growing munitions sector and the transitory population of soldiers *en route* to the fronts. The result were periodic food-supply crises of varying severity in all three cities.

These difficult periods were marked by shortages, the development of substitutes, spiralling prices, speculation, rationing and, in Berlin, a robust black market. All made food supply a matter of uncertainty and increasing difficulty the longer the war went on. Complicating matters was the simple fact that food supply is not simply a matter of quantities; food consumption is deeply embedded in cultural codes and norms of daily life. All were challenged in wartime.

Food supply focused social tensions in these urban areas. Strains were inevitable, given the contradiction between the maintenance of market economies in 1914 and the growing consensus that there must be an equality of sacrifice and hardship in wartime. The imposition of rationing did not solve the problem entirely, because variations persisted both in supply and quality, and in the case of Berlin, illegal supply flourished under conditions of controlled prices.

Here again, the situation in Berlin was more difficult than in the other two capital cities. In neither Paris nor London was the protest movement fostered by growing feelings of unequal access to food as great as in Berlin. Problems of food supply and distribution clearly played a decisive role in the unravelling of the German war effort in the last two years of the war.

To understand the diverse experiences of the three cities, the unequal provision and well-being of urban populations at war and of the role which they played at the end of the war, two forms of political decisions are focused on here. One form, at national or international level, concerned the provisioning of urban districts taken as aggregates, while the other, involving central or local authorities, affected the distribution of food within urban societies.

But this is hardly bureaucratic history pure and simple. The key actors at the heart of these processes were the millions of men and women profoundly affected by their nation's engagement in the war. The success of the nation's defence depended largely on their acceptance of unprecedented and hitherto unimaginable sacrifice. That meant first and foremost the armed conflict, but it came to mean a test of endurance at home as well. The *sine qua non* of that endurance was food supply.

Metropolitan food supplies during the war

The capacity of the authorities to maintain food supplies in the three capital cities on a war economy footing was very unequal. The Allied blockade undoubtedly affected food inflows to Berlin, though the precise effects of global changes on urban inputs is impossible to estimate. It is important to bear in mind that the blockade worked two ways, and that food restrictions marked urban life in London and Paris as well, though to a lesser extent than in Berlin.

Constraints on provisioning

On the eve of the war, the contrast between provisioning London and Paris was obvious. London was enmeshed in a largely international food-supply network. This was inevitable in a country where the national wheat harvest supplied no more than 21 per cent of total domestic consumption (see table 11.1). This dependence on the wheat harvests of other lands and on the empire turned the Thames into the British capital's main food artery. Although higher proportions of dairy products and meat were home-produced, imports were still essential on these essential goods.

Matters in Paris were entirely different. French agriculture was relatively efficient and self-sufficient (see table 11.1), and the capital was doubly privileged. It lay at the heart of one of the nation's finest agricultural regions, a veritable grain store – and at the focal junction of the great railway network. Food supplies in Germany were at an intermediate level between French self-sufficiency and British dependency on overseas supplies. Although responsible for only 60 per cent of fats, fish, and eggs consumed, German agriculture produced 90 per cent of the bread cereals, meat, and dairy products, and almost all the nation's necessary supply of potatoes and sugar.[12] In particular, Berlin profited from the rich arable lands of Brandenburg and West Prussia.

The conditions of war transformed both domestic production levels and the capitals' position of access, as a result of enemy activity and of each state's arrogation of resources for use in waging war. In terms of the strictly national food resources available to metropolitan populations, Paris and Berlin thus appear to have been more comfortably placed than London on the eve of the war. However, with the

[12] The Eltzbacher Commission, charged at the outbreak of war with drawing up a statement of the food-supply situation in Germany, estimated that 27 per cent of proteins and 42 per cent of fats consumed in the country came from abroad. See Paul Eltzbacher (ed.), *Die Deutsche Völksernährung und der Englische Aushungerungsplan* (Braunschweig, 1914). See also Offer, *An agrarian interpretation*, p. 25, and Hardach, *The First World War*, pp. 109–10.

Table 11.1. *Proportion of home-grown produce in national pre-war consumption (%)*

	Great Britain	France	Germany
Cereals[a]	21	90	90
Meat	64	100	90
Dairy produce[b]	38	101	90
Potatoes	96	100	>100
Sugar	0	>100	>100

[a]Wheat in Great Britain, all cereals in France, bread cereals in Germany.
[b]Butter in Great Britain, butter and cheese in France.
Sources: France: J. C. Toutain, *Histoire quantitative de l'économie française* (Paris, 1961), pp. 246, 250; Great Britain: W. Beveridge, *British Food Control* (Oxford, 1928), p. 35; Germany: Hardach, *The First World War*, pp. 109–10.

occupation of ten northern departments of France in 1914, one-fifth of cereal production and more than half of sugar-beet production was lost to the French nation.[13] This military disaster immediately put Paris in a difficult position. Less drastic but still worrying was the situation in London, where the interruption of trade between the combatant powers cut pre-war food-supply networks. The shortage of sugar from Austria-Hungary (two-thirds of British consumption before the war) led to a price rise in London of 63 per cent within one month of the outbreak of war.[14]

The impact of the embargo was far greater on Berlin. Yet it is difficult to distinguish between the blockade's direct and indirect effects on quantities of food available in Germany – and in the capital city. Deprivation of American grain, lack of access to British fodder and fertilizer essential to Germany's own production, and German farmers' and merchants' speculation in newly scarce goods were all related to the embargo. Moreover, aggregate figures for the nation provide a different and more sanguine picture than anecdotal sources for Berlin alone would indicate, particularly as the war dragged on; indeed the latter sources speak to the variability of access within the city itself, still associated indirectly with the effects of the blockade.

In evaluating nutritional deficits compared to peacetime, the Eltzbacher Commission, making its report in October 1914, assessed the shortage of calories nationally at one-quarter, and of protein at one-third.[15] On the one hand, Berlin was less directly affected than other

[13] Pierre Barral, *Les agrariens français de Méline à Pisani* (Paris, 1968), pp. 179–80.
[14] W. H. Beveridge, *British food control* (London, 1928), p. 6.
[15] Eltzbacher and his committee presented these findings first in August 1914, then in revised form in December 1914; though slightly less sanguine in the second report, he

parts of the country because the capital was a hub of supplies which were untouched by the trade barrier. On the other hand, Berlin suffered in many ways more from the indirect effects of the blockade (speculation, black-marketeering, urban–rural strains and tensions between the capital and other parts of the country), as we shall see below. Related to this was the question of appropriate distribution of goods, which was key both to adequate nutrition and to a general sense of equity in the way shortages were shared by the population as a whole.

Finally, the effects of enemy activity such as the blockade must be distinguished from the results of the three nations gearing up for, and maintaining, a major war effort, which affected everything from pre-existing systems of distribution to the availability of resources. The state of war upset all the key relationships in the agricultural production system of 1914. France and Germany felt the drop in agricultural production particularly strongly, as a result of state decrees as well as of enemy activity. The causes are well known, including a drop in the labour force on the land as mobilization affected 60 per cent of agricultural workers, loss of cultivated lands, and a shortage of farm animals.[16]

Industrial requirements upset distribution systems for essential inputs. The use of nitrates by the armaments industry deprived all three nations of fertilizer supplies. The shortage was severely felt by German farmers, deprived of Chilean saltpetre for fertilizer, which before the war used three times more artificial nitrates than did French farmers. The same applied to phosphate fertilizers. The lack of horses due to military requisitioning, the difficulty of replacing agricultural tools, and the unreliable delivery of essential supplies were further constraints. It was in Germany again that the difficulties were greatest, contributing to a series of poor harvests throughout the war.

With domestic production reduced in France and Germany, and with Britain forced to revive a shrinking agricultural sector, provisioning in the three cities also suffered from military demand and the commissariat's view of military provisioning in relation to civilian supplies. In France, a manual published in 1914 bluntly defined the army's subsistence method: 'live off the land', 'live off the home front'.[17] To meet food requirements for front-line soldiers, military authorities had prior claim

continued to maintain the viability of provisioning the population despite the effects of the blockade.

16 See for example Joe Lee, 'Administrators and agriculture', in J. M. Winter (ed.), *War and Economic Development* (Cambridge, 1975), pp. 229–38.

17 G. Nony, *L'intendance en campagne* (Paris, 1914), p. 496, as cited in Pierre Barral, 'L'intendance', in G. Canini (ed.), *Les fronts invisibles: Nourrir, fournir, soigner. Colloque international sur la logistique des armées au combat, 1914–1918, Verdun, 1980* (Nancy, 1984), p. 71.

to available resources, codified by a right of requisition which produced many problems, grievances, and irregularities in France and Germany. The expansion of agriculture in Britain was both later and smoother than in the other two countries.[18]

The priority accorded to food supplies for the armies was both unsurprising and significant for civilian levels of consumption. For many of the men in uniform, army food represented a better standard of diet than in their civilian life, and there were no major complaints in France or Britain about the quantity (let alone the quality) of army food.[19] The situation in Germany was worse, especially after 1917.[20]

Civilians did not object to the fact that the armies received the lion's share of available food. In Britain this included imported meat. When the Board of Trade arranged for Australia and New Zealand to send their surplus to Great Britain, civilian markets had access only to what the army did not claim. *The Times* commented: 'In 1915 the consumption of frozen beef by the Allied armies was so great that there was a reduction of about one-half in the supply of chilled beef for the British population.'[21] This intervention was particularly noticeable in London, where 95 per cent of the meat trade consisted of frozen imports.

In Germany the army's priority over the civilian population set cities at the end of the provisioning chain. Berlin suffered constantly from every delay affecting railway transport, which was primarily routed to suit military requirements. This priority was set by the Kriegsrohstoff-abteilung (War Raw Materials Department, KRA), the system that oversaw the provisioning of military forces.[22] Such an order of priorities was understood and accepted by the civilian population. Indeed the emergence of military control over much of the civilian economy in late 1916 was favourably viewed in Berlin, as an indication of renewed hopes that civilians would be supplied with food as efficiently as the troops.[23]

Although the rhythms of the war effort affected food supplies in all

[18] T.H. Middleton, *Food production in war* (Oxford, 1923), ch. 7.

[19] Barral, 'L'intendance', pp. 75–7.

[20] See for example R. Stumpf, *War, mutiny, and revolution in the German navy*, ed. D. Horn (New Brunswick, 1967), as well as F. Carsten, *Revolution in central Europe, 1918–1919* (Berkeley, 1972), who compares the relatively democratized distribution of food in the army with hierarchized distribution in the navy, in which sailors were given spoiled meat while their officers ate well. See also his *War against war* (Berkeley, 1982), e.g. p. 78, on the embittered exchange of letters between the battle front and home front on the food question. The monthly reports of the deputy commanders also attest to the negative effects on morale of this exchange of correspondence, which wasn't completely censored, despite efforts to do so.

[21] *The Times*, 30 September 1916.

[22] See Gerald D. Feldman, *Army, industry and labor*, pp. 45–52.

[23] See Belinda Davis, 'Home fires burning: politics, identity and food in World War I Berlin', PhD thesis, University of Michigan, 1992, chs. 6 and 7.

three cities, it was in Berlin that they were felt most strongly. Reduced agricultural productivity, uncertain transport, the direct and indirect consequences of the blockade, the army's absolute priority from late summer 1916 on, all combined to create enormous difficulties in the final years of the war.

Accessibility of external agricultural supplies

Although Britain, and through her France, had access to substantial overseas food resources, the way in which this second 'hinterland' was used for the benefit of London and Paris requires elaboration. Until the end of 1916, food imports raised many difficulties. Despite various urgent agreements, the Allies' exploitation of overseas markets remained effectively competitive. The two French missions in London responsible for wheat purchases – one military and one civilian – were in competition with each other and with British buyers. The overlap meant higher prices and freight costs.[24]

The creation of the Wheat Executive in November 1916 was an essential stage in the development of a more efficient pattern of Allied cooperation. Central purchasing was set up for the first time, establishing supply programmes in liaison with available shipping. This essential element in provisioning continued to operate efficiently until the end of the war.

However, the onset of the all-out submarine war and the United States' entry into the war in 1917 produced a drastic drop in shipping capacity available for civilian food supplies.[25] In consequence, the Conseil interallié des transports maritimes was created to organize and coordinate shipping.

To these periodic obstacles were added structural difficulties relating to the new supply systems in London and Paris. The vulnerability of sea lanes across the Channel and the North Sea to the east coast of Britain weighed heavily on London's food supply. The dramatic turn of events affecting these routes at the beginning of 1917 led to the expansion of traffic to ports on the west coast of Britain. The disturbance in the normal channels supplying London inevitably affected the efficiency and regularity of deliveries to the capital.

In Paris the flow of products destined to supply the capital was concentrated in the lower Seine area, as trans-Atlantic imports increased; between 1911 to 1913 and 1916 the quantities of farm produce unloaded in the Department of the Seine rose by 250 per cent. As the port of Rouen became choked with traffic along the river, intensified by

24 Cf. L. H. Hinds, 'La coopération économique entre la France et la Grande-Bretagne pendant la Première guerre mondiale', PhD thesis, University of Paris – I, n.d.

25 Dewey, 'Food production', p. 81.

competition between suppliers, periods of paralysis due to bad weather further restricted the flow of essential goods to the capital. Imports dropped dangerously from 1917 because of the submarine war, although deliveries in 1918 were still 1.5 times greater than those of 1911 to 1913.[26] Of course, such deliveries were not the exclusive property of the civilian population. Consequently, though transport policies mitigated the worst problems, supplies for the city never regained 1914 levels.

This was particularly evident with respect to meat supplies to Paris, which dropped 22 per cent.[27] It was not until November 1918 that figures returned to near pre-war levels (see fig. 11.1). The slow growth in quantities delivered was linked to the import situation, but matters were made worse by the capital's low meat-chilling capacity.

As we have noted, the population of Paris varied considerably in size during the war. In the absence of sufficiently detailed figures to define this development, the reading of figure 11.1 remains uncertain. Balancing the numbers of mobilized men against those recalled to join the labour force and incoming refugees, the drop in the Parisian population may be estimated at roughly 5 per cent. Using figures for 1911 to 1913 as a standard of comparison misses this shift in the target population of food-supply policy.

Even given this margin of error, it is clear that food imports were insufficient to avoid problems in food supply and consequent tensions in wartime Paris and London. To appreciate the character of wartime austerity and sacrifice, we must be more precise about the problems these vast populations faced.

Sacrifice and adaptation in the cities

One way to approach the problem of wartime austerity is to assess consumption in relation to pre-war levels. Such an inquiry may focus on calorific value, establishing energy input available to the individual, but such data are only useful when they can be compared to other parameters, such as individual weight and patterns of cooking. What these quantitative data cannot do is to take account of the cultural dimension of food. Food rations might meet energy needs but still leave consumers unsatisfied because of increasing scarcity of a particularly highly valued foodstuff.[28]

Of the three capitals, it is perhaps in Berlin where such issues loomed largest, unquestionably because resources dropped most precipitously. The two decades preceding the war in Germany were marked by

[26] *Annuaire statistique de la Ville de Paris et du Département de la Seine*, 1911–1919.

[27] Unfortunately sources equivalent to the Paris octroi duties are not available for London and Berlin. [28] Offer, *An agrarian interpretation*, pp. 45–53.

Table 11.2. *Food consumption per head per week in London in 1913–1914 and 1918 (in lbs) and in 1918 as a proportion of 1913–1914 consumption (1913–1914 = 100)*

	Pre-war consumption (1) 1913–14 (lbs)	Wartime consumption	
		(2) 1918 (lbs)	(2)/(1) (1913–14 = 100)
Bread and flour	8.20	7.90	96
Milk	1.55	1.66	107
Butter	0.35	0.05	14
Margarine	0.13	0.28	215
Potatoes	3.19	4.61	145
Fresh meat	1.99	0.93	47
Bacon	0.23	0.51	221
Tinned/frozen meat	0.26	0.25	96
Sugar	1.14	0.61	54

Source: Sumner Report Working Papers, BLPES, 42 (f332), vol. 1, p. 64.

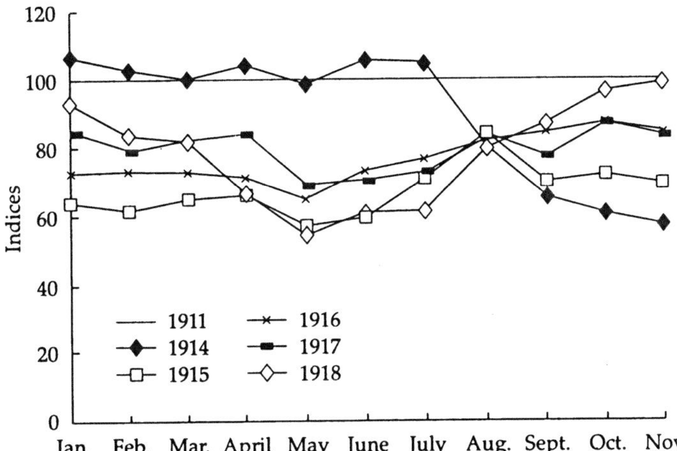

Fig. 11.1 An index of monthly meat deliveries in Paris, 1911 to 1918 (1911 = 100). Source: Conseil municipal de Paris, *Rapports et documents*, 1911–18

transformations in the national diet, for reasons ranging from improved storage technology to urbanization. The changes were perhaps most notable for the urban working class. Thus, although potatoes and bread were still central to the diet of working-class Berlin (and a cornerstone of the national diet, to be sure), pure (domestic) rye bread and rolls had given way to (imported) wheat or wheat-and-rye selections. The consumption of animal fats had also grown considerably, and it is no coincidence that the disastrous drop in the availability of edible fats during the war was a particularly grievous matter. On the eve of the war, pork in some form was an essential part of most Germans' diet; food could not be cooked without fat; and few Germans would eat a slice of bread without some form of fat spread on top. Access to such items were indicators of social integration, and deprivation meant far more than loss of calorific intake.[29] Though to differing degrees, problems of access also played an important role in stirring up social concerns and tensions in the Allied capitals as well.

Other elements of wartime social life complicated food-related grievances. In particular much resentment grew out of the need to devote time to the search for food, and the attendant uncertainties that essential supplies would arrive next week or in a month's time. These are unspecified variables in an equation of wartime well-being. All we can say is that they mattered, and that civilians were intensely aware of them.

Food-consumption patterns touch issues of social identity and self-image. This is why fairness with respect to food supply may matter more than a balanced distribution of other goods. The sensitivity of urban populations in this respect was certainly not invented in 1914, but a new dimension was added: that of the moral discourse of equality of sacrifice in wartime. This ethic required the suspension for the duration of possessive individualism and a free market in food. We have noted that market conditions were controlled but never eliminated; thus tensions were bound to emerge as the war went into its third, fourth, and fifth years.

Such tensions were sharpened by long-standing popular verbal expression of social antagonisms opposing different social categories in terms of physical profile: 'thin' versus 'fat' and 'corpulent' versus 'empty-bellied'.[30] Inequalities in food consumption were time-honoured and therefore conventional, but what was tolerable in peacetime became problematic the longer the war dragged on.

Restrictions on consumption in wartime

All three capital cities experienced some level of shortages as well as price rises for certain basic goods. In each instance the authorities

[29] On the cultural components of diet in Berlin, see Belinda Davis, 'Food scarcity and the empowerment of the female consumer in World War I Berlin', in V. de Grazia (ed.), with E. Furlough, *The sex of things: gender and consumption in historical perspective* (Berkeley, 1995). For Germany more broadly, see e.g. Offer, *An Agrarian Interpretation*; and Alf Lüdtke, 'Hunger, Essens-"Genuss" und Politik bei Fabrikarbeitern und Arbeiterfrauen. Beispiele aus dem rheinisch-westfälischen Industriegebiet 1910–40', *Sozialwissenschaftliche Informationen*, 14, 2 (1985), p. 123.

[30] Maurice Tournier, 'L'envers de 1900, le lexique des luttes et de l'organisation ouvrière en France', *Mots*, 5 (October 1982), pp. 103–26.

Table 11.3. *Consumption per person per week: working-class household in Paris, 1907*

	1907 (g)
Bread	3860
Potatoes	1900
Meat	950
Butter	115
Milk	1.9 (litre)
Sugar	230

Source: M. Hubert and L. Dugé de Bernouville, 'Le mouvement des prix, du coût de la vie', p. 264.

Table 11.4. *Food rations in Berlin as a percentage of pre-war consumption*

	07/1916–06/1917	07/1917–06/1918	07/1918–12/1918
Meat	31	20	12
Fish	51	—	5
Eggs	18	13	13
Lard	14	11	7
Butter	22	21	28
Cheese	3	4	15
Rice	4	—	—
Fried vegetables	14	1	7
Potatoes	71	94	94
Vegetable fats	39	41	17
Sugar	49	61	82
Cereal products	53	47	48

Source: J. Kuczynski, *Geschichte des Alltags des deutschen Volkes, 1600 bis 1945* (Berlin, 1982), vol. IV, p. 450.

intervened in an attempt to regulate distribution of these 'most important goods', certainly with an eye to the importance of keeping up popular morale as well as popular strength. Morale was related not only to availability and price, but also to 'equivalent' and 'equitable' access.

Evidence on wartime variation in levels of consumption is scattered and of inconsistent quality. However, the following provides a sense of where deficiencies were most strongly felt, and how authorities responded. It also provides evidence moreover for redefining the duration of the war. Prices on certain basic food items remained drastically inflated for months after the end of hostilities; while, for Berliners and other Germans, the post-war scarcities proved even more catastrophic than those which prevailed during the war. The evolution of consumption in

Paris can be defined precisely only for products subject to rationing, that is, bread after 29 January 1918 and sugar after 1 March 1917. The bread ration[31] was a little less than the estimated pre-war consumption, assessed at 550g per day for worker[32] apart from those defined as engaged in 'heavy labour'. Overall bread consumption dropped by 22 per cent under rationing. Restrictions on sugar, on the other hand, were much more severe: rationed from 1 March 1917, the allocation was reduced six months later from 750g to 500g per head per month, or from half to one-third of the average pre-war consumption.[33]

Although exact figures are not available, the restrictions on other food products during the last year of the war can be estimated through the impressive list of controls. There was to be no consumption of fresh butter in restaurants (12 February 1918) or milk in cafés (3 September 1917), then in restaurants (12 February 1918) after 9 a.m. 'Meatless days', fixed at two per week between May and October 1917, rose to three from May to July 1918 with purchases limited to 200g every fourth day. These restrictions persisted after the Armistice and were only lifted during the first half of 1919.[34]

The evolution of prices for six food items assessed in a Paris food cooperative (table 11.5) varied greatly. Although the price of bread was held at its pre-war level throughout the war, thus becoming increasingly accessible, this sensitive item was an exception. During the first half of the war the price of sugar, and to a lesser degree meat, rose beyond the capacity of the slenderest purses. After the crisis of spring 1917, it was fats and milk which became too dear. Meat and potatoes were expensive but not out of reach. In July 1919 prices of meat, milk, butter, and sugar were three times higher than they had been five years before.

In London (table 11.2), supplies of essential foodstuffs were reduced severely in a few cases: sugar, fresh meat, and butter. Sugar consumption, affected less acutely than in Paris, was none the less nearly 50 per cent lower than in the pre-war period. Consumption of fresh meat and butter in particular dropped very considerably. Butter, which became virtually unknown in many households, was partially replaced by

31 The bread ration was initially – in February and March – set at 300g per head for all, regardless of age or occupation. This quantity was later designated only for adults between 13 and 60 years of age. Those engaged in heavy labour received 400g, then 500g from October 1918, and old people 200g then 300g. See Robert, 'Ouvriers et mouvement ouvrier', vol. 1.

32 M. Hubert and L. Dugé de Bernouville, 'Le mouvement des prix, du coût de la vie et des salaires en divers pays, de juillet 1914 à janvier 1918', *Bulletin de la Statistique Générale de la France*, 1918, p. 264.

33 Henri Sellier, Bruggeman, and Poëte, *Paris pendant la guerre*, p. 15.

34 The measures restricting the consumption of butter and milk were abrogated on 4 January, those on meat on 5 March. Bread rationing continued until 1 June. See Robert, 'Ouvriers et mouvement ouvrier', vol. IV.

Table 11.5. *Evolution of retail prices in Paris, 1914–1919 (July 1914 = 100)*

	7/1915	7/1916	7/1917	7/1918	7/1919
Bread	106	106	113	113	113
Potatoes	80	160	160	240	200
Meat (steak)	132	132	210	205	289
Butter	126	126	211	242	295
Milk	120	160	200	240	360
Sugar	167	173	227	273	280
Cost of living	119	131	183	217	253

Source: Bulletin de la Statistique Générale de la France, 1915–1920; Robert, 'Ouvriers et mouvement ouvrier', vol. I, p. 150.

Table 11.6. *An index of retail prices in London, 1914–1916 (July 1914 = 100)*

	10/ 1914	1/ 1915	4/ 1915	7/ 1915	10/ 1915	1/ 1916	4/ 1916	7/ 1916	11/ 1916
Bread	111	121	142	144	141	146	152	145	163
Potatoes	93	86	96	102	96	99	111	154	166
Beef[a]	109	116	129	147	149	149	153	174	169
Mutton[b]	115	121	133	151	152	152	159	178	176
Butter	108	110	114	115	127	129	128	129	150
Margarine	123	112	113	111	113	114	123	122	122
Milk	—	—	108	110	115	123	124	136	143
Sugar	163	165	164	166	184	184	203	212	213
Cost of living	110	115	122	125	132	137	143	150	160

[a]British beef (thin flank).
[b]British mutton (breast).
Source: BLPES 42 (f 625), UK Committee on Prices, working papers, Misc.

margarine. Similarly, by the end of the war meat consumption dropped by more than half and was replaced by bacon. The reduced consumption of fats and proteins was obvious, although balanced to a degree by substitute products. In contrast consumption of potatoes rose by 45 per cent.

Class differences did inform the variations in diet to some degree; but consumption patterns were progressively equalized in the course of the war. Apart from the disappearance of a few items such as butter, the overall level of food consumption in London was not reduced drastically. Where the head of the household worked in a war factory, there were even some gains in nutritional intake. The UK Committee on

Prices put it this way: 'The better-off classes eat less meat, many of the working classes eat much more. Families with members in munition works spend more money on meat.'[35] While this may have been true in many cases, it would be rash to generalize here. There is other evidence that meat was very hard to find in London in the later years of the war.[36]

The evolution of London prices confirms this: meat prices rose more steeply than any item except sugar. Although the gap between prices for the best cuts and the more ordinary ones grew smaller (230 per cent in 1914, 175 per cent in July 1917), prices for the latter had none the less increased by 258 per cent between July 1914 and July 1917.[37] Given the uncertainty of the sources, rigorous statements on the food situation in Berlin are hard to substantiate. However, there is considerable evidence that in the German capital the food situation was much worse than in Paris or London. Shortages were numerous and rapid at first, and then became generalized, affecting bread, potatoes, meat, fats, and even vegetables, fruit, and sugar, especially from 1916. Milk, an essential family item, was noticeably absent. From the outbreak of war deliveries dropped steadily in relation to pre-war levels: the deficit reached two-thirds in 1918 and nearly 80 per cent in 1919;[38] in Paris the deficit was real, but it never exceeded 55 per cent.[39]

Official ration allocations in Berlin were far below consumption levels before the war (see table 11.4.). Supplies of meat – for which the ration in 1918 was one-eighth of its pre-war level – fish, eggs, fats, and cheeses were derisory. Sugar and potatoes were virtually the only items for which the ration increased at the end of the winter of 1916 and 1917, and even then it barely reached pre-war levels.

The fundamental problem in this area is the misleading impression gained from solely using official data. Notional or stated ration levels are deceptive; they frequently did not correspond to what was actually allocated according to current availability. Furthermore, there is the difficult question of the black market, which, for those who could afford to use it, made up the shortfall between rations and needs. A few reliable figures for confiscated goods indicated the quantity of goods acquired via this route: probably between one-eighth and one-seventh of potatoes, one-quarter to one-third of dairy produce, and one-third to one-half of the eggs and meat were obtained, at prices up to ten times

35 UK Committee on Prices, working papers, BLPES 42 (f 265).

36 On the latter point, the *Workers' Dreadnought* (19 January 1918) is a notable echo. See this letter: 'I do think it very hard that two old people, 66 years of age, can only get frozen liver or heart.'

37 Board of Trade, *Labour Gazette*, 1917–19.

38 See Aeroboe, *Der Einfluss des Krieges*, p. 90; see also L. Ruge, 'Deutschland- Milch- und Speisefettversorgung im Kriege', *Beiträge zur Kriegswirtschaft*, 47–8 (September 1918).

39 Sellier, *Paris pendant la guerre*, p. 16.

Table 11.7. *Monthly food costs per head in marks, for Berlin workers, 1914 to 1918*

	Estimate		Index (July 1914 = 100)	
	(a)	(b)	(a)	(b)
July 1914	14.07	23.45	100	100
January 1915	16.68	27.80	119	119
July 1915	23.90	39.83	170	170
April 1916	27.40	46.17	195	196
July 1916	28.43	47.38	202	202
April 1917	28.64	47.73	204	204
September 1917	29.44	49.07	210	209
April 1918	33.96	56.60	241	242
October 1918	39.05	65.08	278	278

Note: (a) Cost of foods indicated in Official Price Reports for 51 Prussian cities. (b) Estimates include the total costs of food luxury consumables, and substitute food items for items in estimate (a).
Source: W. Zimmermann, 'Die Veränderungen der Einkommens und Lebensverhältnisse der deutschen Arbeiter durch den Krieg', in Meerwarth, Günther, and W. Zimmermann, *Die Einwirkung des Krieges.*

their pre-war levels.[40] Even if the real drop in consumption was perhaps not as marked for some as rations suggest, the food-supply problem in Berlin was no less acute: use of the black market, socially discriminatory because of its high prices, illustrates the extreme inequality of access to food in the German capital. Those who could afford the black market did not go hungry. But there were few ordinary households capable of improving the official rations to a significant extent by tapping illegal supply networks.

Between July 1914 and October 1918, the monthly food bill for a Berlin worker rose by 178 per cent (table 11.7, index column b). But here, too, the available figures substantially underestimate the increased cost of buying food; they do not take the black market into account and, in addition, they reflect diminishing allocations. It would be fair to say that replacing a pre-war diet in wartime Berlin involved expenditure of a magnitude much higher than official statistics suggest. But it matters not if we settle on a figure of price inflation at 178 per cent or (more likely) at 400 per cent or more; the point is that only the rich and the corrupt could obtain what everyone else had to go without.

Thus the regular shortages experienced in London and Paris – simply

[40] This aggregate figure is from Offer, *An agrarian interpretation*, p. 56. For details on food prices specifically in Berlin and how they changed from week to week, see the columns devoted to the subject which appear in both the liberal *Vossische Zeitung* and the Social Democratic *Vorwärts*, from the end of 1914 on.

a less varied and less attractive form of the pre-war diet – were scarcely comparable with the chronic inequalities and general malnourishment prevalent in Berlin from 1916 onwards. The gravity of the food situation in Berlin, and the state's ultimate lack of success in addressing the situation is part of the story of German failure in the war as a whole.

Urban residents' adaptation and its limits

This overall contrast leaps out of virtually every source on this subject. But this inevitably sketchy view of the metropolitan food-supply situation remains incomplete without reference to the subtle modes of adaptation to the new war-induced austerity.

There were many ways in which city-dwellers got round wartime shortages. One of the most important was the elaboration of links between city and countryside. In this respect, Parisians and Berliners were better placed than Londoners. First, to a far greater extent than London, the continental capitals were immigrant cities: 60 per cent of their residents were born elsewhere, and many retained an active bond with their provincial background. These ties were visible in many localized regional groupings within the cities, particularly (but not only) in Paris. Many Berliners relied regularly on the post to bring in goods from the countryside, even after such practice became illegal in mid-1915. Berliners routinely made excursions out to neighbouring rural areas, where familial connections as well as money might turn up some goods. This activity continued even after being proscribed; police assigned to railway stations often looked the other way, either out of sympathy, or for a share of the goods.

If 'country cousins' were helpful to city-dwellers, so were extended families. Relatives could be exploited in many ways when urban food supplies were found wanting. Children could be sent to stand in food queues; or a family member might spend the day scouting for supplies, which might turn up at any moment, while other family members worked to earn the money to pay for the food. In addition, there was the option of 'free' provisioning, through all kinds of gardening on any plot of land suitable for cultivation. The spectacular development of 'workers' gardens' in Paris is a case in point. By 1916 several towns rented out open lands, either council-owned or made available temporarily by individual landowners, to large families; in return for a modest sum of money used to buy equipment for general use, these families reaped the fruits of their labour. In 1917 there were nearly 2,500 gardens, of between 100 and 200 square metres each, cultivated by about 7,000 people in 21 communes in the Department of the Seine.[41] In Paris itself,

[41] Taken from Ambroise Rendu, Paris municipal counsellor, in a session of the Conseil

the land within the fortifications was used in the same way, at the suggestion of the Ministry of Agriculture; nearly 3,000 gardens were in use there in 1917.[42] Allotments spread in London too. The crowded urban pattern of Berlin provided few such opportunities, though rural excursions for food and fuel were common.

Another major form of subsistence was mutual support. This is a difficult area to document, one which we will investigate on the local level in volume II of this study. Networks of reciprocal support and mutual aid flourished within local communities before the war. They may have been truncated by military mobilization and the movement of urban workers to new munitions works, far from their lodgings. Still, the circulation of information about food and other vital supplies within these close communities was an advantage for Berlin housewives who remained at home. Such networks also helped consumers to maintain a united front against exploitative merchants in a variety of ways. Finally, in Berlin, neighbours helped one another to understand and keep up to date on the myriad regulations regarding pricing and rations which issued forth from one day to the next. Local support groups, based on church membership, were also available for families in need in wartime. This too is a theme we will explore in the second part of this study.

We have more information on *ersatz* strategies. In all three cities the shortages of certain food items, important in the regular diet, encouraged the introduction of substitutes which transformed pre-war dietary habits. Although in London and Paris these substitutes were substantial enough to have left their mark in popular memory (wartime bread or weakened beer, for example), they never reached the scale seen in Berlin after the winter of 1916–17.

In Berlin many substitute products, official or otherwise, replaced missing items. The first true replacement was K bread ('War bread'), the reference 'K' indicating both *Krieg* (War) and *Kartoffel* (potato). This bread, consisting partly of potato flour, was accepted at first without great resistance, at least before it became common knowledge that the more prosperous sections of the population were still able to obtain white bread. Similarly, the shortage of fats was reasonably well accepted at first, as butter or fat was replaced by jam on slices of bread – until jam in turn became unobtainable.

The winter of 1916 to 1917 marked a break with the past in Berlin. Turnips were widely used as a substitute for potatoes during the winter and then as a substitute for most foods, creating the enduring sobriquet

général de la Seine, 19 December 1917: Conseil général de la Seine, Procès-verbaux, 19 December 1917, p. 233.

42 Maurice Quentin, 'Rapport au nom de la 2e Commission sur les jardins cultivés par les parisiens et sur les encouragements à donner aux groupements qui leur sont consacrés', Conseil municipal, Rapports et Documents, no. 66, 8 December 1917.

for the period, henceforth known as the 'turnip winter'. The discomforts of digesting these swede turnips, their bitter taste, the difficulty in preparing them, and their low nutritional value did nothing to reconcile Berliners to the humiliating consumption of what had hitherto been used for animal fodder. Similarly, after this 'turnip winter', the description 'substitute' (*ersatz*) indicated other and even less attractive products. An official project for the extraction of oil from fruit pips and kernels aroused first consternation, then hope, and then disillusionment among residents. On several occasions these substitute products were themselves in short supply, such as the consignment of plum jam which the Ministry of the Interior had promised for Berlin and which never arrived; Berliners accused the authorities of acting in collusion with speculators to send it elsewhere.[43]

At the same time Berlin experienced the ultimate form of replacement, the imitation product. Items under this heading did not aim to counterbalance a nutritional deficiency due to a missing foodstuff but to reproduce the simple physical appearance of the good concerned. Such practices opened the way to many charlatans who offered ash in the guise of pepper or a 'butter' based on carbonate of soda and starch. The constant vigilance needed on the part of the least prosperous consumers to escape such swindles contributed to a climate of distrust towards traders, who were accused of taking illicit profits by adulterating their goods or even adding inedible substances. This distrust of the commercial sector was all the stronger because it revived popular turn-of-the-century representations of salacious trade practices, at a time when the population explosion in the city fostered anxiety over food.[44]

Yet the use of substitute products never resulted in long-term changes in popular tastes. At most it introduced a break in custom together with greater monotony in the diet. Further, many substitute products were easily accepted among the Allied nations, such as bacon in London, where it tended to replace fresh meat.

Tolerance for sacrifices in civilian nutrition was tempered by reminders of front-line hardships. It was the task of propaganda in Paris to recall this fact. One poster by Abel Faivre contrasted the bourgeois sitting down to a well-laden table with the reality of the poilu staggering under his pack and insisting to those at home, 'we don't ask you to die,

[43] 'Marmelade statt Butter?', *Berliner Lokal Anzeiger*, 19 October 1917, and 'Neukölln. Zur Marmeladeverteilung', *Vorwärts*, 30 November 1917.

[44] On these representations, see Eberhard Schmauderer, 'Die Beziehungen zwischen Lebensmittelwissenschaft, Lebensmittelrecht und Lebensmittelversorgung im 19. Jh., problematisch betrachtet', in E. Heischkel-Artelt (ed.), *Ernährung und Ernährungslehre* (Göttingen, 1976). See more generally on the 'food relation' and related transformations in the German diet in the decades before the war, H. Teuteberg and G. Wiegelmann, *Der Wandel der Nährungsgewohnheiten unter dem Einfluss der Industrialisierung* (Göttingen, 1972).

just to live economically.'[45] It was a striking image of this disturbing contrast and introduced the notion of consumers' guilt at the act of consumption while soldiers were dying a mere 100 kilometres away.

The message delivered by this poster was all the more effective because, of the three capitals, Paris was the most closely linked to the front. Paris was on the route of virtually all men going on leave. There were soldiers everywhere in the city. Abel Faivre's poster expressed the position of Paris well, under the anxious gaze of the man who was sacrificing his life.

But the relationship with the front was not unequivocal, nor was the message in the poster. The image of the consumer accentuated feelings of inequality in the face of sacrifice. Which was worse: civilian safety or social inequality? Relations between the home and battle fronts were always complex, moreover, and despondency among soldiers could quickly spread to their families; in the case of Berlin, this despondency was, moreover, sometimes caused by soldiers' concerns over the fate of their families back home. In this instance, such anxiety was closely related to diminishing enthusiasm for and commitment to the war effort, on the part of both civilians and soldiers.

Within this general rubric of home-front austerity at a time of front-line hardships, many forms of adaptation emerged. Cultural patterns and memories entered into the equation of tolerable levels of sacrifice. In Paris the rise in bread prices met a cultural barrier which recalled the capital's subsistence problems and revolutionary traditions. Attitudes in this domain were strongly shaped by past experience, informing decisions to intervene at the outbreak of war. Provisioning in London or Berlin was not affected in the same way.

Other lines of social division, some traditional and some new, appeared and undermined the fragile national unity each state attempted to build; and, in turn, this created controversy over other consumables. Conflicts, erupting in Berlin into demonstrations in the streets, occurred over propaganda, and the systems of special rationing which developed in Germany from late 1915 on. Shortage of milk, the value of which for the sick, for children and pregnant and nursing mothers was underscored by public-health propaganda, created anger in the face of shortages, uncertain or unfair distribution, and what some took to be profiteering.

Meat held an important place in the popular diet of each city. It had a widespread popular appeal as the greatest source of potential energy and was associated with important family occasions. Its standing as a food item from the second half of the nineteenth century symbolized forcefully the recent improvements in popular consumption, long

[45] See ch. 4.

dominated by grains and starches. These advances were brutally interrupted by the war, which changed food culture dramatically, and threatened to undermine progress in nutritional levels widely publicized at the time.[46]

The expert nutritional argument favouring a diet less rich in proteins for the sake of better individual health became more effective with the war. Of British origin, its echoes were perceptible in France in the burgeoning mass of publications, tracts and leaflets on 'Rational diet', on 'Healthy economic cookery' or 'Strength and good health for all, thanks to a rational and economical diet'.[47] Although we must not overestimate the willingness of popular readers to accept these arguments, they still had some force. Their wartime effects could lead to increased tension. Thus the position of German nutritionists, who had favoured a diet rich in proteins, tended to reinforce the popular association of meat with health and to make a modification of dietary custom difficult to accept. Difficulties were redoubled in the case of Berlin, where fats were prominent in the popular diet.

Regulating social tensions

It is a cliché that the 1914–18 war demanded significant material sacrifices from groups and individuals. What was less trivial was recognition of the fact that the unequal nature of these sacrifices challenged their acceptance by a growing number of people in all three cities, but above all in Berlin. The problem of food supply illustrates this point perfectly. Anger produced action, albeit at times very belated action. Various initiatives, intended to sustain the war effort especially after 1916, were specific responses to rising social tensions, visible in the capital cities.

Regulating social tension in Paris and London

A system of food rationing was not introduced in London until February 1918; in Paris, it began closer to the middle of the war. This intervention, though resisted in the case of London, was successful in quelling popular discontent in the Allied capitals: partly because the level of scarcity and price rises remained overall fairly minimal and contained, certainly relative to central Europe; and partly because of the well-managed integration of efforts at various administrative levels. In terms of political intervention, these measures revealed the shift which operated throughout the war: responsibility for key decisions moved

[46] Offer, *An agrarian interpretation*, pp. 39–44.

[47] Many references and advertisements for this kind of publication can be seen in the *Revue de la Société de St. Vincent de Paul:* La correspondance des oeuvres.

from local level to national level then to the international level. In Paris, particularly, the municipality, central powers and international organizations of Allied cooperation worked closely together, but it took three years to get the system to work properly. This vertical integration of the different levels of operation proved decisive in ensuring adequate provisioning in both Paris and London.

In Paris, the war had hardly begun before a commodity seen as particularly sensitive – bread – became the object of close and unremitting attention from the public authorities. Bread's symbolic character, its place in popular Parisian memory, was such that a law of July 1791 was revived in 1914 to hold its price almost unchanged throughout the war.

This radical price-setting measure was complemented by a novel supply system.[48] As a security measure, the military authorities kept close guard over supplies of wheat for Paris until September 1916. The Ministry of War was then responsible, under siege regulations, for all stages in the regular supply of bread for Paris. It requisitioned and stored stocks of wheat, requisitioned flour-mills working for the Paris home front and allocated to each baker a supply miller and a fixed amount of flour for his clientele.[49] This extreme militarization of the food-supply system worked: apart from a few tense moments, evidence of potential popular discontent about bread remained very slight.[50]

However, although the government stepped in quickly to fix the price of bread, other products were left uncontrolled. In general, freedom of trade was uninhibited and public authorities scarcely intervened until 1916, and even then on a very limited scale.[51] The persistence of elements of the free market reflected particular relationships uniting public authorities and an agricultural world which had been the seat of Republicanism since the days of the Paris Commune. The weight of the farming pressure group, represented in particular by the powerful Société des Agriculteurs de France, could not be ignored; for those in political power it was a source of friction in the choice between a policy favouring urban consumers and an alternative inspired by agricultural interests. As usual, the result was a compromise between the two.

In London, public-authority preferences for free-market liberalism were reflected in the absence or low profile of state measures. Reluc-

[48] On this point, see AN F 23 110, 'Ravitaillement du camp retranché de Paris en blé'.

[49] AN F 23 110.

[50] See AN F 23 110 and Archives de la Préfecture de Police, BA/1640, report of 5 August 1918.

[51] The préfecture de police declared during the year a series of maximum prices: for sugar in May, frozen meat in April, potatoes in September, finally milk and butter in February 1917. See Robert, 'Ouvriers et mouvement ouvrier', ch. 23.

tance to break with the policy of freedom from price controls, for example, remained an essential feature of food policy until a very late stage. In February 1918, John Hilton, the civil servant responsible for food policy, still defended this approach to the War Cabinet:

> Practically every unsound notion in regard to food policy comes from regarding food as a stock to be apportioned instead of a flow to be maintained . . . The only sound food policy is one that makes for increased supplies, diminished waste, and economy in use. Free prices would have served these needs; controlled prices are defeating them.[52]

The concern of public bodies was none the less genuine: in August 1914 the government established two monitoring committees – the London Intelligence Committee and the London Sub-Committee for the Prevention and Relief of Distress, responsible for collecting information on food supplies and prices in London. Their activity remained limited: the London Sub-Committee for the Prevention and Relief of Distress was content, for example, to encourage local authorities to distribute free meals to needy children: 73,000 children benefited at first.[53] The creation of the Ministry of Food in December 1916, at a time of significant tension, made little difference to the immediate situation, except for the establishment of a system of voluntary rationing in February 1917.

In both cities the increased cost of food and the first shortages contributed to growing discontent. Paris was very sensitive to the rising cost of living from the second half of 1915: food prices became the object of constant recriminations,[54] particularly from the working classes, among trade unionists and within Socialist party branches,[55] and in the press of the Paris left. The surge in prices was seen in terms of speculation and monopolies, a drama with stock figures, including the speculator and the profiteer, at centre stage. Want versus sacrifice, gold versus blood: more than a description of material problems, such antinomies underlined the inequality of sacrifice among civilians in wartime.

Food had long been a focus of expression of popular protest. Representations of social struggles made the opposition of the bloated and the impoverished the archetype of social divisions *tout court*. The war provided a powerful channel for the display of this popular anger,

52 CAB 24/43 GT 3711, J. Hilton, Memorandum, 23 February 1918.

53 See BLPES Local Government Board, London Intelligence Committee, 'The prevention and relief of distress: memorandum on the steps taken for the prevention and relief of distress due to the war', Appendix C, p. 877, unpublished.

54 This can be seen in the reports prepared for the Ministry of the Interior in each Paris arrondissement in August, September, November, and December 1915. On this point, see Jean-Jacques Becker, *Les Français dans la Grande Guerre* (Paris, 1980), pp. 125–32.

55 Cf. Robert, 'Ouvriers et mouvement ouvriers', vol. 5, pp. 1432–4 and 1440–7.

deepening older representations to which the war contributed a new dimension with the division of front/home front. References to 'those patriots with their backs to the hearth and their stomachs at the table'[56] clearly declared that selfish and conspicuous consumer behaviour was intolerable at a time of collective slaughter on the battlefields and when the families of the men at the front had little to eat.

In London, tension and criticism over prices was lively from 1916 onwards. On 1 January 1916 a meeting of the East London Federation of Suffragettes declared that 'the average working woman housekeeper in East London cannot practice further economies, either in regard to meat or other forms of food, without injuring the physique of their [*sic*] family'.[57] As in Paris, the profiteer and the unscrupulous middleman dominated price rises. A popular and widely read journal like *John Bull* issued a violent challenge to traders in the name of the equality of sacrifice. The traders were accused simultaneously of rejecting their share of the collective burden by transferring the cost of rising prices to consumers, and of creating an artificial rise for their own profit.[58] Again under the heading of equality of sacrifice, the speculative practices of certain middle-class housewives were condemned.

Inequality of access to food was felt primarily in socio-spatial terms in London: the distribution of food products operated to the disadvantage of the city's most crowded districts. Transport costs, multiplied by the war, did not affect the opulent West End shops with their well-heeled clientele; but they handicapped the small traders in the East End and tipped the balance in favour of more prosperous areas. Placed in a difficult situation, 'the small shopkeepers were suffering hardships because while the wholesalers were forcing them to pay high prices, they could not get high prices for their customers'.[59] Elsewhere the same shopkeepers, who had to control their stock carefully, developed a form of unofficial rationing – 'linked sales' – still more prejudicial to popular areas. Under this system, as an item such as sugar became scarce, it could be bought only at the same time as a purchase of tea.[60] Such practices, requiring extra expenditure, were difficult to manage out of smaller incomes.

This socio-spatial dimension of inequality over food, gaining strength through the war, led to various forms of action such as the march of about fifteen women from the 'working-class districts of

56 As cited in Thierry Bonzon, 'Cent quatre vingt dix lettres de pacifistes, juin 1916–octobre 1916', MA thesis, University of Paris – I, 1985, p. 90.

57 *Women's Dreadnought*, 1 January 1916.

58 *John Bull*, 6 May 1916.

59 *Women's Dreadnought*, 6 September 1914.

60 Report from Stepney, July 1916, C0700, Working classes cost-of-living paper. R(0)42 f 332, vol. 1, BLPES.

Hampstead, Camden Town, Bow, Bromley, Poplar, Custom House, and Canning Town' to Harrods, the fashionable department store in the heart of upper-class Knightsbridge, to find sugar.[61]

But it was above all from the spring of 1917, with the appearance of long queues at East End food shops, that social tensions developed in London. At the end of the year they deepened. *The Times* reported in December 1917:

> Over 1,000 people waited for margarine at a shop in New Broad Street in the heart of the City, and in Walworth Road on the south-eastern side of London the queue was estimated to number about 3,000. Two hours later 1,000 of these were sent away unsupplied.[62]

On the last Saturday in January 1918 the Metropolitan Police counted another half million people queuing in the streets of London. Such bottlenecks led the public authorities to introduce rationing for most foodstuffs – bread still excepted – in February 1918. The programme, introduced gradually, aimed to achieve fairer and regular distribution to retailers. By that time, moreover, the Local Food Committees were able to redistribute existing stocks in their own district. The committees in the London boroughs were particularly active, and in Camberwell, Wandsworth, Balham, Hammersmith, and other districts, stocks were taken from the shops which had large supplies and distributed among other retailers who had, for example, no margarine to sell.[63]

The new system reduced the number of Londoners' complaints, as noted by a Ministry of Food report: 'So quick has been the change in the last year that the talk of strikes and revolutions had entirely passed away and trade union conferences ended without a reference to food.'[64]

In Paris, state intervention in favour of urban consumers appeared earlier, following the crisis of the winter of 1916–17. The impotence of local authorities in the face of the food problem was clear. The case of Paris is a powerful illustration of the shift from local to national to international levels of intervention to solve the food problem on the Allied side. This strategy to transfer responsibility to higher levels of supply worked; without this option, the German system was at a great, and perhaps decisive disadvantage.

On the Allied side, bureaucratic obstacles were not unknown. Faced with governmental inertia, consumer cooperatives and municipalities appeared particularly active. From the middle of the winter of 1916–17, and above all in 1918, the defence of civilian well-being in this crucial area was a matter for state authorities and regulations, backed up by inter-Allied cooperation. Although many forms of local protest ap-

[61] *Worker's Dreadnought*, 2 June 1917.

[62] *The Times*, 17 December 1917. [63] *The Times*, 24 December 1917.

[64] CAB 24/67 GT 6036, Ministry of Food, Report for Week Ending 16.10.1918.

peared to precipitate action, their success reflected above all the integration of different levels of decision-making: local, national, and international.

With its membership increased 2.7 times and turnover quadrupled, the Paris cooperative movement[65] enjoyed new vigour during the war. With nearly 170,000 members in 145 societies in 1918, it owed its success to its essential role in maintaining urban food supplies. The expansion of sales of food products was considerable. Compared to the period 1913 to 1914, by 1918 to 1919 cooperative sales of meat and groceries had doubled. Paris cooperatives were pioneers in two areas: the introduction of frozen meat to the Paris market, and the expansion of cooperative restaurants for workers in war factories. The spread of these restaurants was due to the support of Albert Thomas, beginning in the autumn of 1916; by the end of the war there were nearly sixty in the Department of the Seine, offering varied and regular menus at modest prices to munitions workers.

Many socialist or radical municipal councils in the suburbs intervened directly in the distribution of provisions[66] through establishments such as municipal butcher's shops and grocery shops – reflecting traditions of municipal socialism and pre-war ideas on direct supply to consumers, cutting out the middleman.[67] Butchers' shops or municipal shops established during 1916 were strongly promoted in the popular press as a victory of the general interest over that of a small minority seen as responsible for the soaring cost of living. The supposed ill-will of traders and their reluctance to apply official restrictions or regulations on displaying prices were denounced frequently. At times protest led to municipal intervention. In Arcueil, the announcement of the opening of an office d'approvisionnement municipal initiated a campaign of petitions to traders.[68] At Pavillons-sous-Bois meat prices in the municipal butchery, between 25 and 40 per cent lower than in regular butchers' shops, were a silent accusation of the 'attempt at shameless exploitation which the retail butchers had decided to exercise in suburban communities to the detriment of the people'.[69] In Bois-Colombes the Ligue des consommateurs forced the reluctant mayor to promise a municipal operation to supply groceries to traders and impose set prices on sales.[70]

In Paris itself municipal activity remained limited because of hostility from the political right wing of the council to any intervention liable to

[65] See Robert, 'Ouvriers et mouvement ouvrier', vol. III, p. 868–79; and Robert, 'Cooperatives during the war', in Fridenson (ed.), *The French home front*.

[66] Particularly Alfortville, Arcueil, Clichy, Maisons-Alfort, Pavillons-sous-Bois, and Saint-Denis.

[67] See Patrizia Dogliani, 'Un laboratoire du socialisme municipal: France 1880–1920' (PhD thesis, University of Paris – VIII, 1991), pp. 501–20.

[68] *L'Humanité*, 2 December 1915. [69] *La Gazette de l'Est*, 2 April 1916.

[70] *L'Eveil*, 5 June 1916 and *Le Petit Journal*, 19 June 1916.

restrict freedom of trade. There was a broader consensus within the assembly for the policy of aid for the most needy. From December 1916, some 600,000 people, or a quarter of the population of Paris, were able to obtain 4 kg of potatoes per month free of charge during the six winter months.[71]

Following the major turning point represented by the terrible winter of 1916 to 1917, local initiatives appear to have had only limited effect.[72] In the spring of 1917, Parisian workers, particularly women workers, expressed their growing anger at the newly introduced policy of freeing prices from controls. The progressive introduction of rationing thereafter was intended to deflect open revolt over the surge in prices. Sugar was rationed first in March, then bread (the decision taken in August was applied in December); the rationing of coal, operative from 1 September, was widely approved. These measures, accompanied by a policy of restricting purchases of essential products, affected the most sensitive commodity of all – bread – and two scarce essential goods, sugar and coal. The achievements were a lowering of tension over food supplies and feelings of greater social justice.

However, the final year of the war was still marked by tension over food prices. Hardly a day passed when police reports on the state of public morale did not mention 'protests', 'general discontent', or 'numerous and very lively complaints' which increased in intensity as the winter approached.[73] Once again, acceptance of sacrifice was linked to appreciation of its equitable social distribution. This was underlined by a police report of 12 June 1918: 'All conversations [on the topic of restrictions], from the suburbs to the grand boulevards, indicate that the population will accept all that may still be necessary, on condition that no one is spared.'[74]

It was against this particularly tense background that the municipality decided, on 25 March, on the simultaneous creation of *boucheries contrôlées* and of *boucheries municipales* (controlled and municipal butchers). The first were managed by shopkeepers who had agreed to sell their produce at prices set by the préfecture of police. The municipal butchers were to sell meat supplied by the military quartermaster at its requisition price, prepared at a central butchery under préfecture supervision and distributed from butchers' shops rented and managed

[71] Categories recorded as able to benefit from free distributions were as follows: those receiving old-age assistance, large families, newly delivered mothers, recipients of welfare-bureau assistance, recipients of military allowances, unemployment benefit, and refugee aid.

[72] Cf. below, chapter 12.

[73] Archives de la Préfecture de Police (APP), Police report on the state of mind of the Paris public from June 1918 to June 1920, BA 1614.

[74] APP, Reports on 8th district (10th and 19th arrondissements), report of 12 June 1918, BA 1644.

by city authorities. The first public butchers' shops opened on 18 May 1918, in the midst of the German offensive, 'in the most heavily populated arrondissements with the greatest proportion of low-rent housing'.[75] In July, while the German pressure was at its height, there were twenty-five municipal butchers' shops, and forty-four controlled establishments in operation. Together they supplied at least 5 per cent of the meat consumed in Paris, at prices substantially below market prices.

This was undoubtedly a highly successful way of controlling social tensions: 'All the residents demand municipal butchers in every district', stated a police report dated 12 June 1918.[76] Encouraged by this success, socialists made every effort to continue the experiment: by the Armistice, the number of municipal butchers' shops had doubled, with more than 100 in place in April 1919.

Finally, thanks to the support of the prefect and against the majority of the council, in March 1919 the socialists carried the day: a regulation was issued establishing municipal stalls – Vilgrain barracks – functioning in the same way as the butchers' shops. This post-war initiative reflected wartime strategies. They in turn were based on the solid international network behind the provisioning of the city. The inter-Allied purchasing bodies of London and New York were invited to help with provisioning the Vilgrain barracks. Products sold related directly to the typical ration specification established during the war by the Commission scientifique interalliée.[77]

These new systems for checking social tensions arising from worry over the food supply were established after the serious crisis early in 1917 and the spring of 1918. They closely linked local and central powers with international supplies. The feeding of such vast numbers of people was too great a problem for local authorities or merchants alone; solutions were national and, with the development of inter-Allied cooperation, international. In this respect the fate of Berlin was sealed at a level well beyond the reach of even the most well-intentioned and dedicated army officer, local civil servant, labour leader, or businessman.

Berlin: A different scale

The ultimate inability of German authorities to manage the nation's provisioning needs, above all in the capital city, provides a striking contrast with Allied successes; and, as we have suggested, this difference must be figured into the equation both in comparing the outcome of the war itself, and the differing ability of the three regimes to maintain

[75] Conseil Municipal de Paris, *Rapports et Documents*, no. 30, 2 July 1918, p. 2.
[76] APP, BA 1614. [77] Sellier, *Paris pendant la guerre*, pp. 24–5.

legitimacy and wait out the upheaval of war and the shock of demobilization. Measures taken by Reich and Prussian authorities to ensure equitable access to food did not check adequately the deepening crisis; nor, significantly, did they alleviate social tensions and protest. This was in part a question of scale: for whatever the reasons (and many of these are enumerated above), the breadth and depth of scarcity of virtually all foods, the scale of inflation, and the extreme polarization of access rendered the case of Berlin (and, to differing degrees, other areas of the country, particularly urban centres) incomparable to the other two cities. Indeed, one must keep in mind how responsive authorities at all levels were to popular concerns. Though ineffective, their efforts were acknowledged, certainly through most of the war, by the Berlin population.

At the same time, the authorities were ultimately blamed for their failure, whether through lack of leadership, lack of sufficiently focused attention, or 'collusion with profiteers'; and this failure seriously undermined the Wilhelmine regime, even before the war was clearly lost. The widespread expectation that Prussian and imperial authorities would indeed intervene on behalf of urban consumers was itself new. Yet the circumstances of war which reached deep into the home front, well before Hindenburg declared a 'total war' in 1916, coupled with the government's own rhetoric regarding national unity and uniform sacrifice to the war effort (much like British and French propaganda), created this set of expectations, which officials in the end found impossible to meet. German authorities determined through inertia not to pursue pre-war plans for civilian provisioning in the event of a blockade and extended war; but, like the French, the authorities sent out political police to report on morale from the onset of hostilities, anticipating problems precisely on the question of food. Thus, the police note from the first weeks of war that food protests 'have not yet occurred'.[78]

But this quiet was as short-lived as the authorities had feared, and, no sooner had the Battle of the Marne made it clear that the war would not be over by Christmas than flash points began to occur. From October 1914, queues grew in front of bakeries, and consumers – particularly in less prosperous neighbourhoods – complained that by the time they reached their turn no bread was left. These Berliners complained that the limited flour stores were being squandered on cake for the rich, at the expense of their access to the most basic food, thus already raising the spectre of inequitable sacrifice, and sacrifice in the name of someone else's profit, at this early point in the war. The Prussian authorities

[78] See e.g. LA Potsdam, Pr. Br. Rep. 30 Berlin C, Tit. 95, No. 15809, p. 7, Mood Report Kurz, 12.2.15; but one sees this rhetoric regularly, including from the first days of the war.

responded quickly, rationing bread initially in greater Berlin, the first in an endless series of such measures which by the end of 1915 would apply to all 'most important' foods (including potatoes, meat, milk, and butter). At the same time, Prussian authorities supervised the distribution of flour to bakers as well as the method of making the bread; bakers were also limited in the amount of flour they could allocate to cake and pastries.[79]

But rationing on its own proved insufficient in guaranteeing access to basic foods, and Berliner consumers turned their attention away from perceived unfair competition with other consumers to the apparent profiteering of producers, distributors, and merchants. In November 1914, the Imperial Bundesrat responded to popular protest, above all in the capital, with price ceilings on potatoes; and, early in 1916, the link between rationing and price limits extended to direct intervention with producers. While the notion of free trade never played the role in Germany that it did in Britain, the idea of high-level authorities intervening in the affairs of Prussian producers, as well as those of merchants, particularly on behalf of the working urban consumer, was novel indeed.[80] Moreover, defence of property was very much a key ideological tradition in Germany;[81] yet, by 1915, authorities began confiscating foodstuffs directly from producers, to distribute as they saw fit. At the same time, officials remained victim to their own ambivalent allegiances and conflicting goals, as well as to the overlapping hierarchies and crossing jurisdictions of the governing structure, and to the long-standing tensions between city and country, and between Berlin, Prussia, and the other German states.

This hesitant and unsystematic approach to food management seriously compromised the government's efforts in the German case. From late 1914 on, literally tens of thousands of regulations were issued at every administrative level, governing both Greater Berlin and the entire nation, often specifically in the interests of the capital population. Indeed, such edicts, concerning strategies from meatless days, to public meal halls, to proscribed cooking methods, covering every aspect of production, distribution, and consumption, very often contradicted one another; and certainly Berliners, including representatives of the state,

[79] See e.g. Magistrat Berlin (ed.), *Die Versorgung Berlins mit Mehl und Brot im Erntejahr 1914–15* (Berlin, 1915).

[80] Indeed, there were active debates – negative and positive – about the notion of 'war socialism', and what such policy meant for the post-war era. See e.g A. Hesse, 'Freie Wirtschaft und Zwangswirtschaft im Kriege', *Beiträge zur Kriegswirtschaft*, 39 (April 1918); T. Heuss, *Drei Monate Volksspeisung* (Berlin, 1916); and H. Köppe, *Kriegswirtschaft und Sozialismus* (Marburg, 1915). For recent discussions, see G.D. Feldman, 'Kriegswirtschaft und Zwangswirtschaft', and D. Krüger, 'Kriegssozialismus', both in W. Michalka (ed.), *Der Erste Weltkrieg* (Munich, 1994).

[81] See e.g. A. Lüdtke, *Police and State in Prussia, 1815-1850* (Oxford, 1989), pp. 41–5.

had difficulty in keeping track of the changes from day to day, and even frequently in understanding them. It was moreover of little help to the government that, although the greater Berlin public believed itself united in a commitment to equitable distribution, how that common share was constituted varied greatly, from population to population, and from month to month.[82]

Capital residents demanded, in keeping with their role as 'soldiers of the homefront', that military authorities attempted the guarantee of civilian food supply as it did for the armed forces. It was in this spirit that the War Food Office (Kriegsernährungsamt, KEA) was initially conceived in early 1916; and it was for this reason that Berliners were initially quite enthusiastic for the 'military takeover' of the Third Army Command in August 1916. Yet the KEA, ultimately established in May under the auspices of the civilian Bundesrat failed to exercise the requisite 'dictatorial control', and was neither able to coordinate the remarkable tangle of bodies at every administrative level nor to command production, distribution, and consumption. The bureaucratic nightmare was intensified as the division of powers led to even more divided jurisdiction: between civil and military spheres, and between imperial, Prussian, Brandenburger, metropolitan, municipal, and finally communal authorities. Nor was the KEA able effectively to oversee the practices of farmers, merchants, and wealthy consumers, who capably resisted the government's efforts at control. Hindenburg for his part exhibited little interest in civilian nourishment, outside of establishing favourable rations for war-industry workers, and looking the other way as war industrialists acquired food for their canteens on the black market. The appointment of Georg Michaelis as Prussian Commissar for the Provisioning of the People in February 1917, at the depths of the 'turnip winter' – and then as Chancellor – was virtually a symbolic act. In effect, Hindenburg hoped that focusing on accelerating production would win the war; and that a victorious war would justify civilian sacrifice.

Yet Berliners registered their serious concerns over this strategy, even while military circumstances still looked favourable. Indeed, sporadic and increasingly violent street protests occurred from early in the war, leading to the first serious food riots already in October 1915. Localized at first in the working-class districts of Lichtenberg and Wedding, during the ensuing nine months the movement spread to

82 Thus, for example, Berliners moved from widespread demands for absolute equality prior to the turnip winter, to which authorities responded with public kitchens (which were despised on cultural grounds), to common shares determined by particular strengths, weaknesses, and/or contribution to the war effort. Other cities also seem to have undergone transformations in their views of 'equitable distribution'. See Davis, 'Home fires burning', pp. 371–440.

Neukölln, Charlottenburg, and elsewhere. From early 1916 on, police reports indicate that, for a wide population of Berliners, food problems eclipsed interest in news from the front. The ease with which producers, merchants, and wealthy consumers could defy the controlled economy kept the vast majority of consumers in a state of continual agitation, requiring only a nasty interchange with a merchant to create a riot. In a move which differentiates these demonstrations from comparable activity in the preceding century, the broad spectrum of Berlin society sided with poor demonstrators – at least publicly – in the press, through speeches, in published reports, and demanded that the interests of the urban consumer be better served.

Moreover, despite their condemnations, those who could afford to work outside the system continued to do so, procuring products *hintenherum*, by the back way. This only aggravated the failures of the system. Wealthy consumers benefited from the practice of chain-trading, or *Kettenhandel*, whereby franchise retailers moved their products to areas of the city where they could charge higher prices. Out-and-out disposable income was however not the only determinant of how well one was able to 'play the system'. Relatives and other 'connections', and a needed skill which could be bartered, could also prove useful. It must also be noted that many became rich precisely through the circumstances of war, while others were thus impoverished; hence, it was not only a question of polarization of access, but also a rearrangement of position and wealth. Some were able to use the postal system (illegally) to bring in products unobtainable in the city. Of course, some also participated in the flourishing black market, operating at their local merchants, at farms outside the city, at train depots, and in all the hotels and restaurants in the metropolis. Merchants and growers pursued other strategies, moreover, which kept food out of the city altogether. Farmers illegally stockpiled goods until price ceilings were lifted, or made goods into fodder, or simply directed them away from the capital when the ceilings applied only to products sold in the city. Moreover, as against the spirit of mutual sacrifice and collective commitment to the war effort and the German *Volk*, which one heard daily round the country, there was a widespread resentment against both Berlin and Prussia. Thus, for example, imperial officials found it extremely difficult to compel Bavarian officials to oversee Bavarian supplies of pork, and to ensure that proper amounts were sent on to the capital.

The effects of such practices in the unavailability of even basic rations from late 1916 on intensified feelings of intolerable social inequality. Relatedly, the populace registered its extreme distress at the time and effort involved in procuring even minimal supplies. Consumers routinely spent all night in a food queue, only to be met with disappointment, and, often, the knowledge that promised supplies had been delivered elsewhere, or were being held (illegally) for 'special customers'. Berliners expended great energy at weekends in scouring the surrounding countryside, with the decreasing promise of success.[83] Many workers were forced to give up their jobs – even in the better-paying war industries – because they found no food left to buy when they left the factory in the evening.[84] While at work they suffered from the absence of those bits of essential news gathered within the local neighbourhood. In the later stages of the war, prostitutes, exchanging sex for food, were a prominent symbol of deprivation. Severe shortages of fuel for heating, lighting, and cooking (as well as difficulties regarding housing and public transportation) worked in tandem with lack of food to challenge Berliners' ability to weather the wartime experience. Of course, none of this ended with the Armistice: the blockade continued, and severe shortages continued and worsened; witness, the representations, with no small kernel of truth, in for example Döblin's *November 1918*, or G. W. Pabst's *Joyless Streets*.

Demonstrators in the streets – primarily working-class women – directed their anger towards growers and distributors who, they claimed, sacrificed patriotism to profit. From late 1915 on, they began to challenge the legitimacy of the state itself, hoping that the government would vindicate its commitment to 'the German *Volk*'. But, as the months wore on, authorities seemed to have breached the pact between society and the state, a social contract of loyalty and sacrifice in return for adequate and fairly apportioned food supplies. The rupture of this informal but palpable understanding undermined the authority and legitimacy of the state. As one outsider living in Berlin commented:

> Women are realizing the enormous burden imposed upon them . . . Naturally they begin more than ever to say, 'Why should we work, starve, send our men out to fight? What is it all going to bring us? More work, more poverty, our men cripples, our homes ruined. What is it for? . . . The State which called upon us to fight cannot even give us decent food.[85]

The factory strikes of spring 1917 and of January 1918 must be seen in this light; and the tight relationship between factory- and street-centered protest was evident. Indeed, the overlap between these populations and protestors was great.

83 BA Potsdam, 31.01, No. 12183, Abgeordneten haussitzung, 26 April 1918.

84 This naturally greatly disturbed Hindenburg and his subordinates, who began to aid industrialists in their efforts to provide workers' canteens, which were sometimes successful. However, as workers were not in principle allowed to take home food for the rest of their families, this didn't solve the entire problem.

85 Blücher von Wahlstatt, *An English wife*, p. 95. There were daily references to such sentiments in virtually all the newspapers, spanning the political spectrum, as well as in police reports.

It is not that administrators were complacent, but that they worked within a structure that literally could not deliver the goods. During the winter of 1916-17, at a time of extreme social tension, the local authorities launched a vast programme of soup kitchens designed to regulate food distribution in the capital. Municipal efforts notwithstanding, the project was unsuccessful. Despite spreading malnutrition in the city, popular resistance to this reminder of the worst kind of charity won the day. The lack of consistent and regular supplies proved decisive and the scheme was a failure. Here is an important contrast between municipal initiatives of a similar kind in Paris which appeared to flow from an egalitarian commitment of public service. In Berlin, public suspicion and anger embittered an already difficult situation.

This setback is but one indication of the authorities' highly visible inability to resolve the material difficulties of supplying Berlin with food. From 1916 until the end of the war, the food crisis was so serious that no administrative or political solution could be found within existing frameworks of distribution. By the time the soldiers came home, Berlin's food supply situation had deteriorated into near chaos. One indicator among many others reveals this dire state of affairs: the pattern of arrivals of food products in Berlin depots in 1919. In January a few rare items re-emerged at their pre-war level – wheat, rye, flour, and turnips. Deliveries of fruit, meat, fats, and dairy produce were far smaller than in the same month in 1914, more than two-thirds down. In June the situation was even more catastrophic and virtually no products were delivered in quantities remotely related to consumer demand.[86] It was at precisely this bleak moment in provisioning Berlin that the German delegation at Versailles signed the Peace Treaty ending the war.

Conclusion

At the end of this limited survey, several conclusions may be drawn. The first concerns the link between the material difficulties encountered by the populace and the level of discontent inevitably aroused. In effect, no simple and unequivocal relationship existed between the two; the relationship cannot be understood simply by a sort of association linking a given level of material suffering with an equivalent development in social protest.

There is no material threshold for protest, since grievances reflected much more than levels of supply; they arose from a sense of injustice and unfairness in its distribution. Conventional measures of the standard of living cannot illustrate the range of sacrifices suffered in the city or in the nation as a whole. Nor on its own can it be a tool to determine

[86] *Gross-Berlin Statistische Monatsberichte*, Jg. 6. vol. 1/11, pp. 78–9; vol. 11, pp. 44–5.

the maintenance or collapse of the social consensus essential for the mobilization of civilian populations in wartime.

In addition there is no uniform or unitary standard of material deprivation common to all three cities. Urban and national cultures and what some contemporaries called 'collective memory'[87] impose thresholds, zones of tension, and specific limits. In Paris this concerned the most sensitive question, the price of bread. The place of meat in a 'normal' menu in a Berlin household and popular attachment to the 'German diet' are cultural phenomena which cannot be ignored. Early levels of immigration and rapid population growth created a reservoir of anxieties about metropolitan food supplies which resurfaced in wartime discussion and protest. Popular rhetoric had long excoriated the role of middlemen and shopkeepers, against a background of latent anti-semitism in all three cities.

These comments offer a key to the comparative history of consumption, highlighting the need to recreate contemporary opinions on what constituted material well-being in wartime. At the centre of this cluster of popular ideas was the notion of equality of sacrifice. Indeed, it was the unequal distribution of deprivation more than the deprivation itself that annoyed people the most. In all three cities the feeling of unequal access to food, of a growing gap between the excluded majority and a privileged few set a limit on the acceptance of sacrifices endured by individuals, families, and social groups for the sake of victory. The growing significance of this concept of social entitlements during the war related both to the close and long-established link between food and urban social identity and the emergence, with military mobilization, of a resonant moral discourse on equality of sacrifice. In all three capitals, the contradiction grew progressively sharper between this discourse related, on the one hand, to mobilization and thereby to citizenship, and to privilege and profit on the other.

Comparisons among the three cities reveal strong contrasts in the authorities' capacity to achieve a double objective: (1) to negotiate with a wide body of individuals and organizations a consensus as to what constituted an acceptable level of material sacrifice endured for the sake of victory, and (2) to ensure thereafter an equitable distribution of basic foods.

Despite social tensions in London and Paris which should not be ignored (and which largely contributed to the 'mobilization' of public powers on these questions), these two objectives were met. In Berlin both were unreachable. Why was this so? Berlin's problems were everywhere. The absolute priority originally given at the national level to the satisfaction of military needs, then to munitions production,

[87] On the notion of collective memory, see Halbwachs, *La mémoire collective* (Paris, 1932).

seriously undermined strategies to defend the well-being of urban residents. Public authorities, as well as the deputy commanding generals responsible for maintaining public order, were well aware of the problem, but it was one about which at best they could do very little. Next, bureaucratic foul-ups were inevitable given the structure of civil administration in Berlin. The great complexity of regulations, and above all a lack of vertical integration between authorities at different levels, led to confusion, and offered a broad field of action to speculation and the black market.

This kaleidoscopic system became more opaque the longer the war went on. In 1914, it appeared that the balance of administrative incompetence was on the Allied side. Public authorities fled Paris before the German armies reached the Marne. The municipal council did not meet in the first hectic months of the war. But over time, in both cities, administrative order slowly but surely emerged. This meant the messy but ultimately effective integration of the different levels of authority, encompassing district, city, national and inter-Allied cooperation. In Paris particularly, pressure by members of the Socialist party on the municipal council helped ensure the integration of local, national, and international support for the city's population.

The development of the black market in Berlin was no doubt the most visible symbol of the contrast between lived experience in the German capital and that on the other side of the line. Corruption existed everywhere, but only in Berlin did it emerge into a way of life, highlighting the extreme inequality of access to food in the German capital. More than the blockade or the successive bad harvests, the disorganization of the market and modes of distribution (blamed perhaps unfairly on shopkeepers and middlemen), the unequal distribution of essential foods within Berlin society, the link between the access for the most fortunate to the black market and the exorbitant price paid by the majority to obtain no more than reduced rations, all these fuelled public anger and public demand for urgent action by the state.

In Berlin, the authorities' inability to gain a hold on the situation was an essential element in the erosion of the authority of the state. The scale of the process of the unravelling of public confidence on the local level was all the greater because social tensions developed along lines which both highlighted divisions between classes and cut across them. Middle-class people suffered too, but not as much as their poorer neighbours. These social divisions were bad enough; when the news came in 1918 that the war could not be won, they became more serious still. The upshot was the overthrow of the regime and the preparation for a very uncertain future.

12
Coal and the metropolis

Armin Triebel

Introduction

In war the state reveals its essential character . . . It must prove itself capable of awakening and drawing together all of the nation's might. . . The stronger these challenges and burdens become, and the greater their reach into the life of the population, the more the war becomes a test of the entire state's legitimacy.[1]

Problems with the urban distribution of coal were felt from the war's outset in all three cities, and in each case a significant proportion of the population faced both chronic and acute shortages. This chapter tells part of the story of material constraints and administrative reactions in wartime.

The case of coal illustrates well how administrators came up with differing strategies for dealing with wartime shortages in the domestic supply of coal for heating, lighting, and cooking. The measures promulgated in the three capital cities, and their outcomes, shed light on social relations within these cities in the war years and beyond.

The strategies followed by the British and German authorities to supply these populations with coal were antithetical to one another; and just as in other aspects of the economic history of the war, French responses to the problems of coal distribution reflected elements of both German and British policies. These differences may be summarized as follows:

In London: planning and organization under favourable conditions, with a relative abundance of coal, though with some serious short-term shortages. Rationing introduced in London in the summer of 1917, a year before its promulgation in the nation as a whole.

In Paris: more serious shortages controlled by a combination of inter-Allied strategic management and local government initiat-

[1] Erich Kaufmann, *Das Wesen des Völkerrechts und die clausula rebus sic stantibus* (Tübingen, 1911), cited in C. Graf von Krockow, *Die Deutschen in ihrem Jahrhundert 1890–1990* (Frankfurt, 1991), p. 95.

ives; in short, an international solution solved a metropolitan problem. Free and subsidized coal distribution organized by the city for those in need from December 1915 to March 1916, November 1916 to April 1917, and November 1917 to April 1918.

In Berlin: adequate aggregate supply for the city as a whole, but from 1916, chronic and acute shortages in levels of consumption, due to transport problems preventing coal from reaching consumers; in short, an *ad hoc* policy of muddling through, based on a contradictory system: commitment to the maintenance of the 'free market', within a system of complex controls, including rationing from September 1917. This led to a failure to meet civilian needs, especially in the winters of 1916–17 and 1917–18. That problem was primarily one of distribution, not supply.

The social relations of coal consumption in the three cities were set by these parameters. The particular contours of these relations will be examined according to the following questions:

1 What was the distribution policy in each of the three cities? How did the urban administration react to shortages?

2 How did the urban populations respond to the imposition of new regulations?

3 What adaptations were made on the part of the administration or the population in response to coal shortages? Did they learn from their early experiences and change their policies or strategies accordingly?

London and Berlin were best placed with respect to coal supply at the outset of the war, though their respective situations diverged considerably later. The loss of the coal-producing regions of the north of France was bound to have serious consequences for Parisian supplies. But even without this débâcle, Britain and Germany were much better placed than France to find the coal needed both for military and civilian destinations. In 1913, Britain and Germany produced roughly the same amount of coal, though Britain was able to export roughly one-third of its output (see table 12.1). In contrast, French coal production was dwarfed by that of her neighbours, requiring greater imports before the war than either Britain or Germany. In the early days of the war, this was bound to give Germany an advantage.

As the war went on, though, the Allied disadvantage diminished as problems proliferated in Germany. The history of coal supply on the two sides followed quite different paths. Here one can see to what extent the question of resources, which finally would decide the difference between defeat and victory, was determined by political decisions and

Table 12.1. *Coal production, imports and exports, in 1913, Britain, France, and Germany (millions of tonnes)*

Country	Production	Imports	Exports
Britain	287.4	—	94.4
Germany	274.3	10.4	34.0
France	40.2	18.4	1.2

Sources: Imperial Mineral Resources Bureau, The Mineral Industry of the British Empire and Foreign Countries, coal and coke by-products, pt 1 (1921), p. 46; Berlin Chamber of Commerce, *Annual Report,* 1913, p. 170, and J. Hasse-Terheyden, *Die Kohlenversorgung Berlins* (Würzburg, 1922), p. 187, which gives a slightly higher figure of 278.6 million tonnes.

administrative procedures. Patterns of consumption were not primarily a reflection of aggregate supply. Of greater importance was the question, how were these resources managed and distributed? Who would be allowed access to them? The answers to such questions arose out of decisions made concerning the social distribution of the war's burdens.

Early political reactions

Paris

In the early phases of the war, administrative confusion was more evident on the Allied than on the German side. Unlike London and Berlin, Paris was plunged immediately into an acute coal shortage. Initial attempts to deal with the crisis in Paris were hindered by an unwillingness to challenge the principles of free enterprise and a lack of support for state intervention in the economy.

Within a few months it became obvious that there had to be a new source of supply for Parisian coal, as the northern mines near Lille and Mons were behind German lines. The territory occupied by the Germans had previously been responsible for three-quarters of French coal production. Thus, the Department of the Seine immediately lost access to approximately half of the 5 million tons of coal of all kinds which it had consumed annually during peacetime. Britain was forced to provide immediate assistance, and in 1915 some 4 million tonnes of British coal were delivered to the department. These imports made even more vital the water routes along the Seine and the railroad system linked to it: the Seine carried two and a half times more coal to Paris in 1915 than in 1912, and the railroads 70 per cent more. Under such increased pressure, however, there was little spare capacity in these supply lines. High water in winter regularly made the route between Rouen and Paris very slow.[2] In general the channel was very shallow, and the harbour in Paris was old and not up to the task of quickly discharging so many ships. The result was a coal shortage in Paris, even as the fully loaded barges backed up in Rouen. The lack of rolling stock for the trains which serviced the harbours of Caen and Dieppe, which also received British coal, and the one-sided alignment of the rail network outside Paris also led to endless delays.

Above all, the authorities sought to set aside supplies not for civilian use but for the needs of the army and war industry. The list put forth by the municipal customs office every ten days made clear that during periods of increased military activity the trains would cease their deliveries to Paris.[3] This policy, promulgated by the Commission de répartition des combustibles and the Bureau national des charbons in the Ministry of Public Works, provided the orientation for the distribution of the entire French coal supply. It found its expression in dozens of distribution orders and in the establishment of measures which were advantageous to industry. As a result, the proportion of coal which was earmarked for Paris decreased during the war from 37 per cent in 1914 to 28 per cent of the total supply.

After twelve months of insufficient coal deliveries, the Parisian authorities decided on 5 July 1915 to establish their own coal stockpiles. But this measure failed to meet its goals. The stockpiling effort neither increased the availability of coal, nor did it prevent the price explosion which was already under way. In mid-December 1915, the principle of free distribution of coal was adopted. This led to a debate on the limitation of available stocks. The right wing of the Municipal Council, supported by the administration, proposed halting the stockpiling efforts when they had reached 150,000 tonnes, although urban needs were estimated at 400,000 tonnes. This smaller stockpile was gathered by 12 February 1916, supplemented by only a further 50,000 tonnes, bringing the total supply to 200,000 tonnes – still only half of the original target. In the following twelve months, the stockpile would only be replenished, never increased.

In September 1916, when the delivery of coal slowed and prices began to rise accordingly, the prefectural authorities established the Office des charbons du Département de la Seine. Among its other functions was support for a retailers' organization which would

[2] In a proposal for improving the conditions of navigation on the Seine, Georges Lemarchand wrote of two months in the winter of 1916 when traffic was completely stilled on the river. Conseil municipal de Paris, Procès-verbaux, 14 April 1916, p. 173. (Archives de la Seine, D.R. 7/230).

[3] Cf. Archives de la Seine, D.R. 7/232. The reports of the customs office contain many precise and descriptive references to this point.

function as a type of cartel, ensuring a balanced distribution of incoming coal among members, who pledged to respect the price levels set by the Coal Office. In principle, the organization was founded on the basis of voluntary cooperation.[4] Nevertheless, between 24 October 1916 and 1 September 1917 – when it was dissolved – the group received only 878,000 tonnes of coal. This amounted to approximately 2,600 tonnes per day at a time when the prefectural administration estimated the daily needs of the domestic population at 5,000 tonnes.[5] Furthermore, the lack of administrative control over an organization of private businessmen led to misappropriations, profiteering, and eventually, a breakdown in coal distribution.[6] Especially favoured by the situation were those large dealers whose coal yards were located near the major train stations, and whose interests the cartel came to represent.

In the early phase of the war, Paris faced problems unknown in either of the other two capitals. Paris was thus at least as unprepared for the hard winter of 1916 to 1917 as was Berlin. This was not, however, because of insufficient planning and preparation, as was the case in the German war economy. In Paris, the administration had used every possible means at its disposal to avert a coal crisis, but did not have the power to follow these measures through to a successful conclusion. Indeed, the half-heartedness with which their coal policy was implemented often had the opposite effect of that intended, as an example from the high point of the crisis in late January 1917 illustrated. When a portion of the municipal stocks was brought onto the market at a reduced price, retailers with an eye toward future profits took advantage of the lack of public control to replenish their own supplies. From the 45,000 tonnes of coal earmarked for small coal dealers and cooperatives, certain retailers were able to pocket profits of 200 per cent, all the more exorbitant in that they were realized under the auspices of an official municipal policy.[7]

If local authorities were able to limit serious abuse, their intervention remained powerless in the face of rising prices and the disorganized

[4] On the matter of the group's function and the spirit in which it was founded, the Materials Director of the préfecture of the Seine asserted: 'it was taken for granted that, as much as possible, the normal activities of commerce would not be interfered with, that each would retain the freedom of his own initiative', Conseil municipal de Paris, Procès-verbaux, 16 March 1917, p. 35.

[5] Paul Carrau, 'Le ravitaillement en combustibles de la région parisienne pendant la guerre', doctorate in law, Paris, 1924, p. 29.

[6] See the case of the royalist municipal councillor François Froment-Meurice.

[7] 'Aren't those who delivered coal to the city of Paris last winter and who resold it at prices as high as 20 F for a 50 kg. sack just as guilty? And you have permitted them to act in this way . . . in the name of freedom of commerce! Originally the coal had been sold by the municipal service at 6.50 F for a 50 kg. sack,' Conseil municipal de Paris, Procès-verbaux, 21 July 1917, p. 666.

process of coal distribution. Not only were the quantities of municipal stocks insufficient, but partial intervention itself often served to accentuate the crisis. At the end of the winter of 1917 a number of municipal councillors – among them several who would not normally be suspected of advocating state intervention – recognized the problems which had occurred as the result of official indifference. They came to support the view of the socialist Frédéric Brunet, who claimed that: 'The intention was to allow a certain political system to triumph, and in implementing a policy of non-intervention, all in the name of the sacrosanct principle of freedom of commerce, one permitted the freedom to speculate.'[8]

London

A different supply policy was established at the outset of the war in Britain, along lines that made it considerably more effective than the measures implemented in France. The question of coal supply in London can be seen as a classic example of how the need to sustain popular morale led the government to constrain the workings of the free market.

The incremental, but inexorable, extension of the regulation and control of the London coal trade reflected the growing concern in official circles that the well-being and morale of the capital's population was being undermined by constant fuel shortages, by widespread profiteering, and by a growing sense that sacrifices on the home front were not falling equally on rich and poor. As early as March 1915 the British government expressed sensitivity to the potential political consequences of coal shortages and distress in the capital. This can be seen in the speed with which the government sanctioned the creation of two special sub-committees[9] to monitor economic and social conditions in the capital at the outbreak of the war, and also in the government's recognition that special measures would be required to deal with the question of coal supply in the metropolis.

In early 1915, too, the Board of Trade established a committee to investigate the causes of the steep price increases in the domestic coal market during the first winter of war. The winter prices of ordinary quality coal exceeded the summer prices by 14 shillings, while in

[8] Conseil municipal de Paris, Procès-verbaux, 21 July 1917, p. 670.

[9] The two committees were the London Intelligence Committee of the Local Government Board and the London Sub-Committee of the Cabinet Committee for the Prevention and Relief of Distress Due to the War. See PP 1914, Cd 7603, LXXI, p. 877, 'Memorandum on the steps taken for the prevention and relief of distress due to the war', and PP 1914–16 Cd 7763, XXV, p. 299, 'Report on the special work of the Local Government Board arising out of the war: Up to the 31st December 1914'.

ordinary times an increase of only 3 shillings was to be expected. The committee soon determined that the price increases were limited to London. Four causes operated here. First, actual shortages had occurred, despite a decline in overall demand following mobilization, because a greater proportion of coal was being directed to war industries. Secondly, coastal shipping was limited by rising insurance premiums, which increased the cost of ocean transport. Thirdly, the railways were heavily overburdened and subject to delays. Finally, there was a general shortage of coal-yards, which could be stocked in an attempt to balance out the irregularity of new deliveries.[10]

The situation in the capital was especially acute as a result of structural weaknesses in the London coal trade.[11] Before the war much of the working population bought their coal from small dealers and trolleymen who sold only small quantities. These local dealers obtained their stocks from larger wholesale merchants. These few coal merchants possessed a near-monopoly power and played a central role in the city's coal trade. Some merchants only supplied bulk deliveries direct to the middle-class public and to private institutions, but most also carried on their own trolley trade, or supplied the small-scale dealers excluded from railway coal depots and wharfs. During the war, coal merchants preferred to sell to their bulk customers, creating an effective shortage for those whose financial resources did not permit them to buy in more than small quantities.

Once these problems with the coal distribution system were recognized, the administration attempted to bring the coal trade under official supervision. Price levels were set for the trolleymen and retailers, and in the spring of 1916 the coal dealers were required to post the official prices in public view. The Board of Trade and the important London merchants came to an agreement on the limitation of profits in the coal trade and the control of London coal prices. This agreement pledged merchants to withhold supplies from the dealers shown to be charging prices which exceeded the maximum limits set for the different grades and quantities of coal. It also pledged them to maintain a reasonable supply of coal to dealers in times of scarcity.[12]

This voluntary agreement took into consideration not only the distribution of coal as between wholesale and retail merchants but also the role of the coal broker or factor. Although a shadowy figure in the coal-distribution system,[13] the factor often played a vital role as

[10] See *The Times*, 10 March 1915, and PP 1914–16, Cd 7866, XXIX, pp. 3 and 6.

[11] PP 1914–16, Cd 7923, XXIX, p. 13.

[12] See PP 1914–16, Cd 8070, LXI, p. 67, 'List of Coal merchants in the London District who have Accepted an Arrangement for the Limitation of Profits'; and *The Times*, 18 May, 30 Oct., 4, 5, and 6 Nov. 1915.

[13] See PP 1914–16, Cd 7963, XXIX, 'Evidence to 1915 Board of Trade Retail Coal Price

intermediary between mine owner and coal merchant, negotiating bulk orders of pithead coal in advance, and then organizing the delivery of that coal as and when merchants required it. In theory the factor was thus a facilitator, simplifying the trading process for both the coal owner and the London-based merchant. However, he was also the epitome of the unproductive capitalist, able to extract a healthy profit from his control of capital, rather than from his own productive effort. Recognizing that the demands of war rendered the factor's role highly problematic, the Board of Trade agreement (1915) limited the profit which a factor could take for handling coal to 1s 6d per ton. However, this failed to silence criticism of the factors' role because they soon became suspected of operating a secret ring to push up the price of coal between the pithead and London by selling on to fellow factors, rather than direct to a London merchant. In this way, it was alleged, each factor could legitimately take his 1s 6d profit, at the expense of the London merchant and consumer. Significantly, the government did not act to stamp out this practice until the severe coal shortage of 1916–17 had transformed the political significance of the issue.[14]

Berlin

At the outset of the war in Germany, as in Britain, there was no discernible shortage of coal. Unlike the Allies, though, the German government did not pay particular attention to the coal supply until 1916. The experts were unanimous in their opinion that Germany's wealth of coal would preserve them from a coal famine. In fact, German coal production kept on growing in the years preceding the war, and coal stocks increased.[15] It is difficult to be precise about the total coal supplied to Berlin in the years 1913 onwards. The Berlin Chamber of Commerce estimated the whole supply of hard coal and briquettes for Greater Berlin in 1913 at 4.5 million tonnes; the import registers drawn up by the railway administration put it at 6.6 million tonnes in 1913.[16]

Table 12.2 shows that the war brought no significant decrease in coal production in Germany, and especially no decrease in *aggregate* coal supply for Berlin before 1919. Given mass mobilization, this meant that per capita supplies improved in some periods over pre-war levels. Hard

Committee', n. 237–9 Watson; 412–14 (Charrington); 611 (Markham); 1727–30 and 1751–3 (Tebbut); and 1999–2009 (Greig).

14 For complaints about this system see *The Times*, 31 May and 27 July 1916; for the Government's reaction to it see *ibid.*, 2 April 1917.

15 See *Jahresbericht der Handelskammer zu Berlin für 1913*, part 2, pp. 169ff.

16 Josef Hasse-Terheyden, *Die Kohlenversorgung Berlins* (Berlin, 1921), table V. He made use of the import registers of the Reichsbahn (Verkehrskontrolle II) and the shipping companies.

Table 12.2. *Coal production in Germany, and an index of aggregate coal supply reaching Berlin, 1913–1923 (1913=100)*

Year	National production		Supply reaching Berlin		
	Hard coal	Lignite	Hard coal	Lignite	Total (million tons)
1913	100	100	100	100	5.9
1914	84	96	87	105 (107)	5.6
1915	77	101	110	107	6.5
1916	83	108	113	99 (100)	6.4
1917	88 (87)	109 (110)	110	101	6.3
1918	83 (84)	115 (116)	129	103	7.1
1919	61 (56)	107 (106)	85	76 (75)	4.8
1920	69	128	94	96 (93)	5.6
1921	72	141	98	114	6.2
1922	63	157	113	127	7.0
1923	33	136	70	106	4.9

Sources: Walther G. Hoffmann, Franz Grumbach, and Helmut Hesse, *Das Wachstum der Deutschen Wirtschaft* (Berlin, 1965), pp. 342ff.; J. Kürten, *Die Kohlenversorgung in Berlin 1913–1923* in Berliner Wirtschaftsberichte 1,2 (Berlin, 1924), p.9; J. Hasse-Terheyden, *Die Kohlenversorgung Berlins* (Würzburg, 1922), p. 187 and table VB, whose data are indicated in the bracketed figures.

coal was an industrial input, but lignite was the main combustible for private households, and supply remained above pre-war levels nationally, and at or slightly above pre-war levels in Berlin until 1919. Supplies of hard coal for Berlin industry were between 10 and 30 per cent above pre-war levels in 1916–18, despite a decline of about 15 per cent in national production of hard coal in these years. In aggregate terms, Berlin appears to have been slightly worse off than other places for lignite, but better off for hard coal. The role of the war-related industry in the capital helps to account for this difference.

In effect, Berlin was well supplied, but paradoxically, supply sufficiency did not mean that pre-war levels of consumption were maintained. Later in this chapter we will try to resolve this paradox. A number of elements were at work: hoarding, the black market, industrial demand were all important.[17] But above all, urban transport linked supply and demand, and those distribution systems patently failed to bring available coal from depots to domestic customers especially in the second half of the war.

[17] Lignite was the combustible for private households; only small amounts of hard coal were used by them (about 5–10 per cent of the amounts of briquets). On the other hand, some pressed coal destined for private use may have been diverted to industry.

Public authorities never saw the significance of this factor; their blindness may have arisen from the ingrained opposition to state intervention in the economy prevalent in the national and Prussian administrations, especially in the Prussian Ministry of Trade, and among the economists and trade officials who shaped economic policy during the first three years of war. Only in acute emergencies, in temporary situations, or in marginal areas did they contemplate limiting the free production and trade in coal, through stockpiling and some price controls.

In general, city officials were much more willing to dispense with a free-market policy. Nevertheless, the Berlin Magistrates (the executive body of city government) and the members of the Municipal Assembly were, as the director of the City Archives Ernst Kaeber reported, 'a long way away' from pushing through a new economic policy during the war. 'Even the most convinced socialists', he noted, 'are far from eager to make food supply (*Lebensmittel*) a branch of the municipal administration, especially given the acute lack of available personnel.'[18]

In February 1914 an article in the *Berliner Morgenpost*[19] reported that in Paris a flour stockpile had been set aside in case of war. The Director of the Markethalls in Berlin replied in public that such a measure was not necessary in Berlin. Whereas Paris had been transformed into a fortress, he argued, the German capital was a free city and in completely different circumstances. In the matter of coal supply, as in the question of food provision, the city authorities were convinced that free trade would be more effective than any experiment with 'state socialism'. On the occasion of 'long food queues (*Lebensmittelpolonaisen*) in London' the *Berliner Lokal-Anzeiger* smugly cited the parliamentary secretary of the British Ministry of Food, who had rejected the proposal that the British Government take over the food industry, and maintained the view that such would prove impossible for Britain to do. When in May 1916 a special department for coal was created in the Greater Berlin Price Control Office (*Preisprüfungsstelle Groß-Berlin, Fachausschüsse*), the purpose of this office was merely to monitor price movements.

Such surveillance disclosed moderately steep price increases before mid-1916. The price for briquets had gone up the most – 50 per cent since the war's outbreak – but the price for hard coal and gas coke used for central-heating systems had increased only moderately, by about 20 per cent.

In October 1916, the first newspaper articles appeared in Berlin which wrote of coal shortages and the threat of price increases. The articles simultaneously reassured the population, however, by pointing out that it was not a matter of a shortage of fuel, and that on the contrary, coal

[18] Kaeber, *Berlin*, pp. 86ff. [19] 3 Feb. 1914, as cited in Kaeber, *Berlin*, p. 80.

production had risen since the beginning of the war. Such was not the case in France, German journalists patriotically insisted; there hardly any coal at all was available.[20] At this point the coal shortage had not yet reached serious proportions, and it seems that Berliners did not perceive the situation as one of approaching crisis. From September to November 1916 the papers were preoccupied with potato shortages and a lack of milk, but in the *Berliner Lokal-Anzeiger*, a leading daily paper which reported extensively on the supply problems facing the city, there were in the last three months of 1916 eighteen articles on the subject of coal, primarily warnings about price increases and suggestions on how to limit household use. In December 1917, however, there were eighteen such articles in that one month alone.

These reports were based on real evidence of increasing hardship. Shortages in household supply resulted from many sources, but among the most prominent were difficulties in transporting the coal from the mines to the cities. Two-thirds to three-quarters of all coal imports to Berlin arrived by rail.[21] The Prussian Minister for Railways testified in the Assembly that the demand for rolling stock was so great that on average throughout Germany 23 per cent of the locomotives were in repair, compared to an average of 18 per cent in peace time. When the Imperial Commissioner for Coal Distribution was charged with failing to give Berlin priority in the matter of coal supply, he replied:

> I attribute the greatest importance to the supply of Berlin with combustible fuels – and especially the supply of brown coal briquets. The transport of coal to Berlin is as great as the availability of freight cars will permit. Given that only 60 per cent of the normally required freight cars are currently available, then one may conclude that the supply of Berlin is more advantageous than in any other city.[22]

Berlin was given priority, but only in the sense that its shortages were relatively smaller than those registered elsewhere.

Railway traffic was the key to the problem. By 1916 the extension of supply lines into occupied lands forced the German railway to cover 16,000 extra kilometres of rail routes.[23] The conquest of Romania in the second half of 1916 only worsened this problem. In addition, there was a general shortage of transport workers. When the War Office announced in mid-1917 that 100 coachmen and 500 coal workers were ready to work for Berlin coal firms, the newspapers reacted with expressions of relief.[24] The central office for railways assigned special coal trains for the

[20] *Berliner Lokal-Anzeiger* (15 Nov. 1916, evening edition). See also 22 and 29 Nov. 1916, evening editions.

[21] Hasse-Terheyden, *Die Kohlenversorgung*, table 6-F.

[22] LHA, Pr.Br.Rep. 1A, Staatliche Verteilungsstelle, 242.

[23] Cited in *Der Kohlenhändler. Organ des Verbandes der Vereine selbständiger Holz- und Kohlenhändler von Berlin und Umgegend*, 16, 1 (1917), p. 3.

supply of Berlin, but many were unable to move, and they remained inactive in over-loaded freight yards.[25]

In mid-December 1916 the Bundesrat implemented a series of half-hearted conservation measures, including reductions of public transportation, prohibition of illuminated advertising, and the limitation of lighting on the street, in shop windows, and in house corridors.[26] The effectiveness of these measures remained doubtful, however, and on 21 February 1917 the managing board of the price office (Arbeitsausschuß der Preisprüfungsstelle) declined to pursue more radical measures such as strict supply schedules, confiscations of stocks, or quotas on amounts purchased. When wholesale prices for coke, hard coal, and briquets rose by 2 to 3.5 Marks per tonne at the new year in 1917, the only reaction from the government was a moderate appeal to the Mining Producers Association from the Prussian Ministry of Trade. In any case, these increases did not affect the retail prices for coke, and the prices for hard coal and briquets only increased about 10 to 25 pfennigs per 50 kg.

The total breakdown of domestic coal supply did not occur in Berlin until the winter of 1917–18. This crisis proved that the preliminary administrative guidelines were in no way sufficient to deal with the scope of the problem. Above all, the problem was aggravated by poor coordination between officials and a lack of effectiveness in the well-intentioned relief efforts of the Berlin Magistrate. Those responsible for coal policy in Berlin had not learned anything from the earlier (and less severe) crisis of 1916–17; they still retained their commitment to limited controls on coal production and supply.

In spite of the proliferation of committees and offices in 1917, no one among the plethora of authorities proved capable of ensuring effective transport of coal from the mines to Berlin or from depots to consumers in the winter of 1917–18. Consider this maze of administration. In early February 1917 the Imperial Commissioner for Coal Distribution (Reichskommissar für die Kohlenverteilung) was appointed, and in April of that year a Coal Department (Kohlenabteilung der Kriegsamtstelle in den Marken) was established under military authority. The purpose of these new bureaux was to centralize the administration of coal transport, until then the responsibility of separate authorities and the Transportzentrale of the Military Command. Nevertheless, a third bureau, the Greater Berlin Coal Office (Kohlenstelle Groß-Berlin) was

24 *Berliner Tageblatt*, 17 Jan. 1917. 25 *Berliner Lokal-Anzeiger*, 19 Jan. 1917.

26 *Reichsgesetzblatt* 1916 (Brennstoff-Verordnung), pp. 1355f. In the *Berliner Lokal-Anzeiger* of 16 December 1916 (1st supplement) a correspondent calculated that limitations of the street-cars and the city trains would save 11.8 tons of coal daily, worth 260 marks and amounting to 400 freight cars per year. He then asked if such a saving was really in proportion to the disadvantages that such limitations brought to the population.

also created; it was responsible to the Coal Department, and in turn served as the executive board for a fourth authority, the Greater Berlin Coal Association (Kohlenverband Groß-Berlin), founded on 21 August 1917. This latter organization included representatives from most of the communities in the Greater Berlin area and was a more effective office within the regional system of coal administration. On the local level, the Berlin Coal Supply Department (Deputation für die Kohlenversorgung) was founded in June 1917 to oversee the administration of coal-rationing cards and it soon grew to become one of the city's largest offices, with 800 employees. A private enterprise whose shares were completely held by the Magistrate was closely associated with this latter authority – the Berlin Supply Company for Combustible Fuels (Berliner Brennstoffbeschaffungsgesellschaft GmbH). The co-directors of this company were a municipal councillor (Magistratsrat) and a wood merchant. The military authorities too had a word to say since fuel was essential for public order. As these overlapping directorates illustrate, Berlin's coal supply was overadministered; more paperwork never amounted to more coal where it mattered.

Notably, it was the army who first pointed out the signs of the approaching coal supply crisis in September 1917. The provincial command (Oberkommando in den Marken), Generaloberst von Kessel, sounded the alarm to the Reichs Chancellory, noting that only 70 per cent of the promised deliveries of coal had actually arrived in Berlin. Kessel declined to accept any responsibility for social unrest that could arise from the expected coal shortage: 'If the population has not yet exhibited any disorder, it is only because of our continued mild weather.' According to the opinion of the director of the Coal Department, Oberleutnant Körte, Berlin's allottment of 200,000 tons of briquets barely sufficed (*außerordentlich knapp*) to meet the demands of the domestic market in the last autumn of 1917.[27]

If the army was not responsible for the problem, then who was? While the Reich authorities attempted to shift responsibility for the problem, the available supply of hard coal and coke in Berlin sunk to between one-third and one-half of its designated levels, which were themselves below pre-war levels. The allocations discussed here (*Hausbrand*) were determined by the National Coal Commissioner and were destined for the population at large, who would receive the coal in exchange for ration cards. In mid-November only 61 per cent of the briquet allocation actually arrived in Berlin. The new director of the War Office, a central supply office in the War Ministry on the model of the British Ministry of Munitions, ordered the registration of all

[27] LHA, Pr. Br. Rep. 1A, Staatliche Verteilungsstelle, 242.

available stockpiles, whether in official or private hands, and in mid-November an extraordinary session under the chairmanship of the National Coal Commissioner was called. As a result the supply of briquets was improved, so much so that in January 1918 it surpassed its allotted level.

The shortage of hard coal for industry, however, had already surfaced in December 1917, and Körte saw the supply for private central heating endangered as industry sought to substitute coke for coal. By the end of January, following the intervention of the Minister of the Interior, the position with respect to coke improved somewhat, and the supply of hard coal reached the level that had been set for it the previous November. In the meantime, however, the resupply of briquets declined.

Why then this serious undersupply of private households in Berlin, despite evidence in table 12.2 of the maintenance of pre-war levels of output? As this table shows, the National Commissioner for Coal Distribution was correct when he said that the situation in Berlin was *relatively* good compared to other cities, but that was hardly an answer to the problem. To some extent, the situation reflected the diversion of available coal to industrial users. But in essence, the crisis of the winter of 1917/18 was a short-term supply crisis producing anger in a population exhausted by all sorts of shortages and adaptations.

In essence, the critical bottleneck was transportation. The coal was there, and sent from pitheads to depots, as aggregate figures of coal production indicate. From that point on, a Byzantine administrative system could not create vehicles or drivers to unload the depots; like the current 'Butter mountain' in the European community, stocks of supplies and deprivation were parallel, not contradictory, phenomena. For every 2,000 wagons that came to Berlin daily, only 600 to 800 could be unloaded. Both manpower and horsepower were in short supply; hence material inputs to the city reached a barrier created by the overheated nature of the war economy itself. Here in microcosm was the source of the general problem facing Berliners; coal was but one instance of it. Without an effective urban transport network to bring the coal to the consumer, the city's population could not get at the coal which had been allocated to them.

Others, less scrupulous, succeeded. The black market probably relieved these depots of some of their stores. Hoarding was a reality too. But illegality was less the source of the problem than inadequate transport, and this in turn reflected the intensification and bureaucratization of both military and industrial mobilization in the last two years of the war. What Gerald Feldman has called the 'irrationality' of the German economy under the Third High Command of Hindenburg and

Ludendorff[28] has an urban face: it can be seen in the metropolitan coal crisis of the last two years of the war.

Once more we find an eloquent illustration of the strength of Amartya Sen's arguments about entitlements, capabilities, and functionings. Without adequate coal supplies, essential features of urban 'functionings' – lighting, heating, and cooking – were compromised in wartime Berlin.[29] For some, the cold was lethal; for others, it added another component of misery to an already difficult situation. What is remarkable is not the ultimate demise of the German war effort, but the fact that Berliners, and millions of other civilians, carried on as long as they did.

Fair shares in wartime

The coal question highlights both similarities and differences in the metropolitan management of scarcity in wartime. On one level, all three cities faced harsh winter conditions, especially in 1916 and 1917. Despite extraordinarily cold temperatures, one should not overestimate the influence of meteorological factors in the coal crises of the three cities. The winter intensified, but certainly did not cause, the problem of irregular coal supply.

In London the average temperature between November 1916 and March 1917 was 3.6 °C. The coldest spell came between the fourth week in January and the second week in February, where the temperature consistently stayed below freezing (between −0.7 and −9.4 °C). In Richmond the mercury dropped to record levels (−10 °C) on 10 February. In Paris the temperature reached a low of −13 °C in February and −14 °C in April, and was as low as −7 °C in March. The mean monthly temperature in Berlin's inner city Moabit district was between −2 and −3 °C in January and February 1917; in the neighbouring district of Wedding, which was then on the outskirts, still colder monthly mean temperatures were recorded: between −2.3 and −4 °C in January and February 1917, with a average daily low of −18.5 °C in February.[30]

Under similarly difficult weather conditions, each of the capitals dealt with the crisis in a distinct manner, and with varying degrees of success. In Berlin the winter of 1916/17 exhausted the municipal

[28] G.D. Feldman, *Army, industry and labor*, conclusion; see also G. D. Feldman, 'War economy and controlled economy: the discrediting of 'Socialism' in Germany during World War I', in Hans-Jürgen Schröder (ed.), *Confrontation and cooperation. Germany and the United States in the Era of World War I, 1900–1924* (Oxford, 1993), pp. 229–52.

[29] A. Sen, *Poverty and Famines* (Oxford, 1981).

[30] *Statistisches Jahrbuch der Stadt Berlin*, vol. 34 (1915-19), pp. 201, 203, 206, 218ff. *Weekly weather reports at the Meteorological Office* (London), *Annuaire Statistique de la ville de Paris*, 1914–19.

stockpiles and set the stage for the considerably more severe crisis of 1917–18, in which the health and survival chances of the civilian population were seriously impaired. The supply crisis which London experienced in 1916–17 was not the result of shortages: due to greater productivity and a limitation on exports, the amount of coal allocated to private household use (nearly 200,000,000 tonnes) was higher in 1916/17 than in any other war year.[31] The crisis in Paris was also independent of weather conditions. It was rather the concurrence of several unfavourable factors: the flaring up of military operations in Flanders, the increased demand of war industries, as much as intense cold which caused civilian demand in Paris to rise.

London

Let us consider the Allied side first. The London coal crisis arose not out of a shortage of supply, but from imbalances in the market, favouring large over small purchasers, as well as transport problems. There is ample evidence that many working-class families were prepared to pay high prices whenever coal became available in their community. Prices as high as 2s 8d per cwt appear to have been charged by unscrupulous dealers who managed to break the coal famine in the worst-hit working-class districts; there were claims that coal purchased in small quantities was being sold at up to 75 per cent above recommended prices.[32] Sellers tells of visiting the house of a soldier on leave on Christmas Day 1916, to find him, his wife, and his six children living in 'glacial' conditions, having been unable to get any coal for days. She, at least, had no doubts about the cause of their plight:

> Not that there was a coal famine: there was a plentiful supply a few miles away. Not that they themselves were without money: they had money enough to pay for all they needed, could they have bought it [coal] by the hundredweight or sack. It was only because they could not buy it by the ton, as their money came to them weekly, that they were left without coal.[33]

During the summer of 1916 more and more London merchants complained that they were unable to secure sufficient stocks of coal, and that, as a consequence, they could not meet advance orders for winter

31 See Imperial Mineral Resources Bureau, *The Mineral Industry of the British Empire and Foreign Countries, War Period 1913–1919: coal, coke and by-products*, Part I (London, 1921), table vi, p. 66, cols. 1 and 10.

32 *The Times*, 6 Feb. 1917; *Hansard*, 5th Series, XCI, col. 2181 where John O'Connor (MP for North Kildare) claimed that prices reached the equivalent of 3s 6d per cwt at the height of the famine. For official prices see *The Times*, 14 Feb. 1917; carriage costs were recognized to be higher in south London because the main coal depots were all north of the river; shop prices were 1d higher than these trolley prices.

33 E. Sellers, 'On the manufacturing of grievance', *The 19th Century and After*, 481 (March 1917), p. 556.

coal from consumers with substantial bunkering facilities.[34] When the hard winter set in, many middle-class households, fearful that they had insufficient stocks of coal, began to compete directly with working-class consumers trying to meet their daily requirement for fuel. As a result, supplies of coal to small dealers simply dried up in large parts of London.[35] Merchants found themselves under great moral and economic pressure to maintain supplies to their established retail customers at the expense of small dealers who sold coal to poorer consumers. Sellers claimed that the merchants were 'as keenly alive as the rest of us to the inequalities of the present system', but that they could not afford to alienate wealthy customers anxious that their own households might soon be without fuel.[36]

The crisis was exacerbated by the shortage of labour, limiting coal distribution and leaving the streets uncleared of ice and snow. Traditionally much of this labour had been purely casual, relying on the chronic oversupply of unskilled labour in the capital.[37] But now that unemployment and underemployment had all but vanished, merchants found it extremely difficult to secure the services of reliable carters and porters. During the long freeze of early 1917, the clearing of the streets of ice and snow could be done only slowly and so large parts of the capital were effectively cut off from coal supplies for long periods, even when the depots were *not* empty.[38]

Qualitative evidence does suggest that hardship was widespread and profound. In particular, the frequency with which the coal famine of 1916–17 is discussed in the autobiographies of Londoners who lived through the war gives some indication of the impact it had on everyday life. In A. S. Jasper's autobiography we are told that the 'winter of 1917 was the worst I remember as a child'. Jasper recalled that as 'soon as I saw a coal-shop selling coal we would all go and line up and get our seven pounds' which was the maximum purchase allowed in local coal shops (*c.* 3 kgs).[39]

As the cold weather persisted, so the shortage of coal in London grew worse. Interestingly, the government, and others in authority, went to great lengths to insist that all classes were suffering equally during the

[34] See *The Times*, 27 July 1917. [35] *The Times*, 10 Feb. 1917.

[36] Sellers, 'On the manufacturing of grievance', p. 558.

[37] Stedman Jones, *Outcast London*, part 1, especially pp. 35–6, 56–7 and 71.

[38] See *The Times*, 10 Feb. 1917, and *The Coal Merchant and Shipper*, 10 March 1917.

[39] Jasper was about twelve at the time. A. S. Jasper, *A Hoxton childhood* (London, 1969), pp. 88–9; also p. 64 where he discusses similar queues in Hoxton during the winter of 1914–15. See also: A. Linton, *Not expecting miracles* (London, 1982), p. 5 (like Jasper, Linton was brought up in Hoxton, East London), and A. Newton, *Years of change: autobiography of a Hackney shoemaker* (London, 1974), p. 49.

coal famine of 1916/17.[40] It was politically imperative that they should do so, since any widespread sense of the inequality of sacrifice threatened quickly to erode civilian morale. However, the fact that administrative effort was concentrated almost exclusively on guaranteeing that minimum supplies of coal would reach working-class consumers, points to the real nature of the crisis. By February 1917 large parts of East London, including Bethnal Green and Stepney, were said to be almost entirely without coal.[41] When military detachments were brought in to help overcome bottlenecks in the distribution system, they were sent almost exclusively to the poor East End.[42] At the same time, the government relaxed its restrictions which prevented poor boroughs such as Bethnal Green from storing and distributing coal within their communities.[43] When Bethnal Green Borough Council called a meeting of the district's coal merchants and dealers to discover the causes of the recent crisis, there was a general agreement that the monopolization of wharfage accommodation by a few large firms had kept coal out of the hands of smaller East End dealers.[44] Indeed, this problem had been so acute in the neighbouring borough of Shoreditch that the local council bought a barge in order to transport 50 tonne-loads of coal up to its Kingsland wharf, where it was sold to local coal dealers unable to get supplies through normal channels.[45] Stories of scavenging at coal depots and wharves became more common, and there were even reports of women ambushing coal-delivery vehicles and forcing the drivers to sell them their load at a fair price.[46]

The political lessons learned by the London authorities in 1916/17 were clear. The coal-rationing system implemented in the autumn of 1917 compensated poor Londoners for their disadvantaged position with respect to access to coal. Controls applied only to purchases of more than 2 cwt; the poor consumer was excluded from the scheme and could continue to purchase coal without interference.[47] The scheme's

[40] For instance see *Hansard*, 5th series, XCI, col. 2186, where George Roberts, as the Board of Trade minister responsible for civilian coal supply, insists that 'the hardships for once have not been confined to one class'.

[41] See *The Times*, 10 Feb. 1917; *Woman's Dreadnought*, 10 Feb. 1917, and *East London Observer*, 10 March 1917.

[42] *The Times*, 12 Feb. 1917, and *Hansard*, 5th series, XCI, col. 2187 (remarks of the Labour MP Roberts).

[43] See *East London Observer*, 10 March 1917; *The Times*, 14 July 1917.

[44] *East London Observer*, 10 March 1917.

[45] *The Times*, 10 February 1917.

[46] See *The Times*, 6 Feb. 1917; and E. Sellers, 'On the manufacturing of grievance', pp. 550–61, esp. p. 555.

[47] *Manuals of Emergency Legislation, Defence of the Realm Manual (6th Edition) Revised to August 31st, 1918* (London, 1918), pp. 321–43, 'Household Coal Distribution Order, 1917', p. 322; and 'Explanatory Memorandum as to Household Coal Distribution Order, 1917'; and Metropolitan Coal Distribution Papers, BLPES F 196 5; *The Times*, 13 Aug. 1917.

primary purpose was the restriction of middle-class demand during the winter months. Between October and March, coal was not to be delivered to any customer with stocks of more than a quarter ton. There were further restrictions, but none of these applied between April and September.[48] In addition the scheme directed that, throughout the winter, all registered coal merchants maintain adequate stocks of coal at every depot for customers wishing to purchase coal in small quantities of between 25 kg. and 100 kg. The ration itself was not especially strict: a seven-roomed house was allowed one tonne of coal per month or some 33 kg. per day.

There is some scattered evidence that, as a result of this scheme, working-class consumption of coal in the capital increased during 1917–18, even though the winter of 1917–18 was relatively mild.[49] The restrictions were felt chiefly in larger houses, and institutions like hotels and theatres.[50] Compared to the coal situation on the continent, such conditions were paradise. Even in October 1918, when the danger of a real coal shortage loomed in England, and the system of customer lists (already in use in Berlin) was introduced, the implementation of strict conservation measures was never contemplated.

In London, the coal shortage pointed to social inequalities with dangerous potential implications. In Berlin potential became reality: a sense of inequality bred a deepening perception of anger about social injustice. Whereas in London the issuing of coal coupons served to rectify some feelings of social injustice, they did not meet with similar success in Berlin; indeed, the coupon system may even have contributed to greater resentment, since having a piece of paper was no guarantee of finding coal for your home.

Achieving a just distribution of coal in wartime required that the administration determine the amount that each individual should receive. How much coal did a household need? This is an exceedingly complicated question, but some rough orders of magnitude may be suggested. In Germany, where since the early years of the century a large body of advice literature had established the standards for a good and economical household, the average working-class household was said to need between 3.3 and 5.5 kg. per day (28 kg. per week), and middle-class households between 6 and 8 kg. (49 kg. per week). An estimate made for winter conditions arrived at the figure of 5.4 kg. per day (or 38 kg. per week). A household was considered to be two to four

[48] For details of these restrictions on winter purchasing see *Household Coal Distribution Order, 1917*, paras. 9f, 11g, and 12b; also *The Times*, 13 Aug. 1917.

[49] The mean monthly temperature between November 1917 and March 1918 was 5.5 °C.

[50] BLPES, F 332 10, Working Classes Cost of Living Committee, 1918 – Papers [Sumner Committee Papers]; A. S. Oppé (Board of Trade Mines Department) to F. S. Eagles (Secretary of the Working Classes Cost of Living Committee), 24 April 1917.

people in a middle-sized flat: normally one room, a kitchen, and pantry. In order to stay within these limits, only one room was to be heated and never to a temperature that exceeded 15 °C.[51] The boundary conditions in Germany appear to be between 30 and 50 kg. per week per household.

In contrast, a British survey of twenty-one unskilled worker households in the south-eastern district of Kennington put the daily need for coal at 5.9 kg. per day when reckoned over the entire year and 7.6 kg. in the winter months (from October to March).[52] This produces a weekly estimate of 42–50 kg. per week per household, a somewhat higher range of normal fuel supply than in pre-war German estimates. We know that consumption increased in Britain during the war. A survey of 493 London households in the crisis winter of 1916/17 revealed a daily use of 9.2 kg. (calculated over the entire year) in 2–7 room flats – and as much as 14.5 kg. per day in winter. The Sumner Committee calculated in the spring of 1918 that the national average for daily coal consumption in winter was 12.3 kg. – with working-class households averaging 7.25 and salaried employees somewhat more than 10. A French estimate which placed the daily needs of a larger household in winter at 8–12 kg. does not, therefore, seem unrealistic.[53]

Substantial variations existed in coal consumption, but it appears that working-class households in Britain were better stocked with coal than were similar households in Germany. Wartime deprivation pushed down German consumption levels which were already lower than British levels prior to the war.

Paris

In Paris, the implementation of a coal-rationing system (see chapter 10) aimed from the very beginning at a just distribution of coal. Assistance programmes run by charity organizations had been in operation since the first winter of war, although their effectiveness was relatively limited. Since 1915/16 municipal action had supported the neediest sections of the population by distributing more than 100,000 tonnes of coal. Free distribution of coal, introduced under pressure from the

[51] *Wie wirtschaftet man gut und billig bei einem jährlichen Einkommen von 800 bis 1000 Mark?* (Dresden, 1900), pp. 28ff, 46, 51, 67, 74; Julie Ravit, *Wie kommt man mit wenigem aus?* (Kiel, 1908), pp. 13 and 22. (In the above figures 1 cwt = 50 kg. and 1 bushel (*Scheffel*) = 25 kg., A.T.) See also Kürten, *Die Kohlenversorgung*, p. 11, where for 1922 a figure of 4.8 kg. per day is given.

[52] BLPES, F 332 10, *Sumner Committee Papers*, item 96: 'Memorandum on fuel and light'. (In the calculations, 1 cwt = 50.8 kg.)

[53] BLPES, London, *Statement of coal consumption by private households* in: Coal Committee Notes / item 3; BLPES, London, *Sumner Committee Papers*, item 96: 'Memorandum on fuel and light'; socialist municipal councillor Jean Morin, Conseil municipal de Paris, Procès-verbaux, 13 Dec. 1915, p. 712.

socialists in December 1915, as a rule entailed 50 kg. per household per month. Once again, this figure is towards the top end of the pre-war German estimate of household requirements. Eligibility for this programme was decided upon by public-welfare committees (*bureaux de bienfaisance*). Unfortunately, the necessary coal for this programme was not always available. This method of distribution led to conflicts over entitlements, and was the object of numerous protests.[54] Still the effort at equalization through municipal action was significant.

The problem of maintaining the free market for coal in Paris coalesced around the question of distributing the city's own municipal stockpile.[55] The first attempts were restricted to a limited population. Access to reduced-price sales was limited to a specific group of needy people, comprising several categories of recipients from the lists of the welfare committees. The quantities of coal distributed were also reduced to a maximum purchase of 400 kg., and the policy prohibited the accumulation of private stocks by combining such purchases with coal received through free distributions – aimed at the same groups – organized by the municipality. A proposition from the Socialist Reisz which aimed at benefiting a larger population[56] was rejected. It was not until April 1916 that the system became more flexible. Since commercial interests were well-represented on the municipal council, it is not surprising that such small quantities were put on the market.

By the end of 1916, the system of municipal sales of coal at reduced prices was well established, though on a modest scale. A decision of 8 December raised to 30,000 tonnes the amount of coal set aside for sale between November 1916 and April 1917. Given the level of municipal demand, this assistance remained more a form of relief to the poor, complementing the system of free distribution, than a truly effective measure against rising prices. The restricted categories of the population who benefited from the sales, as well as the central role of the welfare committees, whose lack of generosity was frequently an item of contention, tends to point initially towards a relatively small impact on civilian consumption levels.

The Parisian system of late 1916[57] was indeed a departure from the principles of *laissez-faire* government. The number of eligible recipients of the coal allowance was systematically determined, permitting an allocation for each household which corresponded to available

[54] Municipal councillor Alfred Lallement in session of 17 Nov. 1916, Conseil municipal de Paris, Procès-verbaux, 17 Nov. 1916, p. 672.

[55] Conseil municipal de Paris, Procès-verbaux, 27 Dec. 1915, pp. 889–95.

[56] That is, working-class families earning from 4.50 to 5 francs and small shopkeepers, Conseil municipal de Paris, Procès verbaux, 27 Dec. 1915, pp. 891 and 889.

[57] On this system, see Conseil municipal de Paris, Rapports et documents, no. 42, 2 Dec. 1916.

supplies. Thus, for the winter of 1916/17, some 80,000 tonnes of coal were distributed from the city's stockpiles to over 400,000 needy households,[58] or approximately 40 per cent of the Parisian population.[59] This amounted to 1 kg. of coal per day for each household hearth. The neediest households got even more: between 2.2 and 2.7 kg. per day from municipal sources. In June 1916, once the socialists on the city council had taken the matter in hand, support was extended to all women who earned less than 5 francs per day. For each child under sixteen, such women would receive a supplement of 50 centimes per day, so long as the support payment did not exceed 1.5 francs per day.

These new regulations allow us more clearly to determine the population which benefited from municipal allocations. It is apparent that a considerable group, dominated by poor women and workers, benefited from free distribution of coal. Even if the quantities made available were small, they constituted for the most part a guarantee against the worst. Here was a material form of entitlement through which minimal 'capabilities' and 'functionings', in the sense Sen has employed, were ensured.[60]

The response to the Parisian coal crisis of 1916–17 was a system of coal coupons, introduced in Berlin roughly at the same time, but under conditions different from those in Paris. The debate in the Parisian Municipal Council over its implementation lasted seven full days, from 19 to 26 July 1917, and was dominated by the decision announced by the 2nd Commission, to deliver 'a certain base level, such that each household would be assured a warm hearth'.[61] Nevertheless, no minimum guarantees were made; rather, a proportional distribution of available supplies was agreed upon. The principle used was a coefficient based on the number of people in each household. The size of the individual allocation was arrived at by multiplying the coefficient by a base-level quantity subject to change each month; in fact, it remained fixed until February 1920 at 30 kg. According to the size of the household, the allocations varied thus between 120 and 180 kg. per month from November to April, amounting to 4–6 kg. per day.

From the scale used by the Municipal Council we can determine the very slight progression in allocation as the number of people in the household increased. The system thus clearly reflected the overt desire to guarantee each household at least one hot oven. The number of rooms

[58] Eugène Fiancette, in Conseil municipal de Paris, Procès-verbaux, 16 Nov. 1917, p. 801. Fiancette mentions a figure of 390,000 households.

[59] The results of an investigation aimed at assisting the distribution of sugar rations gave a total of 956,000 households for Paris at this time (Archives de la Seine, D.R. 7 141).

[60] See chapter 1, pp. 10–13.

[61] Conseil municipal de Paris, Procès-verbaux, 26 July 1917, p. 716.

to be heated was irrelevant, a matter which led some councillors to complain that standards of bourgeois comfort were in danger, but that was beside the point.

The rationing system was accompanied by price regulation and required the centralization of the entire coal supply network in the hands of the National Coal Office (Bureau national des charbons); both measures gave the public a good reason to believe that there would be a more just distribution of available coal.

Berlin

In the harsh winter of 1916/17, Berlin had edged close to the point of breakdown in coal supply. There was already dissatisfaction among citizens who had encountered empty shelves in the coal shops. But both the newspaper and authorities reassured the public by pointing to the existence of a considerable supply of briquets being stored in the Lausitz region. To the *Berliner Lokal-Anzeiger*, the situation was not so bad, 'so long as the consumer is not too picky about the purchase'.[62]

The decree of 6 July 1917 put forward by the provincial command (Oberbefehlshaber in den Marken) set up a coal-rationing system for private households. The system was to come into force on 5 September 1917.[63] The amount of coal allocated to each Berlin household was determined by using the previous year's consumption (1916–17) as the base. The first surveys of available combustible fuels and the city's estimated requirements took place not earlier than September 1917.[64] The available stockpiles at that point stood at 200,000 tonnes, while the monthly winter requirements for cooking and heating, industry and agriculture, were placed at 350,000 tonnes. Simultaneously, the deliveries of coal to depots in Berlin and even more significantly, to stores throughout the city, were falling well short of their targets. Consumers were getting less than two-thirds of their legal allocation: so much for 'entitlement'. A total breakdown of the system seemed imminent. At the end of October, the delivery of coal to public baths was cut off. By decree, the city limited the heating of water in private houses to specific hours during the day, and heating was restricted to only a few rooms per flat. After considerable protest, however, these measures were lifted in December.

On 20 December the first arrest took place of a coal-coupon thief. Not surprisingly, coal turned out to be a precious black market commodity. By this point, almost every issue of the *Lokal-Anzeiger* contained articles or remarks on the coal emergency. Writing after the war, the city's

62 *Berliner Lokal-Anzeiger*, 8 Oct. 1916, supplement 3.

63 Announcement by the Greater Berlin Coal Association, signed by Lord Mayor Wermuth, 28 Aug. 1917 (LA Rep. 142/2 St.K 508).

64 LHA, Pr.Br.Rep.1A, 242, pp. 5ff; LA, Rep. 142/2 ST.K 352; see also Kaeber, *Berlin*, p. 318.

archivist Kaeber noted the political barriers which prevented Berlin's adoption of a solution along Parisian lines:

A suspension of free trade, which may have seemed advantageous to some, was ruled out by the speed with which the city's conservation measures had to be launched, not to mention the fundamental considerations which spoke against such a policy, and the fact that the National Commissioner for Coal Distribution was in no way in favour of such action.[65]

In the press and elsewhere many called for a system of customer lists, whereby each consumer would be instructed to buy only from one particular retailer, who in turn would receive no more coal than was required by his list of customers. For the consumer such a measure would bring a degree of security, and would dispense with the necessity of waiting in long queues without any guarantee of actually making a purchase. Such a system had already been put in place in Lankwitz, a southern district of the city. On the question of customer lists, however, the authorities were divided over the question of how far to restrict the freedom of commerce. On one side stood the military supply offices and the greater part of the Berlin administration who advocated free trade. On the other side stood the proponents of a municipally run economy, the Social Democrats, the Coal Supply Department of the Magistrate, and to some degree Mayor Wermuth himself. Under the auspices of the Greater Berlin Coal Association, the director of the Coal Department, Oberleutnant Körte, put together a study which concluded that the system of customer lists was impossible to implement. This was the conclusion of the Potsdam Chamber of Commerce, which inveighed against the 'compulsory system where the state directs the customers to the dealers'.[66] Despite these attempts to obstruct the new measure, however, the shortage of coal became so acute that customer lists were introduced in March 1918,[67] just in time for the last major offensive of the war, through which the civilian population of Berlin (and the rest of Germany) collectively held its breath. When the offensive failed, the war was lost.

Sacrifice and exploitation

Allocation and inequality

Shortages reinforced existing social cleavages.[68] Administrative regulations aiming at more just distribution of resources divided the popula-

[65] Kaeber, *Berlin*, p. 318. [66] LHA, Pr.Br.Rep. 1A, 242, Staatliche Verteilungsstelle, p. 167.

[67] *Bekanntmachung über die Einrichtung von Kundenlisten für Braunkohlenbriketts zum Küchen- und Ofenbrand in Gross-Berlin*. Der Kohlenverband Gross-Berlin, 11 March 1918.

[68] For examples on the German case, see Dieter Baudis, 'Vom "Schweinemord" zum Kohlrübenwinter', in D. Baudis (ed.), *Zur Wirtschafts-und Sozialgeschichte Berlins vom 17. Jahrhundert bis zur Gegenwart* (Berlin, 1986), pp. 129–57, and Barrington Moore, *Injustice* (London, 1980).

tion further, between those in need on account of the war and those deemed not to be in need. In all three cities the same question surfaced again and again: who must go without? This question may be reformulated in terms of entitlement: who had a right to public support to limit the hardship imposed by wartime shortages? In Paris coal allocation was modified according to whether meals were taken outside the home, according to the existence of private stocks, and in view of coal allocations provided by employers. In late 1917 allocations were increased for certain groups of the population whose circumstances were especially affected by the war. In this way, households with a young child, an invalid, or an elderly person received a supplement of 100 kg. of coal at the very low price of 15 francs. In both Paris and Berlin, the assessment of individual living conditions thus entailed enormous surveys of the population. The Berlin Coal Supply Department compiled a card catalogue with entries for over a million households.

The leading principle of the different coal rationing systems in the three cities reveals different approaches to the satisfaction of needs. The rationale in London was a 'conservative' one: coal allowances were measured per room or per house respectively. In Paris the unit was not the household but the resident: each person was granted a minimum entitlement to coal. The Berlin system was a mixed one which was further complicated by a great and varying number of special regulations. Coal rations were allowed over the time period of a whole year for the purpose of cooking; these allowances depended on household size, the assumption being that the more persons in the household the greater its need for coal. But additional coal was granted during the winter months, according to the number of rooms, regardless of the number of persons. So, a Berlin four-person household in a two-roomed apartment had an entitlement to 15 kg. per week during the summer and of 15 + 19 (i.e. 34 kg.) from October to March. In Paris, the allocation for heating also depended on the number of persons per household (for up to 3 persons: 7 kg.per week if using gas, 14 kg. if not; for larger households: 14 or 21 kg.). A London family of the same size would get as much as 101.6 kg.

Note the greater importance of the number of rooms per household in Berlin's coal programme. This is clearly an advantage for the wealthy, one not replicated in London or Paris, where per capita allocation was at the heart of the system. In all three cases inequalities were unavoidable, but the way they were treated varied considerably on the two sides of the line.

Adaptation

Adaptation was a matter of ingenuity and stamina. Coping with shortages required a great investment of energy on the part of the population. A considerable amount of time was necessary even to obtain a minimum quantity of heating coal, and this in turn demanded considerable flexibility.

In popular responses to the coal crisis, women played a central role. As much if not more so than in the pre-war period, the working-class woman – 'that eternal gatherer for whom the city is a forest where she tirelessly pursues her needs'[69] – could be found wherever supplies could be obtained. In her quest for combustible fuel, she would take advantage of the smallest opportunity, even the cutting down of a dead tree. One instance took place on 24 November 1915:

> All at once a swarm of women carrying sacks threw themselves at the branches, breaking them into pieces and stuffing them in their bags. One of them, a rather old market woman, could be seen dragging with difficulty a large branch all across the Avenue d'Orléans, where she stuck it under her cart.[70]

Even at the youngest ages, children provided precious help in such efforts, and their role gave them a new responsibility in the household economy. They were sent on errands, often held places in queues, and gathered coal dislodged from passing convoys of supply trucks.

In Paris at the gates of the Maison Bernot on the Avenue d'Orléans queues of women began to form at five in the morning during the freeze of early 1917, and even earlier once the weather became less severe.[71] At this point each sale was limited to 10 kg.

Not all consumers could afford the time and energy for queuing; others – especially the elderly – became lost in the jungle of laws and regulations. The instructions for the Berlin coal ration coupon system ran to twenty-three pages, comprising eighty-four paragraphs. In Berlin it became impossible to obtain anything without carefully reading the newspapers first in order to determine which coupons were valid and what they could be used to purchase.

Certain groups could not compete in the scramble. Which segments of the population suffered most? The poor, whose income gave them little access to the market were no doubt among the most severely affected. Although in Paris such groups were in principle eligible for free distribution or for purchases at reduced prices, the high cost of transporting the coal often ruled out even this assistance. Renting a vehicle for transporting a 50 kg. sack (sold by the municipality at 4.75 francs) became a supplementary expense. With regard to reduced price sales by the local *mairie* in the 14th arrondissement, one observer reported:

[69] Michelle Perrot, 'La femme populaire rebelle', in Christiane Dufrancatel, Arlette Farge, and Christine Faure, *L'histoire sans qualité* (Paris, 1979), p. 142.

[70] A. L'Esprit, *La crise de charbon à Paris pendant la guerre de 1914–18* (Paris, 1924), p. 269.

[71] *Ibid.*, pp. 276ff.

> it was necessary to go to the very edge of the arrondissement, at 205, rue de Vanves in order to obtain the coal. There, men with wheelbarrows offered to transport the coal, and, if an employee of the office is to be believed, they often charged 4.50 or even 6 F to carry the miserable sack home and bring it up to their apartments . . .[72]

The elderly, for their part, were subject to the worst exploitation. The efforts of the Parisian municipality on their behalf were limited, and a proposition to guarantee them a minimum 50 kg. a month was rejected on 8 December 1916.

In Paris, access to the market depended on wage levels, and in this respect the situation of the unemployed was particularly bad. The level of privation was serious, but the municipal guarantee of a minimum level of coal nevertheless constituted a security. That sector of the working population whose salary was just over 5 francs per day, thus making them ineligible for municipal assistance, was placed in a critical situation. Members of this group faced the market from a very disadvantageous position and were forced to rely on the assistance of neighbours and local networks of worker sociability in order to survive.

Even the situation of the urban middle classes was not to be envied. Their access to the market was not obstructed, but the cost was exorbitant, and reflected a drastic reduction in their purchasing power. Faced with shortages, they had little other recourse. Only specific groups were able to avoid hardship. Among the bourgeoisie in Paris, geographical mobility was one way to escape the vicissitudes of the crisis: moving to a country residence, or more simply, obtaining provisions from outside of the city were frequent occurrences.

Shortages did more than simply divide the population into haves and have nots; in some cases it inverted social hierarchies. In Paris middle-class women had to queue in the coal lines as early as 1915, but they quickly became the object of scorn: 'women queuing up for coal will not tolerate the presence of a woman in a hat; it appears that one will go so far as to knock it off her head'.[73] In Berlin, meanwhile, new fortunes were made in war-related businesses; this affluence would have appeared normal during peacetime, but amounted to profiteering, hoarding, and speculating during war.[74]

How could people help one another in the face of these shortages? In the Parisian case we know very little about any forms of solidarity and mutual support beyond the range of the family. If there were neighbourhood networks within the popular and working populations, they were probably disrupted by the departure of mobilized men and changes in work practices. One example is the cooperative La Bellevilloise in the

[72] *Ibid.*, p. 275. [73] *Ibid.*, p. 269. [74] See ch. 4.

poor 20th arrondissement. This organization withered in wartime, when potential members were drawn to work in the suburban war industries.[75]

In London local strategies served to release social tension before they fuelled harsher conflicts. The agreement arrived at in 1915 by the Board of Trade, the London County Council (LCC), and the Association of London Coal Merchants made it possible for independent groups such as trade councils, local 'Vigilance Committees' and the like to monitor prices, and thus highlight abuses of the voluntary agreement entered into by coal dealers.[76]

Contrary to the stereotypical images of communal togetherness fostered by politicians and newspapers, the situation in Berlin bred increased resentment and conflict. We have noted that aggregate supply figures are no guide to civilian consumption. But what was galling to many was not shortages, but inequalities. Official estimates put the supply of pressed coal for the population of Greater Berlin at 1.3 to 1.7 kg. per capita in 1917 and no more than 1.1 kg. in January 1918.[77] Whether or not this is what individual households got is anybody's guess. The least we can say is that such shortages meant real hardship, producing anger against profiteers, speculators, and neighbours. Some respect for officialdom still existed, but the patience of the public was sorely tried. Note the tone of this letter to the Magistrate of Neukölln:

> I humbly ask whether it isn't possible to give to war wives such as myself the names of coal dealers where we really will receive coal in exchange for our coupons . . . anywhere they inform us we must wait for hours in return for coal. I have 5 children, one of whom is sick . . ., and I've been sitting for five days . . . in a cold apartment.[78]

In the autumn of 1917 the newspapers were full of angry complaints about the long queues and the lack of coal. Above all, the anger of the people focused on the 'terrorism of the coal dealer' whose thoughtlessness allegedly knew no limits:

> The customer receives coal coupons, but . . . then they have to find a coal dealer who first, has coal and second, is willing to sell it . . . The customer often must

[75] Robert, 'Ouvriers et mouvement ouvrier', vol. III, p. 872.

[76] LCC, *London Statistics, 1915–20*, p. 182. The LCC made 93,798 inspections of coal trolleys and shops under the May 1915 by-law between 1915 and 1918, discovering 1,770 infringements and making 487 prosecutions. See also the excessive prices discovered by the War Emergency Workers' National Committee in: Workers' National Committee Archive, WNC 3/11 43 and 87 (Museum of Labour History, Manchester).

[77] Calculated on the assumption of some 3,646,000 inhabitants of Greater Berlin in 1917, see *Statistisches Jahrbuch der Stadt Berlin*, vol. 35 (1920). The import data see Hasse-Terheyden, *Die Kohlenversorgung*.

[78] Letter to the Magistrate of Neukölln, Stadtarchiv Neukölln, Coal Supply Section, 5 December 1916.

wander from dealer to dealer, only to have a few miserable pieces of pressed coal to take home with him at the end of it all.[79]

The *Kohlenpolonaisen* – coal queues – which formed at the gates of the coal-yards alarmed the public. The Free Association of Berlin Property Owners (Freie Vereinigung Berliner Hausbesitzervereine) complained to the city administration in October 1917 that 'every day in the present coal shortage . . . long queues of women and men bearing sacks, baskets, and wheelbarrows must wait for hours in the street before receiving anything, or before hearing that the stockpile has been exhausted'. Above all, the Magistrate, the Berlin Coal Supply Department, and the Greater Berlin Coal Office were the target of criticism:

The operation of the Berlin Coal Supply Department is somewhat displeasing. While the entire citizenry is filled with worries and complaints about the insufficient coal supply and while every office and newspaper is overrun by complaints from individuals, the news should have gotten through to the Berlin Coal Supply Department.[80]

The authorities reacted defensively and with some dissimulation. Replying to the concerns of the Chairman of the Prussian Distribution Office (Staatliche Verteilungsstelle), Mayor Wermuth claimed that by 'dint of the efforts of the Greater Berlin Coal Office . . . difficulties in the coal supply have nowhere been in evidence'. The Director of the Greater Berlin Coal Office, Oberleutnant Körte, claimed that reports of 'large gatherings of customers' have not been substantiated by the police. A quasi-public national charity organization, the Nationale Frauendienst, discussed the coal situation in December 1917, and somehow managed to conclude on the basis of its research that the situation was 'not unfavourable'. They claimed that only in a few areas in the north and north-west of Berlin had reports of insufficient deliveries come in.[81] Körte sent the Chairman of the Prussian Distribution Office the results of these investigations, with the assurance that calm was justified.[82] These are all good instances of the authorities and their conservative allies deceiving themselves; it was less likely that they succeeded in deceiving the public.

The Social Democrats suspected an unholy alliance between big business and the bureaucracy in keeping the lid on the story that the coal situation was getting worse and worse. An article in *Vorwärts*, the official party newspaper, castigated the 'criminal indifference of the authorities', and their 'bureaucratic inefficiency'. According to this

[79] *Berliner Lokal-Anzeiger* 35, 639 (16 Dec. 1917), p. 3.
[80] LHA, Pr.Br.Rep.1A, 242, p. 72. [81] *Ibid.*, p. 141f.
[82] The debate continued until the end of the year. See *Berliner Lokal-Anzeiger* (28 Oct. 1917, Sunday edition, and 8 Nov. 1917); also LHA, Pr.Br.Rep.1A, Staatliche Verteilungsstelle, 242, pp. 57ff.

article, the bureaucracy was 'lacking in direction and helpless', and had politely declined all suggestions for remedial action as 'impossible':

> [The bureaucrats] sketch out a distribution plan, ration the individual districts, distribute ration cards to the individual consumers, and then think that they have done their duty. Whether, when, where, and how much coal will be delivered, however, doesn't concern them at all – they give no guarantees and believe that the public has no right to expect any . . . Whoever has connections enough to discover where the coal is arriving, and then queues up for it, or has someone else queue up for it, may actually obtain something. Others come up empty handed, and these are naturally the sick, the old, or those who work throughout the day. Whoever has a cart can easily transport the required amount home, but the weak can only carry a few briquets and must tread the path from the dealer again and again, suffering the queues each time.[83]

The Social Democratic party called for 'energetic controls', and simultaneously lobbied for a complete centralization of coal distribution as well as a linkage between the city and the Prussian administration on the issue. In so doing, they reflected the widespread feeling that only a 'Foodstuffs Dictator' [Lebensmitteldiktator] could manage the difficulties facing the government. Coal profits and trade would be brought under state supervision. 'One should shut the coal trade down, its activities are excessive and harmful'; all coal stockpiles 'should be confiscated, and distributed directly to the communal organizations through a central office'.

On one point, however, such analyses were in error, as the following months were to show. The administration was not acting together with the larger coal dealers. A few offices did not shy away from conflict with private interests, as in the case of the Neukölln Magistrates' struggle with the Neukölln Coal Dealers' Association, or the Berlin Price Control Office's struggle with the Berlin Coke Association.[84] In both cases the administration refused to accept the price increases demanded by the trade organizations; both cases ended with some slight concessions on the part of the suppliers. The conflict with the Coke Association lasted until April 1918, at which point the Association threatened that rising freight costs had made corresponding wage increases impossible. The only way to pay workers more was to increase price levels. Whether or not this was true was beside the point.

By the late spring of 1918 there was little time left for public authorities to act decisively, even if they had wanted to. The shortages among the population, the military defeats on the front, and the rapid currency inflation all combined to bring about the eventual capitulation, and to prolong the effects of the war until well after November 1918. In

[83] *Vorwärts* vol. 34, no. 339 (11 Dec. 1917).

[84] Bezirksamt Neukölln, 24-L-7-6; LHA, Pr.Br.Rep.1A, Staatliche Verteilungsstelle, 242, pp. 183ff.

the post-war period, the coal crisis worsened appreciably, without there being any sense that enduring hardship was necessary for victory.

Conclusion

The specific strategies by means of which the three cities tried to cope with the unprecedented problems of the war revealed different assumptions about state intervention and the freedom of the marketplace. This was decisive in the evolution of administrative responses to shortages, and helps us distance our survey from one which simply reports aggregate supply figures and draws inferences about consumption from them. There were supply constraints in all three cities, but what mattered more was the responses to them, and the assumptions behind those responses.

It was in London – the heart of old free trade and the Mecca of the market – that a collective solution first emerged. This was partly due to British command of the shipping lanes and the capacity of the British economy to coordinate a vast international supply network. But supply advantages do not account for the fact that as early as the summer of 1915 a *voluntary* agreement was reached between the Board of Trade and London coal merchants governing the supply and pricing of metropolitan requirements. Shortages were indeed registered in 1916–17, but thereafter administrators removed the transport and market bottlenecks and ensured that they would not recur.

In Paris there was a mixed response of strict *laissez-faire* policies and respect for industrial interests on the one hand, and relief measures effected by the municipal authorities on the other. Over the war, a process of adaptation can be seen in the suspension of the rules of the market (if only for the duration) and the assertion of collective principles according to which every resident's household had the right to at least a warm hearth.

In Berlin the effort to guarantee fairness through administrative oversight was half-hearted and ineffectual. Totally inconsistent solutions were advanced. On the one hand, retail price controls were general. An effort was made to regulate consumption, and to rally support for solidarity at the local level. On the other hand, freedom of commerce and enterprise remained largely unrestrained, and under war conditions this inevitably meant protection for the freedom to speculate and trade illegally.

Such contradictions made it impossible for public authorities to respond effectively to public protests at unfairness. How could they do so, since bureaucrats remained committed to the concept of the free market, despite their mistrust of the dealers who operated it? In the end, rhetoric mattered little. Given the thriving black market, and soaring inflation, the only arbitrage was through the law of the jungle: those with the money or connections got what they wanted; the rest remained cold or went to the wall.

In Berlin short-term supply and distribution problems, especially linked to transport problems, exacerbated inequalities and increased the sense of injustice associated with them. In Paris and London, shortages and social inequalities persisted, but collective action was undertaken to ensure they did not get out of hand. Supply alone did not provide this solution; it was embedded in a different notion of community in essentially democratic political cultures. In Berlin, illicit trading and rampant inflation made a mockery of appeals for solidarity and fair shares for all. By late 1918, Berliners faced a hard and cold future, with little comfort after four long years of hardship and sacrifice.

13
Housing

Susanna Magri

For the urban historian, 1914 marks the end of a cycle in urban growth that saw the convergence of patterns of living space in the great European cities.[1] Despite differences in building design and style – London with its individual houses, Paris and Berlin with their blocks of flats or *Mietskaserne* – the three capitals had many similarities. The trend since the end of the nineteenth century had been to move residential areas to the outskirts, away from the administrative city centre. Living standards had risen as houses acquired amenities now taken for granted (main drainage, water, and gas), though social inequalities persisted. Housing patterns reflected these inequalities: renting remained the norm, though ownership, together with the tendency to live further out from the city centre, already was spreading beyond the most prosperous. This parallelism in pre-war trends helps account for the similar impact of the war on housing in all three cities. The war's effects differed in intensity, not in kind.

With the outbreak of war, residents of the three cities faced familiar problems in a new guise. Mobilization or unemployment meant difficulty in paying rent for those with reduced or non-existent resources; and low-cost housing was in short supply, either because of demand as inhabitants moved from one sector of the market to another, or because of the large influx of immigrants. Those who suffered most were the socially deprived, the poorest, the least favoured in life. Some social divisions were blurred. Women from all backgrounds were forced to live away from home, although there was still a great gap between the rented room in a middle-class flat and the *garni*, a poorly equipped furnished room. Office employees' families resigned themselves to moving into smaller accommodation while skilled workers managed to move up the scale to more comfort, sometimes even to ownership. The war brought a lower standard of housing to some of the middle classes. These were significant changes, in a brief and unique

[1] Brigitte Yvon-Deyme, keeper of records at the Centre de sociologie urbaine, collaborated in the survey of the Paris daily press.

Table 13.1. *Paris, London, Berlin: net annual change in number of housing units, 1902 to 1918*

Year	Paris	London	Berlin
1902	9,569	—	9,775
1903	10,066	—	13,313
1904	9,341	—	18,802
1905	8,651	—	19,037
1906	8,862	—	20,988
1907	6,031	5,405	12,606
1908	6,047	3,846	9,374
1909	4,840	2,242	5,451
1910	6,065	2,755	4,369
1911	—	1,783	4,552
1912	8,754	625	6,069
1913	10,642	1,608	3,491
1914	11,959	—	1,447
1915	2,258	—	689
1916	2,290	—	123
1917	1,239	—	-8
1918	1,060	-257	5

Source: Annuaire statistique de la ville de Paris, 1902–1918. London County Council, *London Statistics*, vol. 19–vol. 26. *Statistisches Jahrbuch der Stadt Berlin*, vol. 27–vol. 34.

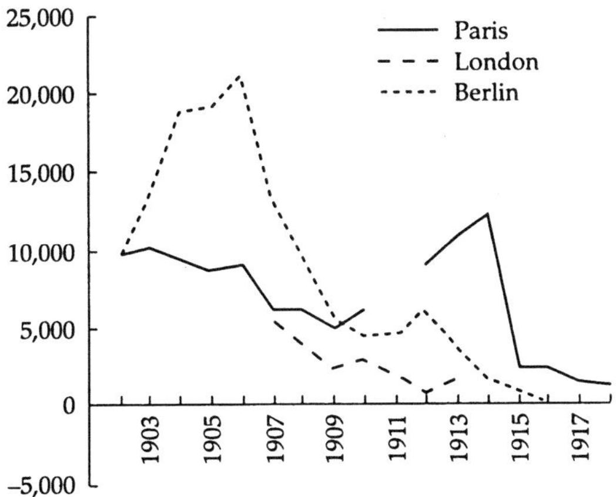

Fig. 13.1 Net annual variation in stock of housing units in Paris, London, Berlin, 1902 to 1918

period which consolidated or modified individual upward or downward mobility. The war reconfigured social stratification, revealing the processes of formation and transformation, permeability and inaccessibility. Community life was affected. The claims of the popular classes to

Table 13.2. *Paris, London, Berlin: housing by size, 1891 to 1921*

	Paris			London			Berlin		
	1891 %	1911 %	1921 %	1891 %	1911 %	1921 %		1905 %	1910 %
1 unit	35.7	32.9	34.7	18.4	13.4	13.2	0 unit	1.1	1.7
2 units	25.6	26.0	26.5	20.2	19.0	21.2	1 unit	49.3	47.2
3 units	17.5	20.0	19.4	16.3	21.3	23.4	2 units	29.8	32.6
4 units	9.5	9.5	8.5	12.3	15.9	18.0	3 units	10.8	10.2
5+units	11.8	11.0	9.7	32.8	30.4	24.2	4+units	8.8	7.3
Nb unknown	0.0	0.7	1.1						
Total	100.0	100.0	100.0	100.0	100.0	100.0	Total	99.8	99

Note: For Paris and London, occupied dwellings on the date the census was counted; for Berlin, dwellings capable of being heated.
Sources: Préfecture de la Seine. Service de la statistique municipale, 'Résultats statistiques du dénombrement de 1891 pour la ville de Paris et le département de la Seine', Paris, 1894; 'Statistique des logements à Paris', *Recueil de Statistique municipale,* 1912; *Recueil de Statistique de la ville de Paris et du Département de la Seine,* 1922. Parliamentary Papers, LXXVII, *Census of England and Wales,* vol. VIII; 1921, 'County of London'. N. Bullock and J. Read, *The movement for housing reform in Germany and France 1840–1914* (Cambridge, 1985), p. 201.

housing and rent expanded, and the middle classes were encouraged to join post-war social movements focused on housing issues.

Difficulties over rent and accommodation challenged public authorities as well as individuals. Forced to intervene on behalf of mobilized tenants to guarantee security of housing for their families, governments were soon faced with a growing rent problem. The mass of tenants affected by the economic fluctuations of the war confronted a group of owners who could not always profit from them. The timing and content of solutions varied from one city to another, resulting in different housing conditions and differing patterns of social tension surrounding these issues. Public-authority responses to uncertainties in the housing market were equally varied – ranging from inactivity to a planned programme for building model housing estates for war factory workers. Common to all was that four years virtually without new building work stored up serious problems for the post-war years. After the war, everything encouraged new local and national housing policies. There were expectations of change, quickly frustrated. There was haste to recover, protect, or gain a good position perhaps for the first time. There was too a new urgency for government to respond to these pressures and simultaneously to return as quickly as possible to the status quo *ante bellum* with respect to common-law lease rights. Whether forced or welcomed, implemented or merely planned, these policies inherited from the war were to mark a turning point in state intervention in housing.

Residents of the three cities therefore had broadly similar experiences, but during the last two years of the war a difference appeared between Berlin on one hand and Paris and London on the other. Berlin's more severe shortages of food and heating intensified housing problems; these were not addressed or mitigated by public authorities, which did not act decisively until the final months of the war. Tensions were therefore all the stronger at the end of the war, and expectations disappointed by local authorities seen as responsible probably contributed to the success of radical Socialists and Social-Democrats in the municipal elections of February 1919, at a moment when the same elections in Paris and London brought success for the political right.

The outbreak of war: variations of change

Domestic accommodation was affected sharply by the exceptional circumstances of the outbreak of war. City-dwellers were dependent on the local housing market and family resources, as well as on public authorities, whose response varied in the early phases of the war. Payment of rent was the main problem, but one whose scale depended on the rate of local unemployment and mobilization when the war began. In Paris and Berlin, governments intervened immediately. Rent policies differed appreciably, however, and Paris was quickly in a category of its own. London did not suffer the effects of a massive call-up and severe employment crisis, but the income of many London families was very soon reduced or threatened, and housing attitudes were modified accordingly.

Many Berlin families were deprived abruptly of income as vast numbers of conscripts left for the front at the outbreak of war, a situation shared in Paris,[2] but aggravated by more widespread and enduring unemployment. Matters were very different in London: there was no conscription and the economic crisis was very short-lived. Only the German and French governments acted immediately to protect tenants. German laws were passed for this purpose on 4 and 7 August 1914, and in France the governmental decree introducing the moratorium on rents was signed on 14 August.

It should be noted immediately that policies in Paris and Berlin varied as much in their categories of beneficiary as in their ways of regulating rent problems. The German laws of August 1914 prohibited landlords from evicting family members or dependants of tenants unable to pay their rent because of mobilization. Most of those called up

[2] See above, ch. 5.

saw this as authorization not to pay rent, and by November the City of Berlin tried to clarify the situation. The city council established Mieteinigungsämter, tenant and landlord arbitrators dealing with accommodation rented at not more than 500 marks per year – about three-quarters of Berlin's accommodation.[3] In October 1914, aid for tenants was introduced. This *Mietbeihilfe* was solely for the benefit of soldiers' families, forming a small part of the city's wider support system for such wives and children. Paid directly to landlords – because it was intended to avoid the accumulation of tenants' debts – and often at the heart of negotiations to achieve lower rents, it was proof of a precautionary local-authority policy towards landlords who were both protected and encouraged to be moderate.[4] Only those Berlin tenants whose immediate family members had been called up were helped, while the system of conciliation and municipal aid protected landlords' interests. Although conflict was checked, these procedures nevertheless created difficulties and severe frustrations for many tenants.

Rent policy in Paris followed the opposite course. Firstly, strong state centralization kept policy exclusively in the hands of the government. The Conseil municipal de Paris and the Conseil général de la Seine offered opinions and 'views' regarding intentions that were wholly determined by the central authority. They had a little idea of intervening themselves, and protested vigorously at a suggestion in the Chamber of Deputies of local contribution to a possible indemnity for landlords.[5] Next, national policy entitled the great majority of Parisian tenants to suspend rent payments. The main concern was with the future of mobilized men and their families, even though the number of beneficiaries was quickly reduced. In order to avoid open conflict with landlords, the government was soon forced to renegotiate a moratorium extended each time for only three months, a quarterly term.[6] Settling the problem of non-payment was therefore repeatedly deferred, and any solution involving public money, in the form of aid to tenants or payment of compensation to landlords, was ultimately rejected. This policy, however, developed only gradually.

Initial decisions were made in an atmosphere of urgency. The 14

[3] See Kaeber, *Berlin*, pp. 446–7, and Heinrich Hirtshiefer, *Die Wohnungswirtschaft in Preussen* (Eberswalde, 1929), p. 107.

[4] On the introduction of this policy, see Kaeber, *Berlin*, pp. 49–50.

[5] Conseil général de la Seine, 'Voeux relatifs aux mesures à prendre en vue de l'organisation du travail au moment de la démobilisation et au projet de loi sur les loyers en instance devant le Parlement'. *Mémoires et procès-verbaux des délibérations, 1ère et 2ème sessions de 1916 (procès-verbal du 12 avril 1916)* (Paris, 1916), pp. 158–82.

[6] This interval can be explained by the fact that rents for unfurnished premises were paid quarterly in Paris, falling due at the end of this period of occupation. Cf. Emile Le Pelletier, *Code pratique des usages de Paris ayant force obligatoire de loi dans les contestations les plus fréquentes entre les habitants de Paris* (Paris, 1890), pp. 87–91.

August 1914 decree established the moratorium of three months for lodgings with an annual rent of less than 1,000 francs – 88 per cent of all housing in Paris – and for all furnished accommodation – 'bed-sitters' and hotel rooms.[7] This general moratorium was authorized by the law of 5 August, and conservative law dictated by the upheavals of general mobilization on 1 August. The German advance and threat of a siege of Paris aggravated problems and led to extension of the initial measures, notably those concerning commercial and banking commitments. In effect, from the first days of August Ministers of Trade and of Justice were pressed to adopt a decree on rents by the Prefect of the Meurthe-et-Moselle and the Procureur général of Nancy. They settled for a 'general measure' rather than recourse to the courts, as the Chancellery had briefly considered.[8] Believing that a siege was imminent, the authorities decided to organize an exodus: from 15 August residents with provincial origins were encouraged to return to their own region, and at the end of the month people from the east and north of the Paris region departed, followed by Parisians themselves.[9] From then on the government undertook to protect the homes of displaced residents; on 1 September, a second decree suspended all notices to quit from landlords and extended the moratorium of payments to tenants with rents over 1,000 francs in the Department of the Seine. The only proviso was that those who were not mobilized had to given notice of their incapacity to honour their debt,[10] a measure unique to the Seine which, like nineteen other Departments, was 'particularly threatened by hostilities'.[11] The danger once passed, the measure was withdrawn: on 17 December, as the January quarter-day approached, a fresh decree removed the Seine from the list of the Departments. Rents over 1,000 francs were returned to common law except where payable by mobilized men – and owners of accommodation with rents under that amount could plead before the magistrate that their tenants were capable of paying all or part of the deferred rent, on condition that the tenant was not serving in the army. But the government immediately changed its mind on this concession to

[7] *Journal officiel*, 19 August 1914, p. 7439. For the distribution of accommodation according to rental value in Paris, see *Annuaire statistique de la Ville de Paris*, 1914 and 1915–18.

[8] Archives nationales (AN), BB30 1535, Ministère de la Justice. Notes of 8 and 9 August 1914 and telegrams from Nancy, same dates.

[9] On the repatriation of provincial French citizens and foreigners and on the exodus, see the detailed account and personal descriptions in *Le Temps*, *Le Matin*, and *Le Petit Parisien*, from 15 August to 22 September.

[10] This declaration was supposed to be presented before the Justice of the Peace but, following popular objections reported on this point by the group of Paris Deputies, the decree of 27 September allowed those concerned to send landlords a registered letter, easing the task for those who had left Paris. On the protests which revealed the scale of the exodus of middle-class residents, see *Le Matin*, 18 Sept. 1914, p. 2, and 20 Sept. 1914, p. 2; *Le Petit Parisien*, 23 Sept. 1914, pp. 1–2.

[11] *Journal officiel*, 2 Sept. 1914, p. 7828.

landlords: the decree of 7 January – the eve of quarter-day – effectively reinstated the full exemption but with the threshold dropped from 1,000 francs to 600 francs. Small tenants and mobilized men benefited henceforward from the same treatment. This ordinance remained in force throughout the war. Governments intended to protect working-class residents and part of the middle classes, since the accommodation covered represented three-quarters of Paris housing (77 per cent) and even more – 84 per cent – in the suburbs.[12]

This policy favouring tenants grew out of the great difficulties facing workers in and around Paris at the outbreak of war. The severe employment crisis which affected Paris – unlike London and Berlin – from August 1914 until at least June 1915 meant that those spared by mobilization were deprived of income. But economic pressures did not operate in isolation. The government was supported by a broad social consensus on a measure which was universally expected to be of short duration. The moratorium on rents was nothing new: it had operated in Paris in 1870 and this precedent, constantly recalled, legitimized state action.[13] During the first months of the war, the politically mixed group of deputies for Paris and its suburbs urged ministers to extend the scope of the moratorium. It was an indirect form of support from property owners. This was also seen in the silence of similar organizations, which continued at least until November, issuing appeals for moderation[14] and individual 'generous gestures' which were proclaimed prominently in the press.

As winter approached, there was calm in Paris between landlords and tenants in popular and normally turbulent districts. Prices had been rising in real terms since the 1860s and on the very eve of the war

[12] In 1915 Paris had 796,000 units of accommodation at under 600 francs, a figure rising to 1,032,524 for the whole of the geographical area covered by the decree – the Department of the Seine and the three communes of the Seine-et-Oise in the province of the police préfecture. Cf. Conseil municipal de Paris, 'Rapport général sur . . . le projet de budget de la ville de Paris pour 1916 présenté par M. Louis Dausset . . .', *Rapports et documents*, 1915 (Paris, 1916), p. 110. To these ordinary units of accommodation must be added the furnished rented rooms in Paris on 31 Dec. 1914 – 13,421 with 120,824 tenants (according to the *Annuaire statistique de la ville de Paris, 1914*, p. 595) and, in the suburbs, 5,900 with 40,000 tenants (according to the Minister of Justice, the Senate, session of 22 December 1915, *Journal officiel*, 23 Dec. 1915, p. 674), who were also affected by this measure.

[13] See for example, *Le Temps*, 6 Aug. 1914 ('Les projets de loi concernant l'état de guerre') and 8 Dec. 1914 ('Le Moratorium et le fonctionnement des tribunaux' by Maxime Leroy).

[14] 'The deadly winter of the unfortunate has arrived. Landlords . . ., do not place the responsibility for your own misfortunes on the unfortunate families of all those brave men who, by fighting for the nation at the risk of their lives, are also fighting for you and your property.' In 'Un appel de la Chambre des propriétaires de Saint-Mandé', *Le Petit Parisien*, 21 Nov. 1914, p. 4.

tenants' agitation had been stirred up by large increases in 'low rents' and by overall inflation. A union was formed, organizing resistance to evictions in Paris and heavily populated suburbs.[15] The moratorium was intended to prevent any revival of this disturbance. It was successful, as noted in *Le Petit Parisien* on 9 October 1914:

> Yesterday was 8 October, quarter-day for the low-paid . . . Contrary to the pattern of events in ordinary times, the streets of popular districts were not full of hand carts transporting the beds, tables, cupboards, chairs and odd ornaments that make up the possessions of the poor. No one was moving. The rent moratorium was functioning normally.[16]

At the beginning of the war, public policy therefore largely assured tenants of security of tenure. Few in the popular districts left their homes, even during the exodus.[17] Even the furnished rooms in eastern Paris arrondissements remained occupied although they were empty everywhere else. They were the standard form of housing for those with little money, and shelter for refugees from the invaded areas.[18]

Matters were different in the other two capitals. Many Berlin families, forced to pay their rent or receiving too little municipal aid, left their accommodation and possibly the city. This is shown in the considerable increase in vacant dwellings, rising from 4.6 per cent of all accommodation in 1913 to 6.6 per cent in 1914.[19] The poorest, particularly wives of mobilized men who remained alone with their children and who needed to find work, probably chose to remain in the city and began sharing accommodation to reduce their rent costs.

In London the absence of public intervention left low-income households to face their problems unaided. They were affected by unemployment which, although short-lived, hit 10 per cent of the active working population in September. There were many shifts from one lodging to another in the popular districts, aided by the local pattern of weekly lettings. Families of volunteer soldiers were no better off; although grants were authorized, the military authorities were slow to organize payments and the Soldiers and Sailors Families Association,

15 Christian Topalov, *Le logement en France. Histoire d'une marchandise impossible* (Paris, 1987), pp. 121–39, and Susanna Magri, 'Les locataires se syndiquent', in Roger Quillot and Roger-Henri Guerrand, *Cent ans d'habitat social. Une utopie réaliste* (Paris, 1989), pp. 98–107.

16 'C'était hier le petit terme . . .' *Le Petit Parisien*, 9 Oct. 1914, p. 2.

17 See *Annuaire statistique de la ville de Paris, 1914*, pp. 645–54 and Robert, 'Ouvriers et mouvement ouvrier', vol. 5, pp. 1310–12.

18 It should be recalled that hotels and furnished rooms were, from 14 August, subject to the rent and dismissal moratorium and that shortly after that date a circular from the Prefect of police to the *Commissaires* specified that 'concerning needy people with accommodation vouchers or lodged by means of requisition, the proprietor is obliged to accept them and in case of refusal the police *commissaire* must enforce acceptance'. Cf. 'Une circulaire pour les logeurs', *L'Echo de Paris*, 23 Aug. 1914, p. 3.

19 Cf. table 13.3 and fig. 13.2.

which distributed aid in this interim period, often insisted that those seeking aid should limit their rent payments in return for the aid sought.[20] For this reason, many soldiers' wives, realizing that the war would not be over by Christmas, decided to move out to cheaper lodgings or to go to their parents.

With their resources reduced, the popular classes saw their fate as depending largely on public authority policy, and therefore varied from one city to another. The middle classes of London and Berlin were not affected materially by the outbreak of war; the contrast with Paris is striking. The end of August 1914 saw a massive middle-class exodus from Paris to the provinces – where the most prosperous returned to their normal holiday areas.[21] Not everyone returned to Paris in the following months. This was shown by the increase in accommodation vacant, noted on 1 January 1915, in lodgings with rents of between 500 and 2,000 francs.[22] Suppression of the rent moratorium for rents over 1,000 francs from 17 December, the loss of income after being called up – irrecoverable when departures became deaths – appears to have encouraged the most prosperous middle-class families to remain in the country rather than move to cheaper accommodation. The increase in empty lodgings continued in 1915, particularly for the dearest accommodation with rent over 1,000 francs per year. Meanwhile, the economic position of the lower middle classes was reduced. Under pressure,[23] the government extended the moratorium on rent for professional premises, established on 27 September, and accorded the full right to 'licensees' whose rent was no more than 2,500 francs per year, the

20 See *Minutes of Evidence taken before the Select Committee on Naval and Military Services (Pensions and Grants)*, PP 1914–16, Iv, p.117.

21 'Il n'en reste plus que quelques uns . . . Les plus heureux', *Le Matin*, 6 Sept. 1914, p. 2, and 'Physionomie de Paris. Les Gares', *Le Figaro*, 29 Sept. 1914, p. 3, which observed people returning to Biarritz, Arcachon, and the Pyrenean resorts.

22 See table 13.3 and fig. 13.2. Comparison with lodgings with rental value lower than 500 francs is not possible, because vacancies for this category of lodging outside taxation aid were not registered during the war. The upper limit of 2,000 francs for accommodation usually inhabited by the lower levels of the middle classes was suggested by Emile Berr who, in his article 'Les loyers' in *Le Figaro* of 28 Aug. 1914, p. 3, considered that 'Two or three thousand francs' rent is in Paris the price of a flat payable to accommodate their family and retain their standing by the civil servant, teacher, officer without private means or the less prosperous doctor.' This comment is confirmed by enquiries into rents by Paris elites at the beginning of the century carried out by Christophe Charle, *Les élites de la République, 1880–1900* (Paris, 1987), pp. 383–6. He states that 3,100 francs was the median rent for university teachers who represented the lower stratum of these elites.

23 'Voeux' of the Federation of retail traders, published in *Le Petit Parisien*, 23 Sept. 1914, p. 2, and Edouard Ignace, Paris deputy, 'Le nouveau décret sur la moratorium des loyers', *Le Petit Parisien*, 21 Dec. 1914, p. 1.

Table 13.3. *Paris: vacant lodgings on 1 January, 1913 to 1919*

	Lodgings with values between:											
	500 and 599 francs			600 and 999 francs			1000 and 1999 francs					
	Total lodgings	Vacant lodgings	%	Total lodgings	Vacant lodgings	%	Total lodgings	Vacant lodgings	%	Total lodgings	Total vacant lodgings	%
1913	40,716	350	0.86	103,784	1,275	1.23	63,411	1,363	2.15	207,911	2,988	1.44
1914	41,749	457	1.09	106,573	1,860	1.75	65,614	1,979	3.02	213,936	4,296	2.01
1915	43,453	1,475	3.39	109,806	5,027	4.58	67,662	3,645	5.39	220,921	10,147	4.59
1916	43,921	1,648	3.75	110,362	5,975	5.41	68,047	5,254	7.72	222,330	12,877	5.79
1917	44,082	1,002	2.27	110,806	4,142	3.74	68,478	4,637	6.77	223,456	9,781	4.38
1918	44,243	456	1.03	111,151	1,524	1.37	68,846	1,939	2.82	224,240	3,919	1.75
1919	44,365	321	0.72	111,373	964	0.87	69,000	896	1.30	224,738	2,181	0.97

Note: For 1919, statistics on lodgings by rentable value are unsafe. We have recalculated 1919 figures by adding to the 1918 statistics an increment equal to half of the average mean variations for 1 Jan. 1918 to 31 Dec. 1919.
Source: Annuaire statistique de la ville de Paris, 1913–1919.

Table 13.4. *Paris: furnished flats and lessees, 31 December, 1899 to 1920*

	Inhabitants	Flats		Inhabitants	Flats
1899	190,617	11,607	1910	191,368	12,155
1900	209,375	12,660	1911	196,945	12,537
1901	185,674	12,175	1912	218,462	12,996
1902	181,015	11,652	1913	231,502	13,266
1903	188,229	11,679	1914	120,824	13,421
1904	183,990	11,657	1915	—	—
1905	185,697	11,589	1916	—	—
1906	185,190	11,510	1917	—	—
1907	183,840	11,571	1918	287,156	14,649
1908	189,177	11,783	1919	331,625	15,243
1909	188,564	11,996	1920	260,416	17,758

Note: Information missing for 1915, 1916, 1917.
Source: Annuaire statistique de la ville de Paris, 1900–1920.

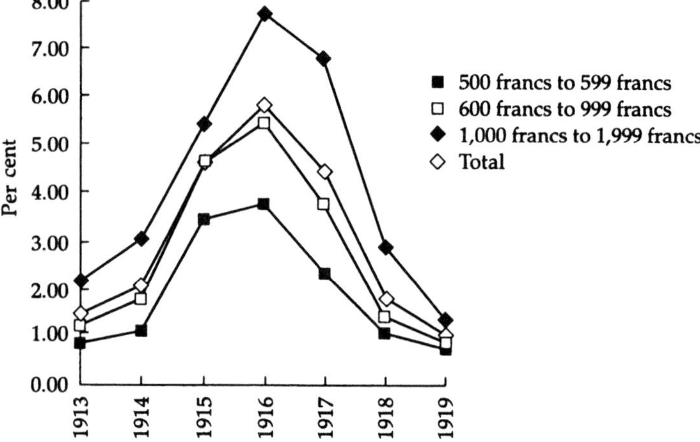

Fig. 13.2 Vacant lodgings in Paris according to their rentable value at 1 January of each year, 1913 to 1919 (percentage of all lodgings vacant)

threshold above which a declaration was required which could be challenged by landlords.[24]

The landlords reacted to this measure, and to others that benefited their tenants. The few early associations, such as the Ligue des petits propriétaires in Paris and its suburbs, founded on 20 October, were joined by further owners' organizations after January 1915. By this time two quarterly rent payments had failed to appear. Often arising from

[24] 'Note concernant les mesures prises depuis le début des hostilités relativement aux loyers. 1 Novembre 1915', AN, Ministère du Commerce, F/12/8022.

suburban groupings – based first in the communes then gathered together in a union of associations of suburban landlords in the Department of the Seine[25] – claims addressed to the public authorities made three repeated demands: restriction of the moratorium to those tenants who genuinely could not pay; state payments to owners to make up for the non-payment of 'small' rents by mobilized or unemployed men;[26] the establishment in their favour of a moratorium on repayment of mortgage borrowings contracted equally for rented and for occupied accommodation, a claim strongly pressed by electors in Paris suburbs.[27] The government met only this final claim, content in other respects to play a waiting game, possibly encouraged by landlords' apparent resignation.[28]

In general terms, middle-class Berliners appear to have been more favoured than their Parisian equivalents. Rent conciliation, operated by the Berlin municipal council, no doubt encouraged most tenants to pay their dues to property owners, and moderated the proprietors' tendency to interfere with tenants' freedom to move. The municipality helped property-owners who were in debt to money lenders: a new conciliation body – the Hypothekeneinigungsamt – was set up in April 1915, charged with helping the defaulting borrower. The latter was thus protected against the threat of losing his possessions, a form of aid that helped loan organizations to avoid a wave of unpaid creditors.[29]

In London too the middle classes felt the effects of the war later than the working classes. In middle-class households, where rent was paid quarterly, the September and December quarter-days were unusually quiet. This was because, in view of the 'general uncertainty as to financial and business affairs',[30] the modest and solid middle classes

[25] AN, Ministère de la Justice, BB/30/1535, 'Réclamations' file.

[26] 'Association des propriétaires suburbains du Département de la Seine à Messieurs le Président du Conseil, à Monsieur le Garde des Sceaux, à Messieurs les Ministres des Finances et du Commerce', undated (November or December 1914), AN, Ministère du Commerce, F 12 8022.

[27] Cf. 'Les Loyers en banlieue', *Le Petit Journal*, 25 Aug. 1914, p. 2, and 'Les loyers en banlieue', *Le Temps*, 27 Aug. 1914, p. 3, 'La question des loyers et des congés', *Le Petit Parisien*, 29 Nov. 1914, p. 2.

[28] Of the 11,289 declarations deposited at the Justice of the Peace in Paris between 20 March and 1 July 1915 by licensed tenants (traders and industrialists), 'who declared themselves unable to pay all or part of the amounts due', only 2,260 (20 per cent) were contested by the owners, with a similar proportion contested in the suburbs (19.4 per cent). Proceedings undertaken against tenants who benefited from full rights to extension of time were very rare: 372 in Paris and 334 in the suburbs over the same period. See Moratorium des loyers. Statistique des déclarations, contestations de déclarations et instances depuis le décret du 20 mars 1915 arrêtée au ler juillet 1915 et dressée d'après le rapport du Procureur Général près la Cour d'Appel de Paris', AN Ministère du Commerce, F 12 8022.

[29] Kaeber, *Berlin*, p. 447.

[30] *The Times*, 24 March 1915.

rejected the cost of a move which would formerly have been easily acceptable. Three months later, however, now convinced of the war's long duration, these families resigned themselves to adjusting their expenditure to reduced – or potentially reduced – income, and housing and servants were the first victims. House agents registered a growing demand for small houses and flats from March, a pressure which set off rises of between 10 and 18 per cent in rents between £45 and £55 per annum in 1914.[31]

The residential housing situation in the three capital cities thus had seen considerable changes by the end of the first wartime spring. Not everyone had been affected, nor had change been equal in scale, for it varied with social class and public policy. But no one was spared uncertainty – a common experience with different causes. In Paris, the policy of successive moratoriums fed landlords' fear of losing their income over long periods, without hope of reparation, of being permanently unable to repay an accumulating debt. Londoners and Berliners anxiously faced the possibility of being forced to sacrifice standards of housing. All three cities' inhabitants saw signs of inescapable problems: sporadic rent rises and an almost complete halt in construction, already at a very low level before the war.

Housing problems: new inequalities and emerging tensions between owners and tenants

The middle of 1915 was a turning point. Now settled into the war, Paris, London and Berlin saw the establishment and development of suburban war production. Where unemployment still existed, it was reabsorbed more rapidly. Workers flooded in and – particularly the women – faced a shift to other sectors of work. As their nations' seat of government and military command, the three capital cities also had increasing civil-service activity as well as industrial employment. The number of wage-earners in the most important services – food supply, sanitation, health – remained constant or increased. Population movements into the capital cities made up for the losses caused by a growing call to arms. This had immediate effects on the housing market. At the same time the tensions between landlords and tenants intensified, the former seeking to profit from the market, the latter seeing their income undermined by inflation. Intervention by public authorities was demanded. In general housing conditions reflected population shifts which led to shortages, but people were affected in different ways. It was particularly bitter for those who lacked any state protection; but in addition life for the most vulnerable was worse in Berlin than in the two Allied capitals.

[31] *Ibid.*

While public-authority policy on rents remained unchanged in Germany, the governments of France and Britain formulated wartime housing policy only at the end of 1915. Differing in the protection they provided, the French and British policies were alike in being based on the same political stakes: preservation of threatened national cohesion when the nation was required to redouble its efforts for the war of attrition. Unlike London, Paris was at the heart of its government's concern. Its position, both strategic and geographically vulnerable, its pivotal role in munitions production after the loss of the industrial Departments of the north and east, the great number of 'small' tenants concentrated in the city, memories of the Paris commune of 1871 – and even of 1793, evoked occasionally in the Chamber of Deputies – made the situation of Parisians one of the main foci for public-policy initiatives and caution. The solution proposed from the spring of 1915 was close to Berlin's: the moratorium would not be extended, and statutory arbitration commissions would order repayment delays and rent rebates in favour of tenants. By the end of the year, however, the contrary had happened and the proposed legislation only came to fruition two years later.

By the winter of 1914 to 1915, the need for a law to remove uncertainty over landlord and tenant finances was unanimously accepted in Paris, by the public as well as in political circles. But many people remained in doubt over the exact measures to take and the timing of their introduction. The first proposals, set down in December by the Paris deputies and examined in February by the Chamber's commission for civil and criminal legislation, envisaged the immediate introduction of arbitration courts. The precedent was the law of May 1871 on rent rebates for tenants, to be compensated partially by indemnities paid to owners by the public authorities.[32] However, opinion did not always follow the lead of elected representatives, and although it prepared the two bills tabled in the Chamber on 6 May and 8 July 1915, the government itself thought that a law of this kind should not take effect until the end of the war.[33] In September this position was abandoned when ministers ranged themselves alongside the Chamber's legislative committee and demanded rapid adoption and application of the measures.[34] However, this was to remain an intention only: in Decem-

[32] On the proposals tabled by Paris deputies, and particularly the Republican deputy of the left, Edouard Ignace, see E. Ignace, 'La question des loyers', *Le Petit Parisien*, 23 Sept. 1914, p. 2, and 'La question des loyers. Une proposition de loi de M. Ignace', *Le Petit Parisien*, 12 Dec. 1914, p. 2. On 12 Aug. 1915, deputy Ignace tabled nineteen proposals. See Robert, 'Ouvriers et mouvement ouvrier', p. 914.

[33] The law of April–May 1871 was studied in order to prepare new legislation. AN, Ministère du Commerce, F 12 8021, 'Dossier général des notes', 'Moratorium des loyers. Propositions tendant à la liquidation de ce moratorium'.

[34] AN, Ministère de la Justice, BB 30 1536, 'Projets de loi du Gouvernement et de la Commission', and Ministère du Commerce, F 12 8021, 'Rapport de M. Albert Tissier'.

ber the government decided to postpone parliamentary debate on the bills.

These twists were dictated by the wartime social context. In September the prefect of police in Paris felt it necessary to indicate to the government that 'antagonism between owners and landlords on one hand and the tenants on the other, is growing' and noted the growing significance of the socialist-inspired tenants' movement.[35] It was this development that helped to spur government action. In July 1915 the socialists had re-established the Federal Union of Tenants, which now joined other bodies of Paris tenants.[36] All clamoured for a law enacting the principle of partial or total rebate of rents due from the beneficiaries of the moratoriums, in opposition to the owners who sought 'the return to common law' without any exemption except for 'tenants actively engaged under arms'. Compensation for these rent rebates for mobilized men would come from indemnities paid by the public authorities.[37] The tenants could count on the support of organizations of the left outside the labour movement, which gave them a wide popular base, even though solidarity was compromised by disaffection over the criteria and extent of the exemptions.[38] The socialists themselves, divided over this suggestion, changed their initial position. From autumn 1915 they sought to delay the final ruling on rents to the end of the war. Finally, the steadily growing tenants' union brought the labour movement together under their maximalist banner. In 1916 the Union demanded full exemption from rent payments for all tenants and therefore ceased to demand immediate legal adjustment.[39] Aware of this developing movement, in November René Viviani, the Garde des Sceaux, withdrew from the Order of the Day in the Chamber of Deputies the proposal prepared by the commission on civil legislation, thereby postponing a discussion which 'on the eve of the loan might – at least in

[35] As cited by Jean-Jacques Becker, *Les Français dans la Grande Guerre* (Paris, 1980), p. 127.

[36] For example the Groupement des Locataires, based in Paris, who issued a 'Petition' dated 4 Nov. 1914, and the Association des Locataires de Paris et des départements, which sent a letter to the Minister on 18 Dec. 1914 (AN BB 30 1535 and 1536). On the Union fédérale des locataires during the war, see Robert, 'Ouvriers et mouvement ouvrier', pp. 927–37.

[37] Chambre syndicale des propriétés immobilières de la ville de Paris, *Au sujet des loyers (Voeu remis aux Pouvoirs publics par nos Délégués)*, AN, Ministère de la Justice, BB 30 1536, 'Protestations'. Cf. also the petition deposited at the Conseil général de la Seine by the Groupe des petits propriétaires de Paris et banlieue, 'seeking the state control of mobilised men's rent terms', in Conseil général de la Seine, *Mémoires et procès-verbaux des délibérations* (Paris, 1915), Procès-verbaux of 28 December 1914.

[38] The tenants were supported in particular by the league of the Rights of Man ('Une belle réunion des ligueurs parisiens', *L'Humanité*, 8 Nov. 1915) and the Socialist municipalities.

[39] The Union fédérale des locataires in the Seine had 18 branches in December 1915, 25 in March 1916, 44 in 1917, 52 in 1918. See Robert, 'Ouvriers et mouvement ouvrier', pp. 929 and 931–7.

Paris – create some unease . . . in the public mind'.[40] This delaying tactic, which increased tenants' determination, introduced a long drawn-out parliamentary debate which only ended on 18 March 1918. In the interim the government returned to its initial temporizing position, bringing with it an extension of the moratorium, thereby defusing a conflict liable to turn into social and political confrontation. This conflict could be expressed without major risk on the parliamentary stage while the legislative text was prepared: it would no doubt have become more difficult if the legislation had spoken plainly. As Viviani stated on 22 December in the Senate, evoking the memory of 1791 as he rejected a demand for suppression of the moratorium of full rights granted to non-mobilized small tenants in Paris, 'the Government's role is not only to foresee; [nor] is it to call on the means of coercion which are not in its thinking, but to try to help this population which had until now shown the greatest calm'. The price of preserving the social fabric, in the absence of an unattainable reconciliation of interests, was to continue sheltering working-class tenants from all their landlords' demands by granting them 'a sort of presumption of social distress'.[41]

In Britain the government's rent policy was also intended to protect tenants of modest means but, unlike the French decision, it faced social conflict instead of avoiding it. Shaped by a broad move to fight the increase of rents for popular accommodation, policy aimed essentially at freezing rents at 1914 levels. The origins and vicissitudes of this movement are well known;[42] starting off in the Clyde valley in Scotland, with its concentration of war manufacture, it was primarily the work of working-class tenants and derived its strength from their long-standing traditions of solidarity. It was also legitimized by their central role in the defence of the nation which made the landlords' demands on them appear particularly unreasonable. The movement grew rapidly with protests from other regions, while the support of the Labour party raised the political stakes.

London was not immune from these problems. Rents rose more or less everywhere during 1915: in Woolwich, with a rapidly growing population drawn in by jobs at the Arsenal before the appearance of the first state-built accommodation, as well as in the boroughs to the north and east of the City, such as Poplar, Bermondsey, Shoreditch, Camberwell, and the neighbouring industrial areas of Ilford and Edmonton. Channelled in Woolwich by the labour movement,[43] popular protest

40 Speech by René Viviani in the Chamber of Deputies, session of 22 Dec. 1915, *Journal Officiel*, 23 Dec. 1915, p. 672, retracing the sequence of events since the summer.

41 Speech by René Viviani to the Senate, session of 22 Dec. 1915, *Journal officiel*, 23 Dec. 1915, p. 675.

42 See Joseph Melling, *Rent strikes: peoples' struggles for housing in West Scotland, 1890-1916* (Edinburgh, 1983), ch. 9, and David Englander, *Landlord and tenant in urban Britain 1838–1918* (Oxford, 1983), ch. 10.

43 *The Times*, 24 Nov. 1915.

was organized elsewhere by tenants' associations and found champions as varied as the local clergy – in Tooting and Poplar – radical town councillors, and bourgeois philanthropists.[44] Rent increases were sometimes modest,[45] but at a difficult time this was enough to turn tenants' frustrations into resistance. Having misunderstood the moratorium concerning commercial dealings, they had begun the war by suspending rent payments;[46] an act reinforced by virtue of the fact that a substantial part of public opinion developed hostility towards landlords.

This set of attitudes was reinforced by wartime patriotism. Using expressions renewed by the Great War – the selfishness of some opposed to the 'sacrifice' of others – this patriotism intensified hostility to owners of property, visible well before 1914. In a venerable radical position, the landlord was denounced as a parasite drawing an inequitable benefit from the value created by the community as a whole.[47] Claims for state intervention against landlords therefore had broad social and cultural foundations. Turning rents into social and political issues drew in some of the middle classes as well, who also, as noted above, suffered increased rents on inexpensive accommodation. Less clamorously displayed than among the workers, the discontent of the lower middle class, which was suffering a lower standard of living, was none the less genuine, and increased pressure on the government.[48] The government responded publicly on 22 November: after receiving a delegation of London tenants, Walter Long, Chairman of the Local Government Board, announced that a bill would immediately be laid before the House of Commons, introducing rent control for the first time in British history. Tabled on 25 November, the bill became law a month later, as the Increase of Rents and Mortgage Interest (War Restriction) Act.[49]

The law consisted of three parts. It set the annual rateable value at £35 for London rents, with rents below that amount held at the level of 3 August 1914, and rents over that sum allowed to fluctuate without restriction. It affected working-class dwellings, defined by municipal statistics as those with an annual rateable value of less than £20[50] – and

[44] *The Times*, 11 oct. 1915, and 16 Nov. 1915. On tenants' associations, see Englander, *Landlord and tenant*, pp. 209–10.

[45] In Poplar they sometimes reached barely 3d per week. See Englander, *Landlord and tenant*.

[46] See Englander, *Landlord and tenant*, pp. 201–2 and 206–7.

[47] For earlier references to this discourse, see Raphael Samuel (ed.), *Patriotism: the making and unmaking of British national identity* (London, 1989, 3 vols).

[48] Englander, *Landlord and tenant*, pp. 185–7.

[49] See Laurence F. Orbach, *Homes for Heroes: a study of the evolution of British public housing, 1915–1921* (London, 1977), p. 26.

[50] Cf. London County Council, *London Statistics*, vol. XXIV, 1913–14, and Marian Bowley, *Housing and the state, 1919–1944* (London, 1945), p. 13.

much of the popular housing in the next category above this, since the gross mean yearly rent per house in 1912 was around £35 in East London.[51] The law was thus generous over small incomes, but it did not protect tenants in furnished rooms or sub-tenants. Landlords benefited from fixed interest rates on their mortgages and were protected against foreclosure in case of difficulty of payment. As in Paris and Berlin, this measure also affected landlords living in their own accommodation. Finally, the Rents Act assured continuity of occupation for tenants affected by the rent freeze, but provided restrictive conditions in favour of landlords recovering property for their own occupation, or using it for a member of their family or an employee.

British and French housing policies thus differed appreciably. The French moratorium largely provided undisturbed occupancy for Parisians in rented accommodation, while simultaneously allowing suspension of rent payments. The British law measured out its protection: above all it satisfied the demands of the working population, which was accustomed to housing stability, except for the most fragile households living in furnished rooms; at the same time it sought to control landlords, with provision for evictions.

The effects of these policies were soon evident. From 1916 the changes in economic activity in the three capitals affected the housing market directly, while inflation added to domestic difficulties. The merits and failings of public policies were visible, depending on the gravity of local conditions. Several factors affected the scale of tensions in the property market, however, including the state of the market before the outbreak of war.

Paris was relatively well placed during the fourteen years leading up to the war, in terms of the property market. Although all three capital cities experienced a brief period of intense activity during the first years of the twentieth century, London and Berlin went on to suffer a sharp and enduring slump in building. The rate of construction and demolition diminished from 1907 onwards, while Paris enjoyed a property boom from 1910 to 1914. Yet this disparity becomes blurred if we look at popular conditions: the stock of housing with a rental value of less than 500 francs diminished from 1906 onwards, with a comparable trend observable in London and Berlin in similar housing.[52]

This situation, universally detrimental to the working classes,was partially offset by suburban construction. Beginning in 1890 at the latest, the supply of housing had grown strongly outside the three cities' administrative boundaries, absorbing part of the popular demand created by demographic growth. This expansion was not uniform; it

51 In Bethnal Green, Stepney, Camberwell and Peckham, as shown in Offer, *Property and politics*, pp. 264–7. 52 Cf. table 13.1.

slowed notably on the outskirts and in the suburbs of London from 1904, while many working-class households remained in the city centre, attracted by its manifold resources.[53] Tension within the housing market therefore remained the norm in all three capitals, hindering improvements in housing conditions which had begun to appear in the 1890s.

On the eve of the war, reformers in all three countries could take justifiable pride in the advances of the previous twenty years in domestic sanitation and comfort. Paris had caught up with London and Berlin by building a main drainage system from 1894 onwards, with 67 per cent of buildings connected to it.[54] Although not all accommodation in all three cities had internal water and gas lighting, these services were at least connected to the great majority of buildings. Coal remained the most widely used fuel for heating and cooking.[55] One- or two-roomed flats, of which there were still many just before the war, were declining in number: between 1891 and 1911 they dropped from nearly 39 per cent to 32 per cent in London and from 61 per cent to 58 per cent in Paris and Berlin, where kitchens were quite often shared in working-class housing. Forty-seven per cent of dwellings had, in 1910, a room capable of being heated, with or without their own kitchen, compared to the roughly comparable figure of 49 per cent five years earlier.[56] Overcrowding was diminishing: calculated for the first time in Paris and London through the 1891 census, it affected 25.6 per cent of Londoners and 14 per cent of Parisians, while in 1911 the proportions were 17.8 per cent and 8.3 per cent respectively. In Berlin 16 per cent of the population lived in overcrowded conditions, thus defined.[57]

This overall pattern of general improvement concealed serious disparities. There was little improvement for many manual workers living in industrial suburbs, or for casual workers, small tradesmen or recent immigrants still living in central areas. Contemporary reformers

[53] Cf. table 13.5. [54] See *Annuaire statistique de la ville de Paris, 1914*, p. 76.

[55] For a general description of these developments in the three cities, see Jean-Luc Pinol, *Le monde des villes au XIXe siècle* (Paris, 1991). [56] See table 13.2.

[57] According to the definition adopted in 1891 in France at the instigation of Jacques Bertillon and in Britain by Charles Booth, overcrowding was 'accommodation occupied by more than two people per room'. We have adopted the same definition to calculate the degree of overcrowding in Berlin, with the 1910 census giving the data for the count but not the result; for London, *Census of England and Wales, 1911*, vol. VIII, 'Tenements', p. 534; for Paris, J. Bertillon, 'Introduction', in Préfecture de la Seine, Service de la Statistique municipale, *Résultats statistiques du dénombrement de 1891 pour la ville de Paris et le départment de la Seine* (Paris, 1894), p. xxxv (this introduction also compares Paris with London, pp. xlii-xliii), and Préfecture de la Seine, Service de la Statistique municipale, 'Statistique des logements à Paris', *Recueil de statistique municipale de la ville de Paris, 1912*. For Berlin, *Statistisches Jahrbuch der Stadt Berlin, 1910*, vol. 32, p. 967.

even noted with distress increased overcrowding in some popular districts, as in the centre of London where it affected more than 33 per cent of the population in 1911. Conversely, other categories of worker had attained housing close to middle-class standards: more consistently in stable employment and therefore with regular income, these workers were able to settle in the suburbs or outlying residential districts with office staff, clerical workers, or primary teachers, or in similar new areas. The separation of home and work, and the long distances travelled daily, the habit of living in the more spacious – even if not more comfortable – accommodation of an independent maisonette, perhaps bought on credit, had become the norm for them too.[58]

These were precisely the workers and office staff for whom the war represented the greatest threat, with the potential destruction of recently acquired or still insecure housing conditions. It can therefore be said that the strongest resistance to the consequences of the war, and the strongest resentment at setbacks, came from these social groups. However, they were not all exposed in the same way and to the same extent. As we shall see, the war created divisions in housing circumstances which did not necessarily coincide with the divisions separating socio-professional categories. The war blurred the contour lines and threw up possibilities for improvement as well as for deterioration.

In all three capitals, density was the prime element of inequality. Residents in central London districts remained unaffected by the changes and experienced little deterioration in their housing. Many of the very badly housed families before 1914 lived in the East End where some benefited from improvements, as shown by the relative decrease in overcrowding between 1911 and 1921.[59] Like those living in modest houses, since the implementation of the Rents Act they were spared the rent increases which landlords, frustrated by the preceding stagnant decade, hastened to impose in 1914-15.[60] Workers' circumstances in other districts were very different; the mass departure of soldiers after the introduction of conscription in 1916 did not match new arrivals drawn in by jobs in war manufacturing. Workers flooded into the south-east of London, adding to the numbers of those employed at the

58 See John Burnett, *A social history of housing 1815-1970* (London, 1980, 1st edn 1978); Alan Jackson, *Semi-detached London Suburban development, life and transport, 1900–1939* (London, 1973); Alain Faure (ed.), *Les premiers banlieusards. Aux origines des banlieues de Paris, 1860–1940* (Paris, 1991). 59 See fig. 13.6.

60 In the East End, particularly in Bethnal Green and Stepney, the significant rise in working-class rents at the turn of the century (12.9 per cent and 24.8 per cent respectively) was followed by a significant decrease (7 per cent and 10 per cent) in the period 1905–12. See Offer, *Property and politics*, pp. 266–7.

Arsenal and other munitions factories.[61] To the west and north, in more socially mixed boroughs, the growth in jobs as a result of the war brought in vast numbers of employees. This influx caused various housing problems, which grew worse from 1917.

Anyone not already living in the city suffered the most insecure living conditions. This was particularly true of women. Giving up their lives as domestic servants in the comfortable houses of the West End, or arriving independently from the surrounding areas to work in factories in Woolwich, Deptford, Greenwich, or Lewisham,[62] many lived in special hostels set up by the government and private associations. The preferred alternative, which avoided the strict hostel discipline, was to lodge with private families. This was popular with parents, who had confidence in the supervision of life in another family home.[63] As demand grew for factory workers, renting a room on a sub-lease increasingly became the norm for women, and also for men. Few new lodgings were available; the residential block built in 1915 by the state for Woolwich employees could not accommodate more than 1,298 workers and remained unique, while few lodgings were built privately.[64] The gap between these mobile workers and those who stuck to their London homes widened under the effect of the Rents Act. The former, lodging with local inhabitants, were effectively outside the housing law and, because of the tensions developing in this sector of the market, paid a high price for mediocre housing; according to a survey carried out by the Ministry of Munitions in May 1917, the average price for full board for men in London and south London reached £50 14s per year in hostels and £66 6s in private lodgings. For women – whose average wage was, according to the survey, 22 per cent lower than that of men – the cost was £43 15s and £46 16s respectively, only 14 and 15 per cent less than housing for men. These prices included all meals and incidental lodging expenses but represented more than twice the annual rent for an ordinary working-class lodging, which was around £20. Even when

61 Numbers employed at Woolwich Arsenal rose from 11,000 at the outbreak of war to 60,000 in June 1916 and reached a peak of nearly 76,000 in November 1917. PRO, SUPP 5/1051, 'Statement of employees in O.F. Woolwich from week ending 1.8.14 to week ending 31.7.1915' and PRO, SUPP 5/63, 'Number of employees – all departments'.

62 The migration of domestic staff from the West End to the munitions factories of the south-east is indicated by the drop of 5-10 per cent in the female population in Westminster, Holborn, and St Pancras and comparable growth in Deptford, Greenwich, Lewisham, and Woolwich. See *Registrar General's Annual Reports for England and Wales, 1914 and 1916.*

63 See Marion Kozak, 'Women munition workers during the First World War: with special reference to engineering', PhD thesis, University of Hull, 1976, ch. 6, and D. Thom, 'Women munition workers at Woolwich Arsenal in the 1914–1918 war', MA thesis, University of Warwick, 1976, ch. 4.

64 Cf. table 13.5. The upward curve in 1915 to 1916 in outer London was due to the construction of the residential Well Hall block, for workers at the Woolwich Arsenal.

Table 13.5. *Greater London: variation in working-class lodgings in different areas, 1902 to 1918*

	Inner London	Outer London	Total London	Extra London 1	Extra London 2	Greater London
1902	−118	17,885	17,767	35,722	—	35,722
1903	440	21,035	21,475	37,534	—	37,534
1904	466	18,550	19,016	32,550	—	32,550
1905	−3,636	17,944	14,308	36,629	—	36,629
1906	−129	14,411	14,282	—	38,473	38,473
1907	−79	8,885	8,806	—	31,211	31,211
1908	−455	6,881	6,426	—	21,815	21,815
1909	−2,247	3,389	1,142	—	20,918	20,918
1910	−974	3,932	2,958	—	17,953	17,953
1911	−1,734	1,969	235	—	14,873	14,873
1912	−2,661	38	−2,623	—	10,961	10,961
1913	−1,418	1,425	7	—	9,155	9,155
1914	−2,268	1,026	−1,242	—	8,947	8,947
1915	−661	4,382	3,721	—	4,052	4,052
1916	−374	9,270	8,896	—	4,631	4,631
1917	−139	592	453	—	1,167	1,167
1918	−603	−438	−1,041	—	−313	−313

Note: Extra London 1 = 35 districts; Extra London 2 = 43 districts after the new definition of 1906.
Source: London Statistics, vol. 24–vol. 27.

comfortably housed and with their rent close to £35 per year, workers living in their own homes were at an advantage: although they had to put up with long daily journeys to work in very uncomfortable conditions,[65] they had at least a home for a fixed expenditure; here we can see to what extent the Rents Act operated to full effect on over-stretched local housing markets.

The same inequality between newcomers and established residents also affected office staff. Those who came to live in London were certainly more likely than incoming factory workers to live independently, in one or two-roomed flats arranged hastily in middle-class homes formerly in sole occupancy. However, they no doubt lived more modestly than before the war and did not always escape high rents despite the legislation in effect since 1915. Landlords knew how to turn the pressure on this market to their own profit; fear of eviction following a sale or the return of a flat to the owner for his personal use often persuaded tenants to accept rent increases.[66]

Further, among the working classes as with the lower middle classes, the uncertainties suffered by one might be of advantage to another. Sub-letting a room covered all or part of the main rent and could supply the necessary extra money to buy an occupied lodging, depreciated by the rent freeze. Those who managed to improve their circumstances in this way no doubt remained in a minority, contrary to newspaper articles emphasizing the social upheavals that accompanied the war. They were however sufficient in number to make sub-tenants, and more generally those who lived in districts heavily affected by incoming residents, aware of the number of people living in small housing units in these districts, and in overcrowded conditions.[67]

The disparities deepened in 1918 as the Rents Act lost some of its effectiveness. Evictions following a change of ownership became more frequent, hitting the lower middle classes hardest. A press campaign stressed this point, though against the difficult background of the final year of the war, it changed its target. Newspapers now paid less attention to the wealth of well-paid workers than to the rapacity of 'panic-stricken plutocrats' or 'opulent conscientious objectors', rich Londoners who escaped air-raids by moving to the outer suburbs or the south coast, throwing out into the street the respectable families of officers who were serving their country.[68] 'Foreigners' were the most heavily criticized among these 'invaders': 'Russian Jews' from the East End, judged as having prospered over the years, were not subject to

[65] *The Times*, 10 Jan. 1916, and 22 May 1916.

[66] Many statements from landlords' court actions to evade the law can be found in *The Times* of 10 Feb. 1916 and of 17 Jan. 1916. [67] See fig. 13.6.

[68] *The Times*, 4, 6, 9, 22, 27, 28 March, 3 April, 7 May 1918.

conscription.[69] The press continued to feed the debate, bringing it to a head over Russian immigrants for whom it suggested the alternatives of 'conscription' or 'expulsion'. The debate was not restricted to London newspapers: the same arguments were used for the French, stirred up in Paris by 'feelings . . .of jealousy and . . . of rivalry' towards Russian and Polish Jews.[70] Both cities had anti-Semitic traditions, but in London they stemmed directly from a campaign which had had some prominence before 1914. After the turn of the century, anti-Semites seized on the surge in rents and increased overcrowding in the East End, coinciding with the wave of immigrants arriving from Eastern Europe. Their call for limits on immigration helped produce the Aliens Act of 1905. The 1918 campaign, building on social tensions in civil society between victims and patriots, British and foreigners, workers and profiteers – once again helped to create a notion of a law-abiding, honest national community, as opposed to those too selfish to work for the commonweal. Once more cohesion was defined by exclusion.[71]

There was no shortage of tensions in 1918. Evictions hit hard at households ill protected by the Rents Act, but even more at those without any form of protection. This often happened among the middle classes, undermined by mobilization which affected them very substantially. After 1916 they received public support: from May of that year the Civil Liabilities Committee supplied mobilized men with a grant towards rent and rates for their houses and commercial premises, annual mortgage loan repayments and insurance premiums. The ceiling was £104 per year, or approximately half employees' pre-war wages.[72] A year later, in March 1917, officers were allocated a grant specifically for their rent, also with a ceiling of £104 per year.[73] These contributions only partially made up for increased rents, however, which during the last two years of the war rose by 25 to 35 per cent for a middle-class maisonette and 100 per cent for flats.[74] The surge in prices introduced a wave of evictions; a harsh challenge for a lower middle

69 *The Times*, 22 and 27 March, 3 April 1918.

70 Becker, *Les Français dans la Grande Guerre*, pp. 128-9.

71 For the pre-war period, see David Feldman, 'The importance of being English: Jewish immigration and the decay of liberal England', in David Feldman and Gareth Stedman Jones (eds.), *Metropolis of London, Histories and Representations since 1800* (London, 1989), pp. 56–84, and 'Les Juifs et la question anglaise, 1840–1914', *Genèses*, 4 (May 1991), pp. 3–22.

72 Susan Pennybacker, 'Les moeurs, les aspirations et la culture politique des employés de bureau londoniens des deux sexes, 1889-1914', *Genèses*, 14 (1994), pp. 87–8. On rents, see Offer, *Property and politics*, pp. 266–7.

73 *Interim Report of the Advisory Committee for the Year Ending 25 May 1918*, PP 1919, Cmd 39, vol. X. See also Gill Thomas, 'State maintenance for women during the First World War: the case of separation allowances and pensions', PhD thesis, University of London 1989, p. 50.

74 *The Times*, 24 Feb. 1919 and 26 March 1919.

class which was not accustomed to being thrown into the street and had already considerably reduced its standard of living. Eviction naturally created deep anger and animosity and prepared the ground for the protest movement of 1918 to 1919.

Inequality in London in the face of these growing difficulties was also evident in Paris. Here too many tenants – manual workers or women of any social class – discovered or rediscovered discomforts and uncertainties of lodgings. For others, more numerous than in London because of the greater protection offered by moratoria on rent or on paid holidays, housing conditions remained unchanged. This applied particularly to the middle classes. As already discussed, moratoria concerned families of mobilized men without limitation on rent, and the non-mobilized with a rent of less than 1,000 francs. However, these families knew well that suspension was not the same as remission of payment, and many were no doubt determined to pay all or part of their quarterly rent at the expense of other items. The problem could be seen in the number of army widows who were forced to move house, knowing that they would not be able to honour their debts; here the government moved quickly to support them. The decree of 17 January 1915 enabled them to move out without having to pay the quarterly rent or indemnities, with payment dates being set by the magistrate. But although such women could still find reasonably cheap housing in 1915 – as seen in the increase in empty accommodation at rents of between 500 and 600 francs – the situation had changed by the following year when the number of lodgings available diminished sharply for all rent values.[75] This imbalance in the market pushed newly deprived families into the most precarious forms of housing. This affected families of widows without savings or any possibility of withdrawing to the country, refugees, workers' wives, teachers, shop-keepers – all of whom had provided numbers of mobilized men.[76]

Furnished rooms, hotels, and rented rooms in private homes thus became the fate of the lower middle class which had generally enjoyed improved living conditions in the 'Belle Epoque'. Working-class women were used to such accommodation. Many women looking for work would no doubt recognize the experience of the refugee woman from the Aisne whose eviction caused a scandal: her husband a prisoner, she was forced to live in a single furnished room in Neuilly with her three children.[77] Taken on at first in offices, banks, transport, or

[75] See table 13.3. [76] See fig. 13.4.

[77] The story of this family was recounted to the Conseil général de la Seine, by councillor M. Vendrin in December 1915. See 'Question de M. Vendrin à M. le Préfet de police au sujet de l'expulsion, d'une chambre de garni, de Mme Sinzot et de ses trois enfants, par le Commissaire de police de Neuilly', Conseil général de la Seine, *Mémoires et procès-verbaux des délibérations. Procès-verbaux du 8 décembre 1915* (Paris, Imprimerie municipale, 1916), pp. 749–52.

tailoring, then from 1917 joining munitions factories in great numbers, these women lived, as in London, in hostels or, if they were working-class, in furnished rooms. The social policy introduced by Albert Thomas had provided canteen nurseries, and breast-feeding rooms, but rarely housing, which was only supplied if the factory was very isolated, such as the Livry-Gargan powder factory far out in the Paris suburbs, which had its own hostel.[78]

Working women therefore often shared the same conditions as men from other areas who came to work in munitions factories. Provincials or foreigners, they frequently took up the nineteenth-century workers' custom of spending a season in Paris, renting a room from a local resident or a bed in a barrack room, and rejecting the few army huts near factories that were subject to military discipline, such as in Boulogne, Puteaux, Saint-Denis, or Ivry.[79] In communes with substantial defence establishments, or their neighbouring communes – particularly to the north, in La Courneuve, Asnières, Epinay, Pierrefitte, and even Enghien, where military reports indicated the presence of workers from the Saint-Denis factories – the increased numbers of lodgers in hotels and furnished rooms was often substantial, exceeding 95 per cent in the period between the census of 1911 and 1921, even where the number was already high in 1911 (see fig. 13.4). Prices rose as a result. The average working woman living in a furnished room in Puteaux had to pay an annual rent of between 420 and 450 francs, or between 40 and 45 per cent more than in July 1914, according to the survey. This represented 23-25 per cent of her wages if, as a skilled metal-worker, she earned 6 francs per day. At the same period the annual rent for a furnished room in Saint-Denis varied between 420 and 720 francs; the turner who was paid 12 francs per day thus spent only 9-16 per cent of his wages on rent, but these rents were two to three times dearer than the pre-war rate. At the Goutte d'or, in the 18th arrondissement in Paris, the rent for an unfurnished room and kitchen was 290-320 francs; in Boulogne, where the number of 'lodgers in furnished rooms' rose from 400 in 1914 to 700 in 1918, the price of a bed in a room with two or three beds was regularly around 5 francs per week, or 260 francs per year.[80]

But the furnished room was not exclusive to the suburbs; there were many in the city itself. The proportion of hotels, furnished flats, and rooms, which doubled in the Seine suburban areas between 1911 and

[78] On Livry-Gargan, see Sellier, Bruggeman, and Poëte, *Paris pendant la Guerre*, pp. 11–12.

[79] The Rapport presented by Lieut. Meurdra and the Rapport presented by Major Dr Landowski. AN, Travail et Sécurité sociale, F22 536. On housing for nineteenth-century seasonal workers, cf. Jeanne Gaillard, *Paris la ville, 1852-1870* (Paris, 1977), and the account of Martin Nadaud, *Léonard maçon de la Creuse* (Paris, 1976), pp. 53–5.

[80] 'Response from the Puteaux construction workshop' in Rapport of Lt Meurdra; for Saint-Denis, Rapport of Lt Meurdra; for Boulogne, Rapport by Major Dr Landowski. AN, Travail et Sécurité sociale, F 22 536.

1921 (4.7 per cent to 8.4 per cent), increased by more than one-third in Paris (11.4 per cent to 15.4 per cent). In existence before August 1914, the furnished room came into its own around 1908 at a time of severe decrease in the stock of 'working-class' lodgings – *les garnis* became commonplace in a few years and continued after November 1918. Its growth was substantial during the war: the annual number of tenants of furnished rooms in Paris increased by one-quarter between 1 January 1914 and 31 December 1918 and can be multiplied by 2.4 if the initial date for calculation is taken as 31 December 1914, the lowest point because of the exodus from Paris.[81] Because the growth in numbers of dwellings was much smaller, overcrowding increased substantially; 15 per cent of people living in Paris in a furnished room or hotel had less than half a room each in 1921, as against 11 per cent in 1911, with the proportion rising from 8 to 16 per cent in the suburbs. In ordinary lodgings, on the other hand, overcrowding increased very slowly during the same period between census counts, from 8 to 9 per cent in Paris and from 7 to 8.7 per cent in the suburbs.[82] The gap between patterns of housing use between these two groups of tenants thus developed during the war. Public authorities did nothing. Although moratoria effectively allowed tenants of furnished rooms to enjoy security of tenure in their rented accommodation, like those who lived in ordinary houses, they could not prevent the imbalance within the market from affecting both rents for new premises and housing conditions. These developments inevitably affected the most insecure accommodation first of all. The remedy would have been a policy of construction which the French state had not even considered; it contented itself with building huts for the foreign and colonial labour force which it was obliged to use.[83]

The imbalance in housing provision and cost divided workers, setting Parisians against provincials and foreigners. Recalled from the front after August 1915 to work in war factories, the workers effectively returned to their pre-mobilization housing and generally benefited fully and as of right from the rent moratorium as 'small tenants'.[84] Targets for the rage of landlords aware that their wages might exceed 3,000 francs per year,[85] these workers no doubt insisted on not paying, hoping for at

[81] Cf. table 13.4.

[82] Préfecture de la Seine, Service de la Statistique municipale, 'Statistique des logements à Paris'; 'Statistique des logements dans les communes du département de la Seine', *Recueil de statistique municipale de la ville de Paris et du Département de la Seine, 1918*; 'Statistiques des logements à Paris', *Recueil de statistique municipale de la ville de Paris et du Département de la Seine, 1922*; 'Statistique des logements dans le département de la Seine', *Recueil de statistique du Département de la Seine, 1923*.

[83] See Rapport presented by Lt Meurdra. AN, F22 536.

[84] As stated by Albert Thomas in a written response to the Minister of Trade on 22 Dec. 1915. AN, Ministère du commerce F 12 8020.

[85] A basic wage of over 3,000 francs was standard for metal-working in 1916.

least a partial remission of their debt until the end of the war and in any case claiming it through the Tenants' Union. Men arriving from the provinces or from other countries, on the other hand, were forced into overcrowded furnished rooms which were more costly than ordinary lodgings. From 1916 these new arrivals saw their right to benefit from the moratorium challenged with increasing frequency, although it applied equally to lettings dating from before August 1914 as after that date.[86] Men from the provinces who were mobilized in war factories at least had the advantage over foreigners in that they did not have to pay two rents, their original home being generally covered by the moratoriums.[87]

Parisian workers thus figured among those spared or even privileged in the capital. True, their living conditions did not improve during the war, nor did the former disparities disappear. Sanitation and standards of housing worsened. After July 1914, the sanitation service no longer required landlords to carry out repairs or to have drainage systems connected.[88] This deterioration meant little to workers who, as in Puteaux or Saint-Denis, lived before 1914 in accommodation without sanitation.[89] Uncomfortably housed, they could at least suspend their quarterly payment without being thrown into the street – possibly a temporary economy, but gained through the sacrifice of other forms of consumption. Other workers, on the other hand – better housed initially and, as skilled workers in munitions factories, better paid – could afford to ignore those office employees whose pay equalled their own and whose rent was no more than 600 or 1,000 francs. These desk-bound wage-earners, more frequently dispatched to the front line than factory

86 This was specified in the Rapport à Monsieur le Président de la République preceding the decree of 28 December 1915. However, this disposition was often challenged by landlords and not accepted by magistrates. Cf. AN, BB 30 1534, Ministère de la Justice, Dossier 'Locations postérieures à la Guerre', *Réponse de la Chancellerie à M. le Ministre d'Etat Léon Bourgeois*, August 1916, and *Proposition de résolution ayant pour objet l'application du moratorium des loyers aux locations contractées depuis la mobilisation, presentée par M. Arthur Levasseur député*, Chambre des députés, minutes of the session of 7 July 1916, Annexe no. 2298.

87 See the written response of Albert Thomas to the Minister of Trade on 22 Dec. 1915, AN, Ministère du commerce F 12 8020, and written reply from the Attorney General to the Minister of Justice dated 21 Feb. 1918, AN, Ministère de la Justice BB 30 1534, Dossier A.

88 Between 1914 and 1919 the proportion of buildings with direct main drainage remained static or increased slightly in popular arrondissements, rising for example from 57 per cent to 58 per cent in the 20th and from 61 per cent to 64 per cent in the 19th arrondissement. Cf. *Annuaire statistique de la ville de Paris, 1914 et seq.*, 'Statistique numérique des divers systèmes de vidange en usage à Paris'.

89 In 1906 in Puteaux only 19.3 per cent of accommodation of less than five rooms, for which information is known, had a lavatory, and 21.5 per cent in Saint-Denis. Cf. Ministère du travail et de la prévoyance sociale, *Enquête sur l'habitation ouvrière (1906)* (Paris, 1908), pp. 78–9.

workers, had, as noted above, less chance of keeping their families in the same living conditions as at the outbreak of war. In reserved office employment, they also lacked the advantages of workers mobilized in factories: covered by the moratoria, they nevertheless lacked the 'full rights' which gave shelter from any owner's challenge – even when their rent was less than 600 francs, under the decree of 30 December 1915 which, as a governmental concession to the Senate, had removed the advantage 'to tenants in receipt of salary or fixed pay of 3,000 francs or more'.[90] Higher social status thus deprived office staff (and those workers in public services who were so close to them and received 'set pay'), if not of a positive advantage, at least of greater latitude in managing their budget during the war and in preparation for the future.

This blurring of the conventional social dividing lines, visible in Paris as in London, was also evident in Berlin. Here, however, the difficulties consequent on the war effort were harsher, and aggravated conditions in the most vulnerable households. This was the situation by the middle of 1916, but public authorities did not respond until the end of the following year, by which time social tensions had deepened significantly.

The housing market in Berlin remained relatively overstretched until the autumn of 1916. The city centre was in good condition when war broke out: the marked reduction in the building industry before 1914 and a drop in the population left a surplus of accommodation available. The outbreak of war made no difference and the number of empty dwellings continued to grow – from 4.6 per cent in 1914 to 6.6 per cent in 1916.[91] The causes, however, had changed. Some families of the most prosperous mobilized men left Berlin; in November 1914, as in May 1916, the greatest concentration of empty accommodation was not in the popular districts of north and east Berlin, but in the middle-class areas of the south and south-west.[92] But after May 1916 this changed completely. Growing numbers of war manufacturing jobs drew people into the city, and although they did not fill the gap left by men at the front, they tilted the relationship back again between accommodation vacant and wanted. In May 1918 the proportion of housing empty in Berlin fell to 3 per cent. The demand was felt throughout the city, except in the centre; more pronounced in the industrial and working-class

[90] This point is important, because it was responsible for the overturning of certain magistrates' decisions affecting workers. Cf. letter from the Procureur Général of the Paris appeal court, 29 October 1915, and his *Rapport*, 9 May 1917, AN, BB 30 1535, Ministère de la Justice.

[91] On the pattern of the Berlin housing market after 1900, see Nicholas Bullock and James Read, *The movement for housing reform in Germany and France, 1840–1914* (Cambridge, 1985), pp. 194–8. For the pattern of empty housing, see table 13.6.

[92] See table 13.7.

Table 13.6. *Berlin: vacant lodgings, 1910–1918*

Year	Total lodgings	Vacant lodgings	%
1 Jan. 1910	576,020	26,617	4.6
1 Jan. 1912	590,062	24,348	4.1
1 Dec. 1912	596,453	26,309	4.4
1 Dec. 1913	599,622	27,811	4.6
1 Nov. 1914	600,827	39,728	6.6
15 May 1916	602,902	39,863	6.6
19 May 1917	602,902	34,574	5.7
31 May 1918	604,006	18,972	3.1

Note: Includes lodgings for both home and work.
Source: Statistisches Jahrbuch der Stadt Berlin, vol. 34, pp. 303.

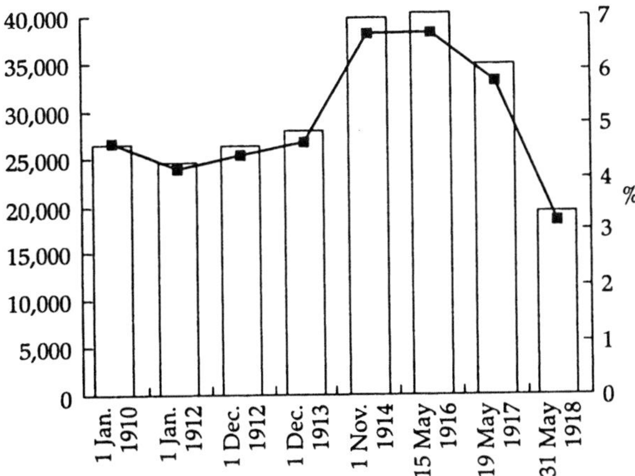

Fig. 13.3 Vacant lodgings in Berlin, and percentage of all lodgings vacant, 1910 to 1918

districts to the north and east of the city (which had 2.5 per cent of its housing empty in 1918, as against 5–6 per cent in 1916), it was also noticeable in the middle-class south and west (empty housing dropped from 8.4 per cent to 4.5 per cent in the south, from 5.5 per cent to 1.8 per cent in the west).[93]

In the suburbs, work available and the consequent imbalance in the market was a powerful attraction to a growing population, intensified by the much smaller stock of housing available than in the city centre before the war; since the end of the nineteenth century, suburban

[93] Cf. table 13.7.

Table 13.7. *Vacant lodgings as percentage of all lodgings in different regions of Berlin, 1914 to 1918*

	North	East	South	South-west	West	Berlin
1 Nov. 1914	6.18	6.51	7.42	7.28	5.27	6.61
15 May 1916	5.16	6.27	8.45	9.34	5.53	6.61
19 May 1917	4.38	5.27	7.77	8.28	4.28	5.74
31 May 1918	2.42	2.62	4.55	4.78	1.84	3.14

Distribution of arrondissements by zone: Centre = I, IX; North = Xa, Xb, Xc, XI, XIIIa, XIIIb; East = VIIa, VIIb, VIIc, VIII; South = IVb, Va, Vb, VI; South-west = II, IVa; West = III, XIIa, XIIb.
Source: Statistisches Jahrbuch der Stadt Berlin, vol. 34, pp. 302.

communes had absorbed the bulk of metropolitan growth. Charlottenburg, the most sought-after residential district for the well-paid staff of large companies like Siemens, installed in the western suburbs since the turn of the century, had only 2.9 per cent of its housing available in 1913, less than the working-class residential commune of Neukölln to the south-east, with 4.5 per cent empty at the same date.[94] As people flooded into these communes from 1916 onwards, housing was quickly taken up and in 1918 none was left empty.

The shortage of housing in the period 1917 to 1918 thus did not spare the middle classes, although they appear to have been more affected in the city centre than in the suburbs. In their favoured southern districts of Berlin, a noticeable drop appeared in the proportion of large dwellings, of five rooms or more: from 36.4 per cent in 1910 to 30.3 per cent in 1918 in Friedrich-und Schöneberger Vorstadt, from 22.5 per cent to 17.8 per cent in Friedrich-und Tempelhofer Vorstadt. Close to the fall registered for Berlin as a whole (15 per cent to 11.9 per cent), this contrasted with the stable proportion of lodgings of the same size in the popular northern and eastern districts and the increase in large lodgings in prosperous suburbs such as Charlottenburg. Required by arbitration more often than the working classes to pay higher rents than in the suburbs, the middle classes of southern Berlin no doubt sought, as in London, to move into smaller accommodation. The demand encouraged owners to divide very large dwellings.

In the suburbs, on the other hand, the housing shortage created by the demand for labour in war factories primarily penalized the working classes. Spandau, the heart of armaments production, was one of the outlying towns which saw its population growing from the begin-

[94] For a fuller discussion, see Maurice Halbwachs, '"Gross Berlin": Grande agglomération ou grande ville?', *Annales d'histoire économique et sociale,* (30 November 1934), pp. 547–70 and Horst Matzerath, 'Berlin, 1890–1940', in Anthony Sutcliffe (ed.), *Metropolis 1890–1940* (London, Mansell, 1984), pp. 230–318.

ning of the war, although its housing supply was among the smallest. The demand for housing grew noticeably following the implementation of the Hindenburg Programme in late 1916, which set off a new influx of labour. But the building programmes initiated in Spandau from 1914 onwards by the Ministry of the Interior, and in 1917 to 1918 by the town council, dealt with barely 1,000 dwellings in all.[95] All possible forms of housing were in demand. Attics and cellars normally considered unsuitable for habitation were let and overcrowding reappeared. In 1918 it affected 13 per cent of the residents, of whom more than two-thirds were living in housing consisting of one or two rooms, not including the kitchen, which was often shared among several households.[96] Similar developments affected other working-class communes, such as Lichtenberg to the east of Berlin, where the scale of overcrowding marked it out from the prosperous communes of the south-west.

Workers were not always condemned to poor housing, however. By using the extended network of public transport they could avoid insecure accommodation near the factories – a sub-let room or bed in a private house, the norm until the end of the nineteenth century.[97] Overcrowding in Berlin's small lodgings dropped considerably between 1910 and 1918, although it reached 14 per cent in one-roomed lodgings and 16 per cent for those with two rooms.[98]

The winter of 1917 to 1918 brought difficulties for most wage-earners, and undermined previous advantages. Lack of heating or lighting encouraged families to get together, and no doubt added to cohabitation.[99] At the same time, the surge in inflation eliminated the advantages of high wages: moving house became more difficult as landlords, who were also affected, tried to increase rents when leases were renewed. This development persuaded the legislators to intervene once more, as will be shown below, but these belated measures were already part of the policy preparing for the transition to peace.

'Crisis' and 'reconstruction': the harsh road back to peace

Whether we emphasize the problems of residents or of buildings, the housing situation in the three capital cities at the end of the war is

[95] See Erich Leyser, 'Gross Berlin Wohnungspolitik im Kriege', in *Grossstadt und Kleinhaus* (Berlin, 1917), p. 39, and R. Eberstadt, *Handbuch des Wohnungswesens und der Wohnungsfrage*, pp. 510–11.

[96] On the shortage in areas with concentrations of the war industry, cf. Eberstadt, *Handbuch des Wohnungswesens*, pp. 189-93; Alfred Kray, 'Die Einwirkung des Krieges auf das Gross-Berliner Baugewerbe', *Beiträge zur Bauwissenschaft*, 25 (1920), pp. 11–12.

[97] 'Boarders' (*Schlafleute*), tenants in a private house, representing 8 per cent of Berlin's population in the 1870s, represented only 5 per cent in 1910, plus another 3 per cent at that date of sub-tenants of a room. *Statistisches Jahrbuch der Stadt Berlin*, vol. 32, pp. 968–75.

[98] See table 13.8.

[99] *Verwaltungsbericht Neukölln*, p. 134.

Table 13.8. *Berlin: population living in overcrowded conditions, 1910 to 1918*

	1910				1918			
	Total population	%	Population in overcrowded lodgings	%	Total population	%	Population in overcrowded lodgings	%
1 unit	57,670	2.89	12,921	22.41	61,171	3.64	8,752	14.31
2 units	592,118	29.65	182,502	30.82	498,568	29.66	81,075	16.26
3 units	713,863	35.75	111,282	15.59	634,489	37.7	46,141	7.27
3 units + kitchen	—	—	—	—	223,949	13.32	4,019	1.79
No. of lodgings	1,996,777	100	323,217	16.19	1,680,725	100	—	8.30

1 Overcrowding is defined as in London and Paris: lodgings occupied by more than two people per room.

2 For size of dwelling, we have followed two definitions: (1) that of 1910, including as 'living quarters' (*Wohnräume*) a room (heated or unheated), a maid's room, an alcove, a private kitchen; and (2) that of 1918, including as 'living quarters' a room, a bedroom, an alcove, but not a kitchen. For comparability, we have included kitchens as 'rooms' in the 1918 statistics, despite the fact that the published statistics have it otherwise.

Source: Statistisches Jahrbuch der Stadt Berlin, vol. 32, p. 967 (our calculations) and *Statistik des Deutschen Reichs*, vol. 287, n. 2, pp. 154–5.

usually described in terms of 'crisis'. This situation continued until at least the early 1920s, together with policies which – according to the terms of a still-continuing debate – at best were incapable of ending it and at worst exacerbated it. Beyond this agreed perspective, it may be recalled that during this period of transition to peace the expectations and claims of civilian society were manifold and contradictory, the reflection of a significant conflict. It is in this light that the different facets of housing policies assume their real significance. Imposing their own hierarchy of issues, they effectively helped to create the problems facing them: policy was part of the problem, not part of the solution. Differing in matters of detail, the policies varied little from one capital to another in their aims: the social inequalities contributing to the housing problem at the end of the war were similar everywhere. The range of solutions available to the three national governments was limited to initiatives and suggestions which before the war had formed part of an international exchange among reformers since the end of the nineteenth century, through international exhibitions and congresses.[100]

The first common issue was the matter of rents. The conflict of interest between landlords and tenants was at its height in 1918, with landlords expecting to minimize their losses and return as quickly as possible to the pre-war common-law system. Everywhere they went on the offensive, seeking to increase their income, and not hesitating to evict. Tenants attempted to retain advantages gained through special public authority measures or, if they had not been affected by them, finally to benefit from them. Under their lessors' onslaught they claimed public protection beyond the end of the war.

Governments faced conflicting demands that were simultaneously political, social, and economic. The protagonists each wore several hats: landlords were also investors on whom the upturn of the building cycle depended, while tenants were the manual and intellectual workers on whom the new expansion of national economies depended. Both were electors, citizens whose discontent could foster and legitimize social disorder, ill-contained since 1917. As they intervened on rents, public authorities were interested primarily in citizens and, of the two parties, selected those with the greater political weight. But they proceeded in stages, according to changing circumstances.

The measures undertaken by Berlin public authorities in 1918 showed that they were facing a particularly arduous task. By May, when the outcome of the war was still uncertain, local authorities were preparing to face a significant human influx – soldiers returning from the front and families returning to their Berlin homes – in a conurbation

[100] Susanna Magri and Christian Topalov, 'De la cité-jardin à la ville rationalisée: un tournant du projet réformateur, 1905-25. Etude comparative France, Grande-Bretagne, Italie, Etats-Unis', *Revue française de sociologie*, 28, 3 (July–Sept. 1987), pp. 417–51.

which, as we have seen, had no spare housing.[101] Large flats divided into smaller units, permission to live in cellars and attics, temporary shelter, barracks, and public buildings – all were planned by the city of Berlin and adjacent towns such as Weissensee, to the north-east of the capital.[102] Profiting from the growing demand, landlords sought to increase their income. To escape the control of municipal arbitration courts they increased rents by changing tenants. The victims of their practices were less the poorest families – whose rent was paid directly to the landlord by the supporting municipality – than the salaried middle classes whose pay lagged far behind inflation, unlike workers' wages.[103] The new decree adopted by the Bundesrat on 23 September 1918 was particularly concerned with these social categories: it required landlords to submit any new tenancy contract to the approval of the Mieteinigungsämter, including cases with rent over 500 marks. The aim was to discourage evictions and rent increases when renewing a lease and it effectively set a general freeze on rents. The effect of central governmental intervention was quickly felt: the number of cases considered by arbitrators in Berlin rose from 6,000 in 1917 to 21,000 in 1918 and 150,000 in 1919.[104]

In London, the frequency of evictions arising from a change of landlord led public authorities to adopt the Increase of Rent and Mortgage (Amendment) Act in April 1918. This removed from owners who had bought an occupied residence since 30 September 1917 the right to recover it for personal occupancy or for the use of an employee. but because it applied to accommodation covered by the law of 1915, the measure, which was to remain in operation until 1920, affected only 'small' tenants.[105] More prosperous tenants were still vulnerable to eviction, finding it difficult to pay their rent because of the inflation eating away at their income. In 1918 their protests increased and were heard more frequently in Parliament,[106] and the following year the campaign organized by the professional associations of the middle classes persuaded the government to give in: the ceiling of the annual rental value with the right to rent control was lifted to £70, or double the limit fixed in 1915.[107]

In Paris, the law of 9 March 1918 regulated the question of rents fixed until 31 March 1918. By retaining the rent level as the principal criterion

[101] *Statistik der Stadt Berlin, 1915–1920*, p. 190.

[102] Stadt Archiv Berlin, Beirat für Städtebau, 16 October 1917, and 13 March 1918.

[103] Kocka, *Die Angestellten in der deutschen Geschichte, 1880–1980.*

[104] Cf. Kaeber, *Berlin*, p. 447; Hirtschiefer, *Die Wohnungswirtschaft in Preussen*; Eberstadt, *Handbuch des Wohnungswesens*, p. 689.

[105] Englander, *Landlord and tenant*, pp. 251–62.

[106] *The Times*, particularly 6 March 1918 and 7 May 1918.

[107] Englander, *Landlord and tenant*, pp. 262–3, 290–3.

for granting tenants partial or complete exemption from payment of their debt, the law maintained the government's orientation throughout the preceding years: it satisfied small tenants, and in particular the well-paid workers in public services and war factories who sought exemption on the basis of the level of rent rather than of income. The legislators were generous to those whose debt had been accumulated without fear of a landlord's action against them: the limit of 500 francs annual rent for a bachelor tenant, or 600 francs for a couple, allowed most workers to come within the exemption clause, while the increase of 100 francs for each child or dependant extended the favour to most of the lower middle classes. However, contrary to the statements of the Ministry of Justice, it was not quite 85 per cent of Parisian tenants who had right to full exemption under the law,[108] but only the poorest households[109] and mobilized tenants under certain income conditions. In all other cases, the lessor was authorized to claim his due before one of the statutory arbitration commissions.[110] Owners who had long claimed the right of recourse against small tenants were satisfied; but the process had the disadvantage of establishing them as aggressors, which contributed to the growing ranks of the intransigent federal tenants union, well established among metal-workers. The union hardened its stance, organized boycotts of arbitration commissions and expanded the movement of tenants against 'predators'.[111] Until September 1918 these committees worked calmly, adjudicating over several months in favour of many of their members from the beginning of the war, particularly among Parisian municipal officers.[112] The result of their labours left no doubt as to the depth of hostility between the two social groups: on 31 December 1918, 102,000 cases had been registered with the arbitration committees in Paris, including the suburbs. Only 43 per cent of all cases

108 After the adoption of the law, René Viviani declared: 'Paris has about one million tenants. Because of the law, 850,000 have full rights to exemption. The arbitration committees will therefore have less to do than is supposed.' *Le Matin*, 'Vote du projet de loi sur les loyers', 22 Feb. 1918.

109 Recipients of military allowances, refugees' allowances, unemployment support, permanent aid from welfare offices, or those on the list of assisted persons, according to article 15 of the law. *Journal officiel*, 12 March 1918, pp. 2271–84.

110 Under title III of the law of 9 March 1918 these commissions were presided over by the magistrate and consisted of two representatives of tenants and owners, with names drawn by lot from lists drawn up by town councils. The decision was a majority one, with the final decision lying with the magistrate.

111 Robert, 'Ouvriers et mouvement ouvrier', pp. 929–36; and Susanna Magri, 'Le mouvement des locataires à Paris et dans sa banlieue (1919–1925)', *Le Mouvement social*, 137, (Oct.–Dec. 1986), pp. 56–76.

112 For example, the budget chairman for the City of Paris, Louis Dausset, who from 1915 was opposed to the renewal of the moratorium. See Conseil municipal de Paris, 'Rapport général sur . . . le projet de budget de la ville de Paris pour 1919 présenté par M. Louis Dausset . . .', *Rapports et documents, 1918* (Paris, 1919), p. 311.

resolved were helped by conciliation; of all cases registered, less than one-third even attempted conciliation. Six months later, the number of cases registered for the city of Paris alone was almost three times greater, but the proportion of conciliations was unchanged.[113]

On 9 March 1918, Paris landlords had reason to feel under attack. Faced with the scale of exemptions accorded to tenants, they had obtained only new facilities for repayment of mortgage loans and remissions on taxes affecting buildings, while the much-demanded state allowances covered only half of the rents for which the tenant was relieved and were only paid to owners whose annual income, allowance included, was no more than 10,000 francs in Paris – an income which was none the less equivalent in 1918 to the pay for a high court judge.[114] Distributed fairly widely, the state's financial support did not satisfy landlords. After 1915 they no longer expected to suffer losses, demanded at least one quarter's rent in advance for agreeing to let vacant premises, and in 1917 announced rent increases of 30 to 50 per cent in the popular districts of northern Paris.[115] Public bodies were braced for massive rent rises and waves of evictions when the final moratorium expired; precautionary measures were included in the law of 5 March. 'Little' tenants, mobilized or non-mobilized but lacking resources, were exempt from rent payment until 24 April 1920. Further, any tenant whose lease had been extended since August 1914 could obtain extension until 24 October 1921.

Thus all three national governments adopted rescue measures to limit social conflict over rent either before or after the Armistice. They had to make protection generally available. Those excluded, such as the middle classes in London, claimed it in their turn: they had paid 'the blood tribute' and were faced with the possibility of losing their home or not finding the equivalent of the one they had lived in before the war. Public authorities were even less inclined to suspend these protective measures because the middle classes, badly protected during the war,

[113] On 30 June 1919 the number of cases registered for Paris alone was 160,007 (as against 59,746 six months earlier), the number of final resolutions was 53,326 (33 per cent) divided into 42.6 per cent conciliations, 2.5 per cent arbitrations, 27.2 per cent judgements and 27.6 per cent abandoned or struck out. Cf. Conseil municipal de Paris, 'Rapport général sur . . . le projet de budget de la ville de Paris pour 1919 présenté par M. Louis Dausset . . .', *Rapports et documents, 1918.*, pp. 328–31.

[114] On allowances to landlords, see articles 29–33 of the law of 9 March 1918, *Journal Officiel*, 12 March 1918.

[115] Cf. Ed. Poisson, 'Observations au sujet de la répartition des secours aux réfugiés à Paris et dans la banlieue', Conseil général de la Seine, *Mémoires et procès verbaux des délibérations* (session of 30 June 1915) (Paris, 1916), p. 312; 'Proposition relative aux mesures à demander au Parlement, . . . presentée par M. Louis Sellier le 28 novembre 1917'; 'Proposition concernant la création d'une taxe municipale sur l'augmentation des loyers, présentée par M. Fiancette le 29 novembre 1918', Conseil municipal de Paris, *Rapports et documents, 1918* (Paris, 1919), p. 311.

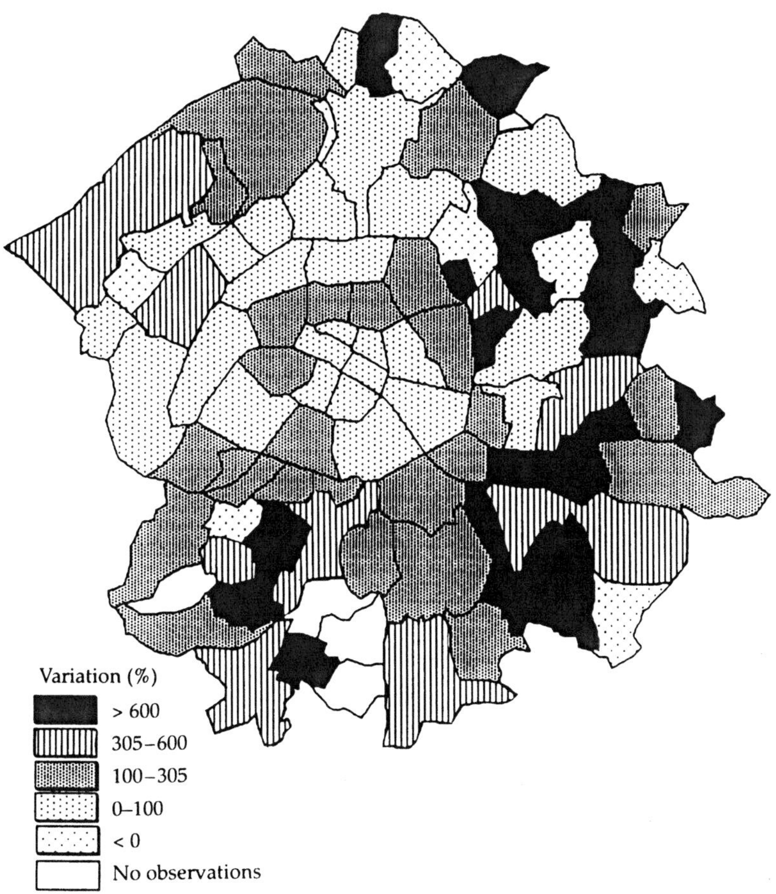

Fig. 13.4 An index of the variation in the population living in furnished rooms or flats in the Département de la Seine, 1911 to 1921 (1911 = 100). Source: Préfecture de la Seine, Service de la statistique municipale, 'Statistique des logements à Paris', 1912, 1922; 'Statistique des logements dans les communes du departement de la Seine', 1918; 'Statistique des logements dans le département de la Seine', 1923

occasionally joined the workers in rent strikes and contributed to the success of labour in the 1919 local elections.

This regulation by exception could not be suspended until the balance of the housing market was re-established. The market was undermined by the halt in building during the war, and further upset by the troops' return home. In Paris in particular demand was also intensified by the predictable growth in the immigrant population, the result of the economic upsurge with the return of peace. The relaunching of the housing sector was hindered everywhere by the dizzy increase in construction costs, the result of lifting controls on prices and

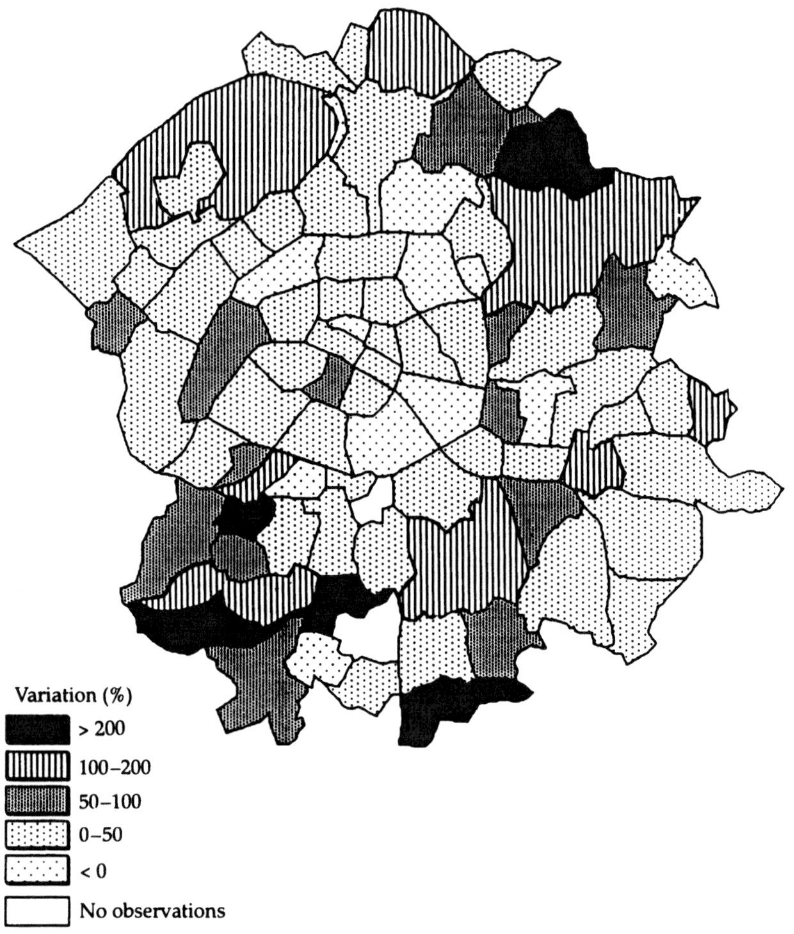

Fig. 13.5 An index of the variation in the population of the Département de la Seine living in overcrowded conditions, 1911 to 1921 (1911 = 100). Source: Préfecture de la Seine, Service de la statistique municipale, 'Statistiques des logements à Paris', 1912, 1922; 'Statistique des logements dans les communes du departement de la Seine', 1918; 'Statistique des logements dans le département de la Seine', 1923

supplies as demanded in business circles. Governments felt that they had to consider, if not effect, new housing policies which would re-launch construction and at the same time respond to various social expectations which were often expressed in protest movements.

Unions, workers' political parties, and tenants' associations in popular districts all demanded the implementation of a housing policy. They considered national needs and demanded a construction programme on a national scale. In Germany they called for national legislation which, although planned before 1914, had not been enacted.[116] Implementation was to be the work of the city councils, sustained by state financial support. Labour unions and progressive industrial leaders both considered that a radical improvement in working-class housing contributed to higher productivity, a new source of national wealth, evidence in Britain and France of the Allies' 'economic victory'.[117] They saw municipal building as one way to achieve this. The workers' associations also wanted to develop residential cooperatives and industrialists had their own staff-housing policies.

Middle classes and working classes did not always share the same demands. Weakened and deprived of the vision of immediate improvement in their housing conditions, driven to seek rent control, the most modest among them looked to municipal construction, from which they had already profited before the war. But the better-off were still hostile; they had to bear their share of local financing of these plans. This applied particularly in London, in the middle-class districts of Islington, Hackney, and Stoke Newington, where middle-class doubts reinforced local authority inactivity, even though the state now offered generous subsidies by virtue of the Housing Act of 1919.[118] In return, this section of the population counted on a revival of private construction, legitimizing a new type of state intervention which would now support private activity alongside municipal programmes.

The governments of the three nations therefore took the initiative in housing, based on experience and planning matured during the war. In Britain, although the model housing built for munitions factory workers had not made up the accommodation shortage during the war, it none the less served as the basis for planning for the post-war period. In 1919 Christopher Addison, in charge of the new Ministry of Health after being Minister of Munitions in 1916 and of Reconstruction in 1917, charged the technical team responsible for wartime housing to set up the Housing and Town Planning Act. He presented the bill to Parliament himself, which was passed in July 1919. The law created a significant state subsidy for municipal construction and to balance this communities were required to fulfil programmes of working-class housing. This policy was completed in December by the Housing (Additional Powers) Act which introduced a subsidy for private builders, paid for each house completed before 1921.

116 On the setback to the establishment of a national housing policy before the war in Germany, see Bullock and Read, *Movement for housing reform*, pp. 248–73.

117 'The military victory, if it is not to be in vain, must be completed by the organisation of the economic victory', stated the Socialist Henri Sellier in a session of the Conseil général de la Seine in 1916. Cf. Conseil général de la Seine, 'Voeux relatifs aux mesures à prendre en vue de l'organisation du travail au moment de la démobilisation et au projet de loi sur les loyers en instances devant le Parlement', *Mémoires et procès verbaux*, p. 178.

118 *The Times*, 2 Sept. 1919.

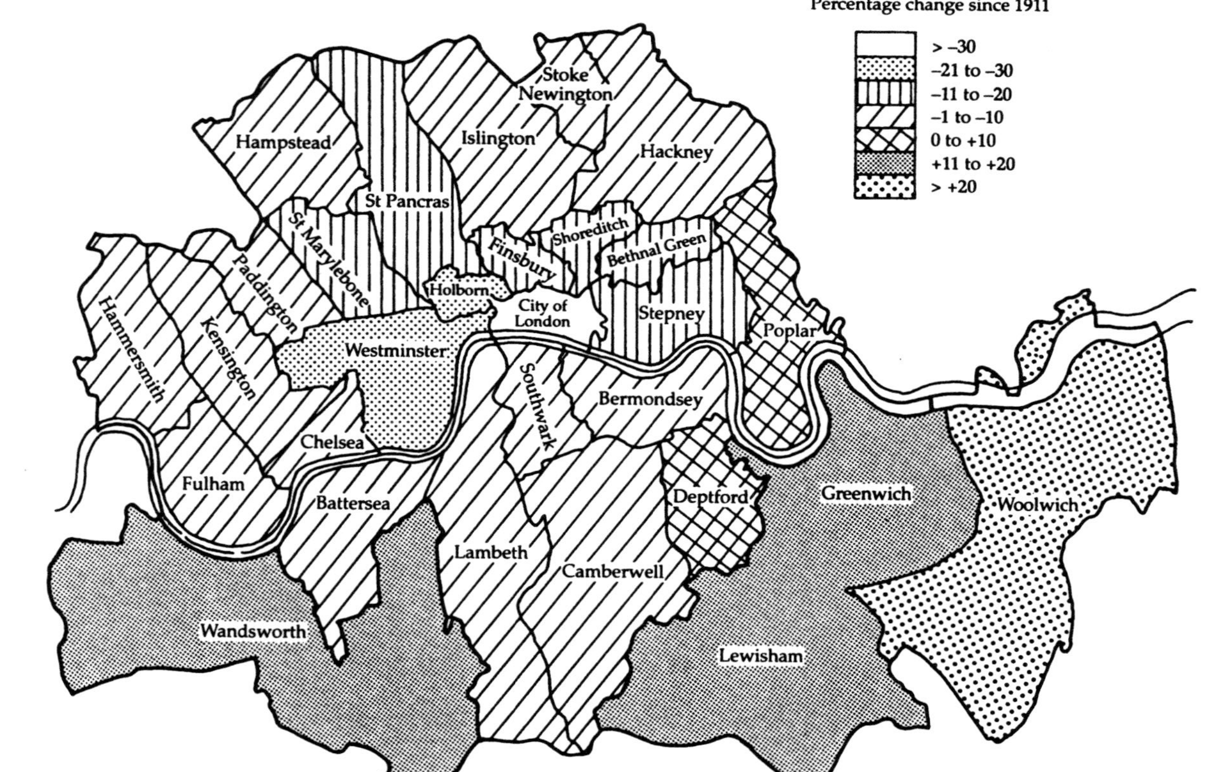

Fig. 13.6 The percentage change in levels of overcrowding in London metropolitan boroughs (City of London and metropolitan), 1911 to 1921. Source: 1911 and 1921 *Censuses of England and Wales.* Note: overcrowding statistics refer to the proportion of the population living more than two to a room

In Germany the state, which had already acted in this domain by building accommodation blocks for war-industry workers, renewed its initiative in 1918. Now it established the prerequisites of a national policy. In May a federal body was created to coordinate the activity of local authorities, hitherto independent. In May 1920 this body was absorbed into the new Volkswohlfahrt Ministerium,[119] while from December the commission on socialization (Sozialisierungskommission) addressed the perennial and intractable question of financing construction.[120]

In France, housing had not been one of Albert Thomas's successfully realized social policies. In 1918 an inquiry set up by his successor as Minister of Munitions, Louis Loucheur, had confirmed the considerable housing needs in the industrial suburbs round Paris. As Minister for Reconstruction until January 1920, Loucheur became chairman in March of that year of a committee for social assistance and protection within the new Ministry of Hygiene, and proposed the introduction of a programme for 500,000 'economical and healthy houses'. Elsewhere, between March 1919 and February 1921, a series of legislative measures modified the system for financing low-rental housing, creating direct state subsidies and loans for municipal construction bodies as well as for low-rent housing associations. In return, the Chamber of Deputies rejected various proposals for laws aimed at creating new tax incentives to re-launch private construction.[121]

Government policy for encouraging new construction was expected by public authorities in all three capital cities. Totally or virtually inactive during the war, all now saw housing as their first priority. Their programmes returned to the grand designs of the early years of the century, when the cities had adopted the principle of urban planning as an expression of social housing policy. The new housing units would be organized in vast planned residential areas, based on a network of public transport, more united and extended than before 1914. It assumed the cooperation of large firms, public or private, capable of creating housing estates round the city centres. This grandiose vision informed attempts at coordinating initiatives in a fragmented local political scene, already disturbed before the war.

In Berlin, a first attempt at unifying municipal policies on transport, land use, and building regulation had led in 1911 to the creation of the

[119] Victor Noack, *Wohnungsnot und Mieterelend. Ein Erbstück des alten Staates* (Berlin, 1918), p. 30.

[120] See *Verhandlungen der Sozialisierungskommission über die Neuregelung des Wohnungswesens* (Vol II, Berlin, 1921), pp. 12-22. The Commission, created in 1918 by the Council movement, was re-established after the revolution had been crushed; it sought solutions to the housing problem in terms of its effects on work and social stability. Cf. Ludovica Scarpa, *Martin Wagner e Berlino* (Rome, 1983), pp. 18–19.

[121] See Magri and Topalov, 'Reconstruire', p. 360.

Zweckverband Gross-Berlin. On 7 November 1918 the new federal administration charged with housing had instituted the Wohnungsverband Gross-Berlin, with the task of coordinating local housing policies, confirming the preeminence of city centre over suburbs which had been established through supply policies during the war.[122] In April 1920 the Socialist and Social-Democratic majority in the Prussian Diet imposed a global and radical solution: the creation of Greater Berlin, attaching 93 adjacent administrative units to the city centre.[123] Set at the head of a vast city, the new local authority had to introduce a varied housing policy based on the operation of public-utility bodies for which it often had to be the principal agent in dealing with unions.[124]

In London, the creation of a Housing Committee to coordinate post-war building was suggested by the city's various local authorities and suburbs in conference between October 1918 and April 1919. But the plan failed, with the London County Council (LCC) wishing to retain full control of what promised to be considerable municipal expenditure.[125] The moderate majority in the LCC, confirmed in the 1919 elections, re-launched the housing policy suspended at the outbreak of war by planning the construction of 39,000 houses. Most were to be in Becontree, an immense housing estate of 24,000 units in the eastern suburbs, for the East End population who would travel into London daily on a new electrified railway line.

In Paris, the municipal council supported by suburban delegates attempted to carry out the long-standing plan to demolish the city's fortifications, an operation which would help to provide work for the immediate post-war unemployed and create space for low-cost housing and accommodation for the middle classes.[126] For its part, the Conseil général de la Seine planned to build eight garden cities as part of the planned urban and suburban expansion adopted in principle by the Paris Conseil municipal in 1911. This task was assigned to the Department's low-cost public housing bureau, set up in July 1914 with the mission to 'reduce congestion in the Paris conurbation and to ease its

[122] See Noack, *Wohnungsnot und Mieterelend*, p. 30.

[123] Eight towns, fifty-nine municipalities and twenty-six administrative districts. See Wolfgang Ribbe, 'Naissance du Grand-Berlin', in Lionel Richard (ed.), *Berlin, 1919–1933* Série Mémoires no. 10 (Paris, 1991), pp. 61–70.

[124] See Matzerath, 'Berlin, 1890-1940', pp. 305-8. Model housing estates in size, layout, and modernity of construction methods, such as the famous *Grossiedlung Britz* of 1925, were built in this way. See Scarpa, *Martin Wagner e Berlino*, pp. 36–46.

[125] The debates were reported in *The Times*, on 31 Oct., 13 and 26 Nov. 1918, and 5 and 28 Feb., 31 March and 11 and 30 April 1919.

[126] Louis Dausset, 'Proposition relative à l'exécution directe et immédiate, dès le vote de la loi, d'une partie de la démolition et de l'aménagement de l'enceinte fortifiée', Conseil municipal de Paris, *Rapports et documents de l'année 1918* (Paris, 1919), 10 December 1918.

expansion by the creation of model developments and garden cities'. The initial work of the bureau had been prepared by 1916 with the Conseil's first allocation of land reserves.[127]

These energetic initiatives were soon to fade, however. In all three nations, the return to social order, the downturn in trade, and the crisis in public finances undermined the ambitions of 1918. By July 1921 the Addison programme had been interrupted. It was eliminated the following year by the new Conservative government which introduced a system of subsidies much less favourable to local authorities.[128] In France, budgetary decisions considerably restricted the effect of the institutional reforms of 1919–20, and the building programme for 500,000 'economic and hygienic homes' proposed by Loucheur was not adopted.[129] In Germany the introduction of public-housing policies only began after 1924, once radical measures against hyperinflation had been adopted. Local projects were naturally affected; the operations planned by public authorities in the three capitals were cut back, put off, slowed down.

Yet new interventionist policies persisted. The war thus inaugurated the central state as director and author of municipal construction, but also as supporter of private construction. This role, paradoxically, could always have been justified by an opposing aim: to restore the free market. Nevertheless, possessive individualism would have to be sacrificed at the altar of rent control, renewed everywhere at the beginning of the 1920s.

[127] Henri Sellier, *La crise du logement et l'intervention publique en matière d'habitation populaire dans l'agglomération parisienne* (Paris, 1921), pp. 163–82.

[128] Johnson, *Land fit for heroes*, pp. 496–9.

[129] *Journal officiel*, Débats, Assemblée nationale, 3 Nov. 1921. The law failed in the Senate.

Part 6
Urban demography in wartime

14
The 'other war' I: protecting public health

Catherine Rollet

'The other war': the phrase comes from the title of George Cahen's book on public health, published in 1920.[1] It refers to the public-health front, the struggle against an invisible enemy capable of sudden and overwhelming attack nullifying the achievements of an entire nation. Images of illness as the enemy within, shadowing everyone at every stage of life, were vivid throughout the war. They expanded vigorously until health care became militarized, not only during but after the war. A Paris obstetrician told midwives in 1922: 'You are the vanguard of the army waging war on the monstrous plagues – gonococcal infection, syphilis, tuberculosis, even cancer.'[2] Before the Armistice, civil and military authorities were faced with the daunting challenge of waging war on disease at the same time as they waged war on the enemy.

Fear of epidemics and the notion of another front line in the nation's defence were universal. This chapter charts reactions to that peril in the three capital cities. This is a story of both successes, examined here, and failures, described in chapter 15.

As we noted in chapter 11, the pre-war system of social assistance in France was less developed than in Britain or Germany. This was also the case with respect to public-health care. Given the city's history of epidemic disease in wartime, Parisians had cause for anxiety about what the war would bring and what help there would be in the event of an outbreak of contagious disease. These fears were present in London and Berlin as well, and we chart efforts to still them in all three capital cities.

Positive responses to the dangers of the war emergency were evident in all three metropolitan centres. Despite fundamental differences in the organization of medical care and social provision, municipal authorities in Paris, London, and Berlin were able in the first half of the war to contain many of the potential hazards of war. Between 1914 and 1916, all

[1] Georges Cahen, *'L'autre guerre'. Essais d'assistance et d'hygiène sociale (1905-1920)* (Paris, 1920), as cited in the *Revue philanthropique*, 43 (15 May 1920), p. 206.

[2] Quoted by Françoise Thébaud, 'Donner la vie: histoire de la maternité en France entre les deux guerres', PhD thesis, University of Paris – VII, 1982, p. 367.

three cities were indeed able to withstand the upheaval of war without incurring a major recrudescence of epidemic diseases previously associated with armed conflict. Public-health authorities were put under severe pressure by the military mobilization, but they performed relatively well during the war. We examine this set of positive achievements in three areas: the control of potential urban epidemics of smallpox, typhoid, cholera; the protection of infant and maternal health; and the defence of adult well-being, with special reference to venereal disease, alcoholism, and work-related health.

In 1918–19, the three cities shared the common catastrophe of the influenza pandemic, discussed in chapter 15. But there the similarity between Paris and London, on one hand, and Berlin, one the other, ends. After 1916, the history of public health in Berlin deteriorated rapidly, and there was little municipal authorities could do to reverse the tide of misfortune progressively engulfing the municipal population.

On both sides, there were groups which did not share the aggregate experience, as we shall see in Chapter 15. But on the whole, the best way to characterize the trend in public health in the Allied capitals is as one of stability in wartime and of resumption of the pre-war downward trend in mortality rates after 1918. The contrast with Berlin is pronounced. From 1916, Berlin suffered a major increase in mortality rates, sufficiently severe to constitute a demographic crisis which continued until the early 1920s. That demographic crisis, described in chapter 16, was not replicated in London or Paris. The sources of this contrast did not lie primarily in the public-health system, but in the organization of the material life of the population as a whole.

Public-health systems 1900 to 1914

Hospital services and medicalization before the war

The adaptation of municipal institutions to the demands of war after 1914 reflected changing pre-war patterns of medical care and social provision. The war experience helped to accelerate already-existing trends towards the medicalization of the population, and towards the separation of public services providing medical care from those providing relief from material distress.

Let us consider medical care first. These three metropolitan centres were unusual in one respect. Each was a centre of medical care, with some of the finest hospital and medical facilities in the world. It should be no surprise, therefore, that the process of medicalization of the population was pronounced in these cities.

Many advances in medical knowledge had been registered there. Robert Koch's work on tuberculosis was conducted in Berlin, with the support of the Imperial Board of Health. He ran two medical research institutes, the Institute of Hygiene of the University of Berlin and the Royal Institute of Infectious Diseases, set up in 1885 and 1890 respectively. The Institut Pasteur illustrated the strength of metropolitan medical research in Paris, as did the great teaching hospitals in London.

Although medical advances in this period were notable, it was still the case that cures for the major endemic diseases were unavailable. Tuberculosis is one such case. Consequently, preventive medicine had as powerful a role to play as curative medicine in the field of metropolitan public health.

London's hospitals catered for both a huge metropolitan population and an international clientele. So did those in Paris. There the entire hospital system was reorganized in 1900, to give greater scope for medical specialization;[3] for example, the speciality of gynaecology and obstetrics became separate from general surgery in 1881. At the outbreak of the war, the Public Health department in Paris oversaw a hospital system of over 30,000 beds.[4]

Berlin had five main hospitals, four of which were managed by the city council and one by the Prussian administration (Charité). By far the largest establishment was the Rudolf Virchow, with nearly 2,000 beds in 1913, followed by the Charité with 1,175 beds. Specialized hospitals also existed for paediatrics and venereal diseases. There were also seven hospitals run by religious denominations and an establishment for lodging the homeless. Here we see the characteristic mix of private and public provision of increasingly sought-after medical services.

One example of rising demand is the increased recourse to hospital delivery of infants. Here the situation in Paris is striking. Of 48,962 births in 1911, nearly half took place outside the home, either in hospital (10,767) or at the midwife's house (10,892).[5] In London, 75 per cent of mothers gave birth in hospital.[6] Medicalization started here.

Elsewhere, the provision of out-patient clinics for both curative and preventative medicine had grown extensively, opening hospitals more fully to the general public. Hospital clinics for infants and municipal and private dispensaries played an important part in educating the public, in the prevention of digestive ailments and the dissemination of basic health information.

The concentration in the three cities of the largest hospitals, the most

[3] Catherine Rollet, *La politique à l'égard de la petite enfance sous la Troisème République* (Paris, 1990), p. 213.

[4] Paul Joanne, *Dictionnaire géographique et administratif de la France* (Paris, 1899), vol. V, article on Paris, pp. 3228-35.

[5] *Annuaire statistique de la ville de Paris*, 1911, pp. 82–5.

[6] J. M. Winter, 'Aspects of the impact of the First World War on infant mortality in Britain', *Journal of European Economic History*, 11, 3 (1980), pp. 713–38.

renowned medical advances, the great research laboratories, and quite simply the greatest number of doctors, inevitably played a role in accelerating medicalization. The concentration of personal wealth in certain metropolitan regions was a powerful force in drawing physicians to these cities. Among the 25,000 general practitioners of England and Wales, a disproportionate number was based in the south-east of the country, notably in London. The British Medical Association even tended to worry about the capital's excess numbers of doctors, attracted to the capital like filings to a magnet.[7]

Social provision and public health

To appreciate the character of pre-war and wartime public health measures, we must consider the forms of social insurance which underlay them. With respect to access to medical care through social insurance, Berliners had a marked advantage over both Londoners and Parisians.

In 1914 more than 40 per cent of the inhabitants of Berlin were covered by medical insurance, as members of the Sickness Fund managed by the Berlin Insurance Office (*Versicherungsamt*).[8] Those insured could arrange to be cared for by doctors recognized by their fund. Part of the remaining population had recourse to private insurance or arrangements with their employer's insurance. Those who remained without insurance had to depend on the city's Health Bureaux. Founded in 1871 as centres of medical reference, these offices became centres where the poor could be given free care and out-patient consultations. At the beginning of the twentieth century Berlin had fourteen centres of this kind operating in close association with the twenty Red Cross First Aid Posts established in industrial districts. These First Aid Posts were originally designed to help victims of industrial accidents; subsequently the Red Cross developed their role and took in all types of patients.[9]

The Berlin system[10] had no equivalent in London or Paris. The essential element in these cities was either individual initiative or public assistance. It should be noted, however, that in London, though hardly at all in Paris, mutual-aid societies partially filled this vacuum of

[7] J.M. Winter, *The Great War*, ch. 5.

[8] In August 1914, 835,782 men and women were registered as affiliated to this Berlin fund, representing, in a population of 2 million inhabitants, a rate of social insurance of 42 per cent (*Gross-Berlin Statistische Monatsberichte*, vol. 5, 1920, n. I/II, p. 44).

[9] Hygienischer Führer durch Berlin, *XIV Internationaler Kongress für Hygiene und Demographie Berlin* (Berlin, 1907), pp. 413–14.

[10] Regarding the laws of 1883–4, and their extension in 1889, see Volker Hentschel, *Geschichte der deutschen Sozialpolitik, 1880–1980* (Frankfurt am Main, 1983), p. 12.

coverage. In the British case in 1911 the National Insurance Act had coopted these groups as approved societies to administer the new system, which provided health and unemployment insurance to a minority (one-seventh) of the working population. Funding was shared in equal parts by wage-earners, employers, and the state. The system offered medical care to those insured through local doctors (Panel Doctors) whose services were paid for by the state. This scheme, however, did not resemble a national health service, and doctors jealously defended their principles of professional freedom. At the same time the 1911 act established free sanatoria for tuberculosis sufferers.[11]

Lacking obligatory or mutual insurance, a substantial proportion of the population was incapable of meeting medical expenses and was therefore forced to turn to social assistance. The scale of the problem in London was vast. Half of London's population of 4,000,000 consisted of manual workers and their families, of which one-third (perhaps 600,000) were families of casual unskilled labourers. Many worked in the environs of the Port of London. For them a visit to a doctor, which cost £1 – a week's wages – was a prohibitive expense. To this financial problem was added the vast social and cultural gap separating the world of the doctors from that of the labouring poor who did not always see medical treatment as particularly beneficial. A minority of Londoners never consulted a doctor in their lives and looked to bone-setters, healers, and abortionists to treat them, from the cradle to the grave. In many instances, who is to say they were the worse off for this unconventional treatment?

Better placed – both financially and socially – were middle-class Londoners. They could count on regular medical care either individually or in hospital. Given the concentration of physicians in the London area, it is safe to conclude that about half the metropolitan population was more than adequately covered in this respect.

Approximately the same system operated in Paris, with divisions into three sectors: individual insurance, mutual-aid societies for wage-earners, and medical aid for the poor. The last option – free medical assistance for the needy – was set up in 1893. A medical consultation in Paris cost between 3 and 5 francs, the equivalent of a day's work for a low-skilled worker or a half-day for a skilled worker. Medical care was thus more easily accessible than in London; and the social gap between a doctor and his patient was probably much smaller than in London.

The history of public health in this period overlaps at many points with the history of philanthropy and private initiatives. Groups and individuals responded to needs that were poorly covered by public

[11] J.M. Winter, 'Le mouvement travailliste en Grande-Bretagne et les problèmes de la santé publique (1900–1948)', *Prévenir*, 19 (1989), pp. 125–40.

assistance. In others, public authorities explicitly delegated projects of general interest to them. At the district level, social assistance and health agencies worked together to provide shelter, food, and clothing for the poor.

The British Poor Law system operated on the same basis, sheltering and caring for the indigent and the ill in workhouses and helping or feeding those who did not live permanently in public institutions. This system, the ultimate recourse for the very poorest and particularly the old, was not abolished until 1929, when hospitals and old people's homes were municipalized. The same mixed functions marked the work of the Bureaux de Bienfaisance in Paris, which put forward lists of the indigent and distributed help in kind, in cash, or through medical care.

In fact if not in law, the different services were combined, at all levels of the institutional pyramid. At the very top of the French hierarchy, there was a 'Directorate of Public Aid and Hygiene', which combined the services previously under the aegis of the Ministry of the Interior and the Ministry of Trade. The simple concept behind this strategy was that it was useless to wish to restore people's health if they lacked the essential minimum material needs for survival.

The same principle underpinned the activities of the many charitable societies of religious or secular origin in the three capital cities. In London the Protestant benevolent tradition inspired many local initiatives, independent of public authorities, backed either by the churches or privately, such as the Charity Organization Society. Directly, through Health Visitors at home and through dispensaries, or indirectly through contributing to hospital fees, these societies played an important part in the health domain, very frequently connecting it with social aid and education. In London, the Jewish or Irish communities had their own system of health and social assistance, concentrating in particular on newly arrived immigrants.[12]

As in London so in Paris medical care and social provision were combined in the public-aid system, the Assistance Publique. Paris occupied a unique status in the French administration,[13] and the number of institutions concerned with public health was large. Consequently the administration of hospitals, the organization of aid for the poor, and the guardianship of children in care in the Department of the Seine was the charge of a unique administrative system, the Paris Public Aid Department. Its director, nominated by the Minister of the Interior, did the work done elsewhere both by mayors, who ran hospitals and aid offices, and by departmental agencies for children in

12 Lara Marks, '"Dear old Mother Levy's": the Jewish Maternity Home and Sick Room Helps Society, 1895–1939', *Social History of Medicine*, 3, 1 (1990), pp. 24–43.

13 On which see Joanne, *Dictionnaire*, pp. 3171–2.

care. Where health and social assistance were concerned, the Paris Public Aid Department acted as a state within a state, run by a 35-member supervisory council. It was required to manage some thirty hospitals and their substantial budgets. it was also responsible for the general area of medical and social care for children, mothers, the poor, the indigent, and the needy.

Whereas the insurance system in Germany was centralized, the system of health care was decentralized, and in Berlin (as elsewhere) entrusted to the private sector. There was no municipal office of public health in Berlin until 1915. The fulfilment of public-health needs depended, therefore, on a wide range of philanthropic institutions. One of the striking features of the history of public health in Berlin was the unique blend of official responsibility and private initiative. Philanthropic and charitable organizations ensured medical care for a significant section of the labouring population and represented the only source of medical treatment for many of them. Protestant, Jewish, and Catholic churches were active at the parish level, particularly in providing aid for families and single mothers. Most parishes also had a system of aid for the poor, and operated soup kitchens.[14] The Jewish community was prominent in the area of child protection. In Berlin alone it supported twenty-four houses and foundations for children, including six orphanages.[15] It also provided houses for the handicapped and old people.

In sum, on the eve of the war, public-health systems in all three cities dealt both with transfer payments for the needy and with medical care for a broad population. The way they did so varied considerably. The French approach did too, until the 1911 National Insurance Act broke new ground. Its nascent provisions on the eve of the war were still not nearly as universal as the German system, covering about half the population.

With respect to medical care, the Parisian system was distinctive. At its centre was the *Assistance Publique*. In contrast, in Berlin and London, provision for the working classes rested in the hands of hospitals and charities; for the middle classes, a prosperous and numerous medical community was at their service.

Public-health authorities

Each of London's boroughs had its own Local Health Committee, as did the County of London as a whole. These committees, made up of elected

[14] *Die Wohlfahrtseinrichtungen von Gross-Berlin, Zentrale für private Fürsorge* (Berlin, 1910), p. 28.

[15] *Handbuch der jüdischen Gemeindeverwaltung und Wohlfahrtspflege*, vol. XXI, Berlin, 1913, pp. 241–3.

councillors, considered essential matters such as drains, roads, and insanitary housing. They worked closely with school doctors, who were concerned with children's physical conditions and health. A central figure was the Medical Officer of Health (MOH), an official of the Local Government Board; apart from the Board of Education, this was the body responsible for questions of the nation's health. The name itself expressed the balance of power in this area. This board had little bureaucratic power; by the war it was more or less moribund, making the creation of the Ministry of Health in 1919 no real surprise. In the midst of the war, there was serious debate on the matter of transferring the functions of the Poor Law Guardians; the theory was that, within a public-health framework, different populations require different treatment. It was absurd to carry on with the old system whereby all the needs were lumped together in a general mixed workhouse. Specialization of care and differentiation of services were pre-war ideas given added force by the war emergency.[16]

From 1855 MOHs were concerned primarily with hygiene and public sanitation. Later their duties were extended and they delegated part of their functions to other municipal officials, who looked after verification of causes of death, disinfection, inspection of public markets, milk supplies, bakeries, unhygienic establishments, and so on. As Anne Wilkinson has shown,[17] the MOHs occupied an unusual position. They were wholly outside the Poor Law system, and therefore avoided the suspicion or opprobrium attached to it. They could challenge the sanctity of private property if they believed it necessary in the campaign to improve public health. Through their deep local knowledge, and the trust they won, many MOHs were able to act to better the well-being of the local community.

In Paris the system of local-health policy through the *Assistance Publique* was much more centralized than in London. State services were widely scattered among the police préfecture, the préfecture of the Seine, and several Commissions. Directly dependent on the Seine Préfecture, inspectors were required to verify deaths or inspect children in care. Three specific services operated under the Préfet's direction, including public assistance. The Seine Préfecture had developed powers of prevention, exercised through the Commission for Assistance and Sanitary Housing with the Préfet acting as its chairman. Also under his direction was the hygienic-housing registry, introduced in the middle of the 1890s, and requiring close supervision. Every house in

[16] Denise Moniez-Terracher, 'La reconstruction sociale en Angleterre', *Revue philanthropique*, 39, 253 (15 Sept. 1918), pp. 369–77.

[17] Anne Wilkinson, 'Disease in the nineteenth-century urban economy: the Medical Officer of Health and the Community', unpublished paper presented to the Society for the Social History of Medicine, meeting, January 1978.

Paris was listed and described, and every death due to transmissible disease recorded with indications of measures taken, supplementary inquiries, etc. Similarly the Commission for Insanitary Housing, with the Préfet as chairman, inspected accommodation and recommended remedial action where necessary.[18]

The police Préfecture was also responsible for several facets of health care: supervision of maternity clinics, crèches, nurseries, inquests on suicides, accidents, and lost children. One division was particularly concerned with matters of sanitation, hygiene, epidemics, and the supervision of midwives. Inspectors were charged with inspecting health clinics, maternity homes, day nurseries, and wet-nursing facilities. Even more significantly, the Préfet de Police was chairman of the Public Hygiene and Sanitation Council for the Department of the Seine. Formerly the Sanitary Council, this body included administrators, scientists, architects, and doctors, and gave advice on all questions of health and hygiene. Dependent on this council, hygiene commissions – one for each arrondissement – collected local information, issued notices and inspected areas suffering from contagious disease. Finally, both the Conseil municipal and the Conseil général had one or more commissions devoted to health and public assistance.

The organization of health and assistance was apparently simpler in London, with powers remaining more firmly in the hands of local decentralized bodies. Under closer inspection, however, the similarities between the London and Paris systems were considerable. The two national bodies, the Direction de l'Assistance et de l'Hygiène publique and the Local Government Board, were very similar in their structure, consisting of parallel departments concerned with various aspects of health and often in dispute with each other.[19]

Berlin resembled both Paris and London. As in London there was a Local Public Health Physician (Kreisarzt), a position introduced following a law of 1899 for towns of more than 5,000 inhabitants. This single civil servant, who was a specialist in social hygiene, presided over a health commission and worked in tandem with the local magistrate on questions of public health.[20] However, Berlin had no true office of health and hygiene (Medizinalamt) until September 1915.[21] Despite repeated demands from the members of the city council for a unified service of

18 Joanne, *Dictionnaire*, p. 3224.

19 Sandra M. Tomkins, 'Britain and the influenza epidemic of 1918–1919', PhD thesis, University of Cambridge, 1989, p. 76. Rollet, *La politique*, p. 293.

20 See E. Dietrich, 'Die Entwicklung der Medizinalverwaltung und der socialen Hygiene bis zur Novemberumwälzung', *Berliner Klinische Wochenschrift*, 56, 2 (27 Jan. 1919), pp. 76–7.

21 Stadtarchiv Berlin, Rep. 00-02/1 1812: Medizinalamt der Stadt Berlin, 1914–1920.

inspection and disinfection, the case for municipal authority was insufficiently strong to gain support before the war.[22]

In other respects, some of Berlin's services were very similar to those in Paris, notably the city's disinfection bureau and bureau of statistics. The former was evidently the equivalent of the French Casier sanitaire des habitations. Founded in 1884, its purpose was to carry out disinfection of housing, furniture, and possessions used by those suffering from contagious diseases. The figures for 1913 give an indication of the bureau's scale of activity: 1,067 housing units disinfected on average each month. In the year as a whole, action was taken with respect to disinfection due to diphtheria (5,452), scarlet fever (5,242 cases) and respiratory tuberculosis (3,240 cases).[23]

The statistical offices in Berlin and Paris[24] resembled each other closely in other respects. Under the management of Heinrich Silbergleit since 1906, the Berlin office published a very substantial statistical report each year, with much detail on mortality rates among Berliners and the illnesses threatening their health. In Paris it was the Bertillon family which presided over the city's statistical office: Louis-Adolphe Bertillon was succeeded by his son Jacques, a convinced populationist and statistician of international repute and author of the first proposal for international classification of causes of death. During the war he directed the army's medico-surgical statistical record.[25] London statistics were prepared both by the London County Council and by the General Register Office, and under T.H.W. Stevenson achieved a standard of professional excellence at least equal to that of any other service in the world.

The collection of statistics is one thing; action to remedy health problems is another. Here we must note the relatively slow pace of development of health policy in these three cities and of the agencies to realize it. Despite the growing role of the state in matters of health, there were still formidable barriers which prevented its full development before the Great War. In the name of individual freedom and the sanctity of the domestic world, intervention by central public powers was restricted and, to a degree, suspect even among those who needed help. Philanthropic agencies and charities (in London and Berlin more than in Paris) filled the gap at the local level.

[22] This delay was linked with a dispute between the Magistrate and the members of the city council; See 'Städtisches Medizinalamt', *Vossische Zeitung*, 24 (23 April 1914); see also Stadtarchiv Berlin, Rep. 00-2/1 1812.

[23] *Statistisches Jahrbuch der Stadt Berlin*, vol. 33 (1912–14), p. 697.

[24] See Joshua Cole, 'The history of demographic statistics in France 1860–1900', PhD thesis, University of California at Berkeley, 1990.

[25] Michel Dupâquier, 'La famille Bertillon et la naissance d'une nouvelle science sociale: la démographie', *Annales de démographie historique* (1982), pp. 293–311.

In conclusion, it is clear that systems of medical care and social provision differed widely among these three metropolitan centres. The Bismarckian system provided Berliners with a form of coverage available to Londoners and Parisians in at best a rudimentary and partial form. But within these parameters, all three populations were able to find more and better medical provision in the pre-war years. On balance, there was little to choose among the three systems of public health. Each had advantages and disadvantages; each was sufficiently flexible to meet the challenges of the first phase of the war.

The shock of war

The shock of the outbreak of war to public-health systems was profound. Within a few weeks doctors and hospital teams in the three capitals were faced with caring for thousands of wounded and mutilated men, as we have seen in chapter 3. Examination of the *Bulletin de l'Académie de Médecine* during the war illustrates what were probably the most urgent medical matters in the three cities.[26] We cite French evidence, but there is a mountain of German and British literature which covers the same ground. The overwhelmingly dominant theme of medical reports and discussions is undoubtedly the treatment of wounded soldiers, with priority for the care, nursing, and rehabilitation of soldiers. The headings in this journal indicate the practical questions doctors had to answer: many articles dealt with wounds and techniques for finding projectiles in the body, the heart, or the lungs. The respective merits of different techniques, such as oxygenated water or radiography, are presented and compared. Doctors debated the treatment of projectile wounds according to sites – nerves, eyes, bladder, larynx, nose, ears, etc. – and the best ways to avoid gangrene and tetanus in wounds. Fractures were the subject of lengthy articles and discussion: how to achieve a good mend, so that the patient would not remain severely handicapped for life? Doctors considered the placing of splints, the materials to be used (rubberized lead, semi-rigid, expanding, etc.), fitting of artificial limbs, functional prostheses, rehabilitation. Amputations were also frequently discussed: which drugs to prescribe, which surgical procedures to use? How to prevent further pathology? Questions of care and rehabilitation for the blind, the deaf, and the handicapped were the subject of many studies.[27]

Equally, there were long debates on health at the front: after an extensive debate on frostbitten feet, a consensus was arrived at in favour of the use of grease and loose-fitting socks. 'Trench diarrhoea', or

[26] *Bulletin de l'Académie de Médecine*, weekly, 1915 to 1918.

[27] Concerning the handicapped, see the *Revue philanthropique*, 39, 247 (15 March 1916).

dysentery, was studied attentively. There was interest too in contagious disease in the army: exanthematous typhus (the battle against lice), tuberculosis, venereal disease, typhoid (water hygiene), diphtheria, scarlet fever. Such concerns illustrate the role of curative medicine and surgery in this period of the war. Medicine's preventative mission was less prominent initially than its rehabilitative and curative work.

Much more clearly, the scientific dimension of medical work took on greater prominence. Experts were needed – specialists in creative dental work, pharmacy, laboratory analysis, and radiology. 'Dental construction', wrote a French Senator, Paul Strauss, 'has acquired a new and tragic element.'[28] It also acquired a new profile as work of national importance.

At the same time that hospitals had to take in wounded men, they had to expel many of those who had come to them before the war for shelter and nourishment; in addition, long-term civilian patients had to make room for soldiers in need. This arose in part due to the serious shortage of beds, medicines, and all forms of manufactured products – but above all of medical staff.

In Paris the army requisitioned nearly 4,500 beds from the public-health sector (out of a total of approximately 33,000 beds), and nearly 1,000 beds outside the capital. Of these, the seaside hospital at Berck-Plage specialized in the treatment of children suffering from scrofula. In August and September 1914 sanatoria, old people's homes, and nurseries were closed in the Paris area. Tubercular invalids, handicapped babies, and healthy or ailing old people were variously returned to their families. The tubercular patients of the Villemin sanatorium, for example, were de-hospitalized, along with many others thereby freed to spread the disease, a phenomenon with consequences outlined in chapter 15. Others were moved to provincial establishments, often under distressing circumstances, like the old people from several homes and nursing homes and the abandoned children from the orphanage at Antony. Some were resettled in Paris establishments.[29] Requisitioned once more by the army in 1916, the Berck hospital with its 400 beds was a severe loss to the Paris public-health department, and the city council insistently demanded its return to civilian use.[30]

The figures for patients treated in the same Paris hospitals for the years 1913, 1914, and 1915 show relative stability, suggesting efficient adaptation to war conditions. But there was a change in the duration of stay of patients. The only marked difference between 1915 and the previous years concerns the number of patients remaining from the

[28] *Revue philanthropique*, 39, 253 (15 Sept. 1918), p. 400.

[29] Henri Rousselle, 'Note sur les travaux de la 5ème commission (Assistance publique – Crédit municipal) pendant la guerre 1914–1919, *Rapport du conseil municipal de Paris*, no. 51 (1916), p. 16. [30] *Ibid.*, no. 51, 26 Dec. 1916.

previous year – four times the normal figure – hence the reduced number of admissions in 1915. In 1915 and 1916 the hospitals admitted fewer civilian patients than before the war (30,000 fewer on average), with the result that the figure for patients treated shows a net deficit in the middle of the war (210,000 patients instead of 240,000). In contrast, 1918 and subsequent years are marked by a very noticeable increase, because of patients already present on 1 January and a rapidly increasing rate of admissions.[31] Earlier in the war, fewer patients were admitted to hospital, because those already there stayed longer; that was no longer the case in 1918.

Towards the end of the war an increase in hospital capacity can be seen. In addition the number of clinics held in welfare centres and the number of patients cared for at home increased appreciably. This is the reality lurking behind the term 'medicalization'.

In all three cities, hospital teams had to operate without the usual medical personnel, chief medical officers and students, with growing problems of supply in a climate of distress which, in the case of Paris, reached a peak in 1918 under daily bombardment. In 1915 in Paris public-health hospitals had 17 unfilled vacancies out of a staff of 105. The situation was worse for surgery, with 36 gaps out of 71 posts. House doctors and non-resident doctors alike, mobilized in large numbers, had to be replaced by retired men and by students.[32]

In London, the pressure of war service was less severe. Mobilization of doctors was supervised by the British Medical Association. The central Medical War Committee estimated that a proportion of approximately one doctor for 3,000 people represented the minimum need in urban areas, but in 1917, after three years of military recruitment, the County of London was still better endowed with physicians than the average. With approximately 1,835 general practitioners in London for a population of over 4 million people, the rate was 1:2,500.[33]

In Berlin, the potential danger in wartime was a shortage of hospital beds for civilians. Across Germany as a whole nearly half the doctors were mobilized[34] and many hospitals were requisitioned by the army.

[31] The figures show discrepancies between the number of patients present on 1 January of one year and those for 31 December for the previous year. Such variance occurred in 1915, 1916, and 1918. See *Annuaire statistique de la ville de Paris*.

[32] Henri Rousselle, *Rapport . . . Conseil municipal de Paris*, no. 60 (1915), p. 22.

[33] BMA Archive, Central Medical War Committee papers, 'Report by the Assessment Sub-committee and the Executive Sub-committee on the Calls Made on LMWCs to Meet the Present Demands of the War Office', January 1917; as cited in J.M. Winter, *The Great War*, pp. 183–5.

[34] This estimate comes from an official of the Ministry of the Interior, Dr Lenz. See Dr Lenz, '*Die Seuchenbekämpfung in Preussen während des Krieges und ihr Ergebnis bis Ende 1915. Veröffentlichungen aus dem Gebiete der Medizinalverwaltung*, vol. VI, no. 3, Berlin, 1916, p. 4.

In Berlin itself the total number of hospital beds available dropped by 6 per cent between 1913 and 1917. Private clinics, together with clinics operated by religious groups, appear to have been even more severely affected by the mobilization of medical staff than the public hospitals (a loss of 24 per cent for the former and an increase of only 1.5 per cent for the latter).[35] In order to avoid the abrupt reduction in medical services and the collapse of public health administration, the government mobilized the forces available and attempted to maintain the existing offices with minimum staff. The chemical and bacteriological research establishments functioned largely because of the contribution of women who had previously only assisted their male colleagues. Nevertheless, on balance, Berlin was well supplied with medical personnel in wartime. On the eve of the war, Berlin had 4,758 physicians, or a ratio of one doctor for 435 inhabitants in a population of 2 million people.[36] Here Londoners and Berliners shared an advantage not enjoyed by the Parisian population.

Defeating the traditional plagues: smallpox, typhoid fever, diphtheria

To what extent did the conflict affect the civilian population's state of health and the ways public authorities faced up to wartime epidemic and endemic disease? The first set of answers to these questions concerns nineteenth-century scourges: smallpox, typhoid fever, and diphtheria.

The need for vigilance in the struggle against the traditional plagues was an urgent issue in Paris and Berlin at the beginning of the war. The memory of the serious smallpox epidemic and the excess number of deaths due to tuberculosis and typhoid fever caused by the siege of Paris and the Commune in 1870 to 1871 was still clear in people's minds.[37] Aware of the health risks to civilians caused by large-scale movement of troops, the inflow of refugees and the creation of new hospitals, the Paris city authorities took various preventative measures from the outbreak of war to combat smallpox and typhoid fever in particular. In the case of smallpox, pre-war plans existed for just such an emergency.

An emergency plan relating to typhoid fever was drawn up at the beginning of the war. It was the second disease (after smallpox) targeted by the decree of 14 August 1914; the plan was concerned with scrupulous surveillance of water sources of all kinds, disinfection

[35] *Statistisches Jahrbuch der Stadt Berlin*, vol. 33, p. 630; vol. 34, p. 621.

[36] *Statistik des Deutschen Reiches*, 1907, vol. 204, p. 92.

[37] The siege of Paris and the Commune had led to nearly 70,000 excess deaths, of which 6,450 were due to tuberculosis, 11,666 to smallpox, 5,060 to typhoid, and 5,600 to violence. See Marcel Moine, *Recherches et considérations générales sur la mortalité à Paris depuis la Restauration* (Paris, 1941), p. 26.

operations (chlorination), supervision of milk and food supplies, and promotion of vaccination.

The dean of the faculty of medicine in Paris, Dr Landouzy, set an example by personally carrying out 600 anti-typhoid injections in the Léon Bourgeois clinic between 19 August 1914 and 13 July 1915. During the same period, Dr Chantemesse administered 3,722 vaccinations in the Ecole Polytechnique.[38] Despite the severe cut in staff numbers, the hygiene laboratory and the disinfection service carried out their work so well that the number of disinfection operations dropped by only 9 per cent in 1914. Similarly, housing-hygiene inspection continued, and seems to have been effective, given the statistics on water-borne infections in wartime. Between 1 January and 15 October 1914 only 1,521 cases of typhoid were registered in Paris instead of the five-year average of 2,069. Twenty-nine deaths from typhoid were registered for the months of May, June and July 1915, as against seventy-three for the same period in 1914. The drop certainly reflected a smaller population, but it also signified a relatively healthy state of sanitation.[39] Subsequently, rates of illness and death from typhoid fever fell without interruption. The war itself appears to have helped, by forcing ahead a range of measures relating to chlorination and vaccination which would otherwise have taken longer to enact.[40]

This did not preclude very real problems concerning other contagious diseases. In 1915, for example, the drop in availability of hospital facilities added to the usual difficulties of the peak periods for some illnesses (the spring and summer), particularly for measles and scarlet fever.[41]

However, the most effective measures undertaken in Paris were in connection with smallpox. The alert was sounded with an outbreak of smallpox between October 1911 and May 1912, with fifty-two cases in the first five months of 1912, including five deaths. From the outbreak of war and under the provisions of the August 1914 decree, a large-scale vaccination operation was undertaken so as to apply the 1902 law[42] fully and to protect the great majority of the population. Propaganda posters and press announcements accompanied the opening of vaccination centres to the public. More than 6,000 posters were plastered on to the city's walls to warn the people of the need for vaccination and re-vaccination, indicating places and dates of sessions. These were organized in settings as varied as welfare offices, war shelters, hospitals,

[38] Léon Bernard, *La défense de la santé publique pendant la guerre*, Publication de la Dotation Carnegie pour la paix internationale (Paris, 1929), pp. 55–85.

[39] Louis Dausset, *Rapport . . . sur . . . le projet de budget de la ville de Paris pour 1916*, 1916, pp. 90–1. [40] Bernard, *La défense de la santé*, p. 65.

[41] Henri Rousselle, *Rapport . . . du Conseil municipal de Paris*, no. 60, 1915, p. 21.

[42] The law made vaccination obligatory under the age of one year, and re-vaccination obligatory between ten and eleven years and between twenty and twenty-one years.

dispensaries, public authority offices, large private offices, charitable establishments in the city of Paris, schools, the Institut Pasteur, the Academy of Medicine, and the headquarters of the Seine ports, as well as in domestic houses, particularly in the *ilôts insalubres* (insanitary accommodation blocks) designated for special attention by the sanitary lodgings registry. The people flocked to these centres, particularly the women, who often resisted vaccination.

Compared to the pre-war period, the achievements in wartime were striking: from less than 190,000 per year,[43] the number of vaccinations and re-vaccinations rose to 614,987 in 1914, falling back to 228,570 in 1915, and stood at approximately 160,000 in 1916, despite the drop in population. The total for 1914–16 was nearly one million as against 854,000 for the five years 1909–13, a figure greater than could have been anticipated from a strict application of the 1902 law. Bureaucratic zeal extended to organizing home vaccination sessions in overcrowded houses with a single case of chickenpox!

The record to be drawn up from these records is indeed highly favourable: in 1914, twelve cases of smallpox were registered, one of varioloid (a variant of smallpox) and one death; in 1915, one case of smallpox, three of varioloid and one death; and in 1916, one death. Noting the figures, the city councillors were able to congratulate themselves on the measures taken: the pleasing results were due, in their eyes, to the intensity of the vaccination service's operations and their methodical application. Dr Roux, the Institut Pasteur's eminent specialist, proclaimed: 'It is the first time that a war has occurred on French soil without an accompanying smallpox epidemic.[44] This prophecy was proved wrong, for although there were no deaths in 1917, smallpox reappeared in 1918 in the form of a minor epidemic which caused twenty-six deaths in Paris, including nine children under the age of ten and seven people over fifty. This was, however, very far from the 11,666 deaths from smallpox during the Franco-Prussian War.

Paris had been relatively backward in the fight against infectious disease when compared with the other two capital cities, but used the war to promote a successful general campaign of prophylaxis against disease. It was therefore a matter of filling a gap which had persisted despite legislation adopted in 1902.

In Berlin smallpox was in effect no more than a distant memory, for legislation adopted as early as 1874 had virtually eliminated it from the German empire by the end of the nineteenth century. The heading

[43] 139,428 in 1908; 159,290 in 1909; 165,575 in 1910; 167,638 in 1911; 186,629 in 1912, and 175,468 in 1913. These statistics are taken from Rousselle, *Rapport . . . Conseil municipal de Paris*.

[44] Emile Deslandres, *Rapport sur le fonctionnement du service de la Vaccination depuis l'année 1914 jusqu'à ce jour*, Conseil municipal de Paris, no. 39, 25 Nov, 1916.

'smallpox' does not appear in German statistics after 1897, although Berlin hospital records show that there were still a few cases on the eve of the war and that smallpox reappeared briefly, indeed twice during the war itself. The first outbreak was in 1915, with 30 cases and 2 deaths; the second, more substantial, was in 1917, with 317 cases and 35 deaths. The absence of statistics for 1918–20 precludes any comment on the subsequent course or control of the epidemic.[45]

In London, although forced to deal with powerful anti-vaccination groups, the public authorities finally managed to convince public opinion of the vaccine's value. Smallpox had not reached epidemic proportions since 1902.[46] During the war itself, three deaths from smallpox were recorded in 1915; but none in 1914, 1916, 1917, or 1918. In the immediate post-war period there were six deaths in 1919 and four in 1920. These were relatively minor incidents in a war against the disease which had already been won.

Treatment of diphtheria in Berlin in certain respects can be likened to Parisian experiences with smallpox and typhoid fever, since Berlin hospital figures reveal a significant epidemic in 1915 and 1916. The number of patients taken into hospital increased by 41 and 85 per cent during these two years, compared to the pre-war levels. Despite this outbreak, however, diphtheria mortality declined slightly; although 14 per cent of patients suffering from this disease died before the war, only 11 per cent died in 1914 and 10 per cent in 1916, at the height of the epidemic.

This outcome is probably attributable in part to the actions undertaken by Berlin's Magistrate and by the City Council. In the autumn of 1915 the councillors, noting the unusual increase in cases of diphtheria, decided to make a stand against the epidemic. In particular it was observed that many women left on their own when their husbands were at the front had to continue working even when they or their children were ill. Extra beds were made available in both general and children's hospitals and the mayor sought funds to help the hospitals take in increased numbers of diphtheria patients. On 11 november 1915 the proposal was accepted and all diphtheria sufferers were able to go into hospital even if they were suffering from only a mild attack and had no money. At the same time a network of nurses was established in collaboration with the new *Medizinalamt* system, in order to carry out home visits to all patients suffering from infectious illness.[47] The system finally managed to isolate diphtheria sufferers almost completely and place them in quarantine. Coverage was not total but it was very

45 *Statistisches Jahrbuch der Stadt Berlin*, vols. 32, 33, 34.

46 Pierre Darmon, *La longue traque de la variole* (Paris, 1986), pp. 386–404.

47 Stadtarchiv Berlin, Rep. 00-02/1 1872, Die auf dem Gebiete der Seuchenbekämpfung getroffenen Maßnahmen, pp. 2–4, 6.

considerable, for a report on statistics gathered by nurses (*Fürsorgeschwestern*) shows that out of 9,367 cases of diphtheria in 1916, 6,684 were taken into hospital.[48] Home visits helped to reduce mortality: there were 647 recorded deaths in 1916, but 595 the following year. Mortality rates stood at 9.7 and 12.5 per cent instead of the 13–14 per cent in the period 1910 to 1912.[49]

The same hospital statistics indicate no appreciable outbreak of typhoid in Berlin for the years 1914 to 1917, and in 1916 it was in decline. Once more we find evidence of relative success in breaking the pattern whereby major war and mass epidemics went hand in hand.[50]

In conclusion, there were varying levels of memory of the link between epidemic and military conflict in the three cities and consequently varying levels of vigilance in August 1914. Paris was particularly attentive to regulation of the smallpox problem and Berlin to that of diphtheria.

Concerning typhoid, Léon Bernard expressed the opinion immediately after the war that 'the conflict hastened a decision which would otherwise have been taken in a more leisurely fashion'. This interpretation could be applied to all the 'classic' infectious illnesses; the war played its part in revealing and instigating, or of accelerating the introduction of prophylactic measures against preventable disease such as smallpox, typhoid fever, and diphtheria. Given the relative backwardness of Paris with respect to public-health structures, and given the seriousness of the military crises in 1914, it is apparent that this 'concentration of minds' enabled the French capital to act in a strikingly innovative way, with beneficial results in terms of the health of the civilian population virtually in the front line.

Protecting infancy: a priority

Initiatives

In all three cities the war created a powerful consensus on the need to enhance the protection of maternal and child health.[51] The struggle

[48] E. Seligman, 'Bericht über die Tätigkeit der Fürsorgeschwestern der Medizinalamtes der Stadt Berlin in Jahre 1917', *Berliner Klinische Wochenschrift*, 55, 25 (24 June 1918), pp. 599–600.

[49] *Statistisches Jahrbuch der Stadt Berlin*, vols. 32, 33, 34.

[50] F. Prinzing, *Wars and epidemics* (Oxford, 1916).

[51] Sigrid Stöckel, 'Die Bekämpfung der Säuglingssterblichkeit im Kaiserreich und in der Weimarer Republik', unpublished thesis, Freie Universität Berlin, 1992. On the war period, see J. M. Winter and J. Cole, 'Fluctuations in infant mortality rates during and after the First World War', *European Journal of Population*, 9 (1993), pp. 235–63. On London, see J. M. Winter, J. Lawrence, and J. Ariouat, 'The impact of the Great War on infant mortality in London', *Annales de démographie historique* (1993), pp. 329–53.

against infant mortality, many thought, was one way of redressing the demographic imbalance created by mass slaughter and thereby of 'saving the race'. To protect children, to provide good conditions for their survival and growth, was a patriotic and humane duty and the best way to share in tomorrow's national defence. The atmosphere favoured highly purposeful slogans celebrating childhood. As 'the Nation's sacred source,[52] childhood had to be protected systematically 'in the name of the Nation'. This rhetoric was shared by men and women of all political persuasions, though some differences persisted as to who should pay for these essential services. We must note that rhetoric and cash only occasionally went hand in hand.

Nevertheless, it is apparent that the pre-war period was one of major initiatives in the defence of child health in all three metropolitan centres. This incorporated better provision for antenatal care and examinations, better perinatal care, and a wide variety of services for mothers and children. In Berlin, for example, municipal authorities and private foundations worked hand in hand to help mothers and children in need.[53] Similar initiatives were launched in Paris and London.

Such initiatives for the protection of mothers and babies – maternity assistance, health care and the distribution of milk and baby food – were severely disrupted from the very beginning of the war. Central authorities took some action to limit the damage the war could cause to family life. This is the origin of family allowances paid to soldiers' wives and graduated according to the size of their families.[54] Two German laws passed in August and December 1914 (*Kriegshilfe* on 4 August 1914 and *Reichswochenhilfe* on 3 December 1914) provided similar allowances in Germany.[55]

Statute was one thing; reality another. The maintenance of these measures by local authorities varied considerably from one capital city to another. In Paris these measures were maintained largely through the drive of central authorities,while in London and above all in Berlin, we see the primacy of private and philanthropic action. Administrative foul-ups were inevitable, leading to real deprivation in the early phase

52 See, for example, W. Clarke Hall, *The state and the child* (London, 1917). For earlier precedents, see Margaret McMillan, *The child and the state* (London, 1911); before that, Florence Davenport-Hill, *Children of the state* (1868).

53 One instance in Berlin was the allocation of milk supplies for children (*Städtische Säuglingsfürsorgestelle*), set up through consultations with a private foundation, Schmidt-Gallisch Stiftung. These allocations were known as *Stillprämie*. See Fritz Rott, *Umfang, Bedeutung und Ergebnisse der Unterstützungen an stillende Mütter* (Berlin, 1914), p. 42.

54 Susan Pedersen, *Family, dependence, and the origins of the welfare state: Britain and France 1914–1945* (Cambridge, 1993).

55 *Reichs-Gesetzblatt*, no. 53, 1914, pp. 332–3.

of the war. After the initial hectic months of war, such problems were reduced, if not resolved.

Positions on financing these services followed political lines in Berlin. While the Social Democratic party was committed to the idea that protection for pregnant mothers and their babies should be paid from municipal funds, the municipal council (Magistrate) won the day with the opposing view, judging that it was a matter for charitable organizations and not public institutions. Moreover, as the non-interventionists pointed out, some doctors believed that children gained from the female unemployment caused by the war because their mothers could stay at home with them.[56]

Such was the level of complacency in some circles at the outbreak of the war. Later, however, and especially from 1916 onwards, awareness of the inadequacy of local efforts grew. It was obvious that centralized state action was required, through the Kriegsfürsorgeamt, empowered to coordinate public and private initiatives. Two measures in particular were introduced: one for the distribution of milk and adequate food for children, and a second for eduction in child-care for mothers and young girls. On 5 September 1918 such instruction began in the prestigious Kaiser und Kaiserin Friedrich Kinderkrankenhaus.

A whole series of initiatives was launched in 1917. Efforts were directed to provide food, child care, help for the poorest. A further 8,000 marks were allocated to extend the protection assured in clinics for infants and children under the age of six. Another sum of 10,000 marks made it possible to devote a clinic to the treatment of syphilitic children. Three other clinics were created, the third opening in 1919. At that point expenditure on the city's ten clinics amounted to 920,400 marks, compared to 450,000 marks in 1913, only partly covering the effects of inflation.[57]

When it came to the care of the children of wage-earning mothers, the solutions adopted were very cautious. Appeals to employers to adapt nurseries and crèches, particularly for the needs of night-workers, and for them to finance these services, produced only poor results. In the autumn of 1917, recognizing that these institutions were still very badly supported and that employers contributed only very small sums, the city council voted an exceptional contribution of 50,000 marks to keep them going.[58]

Another way of protecting children was to send them out of Berlin.

[56] In Paris Dr Pinard of the Académie de médecine asserted similarly that the 'enforced unemployment' of women largely explained the satisfactory state of mothers and children at the beginning of the war. See Dr Pinard, 'De la protection maternelle et infantile pendant la quatrième année de guerre dans le camp retranché de Paris', *Bulletin de l'Académie de Médecine* (17 Dec. 1918), p. 592.

[57] Stadt Archiv Berlin, Rep. 00-02/1 18031. [58] *Ibid.*

This programme, established in the spring of 1917 after an appeal to rural families in eastern Prussia, was open to children aged six to fourteen. A first trainload of 1,000 children left Berlin on 1 May 1917. Similarly, in the autumn, the public authorities created an establishment outside Berlin capable of taking in 600 women and children. This was at Ahlbeck on the Ostsee. Finally, in October 1917, the town council created a special clinic for unmarried mothers.[59]

The record of measures taken reveals delay, decisions taken reluctantly, and solutions which, apart from the education and food programmes, were often incomplete or inadequate. The example of the clinic for unmarried mothers is very enlightening in this respect. Its creation shows the genuine concern of the city councillors for this very vulnerable group of women and children, but the way it was funded meant that it was incapable of having more than a modest effect because the centre was open to clients for only two sessions a week of ninety minutes each![60] Such women in principle had the right to an allowance for childbirth and breast-feeding, should the father be in the army. But many unmarried mothers had difficulty in proving that the mobilized father had indeed contributed to the infant's maintenance, a condition for paying the grant. Furthermore, unmarried mothers had no rights if their partners were killed on active service.[61]

In Paris, pre-war populationist imperatives were strengthened by the war. Both declining birth-rates and staggering death tolls on the battlefields made infant health a priority. The Office central d'assistance maternelle et infantile du Gouvernement militaire de Paris (OCAMI) was at the heart of the struggle against infant mortality during the war. Set up at the beginning of the war, this quasi-private organization, working alongside the military authorities, accepted as its goal the reconciliation of the war effort with the protection of the health of mothers, children, and future mothers. The means consisted of offering to all women without resources, who were pregnant or who had a child under three years dependent on her, the legal, medical, and social protection to which she was entitled. The bureau had important patrons, including Madame Poincaré, wife of the President of the Republic, and was run by the wife of General Michel and by Senator Strauss, an indefatigable advocate of the cause of children and their mothers, co-founder in 1902 of the league against infant mortality. Doctors Lesage and Pinard, of the Academy of Medicine, were highly active too.

In the years 1916 and 1917 the bureau distributed a budget of over 250,000 francs which represented 30 per cent of the state contribution to

[59] *Ibid.* [60] *Ibid.*

[61] F. Rott, 'Die Einwirkung des Krieges auf die Säuglingssterblichkeit und die Säuglingsschutzbewegung', *Zeitschrift für Säuglingsschutz*, 7 (May/June 1915), p. 194.

all children's institutions on French soil.[62] It should be noted that four-fifths of these sums can from individual donations.[63] Once more, we should note the relatively small sums provided by the state for this supposed national imperative. 'Pronatalism' was honoured more through rhetoric than through expenditure.

Contributions from other countries were significant. In this way both American and Australian organizations helped to defend Parisian children. Between 1914 and 1916, the Melbourne Red Cross sent a total of 208,700 francs to Paris. This was the equivalent of a year's budget.[64]

The bureau sponsored places of shelter and supplementary refuge (the future maternity homes) to take in pregnant women and newly delivered women with their babies. By 1915, almost 600 additional beds were available. The effort was also supported by private initiative, such as Mutualité maternelle, Société d'Allaitement maternelle, Société de charité maternelle, Oeuvre nouvelle des crèches parisiennes.

City authorities worked hand in hand with these groups. In 1917 and 1918 the city used some 6,000 beds for pregnant and newly delivered women; relating this figure to the number of live births, this was one bed for every six women who delivered. This undertaking had multiple aims: to prevent accidents to mother or child, to avoid premature births and the birth of sickly children, to sustain the mother in good health despite her work, to reduce the risks of infant mortality, to encourage maternal breast-feeding. These were time-honoured aims, given an urgency by the special conditions of war. According to the statistics gathered by Dr Pinard, the goal established by the bureau was virtually achieved. Over 90 per cent of mothers who were delivered in wartime Paris were helped in one way or another by public authorities.[65]

Great efforts were also made during the war to enable mothers to continue breast-feeding while working in factories. This was the goal of the Comité du Travail féminin from its inception by Albert Thomas, Minister of Armaments, on 21 April 1916. Work conditions for pregnant and breast-feeding women had to be regulated; following in particular the detailed studies of Dr Bonnaire, directives in January 1917 indicated very firmly to management that they should respect certain rules concerning work stations, prohibitions of night work, the creation of part-time jobs, respect for rest periods, setting up health clinics, etc.

[62] Catherine Rollet, 'Le financement de la protection maternelle et infantile avant 1940', *Sociétés contemporaines*, 3 (1990), p. 38.

[63] *Revue Philanthropique*, 39, 250 (15 June 1918) p. 269.

[64] Dr Pinard, 'De la protection de l'enfance pendant la deuxième année de guerre dans le camp retranché de Paris', *Bulletin de l'Académie de Médecine* (3 Dec. 1916), pp. 547–8.

[65] 'Office central d'Assistance maternelle et infantile dans le gouvernement militaire de Paris. Assemblée générale du 23 février 1918', *Revue philanthropique*, 39, 250 (15 June 1918), pp. 265–79.

Provision for rooms for breast-feeding was essential, and its realization was the product of collaboration among bureaucrats, employers, and workers. In this way it was possible to care for the children of thousands of women employed in war factories in a suitably healthy environment and at a reasonable price.

The committee for women's work, the Académie de Médecine and the Ministry of Munitions also cooperated to provide premises offering mothers an acceptable system of care for their small children. During the war, thirteen establishments of this type were created in the Department of the Seine, adding to the nine already in existence. The city of Paris subsidized forty-seven other crèches during the war.[66]

Elsewhere, efforts to prevent childhood diseases and to extend education on health and hygiene expanded considerably. This campaign bore some fruit in increased attendance at baby clinics, Gouttes de Lait (milk dispensaries) and in proliferating home visits. In the Paris region, observations of children in municipal clinics doubled between 1913 and 1918.[67] Disappointingly, however, the proportion of breast-feeding mothers among this population did not increase; from a level of 17–18 per cent in the period 1911 to 1913, the percentage fell to about 11–12 per cent during the war.

Starting in 1917, the American pattern of propaganda by district and by the provision of home visits for mothers expanded rapidly. This challenged the system established in Paris since the 1890s centring on medical clinics. These clinics were increasingly successful during the conflict; but the shortage of doctors, added to some legal problems, undoubtedly favoured the breakthrough of the Anglo-Saxon model of going to the home rather than of the home going to the clinic.[68]

In London, the fight against infant mortality also became a national priority during the war, as is evident in statute and practice. In 1915 the Notification of Births (extension) Act established a register of infants. The milk supply was the concern of the Milk and Dairies Consolidation Act of 1915. The 1918 Maternity and Child Welfare Act and the 1918 Midwives Act provided further services and professional training for those engaged in infant and maternal welfare.[69]

In the midst of the war the Carnegie UK Trust undertook a vast inquiry to find out how it might use its resources to set up programmes of mothers and baby care. It invited MOHs in England and Wales to report on relevant sanitary conditions and resources. In 1917 Dr Hope published the result of the inquiry.[70] This survey disclosed the character

[66] On these points, see many articles in the *Bulletin de l'Académie de Médecine* and in the *Revue Philanthropique*. [67] There were eight in Paris and five in the suburbs.

[68] Rollet, *La politique*, pp. 394–402. [69] J. M. Winter, *The Great War*, ch. 6.

[70] Jay Winter, 'Aspects of the impact of the First World War on infant mortality in Britain', *Journal of European Economic History*, 11, 3 (Winter 1982).

of infant-welfare work, as well as its limited development. Supplies of low-priced sterilized milk were distributed in many infant-welfare centres. Infants fed in this way avoided the risks of dehydration associated with the provision of condensed milk. The report was both encouraging, in showing the effort and imagination involved in this embryonic system of infant welfare, and discouraging, in disclosing the slow pattern of development in this field. The Carnegie Trust was committed to help support these activities, but their effect remained limited during the 1914–18 war.[71]

Outcomes

Wartime conditions threatened to affect adversely the survival chances of the children of all three cities. As we shall see in chapter 16, with some exceptions, that was not the case from 1914 to 1916, and in Paris and London thereafter. Pre-war trends in infant mortality as a whole – the reduction in infant and childhood mortality including an equally great reduction in deaths due to diarrhoea – were not interrupted by the war; they were simply slowed down.

The check on the secular downward trend in infant mortality was particularly noticeable in Berlin, with increased rates of infant mortality in 1914, 1917, 1920, and 1922. We shall deal with the special problems of illegitimate infant mortality in chapter 15. But even when they are included in aggregate statistics, the overall level of infant mortality in Berlin never reached the exceptionally high 1911 level of 173 deaths per 1,000 live births. There was an inflection of infant-mortality rates in London in 1915 and in Paris in 1918, but again the 1911 levels were higher still.

A major crisis in infant health had thus been avoided: how could this be accounted for? One demographic element needs to be noted first. The war brought about a substantial drop in the birth-rate. Between 1913 and 1915 the number of births dropped by one-third in Paris, by 8 per cent in London and by a quarter in Berlin, and stayed at a very low level until the end of the war. This decline in fertility inevitably improved the conditions under which the management of delivery operated and increased the level of care mothers could provide for their families. The drop in admissions into maternity wards, nurseries, and crèches, was a positive factor in sustaining the health of mothers and children alike. Despite the closure of three maternity hospitals in wartime Paris,[72] the percentage of hospital deliveries rose from under 25 per cent before the war to 30 per cent during the conflict.

[71] Winter, Lawrence, and Ariouat, 'Infant mortality in London'.

[72] The drop in the birth-rate also spread unemployment among midwives. The Paris city council voted monthly aid for their maintenance. See Rousselle, *Rapport général . . . budget 1916*, Conseil municipal de Paris, no. 60, pp. 22–4.

Similarly in Berlin, the proportion of women giving birth in hospital increased noticeably (from 18 per cent from the period 1910 to 1913 to 31 per cent in 1917). Contrary to the developments noted in Paris and Berlin, London women – up to 75 per cent of whom gave birth in hospital before the war – made less use of hospitals during the war. There, with few doctors available, babies were more frequently delivered at home with midwives in attendance.

The greatest gains in infant survival chances were registered among legitimate deliveries in Paris and Berlin. It may be that increased hospitalization helped legitimate infants to secure these gains, but that illegitimate infants were not so lucky. In the case of London, where illegitimacy was at much lower levels, the reduction in the hospitalization of delivery may have put a brake on infant-mortality decline. The plateau in infant-mortality rates once more turned into a diagonal after the war, when pre-war practices of childbirth were renewed.

Medical and paramedical care account for only part of the trajectory of infant mortality in this period. Family resources and material conditions had a direct bearing on the survival chances of infants. Women's work was better paid during the war and was supplemented by family allowances for soldiers' families.

There was little evidence of the deleterious effects of women's work in wartime on the survival chances of their children. Such fears were commonplace before the war. It was precisely to refute this argument and to avoid running the slightest criticism of the priority accorded to the war effort that Senator Paul Strauss and Drs Bonnaire and Bar in Paris sponsored studies of the population groups concerned. They investigated whether work in munitions factories had increased the risk of abortion and premature births or reduced the average birth-weight of babies born at full term. Statistics from the Baudelocque clinic,[73] and the Tarnier clinic[74] showed some slight increase in prematurity, but no overall adverse trends. Work itself was not the source of adverse infant health in wartime.

Fewer births, better facilities available, more paid work for women, better nutritional standards for mothers and babies, changes in the conditions for giving birth: these appear to be among the important factors which help to explain the modest reduction in infant mortality in London and Paris throughout the war and Berlin before 1917.[75] As we have seen, there were exceptions, in particular with respect to illegitimate children, but those not on the margins of society were relatively well protected from the potentially disastrous consequences of war.

[73] 'Discussion . . . by Dr Pinard', *Bulletin de l'Académie de médecine* (2 January 1917), pp. 26–42.

[74] 'Discussion . . . by Dr Bar', *Bulletin de l'Académie de médecine* (13 February 1917), pp. 185–207.

[75] Winter, Lawrence and Ariouat, 'Infant mortality in London'.

Problems in adult health

Aside from infant and child health, considerable attention was directed to particular problems of adult health, with a direct bearing on both the sexual behaviour and the efficiency of the wartime labour force. Of special importance were risks conventionally associated with wartime upheavals – notably venereal diseases and health protection in war factories.

Venereal disease

Before the war, the control of venereal disease was a synonym for the regulation of prostitution. Arrangements for the diagnosis and care of patients were embryonic in all three cities. A few clinics and dispensaries existed in the capitals, but they were far from adequate for the needs of populations which feared and concealed these 'shameful afflictions'.[76]

The war encouraged local and national initiatives to avoid the spread of these diseases. Thus, in response to the Act of 12 July 1916 requiring local authorities to prepare plans to combat venereal disease, the Borough Council of the City of London submitted a plan to the Local Government Board for approval. Coming into operation in January 1917, the plan covered the following points: cooperation between twenty-two urban hospitals to cover a vast geographical area (the City of London and its suburbs, and the counties of Middlesex, Buckinghamshire, Hertfordshire, Essex, Kent, and Surrey); treatment and instruction for patients in hospital or attending external clinics, with financial contributions from local authorities in proportion to their numbers of new patients; accommodation in three hostels for infected prostitutes; organization of public conferences and propaganda campaigns by means of posters and leaflets; supplies of medical preparations (Salvarsan) to independent doctors.[77]

The arrangements were subsequently strengthened, extending to sixteen hospitals in 1919. The overall cost reached £79,575 in 1920 to 1921, with 75 per cent coming from the new Ministry of Health. The Campaign resulted in more diagnosis and treatment. Nearly twice as many Wassermann tests were carried out in 1918 as in 1917 (21,360 instead of 12,342); and also nearly twice as many new patients were treated in the special hospital clinics during 1919 compared with 1917 and 1918 (20,908 instead of 12,211 and 12,992); there was also a considerable increase in pathology tests carried out by independent

[76] For Paris, see Corbin, *Les filles de noce* (1982).

[77] *London Statistics*, vol. 26 (1915–20), pp. 104–5.

doctors (2,992 in 1917, 5,122 in 1918, and 8,258 in 1919). In 1919, 240 doctors were engaged in this work, as against 108 in 1917. Other general measures reinforced local arrangements; the Venereal Diseases Act of 1917 prohibited all publicity for anti-venereal medicines without advance permission and also prohibited treatment of venereal disease by anyone without medical qualifications.[78]

The anti-venereal battle intensified in Paris and Berlin as well during the war, although it was not until the Armistice that a specific decree on this issue was adopted in Berlin. The civil and military authorities, already concerned by the pre-war incidence of venereal disease, noted with alarm the fresh outbreak of cases of syphilis during the war. Partial statistics in 1917, for example, revealed a very significant increase in new cases of syphilis in the French army: the increase of 41 per cent between March/April and July/August 1917, indicated at least an increased vigilance among military doctors. However, the annual morbidity rate of primary syphilis, calculated from army statistics, was high during the war; it reached the proportion of 14 men per thousand in 1916, 21 per thousand in 1917, and 20 per thousand in 1918.[79]

Organized prophylaxis began in 1916.[80] The coordination of the military health service, and the Ministry of the Interior's management of public aid and hygiene, opened the way for 'service annexes' in hospitals, special clinics concerned specifically with the diagnosis, care, and instruction of patients suffering from venereal disease. To ensure discretion these services were designated as treatment for 'skin and mucous membrane disorders'. The clinics were free; they were manned at first by mobilized doctors who were specialists in venereology and were then taken over by local civilian doctors. In order to make access easier for patients in employment, the clinics were open in the evenings and on Sunday mornings. As in London, the authorities were concerned to bring the problem to the attention of work inspectors, trade unions, friendly societies, municipal services, doctors, and pharmacists, to prevent ill-informed publicity, and to facilitate access to these services.[81]

In 1916, forty dispensaries of this kind were in operation throughout France, endowed with a grant of 200,000 francs. In subsequent years the budget trebled, and the number of clinics rose from 65 in 1917 to 90 in 1918 and 120 in 1919. Paris had several of these subsidiary services and also was the location of an institute for prophylaxis, established in March 1916 by Senator Chautemps (a doctor who afterwards became a minister) and by Dr A. Vernes, with the support of the Conseil municipal and the Conseil général.

[78] *Ibid.*

[79] Bernard, *La défense*, p. 255.

[80] On this organization, see the chapter on 'La lutte antivénérienne', in *ibid.*, pp. 261–7.

[81] *Revue philanthropique*, 38, 244 (15 December 1917), pp. 601–8.

The tracking-down and treatment of patients, men and women, military and civilian, now took on a systematic pattern. Paris hospital statistics reveal, as in London, a very noticeable increase in the number of patients treated in hospitals between the pre-war period and the war itself: there were 9,565 patients treated in 1917, 9,631 in 1918, 11,434 in 1919, 13,972 in 1920, and 14,847 in 1921, as against 6–7,000 in the period 1913 to 1916.[82]

The struggle was pushed to great lengths, for there were attempts to open 'prevention posts' at a local level. But the failure of the two such posts in Paris was total, linked no doubt to the lack of discretion in such centres; patients had no wish to be identified as infected, in their own neighbourhood and family. Prophylaxis against venereal infection could operate only in the anonymity of a hospital or with the support of systematic visits organized by the army[83] or (as in later years) by employers.[84]

Action in Berlin came later. Only after the Armistice did German authorities adopt a measure on venereal disease, a new general law having been rejected by the Reichstag.[85] As a rapid increase in venereal infections was feared during demobilization, the decree passed in December 1918 introduced strong legislation to avoid the proliferation of syphilis and gonorrhoea. New measures included obligatory hospitalization for patients in the acute phase; a threat of imprisonment for those having sexual relations when aware of personal infection; and compulsory declaration of venereal disease by doctors. These measures ex-tended the widespread diagnosis of syphilis by Wassermann test and treatment with Salvarsan was already common practice.[86]

There was no striking recrudescence of deaths due to syphilis noted in Berlin, London or in Paris. Pre-war levels were not exceeded during the war, though the dispersal of prostitutes to other locations than the capital cities may have had a bearing on this achievement. Once again,

[82] *Annuaire statistique de la ville de Paris.*

[83] The army had set up its own centres for dermatology–venereology in each army corps region. See Bernard, *La défense*, p. 265.

[84] At the beginning of the war it was realized in the United States that the instruction sessions for recruits concerning venereal dangers could usefully be extended to men and women at their place of work. American industrialists initiated meetings, particularly during the dinner break. This method was not however adopted in Europe until after the war. One of the most interesting experiences in France relating to women, between the wars, was that of Dr Germaine Montreuil-Straus, who took her inspiration from the American initiatives. See Catherine Rollet, 'Education et démographie. Reflexions sur l'expérience française d'éducation des mères et des jeunes filles aux XIXe et XXe siècles', *Actes du Séminaire de démographie, l'Université Charles de Prague et l'Université de Paris I, novembre 1992, Les Cahiers de l'IUP* (1994), pp. 1–25.

[85] J. Jadassohn, 'Geschlechtskrankheiten', in F. Bumm (ed.), *Deutschlands Gesundheitsverhältnisse unter dem Einfluss des Weltkrieges* (Stuttgart and New Haven, 1928), vol. I, p. 226.

[86] *Ibid.*

we may conclude that a traditional scourge associated with war was relatively contained in these cities.

Alcoholism

Another risk to adult health was related to what was deemed excessive alcohol consumption. In France several laws were adopted to help limit alcoholic consumption. The best known was the interdiction of absinthe, through the law of 17 March 1915, followed by a restriction on premises selling alcohol (9 November 1915). Then on 6 March 1917 came an amendment to the Labour Code, banning all alcoholic beverages, with the exception of wine, beer, and cider, from factories, and finally a law of 1 October 1917 increased the penalties for public drunkenness. This statute was hardly ever applied: on the eve of the war, there was a total of seven convictions in Paris for this offence.[87]

These measures were echoed by other public gestures, such as the closure of cafés and the strict control of alcoholic consumption by soldiers serving in war factories. Social benefits were denied those 'known to frequent habitually drinking establishments'. Above all, public disapproval of alcoholism was displayed in the considerable increase in the taxation (and thereby the price) of alcoholic beverages.[88]

Some commentators, for instance Léon Bernard, argued that these measures were inadequate, since they did not deal with the source of the problem, namely private distillers especially in the countryside.[89] In the case of Paris, though, there is no doubt that consumption of alcoholic beverages declined in wartime, probably at a steeper rate than in the nation as a whole. Consumption of wine fell by half, from 600 million litres in 1914 to 300 million litres in the period 1916 to 1918. Consumption of spirits fell from 14 million litres before the war to 3 million in 1918. In sum, alcoholic consumption fell by 50 per cent in Paris during the war, as opposed to a 25 per cent drop in the country as a whole.[90]

Statistics on morbidity and mortality further support the view that moral indignation on this issue was simply a waste of time. *Assistance Publique* hospitals treated 534 men for alcohol-related conditions in 1913, 287 in 1915 (after mobilization), but only 95 in 1918. The figure for women fell too, from 268 in 1913 to 58 in 1918. Deaths due to cirrhosis of the liver declined from 599 in 1913 to 317 in 1919. No doubt there are

[87] 'Rapport sur la question de l'alcoolisme présenté à la commission interministérielle de la main d'oeuvre par R. Pinot, secrétaire de l'UIMM, et M. Gervaise, secrétaire de l'Union des travailleurs de l'Etat', *Bulletin du ministère du travail* (June 1917), pp. 275–91.

[88] Robert, 'Ouvriers et mouvement ouvrier', p. 193.

[89] Léon Bernard, 'Lutte anti-alcoolique', ch. 23 of *La défense*, pp. 268–72.

[90] Robert, 'Ouvriers et mouvement ouvrier', p. 195.

many explanations for these trends, but an *increase* in wartime alcoholic consumption is not one of them.[91]

This wartime drop in aggregate consumption of alcohol was a short-term phenomenon, reversed quickly in the 1920s. But in Paris there was a real break in working-class behaviour. Jacques Valdour, an acute observer of working-class life, noted that before the war, a carafe of wine was always on the table in a popular restaurant, and it would have been odd if anyone had refused a drink with his meal. After the war, this was no longer the case. The carafe was no longer on the table, and not to order wine was admissible as an appropriate form of behaviour.[92]

These trends have a bearing on general notions of well-being, though it is difficult to avoid subjectivity in discussing them. The diminution of alcoholism may have been less important to ordinary people than the loss of sociability greater sobriety may have entailed.

In London and Berlin too, the same decline in alcoholic consumption probably took place. In wartime Berlin we also see the deliberate reduction in the production of spirits, and increased prices. The effect of both was appreciable, for the number of patients taken into hospital for alcoholism dropped from an average of 700 cases before the war to less than 100 cases a year in 1916 and 1917.[93] However, during the war only the most severe cases of advanced alcoholism were hospitalized. The end of restrictions after the war brought a fresh rise in morbidity and mortality rates from alcoholism but, according to Dr Bonhoeffer's analysis, the pre-war levels were not reached again.[94]

The effect of the war on lowering alcoholic consumption was even clearer in London. The liquor trade was supervised closely and consumption was restricted. The Liquor Control Board cut opening hours of pubs and limited credit sales. Elsewhere, other ministerial departments decided to raise prices and to reduce the alcohol content of various drinks and the quantity of stocks authorized.[95] The controls were so severe that some pubs had only enough beer to sell at weekends. Once again there is statistical evidence that there was an appreciable reduction in the wartime consumption of spirits and prosecutions for drunkenness. Even if part of this change is attributed to military recruiting, the diminishing proportion of prosecutions for drunkenness

[91] *Annuaire statistique de Paris et du Département de la Seine*, 1913–19.

[92] Jacques Valdour, *Ouvriers parisiens d'après-guerre* (Paris, 1921).

[93] *Statistisches Jahrbuch der Stadt Berlin*, vols. 32, 33 and 34.

[94] Dr Bonhoeffer, 'Geistes- und Nervenkrankheiten', in Bumm (ed.), *Deutschlands Gesundheitsverhältnisse*, pp. 259–88.

[95] M. E. Rose, 'The success of social reform? The Central Control Board (Liquor Traffic) 1915–1921', in M. R. D. Foot (ed.), *War and society: historical essays in honour of J. R. Western, 1928–1971* (London, 1973), pp. 71–84.

per 10,000 of the population (64 in 1905, 47 in 1911, 25 in 1920, and 20 in 1922) points to genuine progress towards a society less devoted to alcohol.[96]

Health at work

Toxic materials and health conditions at work

Everyone knew that increased munitions production involved significant health risks. One of the most dangerous operations was the filling of shells with TNT powder (Trinitrotoluene). In Britain up to 100,000 people, mostly women, were occupied in this work, London being one of the great centres of this essential war work. Seen as less toxic than the powders used previously, TNT powder was none the less the cause of several cases of toxic jaundice. This question preoccupied the two British authorities charged with supervising the health, security, and well-being of workers in war factories: the Health of Munitions Workers Committee and the Medical Research Committee.[97]

The Medical Research Committee established a research programme on this problem in August 1915.[98] The aim was to resolve such questions as how to prolong exposure to TNT without risk of toxic jaundice, how to identify and reinstate those most exposed to poisoning, etc. In general terms, the real dangers linked with handling TNT were recognized without identifying any serious alternative to its use. Neither the trade unions – for example, the National Federation of Women Workers – nor the workers themselves balked at handling these materials, no doubt because of their awareness that this was temporary work and that the risks suffered were far less than those suffered at the front by their friends and relatives.

Some health practices were effective. In the specific case of jaundice linked with the toxicity of TNT, statistics show a very definite drop in new cases and deaths in 1918 (34 cases and 10 deaths in 1918 instead of 170 cases and 52 deaths in 1916 and 190 cases and 44 deaths in 1917). The Medical Research Committee had called for better ventilation and protective clothing, and increased mechanization of the handling of these chemicals. Some of these measures, particularly the wearing of masks and protective clothing, probably did some good.

Of importance in maintaining good health were improved nutrition

[96] G. B. Wilson, *Alcohol and the nation: a contribution to the study of the liquor problem in the United Kingdom from 1800 to 1935* (London, 1940), p. 333.

[97] G. Braybon, *Women workers in the First World War* (London, 1981), pp. 138–49. See also Thom, 'Women and work in wartime', pp. 311–13.

[98] A. Ineson and D. Thom, 'T.N.T. poisoning and the employment of women workers in the First World War', in P. Weindling (ed.), *A social history of occupational health* (London, 1985), pp. 89–107.

levels among women workers in munitions factories. A full programme was sponsored by the Ministry of Munitions relating to canteens, seating provision, ventilation, reduction in hours of work, and the organization of recreational sessions during rest breaks. Without overstating the case, the presence of welfare workers and supervisors may have made a difference.

Similar conclusions may be drawn for Paris.[99] Legislation concerned with insanitary or dangerous premises was put into abeyance by the state of war, which meant increased risks for a population of which one-third consisted of unskilled women. These risks were linked with exposure to toxic dust, gas, and fumes, and contact with corrosive materials (lead, copper, nickel, machine oil). Women worked above all on production lines making shells, cartridges, grenades, and detonators and were less in evidence in foundries or aircraft and car factories. In order to meet increased production rates, hygiene and security safeguards were not always observed or applied rigorously. As in London, however, the Munitions Ministry worked through an under-secretary of state in the health service (created in 1915) and a committee for women's work, charged with examining and improving working conditions for what amounted to 100,000 women workers. A new service of women factory inspectors was also developed along British lines, to watch over the physical and moral well-being of working women.[100]

In some ways, the war inevitably made things worse for industrial workers. It ensured working days of twelve hours or more, night work, few rest days. In July 1917 the Munitions Minister, Albert Thomas, reduced the working day by memorandum, prohibited night work for young women and restored the weekly day off. Until the end of the war these measures were applied with difficulty, judging from the work inspectors' reports.

Elsewhere, certain wartime measures did make a difference in the environment of work. In both London and Paris, working women – at least those working in the largest businesses and when the foremen did not obstruct them systematically – were able to benefit from dispensary services, canteen meals, even women's clubs. This was in addition to health services for pregnant women and young mothers, and the provision of low-cost care for workers' children.

The condition of Berlin workers was no different between 1914 and 1916, though they suffered as did all other inhabitants from the increasing difficulties of the final two years of the war. As in Paris and

[99] Mathilde Dubesset, Françoise Thébaud, and Catherine Vincent, 'Les Munitionettes de la Seine', in P. Fridenson (ed.), *1914–1918, L'autre front*, Cahiers du 'Mouvement social', no. 2 (Paris, 1977), pp. 189–219.

[100] On all these measures, see the *Bulletin des usines de guerre*.

London, shell production drew in large numbers of women workers, many of whom were night workers. In theory, night work required authorization, and was prohibited for those under the age of sixteen. One report for 1917 noted a total of 77,165 women legally authorized to work at night in systems of two or three teams.[101] In fact, night work was frequently undertaken by girls under the age of sixteen and without advance authorization.

The burden of work tended to increase towards the end of the war. One Berlin doctor described exhausted tuberculous women fainting away after working at their metal mould over a period of two years without a daily break.[102] By the summer of 1918, the strain in such factories was palpable.

In view of these conditions it is not surprising that although absenteeism remained stable throughout 1914, 1915, and 1916 (measured by the number of days off work for illness accepted by the sickness bureau), it increased noticeably in 1917 in sectors such as plumbing and metal-working.[103] The measurement of absenteeism is difficult in all cases, and its causality is unclear. Food shortages and the need to spend hours finding food and fuel clearly took their toll on industrial efficiency and the health of war workers in Berlin.

Accidents

Alongside poisoning, accidents were a serious health risk. Statistics collected on a bomb factory outside London between November 1915 and October 1917 showed that a reduction in working hours played a positive role in overcoming risks of accidents. This was particularly true for women workers. Male accident rates increased, though, from 1917 onwards, possibly because they were allocated the most dangerous work. During this period productivity increased very considerably (by 25 per cent in less than a year) while the weekly workload dropped appreciably.

Towards the middle of 1916 men and women were working for less than ten hours per day, instead of more than the twelve hours registered in November 1915. This reduction in working hours helped to eliminate excessive fatigue, and counterbalanced, at least among the women, the risks relating to increased intensity of labour.[104]

The recourse in Paris to a three-shift system, each of eight hours' duration, apparently limited the risks of accident at work. At the beginning of the war, lack of familiarity with new machines and also the

[101] Brandenburg, Landeshauptarchiv, Pr.Br.Rep.Berlin C., n. 1958, Jahresberichte der Gewerbe-Aufsicht, pp. 189–91. [102] *Ibid.*, p. 274. [103] *Ibid.*, pp. 305 and 307.

[104] Ministry of Munitions (Health of Munitions Workers Committee), *Memorandum 21, An Investigation of the factors concerned in the causation of industrial accidents* (PP1918 Cmd 9046, vol, XV, p. 677). I am grateful to Jon Lawrence for help on this point.

frequent use of dangerous products (notably industrial oils) led to a higher accident rate; after a period of adaptation the rate dropped. In general terms, it was lower in factories employing mainly women – possibly because high-risk work was kept for male workers. In Berlin factories with a predominantly male workforce, the accident rate was between 6 and 12 accidents per 100 workers; in establishments with predominantly female workers it was only 3 to 8 per 100 workers.

The specific risks linked to the handling of explosive powders were watched particularly closely by inspectors. Although there were several serious accidents, the total was not high. In a Berlin factory producing 10,000 shells per day, only one accident was recorded for the whole war, resulting in two deaths and four men seriously wounded. In another shell factory employing 2,750 workers (of which 2,200 were women), there were nine accidents, without any deaths. The largest explosion occurred in a Reibzünder factory: one day's entire stock of powder exploded when the ceiling of the depot collapsed, setting fire to an engine on the floor above; thirty-three workers were seriously hurt, of whom five died.[105] Accidents of this kind were a risk in all munitions works; it is all the more remarkable that relatively few disasters of this kind occurred.

Conclusion

In all three cities some traditional health threats associated with armed conflict were avoided between 1914 and 1918. Populations were not swamped by cholera, typhus, smallpox, diphtheria, or typhoid fever. Certain circumstances, paradoxically, had favourable consequences for the health of civilian populations, such as the drop in the birth-rate or the restriction of alcohol consumption.

The rationing of medical personnel as between civilian and military claimants did not on aggregate adversely affect the health of infants, adults in general, or munitions workers in particular. In all three cities social policy directly or indirectly helped defend the well-being of the population at a time when medical care was at a premium.

Before 1914 Berliners enjoyed a fuller system of health insurance than had either Londoners or Parisians. Nevertheless, in the first half of the war, there was little to choose among the ways these cities defended the health of their inhabitants. As we shall see in chapter 15, there were those who fell through the net of social assistance and medical care. But, on balance, these setbacks do not negate the record of accomplishment under very difficult circumstances.

The best way to understand the role of public health institutions in

[105] *Ibid.*, p. 301.

wartime is in terms of damage limitation. They neither caused the crisis nor could they deal with its ultimate causes. In all three cities, they did the best they could. After 1916 in Berlin, everything went wrong. The public-health system suffered from severe restrictions on resources at a time of spiralling inflation. Then came the shock of the last months of the war, political paralysis at the national level, producing the crisis of 1917 to 1919 and beyond. It was not the system of public health which failed, but the German regime itself. Allied populations were more fortunate. But we must not forget those on the margins of all three cities, for whom the war was a misfortune from beginning to end. It is their story we tell in chapter 15.

Before we do so, it may be useful to return to the framework provided by Amartya Sen to help set these developments, both positive and negative in context. In the pre-war period, entitlement to medical care as an element of citizenship was not universal. It was fuller in Germany than in Britain, and better developed in both than in France. The experience of war transformed the issue of universal medical provision, partly because of the numbers of casualties and disabled pensioners who returned home, and partly because of the need to defend the health of the population who provided the weapons of war. Public-health care was an entitlement to a larger population than ever before during the Great War, an element which helps to account for the formation at long last of Ministries of Health in Britain in 1919 and of hygiene in France.

There were other long-term forces working towards this end, but the need in wartime to defend the 'capabilities' and 'functionings' of a population of war workers and soldiers, and to ensure the well-being of their dependants, gave political and social weight to pressure for institutional change. As in the case of housing, demobilization led to a retreat from these state-sponsored experiments. But the experience was there, as a resource on which to draw in later years.

15
The 'other war' II: setbacks in public health

Catherine Rollet

The epidemiology of the war on the Western front marks it out from previous wars, which were accompanied by terrifying increases in diseases such as typhus, cholera, or smallpox. The war on the Eastern front was still, in this sense, a nineteenth-century war, but further west, some plagues traditionally associated with war were avoided. Furthermore, as we have seen in chapter 14, protecting the health of the civilian populations was a priority in all three of the major combatant countries. Children and munitions workers were singled out for special attention, which on balance succeeded in the necessary task of damage limitation throughout the war in the case of Paris and London, and from 1914 to 1916 in the case of Berlin. Thereafter the German capital went through a demographic crisis, the severity of which public authorities could neither contain nor reverse.

At the outset two fundamental points need emphasis. The first is the striking contrast between the successful defence of the well-being of some civilian groups and the conspicuous failure in the case of others. The second point is the significance of internal migration in affecting both the pattern of disease and mortality and other demographic features of these cities.

Let us take these points in turn. In all three cities the medical profession and other social agencies did what they could in wartime to defend civilian health. Unfortunately, some groups benefited more from their efforts than others. Certain sectors of the population suffered higher rates of death or sickness during the war, either in general or in particular periods. Aggregate analyses conceal genuine inequalities in wartime patterns of health. Among those who suffered a recrudescence of mortality rates were the elderly, some young women, and certain groups of very young children.

In addition, there occurred a rise in mortality attributable to some diseases which had been on the decline before 1914. Tuberculosis was the most important – though not the only – cause of deaths among civilians to rise in wartime. In addition, a previously endemic illness became a catastrophic epidemic; this was the so-called 'Spanish flu', which hit soldiers and civilians alike in waves in 1918 and 1919.

The variance in the experience of different groups in wartime precludes either an optimistic or a pessimistic conclusion as to the effects of the war on civilian health. Some did better than others. But the vagaries of disease and survival among civilians in wartime reflected not only their prior material condition but also a fundamental feature of wartime social life, namely high patterns of geographic migration both as between city and provinces and within cities themselves. Military mobilization was one facet of migration; flight from combat another; the growth of munitions industries, a third. All caused massive movements in population, which spread populations and disease in new and significant ways. It is only by highlighting the role of migration that we may appreciate the full cause and character of some of the negative effects of the war on infant health and on patterns of respiratory disease in wartime.

In this chapter we discuss four cases in which setbacks in public health in wartime occurred. The first two describe civilian cohorts whose survival chances were affected negatively by the war: illegitimate children and the elderly. Both were vulnerable groups with direct contribution to the war effort. The third and fourth sections deal with two respiratory diseases, whose lethality increased menacingly among civilians in wartime: tuberculosis and epidemic influenza.

The crisis of mortality among illegitimate children

As we have observed in chapter 14, there was no crisis in aggregate infant mortality in Paris, London, or Berlin. The secular decline in mortality was slowed down by the war, but at least there was no sharp inflection in infant mortality in the period as a whole.

Another picture emerges when we decompose aggregate statistics. It then becomes clear that this suggestion of stability or of a uniformity of fate among the children of the three cities needs to be discarded in favour of a more nuanced interpretation.

Two distinctions are essential here. The first concerns the components of aggregate infant mortality, in particular the divergent death-rates of legitimate and illegitimate children. The second relates to the social composition of illegitimate populations. Some were the product of common-law unions, and their lives differed little from legitimate infants'; others were raised by a single parent, under adverse but adequate conditions; others still were abandoned. It is this last group that suffered most in wartime. Only by reconstructing the complex social history of illegitimacy can we understand the causes and character of the crisis in illegitimate infant mortality in wartime.

The health of legitimate infants was adequately defended in all three cities. This was a remarkable achievement in the German capital. In Paris there was some volatility in infant mortality rates, especially at the end of the war. Problems of estimation require caution in relying on these findings (see chapter 16 and the statistical appendix). It is probably wise to conclude that there was no rise in the risk of survival faced by legitimate infants in these cities in wartime.

The situation regarding illegitimate children is very different. The vulnerability of such babies is well known, relating to the circumstances of the mother's pregnancy, her condition after delivery, and difficulties of child-care. The problem of illegitimacy was a problem of survival in Berlin and Paris, though, due to the very low levels of illegitimacy, not in London. The rise in illegitimate infant mortality is visible in Paris from the beginning of the war, and in Berlin from 1917 onwards. In Paris, infant mortality for babies born out of wedlock in 1918 and 1920 reached the level attained in 1911: nearly 150 per thousand, 8 per cent higher than in the years 1912 to 1914. This was a setback more than a crisis, and one that was over by the mid-1920s.

In Berlin, on the other hand, after 1916 the rate of illegitimate infant mortality regularly exceeded the Berlin figure for 1911 (223 per thousand), reaching the astonishing figure of over 300 per 1,000 in 1920 and 1922. This is catastrophic under any definition. Compared to the pre-war figures, the death-rate had doubled on average for this category of children, proof of the inability of mothers, charities, and public authorities to provide elementary care for these babies.

The full crisis came at the end of the war and extended to 1923; it affected infants at earliest ages in particular and reflected excess mortality due primarily to respiratory infections. Not surprisingly rising perinatal mortality paralleled rising rates of illegitimate still-births. Both probably reflected the poor health and inadequate institutional support of the health of unmarried mothers.[1]

The chronology of mortality rates, and the weight of respiratory infections in it, suggest that patterns of wartime care for illegitimate infants were at the heart of the crisis. These babies died because of a radical disruption of pre-war patterns of aid, both public and private. The system in operation before the war had enabled unmarried mothers to give birth and to find assistance for their infants through grants and institutions such as maternity homes or *Frauenheilstätten*. At the end of the war, and despite the existence of specialized institutions created for them, these infants were effectively abandoned. The older framework of support had broken down under the weight of inflation and social dislocation. Consequently in the German capital illegitimate children and their mothers paid a high price in terms of deprivation and

[1] J.M. Winter and Cole, 'Fluctuations in infant mortality rates', pp. 235–63.

Table 15.1. *Illegitimacy ratios, Paris, London, Berlin in 1913, 1915, and 1917 (illegitimate births as % of all births)*

	1913	1915	1917
London	4.0	4.0	5.4
Paris	24.1	27.8	31.0
Berlin	23.6	22.4	22.0

Sources: London: *London Statistics;* Paris: *Annuaire statistique de la ville de Paris;* Berlin: *Gross-Berlin Statistische Monatsberichte.*

dislocation both during the war and after the armistice. The situation of these young women – always uncertain – was very precarious in the difficult period from 1917 on. In this respect, the crisis of illegitimate infant mortality in Berlin reflected social tensions as well as, in a more general sense, the Central Powers' inability to provide essential support for the most vulnerable elements of the population.[2]

Was the crisis in illegitimate infant mortality a function of rising illegitimacy rates? Illegitimacy rates measure births to unmarried women per 1,000 population. The illegitimacy ratio describes the proportion illegitimate within the total birth cohort. This latter indicator is a more sensitive measure of the incidence of illegitimacy in a population.

A glance at table 15.1 will suffice to show that there was no increase in the illegitimacy ratio in Berlin and only a very slight inflection from much lower levels in London. The increase in wartime illegitimacy was more pronounced in Paris, where the illegitimacy ratio rose from 24 to 31 per cent. It is important to note that the illegitimacy ratio remained stable in Berlin, despite the fact that that city registered the greatest fall of the three in period fertility. The wartime birth-rate was fully 50 per cent lower than that of the pre-war period, but marital and extra-marital fertility fell in tandem. In Paris and London, where the drop in the birth-rate was 33 and 25 per cent respectively, it appears that marital fertility fell more than extra-marital fertility. The crisis in infant mortality in Berlin therefore, does not reflect an upsurge in extra-marital conceptions, but rather a crisis in survival of those born out of wedlock.

Illegitimate infant mortality also rose in Paris. Most vulnerable were foundling children, certainly marginalized in wartime.[3] The rise in their mortality rates began in the period 1914 to 1915, then grew steeper still

[2] *Ibid.*, p. 262.

[3] The term 'assisted children' covers, under the terms of the law passed in 1904, several categories of children, including orphans without kin, abandoned children, children 'in care' or 'placed', children 'morally abandoned' (abused), etc. See Rollet, *La politique*, p. 146.

in 1916 to 1918, and reached its peak in 1920. Statistics of infant mortality – clearly incomplete – for those in the foundling hospital reflect this rise in mortality among these during and after the war.

In Paris this crisis reflected a severe shortage of wet-nurses in the country. The traditional system of wet-nursing which gave abandoned children some chance of survival aimed at three objectives: first, to reduce the time spent on the foundling hospital; then, to place the babies as quickly as possible in country foster-homes; finally, to provide them with a wet-nurse both in the foundling hospital and in the country.[4] The war itself upset all these aims. The authorities had great difficulty in recruiting wet-nurses either to come into hospital to breast-feed babies or to foster them at home, because the nursing women were unavailable in the city or occupied with agricultural labour in the periphery. The movement of children became more difficult too, given problems of transport and the flight of the civilian population out of Paris in 1914.

The number of wet-nurses working in the foundling hospital over the war decade gives a clear idea of the desperate wartime situation. An average of between 1,200 and 1,500 were on call from 1909 to 1913; but in 1914, there were 790; then 442, 193, 158, and 210 between 1915 and 1918. There was a rise in the post-war years, but in 1922, the number of wet-nurses in Paris was still only half the pre-war figure.[5] As we have noted above, the decline in the birth rate in Paris in wartime was about 33 per cent; the decline in wet-nursing was about 75 per cent.

The increase in mortality paralleled the decreasing numbers of wet-nurses because alternatives to breast-feeding in foundling hospitals were not yet available. Given the difficulty in placing these children in provincial homes, it was inevitable that their institutional life was prolonged. Conditions there partially account for the doubling of infant mortality between the pre-war years and the 1920s. But of equal importance were the problems they faced in the countryside. The longer a child stayed in the foundling hospital, the greater the risk; but the sooner an infant was sent to a wet-nurse, the risk rose too. These were expendable children, many of whom were born without a future.

Since only about 3,000 of 50,000 children born annually were placed in the care of public authorities, the effect of this dire situation on overall infant mortality rates in Paris was limited. But we must note too that deaths of children in the care of their rural foster-parents did not appear in the Parisian statistics. Only deaths in the foundling hospitals were registered in Paris, a matter of a few hundred. The crisis in illegitimate

[4] George D. Sussman, *Selling mother's milk. The wet-nursing business in France, 1715–1914* (Urbana, 1982).

[5] Sources for the figures are: Albert Dupoux, 'Sur les pas de Monsieur Vincent, Trois cents ans d'histoire parisienne de l'enfance abandonnée', *Revue de l'Assistance publique* (1962), table IV annexed, and the *Annuaire statistique de la ville de Paris*.

infant mortality was probably worse than aggregate statistics indicate. As in the case of Berlin, so too for Paris we must decompose infant mortality figures to see the full impact of the 1914-18 war.

For this reason, we must treat with some scepticism the triumphalism of Parisian authorities about their achievements during the war. M. Dausset felt justified in claiming that 'While in Berlin the insufficiency and poor quality of scarce nutrition are leading to a greatly increased incidence of illness and mortality in the youngest age-groups, in Paris the state of health of first-born children and of children in general leaves nothing to be desired.'[6] At least with respect to illegitimate children in public care, this statement was wide of the mark.

Dausset's account of conditions in Berlin, while exaggerated for 1914 to 1915, was prescient. The social dislocation of the later phases of the war and its aftermath lay behind the serious rise in mortality among children taken in by the city of Berlin. The traditional pattern of infant feeding and care was disrupted completely. In 1919 only a quarter of the children in care left the foundling hospital for placements in Berlin or in the suburbs with fostering families, instead of over half between 1910 and 1913. Overcrowding was severe in the *Kinderasyl*, the children's home; some doctors spoke of 'institutionalisation' as an illness, a form of listlessness or depression that could kill children.[7] Disease spread rapidly in this environment.

In fact, for these particularly vulnerable infants, there was little hope of public support in wartime. Given the huge pressures on resources, they had some claim on public sympathy perhaps, but less on public funds. We approach here a shadow of the much older treatment of such children, a system of quasi-intentional 'wastage', which cost the lives of illegitimate infants in a war which made their plight simply vanish into the margins of urban social life.

Illegitimate children in London were luckier. They were much fewer in number and did not rely on a traditional system of wet-nursing for their survival. Whether or not 'War is good for babies',[8] it was clearly less bad for illegitimate Londoners than for those born in Paris or Berlin.

The elderly

Among the marginal populations of these three cities at war were the elderly. This section of the population, conventionally designated as those aged sixty and over, suffered both physically and emotionally from the material and psychological conditions of wartime life. Un-

6 Dausset, *Rapport . . . budget . . . 1916*, Conseil municipal de Paris, 1915.

7 J.M. Winter and Cole, 'Fluctuations in infant mortality rates'.

8 Deborah Dwork, *War is good for babies and other young children: a history of the infant and child welfare movement in England, 1898–1918* (London, 1987).

doubtedly more vulnerable than adults in general, old people – like the very young – lacked protection against the constrained conditions of everyday life; during this trying period, they lacked support from public authorities and charitable bodies which previously had provided help. The climate of war was if not hostile to them, certainly indifferent, in the sense that other groups – soldiers, war workers, mothers – took priority. Unfortunately, historians have replicated this tendency to look away from the elderly towards those at the vortex of the war.

The scale of the demographic crisis

Whether we consult the absolute total of deaths among people aged sixty or over, or rates of mortality in this age-group,[9] the demographic crisis affecting older people in the three cities is unmistakable. Comparison between the total number of deaths among those aged sixty and over in 1913 and in 1917 shows an excess of deaths of nearly 4,000 in Paris, 2,500 in London, and 6,500 in Berlin (see table 15.2). The index, from base 100 in 1913, rises very sharply in Paris in 1916 and above all in 1917; in London the peak was reached by 1915, while the crisis in Berlin, severe in 1916, reached dramatic heights in 1917 and continued in 1918 and 1919. Unfortunately statistical gaps in the period 1920 to 1921 preclude any discussion of the possibility that this crisis continued in the early 1920s.

Several features emerge clearly about the deterioration of the survival chances of the elderly in wartime. First, the crisis arose well before 1918, prior to the influenza pandemic. Secondly, conditions deteriorated in London and Paris, but less so than in Berlin where the demographic crisis was not limited to the old. They shared with the civilian population as a whole a heavy price for the continuation of the conflict.

In relation to the pre-war period, the mortality rate of the old during the years 1914 to 1918 rose 5.8 per cent in London and 5.7 per cent in Paris. In Berlin the rise was similar at first, around 5 per cent. From 1917, however, the rise in death-rates in Berlin grew alarmingly. Among women the increase was 48 per cent and 19 per cent in 1917 and 1918, respectively. The inflection in death-rates among male Berliners was higher still, reaching 56 per cent in 1917. We may conclude that the old suffered everywhere, but that the crisis in Berlin was exceptionally severe.

[9] Problems connected with the demographic measurement of mortality (registration of deaths, population groups to be assessed under headings of the rates of death, standardization, etc.), are discussed in Robert and J. M. Winter, 'Un aspect ignoré'. Full statistical information is available there. The following discussion is drawn from this article.

Table 15.2. *Total deaths of population aged 60+ in Paris, London, and Berlin, 1913 to 1920, and an index of deaths (1913 = 100)*

Year	1913	1914	1915	1916	1917	1918	1919	1920
Paris	14,264	15,404	15,643	16,921	18,222	16,421	16,742	15,062
	100	108	110	119	128	115	117	106
Berlin	8,686	9,566	10,074	10,727	15,032	12,584	11,185	n/a
	100	110	116	124	173	145	129	
London	22,929	23,219	26,912	25,236	25,341	25,463	24,857	22,321
	100	101	117	110	111	111	108	97

Source: Robert and J. M. Winter, 'Un aspect ignoré', table 1, p. 304.

Table 15.3. *Standardized death-rates (× 10,000) at ages 60+ in Paris and London and an index of changes 1913 to 1923 (1913 = 100)*

	Pre-war	Wartime	Post-war
Paris	664	702	605
(index)	100	106	91
London	625	661	580
(index)	100	106	93

Sources: Robert and J. M. Winter, 'Un aspect ignoré', pp. 324–8.

The paucity of full statistical data on Berlin precludes extensive analysis and comparison of the demographic position of the elderly in the German capital. Some inferences may be drawn, though, on the fate of the same age group in Paris and London (see table 15.3). It is apparent, first that the upward incidence of mortality at ages 60+ was almost identical in the two capitals. The situation of this cohort was difficult, though not disastrous when compared to the data presented above on illegitimate infants. Secondly, the position of the elderly improved rapidly in the immediate post-war period, even compared to the pre-war situation. By 1923, death-rates for this population were around 8 to 9 per cent below pre-war levels in both Allied capitals.

Thirdly, the deterioration of life chances was marked throughout each capital city. Analysis of the mortality statistic by district shows that the gap between high and low mortality areas narrowed during the war. The mortality rate at ages 60+ dropped more quickly in the poorest districts than in the richer areas.

The most marked periods of difficulty for the elderly were different in Paris and in London. In London, the worst year was 1915, particularly for women. The narrowing of the district differentials in mortality rates began in the same year.

In Paris climate was probably a factor in producing the highest points in mortality rates for the elderly. The crisis was particularly marked in 1917, which began with a severely cold winter. Not surprisingly respiratory illness (and the general category of 'senility') showed the greatest increase in 1917. Deaths from cold, or hypothermia, were registered in a capital city living through a winter of dramatic severity.

Another phenomenon which distinguishes one city from the other is mortality by gender. While in Paris mortality rates for men and women remained in constant proportion throughout the war, in London a very clear difference appeared between male and female rates in 1917 and 1918. During these crisis years it was the male death-rate which increased significantly.

In summary, the secular decline (at least from 1900) in mortality rates among old people was halted and reversed in all three capital cities during the Great War. In contrast to the advances noted for other age-groups, in demographic terms old people suffered more generally during the war than did other age-groups. The decline in life expectancy for the elderly was approximately the same in London and Paris. Proximity to the front, therefore, was not a decisive variable in predicting survival chances among the elderly in Paris and London.

In Berlin the deterioration in survival chances for the elderly was much greater, above all during the demographic crisis in 1917 to 1918. Its early onset suggests that rising death-rates among the elderly were not caused by the influenza pandemic of 1918 but rather by the growing food and fuel crisis in Germany in the second half of the war.

The aged and the war

It is impossible at this stage to give a comprehensive picture of the forces behind the rise in death-rates among the elderly in these three cities in wartime. Privation played its part by denying the old adequate heating, fuel for cooking, food, and other essential supplies. So did exhaustion, through work, the effort to find food and fuel, and the more intangible but no less real psychological pressures of anxiety and bereavement.

The fact that deaths from influenza, bronchitis, and pneumonia rose during the war and that respiratory disease reached a peak in Paris in 1917 indicate that cold was a highly significant cause of death among old people. No doubt the scarcity of coal and oil in the combatant capital cities made the struggle against the cold more difficult for old people. This shortage was chronic throughout the war, particularly in Paris, and many old people probably suffered repeatedly from hypothermia, reducing their resistance to infectious disease; this no doubt explains the Paris crisis of 1916 to 1917, when the very severe winter coincided with a marked increase in mortality. As soon as coal supplies were reorganized after the 1916–17 winter, old people's living conditions improved (see chapter 12).

Calorific intake was also a relevant factor in the struggle against cold; a shortage of calories would add to hypothermia and further undermine old people's already lowered resistance. This would suggest that during the war the older members of the population suffered in the struggle to find food and queue long hours for it.

This brings us to the more general problem of the marginalization of the old during the war. The privations endured by some of the old during the war reflect what Amartya Sen calls 'a caesura' in 'exchange entitlements'.[10] The well-being of the old was not a decisive element in the war effort, and they therefore did not have a strong claim on the allocation of public resources. In fact we know little about the distribution pattern for rationed product according to age and family structure. Even so, it is reasonable to suppose that the queueing and waiting in shops must have added to the strain on the elderly, and increasingly so at more advanced ages.

Marginalization was evident politically as well as materially. In France the grant allocated to those over seventy, the infirm and the incurable, set at a mere 1 franc per day just before war, remained unchanged throughout the war, despite 100 per cent inflation. In ideological terms, the notion of a weak and ageing nation developed by the press, particularly in France, created a negative image of old people.[11] Contemporary voices were silent on the problem of the elderly, in striking contrast to the obsession with the birthrate.[12] In later accounts of the war, the aged were almost completely ignored.[13]

It is therefore hardly surprising that the elderly suffered from the disappearance during the war of many establishments or charitable funds which had helped them. Of forty such institutions in the Paris area, only about ten were still helping old people in 1915. Charitable bodies redirected their aid to refugees, wounded soldiers, widows, orphans. For example, the charity for poor women in Montmartre,

10 A. Sen, *Poverty and famines*.

11 See in particular Patrice Bourdelais, *L'âge de la vieillesse* (Paris, 1993); see also A.-M. Guillemard, 'Transformations du discours sur la vieillesse et constitution d'une "politique française de la vieillesse" durant les trente dernières années', in *Le vieillissement, implications et conséquences de l'allongement de la vie humaine depuis le XVIIIème siècle* (Lyon, 1982).

12 Cf. Rollet, 'Le financement de la protection maternelle et infantile', pp. 33–58; B. Dumons and G. Pollet, 'La naissance d'une politique sociale: les retraites en France (1900–1914)', *Revue française des sciences politiques*, 5 (1991), pp. 627–48; A.-M. Guillemard (ed.), *Old age and the welfare state* (London, 1983).

13 C. Bloch, *Bibliographie méthodique de l'histoire économique et sociale de la France pendant la guerre* (Paris, 1925).

which had distributed bread and clothing to old women every Friday, simply vanished, as did the 19th arrondissement workshop which provided simple work for local elderly women.[14]

At the other end of the social scale, resources were also eroded; elderly middle-class people living off property rents saw their income severely affected by the non-payment of rent by the majority of their tenants and by rent control. We can speculate – and only speculate, given the paucity of current research – on the humbling of those middle-class elderly people whose income from securities or fixed pensions shrivelled as prices skyrocketed in wartime.

In between the well-to-do and the very poor was a large population of elderly working people, whose attempt to contribute to the war effort may well have compromised their health in wartime. Françoise Cribier has demonstrated the importance of exhaustion at work amongst wage-earners in the 1930s.[15] We know for certain that many men over the age of sixty had to carry on working during the war, or had to return to work. In the census of 1921 we find an exceptionally high work-rate among older men.[16] In London, few elderly women were required to work, but in Paris the increase in such numbers was notable from 1917 on. The particularity of excess male mortality in London can reasonably be explained by the severe strain suffered by elderly Londoners who were still required to carry on working in the final part of their lives. The scale of unemployment in Paris in 1915 meant that elderly men were unlikely to work, whereas in London in 1915, they did so to help fill jobs vacated by those who joined the army or war industry.

One striking finding in the analysis of the cause-structure of mortality among elderly men in London was the steep rise in the incidence of heart disease. Without in any way underrating the significance of factors such as exhaustion from work, we should consider linking this phenomenon to other factors, particularly to stress and anxiety. This is not an easy theory to verify, but to ignore it is to depart from the reality of everyday life in wartime.

In Paris, there were periods of collective anxiety, in particular, during the German offensives of 1914 and 1918. In all three cities, anxiety followed those living in retirement homes or public-authority hospitals, torn from their usual domestic surroundings, without the support of some family members, or evacuated to the country, very often in painful circumstances.

The evacuation of the elderly from retirement homes in the Paris area

[14] Cf. *Paris charitable et bienfaisant* (Paris, 1912); *Paris charitable pendant la guerre*, 1 vol. and 3 supplements (Paris, 1915–1918); *Paris charitable, bienfaisant et social* (Paris, 1921).

[15] Françoise Cribier, 'Itinéraires professionnels et usure au travail: une génération de salariés parisiens', *Le Mouvement social*, no. spécial: *'L'usure au travail'*, 124 (1983), pp. 11–44.

[16] *Recensement de la population, 1921.*

illustrates what must have been a genuinely traumatic experience for many frail old people. In September 1914 those to be evacuated were dispersed in several convoys, according to pre-arranged plans. The convoy from the Ménages retirement home at Issy-les-Moulineaux 'formed up at Clamart station, in forty wagons; each old person took his or her luggage containing possessions and a little packet of food and drink for twenty-four hours. Leaving at five a.m., the train was boarded at Versailles and subsequent stations by civilians and soldiers rejoining their units.' The journey continued with difficulties of all kinds; the train reached Le Mans at 9 p.m., and Rennes at 6.30 the next morning. Some of the group left the train, the remainder continued towards Saint-Brieuc (at 1 a.m.), thence to Brest, where the interminable voyage finally ended at 9 a.m. The authorities noted that 'despite hardship and weariness', there had been no untoward incident. The old people from Ivry, who arrived twenty-four hours late and after unbelievable difficulties in finding food, were described as 'prostrate with fatigue and exhaustion'. No doubt this testing journey affected the survival chances of this group of elderly and infirm Parisians.[17]

For Berliners the anguish lasted longer, until well after the Armistice. The blockade continued until the peace treaty was signed in late June 1919. That was a full year after the evaporation of the hopes raised by the spring 1918 offensive. What followed was an autumn of further sacrifice and uncertainty about the future. Then came the revolutionary months, full of crowds, demands, and ultimately gunfire.

For old people with a son away at the front this feeling of isolation became more deep-rooted and diffuse. There was the physical isolation, the deprivation of substantial material and physical support, especially for those who lived with their sons, and a sense of mental isolation which left them feeling worried, abandoned, and distressed.

We can only speculate too over the anxiety of old people over the fate of their sons or grandsons away at the war, an anxiety which drained their energies, even when balanced by a commitment to seeing the war through. But when the news reached a father or a mother, or grandparents, of a death in action, the shock was terrible. Studies show that mortality among the elderly rises considerably in the year following the death of a spouse. Can the same phenomenon be related to the death of a son or grandson? It is hardly illogical to suppose that the deaths in action of relatives, especially members of their immediate families, contributed to the increased mortality rate among the elderly during the war years.

In Père Lachaise cemetery in Paris, there is an inscription in one

[17] Henri Rousselle, 'Note sur les travaux de la 5e commission (Assistance publique – Crédit municipal)', *Conseil municipal de Paris, Rapports et documents*, no. 95, 1919, esp. pp. 16–18.

family crypt in memory of Jules David Lyon, who died aged sixty in 1918. The inscription reads: 'The suffering of his country and the death of his son on the battlefield tore him prematurely from the affections of his family.'[18] The sociologist Emile Durkheim, who died in 1917 a few months after the death of his son, hinted at similar feelings in 1916: 'I cannot explain my anguish to you. It obsesses me the whole time and hurts more than I expected. Now I can see the moment coming when I shall know, I am afraid . . . haunted by the image of that exhausted child, alone at the roadside, in the midst of the night and the fog.'[19]

The universality of such reactions may be presumed, though it is difficult to prove. There were dozens of wartime entries in the socialist newspaper *L'Humanité* announcing the death of elderly people, like the 'former activists, esteemed by all' or the 'outstanding former activist' or again, in November 1917, the 'good old friend Leroy' whose 'son was killed in action'.[20]

Largely ignored at the time, long forgotten by historians, the physical and mental suffering of the elderly become more visible as research on the Great War advances. Even if certain points require clarification, verification, modification, the essential remains: the war brought an infinite number of problems for old people. Some suffered from exhaustion, while others were pushed aside, living as best they could on resources eroded or eliminated by inflation. Everything was difficult, getting hold of essentials such as food or coal; and then, how could they face up to the anxiety, the worry over those in uniform, followed by the shock of the death of a son or grandson, when they themselves felt abandoned and irrelevant?

As in the case of illegitimate infants, it is important to bear in mind that wartime social provision excluded as well as included. Those not at the heart of the war effort had little claims to priority of care. Given the material and psychological pressures of the period, there were those who simply could not survive. Among them were many at the extreme ends of the age structure.

Tuberculosis: migration and public health

Tuberculosis proved to be another area in which there was a setback to urban public health in wartime Paris, London, and Berlin. This was especially the case among adults, and especially among young female adults.[21] This recrudescence in age-specific death rates occurred despite

[18] Robert and J. M. Winter, 'Un aspect ignoré', p. 322.

[19] E. Durkheim, *Textes présentés par V. Karady* (Paris, 1975), as cited in A. Marsauche, 'La question des étrangers à Paris, 1914–18', MA thesis, University of Paris I, 1990.

[20] *L'Humanité*, 9 November 1917.

[21] Linda Bryder, 'The First World War: healthy or hungry?', *History Workshop Journal*, 24 (1987), pp. 141–57.

a major public effort to contain and control the disease. Many agencies addressed the question, how tuberculosis could be avoided, given the high risk of infection from tubercular soldiers returning to the cities, treated in sanatoria cleared of their civilian patients? How could these displaced patients be cared for? The intention to act was there, and yet the demographic evidence suggests that the lethality of the disease increased anyway. Why was this so?

The wartime rise in tuberculosis mortality

First we shall establish the dimensions of this setback to public health; then we shall address its aetiology. Looking first at London, the death rate for respiratory tuberculosis (TB) at ages fifteen to forty-four before the war was approximately 1.27 per thousand. For the years 1914 to 1918 it reached on average 1.53 per thousand. Based on a female population of around 1,200,000 women between the ages of fifteen and forty-four these figures show an increase of deaths from tuberculosis of around 330 per year. Over the war period, there were about 1,650 female deaths from TB over and above the pre-war level. After the war TB mortality fell back to the level for 1911 to 1913: the pre-war trends reappeared quickly once the war was over.

Within the 15–44 age-group there were marked differences in the incidence of TB at various ages. Excess TB mortality was striking in the younger age-groups. In comparison to pre-war levels, the rate increased to 90 per cent for the fifteen-to-nineteen age-group, by 60 per cent for those between twenty and twenty-four, by only 27 per cent for the thirty-to-thirty-four age-group, and remained stable for those between forty and forty-four. It was thus the under thirties who suffered most, although the level of TB mortality at these ages had been particularly low before the war.

This excess mortality was salient in part because it affected the young, particularly young girls with relatively low death-rates. The death of a young girl had become exceptional by 1914; hence the psychological and social significance of these deaths, even though the number never amounted to more than a few hundreds during the war.

All three cities suffered this increased incidence of TB deaths. They were remarkable against the backdrop of major declines in TB mortality in the pre-war period. In Berlin, for example, TB mortality per 10,000 inhabitants dropped from over 30 immediately after German unification to about 20 at the turn of the century and to 16 in 1913. The rate recorded in the capital was slightly higher than in Prussia as a whole.

The war constituted a break in this downward trend in each of these three cities. For young people of fifteen to nineteen the rate of deaths from TB rose sharply between the period 1911 to 1913 and 1916: the increase was 14 per cent in Paris, 19 per cent in Berlin and 53 per cent in

London. After 1916 the increase in Berlin was catastrophic, while in London and Paris it was less marked even though clearly evident.

The Berlin crisis for the years 1917 to 1918 was particularly marked, and continued in 1919; the absence of statistics beyond that date makes it impossible to know if the crisis continued to the 1920s, though all indications are that it did. Young adults were the most severely affected, in particular between the ages twenty to twenty-nine and fifteen to nineteen. In Berlin, for example, the TB death-rate at ages twenty to twenty-nine rose from 198 per 10,000 in 1910 to 1913 to 32 per 10,000 in 1917 to 1918; for the age group fifteen to nineteen, the rise was even more marked: from 14.2 to 31.1 per 10,000. In Berlin (and not in Paris and London) the crisis was generalized: it affected all age groups over the age of one.

In the Allied capitals TB killed more during the war only at certain ages. After the war the rate dropped again in Paris and London, although for the fifteen-to-nineteen age-group it still remained slightly above its pre-war level.

Sources of increased TB mortality

There is a huge literature on the spread of TB during the war. Most authorities referred to one or more of seven factors deemed significant in the aetiology of the disease. They were:

- the harmful effect of women's work in war factories;
- the deterioration in housing conditions;
- malnutrition;
- transmission of the disease by soldiers;
- the spread of the disease through refugees;
- migration, especially to war industry;
- restricted efforts to control the disease and care for those already suffering from it.

Certain factors operated to increase individual vulnerability; others increased the risk of transmission; finally, others hindered systems of prevention and treatment. The simple listing of these factors shows immediately that the causality of excess TB mortality was multi-faceted.

Contemporaries who insisted on the cross-over and accumulation of aggravating causes were not mistaken. Henri Sellier, in his book on tuberculosis published in 1928, commented:

> During the war, men discharged from the army because of tuberculosis went back home; auxiliary troops were crowded together in barracks and camps; munitions factories were full of civilian workers, reserve soldiers and territorials with deferred call-up, refugees from the occupied territories . . . Because

of their poor living conditions, male and female workers in munitions factories were undoubtedly liable to develop tuberculosis through contagion or the re-awakening of a youthful bacillus attack . . . thus, deaths from tuberculosis ensued, to a significant extent, from the considerable growth in the female work-force, the increased population in Parisian industrial centres and suburbs, from overcrowding.[22]

Women's work and TB

Let us consider some of these arguments in detail. The issue of women's work and TB was well worn. Many argued that full-time paid work had a harmful effect on the survival rates of women and on those of their children. TB was the price women paid for factory labour, the argument went, but few calculated the price they would have paid for not working.[23]

Work outside the home was a necessity and not a choice for most women. After 1914 it became a necessity for the nation as a whole. This meant a wholesale transfer of women from one part of the labour market to another, out of domestic service, laundry work, and dress-making to war production. This shift also represented an influx of working women from the suburbs and rural areas to the capital cities.

Many of these new urban workers had been raised in suburban, mixed, or rural environments. Many had not been exposed to the TB bacillus, and had not developed spontaneous immunity; their resistance to the disease when they came to Paris, London, or Berlin in wartime was probably low or non-existent. Here is the link between migration and TB which enables us to understand the significant increase in mortality among young women aged between fifteen and twenty-nine.[24]

Women who had grown up in these cities were no doubt already immune. Others had latent tuberculosis. During the war, working conditions were difficult in munitions factories and workshops: sixty-hour working weeks were not unusual, and the constriction and monotony of the production line in inadequately ventilated premises must have reduced resistance to this and other diseases. In such an environment, a small number of young girls and young women could no doubt spread the illness unhindered. As Dr Clive Rivière of the London City Hospital for Chest Diseases suggested, the problem was

22 Henri Sellier, *La lutte contre la tuberculose dans la région parisienne, 1896–1927* (Paris, 1928), p. 638.

23 C. Dyhouse, 'Working-class mothers and infant mortality in England, 1895–1914', *Journal of Social History*, 12, 2 (1978), pp. 248–67.

24 M. Greenwood, 'Tuberculosis among industrial workers', *British Medical Journal* (15 March 1919), pp. 316–17; A. E. Tebb, *An Inquiry into the prevalence and aetiology of tuberculosis among industrial workers, with special reference to female munitions workers*, Medical Research Council report no. 22 (1920).

partly due to the mixture of exhaustion at work and the revival of latent tuberculosis contracted in childhood.[25] Similarly Major Greenwood, of the Health and Welfare section of the Ministry of Munitions, was convinced that the industrial redistribution of labour prompted by the war was responsible for the inflection in TB mortality rates.[26]

The same comments appear in the reflections of Henri Sellier, when he drew up the balance-sheet of the anti-tuberculosis struggle in the Paris region: 'Large numbers of housewives are engaged in manufacturing munitions. In the years to come, the young women will be paying the price of exhaustion with their deaths.'[27] Stripped of its emotive language, this diagnosis was general: overwork, overcrowding, and an upsurge in a newly-recruited industrial labour force contributed to the recrudescence of tuberculosis in wartime. In effect, the unavoidable change in the sexual composition of the labour force in heavy industry played a major role in the aetiology of this disease.[28]

Housing

Deterioration in the domestic housing stock was often cited at the time as related to rising TB mortality. Women with latent or active tuberculosis had to cope simultaneously with difficult conditions at home and at work. As we have noted in chapter 13, under conditions of rent control landlords had no economic reason to improve housing or to make essential repairs. The rental market was stagnant because of the lack of new building following the rent moratorium. In Berlin there was a housing shortage. Increased overcrowding, especially in the industrial suburbs, no doubt added to the risk of infection. Given the speed of recruitment of labour, housing conditions were bound to be poor for the new wage-earners. The spread of tuberculosis among young women who lived in overcrowded conditions was very often a simple matter of time.[29]

Undoubtedly wartime restrictions on the housing market made improvements in the domestic housing stock impossible. Deterioration, and through it, the spread of disease, were inevitable. At the same time, municipal efforts to inspect inadequate housing were curtailed. Here was an area where public health considerations had to be shelved, in the interests of war production.

[25] In 'Symposium: The arrest of tuberculosis under the after-war conditions', *British Journal of Tuberculosis*, 12, 1 (Jan. 1918), pp. 8–9.

[26] In remarks to the section on epidemiology and state medicine for the Royal Society of Medicine, 24 May 1918. 'Report on industrial tuberculosis', *British Medical Journal* (1 June 1918), p. 618.

[27] Sellier, *La lutte contre la tuberculose*, p. 638.

[28] *Ibid.*, p. 369.

[29] J.A. Miller, 'Tuberculosis among European nations at war', *American Review of Tuberculosis* (Aug. 1919), pp. 337–58.

Nutrition and TB

While poor housing and exhausting work in munitions factories contributed to rising TB mortality in wartime, they did not operate alone. For part of the population inadequate nutrition played an important role in the aetiology of the disease. This was a matter of frequent discussion in Berlin. Journalists attributed the excess tuberculosis mortality to falling nutritional levels, linked to the Allies' economic blockage.[30] Personal accounts point to the same problem. One Berlin clergyman provided a profile of his family's weight loss in this period. He had lost 13 pounds; his wife had lost 17 pounds, and his two daughters had lost 10 and 13 pounds respectively. Only his son, the youngest child had gained weight – 3 pounds – over the two and a half years between August 1914 and March 1916.[31] This was also before the more severe food shortages of the second half of the war set in.

There was considerable debate on how far the population's calorific intake could be reduced without endangering public health.[32] Some held that there was room for enforced slimming; others pointed out that such was the privilege of the comfortable *Bildungsbürgertum* (educated middle class); workers, who had grown up malnourished, could not afford such deprivation. In the working-class areas of Berlin, malnutrition was a stark reality, preparing the ground for turning latent into active TB, and killing those already in the advanced stages of the disease.

There is more debate about levels of nutrition in Paris and London. The consensus is that adequate standards were maintained, and some gains were made by previously disadvantaged groups.[33] But in Berlin, after 1916 there is little doubt that everything got worse, except for those able to exploit the black market. For the rest, poor housing and malnutrition added to overwork and anxiety over the fate of loved ones to form the perfect breeding ground for the spread of TB.

Tuberculosis and the army

Work patterns, housing, nutrition: these were the time-honoured concomitants of TB. But in wartime there were other contributing factors especially evident in capital cities. One was military mobilization and movements.

[30] 'Schädigung der deutschen Volkskraft durch die feindliche Blockade', *Denkschrift des Reichsgesundheitsamtes* (Berlin, 1918), p. 21. On this point of the links between nutrition and tuberculosis, see Knud Faber, 'Tuberculosis and Nutrition', *Acta Tuberculosea Scandinavia*, 12 (1938), pp. 287–333.

[31] BAP Sachthematische Sammlung, Krieg 1914–18, 2.3.1.2.266, entry of March 1916.

[32] See Offer, *An agrarian interpretation*.

[33] J. M. Winter, 'Some paradoxes of the Great War', in R. Wall and J. M. Winter (eds.), *The upheaval of war. Family, work and welfare in Europe 1914–1918* (Cambridge, 1988).

London was the hub of the British military effort. Most of the 9,000,000 soldiers who served in British, Imperial, and Dominion forces during the war passed through the capital at some point in the war. The same was true in Paris: the flow of men from the front or on their way back to it was incessant throughout the war.

There were tuberculous men among both these mass armies. Out of a total of 9 million men mobilized between 1914 and 1919, the French army registered between 400,000 and 500,000 as 'suspected' cases of TB; nearly 150,000 had active forms of the illness. Nearly 100,000 men were discharged because of TB and more than 40,000 died of the disease during the war. Among the 53,897 discharged men who were entitled to a pension and who were alive in 1920, 17,144 gave a Paris home address. These figures show the scale of what constituted a 'constant fear' throughout the conflict, a fact of life which was not new but which was visible because it reached into the armed forces and was spread by them.[34]

At the beginning of the war rapid medical examinations for military service meant that the disease was rarely diagnosed.[35] The rigours of military life probably aggravated cases of latent tuberculosis; hence the numerous discharges. Next came treatment in specialized centres, and then a return home, with a further risk of contagion among the civilian population.

Attempts to control the disease by the armies had little effect beyond slightly restricting the scale and velocity of the spread of TB. From the beginning of the war the military system was specifically concerned with the question of pensions: better to reject an unfit man than to pay him a benefit for the rest of his life. The military tubercular patient would either be discharged 'second rate without pension' if the TB infection was unrelated to his military service, or 'first rate with pension' if the disease had been contracted during his service or aggravated by it. Further, patients had to be cared for and further contagion avoided, which led to a strongly hierarchical and functional system based on complementary and separate centres: *assessment centres* for observation and diagnostic tests, *medical hospitals* where the sick were cared for, fed, and restricted to rest or light work, and *medical posts* (part of the Ministry of the Interior's public hygiene and aid department) where carriers of the TB bacillus were advised and observed for three months.

The armies were breeding grounds of TB, and their passage through

[34] Lion Murard and Patrick Zylberman, ' "L'autre guerre" 1914–1918. La santé publique en France sous l'oeil de l'Amérique', *Revue historique*, 276, 2 (Oct.–Dec. 1986), pp. 369–98.

[35] See the records of R. Murray Leslie, doctor at the Royal Hospital for Chest Diseases, in 'Tuberculosis and the war', *British Journal of Tuberculosis* (April 1915), p. 74.

Paris, London, and Berlin was found to spread the disease. This is one reason why municipal authorities were well aware that, 'of all the evils created by the current war, tuberculosis was undoubtedly one of the most terrible'.[36] But the war brought all existing plans for expanding municipal services to a halt: sanatoria were evacuated, clinics closed, and the army requisitioned 4,500 beds. Further, the system specified at the beginning of the war – the creation of medical posts – was soon exposed as inadequate: because of a shortage of beds – by December 1914, 700 beds had been opened – sick soldiers were discharged at most three months after treatment had begun.

In France, the creation on 1 April 1916 of the 'National Committee for the aid of tubercular soldiers' and the departmental committees strengthened the existing arrangements, but Léon Bernard himself stated in 1917 that only one-quarter of the soldiers discharged because of TB had received treatment. The plan to have each tubercular soldier visited at home by a specialized health visitor, pioneered by Calmette in Lille and strongly recommended by a team of American advisors funded by the Rockefeller Foundation, was realized for only a handful of the soldiers affected.[37]

When Andrew Trimble, responsible for the anti-tuberculosis campaign in Belfast, observed harshly in 1918 that 'a steady stream of discharge tuberculosis soldiers has begun to flow homewards',[38] he was already three years late. In all three armies, tuberculous soldiers were discharged and sent home from the first months of the war.

Refugees and migrants

The numbers of soldier-patients in Paris and London were augmented by many Belgian refugees, including several thousand tuberculous people.[39] Henri Sellier gives a clear picture of the flow into Paris of groups at high risk of tuberculosis: men discharged from the army, workers from munitions factories, refugees. Looking at this huge ebb and flow of high-risk groups, it is easy to understand why TB spread and mortality attributable to it rose in wartime.

[36] Louis Dausset and Henri Rousselle, *Proposition relative à la création dans les hôpitaux de Paris de baraquements spéciaux destinés au traitement des soldats mis en réforme pour raison de tuberculose*, Conseil municipal de Paris, 8 Nov. 1915, no. 48.

[37] Georges Vitoux, 'L'oeuvre des Comités départementaux d'assistance aux soldats réformés', *Revue d'hygiène* (1918), pp. 561–70. Other sources quoted by Murard and Zylberman, 'L'autre guerre', p. 385, indicate only between 4,000 and 5,000 soldiers were treated. There may have been a difference of definition: the *cumulative* number of patients treated from the beginning of the war in the first case; the *annual* number in the second.

[38] 'Symposium', p. 5.

[39] H. M. Biggs, 'A war tuberculosis program for the nation', *American Review of Tuberculosis*, 1, 5 (July 1917), p. 260.

Public-health services

Restrictions on the finance and manning of anti-TB institutions provide a further factor enabling us to account for the wartime recrudescence of the disease. On the eve of the war, civilians could turn to several sources of treatment in the early or advanced stages of TB. London had three sources of public support: the Poor Law system, municipal clinics, and sanatoria. Berlin had two coexisting systems – treatment centres for those with social insurance, administered by the *Landesversicherungsanstalt*; and municipal centres for information and care for sufferers from lung disease, under the management of the Charité hospital, allied to centres for consultation and treatment in the Berlin suburbs.[40] In Paris the anti-TB programme was much less developed than in the other two cities.[41] But in the French capital there were clinics for diagnosis and treatment and a few sanatoria in the suburbs or the provinces.[42]

Financial restrictions and the absence of qualified staff brought these services to a halt; several sanatoria and treatment centres in Paris and Berlin had to close in the autumn of 1914. This happened at Villemin in the Department of the Oise and at Berck in the Pas-de-Calais, which principally took in patients from Paris. Establishments still in operation were requisitioned by the army for its own tuberculous men. In 1916 in Berlin the treatment centres opened once more to civilian patients, but at that time establishments suffered so severely from lack of funds that the treatment provided was singularly ineffective.[43] In London, the same was true. Over the war period, the price level doubled; grants to TB sanatoria were increased by only 25 per cent. The patients being cared for in these institutions received at best only poor-quality care; a service stripped bare had difficulty in preventing the development of mild cases into serious ones. In such conditions, many tubercular patients did not seek treatment: if lucky they were treated at home, but with a very good chance of spreading the disease to their family or the neighbourhood.

The most commonly used method for treating children during the war was to send those threatened with TB to the country. Children from

40 Peter Reinicke, *Tuberkulosefürsorge, Der Kampf gegen eine Geissel der Menschheit, dargestellt am Beispiel Berlins 1895–1945* (Berlin, 1988), pp. 27–9. See also Johannes Rabnow, *Bekämpfung der Tuberkulose in Berlin-Schöneberg* (Berlin, 1913), p. 13; and Hans Rusch, *Die Kommunale Fürsorge für Tuberkulose am Beispiel des Bezirkes Spandau, inaugural conference, Friedrich-Wilhelms-Universität zu Berlin* (Berlin, 1927).

41 On French backwardness, see Edouard Furster, 'L'action nationale contre la tuberculose en Angleterre', *Revue d'hygiène et de police sanitaire* (1916), pp. 289–303. See also the Americans' diagnosis as shown in the studies by Lion Murard and Patrick Zylberman (see nn. 49 and 51 below).

42 On the international position on sanatoria at the outbreak of the war, see F. Rufenacht Walters, *Sanatoria for the Tuberculous* (London, 1913).

43 Bernard Möllers, 'Tuberkulose', in F. Bumm (ed.), *Deutschlands Gesundheitsverhältnisse unter dem Einfluss des Weltkrieges*, vol. 1 (Stuttgart and New Haven, 1928), pp. 215–16.

large families in Paris who were suffering from tuberculosis, or who were threatened by it, were placed in rural sanatoria, eventually paid for out of the funds for additional wartime aid for large families. This measure was administered by the departmental public hygiene office. The so-called Oeuvre Grancher aimed at the placement of very young children at risk of TB contagion in rural families and on supervising them. Indeed, in general the concern to protect children from the risks of catching the disease was met by a great increase during the war of children's rural holidays.

However, the only genuine drive to meet the crisis in TB during the war arose out of a sense of national obligation to discharged soldiers who were TB sufferers. Soldiers took priority everywhere in the allocation of hospital beds, at the expense of civilians. A London docker forced to wait for anti-TB treatment commented severely on this competition between the men at the front whose health had suffered and those at home – in this case in the Port of London – who had also risked their health in the service of their nation. He asked bitterly why he should not benefit from treatment which would enable him to return to work quickly? The reply was clear: he had to wait as long as there were hundreds of soldiers who needed treatment.[44]

Exactly the same attitude towards competing claims can be found in Berlin, where in 1914 and 1915 doctors complained because their patients were evacuated from hospital beds to make room for soldiers.[45] A spokesman for the Ministry of the Interior warned against the harmful effects of a policy which, by sending patients home without medical supervision, risked spreading infection to other members of the family, particularly children. The danger was increased by overcrowded and unhygienic accommodation.[46] Acknowledging the problem, the authorities recommended that patients in an advanced state of the disease should not be sent home. Nevertheless, Berlin hospital statistics suggest that some patients with active TB left hospital without being cured in 1914 and 1915. This unsatisfactory policy no doubt aggravated a situation already beyond the public-health authority's capacity. Their efforts were genuine: in 1916, with the help of the Red Cross, most of the centres of anti-tuberculosis treatment had reopened despite the shortage of medical staff.

We should not underestimate the efforts of municipal authorities in all three cities to cope with the situation. The situation in Paris was very difficult at the end of 1915: the army had nearly 8,000 beds for tubercular

[44] 'Tuberculosis. Colonies for the tuberculous', *Lancet* (4 May 1918), pp. 646–7. According to the statistics of the London Insurance Committee, the waiting list in April 1918 showed 436 patients, of whom 205 were soldiers and 231 civilians.

[45] Medical Reform (1 April 1915), p. 61.

[46] Brandenburg, LHA Pr.Br.Rep.30 Tit. 140, 19544, p. 186.

patients and the city's public health department had 3,000 beds – wholly insufficient to meet the need. Detailed inquiries revealed that the medical services were overburdened with TB patients; nearly one hospital patient in two was suffering from the disease. The moment had come, in the words of councillors Dausset and Rousselle, for 'a fierce fight against tuberculosis', for both humanitarian and hygienic reasons. Treatment had to be provided for soldiers returning from the front with symptoms of the disease who were mostly categorized by army criteria as 'discharge no. 2', that is, without pension. In addition, the nation as a whole had to be protected.

The following spring the city council proposed a full programme of prevention and treatment with the creation of 2,258 beds for TB patients in Paris and the surrounding region. Speed being essential, the plan[47] was based on the provision of temporary 24-bed barrack huts in hospital premises, thus making use of the existing hospital infrastructure and keeping patients reasonably close to home. In all, 718 beds were opened in November 1917, 1,209 in January 1919, and 1,733 at the end of 1919, including 1,100 beds outside Paris. The largest units were opened at Brévannes (the Landouzy Sanatorium with 384 beds), Bicêtre (Georges Clemenceau Sanatorium, 420 beds), and Ivry (the Edith Cavell group, 156 beds). The other units, set up in hospital gardens, consisted of one hundred or fewer beds: Debrousse, La Salpêtrière, Cochin, Laennec, Tenon, La Rochefoucauld, Broussais, Saint-Antoine, Lariboisière, and Garches.

Clearly, the Parisian authorities were struggling with the need to care for discharged soldiers without detracting from the care available to the rest of the city's population. No doubt the plan adopted, as well as general measures adopted at a national level,[48] made it possible to limit the scale of what could have become a much worse calamity. In addition the Ministry of Armaments initiated TB dispensaries and regular check-ups for workers in war factories.

The efforts undertaken, which expanded with American aid after 1917,[49] helped to control the increase in TB mortality during the war,

[47] According to the views of the councillors themselves, 12,000 beds would have been necessary to meet the needs fully; 2,500 fell far below this. See Dausset and Rouselle, *Proposition relative*, p. 9.

[48] In particular the Bourgeois Law of 15 April 1916, concerning the establishment of clinics for social hygiene and protection from tuberculosis, and the Honnorat Law of 7 September 1919, concerning the establishment of one sanatorium per Department or the contracting of agreements. See Pierre Guillaume, *Du désespoir au salut: les tuberculeux aux 19e et 20e siècles* (Paris, 1986), pp. 180–3.

[49] As well as the article already cited by Lion Murard and Patrick Zylberman, see the same authors' 'La mission Rockefeller en France et la création du Comité national de défense contre la tuberculose (1917–1923)', *Revue d'histoire moderne et contemporaine*, 34 (1987), pp. 257–81.

Table 15.4. *Admissions, discharges, and deaths of patients treated in Parisian hospitals for TB, 1913 to 1922*

Year	Admitted	Discharged	Deaths	% deaths
1913	10,991	6,270	4,721	43
1914	10,034	4,954	5,080	51
1915	8,638	4,058	4,580	53
1916	10,875	6,067	4,808	44
1917	12,288	6,976	5,312	43
1918	13,308	8,065	5,243	39
1919	12,200	7,943	4,257	35
1920	10,823	7,682	3,141	29
1921	9,223	6,802	2,421	26
1922	9,773	6,394	3,379	35

Source: Annuaire statistique de la ville de Paris.

with the crisis among young people being less marked than in London or Berlin.[50] It must be accepted, however, that Paris was starting from a much less well-developed system for handling TB than the other two capitals. Analysing the situation in 1917, the Americans estimated that the problem was less scientific than organizational: it was a matter not of medicine but of administration and public response.[51]

Statistics for patients treated in Paris hospitals reflect reasonably accurately the balance-sheet of the struggle against TB (see table 15.4). The drop in the number of patients taken into hospital with TB was very noticeable in 1914 and 1915; during these two years the number of deaths exceeded the number of discharges. Subsequently a healthier pattern was set: more people who entered hospital left alive than died there.

Damage limitation was the best the authorities could hope for in London as well. According to Arthur Newsholme, chief medical officer of the Local Government Board, the diverse arrangements which existed for treating tubercular patients were literally paralysed during the war.[52] The same was true for Berlin, where administrative and fiscal problems merged into the general crisis of the last phase of the war.

50 A graph from the statistician Marcel Moine (*Recherches*, p. 35) illustrates in striking manner, for children between one and five years, the absence of crisis in Paris during the war and the slight rise in deaths from tuberculosis among London children. But the level of tuberculosis mortality in Paris was higher than that in London (250 per 100,000 against 140 per 100,000 children aged between one and four years). The war marks the beginning of the narrowing of the gap between the two capitals.

51 Murard and Zylberman, 'L'autre guerre'.

52 Arthur Newsholme, 'The relations of tuberculosis to war conditions, with remarks on some aspects of the administrative control of tuberculosis', *Lancet* (20 October 1917), p. 592.

Attempts to reorganize the relatively effective pre-war system could not compensate effectively for the increased risks, reflected in rising TB death rates from 1916 on.[53]

In conclusion, we must strike a note of caution. Tuberculosis is a disease with a variable incubation period. Some of those who died of TB during the war had contracted it during the war, others had had it before 1914 and suffered from aggravating conditions such as poverty, insanitary accommodation, and overcrowding, or the rigour of working conditions. The war did not cause their tuberculosis; it reduced their chances of survival if a latent TB infection passed to an active stage or if, already active, it reached an advanced stage. The additional aggravating factor – the influenza epidemic of 1918, to which we shall turn in a moment – further weakened those suffering from TB, and probably increased the death toll attributed to it.

Three features of the war had a special bearing on the trajectory of the disease. The first is migration, which helps to account for its special age-specificity. The second is the deterioration of the urban housing stock under conditions of rent control. The third is the breakdown of administrative structures created to deal with the disease. Even with a better set of policies, and the best will in the world, the Great War set in motion forces which were found to produce a recrudescence of tuberculosis. Once the war was over, and levels of stress and deprivation reduced, the rate of TB deaths fell again, and the secular decline in the disease resumed its earlier pattern.[54]

'Spanish flu'

Whereas the trajectory of TB was determined both by long-term and short-term changes in social conditions, patterns of migration and forms of immunity, the incidence of the greatest killer of all in the war decade was entirely fortuitous. The influenza pandemic probably killed more people than did military action throughout the world. In Western Europe, it 'came like a thief in the night', in the words of Sir George Newman, chief medical officer of the Board of Education.[55] Occurring in several waves in the autumn of 1918 and the spring of 1919, 'Spanish flu' (as it was known) was a violent and irresistible assault on public health, hitting hardest the young and robust. Mortality rates were highest between the ages of fifteen and forty-five.

In a novel published in 1932, entitled *We that were young*, Irene Rathbone depicts a young woman who learns at the Armistice that her young brother is alive and well; but a few days later the young man is in

53 Bernhard Müllers, 'Tuberkulose', vol. I, p. 210.

54 Linda Bryder, *Below the magic mountain. A social history of tuberculosis in twentieth-century Britain* (Oxford, 1988).

55 Ministry of Health Report, no. 4, Preface, p. xiv.

hospital, where he dies of flu following pulmonary complications. Was not this death, comments cousin Jack to the bereaved woman, exactly the same as a death in action?[56]

This conflation of death by disease and death in action recurs in the literature of the period, for the simple reason that the epidemic overshadowed the Armistice. But despite the fact that the pandemic took its course outside of human action, contemporaries still believed that they could contain or control it.[57]

A pandemic of this magnitude undercut the commitment to preventive medicine so central to health policy at the time. This is one of the sources of the relative passivity of medical officers of health (MOHs) in England during the visitation of pandemic influenza. In contrast, general practitioners and local authorities tried to act, but their measures were fruitless in any event. Here was a setback in public health resistant to all efforts to lessen its severity. It took lives at will, and thereby demonstrated the limitations of both preventive and curative medicine.

'Spanish flu' struck in three fairly clear waves. The signs of the first modest wave appeared in March 1918 in US army camps, spreading to Africa and Asia, while the second wave affected Africa, the United States, and reached Brest, the disembarkation port for the American troops, in August and September; by November the pandemic was world-wide; finally, the third wave peaked from February to April 1919.

The full death toll of this pandemic in Paris, London and Berlin is difficult to estimate precisely. Different sources provide different forms of information about the disease. In London, 16,520 influenza deaths were recorded between June 1918 and May 1919, of which 989 came in the summer, 11,898 in the autumn, and 3,633 in the winter. In fact the total might well have approached 23,000 if all deaths from associated causes are included.

In Paris 10,281 people caught 'Spanish flu' (compared with an average annual figure of 166 for the period from 1908 to 1917), of which the majority were sufficiently ill to be admitted to hospital. In a few weeks the number of influenza deaths per week in Paris rose from about 10 to 1,473: the disease accounted for less than 2 per cent of deaths in Paris at the beginning of November and 49 per cent of deaths between 20 and 26 November![58]

[56] Rathbone, *We that were young*, pp. 413–19.

[57] Tomkins, 'Britain and the influenza epidemic'. See also the same author's 'The failure of expertise: public health policy in Britain during the 1918–1919 influenza epidemic', *Social History of Medicine* (1992), pp. 435–54.

[58] The figures for Paris come from a statistical study published in 1919. See préfecture de la Seine, Direction de l'Hygiène, du Travail et de la Prévoyance sociale, *Recueil de Statistiques de la ville de Paris et du département de la Seine, Epidémie de grippe à Paris, 30 Juin 1918–26 avril 1919* (Paris, 1919).

The total number of deaths in Berlin is difficult to establish because of the large number of deaths registered under the general category of 'inflammation of the lungs'. For the whole of Germany, one-fifth of the population probably fell ill.[59] Against a normal average of about 10 deaths per month in summer and about 50 in winter, the number rose to nearly 700 in July and 2,600 in October. For the period from October to December 1918, Berlin recorded 4,732 deaths.[60] Death rates for influenza and respiratory tract diseases rose to 196.27 per 100,000 inhabitants in October 1918, six times the rate for the same month in 1917 and the previous months in 1918.[61]

There were clear similarities in the temporal incidence of the disease and in its age-specificity. The cities' weekly mortality reports show very similar autumn and spring trends, with the peak a few weeks after the beginning of the pandemic – in the week of 9–16 November in London, and in Paris and Berlin at the end of October 1918. Everywhere the climax of the pandemic was devastating.

Especially at risk were the young. Incomplete inquiries showed that morbidity in London schools might reach a rate of 30 to 40 per cent. The only clear correlation with biological and social parameters which can be established for London is that of age: although no age-group was spared, young adults ran the greatest risk of death. This was also true of Paris: adults between twenty and thirty-nine were the most severely affected group. Similarly, in Berlin young adults were the most vulnerable.[62]

Although there was dispute at the time as to the incidence of the pandemic in rich and poor districts, it seems clear that 'Spanish flu' was egalitarian.[63] In a city such as Paris with very wide variations in death rates by arrondissement, this was very striking. But such even-handedness was hardly surprising, given that the pandemic was produced by a mutant virus to which no one had immunity.

'Spanish flu' hit women harder than men. In Paris two-thirds of the victims of the pandemic were women. In London the corresponding proportion was 55 per cent. It should also be noted that pregnant women were particularly vulnerable, with an increased risk of miscarriage. This predominance of female victims was probably due to the

[59] Martin Hahn, 'Influenza, Genickstarre, Tetanus, Weilsche Krankheit', in F. Bumm (ed.), *Deutschlands Gesundheitsverhältnisse unter dem Einfluss des Weltkrieges* vol. I, (Stuttgart and New Haven 1928), p. 331.

[60] The data comes from *Tabellen über die Bevölkerungsvorgänge Berlins* (Berlin 1918).

[61] *Statistisches Jahrbuch der Stadt Berlin*, vol. 34 (1915–19), pp. 4, 144, 889, 896.

[62] Hahn, 'Influenza', pp. 335–7.

[63] L. Hersch, *Pauvreté et mortalité selon les principales causes de décès d'après les statistiques de la Ville de Paris* (Rome, 1932); T. H. C. Stevenson, 'The incidence of mortality upon the rich and poor districts of Paris and London', *Journal of the Royal Statistical Society* (1921), pp. 1–30.

imbalance of the sexes within urban populations. Demobilization came later.

In its suddenness, and its characteristic death-rate, the epidemic confused the public as much as it confused the authorities. A brutal illness which struck swiftly, it affected civilians as much as the military, sparing no age-group, weakening whole populations, leaving them weak even where it did not kill. It was as lethal at home as at the front. The two populations had to confront the illness at the same time, and in the same ways.

In family households, sick mothers were unable to look after sick children. Physicians and funeral services were overwhelmed. The pandemic completely disrupted certain services, such as London's police, fire brigade, and telephone exchange.[64]

Further, the central British authorities (notably the Local Government Board and the Board of Education), convinced that their role was purely one of prevention, intervened very little. They were content to issue recommendations and prescribe ventilation in cinemas. In contrast the public, noting the uselessness of prevention, had recourse to all kinds of treatment, medicaments, potions, and even vaccines. Local authorities took some positive steps, in providing home nursing, soup kitchens, and clinics. One borough even took the step of distributing gargling and disinfection fluids. But all these measures were futile. The illness took its course without interference.

This division between prevention and treatment was much less sharply defined in Paris, where the public authorities were prepared to intervene extensively in order to try to minimize the effects of the pandemic. The first move was to inform the public that this was indeed an asphyxiating form of influenza with cyanosis, and not typhus, cholera, or plague, as had been suggested by certain rumours based on the blueish skin-colour of the victims. This form of influenza was associated with bronchial lesions and broncho-pneumonia, hence its dangers.

Next came various measures concerning notification of the illness, disinfection, isolation of patients, and the banning of gatherings. A solution was sought to the problem of overcrowded hospitals; 300 beds for convalescents were made available to the Paris public-aid authority in Nanterre. The American Red Cross was asked to transport the sick by ambulance. The police helped doctors on their rounds by giving out priority cards for public transport, and the night medical service was enlarged with the help of the army. Emergency teams equipped with quinine and capsules of camphorated oil were ready to rush to patients' homes, and the prefecture of police took on the re-stocking of pharma-

[64] Tomkins, 'Influenza epidemic'.

cies, notably with quinine, and organized night-time manning of dispensaries.

In his report on influenza in Paris, Léon Bernard cited all these measures. But he pointed out that their effects were self-defeating, with hospitalization being far from harmless. It would have been better, he noted to support home nursing care (as happened in Lyon), or to promote the wearing of masks in public.[65] Whether or not such measures would have made the slightest difference to the course of the pandemic is open to question.

The Berlin authorities faced by the pandemic were in an even more difficult situation, in view of the conjunction of the epidemic and the defeat. Their intervention was minimal. Local communities were left to decide for themselves whether or not to close the schools, judging that the children would be deprived of school meals and they might just as easily catch influenza playing in the streets. Their recommendations tended towards the observance of basic hygiene, hand-washing, gargling, and avoiding crowds.[66]

'War and epidemics go together', commented City Councillor Weyl, himself a doctor and member of the Socialist group, meaning that the pandemic also indicated a failed war policy. Perhaps it would have been more accurate to say defeat and apathy go together. Public initiatives were timid and incomplete. This absence of response on the part of the city administration was a fundamental sign of the helplessness of medical authorities faced with the spread of the disease; at the same time, it was the inevitable result of the coincidence of the arrival of a medical catastrophe at a time of defeat, revolution, and demobilization.

One particular incident may highlight the degree to which this visitation united the social history of all three cities at the end of the war. In Paris, as in London and Berlin, men who had survived combat, and the wounds inflicted in it, fell to 'Spanish flu'. One such man was the poet Guillaume Apollinaire. The man who had invented the term 'surrealism' served in the artillery. His mother was always anxious about her son's health: she begged him on 21 April 1915, to

> take care not to be hit by a shell when you are riding through the woods; and take care not to fall into a ditch or a hole. Apparently the shells make enormous deep holes and it would be dreadful if you fell in with your horse, especially if you are alone and there is no one to help you. And I gather too that a bursting shell can bring down trees, take care not to be crushed by a tree. Finally, be careful and pray to the Holy Virgin every night . . . Write to me as soon as possible because I am anxious all the time.[67]

[65] Bernard, *La défense*, esp. pp. 154–8.

[66] 'Mitteilungen über die Grippe (Influenza)', *Ministerial-Blatt für Medizinalangelegenheiten*, 18, 44 (30 Oct. 1918), p. 335.

[67] Guillaume Apollinaire, *Correspondance avec son frère et sa mère*, présentée par Gilbert

Apollinaire was wounded in the head by a shell-burst on 17 March 1917 and had to be trepanned. All this he survived, only to succumb to 'Spanish flu' two days before the Armistice, on 9 November 1918.

The universality of the disaster is reflected in other literary forms. In *Pale horse, pale rider*, written by the American novelist Katherine Anne Porter, the heroine Miranda lies in bed, in the throes of Spanish flu. In her delirium she recalls her childhood and the recent events in her life, her inability recently to pay out 50 dollars for a Liberty Bond, the immense guilt she feels over this, the evening that she spend with Adam, her happiness at seeing him and talking to him, her love for him, a love shadowed by the anxiety of precariousness. Adam is on embarkation leave before his unit departs for the war and nurses her; Miranda is finally taken to hospital and, after long weeks of illness, she escapes death. When she recovers she learns of the death of her lover Adam. He had died of 'Spanish flu'.

Here was a real story retold millions of times. The fate of Apollinaire and these two young fictional characters illustrates the ambivalent legacy of 'Spanish flu'. It was an illness which mocked the efforts of so many people to escape death at the front – and defied the efforts of public-health authorities to protect them from an invisible and all-powerful enemy.

Conclusion

In conclusion, the general reckoning to be drawn from comparison of public-health policy in the three capital cities during the war is a mixed story. In some respects the war left undisturbed some pre-war trends. In a few cases, the war accelerated positive developments, for instance with respect to vaccination against infectious diseases like smallpox or typhoid fever, particularly in Paris. In all three cities sectors of the population were relatively well protected from the vagaries of disease in wartime.

Others were not so fortunate, especially in the second half of the war. Marginal populations were most at risk. There was also the permanent brooding presence of tuberculosis, spread by migration and overwork, and then finally the brutal and overwhelming 'Spanish flu'.

But while Londoners and Parisians weathered these storms relatively well, Berliners went through a much darker chapter in their history. It was a chapter in which illness, deprivation and defeat went hand in hand. Even the Armistice did not end the troubles, for the Allied blockade continued the war against civilians for another six months.

Boudon et Michel Decaudin (Paris, 1987), p. 146. As cited in Michel Cournot, 'L'entière liberté d'écrire d'Apollinaire', *Le Monde* (27 Jan. 1993). I am grateful to M. Cournot for kindly supplying me with the reference.

In London and Paris, on the other hand, public health did not deteriorate markedly after 1916. The major exception was 'Spanish flu', which hit young people and adults everywhere. There were those who suffered increased illness in wartime: illegitimate children and the elderly were particularly at risk. But the bulk of the population of London and Paris weathered the storm of war relatively well. There were the armies of the dead to mourn and the armies of the lame, the halt, and the blind to care for. They were everywhere. But after the Armistice, when the constraints on everyday life lifted, the negative effects of the conflict on civilian heath faded, leaving some positive initiatives and achievements upon which to build in the post-war years.

Policy failures – especially with respect to respiratory infections – as much as the war-time successes surveyed in chapter 14 highlighted the need to improve health-care systems after the Armistice. Full entitlements came only after 1945, but the devastating effects of illness on what Sen calls 'capabilities' and 'functionings' were there for all to see in the 1914–18 war. What could be done after the Second World War was partly a result of lessons learned in the Great War.

16
Surviving the war: life expectation, illness, and mortality rates in Paris, London, and Berlin, 1914–1919

Jay Winter

Introduction

Part of the story of the well-being or ill-being of populations at war is unmistakably demographic. Rates of sickness, death-rates, life expectation at birth describe the rhythms of daily life and the contours of thousands of family histories. But in and of themselves, they do not constitute a summary measure of well-being, let alone an answer to the question as to why one side won the war and the other lost it. Our purpose in the following survey of civilian health is more modest: it is to provide additional evidence about well-being in wartime by rigorously describing its opposite.

Without a comprehensive picture of morbidity, mortality, and survival chances, it is impossible to investigate systematically what Sen has called the 'capabilities' and 'functionings' of populations. When the influenza epidemic of 1918 to 1919 struck, much of life – in and out of the armies – came to an abrupt halt. Illness reduces capabilities and functionings; ultimately to the vanishing point. By studying civilian death-rates, we can see evidence both of the successful defence as well as the progressive erosion of capabilities on the home front during the 1914–18 war.

Our findings offer a clear contrast among these three cities and a clear narrative line within which to set the comparative history of the impact of war. This is the great advantage of demographic analysis. By definition comparative, it enables us to ask the same question of roughly similar sources available for all three cities, a luxury we did not enjoy in many of the earlier chapters of this book.

Interpreting the evidence is even more difficult than gathering it. Much demographic data do indeed reflect aspects of wartime trends in nutrition, housing, fuel supply, and public-health initiatives. But the social processes involved in causality are too complex, and involve so many events of the immediate and the distant past, that we cannot provide a quantitative weighting of the relative significance of one factor over another in the overall pattern of civilian health. We do not view demographic evidence as a culmination or mechanical outcome of the evidence we have surveyed in earlier chapters. It advances the inquiry rather than resolving it.

Our findings may be summarized in the following terms. The fundamental distinction between the pattern of civilian mortality in wartime Paris and London, on the one hand, and in Berlin, on the other, is the difference between loss of progress and loss of life. In the Allied capitals the secular decline of mortality was checked at most ages in wartime. A level trend meant loss of progress, a loss of the annual increment in survival rates likely to have occurred had there been no war. This was the case in Paris and London. A sharply rising trend meant loss of life, an increase in civilian mortality directly attributable to war conditions on the home front. This was the case in Berlin in the latter phases of the war.

This levelling off in the pre-war pattern of declining mortality is evident in both Paris and London in wartime, though recovery was rapid in the post-war period 1919 to 1921. In both cities some increases in death-rates among civilians occurred, especially at the time of the 'Spanish flu' pandemic of 1918 to 1919, but these and other inflections were counterbalanced by declines in other causes of death. The result in the Allied capitals was stability for most age groups, and slight deterioration in survival rates for others. But the sum of upward and downward vectors in the mortality history of Paris and London was close to zero. Given the problems of estimation, it would be wise to conclude that, with a number of exceptions, in the Allied capitals civilian mortality was no better and no worse than it had been on the eve of the war.

There were nearly 1,000 civilian victims of aerial or artillery bombardment in Paris and London;[1] if there ever was an exogenous variable in demographic history, this is it. Leaving aside the incidence of deaths due to enemy action against civilians, it is clear that among those registering rising death rates in these cities in wartime were the elderly, and some adult groups especially vulnerable to respiratory infections. These were of two kinds: pandemic influenza in 1918 and 1919 and endemic tuberculosis, which took an increased toll of civilian life throughout the war.

The public-health picture in wartime Berlin was more sombre than that in Paris and London. The distinction did not become apparent until the second half of the war. During the period 1914 to 1916, there was nothing to choose between the two sides in terms of the capacity of

[1] On the bombardment of Paris and London, see *Paris de jour à jour: le vingtième siècle* (Paris, 1968); for London, see H. G. Castle, *Fire over England: the German air raids of World War I* (London, 1982).

society to organize its wartime life without prejudice to the survival chances of the civilian population. If anything, Berlin was in a more favourable position. Total death-rates rose in Paris in 1914; not in Berlin. The death-rate for civilians rose in London in 1915; not in Berlin. The year 1916 was a relatively good one in terms of civilian death-rates in all three cities. Gains were made in Paris, London, and Berlin in survival rates compared to the pre-war norm. But as soon as we enter the second half of the war, the story is reversed. After 1916, when material pressures increased in all three capitals, it is only in Berlin that we can see unmistakable evidence of a mortality crisis, a substantial and general increase in death-rates in the civilian population as a whole.

All three cities weathered the storm of the influenza pandemic of 1918 to 1919. So did New York and Delhi. The flu and its huge death toll were a product not of the war, but of the (then as now) unknown processes of viral morphology.[2] But in Berlin, the pandemic hit a population in the midst of an independently generated mortality crisis. That crisis was a product of the war and the way it was waged both by the Allies and by the Central Powers.

The structure of this chapter is straightforward. We first describe pre-war demographic trends. Secondly, we specify the amplitude and duration of wartime fluctuations in female mortality rates in Paris, London, and Berlin. Male data are totally distorted by military mobilization. Thirdly, we examine some features of the age-structure and cause-structure of urban mortality in the war decade, and then turn to some aspects of social and spatial inequalities in the trend of civilian mortality rates. Finally, we point out some convergences and divergences in the history of public health in wartime, and try to place these findings within the wider demographic and social history of the war.

Pre-war demographic trends

In chapter 2, we presented some information on the demographic character of these cities. It may be useful to return to some of the salient

[2] The literature on the influenza epidemic is vast. See Tomkins, 'The influenza epidemic'; for other cases see A. Crosby, *Epidemic and peace, 1918* (Westport, Conn., 1976); S. Galishoff, 'Newark and the great influenza pandemic of 1918', *Bulletin of the History of Medicine*, 43 (1969), pp. 246–58; L. Bryder, '"Lessons" of the 1918 influenza epidemic in Auckland', *New Zealand Journal of History*, 16, 2 (1982), pp. 97–121; M. Boyd, 'Coping with the Samoan resistance after the 1918 influenza epidemic', *Journal of Pacific History*, 15 (1980), pp. 155–74; R. Collier, *The plague of the Spanish Lady* (London, 1974); A. Drolet, 'L'épidémie de grippe espagnole à Québec, 1918', *Trois siècles de Médecine québécoise*, Cahiers d'histoire no. 22, La Société Historique de Québec (1970), pp. 98–106; E.O. Jordan, *Epidemic Influenza: a survey* (Chicago, 1927); J.P. McGinnis, 'The impact of epidemic influenza: Canada, 1918–19', *Historical Papers* (1977), pp. 120–40; J. E. Osborn, *Influenza in America 1918–1976* (New York, 1977).

features of this subject, to clarify the later discussion of war-related developments.

We have noted that the most spectacular period of metropolitan population growth in European history occurred in the generation before the outbreak of war in 1914. In this period, Paris added approximately 1 million inhabitants to its numbers, reaching about 2.9 million in 1910. Over the same period, Berlin's expansion was even more remarkable. From a modest city of 800,000 on the eve of the founding of the empire, the Wilhelmine capital was home to over 2 million people in 1910. Greater still was the increase in the population of London. Including its outer ring, Greater London's population rose from approximately 3.9 million in 1871 to over 7 million in 1911. The core London County Council population rose from 3.3 million in 1871 to 4.5 million in 1911. Suburbanization was therefore more rapid than urban growth.[3] Even allowing for inevitable inaccuracies due to changes of boundaries, the overall trend is clear. This unprecedented wave of demographic growth changed the density, the geometry, and the character of these cities, and put an enormous strain on their pre-existing infrastructure.

These cities were not only huge housing districts for permanent residents. They were also stations for temporary residents and for people moving to other destinations. All three cities had large alien populations. Their numbers grew in the two generations before the 1914–18 war, when a strong migratory wave swept westward across Europe and for many, further still across the Atlantic Ocean. Paris, London, and Berlin were frequently points on the way to another destination. As a result, the numbers passing through these cities *en route* added substantially and intermittently to the resident population.[4]

Natural increase was responsible primarily for London's growth in this period. In the case of Paris and to a lesser degree Berlin, migration was of greater importance in this process of metropolitan population growth. Indeed these developments took place against the backdrop of declining fertility rates. From a level of approximately 36 per 1,000 in the 1870s, Berlin's birth rate fell to about 20 per 1,000 in 1910. The same

[3] B. R. Mitchell, *International Historical Statistics. Europe 1750–1988* (Basingstoke, 3rd edn, 1992), table A4.

[4] For recent research and references, see D. Baines, *Migration in a mature economy: emigration and internal migration in England and Wales, 1861–1900* (Cambridge, 1985); D. Hoerder (ed.), *Labor migration in the Atlantic economies: the European and North American working classes during the period of industrialization* (Westport, Conn., 1985); I. A. Glazier and L. de Rosa (eds), *Migration across time and nations: population mobility in historical contexts* (New York, 1986); P. E. Ogden and P. E. White (eds.), *Migrants in modern France: population mobility in the later nineteenth and twentieth centuries* (London, 1989); and the classic study by Brinley Thomas, *Migration and economic growth* (2nd edn, Cambridge, 1972).

secular trend may be observed in the other two capitals, though in Paris, as in the rest of France, fertility rates were lower than in other European countries. French fertility decline after 1870 was the second stage of an earlier process of *dénatalité* beginning a century before.[5]

Mortality rates also declined from the late nineteenth century. But this trend played a smaller role than migration in the pattern of metropolitan growth, largely because the strain of demographic expansion on housing and other urban amenities was so great as to counteract some of the positive effects of municipal improvements in sanitation and water supply. Some facets of urban growth pushed death-rates up while other forces helped contain them.[6]

So far we have pointed to features of demographic history common to all three capital cities. In one respect, though, the demography of London differed substantially from that of Paris and Berlin. Both continental capitals, in contrast to London, registered a relatively high proportion of all births outside of marriage.[7] Family forms clearly differed in these capital cities. These distinctive patterns of family formation and reproduction had dramatic effects on infant mortality, and thereby on metropolitan death rates as a whole.[8]

We noted in chapter 15 that illegitimacy is a cluster of conditions. It covers those born in common-law marriages, those born to women in-migrating to have their children, who then care for them, as well as children abandoned soon after birth. All three groups had mortality rates in the first year of life above those of legitimate infants. Abandoned children were particularly vulnerable. The high proportion of illegitimate births within the overall birth cohort help to account for the fact that in the period 1876 to 1880, the infant mortality rates stood at about 300 per 1,000 live births in Berlin and 200 per 1,000 live births in Paris. The London figure was 154.[9]

Over the years 1870 to 1900, infant mortality rates in London remained stable, but those in Paris declined slightly. The onset of rapid infant mortality decline in both Paris and London came after 1900, starting at a higher level in Paris. In Berlin in contrast, infant mortality

[5] A.J. Coale and S.C. Watkins (eds.), *The decline of fertility in Europe* (Princeton, 1986).

[6] S. Szreter, 'The importance of social intervention in Britain's mortality decline *c.* 1850–1914: a reinterpretation of the role of public health', *Social History of Medicine*, 1 (1988), pp. 1–34. V.Berridge, 'Health and medicine', in F.M.L. Thompson (ed.), *The Cambridge Social History of Britain*, vol. III (Cambridge, 1990), pp. 198–220. On the strains on London, see D. Owen, *The government of Victorian London 1855–1899: the Metropolitan Board of Works, the Vestries and the City Corporation* (Cambridge, Mass., 1982); and J. Davis, *Reforming London: the London government problem, 1855–1900* (Oxford, 1988).

[7] *London Statistics* (1908), p. 46.

[8] Winter and Cole, 'Fluctuations in infant mortality'.

[9] Rollet, *La politique*, ch. 9; R. G. Fuchs, *Poor and pregnant in Paris. Strategies for survival in the nineteenth century* (New Brunswick, N.J., 1992).

began to decline from its dizzying heights in the 1870s, and continued to drop after the turn of the century.[10] Nevertheless, even after thirty years of progress, Berlin's infant mortality rates in 1900 – 202 per 1,000 – were at the level registered by Paris in the years 1871 to 1875, and still well above early Victorian levels in London.

On the eve of the war, London was the healthiest of the three cities. Life expectancy was longest, and adult mortality rates were lowest of the three conurbations. Paris, in contrast, had the highest death-rates, with Berlin located between the two.[11] Berlin's adult mortality levels were lower than those of Paris, but its infant mortality levels remained higher. Levels of infant mortality *registered* in London and Paris had converged, though Parisian infants who were sent out to wet-nurses had much higher infant mortality rates. Consequently, the mortality rates of infants *born* in Paris were significantly higher than those born in London.[12] On balance, it is clear that over the period 1870–1914, the demographic gap between and among these cities had narrowed (see tables 16.1–3).

Within these metropolitan areas, substantial demographic inequalities persisted on the eve of the war.[13] Areas receiving in-migrants, especially of poor labouring families, had substantially higher death-rates than did the city as a whole. This was true of suburban belts surrounding the cities as well as some inner-city districts. The district of Spandau was just outside metropolitan Berlin before the 1914-18 war, and was to become an area of rapid wartime expansion. In 1900 its infant mortality rate stood at 290, while that for Berlin as a whole was about 200.[14] Before its period of rapid growth, Spandau's overall death rate was lower than that for Berlin as a whole. By 1900, the reverse was the case.[15] The poor and overcrowded inner-city quarter of Wedding registered infant mortality rates well above those for Berlin as a whole, though by

[10] Ingrid Stockel, 'Säuglingssterblichkeit in Berlin von 1870 bis zum Vorabend des Ersten Weltkriegs. Eine Kurve mit hohem Maximum und starkem Gefälle', in W. Ribbe (ed.), *Berlin-Forschungen-I* (Berlin, 1986), pp. 219–64.

[11] A. de Foville, 'Enquête sur le dépeuplement de la France', *La revue hebdomadaire*, 5 (1909), pp. 101–29.

[12] C. Rollet, 'Nourrices et nourrissons dans le département de la Seine et en France de 1880 à 1940', *Population*, 3 (1982), pp. 573–604; G.D. Sussman, *Selling mother's milk: the wet-nursing business in France, 1815–1914* (Urbana, Ill, 1982).

[13] R. Spree, *Health and Social Class in Imperial Germany*, trans. S. McKinnon-Evans (Leamington Spa, 1988); J. M. Winter, 'The decline of mortality', in T. Barker and M. Drake (eds.), *Population and society in Britain 1850–1980* (London, 1982), pp. 100–20; L. Hersch, *Pauvreté et mortalité selon les principales causes de décès d'après les statistiques de la Ville de Paris* (Rome, 1932).

[14] R. Gehrmann, 'Zielsetzungen und Methoden bei den historisch-demographischen Auswertungen von Berlin-Brandenburgischem Kirchenbuchmaterial. Das Beispiel St. Nikolai (Spandau)', in Ribbe (ed.), *Berlin Forschungen-I*, p. 285.

[15] Gehrmann, 'Zielsetzungen', p. 282.

the eve of the war this relative disadvantage had narrowed substantially. The relative advantage of the more prosperous Tempelhof quarter remained a constant of Berlin's demographic profile in this period.[16]

The same wide gap was evident when infant mortality rates in poor and affluent quarters of London and Paris were compared. Over the period 1911 to 1913, infant mortality rates in the working-class 20th arrondissement (Belleville) were about four times as high as those in the affluent 8th arrondissement (Elysée). The ratio of total death-rates in the two districts was over two to one.[17] Comparing affluent Hampstead with the poorer working-class district of Shoreditch produces similar inequalities: an infant mortality rate of 72 for the well-off compared to 150 per 1,000 live births for the poor. Tuberculosis death-rates in the two districts varied by a factor of three.[18]

In sum, these cities were patchworks of healthy and unhealthy areas, in which life expectancy varied according to the accident of birth and the advantages of wealth. Those in-migrating chose these mixed urban environments, though to locate pure freedom of choice within the labour or housing markets is an economists' illusion. Most people lived where they had to and in whatever housing they could afford.

On balance, though, on the eve of the 1914–18 war, these city-dwellers had smaller families and lived longer lives than did their forefathers and mothers. Many thousands lived in some of the worst slums in Europe, but despite the stubborn persistence of these *ilôts insalubres*,[19] some real and enduring gains had been made in water supply, sanitation, and other urban amenities.[20] Mortality rates in the

[16] Stockel, 'Säuglingssterblichkeit', p. 246.

[17] L. Hersch, 'L'inégalité devant la mort d'après les statistiques de la ville de Paris', *Revue d'Economie Politique* (1920), p. 297.

[18] T. H. C Stevenson, 'The incidence of mortality upon the rich and poor districts of Paris and London', *Journal of the Royal Statistical Society* (1921), p. 91. On demographic inequality in Britain in general see J. M. Winter, 'The decline of mortality in Britain'; and 'Public health and the extension of life expectancy in England and Wales, 1901–1961', in M. Keynes, D. A. Coleman, and N. H. Dimsdale (eds.), *The political economy of health and welfare. Proceedings of the twenty-second annual symposium of the Eugenics Society* (Basingstoke, 1988), pp. 184–206. On tuberculosis, see G. Cronje, 'Tuberculosis and mortality decline in England and Wales 1851–1910', in R. Woods and J. Woodward (eds.), *Urban disease and mortality in nineteenth century England* (London, 1984).

[19] On which see H. Sellier, *La crise du logement et l'intervention publique en matière d'habitation populaire dans l'agglomération parisienne* (Paris, 1921); and K. Burlen (ed.), *La banlieue oasis. Henri Sellier et les cités-jardins 1900–1940* (Saint-Denis, 1987).

[20] See Spree, *Health and Social Class*, ch. 4; J.-P. Goubert, 'Public hygiene and mortality decline in France in the 19th century', in T. Bengtsson, G. Fridlizius, and R. Ohlsson (eds.), *Pre-industrial population change. Mortality decline and short-term population movements* (Stockholm, 1984); R. H. Guerrand, *Les origines du logement social en France* (Paris, 1967); B. Luckin, 'Evaluating the sanitary revolution: typhus and typhoid in London, 1851-1900', in R. Woods and J. Woodward (eds.), *Urban Disease and Mortality in Nineteenth-century England* (London, 1984).

capital cities were still higher than in the nation as a whole, but conditions had improved. The best way to summarize the demographic profile of Paris, London, and Berlin in 1914 is by emphasizing three features of their recent history: very rapid overall growth, declining fertility and mortality, especially after 1900, and a high degree of variation in vital rates as between districts and social groups.

Populations at risk and mortality rates, 1911 to 1919

Standardized death rates: general comparisons

In the statistical appendix at the end of this volume, we discuss the procedures used to estimate populations and death-rates for the civilian population, and the margins of error produced inevitably by these procedures. Wherever possible, standardized death-rates have been used. Given the scale of military mobilization, we have not provided estimates of male populations. All comments refer to females only, though it is true that the majority of the urban population at home was female. The results must be treated as at best an indication of urban demographic trends in wartime.

The war and its aftermath reordered the demographic history of Paris, London, and Berlin in one important way. Before 1914 mortality rates in Paris were substantially higher than in Berlin. The same gap existed between Berlin and London. The ratio was of the order of 16/14/12 deaths per 1,000, as between Paris, Berlin, and London. Figure 16.1 demonstrates this rank order clearly. The crisis of 1914 in Paris separated the cities further, and the crisis of 1915 in London brought mortality levels up to those of Berlin. The same rank order of the pre-war years is visible in 1916. But thereafter, the crisis in Berlin destroyed the old order, and produced a rough equality between death-rates in Paris and Berlin.

As tables 16.1 to 16.3 show, Berlin death-rates at all ages in the period 1917 to 1919 were slightly higher than those in Paris, and considerably higher than those in London. The contrast with the pre-war period is evident. Berlin death-rates in the period 1911 to 1913 were lower than those in Paris at adult ages (defined due to source limitations as 15 to 44 in London and Paris, 15 to 49 in Berlin). In the period 1917 to 1919, the reverse is true. At the ages of 1 to 4, death-rates in Paris were still higher than those in Berlin in the years 1917 to 1919, but the Parisian disadvantage in survival rates for this age-group was halved during the war.

In effect, the war cost Berlin its demographic advantage over Paris, and widened the gap between Berlin and London. Overall death-rates per 1,000 in the British capital were 1.67 below those in Berlin in the

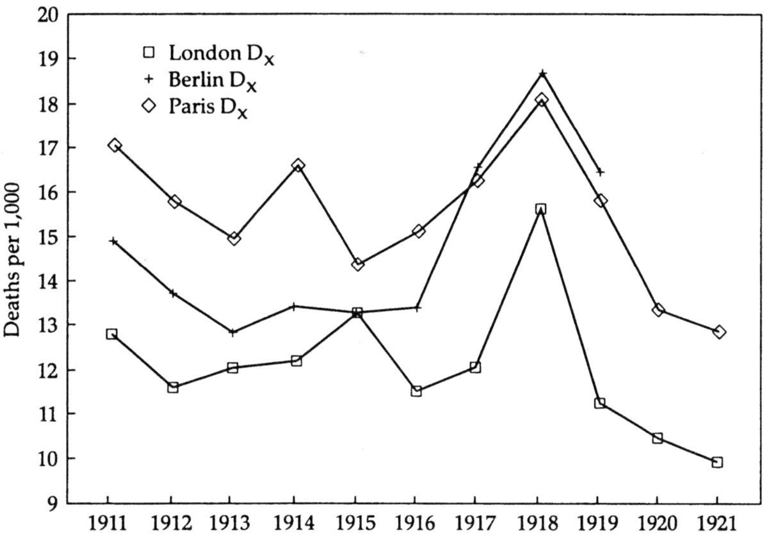

Fig. 16.1 Paris, London, Berlin: standardized female death-rates, 1911 to 1919/21, all ages

Table 16.1. *Standardized death-rates, female population of London, 1911 to 1921 (deaths per 1,000)*

Year	Std D_x[a]	D(0–1)	D(1–4)	Std D(15–44)	Std D(60+)
1911	12.78	125.05	18.43	4.11	57.12
1912	11.63	87.70	13.46	4.03	57.93
1913	12.07	101.69	13.49	3.93	60.29
1914	12.22	100.01	14.13	4.09	60.08
1915	13.29	102.92	18.89	4.26	65.09
1916	11.50	86.24	12.83	3.96	60.05
1917	12.07	94.53	15.53	4.23	59.17
1918	15.58	96.68	23.81	8.69	56.80
1919	11.21	83.40	9.48	4.66	55.87
1920	10.42	82.77	12.56	3.81	49.99
1921	9.89	61.92	11.52	3.61	53.02
1911–13	12.16	104.81	15.13	4.02	58.45
1914–16	12.34	96.39	15.35	4.10	61.74
1914–18	12.93	96.08	17.04	5.05	60.24
1917–19	12.95	91.54	11.19	5.86	57.28
1919–21	10.51	76.03	12.04	4.03	52.96

[a]D_x = standardized female death-rate.

Table 16.2. *Standardized death-rates, female population of Berlin, 1911 to 1919 (deaths per 1,000, mid-year populations)*

Year	Std D_x	D(0–1)	D(1–4)	Std D(15–49)	Std D(60+)
1911	14.91	176.26	15.67	5.80	61.44
1912	13.74	139.11	12.80	5.78	60.77
1913	12.83	132.29	10.10	5.56	57.63
1914	13.45	146.84	12.71	5.38	60.23
1915	13.31	128.67	13.70	5.46	61.25
1916	13.41	111.99	13.67	5.56	62.62
1917	16.55	142.98	14.10	7.02	84.08
1918	18.66	141.72	17.26	11.35	72.10
1919	16.43	177.57	14.70	7.91	65.77
1911–13	13.83	149.22	12.86	5.71	59.95
1914–16	13.39	129.17	13.36	5.47	61.37
1914–18	15.08	134.44	14.29	6.95	68.06
1917–19	17.21	154.09	15.35	8.76	73.98

[a]D_x = standardized female death rate.

Table 16.3. *Standardized death-rates, female population of Paris, 1911 to 1921 (deaths per 1,000, mid-year populations)*

Year	Std D_x	D(0–1)	D(1–4)	Std D(15–44)	Std D(60+)
1911	17.05	165.91	28.84	6.68	64.71
1912	15.81	142.44	25.76	6.38	61.17
1913	14.96	140.1	24.59	6.18	56.53
1914	16.62	151.15	22.43	6.86	69.23
1915	14.39	121.55	22.07	5.53	61.31
1916	15.12	123.26	24.35	5.85	65.92
1917	16.27	129.53	21.11	5.94	69.19
1918	18.05	153.14	21.79	10.27	61.37
1919	15.78	145.17	20.57	7.10	61.20
1921	12.82	103.63	14.75	5.79	56.17
1911–13	15.94	149.48	26.40	6.41	60.80
1914–16	15.38	131.99	22.95	6.08	65.49
1914–18	16.09	135.73	22.35	6.89	65.40
1917–19	16.70	142.61	21.16	7.77	63.92
1919–21	13.98	128.53	18.60	6.23	57.98

period 1911 to 1913; 4.26 below between 1917 and 1919. The gap widened at all other ages, and in particular at advanced years. Even at the ages of 1 to 4, where London death-rates were higher than those of Berlin in the pre-war period, that gap was narrowed during the war.

In sum, the Great War made Berlin an unhealthier city to live in, both absolutely and in comparison with either Paris or London. The change took place after 1916. What of the two Allied capitals? Did the war reorder the survival chances of their populations? On balance the answer is no. Before and after the war, Parisian death rates were about 3.5 per 1,000 higher than those of London. There was some variation as among age-groups, but with the exception of the one to four age-group, where mortality in London was volatile, the two cities' mortality history moved in parallel in the war decade. The real divergence in this period is between the demographic history of Berlin and that of the Allied capitals.

Life expectancy: general comparisons

Another way of expressing the contrast between the wartime demographic history of Berlin, on the one hand, and Paris and London on the other is in terms of life expectancy. These data show very minor changes between 1914 and 1916 in all three cities. Given the fact that estimation problems require us to adopt a 4 per cent margin of error in all cases (see appendix), it is probably best to conclude that female life expectancy was stable in all three cities in the period 1914 to 1916. Only between 1917 and 1919 in Berlin can we report a significant shift in life expectancy among female civilians. In effect the increase in mortality rates between 1917 and 1919 reduced life expectancy at birth in Berlin by 3.7 years. This was the time of pandemic influenza, but the viral infection struck London and Paris, too, and in those cases the overall effect on life expectancy between 1917 and 1919 was negligible.

Here is another way of stating the fundamental point. In Paris and London, female life expectancy stabilized during the war. This entailed a loss of progress. In Berlin female life expectancy fell after 1916. This entailed a loss of life, in the sense that life expectancy fell for both young and older age groups. It is unfortunate that data do not permit an analysis of Berlin's post-war recovery from this wartime crisis. But its severity cannot be disputed. It was not a reflection of an exogenous shock in the form of the influenza pandemic, but of a more general deterioration in the survival chances of the civilian population.

Age-specific mortality

The discussion of age-specific mortality in comparative terms is hampered by different degrees of detail in reporting deaths by age and in estimating populations by age. We have therefore tried to describe differences in the impact of war on the survival chances of different age-groups by clustering the population in four groups: the infant population, under the age of one; the child population under the age of five; the adult population, at the ages of fifteen to forty-four for London and Paris and fifteen to forty-nine for Berlin; and the elderly, at the age of sixty and over for all three cities. This choice of cohort was dictated by the available statistics, and while it would be important to gather further information on those age-groups unrepresented here, the overall trend in civilian health appears sufficiently clear to suggest that these findings apply to the urban population as a whole.

Infancy

There are two ways of measuring the survival chances of the infant population. The conventional one is to divide deaths by the number of live births in a given year. We have repeated this procedure, while smoothing out fluctuations in natality due to military mobilization. The rule we follow is to calculate annual births as the sum of one-quarter of the previous year's registered births and three-quarters of the current year's births. Infant mortality rates have as the denominator this figure, reduced for out-migration due to wet-nursing and to the flight of civilians away from Paris in late 1914. No such correction factor, full of doubtful conjectures, is necessary for London or Berlin. The second measure is to compare deaths in any one year between the ages of nought and one with an estimated population aged nought to one, derived by progression from data on earlier years. We use both procedures here; not surprisingly, they produce very similar results.

Survival rates in infancy: Paris, London, Berlin

Infant mortality in Paris and Berlin moved in parallel, as fig. 16.2 suggests. This is not surprising, given the high levels of illegitimacy in Paris and Berlin, and the entirely different (and lower) illegitimacy ratio in London. But despite this clear differentiation between London and the other two capital cities, there is one feature of wartime demographic history that they share. In all three cities, infant mortality declined in the period 1914 to 1916. The drop was above the 4 per cent margin of error built into all our estimates. The decline was approximately 8, 17, and 20 per 1,000 for London, Paris, and Berlin respectively. London's smaller gains reflect an upward movement in infant mortality in 1915.

In the period 1917 to 1919, infant mortality was more volatile. Increases were registered in 1917 in all three cities, and in Paris and (modestly) in London in 1918. A further rise occurred in Berlin in 1919, but not in the other two cities. In other words, infant mortality in Paris deteriorates until 1918, and then improves. In London, the situation is more stable than in the other two cities. There is some wartime fluctuation, and then a resumption of the pattern of decline during the

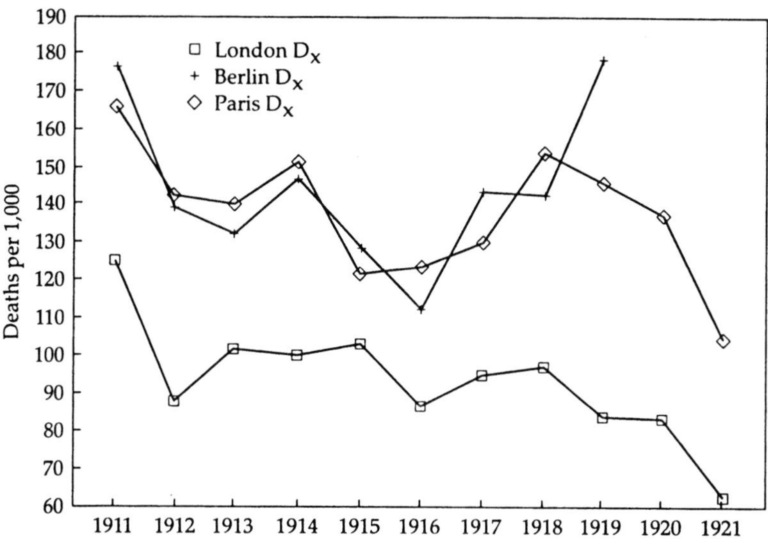

Fig. 16.2 Paris, London, Berlin: female death-rates, 1911 to 1919/21, ages 0 to 1

war. In Berlin wartime volatility continues after the Armistice. It is unfortunate that we do not have adequate data to measure the amplitude and duration of this crisis, but other evidence suggests that it lasted at least until 1922.[21]

On average, in the period 1917 to 1919, despite these fluctuations, London's 0–1 mortality was still well below pre-war levels: from 105 per 1,000 in the period 1911 to 1913, the figure had dropped to 92 per 1,000 in 1917 to 1919. The drop over this period in Paris was smaller – from 150 to 143 per 1,000. Only in Berlin did mortality at youngest ages in the years 1917 to 1919 rise to a point either at or above the pre-war level (see table 16.2).

It is important to accept the limitations of this argument, due to particularly severe estimation problems of the population at risk in 1919. We are dealing only with the female population, since the age-structure of the wartime male population is unknown. But even so, the gross difference between Paris and London, on the one hand, and Berlin, on the other, is clear. After 1916, the contrast is between modest gains in the Allied capitals, and in Berlin, either no gain or loss in survival chances of the infant population.

The case of Berlin requires one further qualification. Rough stability in infant mortality rates masks wide variations in the impact of war on the survival chances of legitimate and illegitimate infants. There was a

[21] Winter and Cole, 'Fluctuations in infant mortality rates'.

very steep rise in illegitimate infant mortality after 1916, much greater in Berlin than in Germany as a whole. Over the next three years illegitimate infant mortality rates in Berlin doubled, from approximately 160 to over 300 deaths per 1,000 live births. In contrast legitimate infant mortality remained stable, at about 120 per 1,000.[22] As figure 16.10 shows, the crisis in Berlin's illegitimate infant mortality continued until 1923 (see p. 513).

The significance of this finding is not in its revelation of the vulnerability of illegitimate infants, which is a universal rule of demographic history.[23] It is rather that in a city where illegitimacy was normal, accounting for over one-quarter of all births, and where the illegitimacy ratio remained high during the war, the deterioration in the survival chances of illegitimate infants should be reflected in infant mortality as a whole. But in fact, legitimate infants were shielded from the worst effects of the war. After an upward inflection in both legitimate and illegitimate infant mortality in 1914, both rates dropped in 1915 and 1916. Thereafter they diverged. The explanation of this pattern of approximate stability in overall infant mortality in Berlin at a time of crisis in illegitimate infant mortality is that there were parallel gains in the survival chances of legitimate infants.

Infant mortality in Berlin, as elsewhere, was a composite of contradictory phenomena. The seriousness of the crisis in illegitimate infant mortality in Berlin after 1916 helps establish the real effects of the war on this vulnerable part of the population. With respect to Berlin, we must, therefore, reject Offer's claim that infant mortality data show 'very little movement during the war'. He has fallen into the trap of aggregate analysis, and throughout his study underestimates the effects of wartime conditions on vulnerable sectors of the German population.[24] Through the close analysis of demographic data, now we can do better.

Because of the contrast between the impact of war on legitimate and illegitimate infants, the overall deterioration in infant survival rates in Berlin in the period 1917-1919 was much smaller than that in the population as a whole (see table 16.2). Considering the evidence on both legitimate and illegitimate infants, it is apparent that infant health was as well defended in Berlin in 1914–16 as in the other two capitals. Thereafter, Berlin's infants were in a vulnerable position, but legitimate infants appear to have been better protected from the pressures producing increased death-rates than were older cohorts.

22 Winter and Cole, 'Fluctuations in infant mortality rates'.

23 See P. Laslett (ed.), *Bastardy. The social history of illegitimacy* (Cambridge, 1984).

24 Offer, *An agrarian interpretation*, p. 36 and *passim*. For a more balanced interpretation, see L. Borchardt, 'The impact of the war economy on the civilian population', in W. Deist (ed.), *The German military in the age of total war* (Leamington Spa, 1985).

The cause-structure of infant mortality

In Paris, the overall decline in infant mortality was due primarily to a drop in the incidence of diarrhoeal-related deaths. About 80 per cent of the total decline in mortality at ages 0 to 1 was caused by this one set of infections. The contribution of respiratory diseases to the overall decline was smaller, about 18 per cent, and it was not maintained after the Armistice. Similarly congenital conditions contributed little to infant mortality decline, and actually worsened after the Armistice.

The overall decline in infant mortality in London masks comparable contradictory movements. Broncho-pneumonia as a cause of infant deaths rose above pre-war levels in 1915, 1917, 1918, and 1920, though on average mortality between 1914 and 1918 was lower than in the period 1911 to 1913. But at the same time, this adverse movement in death rates was overshadowed by an even more powerful decline in deaths attributable to diarrhoeal disease. Over the war years, 60 per cent of overall infant mortality decline is attributable to this one category. It should be noted that this important development was independent of weather conditions.

Evidently a fundamental change in the components of London's infant mortality occurred in the war decade. Before the war diarrhoeal disease contributed more than the cluster of broncho-pneumonial diseases to the overall infant mortality rate. The war reversed this position.[25]

Other factors are also evident in infant mortality fluctuations in London. Measles contributed to the upward surge in infant mortality in 1915 and 1920. Post-war infant mortality rates also reflect an increase in the incidence of deaths due to congenital conditions, probably a shadow effect of the influenza pandemic and its effects on the life chances of children conceived during its visitation. During the war itself, mortality attributable to congenital or prenatal causes fell, along with infant mortality rates as a whole.

In wartime Berlin too, digestive disease-related mortality declined rapidly, while respiratory disease-related mortality remained persistently high. Total infant mortality from digestive diseases declined from the pre-war level of 45 deaths per 1,000 to 33 deaths per 1,000 between 1914 and 1919, a decline of about 27 per cent. Digestive diseases still took a large toll of infant lives in years with hot summers, especially 1914 and 1917. After 1917, however, the decline becomes more readily apparent. Infant mortality from respiratory diseases exceeded that from digestive diseases in 1918 (a year with a relatively cool summer) for the first time, establishing a precedent for what was to become the pattern in the

[25] For a full discussion, see J.M. Winter, Lawrence, and Ariouat, 'Infant mortality in London'.

1920s. Measles mortality rose in the period 1916 to 1917, which may have been related to the triennial cycle of the disease.

In sum, the evidence of stable or declining rates of infant mortality for most parts of the urban populations was a reflection of declining digestive-disease mortality. The drop in the traditional killer of infancy, diarrhoeal disease, was of a sufficient magnitude to counter an upsurge in respiratory infections, leading to gains in infant survival chances in all three cities in the period 1914 to 1916. Some, but not all, of these gains were lost in the period 1917 to 1919, especially among illegitimate infants in Berlin. In Paris and London, the pre-war trajectory of infant mortality decline resumed after the Armistice.

Childhood

Survival rates in childhood (ages one to four)

Data on child and young adult mortality are notoriously hard to handle. By 1914, the number of deaths at ages after the first years of life were very small. Consequently, an increase of a small number of deaths over a brief period can produce massive movements in rates of change. We must beware of this statistical problem of dealing with populations for which death was relatively rare.

It is with some caution that we handle the finding presented in fig. 16.3 that the trend of mortality rates among children aged one to four in the three cities departed from that of infant mortality and from that of other age groups. The first clear distinction is the volatility of London mortality rates at the ages of one to four, not matched in either Paris or Berlin. There were two peaks of mortality in wartime London: the first in 1915, the second in 1918. Overall, the steep rise in 1918 – fully 57 per cent over the pre-war level of about 15 deaths per 1,000 – accounted for a deterioration in child mortality rates in the period 1914 to 1918 as a whole. Thereafter, recovery was very rapid, bringing mortality in this age-group well below pre-war levels.

In contrast, statistics on child mortality (ages one to four) in wartime Paris describe a more favourable trend. From a level of about 26 deaths per 1,000 in the pre-war period, child mortality in wartime reached 22 per 1,000 and fell well below that level in the post-war period. Aside from a brief upward inflection in 1916, there is no evidence of wartime conditions adversely affecting the nearly linear downward slope of child mortality rates.

The case of Berlin appears to be closer to the London than to the Paris pattern at this age-group. Death-rates for the one to four year old population in Berlin were above the pre-war rate in every year after 1914. The overall rise between 1914 and 1916 was small – perhaps 4 per cent – but the figure registered for the period 1917 to 1919 was fully 15

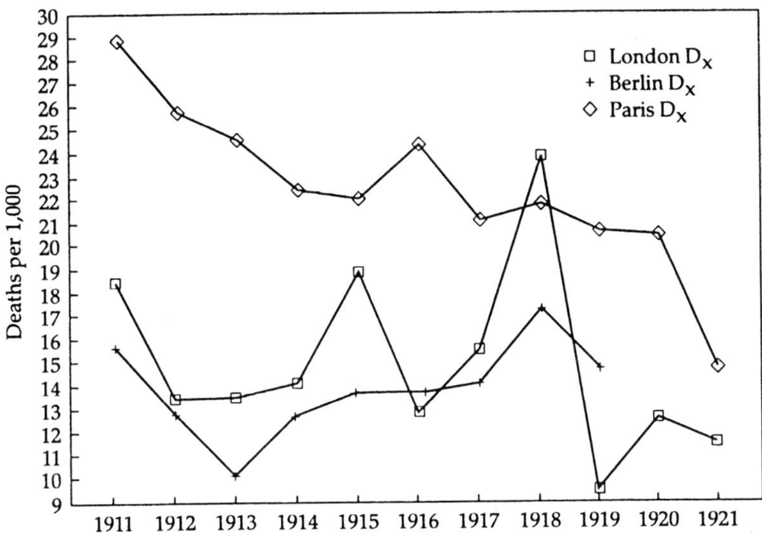

Fig. 16.3 Paris, London, Berlin: female death-rates, 1911 to 1919/21, ages 1 to 4

per cent above pre-war levels. The worst year was 1918, with 1919 not far behind. Again, we are hampered by the absence of statistics on the public-health situation in Berlin between 1920 and 1921.

On balance, the health of young children was compromised in wartime London and Berlin, but not in Paris. The deterioration in London occurred in both 1915 and 1918. In the first two war years, child-mortality rates remained stable in Berlin, and fell in Paris. Between 1917 and 1919, child mortality rose in Berlin and London, and fell in Paris. The deterioration in child health in the years 1917 to 1919 was relatively less severe in London than in Berlin, largely because the London peak of 1918 was followed by a year of very low child mortality. In Berlin, as fig. 16.3 shows, there was an ascending trend of child mortality throughout the war years.

In sum, Paris registered the most favourable record with respect to child health in the war decade. Children in London and Berlin were less fortunate in wartime. In London post-war recovery was rapid and shows few signs of the mercurial conditions of the war years.

The cause-structure of child mortality

Death-rates of female children between the ages of one and four fell more rapidly in Paris than in the other two cities. Why? The Parisian pattern of steady decline in child mortality in wartime was attributable to a mixed set of causes, some of which were related to war conditions and others were probably *sui generis*. Declines were registered in death-rates due to measles, some forms of tuberculosis (of the meninges), pneumonia, and diarrhoea. Together these four sets of causes accounted for two-thirds of the overall decline in early childhood mortality in wartime.

These gains were reduced by slight increases in death-rates due to other causes: pulmonary tuberculosis, whooping cough, and influenza. This latter problem was attributed almost entirely to a rise in 1918, which was probably related to the overall spread of the pandemic form of the disease.

The sources of the more volatile situation in London were varied. In years of high mortality, 1915 and 1918, the incidence of measles and whooping cough was high. In addition tuberculosis death-rates were above pre-war levels. About half the rise in the two difficult years of 1915 and 1918 may be attributed to these causes. Much of the rest was a reflection of pneumonia and, in 1918, of influenza and whooping cough. Diarrhoeal mortality was of little or no consequence.

Some of these fluctuations may have reflected the normal three to four-year periodicity of childhood infections. This may be the explanation for rises in measles or whooping cough in these years. The rise in pneumonia does indicate that more than a 'normal' cycle of children's diseases was operating during the war.

In Berlin, the rise in child mortality after 1916 is similarly due to an increase in endemic childhood diseases such as measles. Influenza, too, took its toll of child lives in Berlin, which also registered deaths due to diphtheria. Even more striking, though, is the increase in deaths due to respiratory tuberculosis. Between 1916 and 1919, this one illness rose to levels double the pre-war norm.

In sum, London and Berlin suffered higher death rates due to common diseases of childhood such as measles. But they also registered higher death-rates due to respiratory infections, in particular pneumonia in the case of London, and tuberculosis in the case of Berlin. The deterioration in the survival rates of children in these two cities was particularly marked after 1916. Child mortality in London and Berlin between 1917 and 1919 was 8 and 19 per cent above pre-war levels. This contrasts sharply with a decline of 20 per cent registered in Paris in this period.

London recovered rapidly from the pre-war increase in child mortality. After the Armistice, most causes of death between the ages of one and four fell rapidly, with the exception of influenza. The flurry of 1918 was probably related to the pandemic of that year. But by 1920, London had joined Paris in registering death-rates at young childhood ages well below those of the pre-war period.

The pattern of child health differed from that of infant health in this period. in Paris, both the nought-to-one and one-to-four age-groups registered gains. In London, death-rates among infants fell; those for children aged one to four rose. In Berlin, there were rising death-rates after 1916 for both infants and young children. The source of these variations was primarily the trajectory of respiratory infections.

Once more it is evident that while upward inflections occurred in the death-rates of infants and young children in the Allied capitals, the period of instability ended in 1918. In Berlin from 1916, a bad situation got worse, and continued to deteriorate after the Armistice.

Adulthood

Survival rates between the ages of fifteen and forty-four

The two phases of the war: 1914 to 1916 and 1917 to 1919 The contrast between the two phases of the war in Berlin's demographic history is evident in adult mortality statistics. Between 1914 and 1916, death-rates declined by about 4 per cent, just on the edge of the margin of error we have adopted in handling these data. A conservative reading of the evidence would posit that adult death-rates in Berlin in the first two years of the war were stable, with some downward drift.

After 1916 adult death-rates in Berlin soared, and did so starting in 1917, before the influenza visitation of the following year. In 1917, death-rates for adult females rose by about 23 per cent. In 1918, death-rates remained elevated, at a point nearly 40 per cent above the 1911 to 1913 average. In effect, adult women in Berlin between 1917 and 1919 suffered death-rates approximately 50 per cent above peacetime levels. The worst increases were registered at younger adult ages.

Given that approximately 650,000 women were in the age-group fifteen to forty-nine, an increase of this magnitude in death-rates was bound to have a significant effect on overall death-rates. The average death-rate for this age-group in the years 1911 to 1913 was about 5.7 per 1,000. In the years 1917 to 1919, the figure was 8.76. In effect, the deterioration in life chances at adult ages was about three per thousand, or about the same as the increase in death-rates as a whole.

Adult mortality rates in Paris were similarly stable in the period 1914 to 1916 and elevated between 1917 and 1919, but the deterioration in the second phase of the war was not as severe in Paris as it was in Berlin. Prior to the war, adult death-rates in Paris were higher than in Berlin. The mortality crisis of 1917 to 1919 reversed that position, as figure 16.4 illustrates.

As we have already noted, in Berlin 1917 opened a difficult period in civilian mortality rates at adult ages. In Paris 1917 was a relatively good year. Death-rates in that year were 7 per cent below pre-war levels. But the upward inflection of the subsequent two years was sufficiently

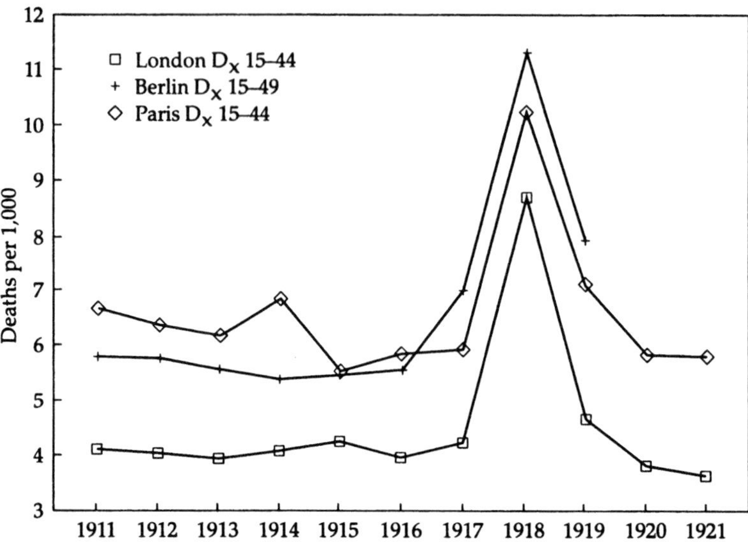

Fig. 16.4 Paris, London, Berlin: female death-rates, 1911 to 1919/21, ages 15 to 44/49

sharp to produce an overall increase in death rates between the ages of fifteen and forty-four, of 21 per cent.

In London the trend in death-rates at adult ages in the war period is less favourable than that of Paris. The pre-war level of about 4 deaths per 1,000 women in this age-group was exceeded in 1914, 1915, 1917, 1918 and 1919. Even allowing for the upward deflection of mortality rates in this age-group in the years 1918 to 1919 due to pandemic influenza, there is still the prior recrudescence in death-rates to account for.

Rising mortality at younger adult ages Within this age-group, it was those aged fifteen to nineteen who were particularly vulnerable to wartime changes adversely affecting their survival chances. Even leaving aside the data on 1918, these young women registered death-rates in London in the period 1914 to 1917 between 14 and 40 per cent higher than pre-war levels. In a moment, we shall examine the cause-structure of mortality to determine the origins of this age-group's special situation. Women in their early twenties also showed a tendency to higher mortality in wartime, in contrast to those in their thirties and forties. Their death-rates fell below pre-war levels between 1914 and 1917.

In effect, adult women in wartime London form two groups: those in their teens and early twenties whose survival chances worsened, and those in their thirties and forties, whose survival chances improved. The same is true after the Armistice: in the years 1919 to 1921, younger adult

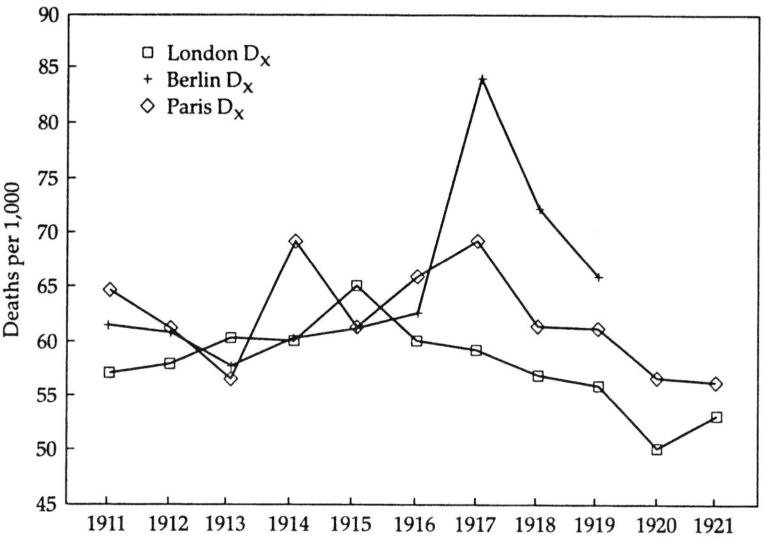

Fig. 16.5 Paris, London, Berlin: female death-rates, 1911 to 1919/21, ages 60+

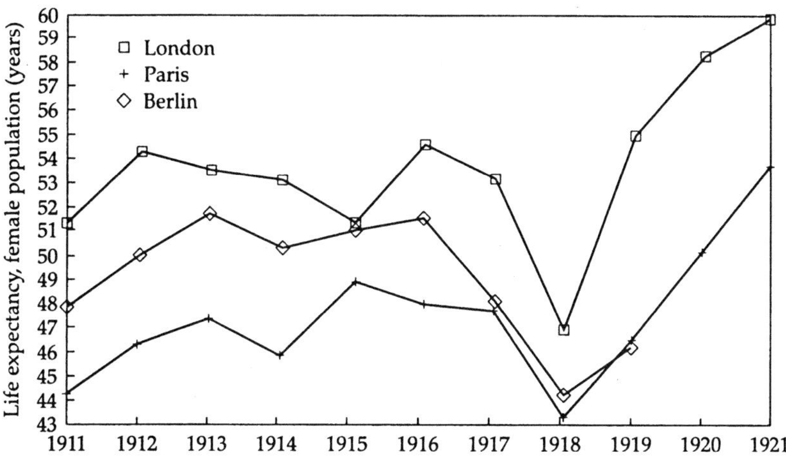

Fig. 16.6 Paris, London, Berlin: life expectancy at birth, 1911 to 1919/21

women registered death-rates above pre-war levels; those in their thirties and forties registered death-rates below pre-war levels.

The same pattern may be discerned in the Berlin data. Younger women suffered the highest increase in death-rates in the period 1917 to 1919. Whereas death-rates between the ages of forty to forty-four were about one-third higher than prior to the war, death-rates between the ages of fifteen to nineteen and twenty to twenty-four were more than double their pre-war levels.

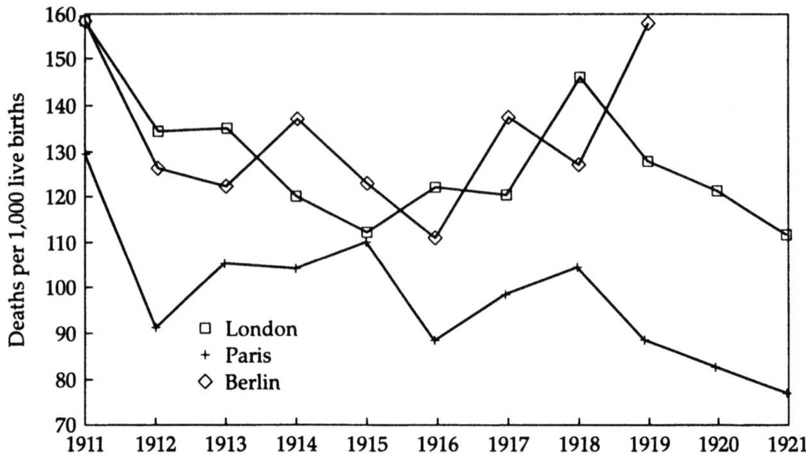

Fig. 16.7 Paris, London, Berlin: female infant mortality rates, 1911 to 1921

What happened in London and Berlin was repeated in Paris. In the period 1914 to 1916, the death-rate for this cohort was stable: about 2 per cent above pre-war levels. But this apparent stability masked a clear divergence between those under and over thirty. Younger women were worse off between 1914 and 1916 than between 1911 and 1913; older women were better off. Everybody was worse off in the period 1917 to 1919, but the increase in death-rates was more marked before the age of thirty than after. Again, the post-war recovery to roughly the same level as in the period 1911 to 1913 masks the fact that while death-rates for women under thirty remained high, those for women over thirty had dropped below pre-war levels.

The cause-structure of mortality: respiratory infections and the waging of war

In all three cases, it is one particular subset of the fifteen to forty-four or fifteen to forty-nine age-group which suffered from war conditions: young women between the ages of fifteen and thirty. To understand this finding, we must turn to the cause-structure of mortality, and in particular to the history of respiratory infections in wartime.

The case of respiratory tuberculosis requires particular emphasis because it demonstrates clearly that the rough stability in civilian death-rates in Paris and London obscures a real deterioration in survival rates among some sections of the population. Among them were young women, whose susceptibility to tuberculosis increased during the war, as did their propensity to die of the disease, once contracted. The war turned some healthy girls and women tuberculous; it turned latent into active tuberculosis among others; and it created conditions in which those suffering from active tuberculosis succumbed

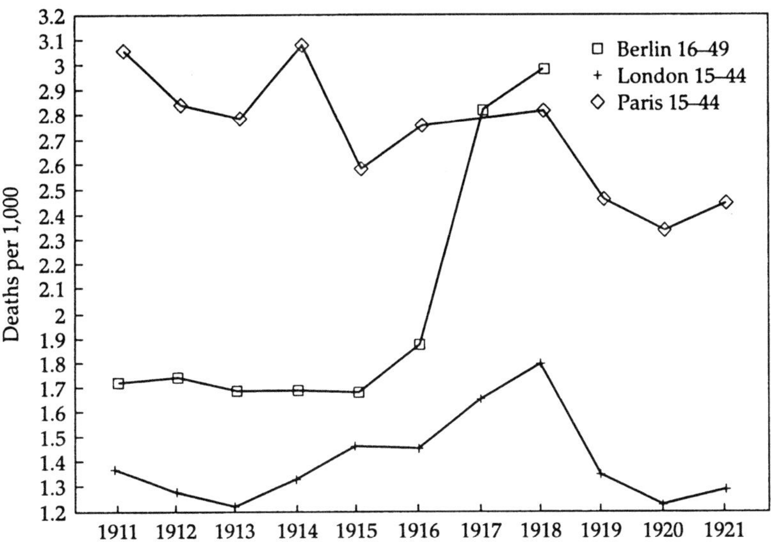

Fig. 16.8 Paris, London, Berlin: female TB death-rates, ages 15 to 44/49

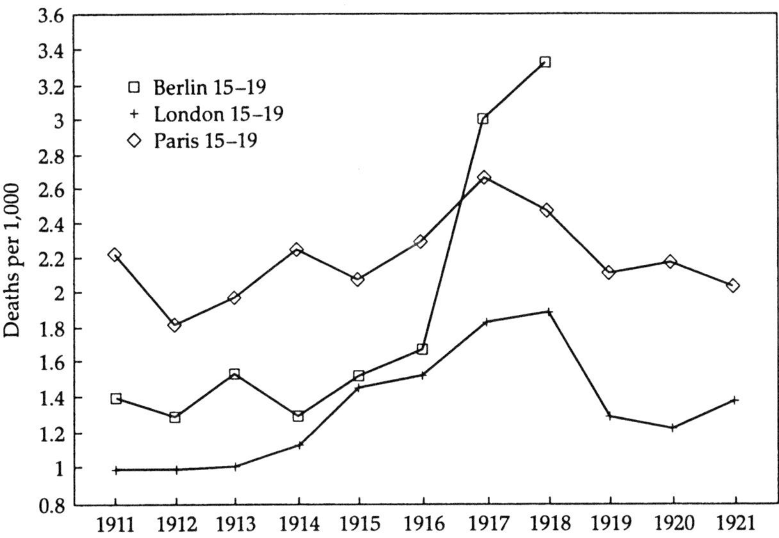

Fig. 16.9 Paris, London, Berlin: female TB death-rates, 1911 to 1918/21, ages 15 to 19

to the disease. The elderly suffered similarly, though death-rates due to tuberculosis at advanced years were relatively slight.

Figures 16.8 and 16.9 show rough parallels in the history of wartime tuberculosis in the three cities. In all three there was a rise in the death-rate due to this disease. The Parisian rise was more modest than that in London, where the pre-war death-rate was much lower than in either continental city. But the rise in Berlin was of an entirely different character. A doubling of tuberculosis death-rates both between the ages of fifteen to nineteen and fifteen to forty-nine contributed substantially to the mortality crisis of the second phase of the war. Some of the peak of 1918 may have been a reflection of influenza contracted by tuberculous women, but the rise in their death-rates began two years before. Once again, what is to be explained varied as between the Allies and Germany: a palpable, though limited, deterioration in urban death-rates due to tuberculosis in Paris and London, on the one hand; and a severe crisis in Berlin, on the other.

Old age

Survival rates at advanced years (sixty plus)

Death-rates for the elderly population of all three cities increased in wartime. Different estimates produce different figures, but they all point the same way. The increases in London and Paris were of roughly the same magnitude: roughly 6 per cent on average.[26] In contrast, the increase which occurred in Berlin was higher still, perhaps 14 per cent, comparing the period 1914 to 1918 with 1911 to 1913.

Once again, the war period is divided into two entirely different phases. In the years 1914 to 1916, death-rates for the elderly rose at roughly the same rate in Paris and London. The rise in Berlin was slight and, given our margin of error, it is possible that a rough stability was maintained in death-rates among elderly Berliners in the years 1914 to 1916. In effect, pressure on the elderly appeared to be less intense in Berlin than in the Allied capitals.

Between 1917 and 1919 the opposite is true. The upward inflection in 1917 was a reflection of a particularly cold winter. The link with cold and coal supply is one we have noted in chapter 12, but it appears that the elderly in Paris and Berlin suffered more from it than did the same age-group in London. Overall, in this period, death-rates in London and Paris at the age of sixty and over are at or below the pre-war level. In contrast, the rise in Berlin in this three-year period was fully 23 per cent. In Berlin the year 1917 was disastrous for the aged. Berlin women aged sixty plus registered death-rates of about 85 per 1,000, fully 40 per cent above the 1911 to 1913 figure. The first year of pandemic influenza, 1918, was less catastrophic, but still poor. Death-rates for this cohort reached about 69 per 1,000, a rise of about 19 per cent over pre-war levels. The

[26] Robert and Winter, 'Un aspect ignoré de la démographie urbaine de la grande guerre: le drame des vieux à Berlin, Londres et Paris', *Annales de démographie historique* (1993), table 2.

death-rate for 1919 was less elevated, but still 9 per cent over peacetime. The average of about 74 per 1,000 in Berlin was higher than any figure registered at advanced aged in any of the three cities.

The cause-structure of mortality

It is unwise to isolate any one cause in the history of mortality at advanced ages. Multiple causes no doubt must be sought for fluctuations in death rates for the over-60 population. Still, it is possible to point to some features of the cause-structure of the mortality crisis of wartime Berlin. After 1916, most causes of death soared. In 1917, there was both an outbreak of diarrhoeal disease among elderly women, increasing deaths due to digestive diseases and a sharp increase in respiratory-disease mortality. The generalized character of the crisis is also reflected in increased death-rates due to heart disease and to the ill-defined category of 'old age'. The years 1918 and 1919 were very bad, too, compared to the pre-war period, but death-rates in 1918 were somewhat lower than 1917. It appears that respiratory infections and heart disease, but not digestive diseases, were responsible for the high death-rates in those years.

A similar set of causes was responsible for the lesser wartime and post-war increases in death-rates for the sixty-plus age-group in Paris and London. In Paris in 1914, deaths attributable to strokes and organic diseases of the heart rose sharply. In 1916 and 1917, respiratory infections and heart disease took an augmented toll of the elderly. In 1918, influenza was active. After the Armistice, heart disease mortality remained above pre-war levels. In London too, respiratory and heart disease mortality remained stubbornly high throughout the war period. This cluster of diseases was substantially responsible for the minor, but real, increase in death-rates registered by the elderly population of both Allied capital cities.[27]

District-level inequalities in mortality rates in Paris and London

In our discussion of infant mortality in wartime, we pointed out the need to disaggregate overall trends to disclose the impact of war on different sections of the population. The same need arises with respect to district-level variations. As we have already noted, it was well established in the pre-war period that some administrative districts were 'healthier' than others.[28] The question remains, what was the impact of war on the variance among death-rates in different urban

[27] For a full discussion, see Robert and Winter, 'Un aspect ignoré'.

[28] For a full discussion, see L. Hersch, *Pauvreté et mortalité.*

districts? In *The Great War and the British people*, the argument was advanced that mortality differentials among occupational and residential groups in Britain were reduced over the period 1911 to 1921.[29] Is this true at the urban level in these three cases?

We can only provide a very tentative answer to the question. The reason is that migration was so substantial in wartime that district-level population estimates are even more notional than are our estimates for the capital cities' total population. It is true that rent control helped to fix populations – and especially those at young and old ages – in their lodgings. To move was to court economic disaster. But informal (or illegal) migration was inevitable for people who had to maintain a fixed address to keep rents down, but who also needed to look after family members or travel long distances to work. Given these unknown variables, the wisest course for us is a cautious one.

In the case of Berlin, we have not even attempted to group urban districts to provide some indication of the wartime variance as between mortality rates in well-to-do and popular quartiers. For London and Paris we can be slightly more daring. It is possible to cluster arrondissements and metropolitan boroughs into groups which describe, in a very general way, very approximate social divisions within the two cities. To do so is partly to lessen the problem of intra-borough migration, as well as to increase the base populations from which vital rates are calculated, thereby minimizing swings reflecting small totals at risk in individual districts.

The turnover of population was so great in the war that we have limited discussion of district-level mortality rates to two sections of the population: infants and the elderly. Estimates of adult populations at district level are probably too imprecise to support this kind of analysis.

Infant mortality

It was well known at the time that the variance among infant-mortality levels as between and among Parisian districts was much greater than those in London. As T. H. C. Stevenson, Registrar General of England and Wales, put it in 1921, 'the contrast between the rich and poor quarters of Paris assumes dimensions which in the light of London experience seem quite fantastic'.[30] Comparing arrondissements and metropolitan boroughs in the pre-war period, the worst infant-mortality rates are roughly four times higher than the best in Paris; in contrast, the London range is in the order of two to one. The effect of the war was to narrow the range of variance among district-level infant-mortality

[29] J.M. Winter, *The Great War*, ch. 4.

[30] T.H.C. Stevenson, 'Incidence of mortality', p. 93.

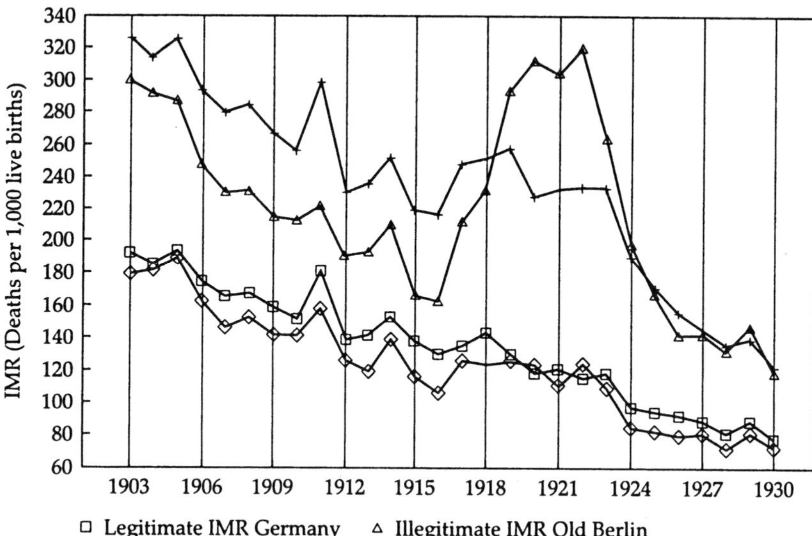

Fig. 16.10 Germany and Berlin, legitimate and illegitimate infant mortality rates (IMR), 1903 to 1930

rates in both Paris and London. This change still left substantial gaps between rich and poor districts, but those gaps were no larger – and probably slightly smaller – than those that had drawn such adverse attention before the war.

We must not exaggerate the weight of evidence supporting the contention that there was a moderate levelling of inequalities in district-level infant-mortality rates; changes are too slight to do more than register a likely inference. For instance, infant-mortality rates in the poorer working-class eastern boroughs fell from 12 per cent above the average for London as a whole in the pre-war period, to 9 per cent above during the war, and seven per cent above in the post-war period. By contrast, infant-mortality rates in the more prosperous western boroughs moved from 3 per cent below the London average in the period 1910 to 1913, to 1 per cent below during the war, and then to 4 per cent above the average in the post-war period. In contrast, the position of the socially mixed south-eastern boroughs and the more prosperous south-western boroughs remained stable in relation to the London average in all three periods.[31] While we must advise caution in dealing with a comparison of Parisian data reflecting the practice of sending infants out of the city for wet-nursing, and London data where wet-nursing was exceptional, some conclusions appear sound. The modest shifts we

[31] For full details, see J.M. Winter, Lawrence, and Ariouat, 'Infant mortality'.

have noted suggest a pattern of greater metropolitan homogenization consistent with the 'levelling-up' hypothesis advanced in *The Great War and the British people*. This held that the worse off was the group or district, the greater were the wartime gains.[32]

The hypothesis of declining inequalities in infant survival chances is supported by evidence on the eight boroughs which experienced the greatest and the least absolute and percentage decline in infant mortality rates between 1910 to 1913 and 1919 to 1923. The boroughs registering the most substantial absolute falls in infant mortality were all poor, central boroughs in east and south-east London. The boroughs registering the least improvement were all in outer London or the West End. With the exception of Woolwich, where war industries may have introduced special factors, they are also all boroughs that can reasonably be characterized as prosperous and predominantly middle-class.

There is some sketchy evidence available supporting the view that a similar levelling of infant mortality rates occurred in wartime Paris. The problem with all such data is that they relate to a period when the traditional practice of sending newborns out of Paris to wet-nurses was coming to an end. It is unclear precisely how many infants in different arrondissements were sent out of Paris to be cared for by *nourrices*. It is very unlikely that the practice was uniform throughout the city. All we can do is to point to some rough indicators consistent with the view that the wide variance in infant-mortality rates as between urban districts lessened somewhat during the war.

For example, the poor, eastern 20th arrondissement registered infant-mortality rates of 156 per 1,000 live births before the war, 147 during the war, and 118 in the period from 1919 to 1923. In contrast, wartime rates rose both in the mixed 4th arrondissement (from about 92 before the war to 100 during the conflict) and in the fashionable 8th (from about 40 before the war to 48 between 1914 to 1918). After the war, infant-mortality rates dropped to pre-war levels in the 4th arrondissement, but continued to rise in the 8th, reaching about 59 per 1,000 in the period from 1919 to 1923. In effect, the gap between the worst and the best districts in terms of the survival chances of infants in Paris had been reduced from a ratio of four to one before the war, to three to one during the conflict, to two to one in the immediate post-war period.

Mortality at ages sixty plus

Given the uncertainties embedded in the data, it would be unwise to rely too heavily on this finding to support the 'levelling-up' hypothesis.

[32] J.M. Winter, *The Great War*, ch. 4.

None the less, these statistics are consistent with other data reflecting a more stable population, that of the elderly.

Using clustered district-level mortality data for the sixty-plus population, we have found some further confirmation of the overall hypothesis that during the war there was a narrowing of the variance as between mortality rates in well-to-do and poorer areas for these cities. For instance, the eastern district of London boroughs registered mortality rates 8 per cent above those of London as a whole between 1911 and 1913, but only 2 per cent above between 1914 and 1918. The seven boroughs of south east London were 3 per cent above London as a whole before the war; 5 per cent below during it. Both of these regions had very poor districts, although there were some better-off neighbourhoods among them as well. In contrast, the more prosperous areas of the northern and western districts, the heartland of the London bourgeoisie, were no better or worse off at the end of the war than before it. Since London's death-rate for the elderly rose during the war, it is apparent that this deterioration was slightly more marked in the (broadly speaking) middle-class north and west of the city than in the working-class east and south.

Clustering data on the mortality of the sixty-plus population in Paris reduces an analogous finding. Here we see that the deterioration in death-rates was greatest in the 4th, 6th, and 10th arrondissements. These were old, central quartiers where impoverished and elegant lodgings existed side by side. What they shared was relatively old housing. In contrast the poorest districts in the pre-war period, like the 19th and 20th, as well as the more prosperous 17th arrondissement, registered lower than average wartime changes in mortality rates among the elderly.[33]

In sum, there appears to be some evidence of a reordering of spatial inequalities of civilian mortality in both London and Paris. We should not make too much of this finding, for the simple reason that our population estimates are too fragile to support any but the most robust findings. The elderly were the least mobile section of the population, but at other ages it is likely that migration helped to produce the small shifts towards a more homogenous demographic profile of mortality rates within these cities as a whole. For this reason alone it is probably safe to conclude that the demographic distance between the mortality rates of different urban districts in Paris and London had narrowed slightly during the 1914–18 war.

One final caveat is needed at this point. Geographic units are not social units. Social links arising from professional, occupational, religious, or ethnic ties, or from shared leisure or personal interest may have

[33] For a detailed discussion, see Robert and Winter, 'Un aspect ignoré'.

mattered more in describing support networks and shared conditions than did an address. Crossing a street could mean moving into a different arrondissement, not a different way of life or social network. Therefore these correlations must be treated as suggesting, rather than proving, that the war helped reduce the social distance between different quartiers.

Conclusions: convergences and divergences in urban demographic history

Divergences: Berlin, Paris, London

Clear conclusions about the impact of war on the survival chances of the civilian population must be limited only to overwhelmingly clear findings. Estimation errors and incomplete statistical data require qualifications of all but the most robust distinctions. Fortunately, the contrast between the history of mortality in the war period in Berlin, on the one hand, and Paris and London on the other, is so sharp that even unavoidable statistical imprecision cannot obscure it.

Demographic trajectories: 1911 to 1921

On balance we can distinguish four periods within the mortality history of the war decade:

1. 1911 to 1913, when mortality differentials among the three cities were clearly visible;
2. 1914 to 1916, when the trajectory of death-rates in the three cities continued to move in parallel;
3. 1917 to 1919, when death-rates diverged, bringing Berlin mortality levels up to or above Paris mortality levels;
4. 1920 to 1921, when in Paris and London major declines in mortality took place.

The two phases of the war

The outline of the story seems clear. First, the chronology: for most soldiers, the war ended in 1918; demobilization took time, and for the disabled the road home was a long one. For civilians too it is only true in the most rudimentary sense to say that the war ended at the Armistice. To use political benchmarks in demographic history is to invite distortion. We have therefore examined the period from 1914 to 1919 (incorporating the period up to demobilization, both military and economic) to identify impacts of the war. Secondly, there is a division in demographic history between 1914 and 1916 and 1917 to 1919. In the first phase, the three cities shared a similar profile in terms of civilian death-rates. Between 1917 and 1919, this important facet of their demographic histories diverged. After 1916, the history of public health in Berlin took a turn for the worse, producing a mortality crisis not registered in Paris or London. Post-war gains contrast in Paris and London with a continuing post-war crisis in Berlin. Here was one facet of the price of Germany's defeat in the Great War.

War-related mortality in Berlin

The dimensions of that mortality crisis have never been measured. In conclusion, it may be useful to provide some rough indication of its amplitude. We have argued that the war brought Berlin death-rates up to Parisian levels. This occurred after 1916. We can document this change over the three years 1917 to 1919. The average death-rate for Berlin in these crisis years was 17 per 1,000. This figure in part reflects pandemic influenza, which, as we have just noted, was mostly probably not a reflection of the demographic costs of war. The years 1917 and 1919 are a better guide to the true increase in civilian death-rates. That average of 16.5 deaths per 1,000 is 3.1 per 1,000 above the level for 1914 to 1916. This is a conservative estimate of the deterioration in death-rates, since it does not take into account the downward slope of mortality rates in the pre-war period. Simply comparing the two periods 1914 to 1916 and 1917 to 1919 with respect to the survival chances of 1,000,000 women in Berlin suggests an annual cost in lives of approximately 3,000 women per year during the crisis period, or a total of 9,000 war-related civilian deaths. It is of course much more difficult to make the same assumptions about the male population, the bulk of which at adult ages were in uniform and subject to much higher death-rates. But even if half the excess civilian mortality suffered by women was suffered by men who lived on the home front, then we reach the figure of 14,500 excess civilian deaths in Berlin during the war. This figure represents roughly 50 per cent of total deaths registered in Berlin in 1913.[34]

[34] It would be foolish to argue that conditions in Berlin were identical to those in Germany as a whole. But if the incidence of war-related civilian mortality in the nation approached that of the capital, then we can use these estimates to provide a rough indication of total war-related mortality in Germany as a whole. Berlin's population was roughly 3 per cent of that of the Kaiserreich. Berlin estimates therefore must be multiplied by a factor of 33, to reach national levels. To do so brings us to the notional total of 478,500 excess civilian war-related deaths in Germany. In other words, a little under half a million German civilians died as a result of conditions attributable to the war.

The absolute figure matters less than the order of magnitude, which is certainly comparable to that produced using other demographic data for Germany as a whole. In 1988 we used life-table estimates to calculate the extent to which civilian deaths in Germany increased during the war over expected pre-war levels. The estimate of total war-related mortality in 1914 to 1918 between the ages of fifteen and fifty-nine was 300,000. This contrasted sharply with the situation in France and Britain, where

Gains and losses in public health in wartime

On balance, aggregate death-rates in the Allied capitals remained stable in wartime. But the history of public health in Paris and London resembled a zero-sum game, that is, increases in death-rates were not uniform. Improvements at some ages were undercut by a deterioration in survival chances at other ages. The elderly and some vulnerable groups at younger ages clearly suffered in wartime. Other groups did better. Together their experience yielded a rough aggregate stability during the war.

Paris

In Paris, stability in overall death-rates is an amalgam of improvements at young ages, volatility at adult ages, and deterioration in advanced ages. The rule appears to be that after 1914 infant and child health were not adversely affected by war conditions; on the contrary, some real gains were registered in wartime. The same may have been true on balance for young women, though the impact of influenza epidemic is extremely difficult to separate from the impact of war. The war adversely affected the health of the elderly, but not that of the rest of the female population.

London

The aggregate data on female death-rates in wartime London describe a stable situation between 1914 and 1917, a crisis year in 1918, followed by three years of declining mortality. But within this pattern, there were sharp differences in the experience of particular age groups. Infant mortality shows a steady decline over the whole period. Child mortality (at ages one to four) shows some worsening of conditions in wartime, followed by major gains between 1919 and 1921. Adult mortality

war-related civilian mortality was either negligible or nil. Our earlier estimates were restricted to 1914 to 1918 and to the age-group fifteen to fifty-nine. Including increased mortality in 1919 at all ages, and earlier increases in the age groups nought to fourteen and sixty plus, would inflate the national estimate by at least 200,000. The figure of just under half a million is, therefore, a very rough and conservative estimate of total war-related civilian deaths in Germany between 1914 and 1919.

Confirmation of the order of magnitude of civilian war-related deaths may be obtained in another way. We have calculated standardized death rates for the population of Germany as a whole from 1914 to 1916 and 1917 to 1919. The difference between the two averages is approximately 3 per 1,000. Applied to a population of 33 million German women, this rate yields a total of 99,000 war-related female deaths for each year 1917, 1918, and 1919. To the sum of 300,000, we should add about half to account for male war-related deaths among the civilian population. The total here is about 450,000 deaths. These estimates fit well with the analysis of Berlin mortality statistics presented here.

For references, see J. M. Winter, 'Some paradoxes of the Great War', ch. 1.

between the ages of fifteen and forty-four is a mixture: apart from the disastrous years of pandemic influenza in 1918 and 1919, death-rates rose in wartime. This deterioration reflected the experience of women aged fifteen to twenty-four, but not those in their thirties and forties. Their death-rates declined during the war, as did that of the age-group as a whole after 1919. Among the elderly, the pattern is clearer: the war years were a time of higher death-rates for women over sixty years old.

In effect, the evidence of age-specific death-rates for females in London shows some adverse effects of war at all ages after infancy. These effects were unevenly distributed throughout the war and throughout the age structure. Children aged one to four suffered in 1915 and 1918; teenagers and women in their early twenties suffered throughout the period under review; so did the elderly. But some other groups were more fortunate. Middle-aged women registered gains in survival rates in every year except during the influenza pandemic, which zeroed in on precisely their cohort. But apart from this extraordinary visitation, the pattern of civilian health reflected in these data is full of contradictory features. Aggregate stability in overall death-rates is simply the sum of positive and negative facets of the impact of war. With respect to London, we must qualify some of the optimistic findings reported for Britain as a whole in *The Great War and the British people*.[35] Further research is necessary before we can determine whether or not the impact of war conditions in London was more severe than in other parts of Britain.

The age-structure of mortality

These complex features of wartime changes in mortality rates point to a rough rule of thumb: the health of young adults and the elderly suffered, but that of other age-groups was better defended. There were exceptions, such as the uneven record with respect to the health of young children in wartime London. But on balance, children's health was not compromised by the war in all three cities. Even in London, the progress made in the immediate post-war years more than compensated for the volatile record of the war period. At older ages, there was also some unevenness, but the trajectory appears clear: two upward inflections for young adults and the elderly within an overall pattern of stability in Paris and London and after 1916 crisis in Berlin.

The cause-structure of mortality

The elderly and some other cohorts paid a price for the war in terms of higher death-rates, especially in the period 1917 to 1919. Why? One

[35] See especially chs. 4 and 7.

major reason for the deterioration in survival changes for some age-groups in wartime was an increase in respiratory infections, in particular influenza and tuberculosis.

The 'Spanish flu'

There are two areas in which the history of public health in Paris, London, and Berlin clearly converged. The first is the propensity in all three cities for pandemic influenza to kill previously healthy young adults. We have noted the exogenous character of this epidemic, which killed millions all over the world between 1918 and 1919. It is difficult to link this killer disease convincingly with war-related developments.[36] Equally unconvincing is the assertion that the 'Spanish flu' hit poorer areas harder than richer ones.[37] As we have noted in chapter 15, the pandemic was an ecumenical disaster, striking at will, especially at the young and robust.[38]

Tuberculosis

The case of tuberculosis is the second instance of wartime convergence, as we have noted in chapter 15. Let us return to a number of points in that discussion. We charted age-specific mortality due to this endemic disease. The data support the argument that in particular young women aged between fifteen and thirty suffered increased tuberculosis death-rates in wartime. Why was this so? It would be unwise to privilege any one cause of this phenomenon, and we surveyed a number of possibilities related to overwork, deteriorating housing, poor nutrition, and the breakdown of public health services.

But we have chosen to highlight one additional factor usually neglected in conventional interpretations of the wartime rise in tuberculosis. It is the effect of wartime migration on the incidence and spread of the disease. We have noted that the war produced substantial migratory flows: millions of men were mobilized; millions of women, as well as men and boys above and below military ages, shifted their jobs and residence. Among them were young women who contracted tuberculosis during the war, or whose latent illnesses became active as a result of wartime conditions.

The move into urban employment of women from the countryside or

[36] See references in note 2.

[37] Liebman Hersch objected to the conclusion of the report on the influenza epidemic in Paris, that 'La richesse a peu d'influence sur la mortalité par grippe' (*Recueil de statistiques de la ville de Paris. Epidémie de grippe à Paris* (Paris, 1919), p. 58). His view was that the flu hit the poorest districts with the greatest ferocity. See the dispute between T. H. C. Stevenson in the *Journal of the Royal Statistical Society* (Jan. 1920), p. 90 and Hersch, in *Pauvreté et mortalité*, p. 97. Stevenson's evidence appears the stronger of the two. [38] See pp. 480–1.

adjacent towns may have increased tuberculosis mortality in another way. Cronje has shown a convergence of rural and urban death rates in the later nineteenth century in the case of England and Wales. She concludes none the less that: 'The statistical data thus bear out the contemporary belief that rural areas escaped more lightly from tuberculosis than urban counties.'[39] It is possible, therefore, that wartime immigration brought into these cities females who had not developed the same degree of immunity as had city-born and bred women. A change in the social and geographic composition of the 15-to-30-year-old age-group helps to account for the upward inflection of wartime death-rates due to tuberculosis.

This migratory factory would weigh more heavily in Paris and Berlin than in London, where the adjacent populations were suburban rather than rural. In the continental cities, fresh waves of workers in war industries probably entered a different disease environment than that of the countryside in which they had been raised. The same was true for Irish migrants to London.[40] In these cases, the very turbulence of wartime population movements may have elevated morbidity and mortality rates due to tuberculosis.

This argument is attractive for another reason. It helps to account for the parallelism of an upward inflection of tuberculosis mortality in the two world wars in areas where nutrition undoubtedly deteriorated as well as in cases where nutritional levels were maintained.[41] In both wars migratory movements were phenomenally high; it seems odd, therefore, that most scholars have neglected to give due weight to this demographic variable in their explanation of the incidence of tuberculosis in wartime.

To emphasize the significance of migration is not to isolate it as the sole cause of increased tuberculosis mortality. Indeed, the mix of factors in each of these three cities probably differed. Nutritional deficits probably mattered more in Berlin; cohort effects and the breakdown of services may have mattered more in Paris, where pre-war death-rates were higher than in the other two cities. Overwork and stress hit residents of all three cities. What is important is to avoid a monocausal explanation of a disease which was clearly the outcome of a complex of wartime events. Not the least important of these was massive population turnover in wartime.

In short, the study of tuberculosis shows the weakness of the

39 Cronje, 'Tuberculosis', p. 91.

40 On Irish immigration and tuberculosis in a later period, see F. C. S. Bradbury, *Causal Factors in Tuberculosis* (London, 1933), ch. 8, unfortunately entitled 'Race'.

41 For the British case, see Bryder, *Below the magic mountain*, p. 228; on the Second World War in Britain, see also *The impact of the war on civilian consumption in the United Kingdom, the United States and Canada* (London, 1945), pp. 26–31.

argument that fluctuations in the disease in wartime were necessarily a reflection of nutritional conditions. This is an element of received wisdom, especially in the medical literature.[42] Diet mattered, but only as one piece in a very elaborate puzzle. With respect to London, we must remain sceptical about Bryder's argument that nutrition was 'a factor ruling mortality from the disease in early adult life'.[43] She has neglected to give due weight to a host of factors, including migration, which dominated these cities' pre-war demographic history and which underlies many of the striking demographic movements of the period of the Great War.

Conclusion

The history of tuberculosis points to features of wartime life which prejudiced the survival chances of some civilians, in particular between the ages of 15 and 30. But other aspects of the cause-structure or mortality point in the opposite direction. Data on digestive-disease mortality, in particular diarrhoea and enteritis, suggest that improved nutrition for some groups ensured the survival of their infants and young children, and blunted the effects of widespread respiratory disease at other ages too.

In effect, wartime mortality rates went up for one set of reasons: rapid migration, poor nutrition, and housing for some groups, which, together with other war-related conditions, aided the spread of respiratory infections. But they were stabilized or reduced by improvements in the nutritional levels of other city-dwellers, helping to limit the lethality of respiratory infections and to bring about a decline in digestive-disease mortality.

These contradictory features of wartime life yielded a rough stability in death-rates in Paris and London. In Berlin, the same was true in the period from 1914 to 1916, but not thereafter, when a generalized economic and social crisis produced a demographic crisis of major importance. We must explain not only why this occurred in the German capital, but also why it did not happen in Paris and London. No one would deny the difficulties, both material and psychological, faced by millions of city-dwellers in the Allied capitals in a period of over 1,500 days of warfare. It is even more remarkable, therefore, that on balance their survival chances were not prejudiced by the waging of war.

What was lost in Paris and London in wartime was some of the

[42] For the older view, on which Bryder relies, see B. R. Clarke, *Causes and prevention of tuberculosis* (Edinburgh, 1952), and A. R. Rich, *The pathogenesis of tuberculosis* (Oxford, 1952), pp. 618–20.

[43] Bryder, *Below the magic mountain*, p. 110. Here she is following Collis and other contemporary writers.

momentum of pre-war mortality decline. However in the immediate post-war years, recovery was rapid and that momentum was restored. Unfortunately, data do not permit a comparison with the history of public health in Berlin after 1919. We do not know how long the crisis of 1917 to 1919 lasted. But whatever its duration, its character distinguished Berlin's wartime history from that of the Allied capitals.

The history of survival, illness, and mortality rates in Paris, London, and Berlin discloses a dense network of social experience and social relations within these cities, bearing on the question of well-being and ill-being in wartime. The evidence of hardship and suffering is unmistakable, though of an entirely different order of magnitude to what the men at the front when through. This contrast did not consign civilian health to the margins of public debate; on the contrary. In a melodramatic film entitled *J'accuse*, made at the end of the war and released in 1919, the French film-maker Abel Gance described the death not only of a pacifist poet turned patriotic soldier but also of his ill mother. 'Civilians too are killed by war', the caption had it, adding another accusation to those responsible for the maledictions of the day. Soldiers cared intensely about the well-being of their families; it was in their defence that the men in uniform had taken up arms in the first place.

It was all the more galling for German soldiers to see in 1918 that everything they and their families had endured was for nought. The unravelling of the German war effort can be seen in many aspects of German social history. Not the least important is the mortality crisis into which the civilian population was flung from 1917 on by the military leadership which brought disaster to the nation they led. The civilian population of the Allied capitals was more fortunate; their hardships had not been in vain; how lasting their victory was an entirely different question.

Part 7

Towards a social history of capital cities at war

17
Conclusions: towards a social history of capital cities at war

Jean-Louis Robert and Jay Winter

The conclusions we present in this volume rest at an intermediary point in our study. We have chosen initially to privilege the material conditions of the lives of the inhabitants of these three cities, the new social relations and hierarchies which they constructed, and the representations they themselves gave to their wartime reality. These matters point forward to the focus of volume II: towards an appreciation of the wartime reactions and perceptions of families, social groups, and social movements.

We offer first in this conclusion some reflections on the historiographical context in which to locate our work. We then consider, from a critical and methodological point of view, the central conclusions of this volume on which rests our understanding of the urban experience of warfare in these three cities. Finally, we anticipate how the material in the second volume of this study in comparative social history will complement and extend what we have presented here.

Introduction: the historiographical debate

Our field of study exists at the junction of a chronological history, that of the Great War, and a thematic history, that of urban history. In these two domains, there is a vast historical literature. On the Great War, entire libraries exist. In the field of urban history, the differences in the levels and rhythms of urban development in British, German, and French cities are well known, as is the dynamics of the organization of urban space. What is rare is any real contact between or overlap of these two fields of study.

Consider for a moment two recent books which have appeared in French on Paris and Berlin.[1] In both the Great War is barely mentioned. Either the war constitutes a convenient political turning point in

[1] Cyril Buffet, *Berlin* (Paris, 1993); Bernard Marchand, *Paris, histoire d'une ville, XIXè–XXè siècles* (Paris, 1993).

national rather than urban history, or the war is located and lost in a longer time span, surrounding the second industrial revolution or the growth of suburbs in the period 1890 to 1930. Does this chronology really help to account for the specificities of urban life, be they Parisian continuities or Berlin discontinuities? The only way to find out is to pose comparative questions in the urban history of this period.

At the same time, the remarkable outpouring of books on the Great War has produced but a trickle of studies of a comparative nature. We have a number of authoritative general histories of the war, especially those which place the war within the history of international relations.[2] Within military or diplomatic history, the war is considered as a series of national confrontations, understood within national frameworks, often presented in series, one after another.[3] Another current of historical thought, originating in the Marxist–Leninist tradition, is equally generalist and serial. Here the war is placed within the double framework of the rise of imperialism and the global history of class conflict. Within this vast tapestry, it was sometimes difficult to see the detail of social history, and rarely possible to confront an explicitly comparative framework.[4]

Within academic history, we also see a double orientation. There is first a history of public opinion, tending towards an appreciation of national sentiment, the rallying of populations for or against war, and more recently, the history of representations in wartime. The studies of Renouvin, Becker, and Mommsen are well known in this context.[5] Largely focusing on the national level, these indispensable monographs and essays tell the story of the war mainly from the point of view of political parties and organized groups, and of the pre-war social stratification (workers, peasants, bourgeoisie) out of which they grew. The history of the men in uniform is also told in this fundamentally national manner.[6]

A second historiographical tendency is more centrally economic,

[2] P. Renouvin, *La crise européenne et la grande guerre* (Paris, 1950); D. Stevenson, *The First World War and international politics* (Oxford, 1988); L. Albertini, *Les origines de la grande guerre* (Paris, 1960); F. Fischer, *German war aims in the First World War* (London, 1963).

[3] G. Pedroncini, *Les mutineries de 1917* (Paris, 1967); J. Keegan, *The Face of Battle* (London, 1978); M. Middlebrook, *The First Day of the Somme* (London, 1971); D. Winter, *Death's Men: soldiers of the Great War* (London, 1978).

[4] An exception of great richness within the Marxist tradition is Eric Hobsbawm, *Age of extremes. The short twentieth century 1914–1991* (London, 1994), ch. 1.

[5] P. Renouvin, 'L'opinion publique en 1917', *Revue d'histoire moderne et contemporaine*, 15 (1968); Becker, *1914*; W. Mommsen, 'The topos of inevitable war', *Central European History*, 6, 1 (1973). See also P. J. Flood, *France 1914–1918* (Basingstoke, 1990); Audoin-Rouzeau, *La guerre des enfants*; and J.-J. Becker, Jay M. Winter, G. Krumeich, and Annette Becker (eds.), *Guerre et cultures* (Paris, 1994).

[6] Audoin-Rouzeau, *Men at War*; Fuller, *Troop morale and culture*.

studying the war from the point of view of changes in the role of the state, in industry, in the organization of work, in the composition of social classes and the social movements which appeared during the war. Prominent in this area are the studies of Haimson, Fridenson, Feldman, and Kocka.[7] If we consider the numerous local studies of the war period, we find by and large that they privilege one or the other of these two approaches, that of public opinion or that of social and economic conflict. These positions have been examined in a number of comparative international colloquia, whose subjects have ranged from wartime culture to comparative social mobilization to the history of strikes and social movements. In virtually every case, comparison reinforced the tendency to isolate national characteristics as dominant features of wartime history.[8]

In addition, it must be noted that within this large and rapidly growing literature the history of these three capital cities is not particularly prominent. Too close to the instruments of government, these cities' histories have rarely been disentangled from the history of the nation state. This is as true in the study of urban strikes as it is in studies of soldiers' morale.[9]

In emphasizing in this volume the comparative dimension, and in privileging the vital parameters of urban life – life and death, work, food – we hope to stimulate a wider historical debate. In the search for the fundamental features of the well-being of the populations of Paris, London, and Berlin, we find a comparative terrain firm enough to locate the common experience of urban societies, at war or at peace. On one level, that experience was unmistakably demographic, relating to military mobilization, military losses, and civilian health. But we have tried to supersede previous demographic studies of the war, which

[7] Haimson (ed.), *Industrial militancy*; Fridenson (ed.), *The French Home Front*; G. D. Feldman, *Army, industry and labour*; Kocka, *Facing total war*. See also: Godfrey, *Capitalism at war*; Kathleen Burk (ed.), *War and the state: the transformation of British government, 1914–1919* (London, 1982); D. French, *British economic and strategic planning*; Kuisel, *Capitalism and the state*; J. Horne, *Labour at war*; D. Geary, 'Radicalism and the war: German metal workers, 1914–1923', in R. J. Evans (ed.), *Society and politics in Wilhelmine Germany* (London, 1978); M. Fine, 'Guerre et réformisme en France, 1914–1918', in L. Murard and P. Zylberman (eds.), *Le soldat du travail*, special issue of the journal *Recherches* (1978).

[8] See the essays in collections such as Haimson, *Industrial militancy* and Fridenson, *The French home front*.

[9] See Robert, 'Ouvriers et mouvement ouvrier'; Bailey, 'The Berlin strike of January 1918'; Moore, *Injustice*; A. Reid, 'Dilution, trade unionism and the state in Britain during the First World War', in S. Tolliday and J. Zeitlin (eds.), *Shop floor bargaining and the state: historical and comparative perspectives* (Cambridge, 1985); essays in Haimson (ed.), *Industrial Militancy*; D. Geary, 'Radicalism and the war: German metal workers, 1914–1923', in R. J. Evans (ed.), *Society and politics in Wilhelmine Germany* (London, 1978); Nolan, *Social democracy*.

have emphasized the costs of war and its long-term effects, but once again located largely within the national framework.[10]

Our study should be seen, therefore, as a comparative examination of a common history within the space of three metropolitan centres. In placing the history of Paris, London, and Berlin within international, national, urban, and local frameworks, and in the exploration of the fundamental material questions of urban life and urban survival in wartime, we hope to have provided some preliminary answers to questions rarely posed in the historiography of the Great War. We also hope to have made some modest progress towards a deeper understanding of urban societies at war.

Continuities and discontinuities: preliminary conclusions

The social relations of the waging of war

In this, the first of a two-volume study of the wartime history of Paris, London, and Berlin, we have sketched the broad outlines of material life in these three metropolitan centres. We have privileged issues of military service and of work, incomes, consumption, and welfare.

Dominating urban life was the fate of the armies. Sacrifice meant first and foremost military service and loss of life and limb. But other questions of well-being had to be addressed at the same time. Civilians needed shelter, jobs, basic commodities. Supply problems loomed large; distribution problems, larger still. But the thorny question of how to provide fair shares for all reflected another dimension of urban history, which was rooted in notions of the social relations of sacrifice.

A new hierarchy of urban citizenship appeared after 1914, highlighting the contribution of soldiers and war workers to the survival of the nation. Everyone had to make sacrifices in wartime, but all claims on the community were a function of the part groups and individuals played in the war effort. The standing of those far from the front, those not provisioning the armies, could not compete with the entitlement of those in uniform, of their families, and of essential war workers. The reordering of rights, the unintended redistribution of incomes in wartime, and the appearance of a language of moral judgement separating the profiteer from the nation at war, arose from these features of the social relations of the waging of war.

In effect, the resolution of material conflicts in wartime only partly

[10] J. M. Winter, *The Great War*, following the earlier work of M. Huber, *La Population de la France pendant la guerre* (Paris, 1931) and M. Meerwarth, Adolf Gunther, and Waldemar Zimmermann, *Die Einwirkung des Krieges auf Bevölkerungsbewegung und Lebenshaltung in Deutschland* (Stuttgart, 1932). But see the rudimentary steps of a comparative history in Richard Wall and Jay Winter (eds.), *The upheaval of war: family, work, and welfare in Europe, 1914–1918* (Cambridge, 1988).

reflected pre-war social stratification. The wartime organization of work, incomes, and consumption both drew upon pre-war norms and procedures and transcended them.[11] What was new was the framework of shared sacrifice, expressed in a multitude of ways, beginning at the front, but extending to every corner of civilian life.

The two phases of the war

Within this overall story, though, there is a clear chronological divide. Between 1914 and 1916, the instabilities arising from the mobilization of armies and the creation of their mammoth lines of supply were more marked in Paris and London than in Berlin. In other words, the proximity of Paris to the front, and the relatively slow pace of industrial mobilization in Britain in 1914 described one phase of the war. In this phase, material conditions and the rhythms of urban life in Berlin were no worse, and in some respects better, than in the Allied capitals.

From 1916, the picture is reversed. Every chapter in this book records the unravelling of the stability conditions of the German war effort in Berlin in the second half of the war. Every chapter records the relative success of authorities in Paris and London in containing the instabilities of the war. It is not that residents of the Allied capitals were spared shortages, blunders, and the grey monotony of wartime life; on the contrary. It is that they had the capacity, both material and administrative, to respond to wartime tensions and conflicts; authorities in Berlin were not so fortunate. The longer the war went on, the more intractable the problems of provisioning the city's population became.

The best way to understand this divide in the chronology of wartime urban history is in terms of crossing vectors. In Berlin, the longer the war went on, the greater the failure to contain the explosive tensions generated by the war. In Paris and London, the longer the war went on, the greater the success in containing them. These two vectors, one of increasing instability, the other of diminishing instability, met in 1916. Thereafter the urban history of Berlin departs completely from that of Paris and London. In this contrast lies one of the key sources of Allied victory and German defeat in the Great War.[12]

Comparative social history has given us, therefore, a more precise chronology of the war, one that reflects lived experience in these metropolitan centres. This framework does not obscure the real difficulties of urban life on both sides of the conflict, but helps us weigh them through comparison.

The fundamental features of this argument are clear. The continuities

[11] See J. Horne, *Labour at War* and B. Waites, *Class society at war*.

[12] This finding confirms the conclusion in Winter, 'Some paradoxes of the Great War', in Wall and Winter (eds.), *The upheaval of war*.

in London's war, supported by a social and political consensus as well as by massive overseas wealth, also helped to shore up the more precarious fortunes of the Parisian population. This achievement was visible only from 1916 on. No such inter-Allied support and coordination was available for the residents of Berlin. They had to make do with much less, and to make do with what was left after the army, heavy industry, and the black market took their share. From 1916, this meant urban insecurity, inflation, deprivation, and injustice on a level Londoners and Parisians never knew. It is this explosive mix which prepared the way for what Alfred Döblin called 'the darkness of defeat and collapse' which 'settled over the teeming city' of Berlin in 1918.[13]

In all three cities, the war did not end at the Armistice. Here too our study has changed our understanding of the chronology of the conflict. When we focus on the urban context, it is evident that 1919 was as much a part of wartime as any of the previous five years. The populations of all three cities were exhausted by the struggle. Lassitude dominated much of public and private life.[14] In Berlin, the blockade continued to make life difficult.[15] The revolution of November 1918 led to uprising and counter-revolution in January 1919. In less dramatic ways, the disruption of traditional forms of employment, earnings, and patterns of consumption in London and Paris carried on well after 11 November, and indeed well after the Peace Treaty was signed on 28 June 1919. Demobilization took months, not days, and the absorption of returning soldiers created tensions which dominated social life throughout 1919 and after.[16]

Above all, 1919 was a year of mourning. The shadow of bereavement, which had been cast on thousands from the earliest days of the war, had spread over millions by 1919. Among these mourners were the pilgrims to the Arc de Triomphe in Paris on Bastille Day 1919 and to Lutyens's Cenotaph in London five days later. These huge crowds turned what was meant to be a festival of triumph into a moment of meditation on suffering and sacrifice. It was the *mutilés de guerre* in Paris, and the

[13] Döblin, *A people betrayed*, p. 6.

[14] See Robert, 'Ouvriers et mouvement ouvrier', vol. VI.

[15] M. C. Siney, *The Allied blockade of Germany* (New York, 1966); Offer, *An agrarian interpretation*; K. Burk, *Britain, America and the sinews of war, 1914–1918* (London, 1985); M. Olson, *The economics of the wartime shortage* (Chapel Hill, N.C., 1970); C. P. Vincent, *The politics of hunger: the Allied blockade of Germany, 1915–1919* (Athens, Ohio, 1985); and the valuable documents in S. L. Bane and R. H. Lutz (eds.), *The Blockade of Germany after the Armistice* (New York, 1938).

[16] See G. D. Feldman, 'Economic and social problems'; R. Bessel, *Germany after the Great War* (Oxford, 1993); A. Prost, *In the wake of war* (Providence and Oxford, 1992); C. Kimble, 'The British Legion and ex-servicemen's politics in Britain', PhD thesis, Stanford University, 1990; and S. Ward (ed.), *The War Generation* (Port Washington, N.Y., 1975).

widows, orphans, and bereaved parents in both 'victorious' capital cities who reminded the men in power that for millions on both sides, the war and the cruel price it exacted would last long after the Armistice. To extend the chronological limits of the Great War to 1919 is simply a recognition of this essential level of reality.[17]

After the war

In order to specify the effects of the war on the three cities, we have to consider a chronological question. Which 'post-war' years do we mean? Until which date do we intend to measure the effects of the Great War? By concentrating on the early 1920s – to use the census of 1921 for instance – we are still in the period of the direct repercussions of the conflict. But to stop there signifies a certain indifference about the longer-term consequences of the war. We are drawn therefore to evidence on the later 1920s and early 1930s, where census material exists, though how to separate the effects of war from those of time is an unanswerable problem. Adding to the difficulty in the case of Berlin, some statistical series were interrupted at the end of the war. At times new categories were adopted in subsequent series describing a different urban space. It is inevitable that conclusions about the post-war years in comparative perspective must remain partial. But on one point there is abundant evidence: the comparative typology of the situation of the three cities in wartime is equally applicable to the 1920s.

London

The degree of continuity we have observed in London as between the pre-war and wartime periods applies to the post-war period too. We noted at the beginning of this book that the growth of Greater London had diminished in the pre-war years. London registered between 1911 and 1921 neither a drop in population like Berlin, nor the growth of the Parisian population. London's population grew in this decade only by 3 per cent, a situation of slow growth maintained in the years 1921 to 1931. London's stability is remarkable, even given the structural stability of its administrative boundaries and bureaucracy in this period.

There were as well striking continuities in the history of the London labour market. Before the war, the British capital went through a reorientation of female labour towards the service sector, a growth of public services and a shift away from the dominance of its older industries – such as clothing and building – and towards more dynamic

[17] See A. Becker, *La guerre et la ferveur* (Paris, 1994); A. Gregory, *The silence of memory. Armistice Day 1919 – 1946* (Oxford and Providence, 1994); D. Lloyd, 'Pilgrimages and British society during and after the First World War', PhD thesis, University of Cambridge, 1994; J. M. Winter, *Sites of memory, sites of mourning* (Cambridge, 1995).

trades like metal-work. The war accelerated these processes only little, with the possible exception of London transport, which benefited from its key role in the inter-Allied war economy.

In demographic terms, London passed through the war without evidence of crisis. Pre-war trends were resumed, and despite some rapid gains in Paris, London maintained its advantage *vis-à-vis* the other two cities in terms of survival rates and expectation of life at birth and at later ages.

Paris

In contrast, the urban history of Paris was marked by a much greater degree of instability in this period. Despite increased mortality rates, especially among men, the population of the Paris region grew by 6 per cent in the 1911 to 1921 decade. This period of growth extended into the mid-1920s, until the total population outstripped that of Berlin, whose expansion was most marked before 1914. The war accentuated the demographic weight of Paris within France, mirroring the unprecedented economic expansion of the war years.

We must look to the war for the sources of the reorganization of Parisian economic activity, and in particular the sharp growth in metalwork, which continued in the post-war period. It was the war too which further limited the growth of older consumer industries like clothing, already stable or shrinking before the war. It was the war which occasioned the striking development of public and banking services. It is clear too that the war contributed to a shift in the sectoral location of women's work, moving the bulk of employees towards commerce and the service sector.

Each of these trends contributed to a spatial reorganization of the Parisian economy. After the war, the core of the region, the city of Paris, shrank numerically for the first time. Demographic dynamism moved to the suburban belt. For political reasons, administrative boundaries were unchanged. This disparity between a demographic shift and bureaucratic stasis inevitably increased the degree of social and spatial heterogeneity in the region as a whole. Added to this was the relatively slow pace of improvement after the war in public health in the popular districts of Paris, where very high mortality rates existed prior to the war.

Berlin

The immediate post-war years are best understood as an extension of the crisis whose onset may be dated from 1917. This crisis was too grave to be contained easily by the new administration of the revolution and the Weimar Republic. On the one hand, given the new constitution, in which executive and parliamentary authority were integrated in new ways, Berlin became more the political capital of Germany than it had been before the war. Though the *Länder* retained authority over police and education, the central state was much stronger than it had been in 1914. The army, postal services, railroads, and taxes were now under centralized control.

The capital city itself was redefined spatially. By a law of 27 April 1920, Greater Berlin absorbed fifty-nine municipalities and twenty-six property-tax districts which had surrounded old Berlin before the war. The provision of universal suffrage – votes for women, the ending of the three-tier Prussian franchise – accentuated the political modernization of Berlin, according to the French sociologist Maurice Halbwachs.[18] It was still the case, though, that the retention of provincial political authority in the *Länder* raised difficult questions about the linkages between city and state in the early Weimar Republic.

Above all, we can see the effects of the war in Berlin's demographic history. Of our three capital cities, only Berlin registered a decline in population between 1911 and 1921. In the pre-war years, the growth of Berlin was much more rapid than that of Paris; post-war Berlin lost ground to Paris in the 1920s. The core of the German capital was not, like Paris, the centre of a rapidly growing metropolitan region. Unfortunately, changes in administrative boundaries preclude a more precise analysis of these economic changes. All we can do is point to the indirect evidence on demographic developments. Here we see in the 1920s few signs of continuity with pre-war trends towards rising life expectancy, bringing Berlin within range of London survival rates. The crisis of 1917 and afterwards was too deep and persisted too long for us to conclude that the war for Berlin was a mere interruption in secular trends.

War and post-war

One clear conclusion is the perpetuation after the Armistice of the character of the impact of war conditions on these three cities: crisis in Berlin; dynamism in Paris; stability in London. The sharp break in Berlin's wartime history between 1914–16 and 1917 and afterwards separates its evolution from that of the other two cities.

The apparent parallels between the histories of Paris and London in wartime mask divergent trajectories. These divergences will become more apparent when we examine the political mutations of the war decade. In London there are signs of growing support for the Labour party, but Paris (like Berlin) becomes a communist stronghold. The degree to which this contrast and other political developments were

[18] M. Halbwachs, 'Gross Berlin: grande agglomération ou grande ville?', *Annales d'histoire économique et sociale*, 30 (Nov. 1934), pp. 547–70.

war-related or built into the long-term history of the three cities will be addressed in the second volume of this study.

Urban life in wartime

The Lost Generation and urban demography in wartime

Statistical limitations

The demographic history of these three cities in wartime can be viewed only through a glass darkly. That prism is the partiality and fragmentary character of the evidence available about the fundamental parameters of population movements. We have only a rough idea of how many people lived in these cities; how many migrants came and went; how these cities' age-structure changed in wartime, and how the sex ratio was distorted by drastic shifts of population.

This last lacuna is of particular importance in this study. Without full demographic data on the male age-structure, it is impossible to discuss urban populations as a whole or to analyse questions related to the balance or relative advantage in terms of life expectancy of urban women over urban men. To explore the critical area of gender and privilege, we must analyse other sources, scrutinized in volume II. But that inquiry is set against the backdrop of the data we have presented here on military losses and on female survival chances in wartime.

The nature of the evidence forced us to divide this part of our study by sex. First, in chapter 3, we presented our findings on military participation and casualties; then in chapter 6, we analysed civilian death rates in terms of statistics on the female population. More general problems of public-health policies and outcomes were explored in chapters 14 and 15. In volume II, we resume the discussion of demographic issues, with respect to nuptiality and fertility.

The Lost Generation

Before summarizing the results of our analysis of casualty statistics, we must consider another preliminary difficulty which has marked all our research. It is the definition of urban boundaries. Published casualty statistics are available only for the larger administrative unit of the Department of the Seine; much of Berlin's data describe only the inner city, within the pre-1920 boundaries. In the case of London, there is an array of references to London casualties, using the definition of the city as: (1) the inner twenty-eight metropolitan boroughs; (2) the overall area within the County of London; or (3) Greater London, co-terminous with the boundaries of the Metropolitan Police District. We have tried to indicate wherever possible the base populations upon which all our demographic analyses rest; the choice of denominator – that is, population at risk – is, therefore, critical.

Equally uncertain is the numerator used in casualty rates – the numbers killed or who died on military services. Casualty statistics are notoriously difficult to handle.[19] The scale of losses made precision impossible; attempts to provide a full list of those who died by Paris arrondissement, for example, are clearly incomplete.[20] Men died of wounds or illness long after the Armistice; hundreds of thousands simply vanished in battle, swelling the category of the unknown, presumed dead. To say the least, a clear margin of error must be accepted here, as in all other areas of demographic inquiry.

Nevertheless, several findings appear sufficiently robust to stand. First, our analysis on the metropolitan level showed, with respect to military losses, a strikingly similar pattern in Paris, London, and Berlin. The direct demographic consequences of the war in these three cities arose from parallel patterns of recruitment and military losses. The fact that until 1916 London's recruitment was voluntary – in contrast to Paris and Berlin, where conscription operated – made little difference to overall casualty rates or the age structure of the 'Lost Generation'.

First, let us consider aggregate losses. Of the three cities, Paris may have lost the most, in terms of total residents killed on military service: of the one million men who went to war from the Department of the Seine, approximately 140,000 were killed or died on active service. This casualty rate is slightly lower than the national figure of one in six killed of those who served. London's much larger population also provided roughly one million men for the army, and about the same number of casualties as did Paris: perhaps 130,000. Here metropolitan casualties are roughly at the national level of losses: one in eight men who served in British forces was killed. Approximately 53,000 Berliners living in the core city were killed or died in uniform. Given the size of the pre-1920 city, this figure is also a bit below, but in line with, the proportion of losses – one in six killed of those who served – suffered throughout the Kaiserreich.[21]

In effect, casualty rates among these three metropolitan populations were slightly below those of the nation as a whole. Men who lived in these cities were privileged: their death-rates were somewhat lower than other male cohorts, though the difference is not as great as previously has been thought.

The mildly 'privileged' position of the male population of Paris, London, and Berlin arose out of the age-structure of military service. Urban populations in uniform were older than the army as a whole.

19 J.M. Winter, *The Great War*, ch. 3.

20 These are hand-written lists held in the Archives Nationales in Paris, in the series F9/17666.

21 J.M. Winter, *The Great War*, ch. 3.

Younger men were in some cases kept back; in others, sent back; and in others still, they stayed put. In other words, rural cohorts lost more men in proportion to their total populations because more of their youngest males eligible for military service were called up or volunteered. The age-profile of metropolitan men who served determined the relative weight of casualties suffered by these three cities' populations.

This is the first surprising finding of our demographic study: metropolitan males in uniform were older, more likely to be married, and also slightly more likely to survive military service, than their compatriots. Male Parisians, Londoners, and Berliners were privileged, in this sense, but only marginally: we must never forget that a quarter of a million men from these three cities died in the war. Loss is never experienced proportionately. Bereavement was everywhere.

A second finding is also surprising. The occupational distribution of metropolitan war losses was mixed. In some cases, we have confirmed received wisdom: Londoners in some middle-class occupations, like banking, suffered much higher than average casualty rates; other non-manual employees were luckier, and men in munitions trades luckiest of all.[22] In Paris, metal-workers had lower than average death-rates. But these indications of a class structure of casualties, in which the better-off suffered higher casualties, is misleading. Parisian printers suffered very high death-rates; intellectuals and students, very low death-rates. The war presented a kaleidoscope of risk, and it would be a mistake to describe the social distribution of casualties in any straightforward or simple pattern.

Civilian health

The same problems of incomplete and problematic evidence hamper our study of civilian mortality and morbidity. In our study of civilian health in wartime, what we have been able to do is to identify certain general trends and divergences with respect to particular age groups and, within them, certain vulnerable categories of people.

On balance, civilian health in Paris and London was maintained at roughly the same levels as in the pre-war period. There was no recrudescence of urban disease, as had occurred in the course of the 1870–1 war in Paris. But it is clear that the pre-war trend of mortality decline was interrupted in the Allied capitals. Their inhabitants suffered a loss of progress; Berliners, in contrast, suffered a loss of life, in that mortality rates soared after 1916.

Within this overall contrast, there were clear divergences with respect to mortality rates in different age-groups and different parts of

[22] For national statistics on Britain, see Winter, *The Great War*, ch. 2; on France and Germany, the older studies of Huber, *La population* and Meerwarth, Gunther, and Zimmermann, *Die Einwirkung*, repeated in many other places.

the community: some suffered more than others. In all three cities, the elderly,[23] illegitimate children,[24] young adult women[25] all registered increased mortality rates in wartime. The reasons were complex, but included, for the elderly and some (but by no means all) infants, a degree of marginalization at a time of scarce resources. Young women were disadvantaged by conditions of work and residence in wartime cities. Their increased death-rates due to tuberculosis were also a function of migration: in-migrants were exposed to a different and more varied disease regime than they had known before their entry into these cities.

This finding points to another important aspect of the demographic history of the war: the reduction of demographic differentials as between different populations. Migration was at the heart of this process. Volatile populations, moving into these cities, or within them, brought their pre-war demographic profiles with them. Their presence in different cities and in different quartiers was mandated by wartime mobilization. These population movements mixed healthier and unhealthier groups, and made it inevitable that mortality differentials would diminish in the war period.[26]

Other sources of the narrowing of demographic inequality, as expressed in death-rates, lay in wartime changes in material conditions. Severe economic difficulties levelled life chances downward in Berlin. In Paris and London, the opposite was the case, due in part to changes in patterns of earnings and consumption. The levelling up of incomes described in chapter 9 and the proliferation of transfer payments described in chapter 10 benefited in particular those who had been worst off in the pre-war years. It would be unwise to posit a clear and unambiguous causal link between incomes and mortality rates, but the direction of the effect of higher and more regular wages on nutritional patterns controlled by rationing and other measures was, for many city-dwellers in Paris and London, entirely positive.

In Berlin, the negative effects of increasingly restricted and uncertain food supplies, the siphoning off of essential goods into the black market, and a mountain of red tape also reduced the distance between the nutritional status of different sectors of the population. Here the thrust was a downward levelling of nutritional differentials, for all except

23 Winter and Robert, 'Un aspect ignoré', pp. 307–28.

24 Winter and Cole, 'Fluctuations in infant mortality rates'. On the more favourable situation with respect to conditions in Britain, where illegitimacy ratios were low, see Winter, Lawrence, and Ariouat, 'The impact of the Great War on infant mortality in London'.

25 See Bryder, *Below the magic mountain* for a discussion of tuberculosis among these young women.

26 This both confirms and offers a more plausible explanation of the demographic data analysed in Winter, *The Great War and the British People*, ch. 4.

those with regular access to the black market. The soaring death-rates from 1917 to 1919 among Berliners had many causes, but for most of the population material shortages underlay them.

Public-health policies in all three cities were strikingly similar. The attempt to ward off the threat of epidemic disease was largely successful, until the influenza pandemic of 1918–19 flattened the meagre and irrelevant barriers set up to cope with it and deal with its ravages.[27] With respect to other, endemic, diseases, the record was mixed, but on balance more positive in all three cities. The exception remains tuberculosis, which rose especially for young women below the age of thirty.

In all three cities, private and philanthropic work carried on in wartime. But its scope was severely restricted, leaving many of those previously assisted without clear means of support. To a degree, municipal and state efforts filled the gap, especially in Paris and London, but in Berlin the scale of the problems faced by some disadvantaged groups was so severe that no one was able to provide adequate assistance.

On balance, the history of public health in wartime was mixed: there were winners and losers on the home front too. But with some important qualifications, we have confirmed the overall argument that, as measured by life chances, there occurred an unintended compression of the demographic distance as between social groups in Paris, London, and Berlin in the period of the Great War.

Within this global interpretation, the stark contrast between Berlin, on the one hand, and Paris and London, on the other, is striking. Only in Berlin did civilians pay a clear price in terms of declining life-expectancy for the waging of war. In Paris and London, conditions were austere and very difficult for some, but on balance civilian health did not worsen. For some groups, especially legitimate infants, life-expectancy rose. The Allies had the material resources and administrative skill to defend the health of the home front. We have found in the case of Berlin abundant evidence of one of the principal failures of the German war effort.

That failure can be dated more precisely, due to the findings we have presented here. The clear divide between the two phases of the war's demographic history also emerges clearly from this part of our study. In demographic terms there were two wars: from 1914 to 1916, when the two sides faced the same pressures and registered the same mixed statistics; from 1917 to 1919, when the demographic crisis in Berlin dramatically departed from the record of rough stability in Paris and London. Rising civilian death-rates in Berlin in the second half of the war bear the unmistakable imprint of Germany's increasingly precari-

[27] On the British case, see Sandra Tomkins's thesis, 'Britain and the influenza epidemic'.

ous economic position, which became untenable after the failure of the 1918 offensives.

In one other respect, demographic evidence opens up new interpretations of the aftermath of the war. The post-war period was strikingly different in the three cities. In London, the difficult conditions of wartime were lifted, providing the basis for a major improvement in life-expectancy at most ages. The gains made in Paris after 1918 were more modest, though real enough. In Berlin, the end of the war inaugurated a difficult phase in the city's demographic history, marked and marred in particular by a crisis in infant mortality, lasting from 1917 to 1923.[28] For many Berlin families the trials of the war continued long after the Armistice. Despite the fragility and lassitude evident among exhausted populations on the other side of the line, the populations of Paris and London faced a less uncertain future.

Work, income, and consumption: social relations and material life

There are problems of evidence which attend all attempts to compare material conditions of daily life in these three cities. Each capital had a different system of social statistics. Categories varied: for example, each city had a different measure of unemployment. It is less our intention to offer precise comparisons than to contrast patterns and trends. With respect to incomes, we come up against difficulties in sorting out different modes of payment not easily converted into time series of wages and earnings. Problems are less severe in the sphere of consumption, since it is possible to separate products and items. On these matters we have adequate data, but they are insufficiently robust to enable us to establish rigorous individual, household, or family budgets.

Work

The comparative social history of labour markets has been a particularly fruitful field; here we have encountered findings which are new, and surprisingly so, given the already abundant literature in this area. Such a comparison has enabled us to outline important features of the impact of war on these three capital cities. We can weight the crisis periods of the war, and distinguish between different urban trajectories. This is particularly true with respect to the first phase of the conflict, in which the special features of the Parisian case are very striking. From 1914 to 1915 there occurred in the French capital a dramatic and extended crisis of unemployment and the suspension of much economic activity. In contrast, the entry into war in London and Berlin was much smoother

[28] See Winter and Cole, 'Fluctuations in infant mortality in Berlin', *passim*.

and more orderly. Here we see the centrality of the military context – the proximity of Paris to the front – and the absolute primacy (not surprisingly) given by public authorities to the army in 1914.

After the end of the war of movement on the Western front in late-1914, the three capitals entered into a common phase of economic mobilization. This was particularly important in Paris from mid-1915 onwards. Labour markets were reoriented towards creating a new labour force, redistributing women workers and newcomers from the provincial hinterlands in Berlin, and from the provinces, dominions, and empire in Paris and London.

Soon contradictions surfaced: how to balance industries oriented towards domestic consumption and war industry? What element of skilled labour should be recalled from the front for service in war factories? These were questions particularly relevant in Paris and Berlin, with early and high rates of military mobilization. In Berlin, production for the domestic sector was largely unprotected from the dominance of military demand. In addition bureaucratic complexity and confusion added to the uncertainty of provisioning the home front. Things got worse after the implementation of the Hindenburg Programme in late 1916, but the origins of the problem of finding a balance between front and home front lay earlier in the war. It is true that war production in Berlin continued at a high pace after 1916, but at the price of stripping the labour force in the domestic sector, and especially in food provision and supply.

In contrast, thanks to a policy of participation of trade-union leaders and the *patronat* (employers), reflecting real civilian control over these questions, the labour force both in London and in Paris was reconfigured to suit the needs both of the army and of the civilian population.[29] This new labour force stood the challenge of the grinding pressure of the war, including the severe test of the German offensive of March–June 1918, when Paris was again under threat.

This contrast between growing integration on the Allied side and growing divisions in Berlin should not obscure the tensions in Paris and London once the war was over. Real instabilities attended the process of demobilization, in particular with respect to the dismissal or redistribution of female labour.[30] But in Berlin these problems were exacerbated by the stresses introduced by inflation, revolution, political instability, the persistence of the Allied blockade, and high unemployment.[31]

[29] For confirmation see J. Horne, *Labour at War*, and Fridenson (ed.), *The French home front*.

[30] On which see F. Thébaud, *Les femmes au temps de la guerre de '14* (Paris, 1980); her essay in Fridenson (ed.), *The French home front*; essays by J.-L. Robert, Ute Daniel, and D. Thom in Wall and J. M. Winter (eds.), *The upheaval of war*, and Daniel's *Women at War in Germany 1914–1918* (Oxford, 1996).

[31] The literature on this subject is vast. For a start see J. P. Nettl, *Rosa Luxemburg* (Oxford, 1966); R. Bessel, *Germany after the Great War* (Oxford, 1993); A. J. Ryder, *The German*

Incomes

At a time when the sacrifices of the front dominate those of the rear, it was not abnormal for there to be a certain reticence about incomes and standards of living. When the consensus was that the war would be short, the sacrifice of wages or dividends was of no great consequence. But once the war of attrition began, and with it the prospect of chronic price inflation, a shrinkage of real assets and a redistribution of income were bound to occur. Those on fixed incomes knew that under these circumstances, they would be the losers. Both in the labour market and in the capital markets, those close to the war economy benefited, those far from it lost. Rentiers were hard hit everywhere. For the less well-off, the state, municipalities, and private philanthropy offered some compensation, through transfer payments incorporating elements of social justice and domestic order.

With respect to wages, the rules of the market governed developments in the three cities: workers in war factories and unskilled labour in general 'profited' from the conflict; their earnings approached or exceeded those of skilled workers. The full account of shifts in the sexual and the skill composition of wages must be placed in the context of the history of social movements in these three cities, a subject treated in detail in volume II.

The same rules applied to middle-class incomes. Rentiers, property-owners, and holders of stock portfolios did worse than shareholders, shop owners, and above all, war industrialists. But on the whole, it is clear that the war had more adverse material effects on the middle classes and the bourgeoisie than on the working-class population. The differential effects of war inflation were fundamental here, though its effects varied in intensity. This issue is of fundamental importance when in volume II we deal with family strategies of survival.

This temporary inversion of the pre-war privileges of the propertied was only one side of the story. Within the working class, there was also a restructuring of material conditions, in which some groups did worse than others. For some of those hard-hit by the war, a set of municipal and national transfer payments eased some of their troubles. In the Parisian case, some material difficulties were ameliorated by a municipal strategy of social consensus and social protection. But despite the fact that urban citizenship was expressed in local initiatives of assistance and material provisioning of the population, large groups of

Revolution of 1918 (Cambridge, 1975); Moore, *Injustice*; A. Rosenburg, *Imperial Germany* (New York, 1959); R. G. Moeller, 'Dimensions of social conflict in the Great War: the view from the German countryside', *Central European History*, 14, 2 (June 1981); Bailey, 'The Berlin strike'; R. Rürup, 'Problems of the German revolution', *Journal of Contemporary History* (1968), pp. 1–18.

people of modest or inadequate means received little or no benefits at all. This was especially true in Berlin, from the middle years of the war, when social problems simply overwhelmed municipal authorities.

Consumption

One of the key contrasts in wartime urban life as between Berlin, on the one hand, and Paris and London, on the other hand, lies in the history of consumption. In the Allied capitals, there were disturbing shortfalls in essential supplies, for instance, with respect to coal in the winters of 1916 to 1917 and 1917 to 1918. But despite the objective difficulties and the tensions these issues generated, solutions were found. Through a series of local and private initiatives, then through state intervention, then through inter-Allied accords, the problem was contained, if not eliminated. The key element was the joint operation of a system of Allied distribution of essential goods drawn from imperial and other sources. Here nation and empire were decisive in terms of stabilizing a difficult situation in the Allied capitals.

In contrast, from the middle years of the war, no authority – municipal, provincial, military, or imperial – could assure regular and adequate food supplies to the population of Berlin. The crisis of the black market – virtually non-existent in Paris and London – flowed directly from price controls and inadequate supply. Aside from the shortfall in agricultural production and the effects of the blockade, our study has shown that the slide towards centralization was not the key difficulty in Germany. On the contrary, the Kaiserreich was an incomplete state in which multiple non-democratic structures took overlapping and at times contradictory decisions about the needs of the same place or region. This administrative and political maze was not the setting in which effective central authority could untangle the complexities of provisioning a city the size of Berlin. The result was a grave crisis of consumption in the German capital, with repercussions of a kind felt only occasionally in Paris and London.

If the problems of coal and food supply highlight clear divergences between the two sides in the war, the question of housing illustrates another set of contrasts. In Berlin, social conflicts over housing did not have the same prominence as they did in Paris and London. In the Allied capitals, many of the problems at the heart of the social relations of housing antedated the war. The tensions which existed between proprietor and occupier were transformed by the rent moratoria of 1914 and 1915 in Paris and London. In Berlin a different system operated, regulated by magistrates' courts, where applications for the deferral of rent payments were processed.

In London and Paris, the loss of proprietors' control over rent was of critical importance, and not only in assuring a smooth military and industrial mobilization. Rent control, which extended after the war, symbolized the suspension of possessive individualism as a whole. The rules of the market did not apply in the search for a roof over your head. Indeed these rules could not apply if soldiers' families were to survive and work in war factories. The interests of the nation clearly took precedence over the interests of private property. Once the war was over, though, the reassertion of the old order was not easy. Wartime changes in tenant–owner relations ensured that after the war housing problems would be a focus for social conflict at the municipal level.[32] This story is addressed in detail in volume II.

The recomposition of urban societies

In the first volume of this study, we have noted many other levels on which the impact of war may be seen. One such level is that of social stratification. Here the effect of war was twofold. First, there is abundant evidence of a break-up of urban society in the sense that conventional pre-war classifications no longer served as a reliable guide to wartime social divisions. This uncoupling process led, secondly, to a reconfiguration arising directly from the demands of the war: there were those who served, at home and at the front, and there were the others. Within this wartime social division, the effects of military mobilization, social policy and social movements (studied in volume II) led to a reordering of social hierarchies particularly evident in the immediate aftermath of the war. In this sense, our three capital cities did indeed constitute communities of common social experience.

Complexities of wartime social divisions

Towards a new hierarchy of privilege

Among civilian populations, there was a complex scale of winners and losers during the war. This hierarchy departed in fundamental ways from pre-war categories of social class. At the positive end of the wartime scale lay all those who contributed directly to war production or who helped maintain the basic material needs of the war industry: workers and management in the war industry, and certain shopkeepers and traders in basic foodstuffs. Whatever their position in the labour market, their incomes, their food situation, and their health, these people at the heart of the war economy were, in a sense, in the best position. They were the clear material winners of the war.

At the opposite extreme were three groups: (1) those employed in

[32] For the British story, see A. Offer, *Property and politics*, and D. Englander, *Landlord and tenant*.

non-essential trades: building, printing, domestic service, some public servants and bureaucrats; (2) a large part of the property-owning middle class, both of substantial and modest means, both those holding real property and portfolios of stocks and shares; and (3) some other marginal groups, such as the elderly, the institutionalized, and dependent unoccupied populations.

Between the two extremes, there was a medley of groups. Public-sector employees and service-sector workers, such as railwaymen, were in a relatively favourable situation. They had regular employment, some social benefits, and they were not subject to new working conditions adverse to their health. But by the end of the war, these workers, especially the more senior among them, were losers in terms of incomes. Others, such as Parisian wine merchants, did better in material terms, but they suffered in other ways, in particular through the closure of their businesses in times of military crisis. The sheer complexity of wartime conditions, the relentless effects of inflation and the uncertainties of material provision lead us to the conclusion that pre-war class formations broke up in wartime. Workers, employees, middle-class people, and property-owners were scattered along the entire spectrum of the privileged and the unprivileged in wartime urban life.

Parallel hierarchies: front/rear; consumers/producers/middlemen

Hierarchies based on material conditions describe some aspects of urban society in wartime. Other hierarchies, visible in images and social representations, appeared too. The first, well known within the historical literature, is the divide between soldier and civilian.[33] In demographic and material terms, soldiers and the social groups from which they came were clearly the losers, and civilians the winners. But in some ways, the situation was more complex. In moral terms, in terms of socially approved images, soldiers were paragons. They formed a 'Lost Generation' no doubt, scarred by the war, but for a brief moment in 1918 to 1919, did not soldiers enjoy universal respect and privileged access to the labour market? Still, the evanescence of this advantage suggests the fluidity of the 'privileged' wartime social status of the men in uniform.

More clear-cut is the divide between consumers and producers and

[33] See E. Leed, *No man's land. Combat and identity in World War One* (Cambridge, 1979); K. Theweleit, *Male Fantasies* (2 vols., Cambridge, 1987–8); R. G. L. Waite, *Vanguards of Nazism. The Freikorps 1919–1933* (Cambridge, Mass., 1964), for the argument for separation of soldiers and civilians. For the opposite view, in which the ties between front and home front are emphasized, see T. Ashworth, *Trench warfare 1914–1918. The live and let live system* (London, 1980); Audoin-Rouzeau, *Men at war*, and Fuller, *Troop morale and popular culture.*

between both and the middlemen who took their cut in wartime. Shortages of food and coal in particular created a heterogeneous bloc of consumers, poor as well as rich, who faced the same problems of everyday life. The pre-war residential divide between different social groups gave way to some degree in wartime, when serious shortages led to common provisioning. People of very different means were seen confronting tradesmen, in queues in and out of butchers' shops, arguing with coal merchants who, it was said, carefully limited their sales, whatever stocks they had in reserve. This image of consumers versus those who exploited serious shortages was hardly new: its parallel was clearly with similar quarrels in urban and rural life in the eighteenth and nineteenth centuries.[34] These historical analogies were not merely academic: they were made during the war and served as sources of popular sentiment at the level of the quartier, which we will examine in volume II.

In wartime there was a dual development: away from pre-war categories of social hierarchies, reflecting the special conditions of the conflict; and at the same time, towards an intensification of pre-war languages of class conflict within urban social movements. The full story of this dialectical process – linking the unusual social structures of wartime and the older categories of social conflict and division, suspended in 1914, but clearly visible towards the end of the war and in its immediate aftermath – will be told in volume II.

Inequalities, social policy, and marginality

In all three cities, there was in wartime a significant expansion of social policy and public intervention in urban life, through state, provincial, and municipal authorities. This concentration effect of services and social action brought into the public domain many activities previously conducted outside it, and placed in the hands of national authorities some services previously provided at the municipal or local level. This finding is consistent with the available literature,[35] though we have shown for the first time precisely how it operated on the metropolitan level in these three cities.

Such social policies were linked to the overall demographic impact of the war. Again, our study follows other work which on the national level juxtaposed the success of Allied governments in defending the

[34] B. Waites, 'The moral economy of the crowd'; J. Horne, 'L'impôt du sang'.

[35] See the classic study of Peacock and Wiseman, *The growth of public expenditure*. On the British case, see J. E. Cronin, *The Politics of State*, for France, see S. Bock, 'L'exubérance de l'Etat, 1914–1918', *Vingtième Siècle*, 1 (1988). Surprisingly, in the light of the strength of the Weberian paradigm, the German literature has not focused on this period in terms of the expansion of state power. For the exception, see Kocka, *Facing total war*.

well-being of their civilian populations with the German failure to do so. Metropolitan demographic evidence has reinforced the hypotheses advanced on the basis of national statistics that there was a compression of the class structure in the sense of reducing the demographic disadvantage of poverty and the demographic advantage of wealth.[36]

In our studies of infants and the elderly in Paris and London, we have also reconfirmed the hypothesis that there was a certain spatial convergence of mortality rates, reflecting a greater commonality of social experience in wartime. Undoubtedly migration, both intra-urban and inter-urban, played a decisive role in this narrowing of demographic differentials. But this finding is consistent with the argument advanced in other parts of this book, on work, wages, and consumption. There was in wartime a narrowing of the range of social situations in societies still harbouring extreme variations of wealth, health, and welfare.

Once again, contradictions abound in wartime social history. Alongside these centripetal forces, other powerful centrifugal forces emerged in wartime, leading to the worsening of the social situation of some marginal groups. These were largely outside the boundaries of social policy. Increased mortality among the elderly in the three cities, the dire circumstances of illegitimate infants in Berlin, and of abandoned children in Paris, the plight of those incarcerated in asylums and prisons in London point to a harsh divide during the conflict. It separated those at the core of society from those at the periphery; it divided those who were deemed deserving of a minimum level of subsistence, and those who, for reasons of age or moral disapproval, did not. We must not forget that there were many who fell through the net created by social policy, and others who were meant to remain outside it. In Paris and London, destitution diminished,[37] but we must not ignore those who were excluded from collective provision in wartime.

Towards a new approach to urban history

City, nation, empire

How do we explain the differing trajectories of the war experience in these three populations? The first point to make is that urban administrations had neither the resources nor the authority effectively to determine levels of well-being in these cities. Virtually all of the key decisions were taken elsewhere.

This had important implications for both sides. The failure of social policy and economic planning to provide an adequate material base

[36] J. M. Winter, *The Great War*, and Wall and J. M. Winter (eds.), *The upheaval of war*, *passim*.
[37] See comments in J. M. Winter, Lawrence, and Ariouat, 'The impact of the Great War'.

for the needs of the Berlin population was not an urban one. When the old regime was swept away and the provisional government leading to the Weimar Republic was established in November 1918, urban administration and politics continued almost without a pause. Everyone could see that the city's problems – and their solutions – were not of their making.

Similarly, the greater capacity of Allied administrators and politicians to adapt to wartime restrictions, and to act when shortages and bottlenecks appeared, did not reflect a greater degree of intrinsic ability or sophistication within the cadre of urban *fonctionnaires*. They simply could pass the message of discontent or shortfall upwards to region, nation, and ultimately to inter-Allied commissioners. The real power lay not in these cities but in the structures of imperial and international wealth and leverage which they controlled.

This finding suggests an approach to both national and urban history which may have some echo in other historical periods. Our assumption is that the only way to write the history of nations without nationalist blinkers is to do so through the study of critical groups within these nations. The metropolis was a huge social formation at the juncture between the national state and civil society, as defined by collectivities of many kinds. The wartime history of these collectivities, at the level of the family, the quartier, social movements, follows in volume II.

At the same time, our study has identified the dangers of the reification of urban history. In wartime, these cities were never for one moment disengaged from the rest of the nation at war. It is true, though, that each had a distinctive cultural life, as the photography of the period suggests. Wartime events also had specifically urban echoes. The taxis of the Marne came from Paris. Karl Liebknecht shouted 'Down with the war' on 1 January 1916 at Circus Busch in Berlin. The Cenotaph was on Whitehall in the heart of administrative London.

These cities were in part symbols of what the war was about. To defend London from the fate of Brussels, thousands of men joined up in 1914. That Paris held out meant (at least symbolically and perhaps materially) that France held out in those early days of combat. The giant statue of Paul von Hindenburg in Berlin's Tiergarten announced to the yet unknowing world that the German military genius was alive and well and living in Berlin or in neighbouring Potsdam.

Crossing boundaries

Here we can see as well that the boundaries between city, nation, and empire, in cultural terms, were porous in wartime. In other ways, these metropolitan centres were imperial meeting grounds. Men and women from virtually every corner of the world met not only in high office, but in cabarets, cinemas, pubs, and clubs.[38] Paris, London, and Berlin were entrepots for itinerant soldiers in search of the front or returning from it. This international *mélange* gave metropolitan life a distinctive taste and colour in wartime. How much remained when the soldiers went home is harder to say.

The indigenous population was highly volatile. Refugees came and went. Men and women on the move included demobilized men, the wounded, relatives in search of family members, recruits to industry, and substitute labour. When coal or food became scarce after 1916 – or just for company, sympathy, and comfort – families moved in together. Grandparents helped keep children out of trouble; adult children invited the vulnerable aged to join them during the harsh winters of the war.

Urban citizenship in wartime

Most city-dwellers were citizens, but the meaning of citizenship varied substantially. The vote was not the decisive issue. Universal manhood suffrage existed only in France; the franchise at municipal level was wider, but eligibility for municipal assistance was not determined by voting rights.

In wartime, there was an egalitarian thrust to social provision. *Habitant* was a much wider and inclusive category than *citoyen*. Those living in cities were able to benefit from many measures new to wartime: rent control, rationing, and the distribution of coal and some foodstuffs were among them. While many individuals fell through the wartime welfare net, it is still true that the meaning of citizenship broadened to include provision for populations especially hit by the war, such as the families of mobilized, wounded, or fallen soldiers, as well as provision for a basic minimum of subsistence. Entitlement rights expanded in wartime, once more linking urban citizenship to the nation under siege.[39]

Realities, representations, social imagery

So far we have concentrated on concrete questions of rights and material entitlements. But in order to enter the world of social movements, and of the associations reflecting family and neighbourhood ties, discussed in volume II, we must consider other more intangible issues. Among them are images of social values and attitudes.

[38] See R. Sweeney, 'Popular entertainments in Paris in the First World War', PhD thesis, University of Berkeley, 1992; P. Martland, 'The gramophone industry in Britain, 1880–1930', PhD thesis, University of Cambridge, 1991, ch. 5, and the programme, 'Cabaret de la grande guerre', broadcast over the Franco-German television channel Arte, 11 November 1993.

[39] Here we follow the formulation of Amartya Sen, *Poverty and famines*.

Taken as a whole the evidence of press caricatures reflects the transmission and reinforcement of a symbolic system of wartime representations. Of course caricatures reflect official propaganda or journalistic preferences. But whatever the source, certain images recur in the wartime press, no doubt with different features and different elaborations over time. In effect there was in wartime a language of social signs recognized by all who read the press. The recurrence of many of these signs points to the existence in wartime of what may be termed a common social imagery, or what in French is termed *l'imaginaire*.

The most striking evidence for this view is the omnipresence of the image of the profiteer, the *nouveau riche*, the tradesman as one of those 'privileged' by the war economy. The first feature of this image is its emotive charge, made more visceral by its juxtaposition with the image of the departing or fallen soldier. During the war, this imagery of social tensions was both powerful and indicative of the contradictions and contrasts of wartime social experience.

The first of these contrasts was between the 'Lost Generation' and the 'shirker'. Always the soldier was represented as the hero, but at times he took on the role of avenger or the man who in time would settle the score. The soldier was portrayed as the common man, occasionally as the elegant officer (depending on the journal), but social distinctions were hardly evident within these two groups. The variations we have found in the social incidence of military service and loss of life were outside this set of symbolic representations.

If the profiteer is first and foremost a man of the rear, a shirker, at times his faults are attributed to women or age. But more central is the merging of wartime images of profiteering with pre-war images of the rich. The profiteer is almost always overdressed, with a vulgarity separating him from the pre-war well-to-do. He disports his wealth, his cigars, his champagne, his car, his holidays, his women. Here we have all the classic signs of a semiology of bourgeois culture, from conspicuous consumption to obesity.

In contrast, other material 'winners' of the war, notably metalworkers, are only rarely caricatured. Some were published in the London press, but never in Paris, despite the unpopularity of *métallos*. This finding suggests that the new social divisions of wartime were comprehensible only in terms of an older set of social signs and images which obscured as much as it illuminated wartime developments. The language of the old suggested some of the tensions of the new. Older tropes about rich and poor, the little man against the boss, the inheritor versus the disinherited were available, and they were the ones that were used.

Closer to wartime realities were the images of consumption in contemporary caricatures. Here consumers were juxtaposed to petty tradesmen, coal merchants, wine merchants, speculators. Once again, though, the continuities with pre-war clichés about such trades, redolent with ethnic or anti-Semitic associations, are evident.

Our conclusion is, therefore, that caricatures as symbolic forms expressed many of the social tensions which arose in wartime, even when these images tried to mask them. They reflected only partially the contrasting material situations and life chances in wartime cities. The opposition between front and rear, to be sure, had a privileged place in these images, but they obscured as much as they illuminated about the complexities of wartime life. Above all we find the continuation of signs of social criticism expressing older attitudes about rich and poor even when these distinctions were remote from much of urban experience. Here we may note a natural propensity to use what is time-honoured to express what is new.

Certainly, representations reinforce the view that moral language flourished in wartime, and not only with respect to the enemy at the gates. Around the notion of sacrifice, there appeared appeals to moral fortitude, material sacrifice, and collective solidarity. Such exertions were, not surprisingly, demanded more of the rich, whose behaviour, be it the indifference or callousness of the industrialist or the merchant, was scrutinized by a metropolitan public used to seeing privilege before their eyes.

In the first volume of this study, we have tried to outline the central features of this complex dialectic between the conditions of material life and social representations only partially reflecting them. It is only by appreciating the subtle interaction between these levels of wartime experience that a full social history, including organization and struggle at the level of the family, the neighbourhood, and the social movement can be written. It is to that task that we turn in volume II of this study.

Towards an urban history of societies at war

This is the first of a two-volume history of Paris, London, and Berlin in the period 1914 to 1919. The findings we have reported here are far from complete. But certain conclusions may be ventured with some authority.

First, we have suggested a way to go beyond the national histories that have dominated the literature of this period. Many of the comparisons we have made show that there was an urban level of the waging of war, attention to which can reveal much about the ways these societies as a whole responded to the pressures of the conflict.

In other words, we have tried to show that an effective way of writing the history of nations in wartime is by isolating a smaller, yet significant, unit of analysis. That unit is the metropolitan centre, in itself an amalgam of very different neighbourhoods and quartiers, extending from an urban core to a suburban belt. Once chosen, the history of this subset of the nation can reveal what was common to similar units in other countries as well as what was specifically national about wartime experience.

The analytical force of the comparison is therefore to revise and rejuvenate, rather than to reject, national histories. For only after discovering convergences in urban histories can true national distinctions be made. We have reported urban similarities, such as the rise in tuberculosis among young women workers or increased mortality among the elderly. But we have also found fundamental differences, such as the unemployment crisis in Paris in late-1914, or the much lower proportion of the labour force occupied in the food trades in Berlin, compared to Paris and London during the war. All these findings are significant, but what matters most is their cumulative effect in identifying both the shared burdens of war and the specific ways the populations of these cities bore them.

That process of adaptation is the central theme of the second volume of this study. It is certainly not our intention to claim comprehensiveness in the treatment presented above. On the contrary, we have provided only the outlines of a full urban history of Paris, Berlin, and London in wartime. To understand the contribution of urban populations themselves to the outcomes we have documented, we must turn to other evidence and other histories. These were lived at the level of the family, the quartier, and the social movement.

In effect, we have studied in volume I the two ends of the urban spectrum: the individual and the collective. In volume II we privilege the intermediary levels of experience, the actions and reactions of groups of urban populations to the daily circumstances of the waging of war.

The second volume focuses on cross-sections of urban life. The contribution of women to family life, to networks of care and support, will loom large in these chapters. So will the emergence and evolution of neighbourhood associations and wider political formations which expressed common sentiment and interests. The history of strikes and other public demonstrations arose out of the rich organizational life of the metropolis at war. It is only by documenting these forms of urban political mobilization at the local level that we can understand how the inhabitants of these cities made their own history in wartime. It is only by attending to their voices at their branch meetings and in their churches, in their daily conflicts and struggles, that we can complete the portrait with which this study began. Only then can we discover the fate of the people Max Beckmann sketched, gazing at the news of the outbreak of war in the local paper. We have only begun to describe their lives in this, the first volume, of our study. The rest of their story is yet to come.

Statistical appendix and tables

Aspects of the history of civilian mortality in Paris, London, and Berlin during the period of the Great War

Estimates of the female population of Paris, 1911 to 1921

The uncertain and the unknown

Establishing reliable estimates of civilian populations in urban districts during the Great War is an onerous, and probably impossible, task. We concentrate here only on the female population, but even eliminating the outflow of men due to military mobilization hardly solves the problem of presenting sound population estimates of females who remained.

The benchmarks of census enumeration occur well outside the period of the Great War, in 1911 and 1921. We have no alternative other than to make some effort to approximate age-structure and aggregate movements of population in the intervening years.

First let us consider the problem of aggregates. We simply do not know with any authority the number of civilians who lived in Paris during the Great War. The primary problem is that migratory flows were both very substantial and unquantified not only during but before and after the war.

Migration was of two kinds: conventional and war related; some can be estimated; much is unknown. Of the conventional kind of migration out of Paris, one in particular separates registered statistics from real populations. Paris was different from London and Berlin in sending out of the city a substantial proportion of its infants to wet-nurses in the countryside. To 'export' one-third of the capital's infants, and most likely the more vulnerable babies among them, artificially lowers Paris's infant mortality rate. This is simply because fewer infant deaths were registered in Paris than actually occurred of infants born in Paris. To make matters worse, the survivors both returned to Paris, and more than occasionally went out again to another bout of wet-nursing. Given the weight of infant mortality in overall mortality patterns, it is obviously necessary to correct the available statistics to make them approximate more closely to lived experience.

In adolescent and adult cohorts, the problems are different. Conventionally, Paris drew thousands of young women into its urban districts and labour force. But here too we confront a fundamental difficulty in accounting for the disturbance to the age-structure due to the war. We know that Paris suffered a severe economic crisis from 1914 to 1915, and that the growth areas thereafter were in the suburbs. The distribution of new workers, men and women, in these new districts and factories is impossible to estimate accurately. The available statistics are simply too scattered and patchy to enable us to make the kind of direct correction we have attempted with the infant and child populations.

To make matters worse, there were the special circumstances of Paris in 1914, and to a lesser degree in 1918. In both those years, the city was adjacent to the theatre of military operations. There was a major outflow of civilians from Paris in 1914, when it appeared possible, if not inevitable, that the German army would reach the capital. We have some very rough estimates of the proportion of people who left: perhaps between 10 and 12 per cent at different age groups; thus some corrections can be made. But other problems are less amenable to adjustment. For instance, there was a flood of refugees streaming south, away from the theatre of military operations. Although we have restricted our scrutiny to statistics of those domiciled in Paris, it is impossible to know how many refugees from the north of France had become 'domiciled' Parisians a few months after their arrival in the capital.

For all these reasons, the aggregates needed to establish death-rates for the female population of Paris are elusive, to say the least. Even more problematic is the question of the age-structure of the population. Here again migration causes havoc to our estimations, for the simple reason that migrants are not randomly distributed throughout the population, but clustered in the younger cohorts. How the war affected these migratory flows is almost impossible to say. For example, the movement of young women into Paris continued, but probably in different directions than in peacetime; war factories rather than domestic service or the textile industries gathered them in. Where did they live? Were they domiciled in the suburbs (and therefore not strictly speaking Parisian) and employed in the city, or did they live and work within the boundaries of the twenty arrondissements? These are questions for which we have no usable answer.

Two implications follow. The first is that any calculations made on Parisian data must be treated with considerable caution. Trends matter more than levels, but even the direction of rates may be flawed by unspecified variables distorting population estimates. The second is that stable population theory, and other tried and true methods, are probably unusable here. The Parisian population had many characteristics in wartime, but stability wasn't one of them. The normal mode of estimation, through the transversal progression of cohorts over time, may work in some cases, but not in all.

Two methods of estimation

For these reasons, we have adopted two different methods in estimating populations. Where precise estimates can be made, in the case of young children, we have used the more precise cohort (or generation) method. That is to say, we moved a population stepwise through the age structure, 'ageing' one-year olds, for instance, in 1914, through their childhood a year at a time over the following seven years, until they reached the age of eight in 1921.

Where no such precise estimates are available, we have used the more rudimentary means of linear interpolation to estimate age-groups at later ages. That is, we calculated the difference between the size of the cohort, for example of those aged thirty to thirty-four, in 1911 and 1921, and then assumed that one-tenth of that difference was registered in each intervening year.

One reason for choosing this method for the cohorts after childhood is that the census enumeration of Paris in 1921 clusters population totals in five or ten-year bands, thus vitiating comparison with the 1911 census, which lists the population at individual ages. To make additional guesses of the distribution of the forty to forty-nine age-group, for instance, at individual ages almost certainly will introduce further error into the calculations.

In using these two approaches, we have tried to make the best use possible of incomplete statistical series. At least this mix of methods is an honest admission of statistical weakness. Where we were able to place some faith on more precise calculations, as in the case of infants aged nought to five, we have used the cohort method, but this is an exception. On the whole, we have tried to accept the weaknesses of the data rather than to pretend that they are better than they are.

Margins of error

A test of the difference between these two methods was carried out on the population of all three capital cities. In the case of young children, aged one to four, linear interpolation seriously distorts population estimates. The reason is obviously the severe fluctuations in the birth-rate occurring in the period of the war. In this instance, the cohort method is both possible and preferable. But in the case of later age-groups, the difference between the two methods is slight. For the twenty to twenty-four age-group, interpolation produced a population 4 per cent below that generated by the cohort method; for the twenty-five to twenty-nine age-group, the difference was also 4 per cent, but this time the cohort method produced higher totals. In the case of London and Berlin, the difference between the two methods was smaller: between 0 and 2 per cent at ages fifteen to thirty. It is not unreasonable to assume that many of these variations cancel each other out, and in any event, the differences in death-rates produced using both methods of population estimation were smaller still: of the order of 0.05 per thousand. To use linear interpolation after the age of five is therefore an acceptable, though flawed, alternative to the more sophisticated, though also flawed, cohort method of constructing population estimates for this turbulent period.

The tests we made on the difference between estimates produced by the interpolation and cohort methods suggest that it would be wise to assume an approximate 4 per cent margin of error in all statistics presented here. Relatively minor changes in the death-rates we have calculated for any one of the three cities, therefore, must be set aside as insufficiently robust. Changes of greater magnitude, above the 4 per cent margin of error, will be the centre of our attention.

The results of these calculations are presented in tables A1–A12 for Paris, London, and Berlin, respectively, listing population estimates, deaths, and age-specific and standardized death-rates. The direct method of standardization was used, the base of comparison being the age-structure of London in 1901.

Estimates of the female population of London, 1911 to 1921

Establishing reliable estimates of London's female population in war-time is also a difficult task, but one which presents fewer difficulties than we confronted in the case of Paris. There are benchmark data available from census enumerations in 1911 and 1921, and total populations for London and for each metropolitan borough for the intervening years. What we do not have are sex ratios and age-structures for the years 1912 to 1920, either for London as a whole or for its constituent boroughs.

To generate these data we have assumed that the age-structure of London was constant at ages over fifteen, and that the totals in the war years 1915 to 1919 were diminished by the male population in the army. If we add the total mobilized by age-group for each district and for London as a whole, and apply the age structure of 1911 and 1921 to the years 1914 to 1919, we can calculate age-specific cohorts of both male and female populations. At young ages, it is necessary to generate the cohorts nought to one and one to four through the same stepwise progression as we adopted in the construction of estimates for Paris. The results may be consulted in Appendices A1 to A3.

Estimates of the female population of Berlin, 1911 to 1919

Of the three capital cities whose demographic history is under review in this study, the one with the most severe estimation problems in the decade of the Great War is Berlin. The first and most intractable problem is that the city itself changed its borders and size in 1920. Greater Berlin was of substantially greater size and more varied social character than the 'old Berlin' of the period prior to or during the Great War. Secondly, data collection was seriously impaired by the revolution of 1919 and the reorganization of civil administration. Whereas mortality statistics were collected and published for Germany as a whole in the period 1920 to 1922, none exists for the city of Berlin. The only available option for this study is to limit our calculations and the inferences derived from them to the period 1911 to 1919.

These generic problems make even more problematic the difficulties already discussed with respect to Paris and London. Once again we have had to fill in the gaps in available census enumeration through estimation procedures. We have followed for Berlin the same procedure with respect to estimating the populations aged nought to one and one to five for London and Paris. We have tried to improve the quality of the data on the age-structure of Berlin at the ages of nought to five by a progression of individual cohorts over time. Thus we 'age' the one-year-old population in 1911 until it arrives at the age of nine in 1919. For older cohorts, we use the method of linear interpolation between 1911 and 1921. The results of these estimation procedures, and the death-rates which use these populations as their denominator, may be found in Appendices A10 to A12.

STATISTICAL APPENDIX: TABLES

Table A1. *Estimates of female population of London, 1911 to 1921*

Year	Estimated P′(0) (0–1)[a]	Estimated P′(1) (1–2)[b]	Estimated P′(2) (2–3)[c]	Estimated P′(3) (3–4)[d]	Estimated P′(4) (4–5)[e]	Estimated P′(1–5) (1–5)
1906						
1907	56,858					
1908	55,982	53,621				
1909	55,601	52,986	52,296			
1910	54,212	52,656	51,547	51,652		
1911	53,602	51,495	51,387	50,993	51,310	205,185
1912	50,529	50,341	49,996	50,735	50,604	201,676
1913	51,478	48,311	49,311	49,488	50,399	197,509
1914	50,814	48,961	47,250	48,860	49,211	194,283
1915	50,531	48,374	47,903	46,760	48,541	191,578
1916	47,063	47,877	46,970	47,234	46,355	188,437
1917	39,854	45,174	46,964	46,524	46,934	185,597
1918	36,969	37,883	44,078	46,417	46,175	174,553
1919	32,355	34,868	36,394	43,212	45,833	160,306
1920	38,152	31,048	34,362	36,071	42,946	144,427
1921	56,086	36,395	30,376	34,016	35,829	136,616

[a] P′(0) in year x = births in year x − 1, minus 2/3 deaths at ages (0–1) in year x − 1.
[b] P′(1) in year x + 1 = P′(0) in year x, minus 1/3 deaths at age (0–1) in year x, minus 1/2 deaths at age (1–2) in year x.
[c] P′(2) in years x + 2 = P′(1) in year x + 1, minus 1/2 deaths at age (1–2) in year x + 1, minus 1/2 deaths at age (2–3) in year x + 1.
[d] P′(3) in year x + 3 = P′(2) in year x + 2, minus 1/2 deaths at age (2–3) in year x + 2, minus 1/2 deaths at age (3–4) in year x + 2.
[e] P′(4) in year x + 4 = P′(3) in year x + 3, minus 1/2 deaths at age (3–4) in year x + 3, minus 1/2 deaths at age (4–5) in year x + 3.

Table A2. *Estimates of female population of Berlin, 1911 to 1919, at ages 0–4*

Year	Estimated P′(0) (0–1)[a]	Estimated P′(1) (1–2)[b]	Estimated P′(2) (2–3)[c]	Estimated P′(3) (3–4)[d]	Estimated P′(4) (4–5)[e]	Estimated P′(0–4) (0–4)
1907	22,489					
1908	22,328	20,905				
1909	21,493	20,786	20,423			
1910	20,301	20,114	20,314	20,208		
1911	19,435	19,014	19,739	20,123	20,053	78,929
1912	18,838	18,005	18,571	19,508	19,959	76,043
1913	18,959	17,732	17,666	18,382	19,369	73,149
1914	18,247	17,946	17,463	17,537	18,286	71,233
1915	16,457	17,169	17,640	17,323	17,421	69,553
1916	13,681	15,600	16,835	17,437	17,190	67,061
1917	10,142	13,026	15,281	16,665	17,314	62,285
1918	8,153	9,534	12,751	15,097	16,531	53,912
1919	8,909	7,571	9,251	12,571	14,956	44,349

[a] P′(0) in year x = births in year x − 1, minus 2/3 deaths at ages (0–1) in year x − 1.
[b] P′(1) in year x + 1 = P′(0) in year x, minus 1/3 deaths at age (0–1) in year x, minus 1/2 deaths at age (1–2) in year x.
[c] P′(2) in years x + 2 = P′(1) in year x + 1, minus 1/2 deaths at age (1–2) in year x + 1, minus 1/2 deaths at age (2–3) in year x + 1.
[d] P′(3) in year x + 3 = P′(2) in year x + 2, minus 1/2 deaths at age (2–3) in year x + 2, minus 1/2 deaths at age (3–4) in year x + 2.
[e] P′(4) in year x + 4 = P′(3) in year x + 3, minus 1/2 deaths at age (3–4) in year x + 3, minus 1/2 deaths at age (4–5) in year x + 3.

Table A3. *Estimates of female population of Paris, 1911 to 1923, at ages 0–4*

Year	Estimated P′(0) (0–1)[a]	Estimated P′(1) (1–2)[b]	Estimated P′(2) (2–3)[c]	Estimated P′(3) (3–4)[d]	Estimated P′(4) (4–5)[e]	Estimated P′(0–4) (0–4)
1907	16,200					
1908	15,877	14,985				
1909	15,948	14,726	14,410			
1910	15,734	14,865	14,210	14,142		
1911	15,800	14,631	14,317	13,911	13,945	56,804
1912	15,553	14,555	14,034	13,984	13,712	56,286
1913	15,633	14,495	13,945	13,683	13,779	55,903
1914	15,445	14,590	13,975	13,623	13,481	55,669
1915	16,271	14,429	14,100	13,690	13,427	55,646
1916	11,158	15,425	14,003	13,891	13,565	56,885
1917	9,822	10,404	14,961	13,732	13,729	52,826
1918	11,486	9,169	9,914	14,684	13,547	47,315
1919	10,427	10,693	8,810	9,646	14,514	43,664
1920	14,193	9,619	10,364	8,630	9,480	38,092
1921	20,515	13,186	9,307	10,211	8,521	41,225
1922	19,310	19,621	12,871	9,150	10,120	
1923	17,524	18,536	19,379	12,781	9,089	
			18,242	19,245	12,718	

[a]Effective births = total births minus total sent out of Paris to *nourrices*. P′(0) in year x = effective births in year x – 1, minus 2/3 deaths at ages (0–1) in year x – 1. Example: P′(0) 1907 = births in 1906 – 2/3 deaths (0–1) in 1906.
[b]P′(1) in year x + 1 = P′(0) in year x, minus 1/3 deaths at age (0–1) in year x, minus 1/2 deaths at age (1–2) in year x.
[c]P′(2) in years x + 2 = P′(1) in year x + 1, minus 1/2 deaths at age (1–2) in year x + 1, minus 1/2 deaths at age (2–3) in year x + 1.
[d]P′(3) in year x + 3 = P′(2) in year x + 2, minus 1/2 deaths at age (2–3) in year x + 2, minus 1/2 deaths at age (3–4) in year x + 2.
[e]P′(4) in year x + 4 = P′(3) in year x + 3, minus 1/2 deaths at age (3–4) in year x + 3, minus 1/2 deaths at age (4–5) in year x + 3.

Table A4. *Age-structure, London, female population, 1911 to 1921*

Age-group	1911	1912	1913	1914	1915	1916	1917	1918	1919	1920	1921
0–1	53,602	50,529	51,478	50,814	50,531	47,063	39,854	36,969	32,355	38,152	56,086
1–4	204,932	202,962	198,406	194,975	191,508	189,062	186,177	174,151	162,603	145,528	136,800
5–9	217,701	215,975	214,250	212,591	212,676	212,179	203,112	198,629	207,882	200,541	200,877
10–14	202,961	203,353	203,743	204,196	206,341	207,949	201,096	198,678	210,081	204,768	207,256
15–19	212,366	212,839	213,312	213,850	216,160	217,909	210,790	208,316	220,336	214,826	217,500
20–4	237,866	236,690	235,513	234,410	235,235	235,426	226,087	221,814	232,908	225,430	226,569
25–9	231,084	229,377	227,670	226,034	226,253	225,853	216,329	211,680	221,675	213,977	214,470
30–4	201,288	200,744	200,199	199,716	200,880	201,509	193,966	190,747	200,761	194,778	196,232
35–9	179,224	179,838	180,450	181,118	183,288	184,905	179,148	177,248	187,689	183,203	185,691
40–4	153,860	155,388	156,915	158,489	161,387	163,881	159,671	158,922	169,276	166,192	169,417
45–9	131,977	134,145	136,311	138,518	141,889	144,916	141,990	142,103	152,174	150,184	153,883
50–4	180,873	110,939	113,003	115,101	118,167	120,952	118,760	119,096	127,790	126,360	129,712
55–9	85,091	86,882	88,672	90,489	93,068	95,427	93,856	94,275	101,315	100,333	103,145
60–4	68,452	69,795	71,136	72,499	74,472	76,268	74,925	75,175	80,701	79,836	81,991
65–9	53,894	54,822	55,749	56,693	58,113	59,394	58,233	58,316	62,488	61,708	63,265
70–4	38,702	39,307	39,911	40,527	41,483	42,339	41,456	41,461	44,371	43,764	44,814
75–9	22,471	22,983	23,495	24,015	24,736	25,400	25,017	25,162	27,076	26,847	27,633
80+	16,503	16,808	17,114	13,423	17,880	18,294	17,955	18,000	19,307	19,084	19,584
Total	2,492,847	2,423,376	2,427,327	2,427,458	2,454,067	2,468,726	2,388,422	2,350,742	2,460,788	2,395,511	2,434,925

Table A5. *Age-structure, Berlin, female population, 1911 to 1919*

Age-group	1911	1912	1913	1914	1915	1916	1917	1918	1919
0–1	19,435	18,838	18,959	18,247	16,457	13,681	10,142	8,153	8,909
1–4	78,797	76,029	72,989	70,982	69,388	67,148	62,355	53,873	44,314
5–9	81,428	82,119	83,023	81,979	79,867	76,638	73,839	70,926	68,680
10–14	81,715	82,404	83,328	82,153	80,760	79,670	80,146	80,276	77,327
15–19	98,855	99,691	100,799	98,462	96,690	93,273	89,959	86,741	84,544
20–9	223,019	224,909	227,413	227,092	225,360	225,392	221,483	217,544	214,103
30–9	182,949	184,526	186,574	188,708	187,748	185,505	187,085	187,551	187,587
40–9	136,346	137,479	139,028	139,421	142,980	146,361	148,344	150,419	151,423
50–9	97,163	98,002	99,040	101,051	103,527	107,079	106,027	105,604	106,469
60–9	59,238	59,746	60,424	62,756	64,689	66,666	67,028	67,020	67,176
70–9	25,228	25,436	25,722	26,909	28,504	29,952	30,223	30,679	30,754
80+	5,642	5,683	5,778	5,952	6,167	6,387	6,768	7,023	7,112
Total	1,089,815	1,094,862	1,103,077	1,103,712	1,102,137	1,097,752	1,083,399	1,065,809	1,048,398

Table A6. *Age-structure, Paris, female population, 1911 to 1921*

Age-group	1911	1912	1913	1914[a]	1915	1916	1917	1918	1919	1920	1921
0–1[b]	15,800	15,553	15,633	13,901	16,271	11,158	9,822	11,486	10,427	14,193	20,515
1–4	56,804	56,286	55,903	48,989	55,646	56,885	52,826	47,315	43,664	38,092	41,225
5–9	82,287	81,046	79,805	69,136	77,322	76,081	74,840	73,599	72,357	71,116	69,875
10–14	85,660	85,413	85,166	74,728	84,672	84,425	84,177	83,930	83,683	83,436	83,189
15–19	116,104	116,496	116,887	105,551	117,670	118,062	118,453	118,845	119,236	119,628	120,019
20–4	165,745	165,336	164,927	148,066	164,109	163,700	163,291	162,882	162,472	162,063	161,654
25–9	174,014	173,975	173,935	156,506	173,857	173,818	173,778	173,739	173,700	173,660	173,621
30–4	157,153	158,232	159,311	144,352	161,470	162,549	163,628	164,708	165,787	166,866	167,945
35–9	136,186	137,942	139,698	127,308	143,210	144,966	146,722	148,478	150,233	151,989	153,745
40–4	116,257	118,084	119,910	109,563	123,563	125,390	127,216	129,043	130,870	132,696	134,523
45–9	102,139	103,271	104,403	94,982	106,667	107,800	108,932	110,064	111,196	112,328	113,460
50–4	84,634	85,447	86,260	78,365	87,886	88,699	89,511	90,324	91,137	91,950	92,763
55–9	63,589	65,082	66,576	61,264	69,565	71,059	72,553	74,047	75,542	77,036	78,530
60–4	51,906	52,941	53,976	49,509	56,045	57,080	58,115	59,150	60,184	61,219	62,254
65–9	38,013	38,611	39,209	35,827	40,405	41,004	41,602	42,200	42,798	43,396	43,994
70–9	41,477	40,764	40,051	35,404	38,625	37,912	37,198	36,485	35,772	35,059	34,346
80+	9,496	9,338	9,179	8,118	8,862	8,704	8,545	8,387	8,228	8,070	7,911
Total	1,497,264	1,503,815	1,510,829	1,361,569	1,525,845	1,529,290	1,531,209	1,534,680	1,537,286	1,542,797	1,559,569

Note: Cohorts 0–1 and 1–4 estimated by generation method; thereafter, for all other cohorts, estimates were obtained by interpolation. Discrepancies in total are due to reordering up of estimates.

[a] 1914 populations were reduced to account for the exodus of civilians from Paris in August–December 1914. At ages 0–1 and 15+, 10 per cent left; at ages 1–5, 12 per cent left.

[b] The 0–1 cohort was reduced by the number sent out of Paris to *nourrices* minus 10 per cent for double counting of those sent out more than once.

Table A7. *Total deaths at selected ages, London, female population, 1911 to 1921*

Age-group	1911	1912	1913	1914	1915	1916	1917	1918	1919	1920	1921
0–1	6,511	4,473	5,201	5,068	5,022	3,748	3,631	3,351	2,940	3,900	3,473
1–4	3,776	2,732	2,676	2,755	3,617	2,426	2,891	4,146	1,542	1,828	1,576
5–9	752	621	627	742	873	648	696	1,205	730	716	649
10–14	419	387	422	476	507	431	441	829	469	436	408
15–19	512	493	526	582	661	606	711	1,329	653	574	591
20–4	644	595	596	634	701	630	673	1,829	870	682	647
25–9	773	743	662	746	777	752	799	2,261	1,017	776	701
30–4	855	852	863	885	827	804	816	1,933	1,065	775	726
35–9	1,078	1,111	1,060	1,022	1,104	1,001	992	1,581	1,071	908	818
40–4	1,286	1,265	1,219	1,275	1,358	1,137	1,133	1,541	1,114	1,003	1,010
45–9	1,445	1,522	1,522	1,498	1,562	1,338	1,313	1,725	1,328	1,212	1,181
50–4	1,579	1,600	1,635	1,732	1,903	1,668	1,540	1,917	1,528	1,380	1,448
55–9	1,737	1,734	1,757	1,797	1,927	1,634	1,771	1,842	1,696	1,616	1,630
60–4	1,913	1,947	1,979	2,125	2,275	2,047	1,969	2,109	1,947	1,753	1,936
65–9	2,137	2,227	2,252	2,336	2,538	2,384	2,405	2,580	2,377	2,142	2,237
70–9	4,617	4,770	4,985	4,974	5,903	5,435	5,318	5,135	5,432	4,843	5,146
80+	2,985	3,094	3,126	3,142	3,699	3,468	3,349	3,164	3,388	3,106	3,394
Total	33,019	30,166	31,108	31,789	35,254	30,157	30,448	38,477	29,167	27,650	27,571

Table A8. *Total deaths at selected ages, Berlin, female population, 1911 to 1919*

Age-group	1911	1912	1913	1914	1915	1916	1917	1918	1919
0–1	3,373	2,629	2,461	2,548	1,939	1,334	1,308	1,209	1,582
1–4	1,214	955	729	895	936	884	819	848	652
5–9	380	379	323	322	353	348	299	387	290
10–14	197	214	161	172	193	197	241	335	219
15–19	333	321	345	315	318	316	505	822	511
20–9	1,081	1,112	1,076	1,008	973	1,095	1,337	2,662	1,637
30–9	1,195	1,211	1,125	1,106	1,145	1,125	1,304	2,070	1,507
40–9	1,214	1,200	1,170	1,182	1,240	1,186	1,502	1,731	1,504
50–9	1,611	1,566	1,503	1,497	1,540	1,582	2,007	2,089	1,827
60–9	2,093	2,037	2,031	2,132	2,157	2,223	2,954	2,887	2,566
70–9	2,017	2,109	2,000	2,269	2,357	2,573	3,516	3,095	2,818
80+	1,088	1,050	1,030	1,103	1,278	1,311	1,859	1,311	1,267
Total	15,796	14,783	13,954	14,549	14,429	14,174	17,651	19,446	16,380

Table A9. *Total deaths at selected ages, Paris, female population, 1911 to 1921*

Age-group	1911	1912	1913	1914	1915	1916	1917	1918	1919	1920	1921
0–1	2,601	2,221	2,177	2,170	1,667	1,293	1,380	1,678	1,787	2,374	2,126
1–4	1,631	1,445	1,372	1,101	1,253	1,348	1,057	991	841	812	608
5–9	424	452	355	332	333	354	371	442	383	371	246
10–14	293	265	275	259	290	288	336	466	304	258	249
15–19	542	483	499	530	479	524	569	1,009	677	615	500
20–4	882	888	889	829	719	827	899	1,679	1,101	986	818
25–9	1,173	1,025	1,039	982	836	895	926	1,918	1,181	1,091	961
30–4	1,102	1,100	1,002	1,032	917	1,005	920	1,867	1,249	1,114	1,020
35–9	1,118	1,202	1,083	1,135	1,060	1,041	1,068	1,553	1,235	1,098	1,092
40–4	1,190	1,102	1,113	1,129	1,103	1,116	1,102	1,330	1,148	1,110	1,117
45–9	1,354	1,284	1,195	1,168	1,201	1,213	1,159	1,369	1,306	1,097	1,205
50–4	1,382	1,311	1,226	1,330	1,327	1,312	1,363	1,518	1,358	1,173	1,167
55–9	1,299	1,386	1,258	1,375	1,368	1,456	1,551	1,492	1,575	1,373	1,302
60–4	1,571	1,506	1,412	1,575	1,475	1,609	1,732	1,595	1,635	1,573	1,679
65–9	1,706	1,686	1,571	1,722	1,680	1,816	1,964	1,972	1,842	1,624	1,682
70–4	1,803	1,839	1,710	1,787	1,903	1,930	2,202	1,941	2,049	1,766	1,860
75–9	1,761	1,593	1,559	1,740	1,801	1,912	2,032	1,821	1,812	1,606	1,651
80+	1,989	1,878	1,741	2,035	2,063	2,378	2,453	2,073	2,154	2,075	2,032
Total	23,821	22,666	21,476	22,231	21,475	22,317	23,084	26,714	23,637	22,116	21,315

Table A10. *Age-specific death rates, female population, London, 1911 to 1921 and standardized death-rates (D_x × 1,000)*

Age-group	1911	1912	1913	1914	1915	1916	1917	1918	1919	1920	1921
0–1	121.47	88.52	101.03	99.74	99.38	79.64	91.11	90.64	90.87	102.22	61.92
1–4	18.43	13.46	13.49	14.13	18.89	12.83	15.53	23.81	9.48	12.56	11.52
5–9	3.45	2.88	2.93	3.49	4.10	3.05	3.43	6.07	3.51	3.57	3.23
10–14	2.06	1.90	2.07	2.33	2.46	2.07	2.19	4.17	2.23	2.13	1.97
15–19	2.41	2.32	2.47	2.72	3.06	2.78	3.37	6.38	2.96	2.67	2.72
20–4	2.71	2.51	2.53	2.70	2.98	2.68	2.98	8.25	3.74	3.03	2.86
25–9	3.35	3.24	2.91	3.30	3.43	3.33	3.69	10.68	4.59	3.63	3.27
30–4	4.25	4.24	4.31	4.43	4.12	3.99	4.21	10.31	5.30	3.98	3.70
35–9	6.01	6.18	5.87	5.64	6.02	5.41	5.54	8.92	5.71	4.96	4.41
40–4	8.36	8.14	7.77	8.04	8.41	6.94	7.10	9.70	6.58	6.04	5.96
45–9	10.95	11.35	11.17	10.81	11.01	9.23	9.25	12.14	8.73	8.07	7.67
50–4	8.73	14.42	14.47	15.05	16.10	13.79	12.97	16.10	11.96	10.92	11.16
55–9	20.41	19.96	19.81	19.86	20.71	17.12	18.87	19.54	16.74	16.11	15.80
60–4	27.95	27.90	27.82	29.31	30.55	26.84	26.28	28.05	24.13	21.96	23.61
65–9	39.65	40.62	40.40	41.20	43.67	40.14	41.30	44.24	38.04	34.71	35.36
70–4	64.26	64.34	66.70	63.71	72.34	65.47	63.34	62.93	61.05	54.43	57.95
75–9	94.79	97.51	98.87	99.60	117.32	104.84	107.61	100.39	100.57	91.67	92.24
80+	180.08	184.08	182.66	234.08	206.88	189.57	186.52	175.78	175.48	162.75	173.30
Crude D_x[a]	13.25	12.71	13.09	13.35	14.37	12.22	12.75	16.37	11.85	11.54	11.32
Standard D_x	12.78	11.63	12.07	12.22	13.29	11.50	12.07	15.58	11.21	10.42	9.89

[a] D_x is a life-table death-rate.

Table A11. *Age-specific death-rates, female population, Berlin 1911–1919 and standardized death-rates ($D_x \times 1{,}000$)*

Age-group	1911	1912	1913	1914	1915	1916	1917	1918	1919
0–1	176.26	139.11	132.29	146.84	128.67	111.99	142.98	141.72	177.57
1–4	15.67	12.80	10.10	12.71	13.70	13.67	14.10	17.26	14.70
5–9	4.65	4.59	3.92	3.98	4.51	4.63	4.13	5.54	4.22
10–14	2.40	2.58	1.95	2.11	2.41	2.47	3.00	4.25	2.83
15–19	3.35	3.20	3.46	3.23	3.35	3.45	5.72	9.60	6.04
20–9	4.83	4.92	4.73	4.46	4.32	4.90	6.09	12.33	7.65
30–9	6.50	6.53	6.00	5.88	6.14	6.04	6.96	11.04	8.03
40–9	8.87	8.68	8.40	8.37	8.57	8.05	10.05	11.47	9.93
50–9	16.51	15.94	15.02	14.64	14.62	14.85	18.97	19.70	17.16
60–9	35.18	33.90	32.98	33.46	32.84	39.81	44.07	43.03	38.20
70–9	79.62	82.45	76.00	81.89	80.64	85.52	115.46	100.76	91.63
80+	192.12	183.21	175.62	182.04	203.60	199.33	269.62	185.51	178.16
Crude D_x	14.46	13.45	12.64	13.19	13.12	13.00	16.43	18.39	15.62
Standard D_x	14.87	13.78	12.85	13.38	13.14	12.77	16.18	18.67	16.43

Table A12. *Age-specific death-rates, female population, Paris, 1911 to 1921, and standardized death-rates ($D_x \times 1,000$)*

Age-group	1911	1912	1913	1914	1915	1916	1917	1918	1919	1920	1921
0–1	164.62	142.80	139.26	156.10	102.45	115.88	140.50	146.09	171.38	167.27	103.63
1–4	28.71	25.67	24.54	22.47	22.52	23.70	20.01	20.94	19.26	21.32	14.75
5–9	5.15	5.58	4.45	4.80	4.31	4.65	4.96	6.01	5.29	5.22	3.52
10–14	3.42	3.10	3.23	3.47	3.42	3.41	3.99	5.55	3.63	3.09	2.99
15–19	4.67	4.15	4.27	5.02	4.07	4.44	4.80	8.49	5.68	5.14	4.17
20–4	5.32	5.37	5.39	5.60	4.38	5.05	5.51	10.31	6.78	6.08	5.06
25–9	6.74	5.89	5.97	6.27	4.81	5.15	5.33	11.04	6.80	6.28	5.54
30–4	7.01	6.95	6.29	7.15	5.68	6.18	5.62	11.34	7.53	6.68	6.07
35–9	8.21	8.71	7.75	8.92	7.40	7.18	7.28	10.46	8.22	7.22	7.10
40–4	10.24	9.33	9.28	10.30	8.93	8.90	8.66	10.31	8.77	8.36	8.30
45–9	13.26	12.43	11.45	12.30	11.26	11.25	10.64	12.44	11.75	9.77	10.62
50–4	16.33	15.34	14.21	16.97	15.10	14.79	15.23	16.81	14.90	12.76	12.58
55–9	20.43	21.30	18.90	22.44	19.67	20.49	21.38	20.15	20.85	17.82	16.58
60–4	30.27	28.45	26.16	31.81	26.32	28.19	29.80	26.97	27.17	25.69	26.97
65–9	44.88	43.67	40.07	48.06	41.58	44.29	47.21	46.73	43.04	37.42	38.23
70–9	85.93	84.19	81.62	99.62	95.90	101.34	54.63	103.11	107.93	96.18	102.22
80+	209.46	201.11	189.67	250.68	232.79	273.21	287.07	247.17	261.79	257.13	256.86
Crude D_x	5.91	15.08	14.22	16.33	14.08	14.60	15.08	17.40	15.38	14.34	13.67
Standard D_x	17.07	15.97	15.18	17.11	14.49	15.56	16.42	18.67	17.23	15.04	13.91

Table A13. *An index of age-specific death-rates, and standardized death-rates (× 1,000), London, female population, 1914 to 1921 (1911–13 = 100)*

Age-group	1911–13	1914	1915	1916	1917	1918	1919	1920	1921
0–1	104.01	96	96	77	88	87	87	98	60
1–4	15.15	93	125	70	84	157	63	83	76
5–9	3.86	113	133	88	99	197	114	116	105
10–14	2.01	116	122	100	106	207	111	106	98
15–19	2.40	114	128	115	140	266	124	111	113
20–4	2.58	105	115	99	110	319	145	117	111
25–9	3.17	104	109	100	110	337	145	115	103
30–4	4.27	104	96	94	99	237	124	93	87
35–9	6.02	94	100	90	92	148	95	82	73
40–4	8.09	99	104	83	85	120	81	75	74
45–9	11.15	97	99	84	84	109	78	72	69
50–4	11.89	127	135	158	149	135	101	92	94
55–9	20.06	99	103	84	92	97	83	80	79
60–4	27.89	105	110	96	94	101	87	79	85
65–9	40.23	102	109	101	104	110	95	86	88
70–4	65.11	98	111	102	99	97	94	84	89
75–9	97.09	103	121	111	114	103	104	94	95
80+	182.55	128	113	105	103	96	96	89	95
Crude D_x	13.02	103	110	92	96	126	91	89	87
Standard d_x	12.16	100	109	95	99	128	92	86	81

Table A14. *An index of age-specific death-rates, and standardized death-rates (× 1000), Berlin, female population 1914 to 1919 (1911–13 = 100)*

Age-group	1911–13	1914	1915	1916	1917	1918	1919
0–1	149.22	107	94	82	104	104	130
1–4	12.86	87	94	93	96	118	101
5–9	4.38	91	103	105	94	126	96
10–14	2.31	91	104	107	130	184	123
15–19	3.34	97	100	103	171	287	181
20–9	4.83	92	89	101	126	255	158
30–9	6.34	92	96	95	109	173	126
40–9	8.65	96	99	93	116	132	114
50–9	15.82	92	92	93	119	124	108
60–9	34.02	97	96	116	128	125	111
70–9	79.36	102	101	107	144	126	114
80+	183.65	98	110	108	146	100	96
Crude D_x	13.52	97	96	95	120	135	114
Standard D_x	13.84	97	96	93	118	136	119

Table A15. *An index of age-specific death-rates (× 1,000), and standardized death-rates, Paris, female population, 1914 to 1921 (1911–13 = 100)*

Age-group	1911–13	1914	1915	1916	1917	1918	1919	1920	1921
0–1	148.89	105	69	78	94	98	115	112	70
1–4	26.31	85	86	90	76	80	73	81	56
5–9	5.06	95	85	92	98	119	105	103	70
10–14	3.25	107	105	105	123	171	112	95	92
15–19	4.36	115	93	102	110	195	130	118	96
20–4	5.36	104	82	94	103	192	126	113	94
25–9	6.20	101	78	83	86	178	110	101	89
30–4	6.75	106	84	92	83	168	112	99	90
35–9	8.23	108	90	87	88	127	100	88	86
40–4	9.62	107	93	93	90	107	91	87	86
45–9	12.38	99	91	91	86	100	95	79	86
50–4	15.29	111	99	97	100	110	97	83	82
55–9	20.21	111	97	101	106	100	103	88	82
60–4	28.29	112	93	100	105	95	96	91	95
65–9	42.87	112	97	103	110	109	100	87	89
70–9	83.91	119	114	121	142	123	129	115	122
80+	200.08	125	116	137	143	124	131	129	128
Crude D_x	15.07	108	93	97	100	115	102	95	91
Standard D_x	16.07	106	90	97	102	116	107	94	87

Bibliography

Primary sources

Unpublished sources

Archives nationales, Paris (AN)
BB30 1534: Ministère de la Justice, Dossier A
Ministère de la Justice, dossier 'locations postérieures à la guerre'
BB30 1535: Ministère de la Justice
BB30 1536: Ministère de la Justice, 'Au sujet des loyers (Voeu remis aux Pouvoirs publics par nos Délégués)'
BB30 1536: Ministère de la Justice, dossiers 'Réclamations'
BB30 1536: Ministère de la Justice, 'Projets de loi du Gouvernement et de la Commission'
F1 12453: Livre d'Or, liste des employés de la Maison Rabaudi Fils, 7 rue du Quatre Septembre, Paris
F 12 8020: Ministère du Commerce
F 12 8021: Ministère du Commerce, 'Dossier général des notes', 'Moratorium des loyers. Propositions tendant à la liquidation de ce moratorium'
F 12 8021: Ministère du Commerce, 'Rapport de M. Albert Tissier'
F 12 8022: Ministère du Commerce, 'Association des propriétaires suburbains du Département de la Seine à Monsieur le Président du Conseil, à Monsieur le Garde des Sceaux, à Monsieur le Ministre des Finances et du Commerce', n.d.
F 12 8022: Ministère du Commerce, 'Moratorium des loyers. Statistique des déclarations, contestations de déclarations et instances depuis le décret du 20 mars 1915 arrêtée au ler Juillet 1915 et dressée d'après le rapport du Procureur Général près la Cour d'Appel de Paris'
F 12 8022: Ministère du Commerce, 'Note concernant les mesures prises depuis le début des hostilités relativement aux loyers, ler Novembre 1915'
F 22 536: Travail et sécurité sociale
F 22 11334: Commission inter-ministérielle de la main d'oeuvre
F 23 110: 'Ravitaillement du camp retranché de Paris en blé'

Archives de la Préfecture de police
BA 1614
BA 1640

Archives de la Seine
D.R. 7 141; D.R. 230; D.R. 7

BLPES (British Library of Political and Economic Science, London School of Economics), London,
Board of Trade, 'Report on the course of employment in the United Kingdom from July 1914 to July 1915'
'Supplementary report on the state of employment in February [1915]'
Board of Trade, 'Report on the state of employment in the United Kingdom in April 1918'
Coal Committee Notes / item 3
Condition of industry after the war, reports
F 196 5, Metropolitan Coal Distribution Papers
F 332 43, vol. 1, 64, Sumner Report Working Papers
Local Government Board, London Intelligence Committee Papers (LIC) (9 vols.): 'The prevention and relief of distress memorandum on the steps taken for the prevention and relief of distress due to the war', Appendix C, p. 877
42 (F 265), UK Committee on Prices, working papers
R(O) 42 (f 332) vol. 1, working classes cost-of-living paper

BMA (British Medical Association) Archive
Central Medical War Committee papers, 'Report by the assessment sub-committee and the executive sub-committee on the calls made on LMWCs to meet the present demands of the War Office', January 1917

Brandenburg, Landeshauptarchiv (LHA), Pr.Br.Rep. 30 Berlin C
n. 1466: Berichte über die Lage der Industrie, 1915–21
Jahresberichte der Gewerbe-Aufsicht, n. 1956 and n. 1958–59
Tit.140, 19 544

Bundesarchiv Potsdam (BAP)
Rep. 39.01, n. 1734; Rep. 32.01.1
2.3.1.2., Sachthem. Sammlung 92, Krieg 1914–18, n. 266

BAP Sachthematische Sammlung
Krieg 1914–1918, 2.3.1.2.266, March 1916

Conseil général de la Seine
Procès-verbaux, April and June 1916, December 1917
Rapports et documents

Conseil municipal de Paris, Procès-verbaux
12 November 1915; 13 December 1915; 27 December 1915; 14 and 15 April 1916; 17 November 1916; 26 July 1917; 16 November 1917

Landesarchiv Berlin, Aussenstelle Breite Strasse
(LAB (STA)) Rep. 00/02-1 2189

Landesarchiv Berlin, Provinz Brandenburg
Berlin C Titel 95, nr. 15813

London County Westminster and Parrs Bank
'Names of members of staff who have given their lives for their country in the great war 1914–1918'

Midland Bank Group Archives
'Salary Register, Midland Bank, Cornhill Branch', Ref. AA 166 1

Museum of Labour History, Manchester, WNC 6/3/3

National Inventory of War Memorials
Registers of Streetham, Mitcham, and Bethnal Green war cemeteries

Potsdam, Archives d'Etat
Province Brandeburg

Préfecture de la Seine, Service de la statistique municipale
'Résultats statistiques du dénombrement de 1891 pour la ville de Paris et le département de la Seine', (Paris, 1894)
'Statistique des logements dans les communes du département de la Seine', Recueil de statistique municipale de la ville de Paris et du département de la Seine, 1912, 1918
'Statistique des logements à Paris', Recueil de statistique municipale de la ville de Paris et du département de la Seine, 1922
'Statistique des logements dans le département de la Seine', Recueil de statistique municipale du département de la Seine, 1923

PRO (Public Record Office)
CAB 24/67 GT 6036, Ministry of Food, Report, October 1918
LAB 2/250/1, November 1917
Ministry of Munitions, 5/93/346/131, 'Reports on hostels . . . May 1917'
SUPP 5/63, 'Number of employees – all departments'
SUPP 5/1051, 'Statement of employees in O. F. Woolwich from week ending 1.8.1914 to week ending 5.2.1916
T 172/1310, Memorandum on the cost of the war, 31 March 1922

Stadtarchiv Berlin
Rep. 00-02/1 18031; 002-02/316

Stadtarchiv Potsdam
BP, Rep. 30, Tit. 35, nos. 1465–6

Women, war and society collection
Reel 41, Adam Matthews publications (Taunton, 1990)

Workers' National Committee Archive
WNC 3/11 43 and 87 (Museum of Labour History, Manchester)

Printed primary sources

Newspapers and periodicals

Banker's magazine, 98, September 1914
La banlieue ouest
La Bataille, February 1915, January, February, March, April, and June 1916
Berliner Börsen-Courier, August and December 1914
Berliner Illustrierte Zeitung, September 1916, April 1917
Berliner Lokal-Anzeiger, November and December 1916; January and October 1917; November and December 1917
Berliner Morgenpost, February and August 1914
Berliner Tageblatt, 1917–18
British Journal of Tuberculosis, January 1918
British Medical Journal, June 1918
Bulletin de l'Académie de Médecine, weekly, 1915–18
Bulletin du centre de recherche de l'Historial de la grande guerre
Bulletin du Ministère du Travail, January–March, May–June 1915, June 1916, June 1917
Charity Organisation Review, February 1916 and May 1917
The Coal Merchant and Shipper, March 1917
Daily Herald, January and August, 1914, February and October 1915, September 1916, February 1917
Daily Mail, August 1914
East London Observer, 10 March 1917
L'Echo de Paris, August 1914
The Economist, July 1919
Estates Gazette, 13 July 1918
L'Eveil, June 1916
Le Figaro, August–September 1914
La Gazette de l'Est, April 1916
Gemeinde Blatt Berlin, 1914
Herald, January 1914; February, March, and October 1915, June 1916, February 1917
L'Humanité, October 1914, November and December 1915, November 1917
L'Image fixe, 1987
L'Intransigeant, May and September 1916, January and March 1917, April, May, and August 1918
Jahrbuch der Gehestiftung, 1903
John Bull, May and July 1915, May and September 1916, June and July 1917
Le journal de St Denis
Journal officiel, 9 August 1914, 2 September 1914, 18 December 1914, 8 January 1915, 22 December 1915, 23 December 1915, 12 March 1918
Kladderadatsch, June and December 1916, February, August, October, and November 1917, March 1918
Der Kohlenhändler. Organ des Verbandes der Vereine selbständiger Holz- und Kohlenhändler von Berlin und Umgegend, January 1917
Korrespondenzenblatt der Gewerkschaften, 1914
Lancet, May 1918

Le Matin, September 1914, February 1918
Medical Reform, 1 April 1915
Militärgeschichtliche Mitteilungen
Monatsberichte Gross-Berlin, 1914
Pall Mall Gazette, September and November 1914, October 1915, January, February, and June 1917, September 1918
Le Petit Journal, August and November 1914, May 1915, June and December 1916, February and April 1917
Le Petit Parisien, September, October, November, and December 1914
Le Populaire, April, June, and September 1918
Punch, August 1914, February 1915, April and November 1916, March and November 1918
Reichsarbeitsblatt, vol. 14, 1916; vol. 17, n.4, April 1919; vol. 17, n.10, October 1919; vol. 17, n.11, November 1919; vol. 1, n.5, May 1920
Reichsgesetzblatt, 1914, 1916, 1918
Revue d'hygiène et de police sanitaire, 1916
Revue philanthropique, 1916, 1918, 1920
Revue de la Société de St Vincent de Paul, 1916
Simplicissimus, March and May 1915, June 1916
Le Temps, August, September, and December 1914
The Times, March, October, and November 1915; January, February, May, July, August, September, and November 1916; February, April, May, July, August, and December 1917; March–May 1918, August and November 1918; February–April 1919
Toynbee Record, November 1914
Ulk, March 1915; June, August, October, and November 1918
Verwaltungsbericht Neukölln, 1917
Vorwärts, November and December 1917
Vossische Zeitung, 1917–18
War and Society Newsletter
Women's Dreadnought, September–December 1914; January 1916; March and June 1917

Official publications

Annuaire statistique de la ville de Paris et du Département de la Seine, 1902–19
Archives de la ville de Paris, *Paris démuré* (Paris, 1990)
Berlin Chamber of Commerce, *Annual Report*, 1913
Board of Trade, *Labour Gazette* (Feb. 1914–Jan. 1919); August 1919
Board of Trade, *State of employment reports for January 31st 1919 and the end of April 1919*
Bulletin de la Statistique générale de la France, 1913–19; 1915–20
XIV, 1915, 'Progression des impôts de 1913 à 1925 en France et en divers pays'
Bulletin de statistique et législation comparée, Ministry of Finance, Paris (1913, 1915, 1927, 1928, 1977)
Bulletin des usines de guerre, no. 5, 29 May 1916 and no. 49, 2 April 1917
Census of England and Wales, 1911, 1921
Commission mixte chargée d'étudier les questions relatives au maintien du travail dans

le Département de la Seine (Paris, 1915–18)

Conseil général de la Seine, 'Question de M. Vendrin à M. le Préfet de police au sujet de l'expulsion, d'une chambre de garni, de Mme Sinzot et de ses trois enfants, par le Commissaire de police de Neuilly', *Mémoires et procès-verbaux des délibérations. Procès-verbal du 8 décembre 1915*, Paris, Imprimerie municipale, 1916

'Voeux relatifs aux mesures à prendre en vue de l'organisation du travail au moment de la démobilisation et au projet de loi sur les loyers en instance devant le Parlement', *Mémoires et procès-verbaux des délibérations, 1ère et 2ème sessions de 1916 (procès-verbal du 12 avril 1916)*, Paris, Imprimerie municipale, 1916, pp. 158–82

Conseil municipal de Paris, *Rapports et documents*, no. 30, 3 July 1918

Dausset, Louis, *Rapport . . . sur . . . le projet de budget de la ville de Paris pour 1916* (1916)

Dausset, Louis, *Rapport . . . sur le projet de budget de la ville de Paris pour 1916*, 1916

Dausset, Louis and Rousselle, Henri, *Proposition relative à la création dans les hôpitaux de Paris de baraquements spéciaux destinés au traitement des soldats mis en réforme pour raison de tuberculose*, Conseil municipal de Paris, 8 November 1915, no. 48

Decennial Supplement to the Census of England & Wales, 1921.

Deslandres, Emile, *Rapport sur le fonctionnement du service de la Vaccination depuis l'année 1914 jusqu'à ce jour*, Conseil municipal de Paris, no. 39, 25 November 1916

Dokumente aus geheimen Archiven, vol. IV (Berlin, 1914–18)

Gross-Berlin Statistische Monatsberichte, 1914–18

Handbuch der jüdischen Gemeindeverwaltung und Wohlfahrtspflege, vol. 21, Berlin, 1913

Hansard, 5th Series, XCI

History of the Ministry of Munitions, 1922: vols. V-VI-VIII; 1923: vol. VIII

Household Coal Distribution Order, 1917

Imperial Mineral Resources Bureau, *The Mineral Industry of the British Empire and Foreign Countries, War period 1913–1919: coal, coke, and by-products*, part I (London, 1921)

Industrial Unrest: reports of the Commission of Enquiry into Industrial Unrest, London and South-Eastern Area, 1917–1918, Cd 8666, vol. XV

Institute of Electrical Engineers Roll of Honour

Jahresberichte der Gewerbeaufsichten, 1914–18

Jahresberichte der Handelskammer zu Berlin für 1913

Jahresberichte der Preussischen Gewerberäte

Jahres- und Kassenberichte der Gewerkschaftskommission Berlins und Umgegend, vol. 25, 1914; vol. 26, 1915; vol. 27, 1916; vol. 28, 1917

Kommission zur Erforschung der Geschichte der örtlichen Arbeiterbewegung, *Geschichte der revolutionären Berliner Arbeiterbewegung. Band 1 von den Anfängen bis 1917; Band 2 von 1917 bis 1945* (Berlin, 1987)

Lloyds of London Roll of Honour

London County Council (LCC), *London Statistics* 1904–14, 1908, 1913–14, 1915–20, 1921, 1923–4

The London County Council (LCC) Roll of Honour, London, 2 vols. 1915–16 and

1919–20 (originally published as weekly volumes)
Manuals of Emergency Legislation, Defence of the Realm Manual (6th Edition) Revised to August 31st, 1918 (London, 1918).
Ministère du travail et de la prévoyance sociale, *Travaux des Commissions mixtes départementales pour le maintien du travail national* (Paris, 1916–18), vols. I–V, *1915–1918*
Ministère du travail et de la prévoyance sociale, *Enquête sur l'habitation ouvrière* (1906), Paris, 1908
Ministry of Munitions (Health of Munitions Workers Committee), Final Report. Industrial Health and Efficiency, Cd 9065, 1918, vol. XII
Ministry of Munitions (Health of Munitions Workers Committee), *Memorandum 5, Hours of Work*. Cd 8186, 1916, vol. XXIII
Ministry of Munitions (Health of Munitions Workers Committee), *Memorandum 21, 'An Investigation of the factors concerned in the causation of industrial accidents'*
Monatsberichte Gross-Berlin, 1913–14, 1914–18
National Provincial and Union Bank Roll of Honour
National Roll of Honour (London, 1915–22)
National Westminster and Parrs Bank Roll of Honour
Poisson, Edouard, 'Observations au sujet de la répartition des secours aux réfugiés à Paris et dans la banlieue', Conseil général de la Seine, *Mémoires et procès-verbaux des délibérations (séance du 30 juin 1915)* (Paris, 1916)
Port of London Authority Roll of Honour
PP 1914, Cmd 8335, vol. XI, *Second interim report on an investigation of industrial fatigue by physiological methods*
PP 1914–16, LXXI, 'Memorandum on the steps taken for the prevention and relief of distress due to the war'
PP 1914–1916, XXV, 'Report on the special work of the Local Government Board arising out of the war up to 31st December 1914'
PP 1917–1918, Cmd 8666, vol. XV, *Industrial unrest: reports of the Commission of Enquiry into Industrial Unrest, London and South-Eastern Area*
PP 1918, Cd 8980, VII, *Report of the Committee appointed to enquire into and report upon (i) the actual increase since June 1914 in the Cost of Living to the working classes and (ii) any counterbalancing factors (apart from increases of wages) which may have arisen under War conditions*
PP 1918, Cmd 9065, vol. XII, Ministry of Munitions, Health of Munitions Workers Committee final report: 'Industrial health and efficiency'
PP 1918, Cd 9017, vol. VII, 'Conciliation and Arbitration Board for Government Employees: Record of Proceedings for 1917'
PP 1919, Cmd 39, vol. X, 'Interim Report of the Advisory Committee for the Week Ending 25 May 1918'
PP 1919, Cmd 135, vol. XXXI, 'Report of the War Cabinet Committee on Women in Industry'
PP 1919, Cmd 504, vol. XXVI, 'Report on the physical examination of men of military age by National Service Medical Boards'
PP 1921, Cmd 1188, vol. IX, 'Report of the Committee Appointed to Advise as to the Salaries of the Principal Posts in the Civil Service'
PP 1919, Cmd 9978, vol. VII, Report from the Select Committee on Transport

(Metropolitan Area)'

Préfecture de la Seine, Service de la Statistique municipale, *Résultats statistiques du dénombrement de 1891 pour la ville de Paris et le département de la Seine*, Paris, 1894

Préfecture de la Seine, Statistique Générale de la France, *Statistiques des familles et des habitations en 1911*, Paris, Imprimerie nationale, 1918

Quentin, Maurice, 'Rapport au nom de la 2ème Commission sur les jardins cultivés par les Parisiens et sur les encouragements à donner aux groupements qui leur sont consacrés', Conseil municipal, *Rapports et Documents*, no. 66, 8 Dec. 1917

Recueil de Statistiques de la ville de Paris et du département de la Seine, Epidémie de grippe à Paris, 30 juin 1918–26 avril 1919, Paris, 1919

Registrar General's Annual Reports for England and Wales, 1914–21

Report from the Select Committee on Transport (Metropolitan Area), 1919, vol. VII

Résultats statistiques du Recensement Général de la population effectué le 6 mai 1911 (Paris, 1913–16)

Rousselle, Henri, 'Note sur les travaux de la 5ème commission (Assistance publique - Crédit municipal) pendant la guerre 1914–1919', *Rapport du conseil municipal de Paris (1919)*, nos. 51, 60, 95

Second Interim Report on an Investigation of Industrial Fatigue by Physiological Methods, 1916, Cd 8335, vol. XI

South Metropolitan Gas Company Roll of Honour

Statistics of the military effort of the British Empire during the Great War (London, 1922)

Statistik des Deutschen Reichs

Statistik der Stadt Berlin, 1912–14, 1915–20

Statistisches Jahrbuch der Stadt Berlin, vol. 32, vol. 33, 1912–14; vol. 34, 1915–19

Tabellen über die Bevölkerungsvorgänge Berlins (Berlin, 1918)

Die Wirtschaftliche Demobilmachung, 21 February 1919

Contemporary studies and pamphlets

Aeroboe, F., *Der Einfluss des Krieges auf Bevölkerungsbewegung und Lebenshaltung in Deutschland* (Stuttgart, 1927)

Angell, N., *The great illusion: a study of the relation of military power in nations to their economic and social advantage* (London, 1910)

Apollinaire, Guillaume, *Correspondance avec son frère et sa mère*, présentée par Gilbert Boudon et Michel Decaudin (Paris, 1987)

Barton, D. M., 'The course of women's wages', *Journal of the Royal Statistical Society* (July 1919), pp. 529–33

Baumer, G., *Heimatchronik während des Weltkriegs* (Berlin, 1930)

Bekanntmachung über die Einrichtung von Kundenlisten für Braunkohlenbriketts zum Küchen- und Ofenbrand in Gross-Berlin (Der Kohlenverband GrossBerlin, 11 March 1918)

Berliner Fürsorge-Arbeit während des Krieges (Berlin, 1910)

Bernard, Léon, *La défense de la santé publique pendant la guerre*, Publication de la Dotation Carnegie pour la paix internationale (Paris, 1929)

Bernstein, E., *Die Geschichte der Berliner Arbeiterbewegung* (Berlin, 1910)

Beveridge, W., *British food control* (London, 1928)
Biggs, H. M., 'A war tuberculosis program for the nation', *American Review of Tuberculosis*, 1, 5 (July 1917)
Bloch, C., *Bibliographie méthodique de l'histoire économique et sociale de la France pendant la guerre*, Publications de la Dotation Carnegie pour la paix internationale (Paris, 1925)
Blücher von Wahlstatt, Evelyn, *An English wife in Berlin* (New York, 1920)
Bonhoeffer, Dr, 'Geistes- und Nervenkrankheiten', in F. Bumm (ed.), *Deutschlands Gesundheitsverhältnisse unter dem Einfluss des Weltkrieges* (Stuttgart and New haven, 1928), vol. 1, pp. 259–88
Booth, Charles (ed.), *Life and labour of the people of London*, 9 vols., 1892–7
Bowley, A. L., *Prices and wages in the United Kingdom, 1914–1920* (Oxford, 1921)
'The survival of small firms in London', *Economica*, 1 (1921)
Brittain, Vera, *Testament of youth* (London, 1933)
Cadoux, Gaston, *La vie des grandes capitales, études comparatives sur Londres, Paris, Berlin* (Paris, 2nd edn 1913)
Cahen, Georges, *'L'autre guerre'. Essais d'assistance et d'hygiène publique (1905–1920)* (Paris, 1920)
Céline, Louis Ferdinand, *Voyage au bout de la nuit* (Paris, Gallimard, 1952); trans. R. Manheim, *Voyage to the end of the night* (London, 1988)
Centre de Documentation d'Histoire des Techniques, *Evolution de la géographie industrielle de Paris et la proche banlieue au XIXème siècle* (Paris, 1991)
Clarke Hall, W., *The State and the Child* (London, 1917)
Confédération Générale du Travail (CGT), *Compte-rendu des travaux du Congres de 1918 de la CGT* (Paris, 1919)
Cook, Arthur G., 'Londres et la gestion de ses affaires municipales', *Journal de la société de statistiques de Paris* (1914), pp. 345–55
Cooper, C. E., *Behind the lines: one woman's war, 1914–1918* (London, 1982)
Davenport-Hill, Florence, *Children of the State* (1868)
Dearle, N. B., *Problems of unemployment in the London building trade* (London, 1908)
The labor cost of the world war to Great Britain 1914–1922. A statistical analysis (New Haven, 1940)
Deschamps, Paul, *La formation sociale de Prussien moderne* (Paris, 1916)
Desormeaux, A., *Clichy pendant la guerre* (Paris, 1920)
Dietrich, E., 'Die Entwicklung der Medizinalverwaltung und der sozialen Hygiene bis zur Novemberumwälzung', *Berliner Klinische Wochenschrift*, 56, 2 (27 January 1919)
Döblin, A., *A people betrayed. November 1918: a German revolution*, trans. by J. E. Woods (New York, 1983)
Drake, B., *Women in the Engineering Trades* (London, 1917)
Dugé de Bernonville, L., 'Les revenus privés, 1913–1936', *Revue d'économie politique* (June 1937)
Eberstadt, R., *Handbuch des Wohnungswesens und der Wohnungsfrage*
Eildermann, W., *Jugend im ersten Weltkrieg. Tagebücher, Briefe, Erinnerungen* (Berlin, 1972)
Eltzbacher, Paul (ed.), *Die Deutsche Volksernährung und der Englische Aushungerungsplan* (Braunschweig, 1914)

L'Esprit, A. L., *La crise de charbon à Paris pendant la guerre de 1914–18* (Paris, 1924)
Fontaine, A., *French industry during the war* (New Haven, 1926).
Fonville, A. de, 'Enquête sur le dépeuplement de la France', *La revue hebdomadaire*, 5 (1909), pp. 101–29
Lord Fraser of Lonsdale, *My story of St Dunstans* (London, G. Harrap, 1961)
Fuchs, Eduard, *Die Karikatur der europäischen Völker von 1848 bis zur Gegenwart* (2 vols., Berlin, 1904)
Der Weltkrieg in der Karikatur (Berlin, 1916)
Fuster, Edouard, 'L'action nationale contre la tuberculose en Angleterre', *Revue d'hygiène et de police sanitaire* (1916), pp. 289–303
Gibbs, P., *Realities of War* (London, 1929)
Gide, Charles and Oualid, William, *Le bilan de la Guerre pour la France* (Paris and New Haven, 1931)
Gladstone, F. M., *Aubrey House Kensington 1698–1920* (London, Arthur Humphreys, 1922)
Glatzer, R. and G. (eds.), *Berliner Leben 1914–1918* (Berlin, 1983)
Gray, J., *Gin and bitters* (London, 1938)
Greenwood, M., 'Tuberculosis among industrial workers', *British Medical Journal* (15 March 1919)
Güther, A., *Kriegslöhne und Preise und ihr Einfluss auf Kaufkraft und Lebenskosten* (Jena, 1919)
Hahn, Martin, 'Influenza, Genickstarre, Tetanus, Weilsche Krankheit', in F. Bumm (ed.), *Deutschlands Gesundheitsverhältnisse unter dem Einfluss des Weltkrieges*, vol. I (Stuttgart and New Haven, 1928)
Halbwachs, Maurice, *La classe ouvrière et les niveaux de vie* (Paris, 1912)
'Budget de familles ouvrières et paysannes en France en 1907', *Bulletin de la Statistique générale de la France* (October, 1914)
'Prix de détail', *Bulletin de la Statistique générale de la France* (October 1915–July 1920)
Les cadres sociaux de la mémoire (Paris, 1925)
'"Gross Berlin": grande agglomération ou grande ville?', *Annales d'histoire économique et sociale*, 30 (Nov. 1934), pp. 547–70
La mémoire collective (Paris, 1932) transl. by F. J. and V. Y. Ditter as *On collective memory* (New York, 1980)
Hammond, M. B., *British labour conditions and legislation during the war* (Oxford, 1919)
Hasse-Terheyden, Josef, *Die Kohlenversorgung Berlins* (Berlin, 1921)
Hauser, Henri, *Le problème du régionalisme* (Paris, 1924)
Henry, Marc, *Trois villes: Vienne, Munich, Berlin* (Paris, 1917)
Hersch, L., 'L'inégalité devant la mort d'après les statistiques de la ville de Paris', *Revue d'Economie politique* (1920)
Pauvreté et mortalité selon les principales causes de décès d'après les statistiques de la Ville de Paris (Rome, 1932)
Hesse, A., 'Freie Wirtschaft und Zwangswirtschaft im Kriege', *Beiträge zur Kriegswirtschaft*, 39 (April, 1918)
Hessel, Franz, *Spazieren in Berlin* (Berlin, 1929), transl. by Jean-Michel Beloeil as *Promenades dans Berlin* (Grenoble, 1989)
Heuss, T., *Drei Monate Volksspeisung* (Berlin, 1916)

Hirtshiefer Heinrich, *Die Wohnungswirtschaft in Preussen* (Eberswalde, 1929)

Histories of two hundred and fifty one divisions of the German army which participated in the war (1914–1918) compiled from the records of the intelligence section of the general staff, American Expeditionary Forces (Chaumont, 1919, repr. London Stamp Exchange, 1989)

Hogge, J. M. and Garside, T. H., *War pensions and allowances* (London, 1918)

Huber, M., *La population de la France pendant la guerre* (Paris, 1931)

Huber, M. and Dugé de Bernouville, L., 'Le mouvement des prix, du coût de la vie et des salaires en divers pays, de juillet 1914 à janvier 1918', *Bulletin de la Statistique Générale de la France* (1918)

Huret, Jules, *En Allemagne, Berlin* (Paris, 1909)

'Hygienischer Führer durch Berlin', *XIV Internationaler Kongress für Hygiene und Demographie Berlin* (Berlin, 1907)

Ignace, E., 'La question des loyers', *Le Petit Parisien* (23 Sept. 1914)

'La question des loyers. Une proposition de loi de M. Ignace', *Le Petit Parisien* (12 Dec. 1914)

The impact of the war on civilian consumption in the United Kingdom, the United States and Canada (London, 1945)

Jadassohn, J., 'Geschlechtskrankheiten', in F. Bumm (ed.), *Deutschlands Gesundheitsverhältnisse unter dem Einfluss des Weltkrieges* (Stuttgart and New Haven, 1928), vol. I, pp. 223–58

Joanne, Paul, 'Paris', in *Dictionnaire géographique et administratif de la France*, vol. V (Paris, 1899)

Jordan, E. O., *Epidemic influenza: a survey* (Chicago, 1927)

Kaeber, E., *Berlin im Weltkriege: fünf Jahre stätdtischer Kriegsarbeit* (Berlin, 1921)

Kaufmann, Erich, *Das Wesen des Völkerrechts und die clausula rebus sic stantibus* (Tübingen, 1911)

Köppe, H., *Kriegswirtschaft und Sozialismus* (Marburg, 1915)

Kray, Alfred, 'Die Einwirkung des Krieges auf das Gross-Berliner Baugewerbe', *Beiträge zur Bauwissenschaft*, no. 25 (Berlin, 1920)

Kürten, J., *Die Kohlenversorgung in Berlins, 1913–1923* in Berliner Wirtschft-Berichte, 1, 2 (Berlin, 1924)

Labour Research Department, *Wages, prices and profits* (London, 1922)

Lawrence, D. H., *Sons and lovers* (London, 1913)

Women in Love (London, 1922)

Lenz, Dr, 'Die Seuchenbekämpfung in Preussen während des Krieges und ihr Ergebnis bis Ende 1915', *Veröffentlichungen aus dem Gebiete des Medizinalverwaltung*, vol. VI, no. 3 (Berlin, 1916)

Le Pelletier, Emile, *Code pratique des usages de Paris ayant force obligatoire de loi dans les contestations les plus fréquentes entre les habitants de Paris* (Paris, 1890)

Leyser, Erich, 'Gross-Berlin Wohnungspolitik im Kriege', in *Grossstadt und Kleinhaus* (Berlin, 1917)

McDonagh, M., *In London during the Great War* (London, 1935)

McMillan, Margaret, *The child and the state* (London, 1911)

Macpherson, W. G., *Official history of the medical services* (London, 1921)

Martin du Gard, Roger, *L'été 1914* (Paris, 1932)

Martin Saint-Léon, E., 'La bourgeoisie française et la vie chère', *Le Musée Social* (1 Jan. 1921)

'La bourgeoisie française et la vie chère', in *La vie chère et les classes moyennes*, Bibliothèque du Musée social (Agen, 1921), pp. 35–41

Masche, W., *Kriegsgeschichte der Schüler und Lehrer des Kaiser-Wilhelm-Real-Gymnasiums zu Berlin* (Berlin, 1919)

Meuriot, Paul, 'Dans quel sens se développent at les métropoles européennes', *Journal de la société de statistiques de Paris* (1913), pp. 238–50

'Le Reichstag impérial, 1871–1912, étude de démographie politique', *Journal de la société de statistiques de Paris* (1914)

'De la valeur du terme de banlieue dans certaines métropoles: Paris, Berlin, et Londres', *Bulletin de l'Institut International de Statistiques* (1915), pp. 320–30

Middleton, T. H., *Food production in war* (Oxford, 1923)

Miller, J. A., 'Tuberculosis among European nations at war', *American Review of Tuberculosis* (Aug. 1919), pp. 337–58

Mitchell, P. (ed.), *Memoranda on army general hospital administration* (London, 1917)

'Mitteilungen über die Grippe (Influenza)', *Ministerial-Blatt für Medizinalangelegenheiten*, 18, 44 (30 October, 1918)

Moniez-Terracher, Denise, 'La reconstruction sociale en Angleterre', *Revue philanthropique*, 39, 253 (15 Sept. 1918)

Müllers, Bernard, 'Tuberkulose', in F. Bumm (ed.), *Deutschlands Gesundheitsverhältnisse unter dem Einfluss des Weltkrieges*, vol. I (Stuttgart and New Haven, 1928)

Murray, F., *Women as army surgeons* (London, 1920)

Newsholme, Arthur, 'The relations of tuberculosis to war conditions, with remarks on some aspects of the administrative control of tuberculosis', *Lancet* (20 Oct. 1917)

Noack, Victor, *Wohnungsnot und Mieterelend. Ein Erbstück des alten Staates* (Berlin, 1918)

Nony, G., *L'Intendance en campagne* (Paris, 1914)

Orwell, George, *Coming up for air* in *Collected Works* (London, 1986)

Ostwald, Hans, *Berlin und die Berlinerin. Eine Kultur- und Sittengeschichte* (Berlin, 1911)

Paris charitable et bienfaisant (Paris, 1912)

Paris charitable, bienfaisant et social (Paris, 1921)

Paris charitable pendant la guerre, 1 vol. and 3 supplement (Paris, 1915–18)

Parkinson, H., *Ordinary shares: a manual for investors* (3rd edn, London, 1948)

Parst, Julius, *Gesetzliche Kriegsfürsorge Invaliden – und Hinterbliebenen – Fürsorge* (Berlin, 1915)

Pasquet, D., *Londres et les ouvriers du Londres* (Paris, 1913)

Pember-Reeves, M., *Round about a pound a week* (London, 1979)

Pesl, L. D., 'Mittelstandsfragen. Der gewerbliche und kaufmännische Mittelstand', in *Grundrisse der Sozialökonomie*, vol. IX (Tübingen, 1926)

Pinard, Dr, 'De la protection de l'enfance pendant la deuxième année de guerre dans le camp retranché de Paris', *Bulletin de l'Académie de Médecine* (3 Dec. 1916)

'Office central d'Assistance maternelle et infantile dans le gouvernement militaire de Paris. Assemblée générale de 23 février 1918', *Revue philanthropique*, 39, 250 (15 June 1918), pp. 265–79

'De la protection maternelle et infantile pendant la quatrième année de guerre dans le camp retranché de Paris', *Bulletin de l'Académie de Médecine* (17 Dec. 1918)

Pinot, Robert, *Le comité des Forges au service de la nation* (Paris, 1919)

Poëte, Marcel, 'La physionomie de Paris pendant la guerre', in H. Sellier, A. Bruggeman, and Marcel Poëte (eds.), *Paris pendant la guerre* (Paris, 1926), pp. 69–87

Porter, Katherine Anne, *Pale horse, pale rider* (New York, 1936)

Prinzing, F., *Wars and epidemics* (Oxford, 1916)

Quante, P., *Lohnpolitik und Lohnentwicklung im Kriege* (Berlin, 1920)

Rabnow, Johannes, *Bekämpfung der Tuberkulose in Berlin-Schöneberg* (Berlin, 1913)

Ravit, Julie, *Wie kommt man mit wenigem aus?* (Kiel, 1908)

Reichardt, Friedrich, *Die Entlassung Auswärtiger* (Berlin, 1919)

Romains, Jules, *Les Hommes de bonne volonté. Le 6 Octobre 1908* (Paris, 1st edn 1932, 2nd edn 1958)

Verdun (London, 1940)

Rott, Fritz, 'Die Einwirkung des Krieges auf die Säuglingssterblichkeit und die Säuglingsschutzbewegung', *Zeitschrift für Säuglingsschutz*, 7 (May–June 1915)

Umfang, Bedeutung und Ergebnisse der Unterstützungen an stillende Mütter (Berlin, 1914)

Rufenacht Walters, F., *Sanatoria for the tuberculous* (London, 1913)

Ruge, L., 'Deutschlands Milch- und Speisefettversorgung im Kriege', *Beiträge zur Kriegswirtschaft*, 47-8 (Sept. 1918)

Rusch, Hans, *Die kommunale Fürsorge für Tuberkulose am Beispiel des Bezirkes Spandau, inaugural conference, Friedrich-Wilhelms-Universität zu Berlin* (Berlin, 1927)

'Schädigung der deutschen Volkskraft durch die feindliche Blockade', *Denkschrift des Reichsgesundheitsamtes* (Berlin, 1918)

Schmoller, G., *Was verstehen wir unter dem Mittelstand?* (Göttingen, 1897)

Schreiner, George, *The iron ration* (New York, 1918)

Schuster, Felix, 'Foreign trade and the money market', *Journal of the Institute of Bankers*, 25 (1904), pp. 55–81

Seligman, E., 'Bericht über die Tätigkeit der Fürsorgeschwestern des Medizinalamtes der Stadt Berlin im Jahre 1917', *Berliner Klinische Wochenschrift*, 55, 25 (24 June 1918)

Sellers, E., 'On the manufacturing of grievance', *The 19th Century and After*, 481 (March 1917)

Sellier, H., *La crise du logement et l'intervention publique en matière d'habitation populaire dans l'agglomération parisienne* (Paris, 1921)

La lutte contre la tuberculose dans la région parisienne, 1896–1927 (Paris, 1928)

Sellier, Henri, A. Bruggeman, and M. Poëte, *Paris pendant la guerre* (Paris, 1926)

Siemens, G., *Der Weg der Elektrotechnik* (Munich, 1961)

Soldiers died in the Great War Volume 76r: London Regiment, Inns of Court OTC and the Honourable Artillery Company (London, 1920; repr. Polstead, 1988)

Spears, E., *Statistics of the Military Effort of the British Empire* (London, HMSO, 1922)

'Städtisches Medizinalamt', *Vossische Zeitung*, 24 (23 April 1914)

Stevenson, T. H. C., 'The incidence of mortality upon the rich and poor districts of Paris and London', *Journal of the Royal Statistical Society* (1921)
'The social distribution of mortality from the different causes in England and Wales, 1910–12', *Biometrika*, 15 (1923), pp. 382–400
Tebb, A. E., *An inquiry into the prevalence and aetiology of tuberculosis among industrial workers, with special reference to female munitions workers*, Medical Research Council Report no. 22 (1920)
Tobis, H., *Das Mittelstandsproblem der Nachkriegzeit und seine statistische Erfassung* (Grimmen in Pommern, 1920)
'Tuberculosis. Colonies for the tuberculous', *Lancet* (4 May 1918), pp. 646–7
Tucker, John, *Johnny get your gun* (New York, 1958)
Unwin, S. (ed.), *The work of V.A.D.* (London, 1919)
Valdour, Jacques, *Ouvriers parisiens d'après-guerre* (Paris, 1921)
Verhandlungen der Sozialisierungskommission über die Neuregelung des Wohnungswesen (Berlin, 1921)
Victor, M., *Verbürgerlichung des Proletariats und Proletarisierung des Mittelstandes* (Berlin, 1931)
Vitoux, Georges, 'L'oeuvre des comités départementaux d'assistance aux soldats réformés', *Revue d'hygiène*, (1918), pp. 561–70
Vivian, E., Charles and Hodder Williams, J. E., *The way of the Red Cross* (London, 1915)
Wermuth, Adolph, *Ein Beamtenleben* (Berlin, 1922)
Wie wirtschaftet man gut und billig bei einem jährlichen Einkommen von 800 bis 1000 Mark? (Dresden, 1900)
Wie wirtschaftet man gut und billig bei einem jährlichen Einkommen von 1400 bis 2000 Mark? (Dresden, 1900)
Die wirtschaftliche Demobilmachung (9 Jan., 21 Feb. 1919)
Die Wohlfahrtseinrichtungen von Gross-Berlin, Zentrale für private Fürsorge (Berlin, 1910)

Secondary sources

Books and articles

Abel-Smith, B., *The hospitals, 1800–1948* (London, 1963)
Adams, R. J. Q. and Poirier, Philip P., *The conscription controversy in Great Britain, 1900–1918* (Basingstoke, 1987)
Albertini, L., *Les origines de la grande guerre* (Paris, 1960)
Anderson, Benedict, *Imagined communities. Reflections on the origins and spread of nationalism* (London, 1983, 2nd edn 1991)
Armitage, Susan, *The politics of decontrol: Britain and the United States* (London, 1969)
Ashworth, T., *Trench warfare 1914–1918. The live and let live system* (London, 1980, 2nd edn 1986)
Audoin-Rouzeau, Stéphane, *A travers leurs journaux: 14–18, Les combattants des tranchées* (Paris, 1986)
Men at war. National sentiment and trench journalism in France, 1914–1918, transl. H. MacPhail (Oxford and Providence, 1992)

La guerre des enfants, 1914–1918: essai d'histoire culturelle (Paris, 1993)
Bailey, Stephen, 'The Berlin strike of January 1918', *Central European History*, 13, 2 (June 1980), pp. 158–74
Baines, Dudley, *Migration in a mature economy: emigration and internal migration in England and Wales, 1861–1900* (Cambridge, 1985)
Bairoch, Paul, *De Jéricho à Mexico. Villes et économie dans l'histoire* (Paris, 1985)
Bane, S. L. and Lutz, R. H. (eds.), *The blockade of Germany after the Armistice* (New York, 1938)
Barral, Pierre, *Les agrariens français de Méline à Pisani* (Paris, 1968)
'L'Intendance', in G. Canini (ed.), *Les fronts invisibles: Nourrir, fournir, soigner. Colloque international sur la logistique des armées au combat, 1914–1918, Verdun, 1980* (Nancy, 1984)
Barrows, Susanna, *The deforming mirror* (New Haven, 1984); *Miroirs déformants* (Paris, 1990)
Baudis, Dieter von, Vom 'Schweinemord zum Kohlrübenwinkeer', in D. Baudis (ed.) *Zur Wirtschafts- und Sozialgeschichte Berlins vom 17. Jahrhundert bis zur Gegenwort* (Berlin, 1986) pp. 129–57
Bay-Heard, F., *Haupstadt und Staatsumwälzung – Berlin 1918. Problematik und Scheitern der Rätebewegung in der Kommunalverwaltung* (Stuttgart, 1969)
Becker, A., *La guerre et la ferveur* (Paris, 1994)
Becker, Jean-Jacques, *Le carnet B: les pouvoirs publics et l'antimilitarisme pendant la guerre* (Paris, 1973)
1914. Comment les Français sont entrés dans la guerre (Paris, 1977)
Les Français dans la grande guerre (Paris, 1980); English transl., *The Great War and the French people* (Oxford and Providence, 1985)
Becker, Jean-Jacques, Winter, Jay M., Krumeich, Gerd, Becker, Annette, and Audoin-Rouzeau, Stéphane (eds.), *Guerre et cultures 1914–1918* (Paris, 1994)
La très grande guerre (Paris, 1994)
Beckett, Ian, 'The territorial force', in Ian Beckett (ed.), *A nation in arms* (Manchester, 1985), pp. 128–63
Bédarida, François, 'Urban growth and social structure in nineteenth century Poplar', *London Journal*, 1, 2 (November 1975), pp. 159–88
Bell, A., *A history of the blockade of Germany and the countries associated with her in the Great War, Austria-Hungary, Bulgaria, and Turkey, 1914–1918* (London, 1937)
Bellanger, C. *et al.* (eds.), *Histoire générale de la presse française*, 5 vols. (Paris, 1976)
Benjamin, Walter, *Reflections. Essays, aphorisms, autobiographical writings* (ed. by P. Demetz) (New York, Schocken Books, 1986)
Benjamin, Walter, *Passagen: Walter Benjamins Urgeschichte des neunzehnten Jahrhunderts*, ed. Norbert Bolz and Bernd Witte (Munich, 1984)
Berghahn, Volker Rolf, *Germany and the approach of war in 1914* (London, 1973)
Imperial Germany (Providence, 1994)
Berlanstein, Lenard R., *The working people of Paris 1871–1914* (Baltimore, 1984)
Berridge, V., 'Health and medicine', in F. M. L. Thompson (ed.) *The Cambridge social history of Britain*, vol. III (Cambridge, 1990)
Bessel, Richard, 'Unemployment and demobilization in Germany after the First World War', in Richard John Evans and Dick Geary (eds.), *The German unemployed, experiences and consequences of mass unemployment from the*

Weimar Republic to the Third Reich (New York, 1986; London, 1987)
Germany after the Great War (Oxford, 1993)
Bey-Heard, F., *Hauptstadt und Staatsumwälzung Berlin 1919. Problematik und Scheitern der Rätebewegung in der Kommunalverwaltung* (Stuttgart, 1969)
Bieber, H. J., *Gewerkschaften in Krieg und Revolution. Arbeiterbewegung, Industrie, Staat und Militär in Deutschland, 1914–1920* (Hamburg, 1981)
Bock, S., 'L'exubérance de l'Etat, 1914–1918', *Vingtième siècle*, 1 (1988)
Bonnefous, G., *La Grande Guerre* (Paris, 1957)
Borchardt, L., 'The impact of the war economy on the civilian population', in Wilhelm Deist (ed.), *The German military in the age of total war* (Leamington Spa, 1985)
Boswell, J. S. and Johns, B. R., 'Patriots or profiteers? British businessmen and the First World War', *Journal of European Economic History*, 11, 2 (1982), pp. 423–46
Bouille, Michel, 'Les congrès d'hygiène des travailleurs au début du siècle 1904–1911', *Le Mouvement social*, 161 (Oct–Dec. 1992), pp. 43–66
Bourdelais, Patrice, *L'âge de la vieillesse* (Paris, 1993)
Bourke, Joanna, *Working-class cultures in Britain 1890–1940* (London, 1993)
Bowley, Marian, *Housing and the State, 1919–1944* (London, 1945)
Boyd, M., 'Coping with the Samoan resistance after the 1918 influenza epidemic', *Journal of Pacific History*, 15 (1980), pp. 155–74
Bradbury, F. C. S., *Causal factors in tuberculosis* (London, 1933)
Braybon, Gail, *Women workers in the First World War* (London, 1981; 2nd edn 1989)
Brewer, J., *The sinews of power: war, money and the English state, 1688–1783* (London, 1989)
Broadberry, Stephen N., *The British Economy Between the Wars: a macroeconomic survey* (Oxford, 1986)
Bry, G., *Wages in Germany, 1871–1945* (Princeton, 1960)
Bryder, Linda, '"Lessons" of the 1918 influenza epidemic in Auckland', *New Zealand Journal of History*, 16, 2 (October 1982), pp. 97–121
'The First World War: healthy or hungry?', *History Workshop Journal* (1987), pp. 141–57
Below the magic mountain. A social history of tuberculosis in twentieth-century Britain (Oxford, 1988)
Buenger, B. C., 'Max Beckmann in the First World War', in R. Rumold and O. K. Werckmeister (eds.), *The ideological crisis of expressionism. The literary and artistic German war colony in Belgium 1914–1918*, Studies in German Literature, Linguistics and Culture, vol. 51 (Columbia, S.C., 1990)
Buffet, Cyril, *Berlin* (Paris, 1993)
Bullock, Nicholas and Read, James, *The movement for housing reform in Germany and France, 1840–1914* (Cambridge, 1985)
Burchardt, Lothar, *Friedenswirtschaft und Kriegsvorsorge* (Boppard am Rhein, 1968)
Burk, Kathleen (ed.), *War and the state: the transformation of British government, 1914–1919* (London, 1982)
Britain, America and the sinews of war, 1914–1918 (London, 1985)
Burlen, K. (ed.), *La banlieue oasis. Henri Sellier et les cités-jardins 1900–1940*

(Saint-Denis, 1987)
Burnett, John, *A social history of housing, 1815–1970* (London, 1980; 1st edn Newton Abbot 1978)
Bush, Julia, *Behind the lines. East End Labour, 1914–1919* (London, 1984)
Carsten, F., *Revolution in central Europe, 1918–1919* (Berkeley, 1972)
War against war (Berkeley, 1972)
Carter, Harold and Lewis, C. Roy, *An urban geography of England and Wales in the nineteenth century* (London, 1990)
Cassis, Youssef, *La City de Londres, 1870–1914* (Paris, 1987)
(ed.), *Finance and financiers in European history 1880–1960* (Cambridge, 1992)
Castle, H. G. *Fire over England: the German air raids of World War I* (London, 1982)
Centre de Documentation d'Histoire des Techniques, *Evolution de la géographie industrielle de Paris et la proche banlieue au XIXe siècle* (Paris, 1991)
Charle, Christophe, *Les élites de la République, 1880–1900* (Paris, 1987)
Histoire sociale de la France au XIXe siècle (Paris, 1991)
Clarke, B. R., *Causes and prevention of tuberculosis* (Edinburgh, 1952)
Coale, Ansley J. and Watkins, Susan Cott (eds.), *The decline of fertility in Europe: the revised proceedings of a conference on the Princeton European Fertility Project* (Princeton, 1986)
Cohen, Jean-Louis, 'Les réformes urbaines à Berlin: deux siècles de chantier', *Critique*, numéro spécial: *Berlin n'est plus une île* (Aug. 1991), pp. 580–95
Collier, R., *The plague of the Spanish lady* (London, 1974)
Collingworth, J. B., *Town and country planning in Britain* (London, 1982)
Collins, R. F., 'The development of censorship in World War I France', *Journalism Monographs*, no. 131 (Columbia, S.C., 1992)
Comfort, R. A., *Revolutionary Hamburg. Labor politics in the early Weimar Republic* (Stanford, Calif., 1966)
Corbin, Alain, *Les filles de noce. Misères sexuelles et prostitution* (Paris, 1978, repr. 1982)
Costas, Ilse, 'Management and labor in the Siemens plants in Berlin, 1896–1920', in L. Haimson and G. Sapelli (eds.), *Strikes, social conflict and the First World War. An international perspective* (Milan, 1991)
Cournot, Michel, 'L'entière liberté d'écrire d'Apollinaire', *Le Monde* (27 Jan. 1993)
Cribier, Françoise, 'Itinéraires professionnels et usure au travail: une génération de salariés parisiens', *Le Mouvement social*, no. spécial: *L'usure au travail*, 124 (1983), pp. 11–14
Cronin, James E., *The politics of state expansion: war, state and society in twentieth-century Britain* (London, 1991)
Cronje, G., 'Tuberculosis and mortality decline in England and Wales, 1851–1910', in Robert Woods and John Woodward (eds.), *Urban disease and mortality in nineteenth century England* (London, 1984)
Crosby, A., *Epidemic and peace, 1918* (Westport, Conn., 1976)
Cross, G., 'Worktime in international discontinuity', in G. Cross (ed.), *Worktime and industrialization. An international history* (Philadelphia, 1988)
Crowther, Margaret Anne, *The workhouse system, 1834–1929, the history of an English social institution* (London, 1983)
Cullingworth, J. B., *Town and Country Planning in Britain* (London, 1982)

Dallas, Gloden and Gill, Douglas, *The unknown army* (London, 1985)
Daniel, Ute, *Arbeiterfrauen in der Kriegsgesellschaft: Beruf, Familie und Politik im Ersten Weltkrieg* (Göttingen, 1989), transl. as *Women at war in Germany 1914–1918* (Oxford, 1996)
Dare, R., 'Australie et l'éclatement de la guerre de '14', *Guerres mondiales et conflits contemporains* (1995), pp. 323–54
Darmon, Pierre, *La longue traque de la variole* (Paris, 1986)
Daumard, Adeline, 'La bourgeoisie', in G. Duby and E. Labrousse (eds.), *Histoire économique et sociale de la France* (Paris, 1980)
Dauton, M. G. (ed.), *Housing the workers: a comparative history, 1850–1944* (Leicester, 1990)
Davis, Belinda, 'Food scarcity and the empowerment of the female consumer in World War I Germany', in V. de Grazia (ed.), with E. Furlough, *The sex of things: gender and consumption in historical perspective* (Berkeley, 1996)
'"Legitimate beefs" and "just desserts": women's strategies and the female consumer in World War I Berlin', in V. de Grazia (ed.), *Conspicuous constructions: essays on gender and consumption* (Berkeley, 1996)
Davis, John, *Reforming London: the London government problem, 1855–1900* (Oxford, 1988)
Dewey, Peter E., 'Food production and policy in the United Kingdom, 1914–1918', *Transactions of the Royal Historical Society*, 5th ser., 30 (1980), pp. 71–89
'Military recruiting and the British labour force during the First World War', *Historical Journal* 27, 1 (March 1984), pp. 199–223
'The new warfare and economic mobilization', in John Turner (ed.), *Britain and the First World War* (London, 1988)
Dodds, F. H. and Colls, C., *Englishness* (London, 1992)
Dogliani, Patrizia, *Un laboratorio di socialismo municipale: La Francia (1870–1920)* (Milano, 1992)
Dowie, J. A., '1919–1920 is in need of attention', *Economic History Review*, 2nd ser., 28 (Aug. 1975)
Draw! Political cartoons from left to right (Washington, 1991)
Dreyfus, F. G., 'Berlin, capitale du Reich, 1871–1933', in Etienne François and Egon Westerhalt (eds.), *Berlin: capitale, mythe, enjeu* (Nancy, 1987)
Drolet, A., 'L'épidémie de grippe espagnole à Québec, 1918', *Trois siècles de Médecine québécoise*. Cahiers d'Histoire no. 22, La Société historique de Québec (1970), pp. 98–106
Dubesset, Mathilde, Thébaud, Françoise, and Vincent, Catherine, 'Les munitionnettes de la Seine', in Patrick Fridenson (ed.), *1914–1918, L'autre front*, Cahiers du 'Mouvement social', no. 2 (Paris, 1977), pp. 189–219, transl. as *The French home front* (Oxford, 1992)
Dumons, B. and Pollet, G., 'La naissance d'une politique sociale: les retraites en France (1900–1914)', *Revue française des sciences politiques*, 5 (1991), pp. 627–48
Dupâquier, Michel, 'La famille Bertillon et la naissance d'une nouvelle science sociale: la démographie', *Annales de démographie historique* (1982), pp. 293–311
Dupoux, Albert, 'Sur les pas de Monsieur Vincent. Trois cents ans d'histoire

parisienne de l'enfance abandonnée', *Revue de l'assistance publique* (1962)
Durkheim, E., *Textes présentés par V. Karady* (Paris, 1975)
Dwork, Deborah, *War is good for babies and other young children: a history of the infant and child welfare movement in England, 1898–1918* (London, 1987)
Dyhouse, C., 'Working-class mothers and infant mortality in England, 1895–1914', *Journal of Social History*, 12, 2 (1978), pp. 248–67
Dyos, H. J. and Wolff, Michael (eds.), *The Victorian city: images and realities* (2 vols., London, 1973)
Englander, David, 'Die Demobilmachung in Grossbritannien nach dem Ersten Weltkrieg', *Geschichte und Gesellschaft*, 9 (1983), pp. 195–210
Landlord and tenant in urban Britain, 1838–1918 (Oxford, 1983)
Evans, Richard and Geary, Dick (eds.), *The German unemployed, experiences and consequences of mass unemployment from the Weimar Republic to the Third Reich* (London, 1987)
Evenson, Norma, *Paris: a century of change, 1878–1978* (New Haven, 1979)
Faber, Knud, 'Tuberculosis und Nutrition', *Acta Tuberculosea Scandinavia*, 12 (1938), pp. 287–333
Faure, Alain (ed.), *Les premiers banlieusards. Aux origines des banlieues de Paris, 1860–1940* (Paris, 1991)
Faure, Olivier, 'Les historiens face à la médicalisation', in *La société inquiète de sa santé* (Lyons, 1988)
Feinstein, C., *National income, expenditure and output of the United Kingdom, 1855–1965* (Cambridge, 1972)
Feldman, David, 'The importance of being English: Jewish immigration and the decay of Liberal England', in David Feldman and Gareth Stedman Jones (eds.), *Metropolis London. Histories and representations since 1800* (London, 1989)
'Les Juifs et la question anglaise, 1840–1914', *Genèses*, 4, (May 1991), pp. 3–22
Feldman, David and Stedman Jones, Gareth (eds.), *Metropolis London. Histories and representations since 1800* (London, 1989)
Feldman, Gerald D., 'Economic and social problems of the German demobilization, 1918–1919', *Journal of Modern History*, 47 (March 1975)
'The political economy of Germany's relative stabilization during the 1920/21 world depression', in G. Feldman, C.-L. Holtfereich, G. A. Ritter, and P.-C. Witt (eds.), *Die Deutsche Inflation. Eine Zwischenbilanz* (Berlin, 1982)
'Die Demobilmachung und die Sozialordnung der Zwischenkriegszeit in Europa', *Geschichte und Gesellschaft*, 9 (1983), pp. 156–77
'Das deutsche Unternehmertum zwischen Krieg und Revolution: Die Entstehung des Stinnes-Legien-Abkommens', in G. D. Feldman, *Vom Weltkrieg zur Weltwirtschaftskrise. Studien zur deutschen Wirtschafts- und Sozialgeschichte 1914–1932* (Göttingen, 1984). pp. 100–27
'Saxony, the Reich, and the problem of unemployment in the German inflation', *Archiv für Sozialgeschichte*, 29 (1989)
Army, industry and labor in Germany 1914–1918 (Oxford and Providence, 1992 1st edn Princeton, 1966)
'War economy and controlled economy: the discrediting of "socialism" in Germany during World War I', in Hans-Jürgen Schröder (ed.), *Confrontation and Cooperation. Germany and the United States in the Era of World War I,*

1900–1924 (Oxford, 1993), pp. 229–52

The great disorder. Politics, economics, and society in the German inflation 1914–24 (Oxford, 1993)

'Kriegswirtschaft und Zwangswirtschaft', in W. Michalka (ed.), *Der Erste Weltkrieg* (Munich, 1994)

Feldman, Gerald D., Holtfrerich, C.-L., Ritter, G. A., and Witt, P.-C. (eds.), *Die Anpassung an die Inflation* (Berlin, de Gruyter, 1986)

Fine, M., 'Guerre et réformisme en France, 1914–1918', in L. Murard and P. Zylberman (eds.), *Le soldat du travail*, numéro spécial de *Recherches* (1978)

Fischer, F., *German war aims in the First World War* (London, 1963)

Flemming, J., *Landwirtschaftliche Interessen und Demokratie* (Bonn, 1978)

Flood, P. J., *France 1914–1918: public opinion and the war effort* (Basingstoke, 1990)

Floud, R. and McCloskey, D. (eds.), *An economic history of modern Britain* (2nd edn, Cambridge, 1994)

Forster, E. M., *Howard's End* (London, 1908)

Fourcaut, Annie, *La banlieue rouge 1920–1960* (Paris, 1992)

François, Etienne, 'Berlin au xviii siècle: naissance d'une capitale', in François and Westerhalt (eds.), *Berlin: capitale, mythe, enjeu*

François, Etienne and Westerhalt, Egon (eds.), *Berlin: capitale, mythe, enjeu* (Nancy, 1987)

French, David, 'Allies, rivals and enemies: British strategy and war aims during the First World War', in John Turner (ed.), *Britain and the First World War* (London, 1988)

British economic and strategic planning, 1905–1915 (London, 1982)

'The rise and fall of "Business as usual", in Kathleen Burk (ed.), *War and the state: the transformation of British government, 1914–1919* (London, 1982)

Fridenson, Patrick, *Histoire des usines Renault. Naissance de la grande industrie, 1898–1939* (Paris, 1972)

(ed.), *1914–1918, L'autre front*, Cahiers du 'Mouvement social', no. 2 (Paris, 1977); English transl.: *The French Home Front, 1914–1918* (Providence and Oxford, 1992)

Fuchs, R. G., *Poor and pregnant in Paris. Strategies for survival in the nineteenth century* (New Brunswick, 1992)

Fuller, J. G., *Troop morale and popular culture in the British and Dominion armies, 1914–1918* (Oxford, 1990)

Gaillard, Jeanne, *Paris la ville, 1852–1870* (Paris, 1977)

Galishoff, S., 'Newark and the great influenza pandemic of 1918', *Bulletin of the History of Medicine*, 43 (1969), pp. 246–58

Garside, W. R., *British unemployment policy, 1919–1939: a study in public policy* (Cambridge, 1990)

Geary, D., 'Radicalism and the war: German metal workers, 1914–1923', in Richard J. Evans (ed.), *Society and politics in Wilhelmine Germany* (London, 1978)

Gehrmann, R. 'Zielsetzungen und Methoden bei den historisch-demographischen Auswertungen von Berlin-Brandenburgischem Kirchenbuchmaterial. Das Beispiel St. Nikolai (Spandau)', in Wolfgang Ribbe (ed.), *Berlin Forschungen-I* (Berlin, 1986)

Geist, Johann Friedrich, *Das Berliner Mietshaus* (3 vols., Munich, Prestel, 1980)

Gérôme, N. (ed.), *Archives sensibles. Images, et objets du monde industriel et ouvrier* (Paris, 1995)
Gilbert, B., *British social policy, 1914–1939* (London, 1970)
Glazier, Ira A. and di Rosa, Luigi (eds.), *Migration across time and nations: population mobility in historical contexts* (New York, 1986)
Godfrey, John, *Capitalism at war: industrial policy and bureaucracy in France, 1914–1918* (Leamington Spa, 1987)
Goubert, Jean-Pierre, 'Public hygiene and mortality decline in France in the 19th century', in T. Bengtsson, G. Fridlizins, and R. Ohlsson (eds.), *Pre-industrial population change. Mortality decline and short-term population movements* (Stockholm, 1984)
Graubard, S., 'Military demobilization in Great Britain following the First World War', *Journal of Modern History*, 19, 4 (1947), pp. 1–18
Gray, J., *Gin and bitters* (London, 1938)
Gregory, Adrian, *The silence of memory. Armistice Day 1919–1946* (Oxford and Providence, 1994)
Grzywalz, B., *Arbeit und Bevölkerung im Berlin der Weimarer Zeit* (Berlin, 1988)
Guerrand, R. H., *Les origines du logement social en France* (Paris, 1967)
Guillaume, P., *Du désespoir au salut: les tuberculeux aux 19e et 20e siècles* (Paris, 1986)
Guillemard, Anne-Marie (ed.), *Old age and the welfare state* (London, 1983)
'Transformations du discours sur la vieillesse et constitution d'une "politique française de la vieillesse" durant les trente dernières années', in *Le vieillissement, implications et conséquences de l'allongement de la vie humaine depuis le XVIIIème siècle* (Lyon, 1982)
Guiral, P., *La vie quotidienne des domestiques en France au xixè siècle* (Paris, Hachette, 1978)
Haimson, L. (ed.), *Industrial militancy in Europe during the First World War* (Cambridge, 1993)
Haimson, L. and Tilly, Charles (eds.), *Strikes, wars and revolutions in international perspective* (Cambridge, 1992)
Hall, P. G., *The industries of London since 1861* (London, 1961)
Hardach, Gerd, *The First World War, 1914–1918. An Economic History* (London and Harmondsworth, 1987)
Harling, P. and Mandler, P., 'From "fiscal-military" state to laissez-faire state. 1760–1850', *Journal of British Studies*, 32, 1 (Jan. 1993), pp. 44–70
Harris, José, *Unemployment and Politics: a Study in English social policy 1886–1914* (Oxford, 1972)
Public lives, private virtues (Oxford, 1993)
Haxthausen, C. W., 'Beckmann and the First World War', in C. Schulz-Hoffman and J. C. Weiss (eds), *Max Beckmann retrospective* (Munich and New York, 1985), pp. 69–80.
Heischkel-Artlet, E. (ed.), *Ernährung und Ernährungslehre* (Göttingen, 1976)
Hentschel, Volker, *Geschichte der deutschen Sozialpolitik, 1880–1980* (Frankfurt am Main, 1983)
Hesse, Friedrich, *Die Deutsche Wirtschaftslage von 1914 bis 1923* (Jena, 1938)
Hiley, N., 'British propaganda and the First World War', in J.-J. Becker, J. M. Winter, G. Krumeich, A. Becker, and S. Audoin-Rouzeau (eds.), *Guerre et*

cultures 1914–1918 (Paris, 1994)

Hobsbawn, Eric J., *Age of extremes. The short twentieth century 1914–1991* (London, 1994)

Hobsbawn, Eric J. and Ranger, T. (eds.), *The invention of tradition* (Cambridge, 1983)

Hoerder, D. (ed.), *Labor migration in the Atlantic economies: the European and North American working classes during the period of industrialization* (Westport, 1985)

Hoffmann, Walther G., Grombach, Franz, and Hesse, Helmut, *Das Wachstum der Deutschen Wirtschaft* (Berlin, 1965)

Horn, Pamela, *The rise and fall of the Victorian servant* (Gloucester, 1986)

Horne, A., *The price of glory. Verdun 1916* (London, 1962)

Horne, John, *Labour at war: France and Britain 1914–1918* (Oxford, 1991)

'"L'impôt du sang": republican rhetoric and industrial warfare in France, 1914–1918', *Social History*, 14, 2 (May 1989), pp. 201–23

Howard, N. P., 'The social and political consequences of the Allied blockade of Germany, 1918–1919', *German History*, 11, 2 (June 1993), pp. 161–88

Howson, S., *Domestic monetary management in Britain, 1919–1938* (Cambridge, 1975)

Ineson, A. and Thom, D., 'T.N.T. poisoning and the employment of women workers in the First World War', in P. Weindling (ed.), *The social history of occupational health* (London, 1985), pp. 89–107

Jackson, Alan A., *Semi-detached London. Suburban development, life and transport, 1900–1939* (London, 1973)

Jacquemet, P., 'Belleville aux XIXème et XXème siècles', *Annales–Economies, sociétés, civilisations*, 30, 4 (1975), pp. 819–43

Belleville au XIXème siècle (Paris, 1984)

Jasper, A. S., *A Hoxton childhood* (London, 1969)

Jeffery, K., 'The post-war army', in Ian Beckett and K. Simpson (eds.), *A nation in arms: a social study of the British Army in the First World War* (Manchester, 1985)

Jefferys, J. B., *The story of the Engineers, 1800–1945* (London, 1946)

Johns, B. R., 'Patriots or profiteers? British businessmen and the First World War', *Journal of European Economic History* (1982)

Johnson, Paul Barton, *Land fit for heroes: the planning of British reconstruction, 1916–1919* (Chicago, 1968)

Jones, Gareth Stedman, *Outcast London. A study in the relationship between classes in Victorian society* (Oxford, 1971, repr. 1984)

Keegan, John, *The face of battle* (London, 1976)

Keers, Robert Young, *Pulmonary tuberculosis. A journey down the centuries* (London, 1978)

Kermode, Frank, *D. H. Lawrence* (London, Fontana, 1973)

Kluge, Ulrich, *Die Deutsche Revolution 1918–1919: Staat, Politik und Gesellschaft zwischen Weltkrieg und Kapp-Putsch* (Frankfurt am Main, 1988)

Koch, Ursula, *Der Teufel in Berlin. Von der Märzrevolution bis zu Bismarcks Entlassung. Illustrierte politische Witzblätter einer Metropole, 1840–1890* (Cologne, 1991)

Kocka, Jürgen, 'Weltkrieg und Mittelstand. Handwerker und Angestellte in Deutschland, 1914–1918', *Francia*, 2 (1975)

Klassengesellschaft im Krieg, English trans. by B. Weinberger: *Facing total war: German society, 1914–1918* (Leamington Spa, 1984)

Die Angestellten in der deutschen Geschichte, 1850–1980: vom Privatbeamten zum angestellten Arbeitnehmer (Göttingen, 1981); French trans. *Histoire d'un groupe social. Les employés en Allemagne, 1850–1980* (Paris, 1989)

Koszyk, K., *Deutsche Pressepolitik im Ersten Weltkrieg* (Hamburg, 1978)

Kriegel, Annie, *La croissance syndicale* (Paris, Mouton, 1967)

Krockow, C., *Die Deutschen* (Frankfurt, 1991)

Krüger, D., 'Kriegssozialismus', in W. Michalka (ed.), *Der Erste Weltkrieg* (Munich, 1994)

Kuczynski, Jürgen, *Geschichte des Alltags des deutschen Volkes, 1600 bis 1945*, vol. IV (Berlin, 1982)

Kuisel, Richard F., *Capitalism and the state in modern France: renovation and economic management in the twentieth century* (Cambridge, 1981)

Laslett, Peter (ed.), *Bastardy. The social history of illegitimacy* (Cambridge, 1984)

Lawrence, Jon, Dean, Martin, and Robert, Jean-Louis, 'The outbreak of war and the urban economy: Paris, Berlin, and London in 1914', *Economic History Review*, 2nd ser., 45, 3 (August 1992), pp. 564–93

Lee, Joe, 'Agricultural production and supply', in J. M. Winter (ed.), *War and economic development* (Cambridge, 1975)

Leed, Eric J., *No man's land. Combat and identity in World War One* (Cambridge, 1979; repr. 1981)

Lindenberger, T., 'Die Fleischrevolte am Wedding. Lebensmittelversorgung und Politik in Berlin am Vorabend des Ersten Weltkrieges', in Manfred Gailus and Heinrich Volkmann (eds.), *Der Kampf um das tägliche Brot* (Opladen, 1994), pp. 282–304

Linton, A., *Not expecting miracles* (London, 1982)

Lohmann, Georg, 'La confrontation de Georg Simmel avec une métropole: Berlin', *Critique* (1991), pp. 623–42.

Lowe, Rodney, 'The erosion of state intervention in Britain, 1917–1924', *Economic History Review*, 2nd ser., 31, 2 (May 1978), pp. 270–86

Luckin, B., 'Evaluating the sanitary revolution: typhus and typhoid in London, 1851–1900', in Robert Woods and John Woodward (eds.), *Urban disease and mortality in nineteenth-century England* (London, 1984)

Lüdtke, Alf, 'Hunger, Essens-"Genuss" und Politik bei Fabrikarbeitern und Arbeiterfrauen. Beispiele aus dem rheinisch-westfälischen Industriegebiet 1910–1940', *Sozialwissenschaftliche Informationen*, 14, 2 (1985)

Police and state in Prussia, 1815–1850 (Oxford, 1989)

McBride, Theresa, *The domestic revolution, 1820–1920* (London, 1976)

McGinnis, J. P., 'The impact of epidemic influenza: Canada, 1918–1919', *Historical Papers* (1977)

McKibbin, Ross, *The ideologies of class: social relations in Britain 1880–1950* (Oxford, 1990)

Magri, Susanna, 'Le mouvement des locataires à Paris et dans sa banlieue (1919–1925)', *Le Mouvement social*, 137 (Oct.–Dec. 1986), pp. 56–76

'Les locataires se syndiquent', in Roger Quillot and Roger-Henri Guerrand (eds.), *Cent ans d'habitat social. Une utopie réaliste* (Paris, 1989)

Magri, Susanna and Topalov, Christian, 'De la cité-jardin à la ville rationalisée:

un tournant du projet réformateur, 1905–25. Etude comparative France, Grande-Bretagne, Italie, Etats-Unis', *Revue française de sociologie*, 28, 3 (July–Sept. 1987), pp. 417–51

'"Reconstruire": l'habitat populaire au lendemain de la première guerre mondiale. Etude comparative France, Grande-Bretagne, Italie, Etats-Unis', *Archives européennes de sociologie*, 29 (1988), pp. 319–70

Mai, Gunther, *Kriegswirtschaft und Arbeiterbewegung in Württemberg 1914–1918* (Stuttgart, 1983)

'Arbeitsmarktregulierung oder Sozialpolitik? Die personelle Demobilmachung in Deutschland 1918 bis 1920/1924' in G. D. Feldman, C. L. Holtfrerich, G. Ritter, and P.-C. Witt (eds.), *Die Anpassung an die Inflation* (Berlin, 1986), pp. 202–36.

Maier, Charles S., *Recasting bourgeois Europe: stabilization in France, Germany, and Italy in the decade after World War I* (Princeton, 1975; repr. 1988)

Marion, M., *Histoire financière de la France depuis 1715* (6 vols., Paris, 1927–31)

Marks, Lara, '"Dear old Mother Levy's": the Jewish Maternity Home and Sick Room Helps Society, 1895–1939', *Social History of Medicine*, 3, 1 (1990), pp. 24–43

Marquis, H. G., 'Words as weapons: propaganda in Britain and Germany during the First World War', *Journal of Contemporary History*, 13, 3 (July 1978), pp. 467–98.

Martin-Fugier, Anne, *La place des bonnes. La domesticité féminine à Paris en 1900* (Paris, 1979)

Masur, Gerhard, *Imperial Berlin 1871–1918* (London, 1971)

Matzerath, Horst, 'Berlin, 1890–1940', in Anthony Sutcliffe (ed.), *Metropolis 1890–1940* (London, 1984), pp. 290–318

Urbanisierung in Preussen, 1815–1914 (Berlin, 1985)

Maurin, J., *Armée, guerre, société: soldats Languedociens, 1889–1919* (Paris, 1982)

Meerwarth, M., Gunther, Adolf, and Zimmermann, Waldemar, *Die Einwirkung des Krieges auf Bevölkerungsbewegung und Lebenshaltung in Deutschland* (Stuttgart, 1932)

Melling, Joseph, *Rent strikes: peoples' struggles for housing in West Scotland, 1890–1916* (Edinburgh, 1983)

Merrett, S., *State housing in Britain* (London, 1979)

Michaud, Stéphane, Mollier, Jean-Yves, and Savy, Nicole (eds.), *Usages de l'image au XIXe siècle* (Paris, 1992)

Middlebrook, Martin, *The First Day of the Somme: 1 July 1916* (London, 1971)

The Kaiser's battle: 21 March 1918: the first day of the German spring Offensive (London, 1978; repr. Harmondsworth, 1983)

Mitchell, B. R., *International historical statistics. Europe 1918–1976* (3rd edn, Basingstoke, 1992)

Moeller, R. G., 'Dimensions of social conflict in the Great War: the view from the German countryside', *Central European History*, 14, 2 (June 1981), pp. 142–68

Moine, Marcel, *Recherches et considérations générales sur la mortalité à Paris depuis la Restauration* (Paris, 1941)

Mommsen, Wolfgang J., 'The topos of inevitable war', *Central European History*, 6, 1 (March 1973), pp. 3–43

(ed.), 'Die Organisierung des Friedens: Demobilmachung 1918–1920', *Ge-*

schichte und Gesellschaft 9 (1983)
Moore, Barrington, *Injustice: the social bases of obedience and revolt* (London, 1980)
Morgan, Kenneth Owen and Morgan, Jane, *Portrait of a progressive: the political career of Christopher, Viscount Addison* (Oxford, 1980)
Moriarty, C., 'Christian iconography and first world war memorials', *Imperial War Museum Review*, 6 (1990), pp. 63–75
Morris, A. J. A., *Radicalism against war, 1906–1914: the advocacy of peace and retrenchment* (London, 1972)
Mosse, George L., *Fallen Soldiers. Reshaping the Memory of the World Wars* (Oxford and New York, 1990)
Muellbauer, John, 'Professor Sen on the standard of living', in Geoffrey Hawthorn (ed.), *The standard of living: the Tanner lectures, Clare Hall, Cambridge* (Cambridge, 1987)
Müller, Dirk H., *Gewerkschaftliche Versammlungsdemokratie und Arbeiterdelegierte vor 1918: ein Beitrag zur Geschichte des Lokalismus, des Syndikalismus und der entstehenden Rätebewegung* (Berlin, 1985)
Murard, Lion and Zylberman, Patrick, '"L'autre guerre", 1914–1918. La santé publique en France sous l'oeil de l'Amérique', *Revue historique*, 276, 2 (Oct.–Dec. 1986), pp. 367–97
'La mission Rockefeller en France et la création du Comité national de défense contre la tuberculose (1917–1923)' *Revue d'histoire moderne et contemporaine*, 34 (1987), pp. 257–81
Nadaud, Martin, *Léonard maçon de la Creuse* (Paris, 'La mémoire des peuples', 1976)
Nettl, J. P., 'The German Social Democratic party as a political model', *Past & Present*, 30 (April 1965), pp. 65–95
Rosa Luxemburg (2 vols., Oxford, 1966)
Newton, A., *Years of change: autobiography of a Hackney shoemaker* (London, 1974)
Nipperdey, Thomas, *Deutsche Geschichte 1866–1918* (2 vols., Munich, C. H. Beck, 1991–2)
Noiriel, Gérard, *Les ouvriers en France aux 19ème et 20ème siècles* (Paris, 1988)
Nolan, Mary, *Social Democracy and Society. Working-class radicalism in Düsseldorf 1890–1920* (Cambridge, 1981)
Norman Meachen, G., *A Short History of Tuberculosis* (London, 1936)
O'Brien, P. K. and Hunt, P. A., 'The rise of the fiscal state in Britain, 1485–1815', *Historical Research* (June 1993)
Offer, Avner, *Property and politics, 1870–1914: landownership, law, ideology and urban development in England* (Cambridge, 1981)
The First World War. An agrarian interpretation (Oxford, 1989)
Ogden, Philip E. and White, Paul E. (eds.), *Migrants in modern France: population mobility in the later nineteenth and twentieth centuries* (London, 1989)
Olsen, Donald J., *The city as a work of art: London, Paris, Vienna* (New Haven and London, 1986)
Olson, M., *The economics of the wartime shortage* (Chapel Hill, N.C., 1970)
Orbach, Laurence F., *Homes for heroes: a study of the evolution of British public housing, 1915–1921* (London, 1977)
Osborn, J. E., *Influenza in america 1918–1976* (New York, 1977)
Owen, David, *The government of Victoria London 1855–1899: the Metropolitan*

Board of Works, the Vestries and the City corporation (Cambridge, Mass., 1982)
Ozouf, J. and Furet, F., *Reading and writing* (Cambridge, 1982)
Ozouf, Mona, *L'Ecole, l'Eglise et la République: 1871–1914* (Paris, 1982)
Panayi, P., *The enemy in our midst. Germans in Britain during the First World War* (Oxford, 1991)
Paret, Peter, Irwin Lewis, Beth, and Paret, Paul (eds.), *Persuasive images: posters of war and revolution from the Hoover Institution Archives* (Princeton, Princeton University Press, 1992)
Paris–Berlin, 1900–1933: rapports et contrastes France-Allemagne (Paris, 1978)
Paris de jour à jour: le vingtième siècle (Paris, 1968)
Paris démuré (Paris, 1990)
Peacock, A. J. and Wiseman, J., assisted by Jindrich Vevenka, *The growth of public expenditure in the United Kingdom* (Princeton, 1961; repr. Cambridge 1970)
Pedersen, Susan, 'Gender, welfare and citizenship in Britain during the Great War', *American Historical Review*, 95, 4 (1990), pp. 983–1006
Family, dependence, and the origins of the welfare state: Britain and France 1914–1945 (Cambridge, 1993)
Pedroncini, G., *Les mutineries de 1917* (Paris, 1967)
Pennybacker, Susan, 'Les moeurs, les aspirations et la culture politique des employés de bureau londoniens des deux sexes, 1889–1914', *Genèses*, 14 (Jan. 1994), pp. 83–104.
Perrot, Michelle, 'Les classes populaires urbaines', in F. Braudel and E. Labrousse (eds.), *Histoire économique et sociale de la France* (Paris, 1979)
'La femme populaire rebelle', in Christiane Dufrancatel, Arlette Farge, and Christine Faure, *L'histoire sans qualité* (Paris, 1979)
Peukert, Detlev, *Die Weimarer Republik. Krisenjahre der klassischen Moderne* (Frankfurt, 1987); English trans. *The Weimar Republic: the crisis of classical modernity* (London, 1991)
Phillips, G. and Whiteside, N., *Casual labour. The unemployment question in the port transport industry 1880–1970* (Oxford, 1985)
Picard, R., *Le mouvement syndical pendant la guerre* (Paris, 1927)
Pigou, A. C., *Aspects of British economic history, 1918–1925* (London, 1947)
Pinol, Jean-Luc, *Le monde des villes au XIXe siècle* (Paris, 1991)
Pollard, Sidney, *The development of the British economy, 1914–1980* (3rd edn, London, 1983; 4th edn 1992)
Pourcher, Guy, *Le peuplement de Paris, origine régionale, composition sociale, attitudes et motivations*, Cahiers de l'INED no. 43 (Paris, 1963)
Prion, W., 'Die Finanzen des Reiches (Kriegsanleihen, Inflation)', in G. Anschütz, F. Berolzheimer, *et al.* (eds.), *Handbuch der Politik, V, 4, Der Wirtschaftliche Weideraufbau* (Berlin and Leipzig, 1921)
Procacci, Giovanna, *Stato e classe operaia in Italia durante la prima guerra mondiale* (Milan, 1983)
Prost, Antoine, *Histoire de l'enseignement en France (1800–1967)* (Paris, 1975)
Les anciens combattants et la société française, 1914–1939 (3 vols., Paris, 1977); abr. transl. *In the wake of war: 'les anciens combattants' and French society, 1914–1940* (Providence and Oxford, 1992)
Rasmussen, S. E., *London. The unique city* (London, 1937)
Read, J. M., *Atrocity propaganda* (London, 1958)

Reid, Alistair, 'Dilution, trade unionism and the state in Britain during the First World War', in Steven Tolliday and Jonathan Zeitlin (eds.), *Shop floor bargaining and the state: historical and comparative perspectives* (Cambridge, 1985)

Reulecke, Jürgen and Huck, Gerhard, 'Urban history research in Germany: its development and present condition', *Urban History Yearbook* (1981)

Renouvin, Pierre, *La crise européenne et la grande guerre* (Paris, 1950)

'L'opinion publique en 1917', *Revue d'histoire moderne et contemporaine*, 15 (Jan.–March 1968), pp. 4–23

Reinicke, Peter, *Tuberkulosefürsorge, Der Kampf gegen eine Geissel der Menschheit, Dargestellt am Beispiel Berlins 1895–1945* (Berlin, 1988)

Rials, Stéphane, *Nouvelle histoire de Paris. De Trochu à Thiers, 1870–1873* (Paris, 1985)

Ribbe, Wolfgang, 'Naissance du Grand-Berlin', in Lionel Richard (ed.), *Berlin, 1919–1933* (Paris, 1991)

Ribbe, Wolfgang (ed.), *Geschichte Berlins, zweiter Band. Von der Märzrevolution bis zur Gegenwart* (Munich, 1988)

Rich, A. R., *The pathogenesis of tuberculosis* (Oxford, 1952)

Richard, Lionel (ed.), *Berlin, 1919–1933. Gigantisme, crise sociale et avant-garde: l'incarnation extrême de la modernité* (Paris, 1991)

Richard, Lionel, 'Identité contradictoire', in L. Richard (ed.), *Berlin 1919–1933. Gigantisme, crise sociale et avant-garde: l'incarnation extrême de la modernité* (Paris, 1991), pp. 14–43

Ritter, Gerhard A. and Miller, Susanne (eds.), *Die Deutsche Revolution 1918–1919. Dokumente* (Frankfurt, 1983)

Robert, Jean-Louis, *La scission syndicale de 1921* (Paris, 1980)

'La C.G.T. et la famille ouvrière, 1914–1918: première approche', *Le Mouvement social*, 116 (July–Sept. 1981), pp. 47–66

'Banlieue rouge sang', in Annie Fourcaut (ed.), *La banlieue rouge* (Paris, 1992), pp. 146–59

'Cooperatives during the war', in P. Fridenson (ed.), *The French Home Front* (Oxford, 1992)

'Cours sur Culture et société en France 1880–1929', University of Orléans, 1992

'Mobilisations militantes à Paris pendant la grande guerre', communication to conference on 'Mobilizing for total war: society and state in Europe, 1914–1918', Dublin, 23–25 June 1993

Les ouvriers, la patrie et la Révolution, Paris 1914–1919 (Besançon, 1996)

Robert, Jean-Louis and Winter, Jay M., 'Un aspect ignoré de la démographie urbaine de la Grande Guerre: le drame des vieux à Berlin, Londres et Paris', *Annales de démographie historique* (1993), pp. 303–29

Robson, B. T., *Urban growth: an approach* (London, 1973)

Rodger, Richard, *Housing in urban Britain 1780–1914* (London, 1989)

Roerkohl, Anne, *Hungerblockade und Heimatfront* (Stuttgart, 1991)

Rollet, Catherine, 'Nourrices et nourrissons dans le département de la Seine et en France de 1880 à 1940', *Population*, 3 (1982), pp. 573–604

'Le financement de la protection maternelle et infantile avant 1940', *Sociétés contemporaines*, 3 (1990), pp. 1–40

La politique à l'égard de la petite enfance sous la IIIe République (Paris, 1990)
'Education et démographie. Réflexions sur l'expérience française d'éducation des mères et des jeunes filles aux XIXe et XXe siècles', *Actes du Séminaire de démographie, l'Université Charles de Prague et l'Université de Paris I, novembre 1992, Les Cahiers de l'IOUP* (1994), pp. 1–25
Rose, Michael E., 'The success of social reform? The Central Control Board (Liquor Traffic) 1915–1921', in M. R. D. Foot (ed.), *War and Society: historical essays in honour of J. R. Western, 1928–1971* (London, 1973), pp. 71–84
Rosenburg, A., *Imperial Germany* (New York, 1959)
Rothstein, Andrew, *The Soldier's Strikes of 1919* (London, 1980)
Routh, G., *Occupation and pay in Great Britain, 1900–1960* (Cambridge, 1965)
Rubin, G., *War, law and labour: the Munitions Acts, state regulation and the unions* (Oxford, 1987)
Rubinstein, W. D., *Wealth and the wealthy in modern British history: essays in social and economic history* (Brighton, 1987)
Rürup, R., 'Problems of the German revolution', *Journal of Contemporary History* (1968), pp. 1–18
'Demokratische Revolution und "dritter Weg". Die deutsche Revolution von 1918/19 in der neueren wissenschaftlichen Diskussion', *Geschichte und Gesellschaft*, 9 (1983), pp. 278–301
Ryder, A. J., *The German Revolution of 1918* (Cambridge, 1975)
Samuel, Raphael (ed.), *Patriotism. The Making and Unmaking of British National Identity* (3 vols., London, 1989)
Sanders, M. L. and Taylor, Philip, *British propaganda during the First World War 1914–1918* (London, 1982)
Scarpa, Ludovica, *Martin Wagner e Berlino. Casa e citta nella Repubblica di Weimar, 1918–1933* (Rome, 1983)
Scholz, Robert, 'Die Auswirkung der Inflation auf das Sozial- und Wohlfahrtswesen der neuen Stadtgemeinde Berlin', in Gerald Feldman, C.-L. Holtfrerich, G. A. Ritter, and P.-C. Witt (eds.), *Konsequenzen der Inflation* (Berlin, 1989), pp. 45–75
Schröder, Hans-Jürgen (ed.), *Confrontation and cooperation. Germany and the United States in the Era of World War I, 1900–1924* (Oxford, 1993)
Schultz-Hoffman, C. and Weiss, J. C. (eds.), *Max Beckmann retrospective* (Munich and New York, 1985)
Schwippe, H. J. 'Zum Prozess der sozialräumlichen innerstädtischen Differenzierung im Industrialisierungsprozess des 19. Jahrhunderts: eine faktorialökologische Studie am Beispiel der Stadt Berlin, 1875–1910', in H. J. Teuteberg (ed.), *Urbanisierung im 19. und 20. Jahrhundert. Historische und geographische Aspekte* (Cologne, 1983), pp. 284–307
Sen, Amartya, *Poverty and famines: an essay on entitlement and deprivation* (Oxford, 1981)
'The standard of living: Lecture I, concepts and critiques', in G. Hawthorn (ed.), *The standard of living* (Cambridge, 1987)
'The standard of living: Lecture II, lives and capabilities', in G. Hawthorn (ed.), *The standard of living* (Cambridge, 1987)
Simkins, Peter, *Kitchener's army: the raising of the New Armies* (Manchester, 1988)
Simmel, G., 'Les grandes villes et la vie de l'esprit', trans. by J. L. Vieillard-Baron,

in *Philosophie de la modernité: la femme, la ville, l'individualisme* (Paris, 1989)
Siney, M. C., *The Allied blockade of Germany* (New York, 1966)
Siwek-Pouydesseau, Jeanne, *Le corps préfectoral sous la Troisième et la Quatrième République* (Paris, 1969)
Smith, D. H., *The industries of Greater London: being a survey of the recent industrialisation of the northern and western sectors of Greater London* (London, 1933)
Smithies, Edward, *The black economy in England since 1914* (Dublin, 1984; Atlantic Highlands, N.J., Humanities Press, 1984)
Spiers, E. M., 'The regular army in 1914', pp. 37–62, in Ian Beckett (ed.), *A nation in arms* (Manchester, 1985)
Spree, Reinhard, *Soziale Ungleichheit vor Krankheit und Tod* (Göttingen, 1981); English transl. *Health and Social Class in Imperial Germany: a social history of mortality, morbidity and inequality* (Oxford, 1988)
Stamp, J. C., *Taxation during the war* (London, 1932)
Stephen, Martin (ed.), *Never such innocence: a new anthology of Great War verse* (London, 1988)
Stevenson, D., *The First World War and international politics* (Oxford, 1988)
Stockel, Sigrid, 'Säuglingssterblichkeit in Berlin von 1870 bis zum Vorabend des Ersten Weltkriegs. Eine Kurve mit hohem Maximum und starkem Gefälle', in W. Ribbe (ed.), *Berlin-Forschungen-I* (Berlin, 1986), pp. 219–64
Stovall, T., *The Rise of the Paris Red Belt* (Berkeley, 1990)
Stumpf, Richard, *Warum die Flotte zerbrach? Kriegstagebuch eines christlichen Arbeiters* (Berlin, 1927)
War, mutiny, and revolution in the German navy, ed. D. Horn (New Brunswick, 1967)
Sussman, George D., *Selling mother's milk: the wet-nursing business in France, 1715–1914* (Urbana, 1982)
Szreter, S., 'The importance of social intervention in Britain's mortality decline *c.* 1850–1914: a reinterpretation of the role of public health', *Social History of Medicine*, 1 (1988), pp. 1–34
Tawney, R. H., 'The abolition of economic controls, 1918–1921', *Economic History Review*, 13 (1943), pp. 1–30
Teuteberg, H. and Wiegelmann, G., *Der Wandel der Nährungsgewohnheiten unter dem Einfluss der Industrialisierung* (Göttingen, 1972)
Teuteberg, H. and Klemens Wischermann, J., *Wohnalltag in Deutschland 1850–1914. Studien der Geschichte des Alltags* (Munich, 1985)
Thébaud, Françoise, *Les femmes aux temps de la guerre de 14* (Paris, 1980)
'La Grande Guerre', in Françoise Thébaud (ed.), *Histoire des femmes en occident. Le XXe siècle* (Paris, 1992)
Theweleit, Klaus, *Männerphantasien*; English trans. *Male Fantasies* (2 vols., Cambridge, 1988)
Thom, D., 'Free from chains? The image of women's labour in London, 1900–1920', in David Feldman and Gareth Stedman Jones (eds.), *Metropolis London. Histories and Representations since 1800* (London, 1989), pp. 85–99
'Women and work in wartime Britain', in Richard Wall and Jay M. Winter (eds.), *The upheaval of war: family, work and welfare in Europe, 1914–1918* (Cambridge, 1988)

Thomas, Brinley, *Migration and Economic Growth* (Cambridge, 1954; 2nd edn, 1972)

Thompson, F. M. L., *English landed society in the nineteenth century* (London, 1963)

'Britain', in D. Spring (ed.), *European landed aristocracy* (Baltimore, 1980)

Tilyard, F., *Unemployment insurance in Great Britain, 1911–1948* (Leigh-on-Sea, 1949)

Tobin, Elizabeth H., 'War and the working class: the case of Düsseldorf 1914–1918', *Central European History*, 18 (1985), pp. 257–98

Tomkins, Sandra M., 'The failure of expertise: public health policy in Britain during the 1918–1919 influenza epidemic', *Social History of Medicine* (1992), pp. 435–54

Topalov, Christian, *Le logement en France. Histoire d'une marchandise impossible* (Paris, 1987)

'De la cité-jardin à la ville rationalisée: un tournant du projet réformateur, 1905–1925. Etude comparative France, Grande-Bretagne, Italie, Etats-Unis', *Revue française de sociologie*, 28, no. 3 (1992), pp. 417–51

Tournier, Maurice, 'L'envers de 1900, le lexique des luttes et de l'organisation ouvrière en France', *Mots*, 5 (Oct. 1982)

Toutain, J. C., *Histoire quantitative de l'économie française* (Paris, 1961)

Trebilcock, R. C., 'War and the failure of industrial mobilisation, 1899 and 1914', in J. M. Winter (ed.), *War and economic development: essays in memory of David Joslin* (Cambridge, 1975)

Turner, John, *British politics and the Great War: coalition and conflict, 1915–1918* (New Haven and London, 1992)

Ullrich, V., *Kriegsalltag: Hamburg im Ersten Weltkrieg* (Cologne, 1982)

Vettraino-Soulard, Marie-Claude, *Lire une image* (Paris, 1993)

Vincent, C. Paul, *The politics of hunger: the Allied blockade of Germany, 1915–1919* (Athens, Ohio, 1985)

Waite, R. G. L., *Vanguards of Nazism. The Freikorps 1919–1933* (Cambridge, Mass., 1964)

Waites, Bernard, 'The moral economy of the crowd in the First World War', in P. H. Liddle (ed.), *Home Fires and foreign fields: British social and military experience in the First World War* (London, 1985)

A class society at war. England 1914–1918 (Leamington Spa, 1987)

Wall, Richard and Winter, J. M. (eds.), *The upheaval of war: family, work, and welfare in Europe, 1914–1918* (Cambridge, 1988)

Waltner, G. and U. A. Hoffmann, *Das Wachstum der deutschen Wirtschaft* (Berlin, 1965)

Ward, S. R. (ed.), *The war generation* (Port Washington, N.Y., 1975)

Weber, Eugen, *Peasants into Frenchmen: the modernization of rural France, 1870–1914* (London, 1979)

Wehler, H. U., 'Wie bürgerlich war das deutsche Kaiserreich?' in Jürgen Kocka (ed.), *Bürger und die Bürgerlichkeit im 19. Jahrhundert* (Göttingen, 1987)

Weinroth, H. 'Norman Angell and *The great illusion*: an episode in pre 1914-pacifism', *Historical Journal*, 17, 3 (Sept. 1974), pp. 551–74

Whalen, Robert W., *Bitter wounds: German victims of the Great War, 1914–1939* (Ithaca, N.Y., 1984)

White, J., 'Campbell Bunker: a lumpen community in London between the

wars', *History Workshop Journal* (Autumn 1979), pp. 1–49
Whiting, R. C., 'Taxation and the working class, 1915–1924', *Historical Journal*, 33, 4 (December 1990) pp. 895–916
Wilde, Oscar, *The importance of being earnest* (London, 1898)
Wilkinson, Anne, 'Disease in the nineteenth-century urban economy: the Medical Officer of Health and the Community', unpublished paper presented to the Society for the Social History of Medicine, meeting, Jan. 1978
Williams, B., 'The standard of living: interests and capabilities', in G. Hawthorn (ed.), *The Standard of Living* (Cambridge, Cambridge University Press, 1987)
Wilson, G. B., *Alcohol and the nation: a contribution to the study of the liquor problem in the United Kingdom from 1800 to 1935* (London, 1940)
Wilson, Trevor, *The myriad faces of war* (Cambridge, 1986)
Winkler, Heinrich August, *Von der Revolution zur Stabilisierung. Arbeiter und Arbeiterbewegung in der Weimarer Republik 1918 bis 1924* (Berlin, 1984)
Winter, Denis, *Death's men: soldiers of the Great War* (London, 1978; reissued Harmondsworth, 1979)
Winter, Jay M., *Socialism and the challenge of war* (London, 1974)
'Aspects of the impact of the First World War on infant mortality in Britain', *Journal of European Economic History*, 11, 3 (Winter 1982), pp. 713–38
'The decline of mortality in Britain, 1870–1950', in Theo Barker and Michael Drake (eds.), *Population and society in Britain 1850–1980* (London, 1982), pp. 100–20
The Great War and the British people (Basingstoke, 1986)
'Some paradoxes of the Great War', in Richard Wall and Jay M. Winter (eds.), *The upheaval of war. Family, work and welfare in Europe 1914–1918* (Cambridge, 1987)
'Public health and the extension of life expectancy in England and Wales, 1901–1961', in Milo Keynes, David A. Coleman, and Nicholas H. Dimsdale (eds.), *The political economy of health and welfare: proceedings of the twenty-second annual symposium of the Eugenics Society* (Basingstoke, 1988), pp. 184–206
'Public health and the political economy of war', *History Workshop Journal* (1988), pp. 163–73
'Le mouvement travailliste en Grande-Bretagne et les problèmes de la santé publique (1900–1948)', *Prévenir*, 19 (1989), pp. 125–40
'Nationalism, the visual arts and the myth of war enthusiasm', *History of European Ideas* (1992)
Sites of memory, sites of mourning. The Great War in European cultural history (Cambridge, 1995)
(ed.), *War and economic development: essays in memory of David Joslin* (Cambridge, 1975)
Winter, Jay M. and Cole, J., 'Fluctuations in infant mortality rates in Berlin during and after the First World War', *European Journal of Population*, 9 (1993), pp. 235–63
Winter, Jay M., Lawrence, J. and Ariouat, J., 'The impact of the Great War on infant mortality in London', *Annales de démographie historique* (1993), pp. 329–58
Witkop, P. (ed.), *Kriegsbriefe gefallener Studenten* (Munich, 1928)

Witt, Peter Christian, 'Staatliche Wirtschaftspolitik in Deutschland 1918 bis 1923: Entwicklung und Zerstörung einer modernen wirtschaftspolitischen Strategie', in G. Feldman, C.-L. Holtfrerich, G. A. Ritter, and P.-C. Witt, (eds.), *Die Deutsche Inflation, Eine Zwischenbilanz* (Berlin, 1982), pp. 153–79

Wohl, Anthony S., *The Eternal Slum. Housing and Social Policy in Victorian London* (London, Edward Arnold, 1977)

Wohl, R., *The generation of 1914* (London, 1979)

Young, M. and Willmott, P., *Family and kinship in East London* (London, 1957)

Zilch, Reinhold, *Die Reichsbank und die finanzielle Kriegsvorbereitung, 1907 bis 1914* (Berlin, 1987)

Zimmermann, Clement, *Von der Wohnungsfrage zur Wohnungspolitik: die Reformbewegung in Deutschland 1845–1914* (Göttingen, 1991)

Zimmermann, W., 'Die Veränderungen der Einkommens- und Lebensverhältnisse der deutschen Arbeiter durch den Krieg', in Meerwarth, Gunther, and W. Zimmermann, *Die Einwirkung des Krieges*

Theses and dissertations

Bonzon, Thierry, 'Cent quatre vingt dix lettres de pacifistes, juin 1916–octobre 1916', master's thesis, University of Paris – I, 1985

'La politique sociale du Conseil Municipal de Paris et du Conseil Général de la Seine pendant la Grande Guerre', DEA, University of Paris – I, 1990

'La politique sociale du Conseil municipal de Paris et du Conseil général de la Seine, 1910–20', PhD thesis, University of Paris – I, forthcoming, 1997

Bott, J. P., 'The German food crisis of World War I: the cases of Coblenz and Cologne', PhD thesis, University of Missouri, 1981

Carrau, Paul, 'Le ravitaillement en combustibles de la région parisienne pendant la guerre', doctoral thesis in law, University of Paris, 1924

Chilly, L. de, 'La classe moyenne en France après la guerre, 1918–1924. Sa crise: causes, conséquences et remèdes', doctoral thesis, Paris Faculty of Law, 1924

Cole, Joshua, 'The history of demographic statistics in France 1860–1900', PhD thesis, University of California at Berkeley, 1990

Collins, R. F., 'Newspapers of the French left in Provence and Bas-Languedoc during the First World War', PhD thesis, University of Cambridge, 1990

Davis, Belinda, 'Home fires burning. Politics, identity and food in World War I Berlin', PhD thesis, University of Michigan, 1992

Dettmer, Klaus, 'Arbeitslose in Berlin. Zur politischen Geschichte der Arbeitslosenbewegung zwischen 1918 und 1923', PhD thesis, Free University of Berlin, 1977

Dogliani, Patrizia, 'Un laboratoire du socialisme municipal: France 1880–1920', doctoral thesis, University of Paris – VIII, 1991

Fonvieille, A., 'Etude critique du régime des allocations aux familles des militaires soutiens indispensables', doctoral thesis in law, University of Montpellier, 1919

Hinds, L. H., 'La coopération économique entre la France et la Grande-Bretagne pendant la première guerre mondiale', PhD thesis, University of Paris – I, 1982

Isobe, Kaizo, 'Problèmes d'évolution économique et d'urbanisme dans la banlieue ouest de Paris: Puteaux et Suresnes pendant la guerre de 1914–1918 et pendant l'entre deux-guerres', PhD thesis, University of Paris – IV, 1982

Kimble, C., 'The British Legion and ex-servicemen's politics in Britain', PhD thesis, Stanford University, 1990

Kozak, Marion, 'Women munition workers during the First World War: with special reference to engineering', PhD thesis, University of Hull, 1976

Lloyd, D., 'Pilgrimages and British society during and after the First World War', PhD thesis, University of Cambridge, 1994

Marsauche, A., 'La question des étrangers à Paris, 1914–1918', MA thesis, University of Paris – I, 1990

Martland, P., 'The gramophone industry in Britain, 1880–1930', PhD thesis, University of Cambridge, 1991

Mathews, William C., 'The German Social Democrats and the inflation: food, foreign trade and the politics of stabilization, 1914–1920', PhD thesis, University of California, Riverside, 1982

Pedersen, Susan, 'Social policy and the reconstruction of the family in Britain and France, 1900–1945', PhD thesis, Harvard University, 1989

Peiter, Henry Donald, 'Men of good will: French businessmen and the First World War', PhD thesis, University of Michigan, Ann Arbor, 1973

Pennybacker, Susan, 'The labour policy of the London County Council, 1889–1914', PhD thesis, University of Cambridge, 1981

Robert, Jean-Louis, 'Ouvriers et mouvement ouvrier parisien pendant la grande guerre et l'immédiat après-guerre. Histoire et anthropologie', state doctorate , University of Paris – I, 1989

Schweitzer, Sylvie, 'Organisation du travail, politique patronale et pratiques ouvrières aux usines Citroën, 1915–1935', PhD thesis, University of Paris – VIII, 1980

Stöckel, Sigrid, 'Die Bekämpfung der Säuglingssterblichkeit im Kaiserreich und in der Weimarer Republik', PhD thesis, Free University of Berlin, 1992

Sweeney, R., 'Popular entertainments in Paris in the First World War', PhD thesis, University of California, Berkeley, 1992

Thébaud, Françoise, 'Donner la vie: histoire de la maternité en France entre les deux guerres', Phd thesis, University of Paris – VII, 1982

Thom, D., 'Women munition workers at Woolwich Arsenal in the 1914–1918 war', MA thesis, University of Warwick, 1976

Thomas, Gill, 'State maintenance for women during the First World War: the case of separation allowances and pensions', PhD thesis, University of London, 1989

Tomkins, Sandra M., 'Britain and the influenza epidemic of 1918–1919', PhD thesis, University of Cambridge, 1989

Topalov, Christian, 'Formes de production et formes de propriété du logement en France', PhD thesis, University of Paris – V, 1984

Index

Printed in the United Kingdom
by Lightning Source UK Ltd.
121487UK00001B/20/A

9 780521 668149